CONTEMPORARY FAMILIES AND RELATIONSHIPS

Reinventing Responsibility

CONTEMPORARY FAMILIES AND RELATIONSHIPS

Reinventing Responsibility

John Scanzoni

University of Florida

McGraw-Hill, Inc.

New York   St. Louis   San Francisco   Auckland   Bogotá   Caracas
Lisbon   London   Madrid   Mexico City   Milan   Montreal   New Delhi
San Juan   Singapore   Sydney   Tokyo   Toronto

This book was set in Palatino by Ruttle, Shaw & Wetherill, Inc.
The editors were Jill S. Gordon, Robert Greiner, and Sheila H. Gillams;
the production supervisor was Richard A. Ausburn.
The cover was designed by John Hite.
R. R. Donnelley & Sons Company was printer and binder.

Cover photo credits:
Donna Day/AllStock
Myrleen Ferguson
Nicole Katann/Tony Stone Images
Jo Browne/Nick Smee/Tony Stone Images

CONTEMPORARY FAMILIES AND RELATIONSHIPS
Reinventing Responsibility

Photo Credits appear on page 451 and on this page by reference.

 This book is printed on recycled, acid-free paper containing 10% postconsumer waste.

1 2 3 4 5 6 7 8 9 0   DOH DOH   9 0 9 8 7 6 5 4

ISBN 0-07-055133-2

Library of Congress Cataloging-in-Publication Data

Scanzoni, John H., (date).
    Contemporary families and relationships : reinventing
responsibility / John Scanzoni.
        p.   cm.
    Includes bibliographical references and index.
    ISBN 0-07-055133-2
    1. Family—United States.   2. Marriage—United States.   I. Title.
HQ536.S335   1995
306.8'0973—dc20   94-40493

ABOUT THE AUTHOR

JOHN SCANZONI is Professor and Chair of Sociology at the University of Florida. He has conducted a great deal of research, and has published widely in the area of families and primary (close) relationships. Some of his research interests include gender and paid employment, fertility control, comparisons between black and white husband-wife families, conflict, negotiation and decision-making, and, most recently, the formation of social family networks across several solo-parent black households. He has a strong interest in theories about families, as well as public policies for families. Professor Scanzoni is a member of the American Sociological Association, and the National Council on Family Relations.

Among other places, he has published articles in the *American Sociological Review, American Journal of Sociology, Journal of Marriage and Family, Journal of Family Issues,* and *Policy Studies Review.* Some of his book titles include *The Black Family in Modern Society, Family Decision-Making, Shaping Tomorrow's Family—Theory and Policy for the 21st Century,* and, most recently, *The Sexual Bond: Rethinking Families and Close Relationships.* He was also co-author of the earlier and very popular McGraw-Hill book, *Men, Women, and Change.*

CONTENTS IN BRIEF

CONTENTS

PREFACE

Margaret Mahoney, president of the Commonwealth Fund, recently observed that

> The endurance and universality of the concept of family testify to its strength and vitality. Family patterns vary and compositions alter, but the need to belong to something larger than oneself is innate and compelling. This need is demonstrated over and over again by groups that refer to themselves as "family." . . . Children play "family," and *elders reinvent it when it does not exist*.[1]

This book is all about what Mahoney calls *reinvention*—reinvention of the concept of family. Family is found in every society, it is universal. And that, says Mahoney, proves its endurance, strength, and vitality. She adds that people *need* family—human beings need to belong to something "larger than oneself." But just as powerful as the need to belong to family is the demand to create its varied social expressions. Family is a social reality, and in every society, says Mahoney, people invent and later reinvent the kinds of family patterns that "work" and make sense for them. Societies never stand still; cultures are forever shifting. Family is part of society and of culture. Citizens who are reinventing society and culture are also reinventing family at the same time.

Reinvention of family is an ongoing, never-ending thing. Reinvention demands that people face complex sets of challenges that never seem to let up. During the ongoing reinvention, people invariably make mistakes. They get it wrong, they stumble. But then they start over again and try to get it right. Very often the parents and children doing the reinventing hurt themselves, and sometimes they hurt one another.

But in most cases they don't intend to. People hope to reinvent and be responsible at the same time.

And sometimes, they do get it right—the reinvention of family works! At least for a while. And when it works, people are pleased and wish they could finally cease reinventing. That's how most North Americans felt during the late 1940s and the 1950s. After centuries of struggling to get it right, they'd finally invented the Modern Family for modern times, and it seemed ideal.[2] Following the gigantic upheavals of World War II, America stood astride the world politically and economically. Internally, North America invented a new society of suburbs and freeways, and prosperity for everyone—that is, for almost everyone who was white and male and had a high-school diploma. People who were poor, or black, or Hispanic, or Native American, didn't have it so good. And many white women were afflicted by a strange malady: Betty Friedan called it "the problem that has no name."[3] After a while, some of the people who didn't have it so good got restless and started trying to reinvent society all over again. During the 1960s they were joined by some young white men who'd had it pretty good but felt the need to reinvent anyhow.[4]

Alongside trying to change many aspects of American society, they also began to reinvent family. The hope that the 1950s' family marked the climax of hundreds of years of reinvention was false, and they realized it. "The times they are a-changing," sang Bob Dylan in the sixties. Among the things that have kept on changing ever since is family.

Family change worries many citizens, as in fact it always has.[5] Turn on the television and we hear about family "breakdown, decay, collapse, disappearance, decline, disorganization," and worse. We also learn that family, and especially its children, are in "crisis." What to do? Many solutions are offered. Among the most prominent is to resurrect what some citizens believe was the Golden Age of the Family—the 1950s.[6] But that's an impossible dream.

By contrast, asserts Mahoney, the twenty-first century calls for creative thinking that looks forward—not backward. The task ahead of us, she says, is to think up new ideas and fresh ways to reinvent family. During the past thirty years of reinvention, mistakes have been made—many adults and children have suffered and indeed are suffering now. But the Golden Age family had its own share of suffering. Reinvention can never totally eliminate hard times. Nevertheless, people keep on trying to make life better and that, after all, is what reinvention is all about. People must live in family, and so they try to make it the very best they can. And as they try to make it better, most people want to be responsible to themselves, to the adults and children who are with them in family, and to their community.

This book is about reinventing family—about how difficult it is to reinvent and be responsible at the same time. Reinventing responsible families is part of a much broader theme that concerns growing numbers of today's sociologists. Many sociologists want to study how people go about changing all aspects of their society.[7] Sociologists want to discover the social conditions that help and/or hinder people as they engage in continual struggles to reinvent society, including family. And sociologists want to investigate how people's struggles impact on what's known as the *social fabric*, or the *public household*.[8] In plain English, how do people's reinventions harm themselves or others in their community and society? How might people's reinventions be beneficial?

One example of what some might call a reinvention that concerns just about everyone is the practice of adolescents having babies. Does this growing trend harm or help the social fabric? Or is it neutral? How responsible are these young women and men being to themselves? How responsible to their offspring? And how responsible to others who must help care for them and their offspring? These questions are tough because the solutions are so complex.

This book is full of tough questions like this for which there are no pat answers. My hope is that students will grapple with the questions and debate their complex solutions both in and out of class. And as they do so, my further hope is that they will come to view contemporary sociology as a stimulating and exciting intellectual pursuit. At the same time, I hope just as strongly that the intellectual debates will translate into practical, everyday behaviors. This book is designed to assist students in reinventing family for the twenty-first century—reinventing it, moreover, in a fashion that benefits not merely themselves, but the social fabric as well.

I am deeply indebted to the many colleagues and friends who at various times have engaged me in discussion or in vigorous debate over one or more of the ideas of this book, and thus contributed greatly to it. These include: Joanne Aldous, Joyce Arditti, Pauline Boss, Peter Carter, Deborah D. Godwin, Jay Gubrium, Mary Joyce Hasell, Nancy Kingsbury, David Klein, Ralph LaRossa, Gary Lee, Geoffrey Leigh, William Marsiglio, David Mitchell, Karen Polonko, Rose Rivers, Hyman Rodman, David Scanzoni, Constance Shehan, Jetse Sprey, Gordon Streib, Jay Teachman, Linda Thompson, and many others too numerous to mention. In addition, I would like to express my thanks for the many useful comments and suggestions provided by the following reviewers: Benigno E. Aguirre, Texas A & M University; Lee K. Frank, Community College of Allegheny County; Karen Hossfeld, San Francisco State University; Jan E. Mutchler, State University of New York at Buffalo; Ellen Rosengarten, Sinclair Community College; and Roger H. Rubin, University of Maryland.

It goes without saying that apart from the dedicated and talented staff at McGraw-Hill this book would never have come into being!

Many thanks are due Jill Gordon (sponsoring editor), Robert Greiner (editing supervisor and proofreader), Sheila H. Gillams (editing supervisor), Richard Ausburn (production supervisor), Anne Manning (photo researcher), Leslie Reindl (copyeditor), and Caroline Iannuzzo (front matter editor), for their tireless efforts on behalf of this project.

Finally, last but really first, I am grateful to the many students in scores of classes who over the years have remained a constant source of stimulation and correction. The lively classroom discussions generated by earlier drafts of this book were gratifying indeed. My hope is that instructors and students will have as much satisfaction in using it as I've had in writing it!

John Scanzoni

NOTES

1. Mahoney, Margaret E. 1986. Cited in *Work and Family Responsibilities: Achieving a Balance.* New York: Ford Foundation, 1989, p. 3; italics added.   2. Bell and Vogel, 1960.   3. Friedan, 1963.   4. Gitlin, 1987. 5. Mintz and Kellogg, 1988, pp. 177ff.   6. Ibid.   7. Alexander, 1988. 8. Bell, 1990; Etzioni, 1991; Avineri and De-Shalit, 1992.

CONTEMPORARY FAMILIES AND RELATIONSHIPS

Reinventing Responsibility

PART ONE

CENTRAL IDEAS

CHAPTER 1

INTRODUCTION: WHAT THIS BOOK IS ABOUT

A GREAT DEBATE

In August 1993, the *Journal of Marriage and Family* featured a lively debate called "The decline of the American family." Marilyn Coleman, the journal's editor, said that the debate had three sides.[1] On one side, David Popenoe claimed that since 1960, "people have become less willing to invest time, money, and energy in family life, turning instead to investments in themselves. Recent family decline is . . . serious . . . because what is breaking up is the nuclear family. . . ."[2] In support of that viewpoint, Norval Glenn adds that "much of Popenoe's account of family decline is undeniably correct."[3]

Judith Stacey places herself at the opposite extreme from Popenoe and Glenn by saying, "Good riddance to 'the family.'"[4] She adds that Bill Clinton, like George Washington, was reared by a single parent and that that fact "provides an excellent opportunity to end the scapegoating of unconventional families."[5] She argues that we should "bury the ideology of 'the family' and . . . rebuild a social environment in which diverse family forms can sustain themselves with dignity and mutual respect."[6]

The third voice in this debate is Philip Cowan's, "whose perspective falls somewhere in between" the two extremes.[7] Cowan disagrees with Popenoe that persons are no longer interested in "family making. I see men and women struggling hard . . . to make decent families."[8] Cowan adds that a big reason people find family making so difficult is because of "great political, economic, and social barriers to the creation of a child- and family-focused life."[9]

In spite of their genuine differences, all three sides agree on one central theme: During the 1990s and beyond, it is hard work to achieve "effective" families (places where primary human needs are being met), and all sides agree that many of today's families do not achieve that goal. Nevertheless, they disagree sharply on how to do so, their disagreement revolving around what it means to be "responsible."

Interestingly enough, Daniel Yankelovich's research turned up these same three view-

Process-oriented	Majority	Fixed-philosophy
20%	60%	20%

FIGURE 1-1   A Continuum of Three Perspectives on Families
The range is measured by the approximate proportions of U.S. citizens holding each viewpoint. (*Adapted from Yankelovich, 1981; Francoeur, 1983; and Coleman, 1993.*)

points as early as the 1970s.[10] Figure 1-1 shows that he, along with others, found some 20 percent of the U.S. population held what Robert Francoeur calls a "fixed-philosophy" outlook. These citizens are "conservative in their cultural outlook, oriented to preserving the 'good old days.'"[11] Like Popenoe and Glenn, Yankelovich, Francoeur, and Coleman believe that the American family of yesteryear is in decline. To reverse the decline (Popenoe says it began around 1960), they argue that adults should behave more *responsibly*. "Behaving responsibly" means doing what people used to do before the family fell into its alleged decline. People, says Popenoe, should start investing more "time, money, and energy in family life," and invest less "in themselves."[12] Examples of investing in family life would include, but not be limited to, the following: People should stop having sex—and especially stop having babies—outside of marriage. And people should get married; they should stop living together if they're not married. And they should have children. And parents should put the well-being of their children ahead of their own interests. Among other things, that means that mothers of preschoolers should stay home and take care of their children. And married couples with resident children should not divorce.

At the other end of the Figure 1-1 continuum, is another 20 percent of the population that Francoeur labels "process-oriented." These citizens hold viewpoints similar to Stacey's. They "were deeply and openly com-

mitted to the emerging new person-oriented values. . . . [But they] often agonize over their commitment to the quest for self-fulfillment in an ever-changing world."[13] These people want to "invest in themselves" (self-fulfillment) but they want to do so in a *responsible* manner. For them, "responsible" means *helping* (and not hurting) their partner (whether spouse, cohabitor, boy/girlfriend), children, parents, or other family members. It means investing in others *and* in oneself at the same time. Francoeur shows that whether or not people in the "process" camp are actively religious, they take seriously the Judeo-Christian precept, "Thou shalt love thy neighbor as thyself." That is, one should not love one's neighbor (partner, parent, children) *more* than oneself. Underlying this idea are two assumptions. First, anyone who doesn't love and take care of herself or himself doesn't have much to give to others. Second, the most reasonable way to overcome people's selfishness and irresponsibility is to create situations where people feel cared for at the same time that they are caring.

Critics in the "fixed" camp charge that works fine for adults, but what about children who don't have the emotional and economic wherewithal to take care of the adults in their lives? People in the "process" camp are very sensitive to that criticism and that's why they "agonize" over being responsible to themselves as well as to others—especially children. For example, some husbands refuse to allow their wives to seek outside employment.[14] But very often the wife (let's call her Cindy) believes she needs a job to "feel good" about herself. And the extra money, she thinks, would help out with their children's expenses. Cindy has tried long and hard to work out a compromise with her spouse, but he's adamant: "A mother belongs at home with her children." What is the responsible thing for her to do? She believes that if she continues to stay home, she'll feel worse and worse about herself. That, she reasons, would make her an ineffective mother and wife. So she goes out and gets a part-time job. Her husband is so furious that he threatens to leave unless she quits. She doesn't, and he does.

How does Cindy feel about herself now? Her husband has walked out on her, and her children now have fewer household dollars than before she went to work. She doesn't like being alone, and she's sorry her children don't have a resident father. Nonetheless, Cindy does feel better about herself than she did before. She also feels that she's a better parent even though she has less money and spends less time with her children. She defines herself as behaving in a way that's responsible both to herself and her children. She's upset that her husband doesn't share her definition. Quite the contrary—he charges she's being irresponsible. But she countercharges that he is the irresponsible one by not "allowing" her to work outside the home. Who's right? Who's wrong? Citizens in the fixed category of Figure 1-1 would tend to say he's right. Those in the process category would tend to say she is.

And what do citizens say who are found in what Francoeur calls the "majority" (60%) category of Figure 1-1? For these citizens, according to Francoeur, "Self-fulfillment with the freedom to choose from many options and lifestyles is . . . a reality. Although they worry about the death of old values and goals, they question these traditions and wonder where to draw the line."[15] Hence, these citizens might tend to say he's right, but if they were in Cindy's situation they'd behave just like her. Francoeur concludes that the majority of citizens are uneasy and anxious because throughout their lives they experience a great deal of tension between what they *believe* and how they *behave*. What they believe is much closer to the fixed than to the process position. By contrast, how they behave is much closer to the process than to the fixed position.

One need look no further than parents of today's adolescents to spot the paradox. When

they themselves were adolescents and young adults, most 1990s' parents were sexually active, that is, they were violating the cultural norm that unmarried persons should refrain from sexual intercourse. Further, some of today's parents may be sexually active right now with someone othe than their current spouse. In particular, parents who are separated or divorced from their spouse, or who were never married, are very likely to be sexually active. But in spite of their past and/or present sexual behaviors, research evidence indicates that the vast majority of today's parents do not speak candidly with their adolescents regarding their own or their adolescents' sexuality.[16] And needless to say, few parents endorse adolescent sexual activity. At most, parents tacitly communicate the ideas that, "I hope you're not having sex; but if you are I really don't want to know about it; and if you are please protect yourself from getting AIDS or getting in trouble."

THE DEBATE THROUGHOUT RECENT HISTORY

It turns out that many citizens have worried about family changes long before now. Over 200 years ago, one of the first things that puzzled social observers as West European societies began to industrialize was family change. Childbearing was a striking example of change. Families that moved to the cities to work in factories and businesses had fewer children than families remaining in the countryside. Many more changes surfaced toward the end of the nineteenth century when researchers discovered that, compared with rural folk, urban dwellers not only had fewer children, they also experienced more divorce, alcoholism, poverty, violence, and juvenile delinquency.[17]

Many citizens became alarmed at trends that, in their view, demonstrated that people were becoming irresponsible. Researchers began to study urban families to find out what was "going wrong." Social workers and counselors began to try to help families. From the anxieties felt by citizens regarding what was happening to families sprang "family sociology."[18]

From the onset of those alarms and worries, women's alleged selfishness and irresponsibility were viewed with considerable ambivalence and suspicion.[19] By the end of the nineteenth century, feminism had been a vocal social movement both in the United States and parts of Europe for almost a hundred years.[20] A number of social critics believed that feminism and industrialization fed on one another, leading to the irresponsible patterns springing up around them. Mostly, the critics complained that as women were getting jobs, they were having fewer children and more divorces. They viewed these trends as bad for the family in general, and as especially harmful to children.

And today? Probably everyone agrees (no matter where they're located on the Figure 1-1 continuum) that relationships and families aren't what they used to be—they're very difficult for both children and adults. But what to do about it depends a lot on what social scientists call "theoretical perspective."

OLD ACTION THEORY—PRESERVING THE FAMILY

People on the "fixed" side of Figure 1-1 tend to hold a perspective known as *structural-functionalism*.[21] Jeffrey Alexander calls it "old action theory."[22] One of the ideas of old action theory is that society has norms, or rules of behavior, that are necessary to have a good society. A few paragraphs ago I referred to the norm that people should have sex solely within marriage. The "action" (or behavior) comes about when people conform to the norm—they do what they're *supposed* to do. And if people do what they should, then society is better off. In the current welfare reform debate, a lot of politi-

cians and citizens are saying that if couples would wait until marriage to have sex and babies, and also stay married, then they'd never have to live off taxpayers and run up the national debt.[23]

Sociologists who are functionalists believe that certain norms get clustered together and form what they call "institutions." The family, they say, is an *institution* made up of certain norms that are bound up with the norm telling people when to have sex. Some of these clustered norms are: one should marry, one should have children, one should not divorce, and so on.

The next logical step in functionalist theory is that institutions do good things for society, called "functions." For example, the family is an institution that controls sex and produces new recruits for society. Functionalists add that the family then trains (i.e., "socializes") infants and children to fit into society. In short, functionalists believe that when the family does these *core functions*, it contributes to a good and healthy society.

Both Popenoe and Glenn worry about the "recent decrease in how well the family is performing its core functions."[24] For example, if unwed women have babies or if married women get divorced, no father is around to be a male role model for the children. Or if there are two adults in the household but they're both employed, then they don't pay enough attention to their children, especially if they send their preschoolers to daycare. And if solo parenthood and dual-earner parenthood hurt children, then society will hurt as well. During 1993–1994, for example, politicians were talking a lot about violent crime and blaming it in part on "family breakdown." In other words, the family is no longer doing its core functions for society such as training children to respect authority and obey the law.

Defining the Nuclear Family When functionalists define the family, or what Norman Bell and Ezra Vogel called the "nuclear" fam-

The Nuclear Family—also described as the Modern Family. In North America it remains as the benchmark against which the many emerging varieties of household and family arrangements are measured.

ily, they usually mean the "sexually exclusive, legally sanctioned married couple that lives together [with their children] in a joint household."[25] Sandra Hofferth coined the term *Benchmark* to describe how most citizens (fixed and majority in Figure 1-1) feel about the nuclear family.[26] A benchmark is like the ultimate yardstick that the U.S. government keeps at the Bureau of Standards in Washington, D.C. Someone comparing her warped ruler with the ultimate yardstick discovers that hers is only 35 and 31/32 inches long. Alas, her yardstick is simply not as good as the ultimate! In similar fashion, numerous studies report that most U.S. citizens believe it's *better* to live in

the Benchmark Family than any other way.[27] On the basis of her research, Canadian sociologist Dorothy Smith uses the label "Standard North American Family" (SNAF) to capture the same idea.[28] If something is the "standard," it's like a benchmark against which other things are measured. And by definition, the standard must be the best. And the chief reason many believe that the Benchmark Family is best is because of the core functions it does for society.

But asserting that the Benchmark is actually better than, say, a solo-parent family, or a family with two employed adults, or a cohabiting family, is open to question, a question that is considered repeatedly throughout this book. S. B. Taubin and E. H. Mudd remarked that when a huge bronze sculpture of a family group—nudes of a mother, father, daughter, son—was placed in a downtown Philadelphia street, a local art critic praised it as "a moral statement, a celebration of the family." The critic quickly added, however, that the sculpture also conveys a "disquieting element" because it implies that other varieties of families may be "less than ideal . . . less acceptable."[29]

NEW ACTION THEORY—
REINVENTING FAMILIES

Your college adviser tells you that you need a suit for your job interview. So you go to a store that advertises, "One size suit fits all!" But when you try the suit on, it doesn't quite fit. Perhaps it's a bit tight there, or too big here, or the pants are too short, or the sleeves too long. Perhaps you don't like the color, or the cut. But no matter; you must have a suit so you buy it anyhow, and you work very hard to change yourself (e.g., lose or gain weight) to make it fit.

But suppose instead you visit a tailor, and together you and she construct a suit made precisely for you. The material, the color, the cut, and especially the size are exactly what you want. Now you feel comfortable—and you're ready for that job interview. The contrast between conforming to a suit that's handed to you, versus creating your own suit, is one way to illustrate an important distinction between *old* action theory and *new* action theory. According to Alexander, and many other contemporary social scientists, new action theory is all about people's behaviors in constructing fresh ways of doing things, including creating families.[30]

Everyone agrees with Mahoney that people can't get along without families.[31] But she adds that people are struggling to *reinvent* families, and most try to do so in a responsible manner.

Cowan calls it "family-making."[32] Unlike suits, there is never a "final-product" family. You can't ever stand back and admiringly say, "It's done!" "If it ain't broke, don't fix it," goes the old saw. But it seems that many of today's citizens are tinkering with families in hopes somehow making them work better, and like Cindy, they're discovering that the task is very difficult and often painful. But they keep on struggling because *they're trying to make life better for themselves and the people they care about.* Families and relationships are after all social patterns that people created in the first place. And because people constructed those patterns, people can keep on changing them if they wish. Or if they want to preserve those patterns just the way they are, that's okay too. The point is that people have choices—they can fit themselves anywhere they wish on the many points along the entire Figure 1-1 continuum.

But someone once quipped that sociology is all about people *not* having choices. Functionalists, for instance, say that children are socialized into certain norms. They learn what they're supposed to do from parents, teachers, and clergy. And when they're adults, they should do what they've learned. Alongside cultural restaints on choices, other sociologists say that the *structure* of society severely limits people's choices. For instance, how can Andrea—who grows up in poverty and is physically abused by her mother and sexually abused by her mother's boyfriend, and whose neighborhood is filled with violent drug dealers and sleazy pimps, and who attends an inferior school where the boys continually harrass her—choose to attend and graduate from university? Don't the structural conditions that surround her pressure her into following her mother's example? At age 16 a high-school dropout and an unmarried mother receiving welfare?

Sociologists who are *new* action therorists pay close attention to cultural and structural constraints on people's choices. But they also

A large part of reinventing families revolves around men's behaviors. For example, although the majority of solo parents are women, some men such as Rick Smith, a solo parent with custody, gets Ashley, 5, and Holland, 8, off to school every morning before he goes to work.

believe that we should study people like Andrea. Sometimes people in her social circumstances do in fact "make it." How come? New action theorists want to find out how people struggle "to try to make life better" within the context of their life circumstances.[33] How, for instance, does a dual-employed, working-class couple decide who's going to take the kids to daycare, or to youth soccer practice? Or who's going to scrub toilets or vacuum floors?

New action theorists also pay a lot of attention to how people's struggles might change the cultural and structural conditions that surround them. For example, during the late 1980s and early 1990s, people in the Soviet Union and Eastern Europe struggled to rid themselves of oppressive communist regimes. Although they succeeded beyond anyone's imagination in changing their societies, many now don't like what they got—high inflation and unemployment, and a lot less economic security than they had before. So are they going back to the old ways? No one can be sure, but it doesn't seem likely. What seems more certain is that as they try to make life better they're going to continue struggling and thus changing, perhaps in ways that they never expected.

PLAN OF THE BOOK

Part One connects some of the key ideas of new action theory with the study of families. In doing so it supplies the foundation for the remainder of the book. Chapters 2 and 3, for example, force us to think carefully about what we mean by the term *family*. These two chapters discuss families beyond the nuclear family, families that may include quite a number of relatives and/or friends. Chapters 4 and 5 narrow the focus to two-person groups, called "dyads." Sometimes dyads can be described as just friends. At other times, dyads are what Chapter 5 calls erotic friends. These latter couples, in contrast to just friends, are said to have a "relationship." In sum, Part One shows how some people are trying to reinvent families that include a number of persons, who often reside in several households. And it also talks about how some people are struggling to redefine sexuality, and to reinvent two-person families (i.e., dyads). And it describes the difficulties in trying to do those things in a responsible manner.

Part Two provides a brief historical perspective on families. Chapters 6 and 7 trace the reinvention of families that has been occurring during the last 200 years. Families of the past were not static entities, and these chapters trace some of the paths that have led to where we are today. Chapter 7 pays particular attention to the 1960s—the decade that Popenoe and others claim ushered in the decline of the nuclear family.

Part Three discusses a number of contemporary examples of how people are struggling to reinvent relationships and families, often responsibly, sometimes not. These examples include redefinitions of singleness, and the spread of cohabitation (also known as "informal marriage"). Part Three also makes the point that living in nuclear families does not make persons automatically responsible to their partners and/or children. Perhaps the chief example of that reality is how much physical violence and sexual abuse occurs within many North American families.

Finally, Part Four connects people's struggles to reinvent and be responsible with public policies. One reason we pay close attention to how people's struggles might change society is that we see a close fit between research and public policy. For example, if Andrea does make it, let's find out why and then create a fresh set of cultural and structural conditions that might help other women and men to make it too.[34]

Social research is similar to most biological research. Probably every biologist believes that she or he could help make life better by discovering a cure for cancer, or a vaccine against the HIV virus that causes AIDS. And what do social scientists believe? We believe that we help to make life better by helping people construct effective families. An "effective" family (meeting primary human needs) benefits not only its members but society as well. Achieving that social goal requires changes in public policies. For instance, as part of its goal to reduce cancer, the federal government during the 1960s began antismoking programs. And as part of their goal to control AIDS, some government officials publicize the idea of "safe sex" and distribute free condoms.

What changes in public policies throughout North America would help bring about effective families? Although Chapter 18 considers this question in detail, every chapter is to one degree or another tied to it. *Every chapter approaches families from the viewpoint of new action theory.* Each chapter wants to know: What are people doing to construct, that is, reinvent, their families? Their relationships? Whether the topic is employment, or relatives, or money, or heterosexuality and homosexuality, or housework, or marriage, or singleness, or problem-solving and negotiation, or cohabitation, or rape and violence, or children, or aging, or whatever—the basic question is, *How are people trying to create families?* Moreover, how effective are those families? How do cultural and structural conditions help or hinder their efforts? Answering this last query speaks to the paragraph's first question: Changing public policies to help people make effective families requires serious rethinking of

Participation in extended families—a series of households connected by blood ties—is very much a part of the lives of most present-day Japanese.

surrounding cultural and structural conditions.[35]

DIVERSITIES AMONG FAMILIES

Contained within the idea of people constructing families is the notion of *diversity*. People have the option, at varying points throughout their life courses, of creating different kinds of families besides the Benchmark Nuclear Family. African-Americans, for instance, have for a long time constructed what Chapters 2 and 3 call "social families." And people in different social classes (upper, upper-middle, middle, working, and lower) have also created families that are not merely carbon copies of one another. In addition, the families of Hispanics are not identical to those of Anglos or blacks. And recently, researchers have begun paying attention to families constructed by gays and lesbians.[36] Moreover, there are many distinctions between families in North America and, say, families in Latin America, or Africa, or the Pacific Islands.

When sociologists talk about Western societies or the West, they generally mean North America and European countries such as Great Britain, France, Germany, Italy, the Scandinavian lands, and so on. Although there are many important differences among them, they are all heavily industrialized. Some sociologists add that, culturally speaking, they are "modern" societies. According to Daniel Bell, modern societies value individual self-fulfill-

Youngsters participate in a demonstration to show support for Ayatollah Ruholla Khomeini in Qom, Iran's holy city.

ment, that is, individualism.[37] Persons holding the process view in Figure 1-1 are said to be highly individualistic. But their critics (persons holding the fixed view) often charge them with having no sense of duty or obligation to others. By contrast to Western societies, Japan is an example of a powerful industrial society that resists the label "modern."[38] In Japan, obligations to one's group (whether family or occupation) tend to take precedence over the idea of taking care of oneself.

David Cheal adds that modern societies also tend to be characterized by "struggles for emancipation of oppressed and disadvan-

taged groups."[39] For 200 years, some Western women have defined themselves as oppressed, and have struggled for greater self-fulfillment and individual rights. By contrast, Japanese feminists are a tiny minority, and not politically powerful.[40] In the same vein, many Americans were astonished by 1991 TV Gulf War coverage of Saudi Arabia revealing that women, no matter how well educated, were not allowed to drive! Some Saudi women may view themselves as oppressed and disadvantaged. But as yet there is no evidence that they're struggling for emancipation. Even though Saudi Arabia has great wealth, and even though the capital city Riyadh is an urban center, and even though the society may be industrializing, we would not consider Saudi Arabia to be a modern society. This book primarily targets families in modern societies, and looks at diversities among them. We are particularly interested in the differences between North America and, say, Scandinavian societies such as Sweden. At the same time, we pay attention to cultural differences between the West and industrial societies such as Japan.

Today, most sociologists believe it's impossible to understand Western families and their diversities without grasping what *gender* is all about.[41] Gender is a social category like race and social class. Hence, men are different from women in more than just the obvious biological ways. Both as children and adults the genders face sharply different life experiences, analogous to the contrasting experiences of blacks and whites, or of upper- and lower-class persons. Men's and women's divergent life experiences mean that they often approach the reinvention of families in very different ways.

Labels such as "gender" and "feminism" sometimes cause discomfort and uneasiness. Part of the problem is that we're not always certain what the labels mean even though they appear frequently in the mass media. Recently, Pulitzer Prize winner Anna Quindlen tried to sort out the meanings of feminism in a way that would make sense for the majority of citizens: "Feminism is no longer a group of organizations or leaders. It's the expectations that parents have for their daughters, and their sons, too. It's the way we talk about and treat one another. It's who makes the money and who makes the compromises and who makes the dinner. It's a state of mind. *It's the way we live now.*"[42]

During the late 1960s and early 1970s, when the idea of family diversity was first seeping into the consciousness of many North Americans, Herbert Otto asked a question that's even more relevant today than it was back then: "To what extent does the American family structure contribute to the optimum development of the human potential of its members?"[43] That is *not* a functionalist type of question. Instead it is a new action theory kind of question. Otto wanted to know how families help people help themselves. He assumed that the more people are helped, the better off society will be. This book assumes the same idea. The following pages try to help us figure out how society can help people reinvent effective families that in turn make for better socieites.

METHODS OF RESEARCH ABOUT FAMILIES

Researchers studying families get their information in many different ways. One of the most widely used methods is the *sample survey*. For example, in the Yankelovich survey described previously, researchers drew a sample of respondents that was as representative as possible of the entire U.S. population in terms of, say, education, income, age, gender, race, urban/rural residence, and so on. Next, an interviewer asked (either by telephone or in a face-to-face setting) each respondent to answer a sequence of carefully worded (standardized) questions regarding her or his norms and behaviors. Finally, each respondent's answers were tabulated either into percentages (as in Figure 1-1) or into more complex kinds of statistics. The following chapters frequently make use of percentages to show changes (or lack of them) over time in people's beliefs and behaviors regarding families. Sample surveys belong to what is called a *quantitative* approach to social research.

In addition, the following chapters also make use of what's known as a *qualitative* approach. Researchers using these approaches pay less attention to carefully worded questions and statistics than they do to unraveling "what's actually going on" in particular social situations. For example, these researchers believe that to help people such as Andrea to make it, we must understand her social situation from her standpoint. Doing that may require observing Andrea at school or home, and it may also demand what are called *in-depth* interviews. Unlike standardized interviews, the interviewer is free to explore in detail the twisting paths that might emerge in the course of talking with the respondent. In Andrea's case, for instance, one might ask, "What's it like to be bombarded by TV commercials about material success and yet be surrounded by so much deprivation and poverty?" Some researchers use the label "case study" as a general means to describe the many different styles of qualitative research.[44] By that label, they mean that in order to figure out what's going on, we must target "cases" such as Andrea as well as other women and men in similar circumstances.

There is no one best way to study the reinvention of families. Most researchers agree that if at all possible, both quantitative and qualitative approaches should be utilized at the same time. Because sample surveys and case studies complement each other, both should be used in trying to figure out, for example, why some deprived adolescents "make it" and some don't.

NOTES

1. Marilyn Coleman, 1993, p. 525.
2. Popenoe, 1993, p. 527.
3. Glenn, 1993, p. 543.
4. Stacey, 1993, p. 545.
5. Ibid., p. 547.
6. Ibid.
7. Coleman, p. 525.
8. Philip Cowan, 1993, p. 550.
9. Ibid.
10. Yankelovich, 1981.
11. Francoeur, 1983, p. 381.
12. Popenoe, p. 527.
13. Francoeur, p. 381.
14. Scanzoni, 1978.
15. Francoeur, pp. 381–382.
16. Nathanson, 1991.
17. Mintz and Kellogg, 1988.
18. Ronald Howard, 1981; Bahr, Wang, and Zhang, 1991.
19. Mintz and Kellogg.
20. William O'Neill, 1967.
21. Merton, 1957; Kingsbury and Scanzoni, 1993; Stacey, p. 545.
22. Jeffrey Alexander, 1988.
23. Kimberly J. McLarin, *The New York Times*, December 9, 1993, p. A14.
24. Glenn, p. 544.
25. Buunk and van Driel, 1989, p. 19. See also Bell and Vogel, 1960, p. 1.
26. Hofferth, 1985.
27. Montgomery, 1988; Yankelovich; Ganong, Coleman, and Mapes, 1990.
28. Dorothy Smith, 1993.
29. Taubin and Mudd, 1983, p. 258.
30. Jeffrey Alexander; Jonathon Turner, 1988; Ralph Turner, 1962, 1985; Ira Cohen, 1989. Alexander argues that what he means by "new action theory" includes a wide range of perspectives such as symbolic interaction, exchange, conflict, ethnomethodology, critical and feminist theories, and so forth. Walter Buckley (1967) used the term *process theories* to distinguish the thread that is common to those several perspectives vis-a-vis functionalism.
31. Mahoney, 1986. See note 3 in the Preface to this book.
32. Cowan, 1993.
33. Warren Brown and Waln Brown, 1991.
34. Cowan, 1993.
35. Stacey.
36. Weston, 1991.
37. Daniel Bell, 1990.
38. Condon, 1985; Kondo, 1990. Other Asian countries in this category include Taiwan, People's Republic of China, Singapore, and Malaysia.
39. Cheal, 1991.
40. Bornoff, 1991.
41. Scanzoni and Marsiglio, 1993.
42. Anna Quindlen, "And Now, Babe Feminism," *The New York Times*. January 19, 1994, p. A19. Italics added.
43. Otto, 1970, pp. 4–5.
44. Feagin, Orum, and Sjoberg (eds.), 1991.

CHAPTER 2

FAMILIES WE CHOOSE

If there are many different varieties of families, how can we identify what is "family" and what isn't? The goal of this chapter is to help us answer that question. During the Middle Ages, researchers searched diligently for a substance called "phlogiston." They believed that phlogiston inhabited anything that burned. Its absence, they thought, was the reason rocks didn't burn. During that same period, alchemists hunted for the elusive formula that could turn copper and other metals into gold. Today, some men and women are scouring the ice flows of Turkey's Mount Ararat for the remains of Noah's ark. *Contemporary Sociology*, the official book review journal of the American Sociological Association, published a set of reviews about recent studies of families. In commenting on the reviews, one sociologist said, "These authors make clear that we are now dealing with the sociology of families rather than family sociology."[1]

But what are families? What are *not* families? How can we tell the difference? In response to a reporter's question probing why his team was so successful, the quarterback said, "Hey, man, this is my family!" What does

he mean? Watching the team in action, we notice that every time the team scores a touchdown the players laugh, hug, and jump on each other, and especially on the guy who scored. Since laughter, hugging, embracing, and patting behinds are behaviors associated with families, does that make the team a family?

Soldiers returning from combat zones are asked how they managed to survive. "My family got me through," they say. What does that mean? Civilians seldom, if ever, think of families as a way to help survive combat. Why do soldiers feel that way? How could the life-and-death struggles of combat have anything in common with the glitz of big-time sports? And then the TV News switches to an account of a 30-year-old man with a history of physical abuse who shoots and kills his wife, their two young children, and her parents. The reporter says the incident occurred because as the man beat up the children his wife ran to get a gun. But he wrested it from her and started shooting. None of us likes to imagine that murderous violence is part of families. Nevertheless, the reporter goes on to talk about recent in-

Embracing, team members exclaim, "These guys are my *family!*"

creases in family murders in the United States. And in the next scene, that same reporter is interviewing a neighbor who alleges, "They weren't a 'real' family anyhow. They never did anything together. . . . Whenever he was home he was always knocking them about, and most of the time the kids lived with her parents."

DEFINING "FAMILIES"

What *is* a real family? Will the real family please stand up? Does a *real* family exclude situations where the husband abuses the wife and children? What about when the woman abuses the children? Can that be a family? Is a sports team or combat unit a family? How about a sorority or fraternity? Why do the members call each other brothers and sisters? Can a lone-parent household be a real family? What about a homosexual household? In a recent national survey, 75 percent of Americans

agreed with the statement that "a family is a group of people who love and care for each other."[2] By that definition the neighbor is correct—the abusing household would not be a family.

But how does that conclusion square with the classic definition of the family: "a group of people related by blood, marriage, or adoption"? Incidentally, 22 percent of Americans from that same survey selected the classic definition. But do abuse and violence actually sunder those legal and formal ties? And if the classic definition is valid, how can groups such as sports teams, combat units, sororities, and so on, be families? Do the sport and combat groups qualify as families because the love and caring identified by 75 percent of Americans are more important than the connection by blood or marriage?

Social Families in a Women's Factory

In her 1960s study of a federal women's prison, Rose Giallombardo was curious how women survived the ordeal and indignities of being deprived of their liberty.[3] Although men's prisons had often been studied, not much was known about women's prisons. Giallombardo became interested in women's prisons by reading about unmarried Chinese women factory workers.[4] According to Ju-K'ang T'ien, the women had to travel great distances to get to the centrally located factories. Once they arrived, they lived in onsite dormitories provided by management for as long as they remained workers. The women formed what T'ien called "imaginery" families. They used labels such as "mother," "father," "son," "daughter," "aunt," "stepmother," "second uncle," and "son/daughter-in-law" to describe the role relationships that they carried out among themselves. In the eyes of the outside world they were all unmarried women. Nevertheless, they viewed themselves and also behaved as if they were married and had children, or brothers, or resident parents, or resident kin such as uncles or in-laws.

In trying to figure out why those factory women formed imaginary families, Giallombardo pointed first to the social conditions under which they were living. The factory living arrangements had cut them off from their blood families for lengthy periods of time. No longer could they receive or give the affection, love, favors, help, material needs, loyalty, and support they'd experienced within their blood families. They no longer felt they belonged to a group they cared about, and that cared about them. They lacked the "interdependence . . . out of which a primary group is made."[5]

The term *interdependence* in Giallombardo's study refers simply to the *social exchanges* that the Chinese factory women had previously shared with their blood families. They were no longer giving and receiving things that were extremely important to them. Giallombardo described a *primary group* using an illustration from the noted philosopher Alfred North Whitehead. Whitehead remarked that trees in a forest require one another for the best possible development. Forest trees (along with forest animals) are "interdependent" with one another not merely for survival, but also for flourishing. No one tree or animal can survive very well by itself—it does its best in a situation of mutual giving and receiving of the things that all the creatures and trees need and want.

Similarly, the Chinese women living with their blood families were trees located in a forest that enabled them to survive and perhaps to flourish. Once transplanted to the factory, they lost their "forest." Thus, to survive and perhaps to flourish, the factory women had to create, or *reinvent*, their own patterns of social exchange. They had to think up new and innovative ways of giving and getting the things that mattered to them. Part of their construction was the labeling of certain women as "fathers," "daughters," "sons," and so on. A

woman worker who was a "father" behaved just like one, giving benefits to "his children." In turn, a "child" provided things to his or her "parents" that were important to them, such as affection, companionship, doing chores, and so on.

Social Families in a Women's Prison

Primary Groups   Giallombardo found comparable patterns among the women prisoners she studied. Having been forcibly ripped from the outside world, they created their own "substitute universe"—their own primary groups.[6] Since they'd been sentenced to "do time," the prisoners' uppermost concern, she says, was that the time be as tolerable, and perhaps pleasant, as possible under the circumstances. To make the time pleasant, new prisoners soon learned they had to become part of a primary group—a *family*. The primary group was, first, the only means to meet needs for emotional support and companionship. Second, it was the sole mechanism to get more than the meager allotment of material things (money, cigarettes, clothing, reading materials, personal items) doled out by the authorities. The family consisted of prisoners labeled as "fathers," "mothers," "daughters," "sons," and so on.

As in the Chinese factory, women prisoners had to behave according to their labeled role. The prison contained several different families of this sort. Families A, B, and C were social families. The members of each family maintained shared exchanges among themselves. Furthermore, family A members were discouraged from exchanging benefits with members of families B or C, and vice versa.[7]

Interestingly enough, some studies of blood families reveal the same thing.[8] Persons who belong to a particular blood family are often advised not to exchange certain benefits (e.g., money) with "outsiders." Family members are told not to incur social obligations to outsiders.

The idea is to try to avoid owing anything. The message is that, after all, "outsiders are not family."

Erotic Friendships Giallombardo described a number of dyadic (two-person) primary groups existing within each larger social family.[9] (T'ien didn't mention such a finding.) These were couples maintaining what Chapter 5 calls *erotic friendships*. Erotic friends can be either heterosexual or homosexual, but in this case, the relationships were necessarily homosexual. However, the wider family did not view them merely as girlfriend/girlfriend. They were perceived as married, and were assigned the roles of "husband" and "wife." In the prison Giallombardo studied, the husband and wife played the roles of the steoreotypical lesbian couple in extreme fashion. The stud or *butch* was identified by hairstyle, clothing, and boldily demeanor that let everyone in her social family, and in other families, know that she was the man. The *femme* adopted the kinds of outward symbols, including deference, that let everyone know she was "his woman."

Giallombardo's study was done during the early 1960s, and thus the prisoners copied the only everyday husband and wife behaviors they knew about, those of the nuclear families outside the prison. That was the world from which they had come, and to which most would eventually return. Research shows that heterosexual persons will sometimes engage in homosexual behaviors if they find themselves in a social setting that encourages it.[10] Giallombardo said that most of the women she studied were heterosexuals; before coming to prison they'd been interested only in men. And after leaving it, they would once again restrict their sexual interest to men. But for the time being, many of them were involved in prison "marriages." In those 1950s-style marriages, the "man" was expected to provide for and defend his woman. She was expected to "keep house" for him and, practically speaking, be his domestic servant. Sexually, "he" was expected to be the aggressor, she the more passive, coy, and reticent.

According to Giallombardo, the marriage of the two partners had many of the same features as a marriage in the outside world. First, it was based on public recognition. A couple was not legitimate unless their families approved of it. Once that approval was publicly accorded, everyone in the prison knew that Sandy and Jane were partners. Second, the prisoners adhered to a clear incest taboo. That is, persons in family A seldom picked brothers, sisters, first cousins, or parents be to their erotic friend. Such persons were not eligible to be their spouse. Instead, they picked a spouse from members of family B or C.

Third, partners held strong feelings of sexual jealousy and possessiveness, as well as norms of exclusivity and monogamy. Once Sandy and Jane got married, they were no longer supposed to "fool around." Most prisoners were highly suspicious of their partners if they spent a lot of time with any other prisoner with whom they might have either casual sex or an ongoing relationship. Giallombardo said that the way a prisoner defused that fear was to convince her partner that she was merely spending time with a "blood relative": "This is my sister. How could I have sex with her?"

Some prisoners did not wish to engage in homosexual behavior. Nevertheless, they did want to be part of a social family because of the benefits they could get in no other way. To walk that tightrope, the woman had to first adopt a wider family role (e.g., sister, brother, cousin). Second, she had to make it known to her family and to outsiders that she did not wish ever to play a husband/wife role. Usually, only short-term prisoners adopted this celibate option.

Giallombardo reported that one major difference from outside marriages of the 1950s was that prisoners placed considerably less importance on the idea of permanence. When one or both partners wanted out of their relationship, they got "divorced." It became publicly recognized that they were no longer erotic friends, that is, a couple. Although the roles (brother, mother, and so on) they played in their wider family remained quite constant, couples frequently changed "husbands" and "wives."[11]

African-Americans and Social Families

The peculiar environments of the factory and the prison were the catalysts for women to create their own social families—their primary groups. Sociologists use the label "macro-level" to identify the broader economic and political forces under which people live. The United States, for example, is a political democracy that follows a form of modified capitalism. China, on the other hand, is a communist state that is evolving toward a different brand of capitalism. Macro forces might also include the structure or framework of an organization such as the military, a factory, a university, or a prison.

It is well known that blacks have encountered vastly different economic and political (macro) conditions than have whites. The most drastic difference, of course, was slavery, followed by a stormy Reconstruction period. Next came the legal segregation and economic discrimination of Jim Crow laws. As Jim Crow disappeared, it was replaced by more subtle but nonetheless powerful informal patterns of racism.[12] Perhaps the most significant impact of the macro conditions for blacks was the way they limited the choices of black men. When white boys and men were learning to be what Jessie Bernard calls a "good provider," most black males were still in slavery.[13] After Emancipation, black women could get jobs as domestics, but except for sharecropping most black men were denied most other kinds of jobs.[14] Although working- and lower-class

white men faced many more difficulties than middle-class white men in being good providers, they never faced the same kinds of barriers to education and employment encountered by black men. Even though black men themselves believed they should provide material things to their families, and thus earn the respect that comes from being a good provider, the social conditions under which they lived made that goal very difficult.

If we think about it, the situation of African-Americans has in many respects been analogous to that of the Chinese factory workers and the prison inmates. The broader situation—the macro social conditions under which they lived—has kept them from giving and receiving benefits in ways they might prefer. And just as the factory workers and the inmates in response to their conditions created their own families, so blacks in response to their environment have created, or reinvented, theirs.

Black Reinvention What kinds of families did blacks create? What they constructed has been studied by many investigators.[15] Sue Jewell says that blacks constructed "unique family arrangements."[16] What was unique? Since blacks couldn't count consistently on the husband-father to be the good provider in the same sense whites could, they had to look elsewhere for economic survival. And survival often meant looking outside the confines of their own household.

Historians tell us that a "helping tradition" existed among Africans that persisted during slavery and continued beyond its end in 1865.[17] That tradition meant that persons felt obliged to help others beyond their own households and beyond their blood kin. Jewell states that during the century after slavery's end blacks constructed social families that spilled over household boundaries. Black churches often served as focal points for these families.[18]

For example, let us imagine ten apartments,

or what the Census Bureau calls "households." The households may be located in a number of different buildings scattered, say, over a 5-mile radius in a particular town or city. Some households may contain a man, woman, and children; others a woman and children; still others some differing combinations of genders and ages. Not all the persons in any one household are necessarily linked to each other by ties of blood, marriage, or adoption. For instance, some adults may be cohabiting; some children may not be biologically linked to any of the household adults. Similarly, some persons in one household may have a blood tie to one or more persons in another household, but most of the persons do not have blood ties across households. And even where blood ties exist, they tend not to be more significant than the social ties that are described in the following.

Social Exchange Processes Let's say that at least one adult woman from each of these households attends church X.[19] After a time, these women become friends. During the course of their ongoing mutual self-disclosure they talk about many things, including their everyday material needs as well as their needs for services such as babysitting or elderly personsitting.[20] For instance, they may discuss the fact that household 4 has come up short in meeting the current month's rent. But households 6, 7, and 10 have some dollars they can pool to make up 4's deficit. The month following, household 4 is able to meet the rent, but 7 lacks not only rent but also money for certain clothing needs. So households 4, 6, 10, and 2 provide additional rent dollars for 7. In addition, they canvas households 1, 3, 5, 8, and 9 for some of the needed clothing.

In a few weeks, household 3 finds itself short of food. Households 8 and 5 are able to bring groceries to 3, and someone in 3 learns that 5 needs to get one of its older members to

a physician on Friday. A person from household 3 then performs that service for 5. Household 8 needs a babysitter on Saturday, so yet another person from 3 supplies that service. Household 1 may lose its apartment, and several of the other households take in its various members until 1 can find new shelter. The giving and receiving of material and service needs, along with emotional needs, continues indefinitely among these ten households. Jewell describes these giving and receiving behaviors as processes of *social exchange*.[21] Similar kinds of exchange processes took place in the prison Giallombardo studied, and in the Chinese women's factory.

These ten households form a "mutual aid network," and a "social support system."[22] Quite apart from any official government program, the households provide an ongoing flow of emotional, material, and service needs to one another. Because no one household is quite able consistently to "make it" on its own, the ten bind together so that all can at least "get by." Within the broader social context of very difficult and stringent economic conditions, these households have forged their own family—family Y.

Studies by Carol Stack and many others indicate that over time certain households in these situations of mutual exchange indeed begin to define themselves as family.[23] Quite apart from any blood ties that may exist across households, persons in this kind of wider family begin to use kinship labels such as "sister," "brother," "mother," "child," and so on to describe their relationships.[24] R. Rivers and J. Scanzoni studied a social family of blacks consisting of five women and one man. One of their respondents said that " 'we are closer than blood relatives.' "[25] In the respondent's opinion, "being blood relatives does not guarantee personal closeness or help in time of need."

This is precisely the same thing that happened in the factory and prison. Because broader social conditions prevented workers and prisoners from *reproducing* the kinds of families they'd enjoyed previously (or in the case of blacks, learned about as cultural ideals), they *reinvented* families using familiar terms. Certain persons behaved *as if* they actually were an aunt, brother, uncle, son, and so on. As a result of acting *as if* they were one of those roles, over time they became defined by the label appropriate to it.

Comparing Black, Prison, and Factory Social Families   Jewell states that labels such as "restructuring," "fluidity," "fluctuation," "reshaping," and "malleability" characterize disadvantaged urban black families.[26] What does Jewell mean by those labels? If we think about factories and prisons, it's plain that resident workers and inmates hope their stay on the premises will be as brief as possible. They enter a social family while they're there, and most leave it afterward.[27] When we compare the factory and prison social families with black social families, we find two important similarities, but one major difference.

One similarity is found by looking at Rivers and Scanzoni's study of six households. Persons from additional households may over time become part of that family. There is no fixed limit regarding how many households may enter the social family. The family grows as material and emotional bonds are formed with additional households. If the family got too big for the social exchanges to be carried out effectively, however, current family members would probably not let any new households into the loop. In fact, Rivers reports that although some other persons in the community wanted "in" to the family, current members were not keen on it. They felt the family might get too big to provide the attention to material needs as well as emotional closeness that they now enjoyed.

A second similarity with prisons and factories is that a social family may also decline in size. Say that one household in the family consists of a cohabiting couple (Sheron and Brian) who are unemployed and living with her sister and the sister's child. After a while Sheron and Brian find jobs in a suburb a considerable distance from the part of the city in which their social family is located. They move to that suburb and gradually cease to exchange emotional and material benefits with their social family. Given enough time, Sheron and Brian are no longer close friends with their family members, and they don't give and receive any material and service benefits. The couple withdraws from the family, and the family shrinks in size.

Thus, when Jewell says that urban black families are malleable, and are being reshaped and restructured, she means their boundaries are continually expanding or contracting. At a certain point in time, household 7 (above) and Fran, its head, may be located in the exchange loop of family Y. Several years later she may no longer be in the loop, although other members of household 7 may still be in it. During that time another household (11) may have become part of the social family by entering the exchange loop.

A major difference between disadvantaged urban black families and families of resident workers and prisoners is that social conditions are not temporary for most urban blacks. Current econmic conditions make it extremely difficult for most blacks to escape to a comfortable suburb. Consequently, when Jewell says that black families are fluid—they "expanded and contracted as members, both [blood kin] and [non-blood kin], arrived and departed," the fluidity is not as great as for families in resident factories or women's prisons.[28] Blacks in family Y count on each other to "be there for them over the long haul" because most of them have neither alternative sources of benefits nor a viable option enabling them to exit their circumstances.

Comparisons with the Benchmark Nuclear Family

The overall image of disadvantaged urban black families that Jewell conveys is very different from the prevailing cultural image of the Benchmark Family. Jewell criticizes white social scientists who compare the social families of blacks with the Benchmark Family and conclude that because these families lack formal ties of marriage and/or blood, they are somehow not as "good."[29] Comparing social families with benchmark families is like comparing bananas with cucumbers—they're very different. And one is not necessarily any better or worse than the other.

Most U.S. whites conceive of the family as encompassed within the boundaries of a single household in one physical dwelling unit.[30] If pushed, whites may acknowledge that "my children and I live in one dwelling unit, but my parents who are also 'my (wider) family' live in another." However, using "my wider family" in that specific sense limits its meaning to blood kin. It overlooks entirely the idea of "social kin" discovered by many researchers among both ubran and rural blacks. (Remember that Giallombardo compared members of primary groups to trees, and the group itself to a forest. The trees and the forest depend on each other to survive and thrive.) Most sociologists are white and thus usually focus mostly on white families that are relatively well-off economically and living with their own households. Not only that, Patricia Wilson and Ray Pahl charge that sociologists have paid little attention to each household's connections with the "forest" of other households, whether blood or social.[31] Among blacks, however, the interconnections across households become much more readily apparent. Instead of seeing a number of *independent* households each con-

taining the Benchmark Family, what we see instead is something like family Y. Family Y is a *forest*—a primary group consisting of a number of *interdependent* households.

Comparisons with Support Networks and Friendships

Recall that Jewell used terms such as *social support networks* and *mutual aid systems* as being synonymous with families. However, social networks supplying mutual aid are not necessarily the same as families. For example, alongside the six households in Rivers' study, there may be a separate cluster of households in their community that are also receiving and giving material aid and services. That cluster is clearly a mutual aid network, but they may not be family. Why not? Because they do not perceive of themselves as a family.

If we go out to the integrated suburban church that Sheron and Brian now attend, we find that they have become part of a friendship network. This is a group of couples who do activities together during leisure time. Although they are a *network*, these couples do not define themselves as family.[32] Since each household in the friendship network is economically self-sufficient, the couples do not exchange material aid. If they need services such as babysitting they usually hire someone. If one of them lands in a sudden time squeeze or has some other similar problem, an available network member may, or may not, help out. Finally, shared emotional intimacy is not something that is part of their network of companionship, although three of the women have begun to get quite close.

REDEFINING FAMILIES

If neither mutual support networks nor friendship networks are necessarily families, then what are families? That's the same question we raised earlier when we talked about sports teams, combat units, and sororities. If you're tempted to throw up your hands and exclaim in exasperation that it's useless to try to define what "family" means, then you're in the company of at least one British sociologist. Jon Bernades argues that trying to define "family" is like trying to define the winds and the waves. We all have an intuitive feeling of what these terms imply, but being precise about them is quite another matter. He says it's better to drop the label "family" altogether.[33]

Additionally, Bernardes is worried about the issue we discussed in connection with the social families of urban blacks. When people today try to define family, they usually illustrate their definition by pointing out the numerous types of households that have begun to proliferate: Lone-parent households, cohabiting households, households with blended families, households with divorced families, and so on, and on. That strategy aims at the goal of defining family by coming up with a typology that includes every possible permutation of living arrangements and households.

Inevitably, says Bernardes, that strategy triggers in the reader's mind the dichotomy between the Benchmark Family and everything else. And as Jewell noted in the case of blacks, the alternatives are always compared with the ideal and found wanting. But since increasing numbers of whites are also constructing all kinds of families, they too find themselves being compared with the Benchmark and found lacking. In other words, says Bernardes, keeping the label "family" implies that what increasing numbers of persons are doing throughout Western societies is *deviant*.

Bernardes' solution is to banish the label altogether and to come up with a new term that is more precise and that does four things: (1) It erases the confusion and ambiguities that arise when one tries to define it. (2) It makes it explicit that the Benchmark is not necessarily any better or any worse than any other arrangements. (3) It emphasizes that families are not

limited to one household (an apartment or other dwelling space). (4) It helps us grasp the idea that families are not limited to ties of blood and the law (marriage and adoption).

Our solution is different from Bernardes' solution, although we have the same four goals. We shall retain the label "family" but make it plural, "families." We think of the label as a way for most citizens to communicate about primary groups. Let's say that a parent or friend asks what you're learning in your chemistry course, and you happen to be studying water compounds. Rather than be technical and tedious and watch his or her eyes glaze over, you try to summarize in plain English some interesting things you've learned about a substance that everybody deals with everyday. PBS programs such as *Nova* and *Scientific American Frontiers* do a superb job of communicating technical notions in a plain and appealing manner. Similarly, if someone asks what you're learning in this course you might respond by talking about families in the *plural* sense, another reality that most people deal with everyday.

We-ness and Bonding

To help us understand what we have in mind when we talk about families (plural), let's return to Giallombardo. What precisely did she mean when she said her women prisoners belonged to primary groups? The debate over what Charles Cooley had in mind in 1909 when he coined the term *primary group* is almost as fierce as the debate over *family*.[34] But Cooley helps us see why the prisoners' groups were called "primary." He asserted that a primary group "is a 'we'; it involves the sort of . . . mutual identification for which 'we' is the natural expression."[35]

Ellsworth Faris agreed with Cooley that the essence of a primary group is that it generates a powerful sense of *we*, or *we-ness*.[36] That sense of bonding supplies its members with identity,

A two-person primary group bonded by a sense of "we-ness"—each one feeling that "I belong" and that "I matter."

security, and belonging. Let's say that a person who belongs to a primary group feels something like this: "I matter to other group members—I'm important to them. What is more, they matter to me—they're important to me. Who I am as a human being is substantially influenced by my group. What is more, I have some degree of influence over others in my group." Thomas Scheff and Suzanne Retzinger put it this way: "Everyone requires a minimal sense of belonging, a web of secure bonds."[37] And Morris Rosenberg and Claire McCollough added that when a person feels that he or she *matters* to another person or persons, that feeling contributes greatly to his or her mental health.[38]

Alan Bates and Nicholas Babchuck agree that feelings of we-ness or bonding, and mattering, are the very essence of a primary group.[39] A person is like Whitehead's tree, re-

quiring the forest of *significant others*. Together the persons share the definition of *we*—a we that is separate and distinct from *they*. "They" refers to everyone who is not part of "*my* we-group." In the closed environment of the women's prison, it was not possible to belong to more than a single we-group (social family) at a time. But in the broader world that most of us inhabit, it is quite possible to participate simultaneously in several we-groups.

Clara, the newly arrived prisoner, was not part of any we-group; she could think of herself only as *me*. Being socially isolated meant great emotional emptiness and suffering. It also resulted in material deprivation and lack of social prestige. To meet these several needs, Clara had to become part of one of the prison's primary groups, or families. As she became family, she began increasingly to perceive herself as *we*—she was no longer merely *me*. And not only did she begin to perceive herself that way, other members of her family did too. They began to share the definition that indeed Clara belongs to *our* we-group, to *my* we-group. What accounted for Clara's transition from being *me* to being *we*? Giallombardo called it *interdependence*—the giving and receiving of emotional and material benefits with her family members. As both Clara and the other members continued exchanging, the sense of we-ness kept on developing for both her and the other family members. Correspondingly, the sense of *they* emerged from the fact that Clara was not exchanging with other prisoners—outsiders—in the same ways she was with her social family.

But what about Sheron and Brian's suburban friendship network of couples? Is that a primary group? Probably. But is it like family Y? Probably not, because it merely supplies companionship. What is missing from their network are *help patterns*—ongoing and predictable exchanges of good, services, money, and so on. In short, groups that exchange a great array of benefits are more likely to have a stronger sense of we-ness and belonging than groups exchanging fewer benefits. Family Y is like the families in the prison. They depend on one another for a wide range of money, goods, services, companionship, and emotional closeness. They are much more dependent on one another than couples in the friendship network. Those suburban couples are highly independent of one another except in the area of companionship.

A primary group, we say, is like a forest and its members are like the trees. The more the members depend on each other the more they feel like a forest. "Feeling like a forest" means they feel bonded to, and a part of, one another, of some larger whole. In other words, greater *inter*dependence in the form of a greater number of exchanges (carried on frequently) develops the sense of we-ness that Cooley talked about. By contrast, the more the trees are *inde*-pendent, the less like a forest (less bonding) they will feel.

When Does "Being in Family" Begin?

On the *Fahrenheit* scale, water hardens into ice at 32 degrees. Is there some point where it slowly begins to dawn on persons who are part of an in-group that they are family?[40] When does a sense of social bonding get so strong that persons gradually begin to think of themselves as "being in family?" When do they say it out loud to one another, as well as to outsiders?

Outsiders and Families In the women's prison and in studies of black families, the outsiders (the *they*-groups), played an important part in answering that question. In the prison, for example, family B members knew that family A members viewed them as "different." And persons who were outside the social family that Rivers studied also thought of that family as being "different." In both settings, outsiders viewed the families as more than merely friendship or mutual support networks. And knowing that outsiders think of the group as different helps to reinforce the in-group's sense of belonging, bonding, and we-ness.

Homosexuals and Families Kath Weston says that the "families I saw gay men and lesbians creating . . . [were like certain] African-American" families.[41] It is no secret that being homosexual in America means being marked as very different from outsiders—the majority of the citizens. And as part of their response to outsiders thinking of them as "different," many homosexuals create their own families.

Weston is quick to add, however, that there is no such thing as " *'the* gay family' "[42] What she means is that the families homosexuals create are fundamentally the same as families created by heterosexuals. Numerous studies, for example, show that gay/lesbian parents fare no better nor worse than straight parents in raising children (see Chapter 16). Moreover, homosexual couples struggle with conflicts and negotiations in the same ways as today's heterosexual couples (see Chapter 11). The major distinction between them, of course, is that outsiders resist the efforts of homosexuals to create families. Heterosexual efforts are supported—but only to fashion the Benchmark Family. For example, in 1993 the government endorsed a "don't ask–don't tell" policy regarding gays in the military. Under that policy, if a group of gays on a military base gradually developed from a covert mutual-support network to a public social family, they could be discharged. They could be penalized even though their social family provided them with the same kinds of emotional and material benefits as, say, the social families of urban blacks or women prisoners.

Nevertheless, because homosexuals, like heterosexuals, need a sense of belonging, they too create social families. Weston is an anthropologist, and so she became a "participant observer" in her study of how homosexuals create social families. And what she found is remarkably similar to what other researchers had previously reported about prisoners and blacks. First, the group of persons (mostly women, a few men) she was "hanging around with" became friends. Friendship has at least two dimensions, the first of which is called "companionship." Companions do things together (movies, hiking, sports, meals, etc.). And so Weston and her group first became friends in the sense of being companions. Second, after a few months as companions, her group gradually moved to a second, and deeper, level of friendship known as intimacy, self-disclosure, sharing of feelings, and so on. Finally, she remarks that after a while "we

began to apply the terms 'family' and 'extended family' to one another.[43]

Like family Y and the social family Rivers studied, they maintained their own separate residences. And says Weston, about the time that her group "began to classify ourselves as family," something else surfaced: The family members began to "provide one another with material assistance."[44] That is, they began to help each other out with services, goods, and money. If someone's car broke down, or someone got injured and required care, or if cleaning or childcare services were needed, or something else, someone from the family was there to lend a hand. Weston says that this sort of material assistance is a large part of what families are all about, as urban blacks have long known. The "bottom line" of families, says Lillian Rubin, is that members help each other out whenever there's a tangible or material need.[45]

"Fictive" Kin? For a long time, says Weston, anthropologists were fond of talking about "fictive kin."[46] For example, a tribal member might behave "as if" he were a father when in fact he is merely a family friend. He might treat a young boy with great warmth and affection, shower him with gifts, and provide many services. The man is behaving just like a father, but he is not, say many anthropologists. Rather, he is a "fictive" father. Many social scientists believe that only the biological, or blood, father is the *real* father.

Weston disagrees.[47] She says that the social ties of emotional bonding and also material assistance that give rise to feelings of bonding, belonging, and we-ness are what families are all about. That is true, she argues, whether the family is made up of persons who are heterosexual, homosexual, or a sprinkling of both. Weston says that those social ties are *at least as important* as the blood, or genetic, tie. The families she studied are not fictive, any more than

An AIDS victim is comforted by a longtime friend in a hospital room.

cohabitors are a fictive couple when compared with a married couple (see Chapter 9).

AIDS and Social Families   Striking evidence that social families can sometimes be even *more* important than blood families comes from recent studies of AIDS victims.[48] As in the 1990 film, *Longtime Companion*, these studies suggest that when homosexual persons (usually men) begin to manifest the symptoms of the HIV virus, their natural (i.e., blood) families become appalled or repulsed, or both. In any case, their families sometimes fail the bottom-line test of what a family is all about—being there when a member needs help.

However, the patient's social family is there. Sometimes the person has been part of a social family before the emergence of symptoms. At other times the victim's needs stimulate his friends into becoming, first, a mutual aid network, and next, a social family. As they care for both his physical and emotional needs, they tend to behave toward each other, and also view one another, as *family*.

When Does "Being in Family" Cease?

But there's a flip side to asking when in-groups begin to think of themselves as families: How low must feelings of belonging and bonding drop before the idea that "we are family" begins to evaporate and eventually cease to exist? When do persons who used to think of themselves as family no longer feel that way? Faris remarked that if the we feeling is pivotal, then "not every family is a primary group and . . . a school group may or may not be so defined."[49] When Faris used the word *family*, he meant the Benchmark Family of the 1930s and

1940s. Although its members might have ties of marriage and blood, Faris nonetheless realized they might *not* consider themselves a we-group. Their level of giving and receiving might be so low, and/or so unsatisfactory, that they no longer imagine themselves as a forest, as belonging to a we-group.

Remember that Jewell spoke of many black families as being "fluid" because persons such as Sheron and Brian enter and exit over time. At one point, that couple felt a strong sense of we-ness with family Y. But gradually their sense of we-ness dropped so much that neither they nor their family felt they "belonged" anymore. Similarly, once women left the prison and were no longer giving and receiving with persons who had been their family, most of them no longer maintained those family ties.[50]

Persistence of Social Families Over Time
But the situation of U.S. blacks, we said, is different from that of prisoners who are eventually released. Since their social and economic conditions are not easily overcome, their social families apparently tend to have longer histories. The same conclusion applies, says Weston, to homosexuals.[51] They must live in the midst of hostile social and political conditions from which there simply is no escape. There is no magical prison door through which they easily pass back into the "normal heterosexual" world.[52] Hence, as with African-Americans, some homosexuals experience social families that have what Weston calls a lengthy "shared past."[53]

For example, given enough time, all of the households in a family such as Y could be replaced either by death or by withdrawal from the exchange loop. Nevertheless, family Y could remain as an identifiable in-group. How is that? When we last looked, family Y consisted of ten households. Let's say that over several years, households 3, 7, and 9 cease to maintain exchanges with the other seven, and family Y shrinks to seven households. But

slowly household 11 becomes part of family Y, which expands it to eight households. Given still more time, households 2, 4, and 10 cease to belong to family Y but the family gradually adds households 12, 13, 14, and 15, which enlarges family Y to nine households. Again over time, households 1, 5, 6, and 8 are no longer perceived as part of family Y, and so it shrinks to five households. Now all of the original ten households are gone, but everyone in church X still thinks of the family as family Y, and so do its current members. Why?

If family Y had consisted originally of ten blood-linked households that shared the same surname (e.g., Washington), we would readily understand that even though the original ten had disappeared as a result, say, of death, the Washington family continues via the current five households. But since family Y households are *not* blood linked, and do not share a common surname, how does that family manage to maintain its identity over time?

Keeping Up the Exchanges   The basic reason family Y stayed "alive" was because they kept up their exchange patterns. As a result, they continued thinking of themselves as a distinctive we-group no matter which households were or were not currently in the exchange loop. As long as they carried on the giving and receiving of valuable benefits, their sense of belonging and bonding persisted. Maintaining their identity as an in-group stimulated outsiders to keep on defining them as a family even though they lacked blood ties and a shared surname.

Several social and/or blood families may exist in the same social space (church X). The fact that each maintains its distinct boundaries helps to reinforce each family's unique identity. The boundaries, of course, are the exchange patterns. Households participating in family K's exchanges are divided from households participating in, say, family Y's exchanges, or in the exchanges of family M.

Whether in black communities, or in women's prisons, or in homosexual communities, those divisions, although informal, are socially meaningful and very powerful. And even though the boundaries may expand and contract over time, both insiders and outsiders perceive that certain households belong to a particular family, but others do not.

CONCLUSION—SOCIAL FAMILIES AND SOCIAL RESPONSIBILITY

"You can pick your friends, but you can't pick your relatives," goes the old cliché. But Weston talks about the freedom to "choose" one's family. And so do studies of African-Americans and inmates of a women's prison. A major theme of this book is the spread of choices and options throughout Western societies. Increasingly, the freedom to fashion, and thus reinvent, one's social family—whether one is white or black, straight or gay—is becoming a live option. With more choices come greater opportunities for a sense of control over one's life. And a sense of control contributes to a person's mental, and even physical, health (see Chapter 14).

Primary groups are like a forest. They provide a sense of we-ness, belonging, bonding, and mattering. They supply a context of opportunities both to give and receive material and emotional benefits. Trees (individual persons) require membership in some sort of primary group (forest) to be fully human. To be part of a primary group is often to have a sense that one is "in family." Some persons belong simultaneously to more than one family. But others may belong to none, even though they have ties of blood and/or marriage.

Throughout Western societies, the definitions of *family* have become extraordinarily complicated. However, it turns out that a large part of what families are all about is the giving and receiving of material and emotional benefits. And the more consistently the members give and receive those benefits, the stronger is their sense of we-ness. The result is that persons can, if they wish, create *social* families. Social families may have profoundly positive effects for the persons who construct and maintain them. Hence, creating social families may be an extraordinary responsible thing to do for both adults and their children. On the other hand, social families might have painfully negative effects. But no more so than biological families. And just as biological and social families are similar in those ways, Chapter 3 reveals that they share many other similarities as well.

NOTES

1. Aldous, 1991, p. 660.
2. Jean Seligmann, 1989. "Variations on a theme." Special supplemental issue of *Newsweek*, p. 38.
3. Giallombardo, 1966.
4. T'ien, 1944.
5. Giallombardo, p. 16.
6. Ibid., p. 103.
7. Ibid., p. 166.
8. Firth, 1936.
9. Giallombardo, pp. 136ff.
10. Money, 1988.
11. Giallombardo, p. 162.
12. Vera and Feagin, in preparation.
13. Bernard, 1981.
14. Jewell, 1988, p. 39.
15. The classic is Carol Stack, 1974. See also Liebow, 1967; Billingsley, 1968; Staples, 1976; Berry and Blassingame, 1982; McAdoo and Peters, 1983; Hatchett, Cochran, and Jackson, 1991.
16. Jewell, p. 13.
17. Cheatam and Stewart, 1990.
18. Jewell, p. 40.
19. Caldwell, Greene, and Billingsley, 1992.
20. Gerstel and Gross, 1987.
21. Jewell, pp. 41–42.
22. Ibid., p. 13.
23. See note 15.
24. Allen, 1991.
25. Rivers and Scanzoni, 1994.
26. Jewell, pp. 15–19.
27. Giallombardo, p. 176.

28. Jewell, p. 21.
29. Ibid., pp. 13–17.
30. Wallerstein and Smith, 1990.
31. Wilson and Pahl, 1988.
32. Babchuck, 1965.
33. Bernardes, 1986.
34. Faris, 1937; Bates and Babchuck, 1961; Lee, 1964.
35. Cooley, 1909, p. 23.
36. See note 34.
37. Scheff and Retzinger, 1991, p. 14.
38. Rosenberg and McCollough, 1981.
39. Bates and Babchuck, p. 82.
40. Gubrium and Holstein, 1990.
41. Weston, 1991, p. 108.
42. Ibid., p. 3, italics added.
43. Weston, p. 104.
44. Ibid., p. 105, pp. 196ff.

45. Rubin, 1985.
46. Weston, pp. 105ff.
47. Ibid., p. 106.
48. Levine, 1990; Lovejoy, 1990. Sklar and Hartley, 1990, do not deal directly with homosexuals, but their insights are valuable in understanding grieving among homosexuals who, for example, are denied access by the blood family to partners who have suddenly died.
49. Faris, p. 302.
50. Giallombardo, pp. 117–119.
51. Weston, p. 114.
52. Later chapters note that some homosexuals enter heterosexual marriage as a "possible way out."
53. Weston, p. 114.

CHAPTER 3

FAMILIES WE'RE BORN WITH

THE IMPORTANCE OF BLOOD TIES

"Blood is thicker than water," goes the old cliché, but what does it mean? This chapter explores the connections between blood ties and what Chapter 2 called "being in family." David Schneider says that the cliché means that blood, or biological, ties are stronger than any other ties, and take priority over them.[1] He adds that genetic, or kinship, ties have nothing to do with behavior or performance. People are kin because of *who* they are, not *what* they do. Kin folk help each other out, Schneider states, simply because they're kin. If other reasons exist for helping out, they are secondary. Schneider adds that some kin are closer to each other than other kin, and thus more likely to help one another. The closest kin are parents and children, because according to Schneider sexual behavior and reproduction are the centerpiece of kin relations. The bond of kinship is "biologically determined. . . . [It] derives directly from the nature of human nature."[2] Schneider also points to the recent and highly publicized work of re-searchers known as "sociobiologists."[3] They too believe that kinship is biologically, or innately, determined.

If Schneider and the sociobiologists are correct, what accounts for behaviors such as "granny-dumping?" According to a 1991 Associated Press report, emergency room workers say that growing numbers of elderly persons are being abandoned by children unwilling or unable to care for them. "One elderly woman was left sitting in a hospital driveway as a car sped away. Another was wheeled into an emergency room with a note saying, 'Please take care of her,' pinned to her purse."[4] A survey done by the American College of Emergency Room Physicians of 169 hospitals throughout the United States reported an average of eight abandonments per week.[5] Furthermore, Chapter 14 shows that the physical abuse of elderly persons by their children and other relatives is far more common than anyone previously realized. And flipping the coin, Chapter 17 shows how some parents and other adults neglect children, as well as physically and sexually abuse them.

Formal Families

Patricia Wilson and Ray Pahl are British sociologists who have done a lot of research on urban families linked by blood, marriage, and adoption, that is, *formal* families.[6] Their research strategy was not to conduct one-time surveys, such as those done by the Census Bureau, but rather to spend months, and even years, living in the communities they studied. While living there they carried out in-depth field work, much like anthropologists. Consequently, they were able to observe formal families over a considerable period and record what happened to them.

As a result of their work, Wilson and Pahl came to the following important conclusions:

1. Families cannot be "neatly specified" by ties of blood and marriage. The realities of modern societies have become far too complex for that simple formula.
2. Households and families are not necessarily the same thing. Families can and do spill over the physical walls of particular dwelling units (as in the case of the social families described in Chapter 2).
3. Families must be understood chiefly in terms of their social *processes,* and only secondarily in terms of their genetic connections.

For instance, we understood social family Y in Chapter 2 because of the giving and receiving (called interdependence) that bound them together. That same giving and receiving also held them together for an extended period. They had a shared sense of we-ness, bonding, and belonging. Wilson and Pahl claim that the same thing applies to formal families. These two researchers suggest that the dynamics of giving and receiving are actually more crucial than the blood tie itself.

What is remarkable about Wilson and Pahl's three conclusions is that they emerged from their studies of families connected by blood and marriage. The conclusions are strikingly similar to those just described in Chapter 2, for *social* families. The Wilson and Pahl research suggests that formal and social families may sometimes be more alike than unlike.

White and Working Class The families Wilson and Pahl examined were white and working class. Since many of the adults held steady jobs, the families were neither poor nor near-poor, as were many of the African-Americans described in Chapter 2. Nevertheless, Wilson and Pahl found that the material help patterns exchanged across their households were extremely important.[7] For instance, the households provided shelter and food to any family members needing them. These might include newly married couples, or relatives of any age (including young single adults) not currently able to find a place to live. Second, households provided actual financial support as well as services such as sitters for children and for adults who might be ill or infirm. Third, they tracked down pipelines to employment: "If someone needed a job or heard of a job he or she contacted the family . . . first."[8]

Giving and Receiving as Obligations Those exchange patterns hold many features in common with patterns found among women prisoners, African-Americans, and gay/lesbian social families. Furthermore, some recent studies suggest that they also exist among social families that include senior citizens, mid-life persons, and younger persons as well.[9] The basic idea governing the giving and receiving is the same whether the families are formal or social. The essence of being in family means that, if they are able, everyone has a responsibility to *give* to other members in need, and also to *receive* whenever they have a need. For example, if household 1 can't afford to replace the car engine that just blew, and household 9 can, that's what 9 does. Moreover, 9 does so even if 1 has not done anything recently, or ever, for 9.

Instead, persons in 9 may think, "Hey, when we need something, the family helps us out, so we're just doing the same thing."

Furthermore, 1 has the obligation to take the rebuilt engine. It might be polite to exclaim, "Oh, you shouldn't have," but 1 has been made an offer it can't refuse. Why not? Because that would place 1 outside the exchange loop. If the household does not take the engine, they have less obligation to help out the family sometime in the future. Refusing the engine is a way of tacitly communicating, "I don't want to be part of what being in family is all about."

Importantly, Wilson and Pahl found that these kinds of material exchange processes gave formal family members a strong sense of "social identity."[10] Because of their continual giving and receiving, family members developed a powerful sense of we-ness and belonging. They were a primary group. They sensed they belonged to a special in-group, and that ousiders with whom they did not exchange belonged to they-groups.

The Constraints of Formal Families

Violent behavior is likely to depress a sense of we-ness. Wilson and Pahl note that most earlier studies "glamorised [mate-working-class] camaraderie." However, the studies failed to mention the "physical violence and the containment of violence so typical of working-class family life."[11] Wilson and Pahl report that fistfights and physical aggression were part of their respondents' everday lives. At any time, violence might explode between members of the same household, across households, or with outsiders. In particular, Wilson and Pahl found that male control over the romantic and sexual behaviors of the women in those families often precipitated severe aggression.

Taking a U.S. example, in the 1991 film *Jungle Fever*, a white working-class man is innocently dating the white working-class woman who is the film's female lead. Her two brothers

continually harass him, and in no uncertain words threaten violence if he so much as thinks about robbing her virginity. Similarly, Wilson and Pahl report that threats as well as actual violence toward outsiders on the part of male sibs and cousins trying to protect "their women" are constant realities. The scene is very much like the constantly skirmishing young males in Shakespeare's *Romeo and Juliet*. Not only are men at risk of violence, women in contemporary white working-class British and U.S. families who dare to cross sexual lines drawn by male relatives are also in danger of getting beaten up. In *Jungle Fever*, when the female lead's father discovered she had slept with her black boss, he beat her ferociously until his sons finally restrained him.

Wilson and Pahl remark that those kinds of situations emphasize that formal families can be highly oppressive, especially of women. The younger women in their studies did not feel free to pursue the romantic aspects of their lives. They were constrained because of the potential and/or actual violence that could occur to themselves as well as to outside men. Besides violence, there are many other ways in which formal families may constrain their members, and thus be perceived as oppressive. For instance, an elderly person requires constant care but none of the male family members feels he can provide that service. Yvon, a family member, has just been graduated from high school. Other family members let Yvon know in subtle, and sometimes not so subtle, ways that it is her obligation to take care of the elderly member. But Yvon wants to go to college, and indirectly fingers her same-aged unemployed male cousin who could do the caregiving as well as she. Nonetheless, Yvon is pressured into doing so. She feels resentful about it. She feels that she is being oppressed merely because of her gender. As with violence, a sense of oppression is likely to have a dampening effect on any person's perceived we-ness with her or his primary group: Yvon wonders, "How much do I actually *matter* to my family since they treat me like this?"

Constructing Family Boundaries

Chapter 2 showed that social families expand and contract as persons move in and out of the exchange loop. The boundaries surrounding social families consist of the exchanges that occur across households: Households in the exchange loop are within the boundaries. Households outside the loop are not in the boundaries. Boundaries expand as the number of households in the loop increases. Boundaries shrink as the number in the loop goes down.

In contrast to saying that the boundaries of families are socially constructed, Schneider asserts that the boundaries of formal families are biologically determined. Some sociologists also believe that "membership in a [formal] family is involuntary . . . terminated only by death."[12] From that viewpoint, persons have neither autonomy nor choice in selecting their family. They're "born with" their family—and that's that! Wilson and Pahl found something different. They discovered that the persons in their studies drew *social* boundaries around their formal families. What is more, those social boundaries meant much more to them than the boundaries based on "merely biological or legal terms." The researchers discovered that the boundaries of formal families are established on many of the same bases as those of social families. Wilson and Pahl illustrate their point by information they gathered from persons in a certain formal family. The specific question they were examining was whether a pair of young women twins, related by blood to their respondents, *"are*, in fact 'family.' "[13]

First, it's vital to note that it made perfectly good sense to the respondents to discuss whether a blood relative is "in fact" family. Respondents could very well have laughed at the researchers and said, "Well of course they're family—they're biological kin!" Furthermore, it made equally good sense for the respondents to draw a sharp distinction between the twins and the twins' sister who had grown up in a different household. The twins' sister was said to be "firmly in the family, and . . . [was] clearly recognised as such."[14] *Firm* is a variable like temperature or a sense of we-ness. "Firmness," "temperature," "we-ness," can each range greatly from very high to very low. Saying the sister was clearly recognized as being firmly in the family meant that she was high on the firmness variable. There was no doubt she *belonged*. But not because of her biological tie. A biological tie is not a variable. A person either is biological kin or is not.

Expelled from Family   How then could the twins be expelled from the family? How could the respondents say the twins " 'did not belong in the family,' " since they had the same biological tie as their sister? Compared with her, why were the twins so low on the firmness variable? Wilson and Pahl report that the reason the family had expelled the twins was because they had become "marginalised [from] the family" loop of exchanges.[15] The "real problem," or the "crucial factor," leading to their being outside the loop was the twins' "rejection of family support." They had violated half of the cardinal rule of being in family—the obligation to *receive*. And by not *taking*, they simultaneously made the other half of the rule null and void—the obligation to *give*.[16]

The twins had chosen to place themselves outside the network of family exchanges. They were living apart from the kind of mutual interdependence that gives rise to a sense of we-ness. The twins shared little if any sense of bonding with or belonging to the family. And neither did family members share any sense of we-ness with the twins. But the twins' sister was in the exchange loop, and family members affirmed that "she belongs to our family—our primary group."

Wilson and Pahl acknowledge that discussing these sorts of matters with their respondents "raised delicate issues." The first was the matter of family oppression and having control over one's own life. The twins had chosen to behave in ways that suited them as individuals. Since their lifestyles were highly unconventional, they apparently felt that being in family cramped their styles. Not surprisingly, younger respondents in the study were sympathetic with the idea that the twins had "openly rebelled against the family."[17] They saw the twins as exercising their right to freedom. In contrast, older respondents were much more critical of the twins' choices.

The second delicate issue was how the respondents felt about excluding the twins from the family loop. Family members had "ambivalent feelings" about no longer sensing any obligations to "accommodate and provide some support for its wayward members."[18] Wilson and Pahl report that the respondents recognized that they were in fact discussing the core of what family is all about: They were wrestling with the "true boundary of the family and what its social significance is in their daily lives."[19] One respondent, for instance, "confesses [that] she 'didn't have the same feelings [she once had] for the twins.'" By "feelings" she seemed to mean the sense of bonding she once shared with them. Previously, she had perceived the twins as "belonging to us—as being part of our in-group." But now she defined the twins as outsiders, as *they*.

Wilson and Pahl conclude that their study shows there is no "mechanistic" way of determining the social boundaries of formal families.[20] A map reveals the Rio Grande River as the political and physical boundary between Texas and Mexico. However, the social reality is that Mexican and U.S. citizens cross it in either direction virtually at will. Artificially mapping kin ties on the basis of blood and marriage, as many anthropologists do, is one thing, but knowing who is presently *in* family

and who is currently *out* may be quite another.

Wilson and Pahl add that formal families are "socially constructed," and because they are, they "grow and decline over time." Persons may enter and exit primary groups known as families by means other than birth and death. For example, if they eventually choose to do so, there seems nothing to prevent the twins from gradually reentering the same exchange loop they once belonged to. By the same token, there seems nothing to prevent one of the current members of households of that same loop to cease their receiving and giving. Eventually they would be perceived in the same way as the twins are now. Thus, Schneider is correct by asserting that kin ties are biologically determined: Indeed, a person cannot choose her or his blood relatives. But what persons can and do choose is how much they will *participate with* their blood kin. Family, in other words, is not necessarily the same thing as blood kin. Family is socially constructed—it is by no means biologically determined.

SOCIAL CONDITIONS, FAMILIES, AND FRIENDS

Karen Lindsey has asserted that the matter of which formal and social families to belong to, and how fully to participate in the exchange networks of those families, are choices that people make and remake throughout their life course.[21] (See also Chapter 14). Remember, of course, that persons' choices are significantly affected by their broader social context, as in the case of Chinese resident-factory workers, women prisoners, African-Americans, and gays/lesbians. It seems plain, however, that persons look first to their blood kin—especially their parents and their children—for material help when they need it. But if no help is available, then persons get it where they can. Chapter 2 showed that when several friends help each other out over an extended period, the potential exists for their group to become more than just-friends—they could develop into "being family."[22] And that brings us back to the question posed at the start of Chapter 2—"What are families?" In trying to figure out the answer, we're now forced to ask, "What is the difference between friends and families?"

Being Just-Friends

In her book *Just Friends*, Lillian Rubin studied women and men enjoying varying degrees of both companionship and intimacy.[23] Since most of her respondents were white, and middle class or upper working class, they were relatively well-off. Rubin found that persons carry around distinctive images of their kin versus the images they hold of their friends. She says that in North American culture formal families hold a certain mystique—almost a sacred character.

In her book *Friends As Family*, Lindsey agrees with Rubin. However, she adds that the mystique surrounding blood kin can be characterized by the term *myth*.[24] A myth is not a lie. Lindsey says that stories about George Washington freely mix objective fact with legends and myths. Myths, such as his silver dollar toss and his cherry tree encounter, convey positive emotional feelings about Washington that serve to enhance our admiration for him. Similarly, when Rubin uses the term *family metaphor* she means myths that touch both our emotions and our minds in ways that enhance our admiration for formal families. "I'll be home for Christmas" is a popular song that with great passion conveys myths about the virtual necessity of visiting blood kin at Christmas. The song causes the listener to reflect on all the warm, wonderful, and cozy things that supposedly happen as the kin gather 'round the Tree. No comparably suggestive or evocative myths exist about friends.

Nevertheless, in spite of powerful family myths, many of Rubin's respondents said,

"'I'd go to my friends for anything, with any kind of problem.'"[25] The "problems" those persons shared with their friends fell under the heading of *intimacy*. They told Rubin that they and their friends self-disclosed about deeply felt concerns, sorrows, joys, fears, aspirations, disappointments, and anxieties. In short, those friends intertwined their innermost selves. And they also shared good times together— they were companions. In view of such positive intimacy and sociability, why does Rubin report that "there's a limit to what we expect from friends, a certain amount of care with which we . . . ask for their help?" If her respondents had such deep friendships, it appears contradictory to add, " 'The family is the bottom line, the people you know you can always count on, no matter what.' "[26]

The Bottom Line—Services, Goods, and Money

What does Rubin mean by the "bottom line"? What do kin generally supply that friends typically do not? Evidently not intimacy and/or companionship, since Rubin's respondents were receiving generous amounts of those intrinsic benefits from friends. Indeed, many studies of formal families reveal that the myths about having good times with kin are often more fancy than fact.[27] There is, for example, evidence to suggest that the Christmas–New Year period is a time of heightened formal family abuse and violence, as well as suicide.[28]

In the Wilson and Pahl study, women's intimacy and male camaraderie were certainly present, but by no means were they the bottom line. The bottom line in that study was the complex loop of material exchanges shared across households—goods, services, and money. And recall from Chapter 2 that the households in family Y, and in Rivers' study, and the Chinese factory workers and women prisoners, and blacks and gays/lesbians, exchanged both friendship behaviors and the bottom line of services, goods, and money. As a result of that bottom line, each of those groups perceived themselves as being family.

By contrast, the friendships studied by Rubin lacked that bottom line. They were not exchanging tangible or *extrinsic* benefits. Of course, they didn't need to. The friends Rubin studied were relatively well-off. They represented households that were economically *independent* of one another. Thus they had no particular need to be economically *inter*dependent. As a result, Rubin's respondents drew a sharp distinction between their friends, who were not perceived as family, and their blood kin, who were family. And even though they might not need any material things just now from their formal families, they felt that if they ever did need money, goods, or services, their kin would give them whatever they needed. They expected neither to *give* nor to *receive* that sort of bottom line help from their friends.[29]

Friends Reinventing Families

One way or another, most social scientists usually find what they set out to discover. Rubin, for instance, wanted to demonstrate that friends are uniquely distinct from family. But Lindsey had another objective—she wanted to show how friends in modern societies might create families. Her argument is that just as persons are free to make choices about their spouses, they also have additional options: "We can choose *all* of our family," she says.[30] Like Rubin's respondents, the people Lindsey studied were neither poor nor near-poor. The question she explored was: How do heterosexual friends who are upper-working-class or middle-class construct families?

Lindsey reports that very often friends do not set out with the intention to create family. Sometimes, however, that may be their goal.[31] In either case, she wanted to find out how her respondents came to the perception that they were more than just-friends. Lindsey says that most of her respondents told her that the most important criterion for being part of a social family is the bottom-line exchange of extrinsic benefits.[32] If Chip, for instance, finds himself in an emergency, he must be able to rely on his family. Chip, who is a heterosexual cohabitor, might have a formal family, or he might not. If he does, it might be unable and/or unwilling to assist him.

Even if it could help him, he, like the twins in the Wilson and Pahl study, might choose to live outside his formal family exchange loop. Although he remains tied to them by blood, he is not, in terms of *social* reality, part of their we-group. But Chip is an active participant in a social family that includes other cohabitors as well as some married persons. He gives and receives both extrinsic as well as friendship-type benefits.

It's instructive that many of Lindsey's respondents used the term *emergency* to describe their extrinsic exchanges. Unlike lower-class and many working-class households, middle-class households (white and black) are able to be materially self-sufficient most of the time. When a pressing need for money, goods, or services does arise, it tends to be out of the ordinary (i.e., an emergency). The bottom line of being part of a family—formal or social—means that that pressing need will likely be met. In contrast to economically disadvantaged persons, persons who are middle class (or even upper working class) have the option of turning to formal families that tend to have the material resources to help. So why not do that? Why bother creating families out of clusters of friends?

Lindsey's response to this question is illustrated by the example of the twins from the Wilson and Pahl study. The twins could have gotten extrinsic benefits from their formal families, but they definitely were not receiving friendship, or what sociologists call *intrinsic* benefits. The twins were not getting acceptance, nurture, support, affirmation, and so on, for their lifestyle. Similarly, Lindsey observes that some persons (such as Chip) may not get the levels of intimacy and acceptance they desire from their formal families. Conversely, they do get friendship, affirmation, and emotional support from their friends because that's what friends are all about. And persons who do share intimacy and/or companionship sometimes have the option to add something else to their friendships. They can choose to add extrinsic exchanges. The combination of both sets of exchanges is likely to generate a strong sense of we-ness—of family—that does not occur with merely one set of exchanges. Being friends alone does not seem to do it, nor does simply being part of a material support network. It is not sufficient even to be linked by blood. But put the intrinsic and the extrinsic

together, and something unique tends to emerge: a sense of being in family, of belonging to a special primary group.

Just-Friends, Erotic Friends, and Families
Chapter 2 implied that the special thing that marked an erotic friendship from a platonic friendship was the sharing of a sexual partnership. In like manner, what distinguishes friends from family is the bottom-line sharing of goods, services, and money. In both instances, friendship (either as companionship and/or intimacy) is the springboard to something else. Friendship is a necessary (but never a sufficient) condition for both an erotic friendship and a family. By itself, "mere" friendship is never the same as an erotic friendship or a family.

A group of friends who do *not* perceive themselves as family.

Belonging to More than One Family It's quite possible, of course, for someone such as Chip to belong to his social family and to participate in his formal family at the same time. However, given what we know about him, he probably feels a stronger sense of we-ness and bonding with his social family than he does with his formal family. Similarly, Chip's social kin probably feel more strongly than his blood kin that "he belongs to and is one of us."

Moral Obligations

Let's say that Chip does indeed feel a much stronger sense of we-ness with his social family than he does with his formal family. If they're no fun, and he doesn't need them in a crunch, then why does he spend any time at all with his blood kin? It turns out that the only kin with whom Chip ever maintains any contacts are his mother and father and one of his brothers. When he visits his kin he informs his social family that he is making his yearly *obligatory* kin look-in. According to a number of anthropologists and sociologists, Chip has highlighted the basic reason he continues to participate in his formal family. Even though he feels he doesn't need them, nor does he particularly enjoy them he visits them annually out of a sense of obligation.[33] But not just your common garden-variety obligation such as paying a bank loan, or sharing class notes with a friend who did it for you.

Janet Finch talks about *moral* obligations, or what Desmond Ellis calls moral norms.[34] By "moral" sociologists mean something that is distinctively ethical and elevated—something that is *right* in and of itself. Some examples of moral norms are: "Blacks and whites should have equal employment opportunities." "Women and men should be paid equally for the same job." "A man should not force a woman to have sex."

According to Finch, the moral norm that makes families (both social and formal) special

is the obligation to "share without reckoning."[35] Chapter 2 said that if household 4 in family Y lacks current rent money, then households 6, 7, and 10 might pool dollars to make up the deficit. But in no way did that imply that 6, 7, and 10 calculate that 4 then owes each of them, say, 20 dollars each. Nor does 4 feel obligated to come up with 20 dollars to repay each one. Nor was there any hint that 4 had given those three households 20 dollars each for their own rents last month. Importantly, neither did any of the remaining households in the family feel that a quid pro quo was occurring or was necessary between 4 and the other households.

General Exchange Then what *is* going on within family Y? Although Sue Jewell called them exchange processes, she wasn't quite specific enough. More precisely, Peter Ekeh says they are *general* exchange processes.[36] "General exchange" usually involves three or more persons or households joined in a loop such as the one in which family Y is located. As we learned from the Wilson and Pahl study, the moral obligation of all persons in the loop is, as far as they are able, to give to all other needy persons in the loop, and also to receive from all other persons in the loop.

But an additional feature is that family members are supposed to give and receive without *reckoning*—apart from any rational calculus. For example, households are obliged to give (if they are able) regardless of whether the household they are helping has ever specifically helped them in the past. Thus, household 5 might assist 8 but does not expect that 8 will repay it as soon as possible. What 5 does expect is that 8 will assist other households in need. Moreover, if 5 ever has a need in the future, it expects that 8 will come to its aid. And 5 also expects other households to assist it when in need, including those that might in the past have been helped by 8.

In short, what's going on in family Y is that

each household thinks of all other households as interchangeable, or general.

Universal Reciprocity   Alongside general exchange, people in families have the moral obligation to engage in what can be called *universal reciprocity*.[37] It's universal because everyone in the family is expected to exchange with everyone else, insofar as they are able. The opposite of universal reciprocity is *mutual reciprocity*. Mutual reciprocity means that only A and B are expected to exchange with each other. An erotic friendship between A and B is a chief example of mutual reciprocity and what sociologists call restricted (as opposed to general) exchange: Persons A and B are not interchangeable with D, E, or F when it comes to exchanging sexual behaviors.

Finch acknowledges that although family exchanges are supposed to be general and universal, giving and receiving between parents and offspring are commonly the most frequent. Next in frequency are exchanges among siblings. Parents, children, sibs, and grandparents typically feel differently about their relationships than they do about relationships with other family members such as cousins, aunts, and uncles. It's as if parents and children have a special core of we-ness, or bonding. Those kinds of relationships make up a unique and intense primary group within the wider family. Interestingly enough, Giallombardo discovered a similar pattern among her women prisoners.[38] Relationships within the inner core of parents, children, and sibs tended to be much more intense and frequent than relationships with other relatives in the same broader family. Christmas gift-giving illustrates these kinds of differences.[39] Although family members across several households may exchange presents with one another, persons tend to make distinctions among their exchange partners. Angela, for instance, gives very different sorts of gifts to her cousins and her sisters' husbands than she does to her parents, her children, and her cohabiting partner.

Lindsey points out that in both social and formal families, feelings of moral obligation and debt tend to be very powerful among that inner core of parent–child. For example, Chip feels that if either of his parents had any extrinsic needs, he would be obliged to meet those needs. He feels that way even though they wouldn't use any of their material resources to meet needs of his that might arise. But Chip does not feel that way toward his cousins, nieces, uncles, nephews, and so on. He does not feel that they and he are "family."

Parents as Front Line

The reason Chip feels so intensely indebted to his parents highlights the following point: Although family exchanges are general and their obligations universal, parents and children have special—many would say unique—obligations. The parent-child connection need not be biological to be special. In many tribes, a man other than the biological father is designated as the social father.[40] By assuming the duties of fathering, that man actually becomes more obligated to meet the son's needs than does the natural father.

And in studies of African-Americans, as well as in the women's prison and the Chinese factory, persons designated as social parents had a special relationship to persons designated as their children. In all those cases, what is special is that parents have the front-line responsibility to children. Whether biological or social, other members of the family expect parents to take the prime responsibility of caring for their children. Of course, most parents also feel that way themselves, and so do most persons in the larger society.

However, families (formal, social), to the extent that they are able, seek to assist parents in meeting their children's material and emotional needs.[41] Very often, when parents are unable and/or unwilling to meet those needs, other family members surface gradually as social parents.[42] Sometimes those social parents legally adopt offspring of other family members. For example, Ernest's social daughter Camella (whom he's not adopted) is the 18-year-old natural parent of 2-year-old Nadia. Camella is a solo mother, and almost since Nadia's birth Ernest has been Nadia's social father. Since Camella is steadily losing interest in parenting Nadia, she allows the child to move to Ernest's household. Ernest replaces Camella as the lone parent. After a time he decides to adopt Nadia formally, and Camella does not object.

Paying Debts from the Past   One reason parents are defined as having front-line obligations to their children is because of the obligations they themselves incurred earlier as dependent children. When adults were children, their parents often generously fulfilled the moral norm of sharing without reckoning. Most parents expend enormous amounts of resources—material and emotional—for their children (biological or social). What parents receive in return rarely matches the sacrifices they made, especially in material terms. Parent–child exchanges tend to have enormous built-in inequities. Why doesn't that reality bother most parents? One reason most parents don't care about the huge inequities is that they are part of a general exchange loop governed by the norm of universal reciprocity. For instance, Ernest's social mother, Martha, gave abundantly to him when he was a child with no reckoning on her part whatsoever. "If I lived a hundred years," he thinks, there is no way Ernest could ever repay the enormity of his debt directly to Martha, although he might try.

The important thing to remember is that his debt is not solely to Martha but also to his broader family, his we-group, some of whom assisted Martha in caring for him. Consequently, Ernest has obligations to those family members as well as to Martha. And Ernest feels obliged to discharge those obligations by helping out both Camella and Nadia, even

though they never did anything for him or for Martha. Because they are part of the broader we-group that has benefited him, he feels a moral obligation to try to meet their needs as best he can. Because he was parented, he feels an obligation to parent. Because he got so much from his parents, he wants to give all he can to his children.

The keenness of obligations that mid-life parents feel to their children even when the children are adults, and the duties that those same mid-life adults feel to their older parents, can be seen in a number of ways. For example, Gerdt Sundstrom investigated century-long trends in both the United States and Sweden regarding the extent to which adult family members from different generations co-reside, that is, share the same household.[43] She found that over time the trend lines reveal repeated valleys and peaks. That is, at certain times young adults (under age 35) may be more or less likely to be living with their parents than at other times. Sundstrom concludes that the reason for the valleys and peaks is economic conditions in the broader society. If times are good, young adults are better able to make it on their own; if times are bad, their parents feel obligated to shelter them.[44]

Similarly, depending on economic conditions, elderly parents may be more or less likely to be living with their mid-life children. Whether it's young adults or senior citizens, the point is that the obligations to provide and receive extrinsic benefits such as shelter are lifelong. Mid-life persons are mostly on the giving end to both their adult children and their parents. But as they age, their children will in turn likely feel constrained to discharge the obligations they themselves are now incurring.

Another example of parents feeling powerful obligations to their adult children comes from a study of persons requiring kidney transplants to avoid death.[45] When told they needed transplants, the patients announced their need for kidney donors to all of their

Generations stretch out over time because of enduring obligations that can never be fully repaid.

blood kin. They did not ask any one relative in particular to donate. Most kin responded by saying, "I would like to help, but I cannot for these reasons: . . . ." No kin refused outright because a straightforward "no" violates the norm of universal reciprocity. Among kin who said they would be volunteers, the great majority were the parents of the patients. The second largest proportion of volunteers were the sibs of the patients. Nevertheless, sibs ranked considerably behind parents in terms of wanting to be a volunteer. It turns out that sibs are much less likely than parents to have their kidneys rejected by patients' bodies. As a result, their kin began to transmit subtle signals that sibs had the strongest moral obligation to volunteer even though they might not wish to. Many sibs got the "delicate message." Although no one never directly and explicitly asked them to volunteer a kidney, they did so anyhow.

Thus, even though parents felt stronger obligations than anyone else to volunteer a kidney, they were not always able to do so because they were less medically acceptable. And although sibs were less likely than parents to feel the duty to volunteer, precisely because they were *able* to help they eventually responded to their perceived obligations. The sibs' "gifts of life" aptly illustrate the character of universal reciprocity and general exchange: notions of quid pro quo were never relevant to donors, patients, or other family members. All that mattered was that the sibs were *able* to meet a pressing need. Importantly, the sibs' obligations were not merely to the patients but also to their families. First, the sibs had obligations to discharge regardless of what the patients may or may not have done for the sibs in the past. Second, the sibs had obligations to the patients regardless of whether they thought the patients would ever do anything for them in the future. What sibs could look forward to was the approval of their families (including the patients), as well as their family's help down the road should they ever need it.

Families, Obligations, and Histories

In virtually every study of friendship, the authors say that although formal families have ongoing histories and continuities, friendships are likely to be limited in time. Friendships end, but families do not, says Rubin. The basic reason blood families tend to have ongoing histories is that moral obligations can never be fully discharged. When parents give to children without reckoning, children become obliged to give to their own children, as well as to their parents. These children in turn incur obligations to their parents, to their grandparents, and to their own children, and so on, over time. No one can ever say when either intergenerational or sibling moral obligations have been fully discharged. It's totally different from having a sixty-month car loan and knowing your debt to the bank is over when it's over! Family obligations are *never over*. Parents, grandparents, and children (and to a much lesser degree sibs, cousins, uncles, aunts) are caught in the loop of never-ending general exchanges governed by universal reciprocity. Family members may choose to ignore their duties, but that doesn't make the obligations go away.

Lindsey contends that friends who are able to advance beyond being just-friends and to construct social families may experience family histories in many of the same ways as formal families. Chapter 2 showed that in the case of family Y, certain households dropped out of

the loop over time either because they wanted to or because of death. But because other households gradually replaced them, the giving-and-getting patterns continued. Outsiders recognized the continuity of family Y over the span of many years.

Social Generations Just as in the Washington's formal family, persons in the Y social family loop never felt they had completely discharged their moral obligations to other family members, especially to children. Discharging those obligations meant that a "family history" developed over time. In effect, they were developing a series of *social* generations, or lines of social descent. The exchanges were never over because they were never over! There was never an umpire to decree that the game was concluded, that everyone has finally discharged all of their moral obligations.

Rubin claims that a major difference between friendship and family is that friends are voluntarily chosen, whereas one's formal family is simply *there* (she says you can't "unchoose" it). But when it comes to friends, she says, "If we can be chosen, we can also be '*un*chosen.'"[46] Nevertheless, we learned form the Wilson and Pahl research that persons in formal families can and do choose to cease exchanging with one another. The twins chose to violate the kinds of moral obligations that maintain family histories. The only way they can "become family" again is to participate actively once more in the exchange loop. In that case the twins would probably have to make amends for their unfulfilled obligations to give and receive.

In short, to one degree or another, the element of choice is always present in friendships on the one hand, and in formal and social families on the other. What makes formal and social families different from friendships is not so much choice as it is the presence of bottom-line extrinsic exchanges. Friendships may indeed have shorter histories than families, but not because friends have choices and family members do not. Friendships are briefer because they do not include the range of powerfully intense moral obligations that make families families. The open-endedness of those obligations contributes to the shared histories of families, whether they be formal or social.

LIMITING OBLIGATIONS TO CHILDREN

Neglect and Abuse

If parents are unable to meet their children's material needs, or are unwilling to do so, family members tend to step in. If parental neglect is extreme, family members often enlist the help of outside authorities such as social workers. Shortly after Nadia's birth, for example, Ernest got a court order giving him temporary custody of her, because Camella was neglecting the infant's basic material needs. In short, family members, as well as the authorities, feel keen obligations to try to meet the material and physical needs of children if parents don't do what they're supposed to do. However, it's quite a different story if the parents do what they're *not* supposed to do, namely, *abuse* their children physically and/or sexually (see Chapter 17). Family and friends living outside the household, as well as the authorities, hesitate to interfere with parents as long as they're giving their children shelter, clothing, food, and so on. The sense of moral obligation held by the wider family to children living in any of its various households tends to be limited to helping out with the children's material needs. Family members may feel pained—even outraged—but few of them take the kinds of steps necessary to end the abuse. They will rarely confront the abusing parents, and they are even less like likely to report the parents to the authorities.

Part of the issue, of course, is that the abusing parents seek to conceal their behaviors from wider family members. (Incidentally, in the same furtive manner, many adult women victims of physical and sexual abuse tend not to reveal it to family, friends, or authorities.[47]) However, when abuse and violence become known (toward women as well as children), a major reason wider family members fail to intervene is that currently there is no moral norm comparable to "share without reckoning" that would justify their doing so.

Family exchange loops exist to provide tangible help, not to change individual household patterns. Wider family members are probably aware that if they intervene in an abusing household, its adults are likely to resent it and to view it as interference. The perceived interference could lead to overt conflict, and to avoid that the adults might begin to withdraw from the exchange loop. Finch reports that formal families tend to place great value on peace, stability, harmony, order, and tranquility. According to her, open conflict is something that wider families seek to avoid lest the "unpleasantness" disrupt the flow of ongoing giving and receiving. To intervene in an abusing household is to run the risk of upsetting the entire wider family. On the other hand, failing to intervene risks serious damage to the children. On balancing the two sets of risks, it appears that wider families would rather take the risk of harming children, since it appears to them as less disruptive of family order. But it's not just families that hesitate to interfere in household violence and abuse. Authorities such as social workers, school teachers, medical personnel, and police also hate to "meddle" in such "private" matters. In short, the larger society too places limits on its perceived obligations to *all its children*.

Distribution of Tangible Benefits

A second way the larger society places limits on its defined obligations to all its children has to do with the distribution of tangible or extrinsic benefits—money, goods, and services. In the event the front line of parents cannot adequately meet children's material needs, and the secondary line or backup of other family members (formal or social) cannot or will not step in to do so, where is the children's safety net? In many Western societies, citizens believe that all children are ultimately the obligation of all citizens.[48] In other words, the idea of a broader family based on general exchange and universal reciprocity is enlarged to include the entire society. Obviously, the "whole society as family" cannot be a primary group. Instead, formal government programs are designed to assist families and children in need. Up to this time, the United States is the modern society *least* likely to feel those kinds of general obligations to all its children.[49]

For the most part, the United States imposed limitations because most of the children left outside exchange loops in the past were poor whites and blacks.[50] For almost 200 years, the majority of whites have held tenaciously to Horatio Alger myths that any American man who works hard can support his family (see Chapter 6). Most middle-class Americans believe that if some children lacked material things, it was because their families—especially fathers—were shirking their obligations. Middle-class citizens have feared that if U.S. society does "too much" for children, family members will have little motivation to discharge their front-line, as well as their secondary-line, obligations.

More recently, however, the picture has gotten more complex. For many years, major economic shifts have been taking place throughout Western societies. One of the most crucial shifts is that from a base of heavy and dirty industry to light and clean manufacturing and services[51] (see also Chapters 14 and 15). Central to the changes are computers and automation. One of the results of these momentous structural shifts is that many jobs requiring brawn that white and black men from the working

classes used to perform are gradually disappearing. In addition, events such as the 1991 recession forced unemployment on many men from these social classes, making it more difficult for them to fulfill keenly felt moral obligations to provide for their children. Seldom, however, are families from the working classes eligible for government safety-net programs to assist their children. Many persons in those families wonder why, since they've always paid their taxes and thus fulfilled their general obligations to the larger society, they're not now eligible for some sort of universal reciprocity from their society. Why, they puzzle, are they being left out of exchange loops that they believe benefit poor (often black) children, but not their children.

Women, Paid Labor, and Children The growing participation of women in paid labor has many consequences for families.[52] One is that it provides money that enables households to discharge their front-line obligations to children. The woman's employment is particularly significant if the man's earnings don't stretch far enough, or if he becomes unemployed. However, another consequence is that the woman has less time available to carry out her traditional role as her children's chief caretaker. Thus, many Americans face thorny issues that never confronted the 1950s' Benchmark Family. These complexities include maternity/paternity leaves, daycare, time off when children (or other family members) are ill, and so forth. In the realm of children's services for employed parents, the United States is the *most* likely of all Western nations to limit universal obligations to its children.[53] Family members themselves are expected to provide those services.

Advocates for government programs aimed at addressing these kinds of issues say that all citizens have an obligation to see that "all our children" are not shortchanged as a result of the increasing participation by women in paid labor.[54] The issue, say the advocates, is the degree to which the larger society has the obligation to assist in providing services to the children of middle- and working-, as well as lower-class, families. For example, when a woman entered paid labor in the past, she could generally expect that her mother, mother-in-law, or some other woman family member would assist with most aspects of child care. But now those other women are just as likely as she to be employed!

Lone Parents and Obligations to Children

The question of services to children is particularly important if only one adult resides with them in the household. Although at one time uncommon among Europeans and white North Americans, in recent years lone-parent households have grown at a very rapid pace throughout all Western societies.[55] Although we say a great deal more about lone parents in Chapter 16, we mention them here briefly to make several points. One is that no matter how difficult it is for two employed parents to cope with the numerous demands of parenting, studies reveal that combining parenting and employment is extraordinarily strenuous for lone parents.[56] Most lone parents are employed women earning considerably less than men with comparable education. A second point is that some white lone parents have recently begun coping by means of strategies devised decades ago by African-Americans. Although the incidence of lone parenting is proportionally higher among blacks than whites, the rate of increase is greater among whites than blacks (see Chapters 13 and 16). One of the most significant reasons for this is high divorce rates followed by extended periods of singleness. Another reason is the increased tendency of unmarried white women to have babies.

Mutual Support Networks among Whites
In the wake of recent increases in white lone-parent households, Cochran and colleagues report that some of them are forming mutual aid and mutual support networks in the same ways blacks have for many decades.[57] Clusters of white women who are lone parents are forming networks in which they exchange not only friendship behaviors but also goods, services, and money. In some instances, the women formed what the researchers called "primary networks."[58] These kinds of networks were very much like the social families described in Chapter 2. They engaged in the giving and receiving of many kinds of benefits that were very helpful for struggling parents.

Increasingly, white women parents are facing social conditions making it difficult for them to maintain households on their own. Those conditions, as mentioned, include divorce and limited earnings potential, as well as unwed motherhood. Unlike black women, who are much more accustomed to expecting transitions in their relationships (including marriage), most white women still expect their marriages to be stable. And because they do not ever expect to be sole earner-parents, the women see little need to become economically self-sufficient, or what some call "economically autonomous."[59] They don't anticipate being able to take care of themselves and their children in the same ways that men do.

CONCLUSION—SOCIAL FAMILIES AND THE TWENTY-FIRST CENTURY

In view of these rapidly developing trends, Cochran and co-workers suggest that the *responsible* thing to do is to make social families a national policy goal. In their view, social families would benefit dual-earner parents as much as solo parents, to say nothing of the benefits for adults of all ages living entirely alone. Indeed, the networks they studied contained dual-earner as well as solo parents. Right now, most North Americans believe that the most responsible way to take care of children is in the context of the Benchmark Family. Cochran and colleagues are quick to state that they're not challenging that assumption. They add, however, that for growing numbers of black, white, and Hispanic citizens who are located in the middle classes as well as in the working and lower classes, that ideal is proving increasingly elusive.

As a result, one means to reinvent family is to update an idea that's been part of the African-American community for a long time. Being part of a social family demands responsibility. In that setting, each member has a moral obligation to fulfill her or his duties to other family members, both adults and children. But because one must give, one is entitled to receive as well. To be sure, as Rivers and Scanzoni state, it's hard work to be part of an effective social family. But advocates who want to make social families a public policy goal believe that social families would benefit a lot of parents who are now tryng to make it on their own. They genuinely wish to be responsible parents and partners, but find it exceedingly difficult to do so. For many of those persons, "chosen" families might supply just the impetus they need to fulfill their responsibilities.

NOTES

1. David Schneider, 1984, pp. 164–165.
2. Ibid., pp. 166, 170.
3. P. S. Wilson, 1980.
4. Michelle Locke, 1991. "Associated Press News." *The Gainesville, Florida, Sun,* November 28, p. A7.
5. Ibid.
6. Wilson and Pahl, 1988.
7. Ibid., pp. 249ff.
8. Ibid., p. 251
9. Jaffe, 1989; Danigelis and Fengler, 1991.
10. Wilson and Pahl, p. 253.
11. Ibid., p. 255.
12. McChesney and Bengston, 1988, p. 19; see also James White, 1991.
13. Wilson and Pahl, p. 257, italics in original.
14. Ibid.
15. Ibid.
16. Ibid., p. 258.
17. Ibid.
18. ibid.
19. Ibid.
20. Ibid.
21. Lindsey, 1981, p. 12.
22. Ibid.
23. Rubin, 1985.
24. Lindsey, p. 2.
25. Rubin, p. 22.
26. Ibid.
27. Allan, 1989.
28. Gelles, 1972.
29. Rubin, p. 33.
30. Lindsey, p. 12.
31. Ibid., pp. 108–109.
32. Ibid., pp. 113–114.
33. Levi-Strauss, 1957; Fortes, 1969; Ekeh, 1974; Firth, 1936.
34. Ellis, 1971; Finch, 1989, p. 230.
35. Finch, pp. 220, 231.
36. Ekeh, p. 205, See also Jean Peterson, 1993.
37. Ibid.
38. Giallombardo, 1966.
39. Moschetti, 1979.
40. Finch, p. 220.
41. Wilson and Pahl, 1988.
42. Billingsley, 1968.
43. Sundstrom, 1987.
44. See Melynda Dovel Cox, 1993. "Life with the 'boomerang generation.'" *The Gainesville, Florida, Sun,* January 6, p. 1D.
45. Simmons, Klein, and Simmons, 1977.
46. Rubin, p. 22.
47. Pirog-Good and Stets, 1989, p. 108.
48. Moen, 1989.
49. Fuchs, 1988.
50. Jewell, 1988.
51. Fuchs.
52. Ibid.
53. Moen.
54. Hewlett, 1991.
55. Ermisch, 1990.
56. Joshi, 1990; Hardey and Crow, 1991.
57. Cochran et al., 1990.
58. Ibid., p. 266.
59. Thompson and Gongla, 1983.

CHAPTER 4

SOME CONTEMPORARY SEXUAL SCENES

Chapters 2 and 3 talked about families in a broad sense. Families consist of several persons bound together in one or more ways, and usually residing in several households. They are a primary group, that is, a we-group. The bottom line of a family is the exchange of tangible benefits such as services, goods, and money. Sometimes families also share ties of friendship—companionship, intimacy, emotional support. Families may have blood ties, but not necessarily. A particular family may include older persons, solo parents and their children, dual-earner couples with children, and persons who are black or white, Hispanic or Anglo, straight or gay. "Effective" families are made up of responsible persons, that is, persons who fulfill their obligations to one another.

Chapters 4 and 5 shift our focus from families to dyads, or two-person groups. Thus far we've mentioned sexual ties simply in passing. But now sexual behaviors and bonds take center stage. Critics holding the fixed-philosophy position in Figure 1-1 charge that many of today's family problems stem from irresponsible sexual behaviors. In fact, they connect irre-sponsible parenthood to sexual irresponsibility: "If persons would wait till marriage to have sex and babies (and then stay married), they'd be able to take care of their children properly," is the frequently heard complaint. But what does it actually mean to be "sexually responsible"? And can we reinvent dyads so as to make them sexually responsible, similar to the ways in which reinventing social families contributes to shared responsibility?

SEXUAL NORMS AND BELIEFS

The First Kinsey Reports

Alfred Kinsey's investigations of human sexual behaviors were truly path breaking. Based on people living during the 1930s and 1940s, his studies supplied facts and figures that scandalized Americans and became overnight media sensations.[1] But when this evidence about men's and women's sexual behaviors was published during the 1940s and 1950s, it was greeted with incredulity and disbelief. Certain religious leaders refused to acknowledge the reports as valid. Kinsey was accused of falsifying the numbers to sell books. Worse, his critics charged that by giving people the allegedly flawed idea that "everybody's doing 'it,' " he was leading people to conclude that "I can do 'it' too." As a result, many religious leaders accused Kinsey of corrupting America's morals, and thus of undermining the foundations of the Benchmark Family and society.

Those leaders feared that the cultural gap between norms prohibiting premarital sex and persons' actual behaviors would be narrowed if ordinary citizens began realizing how many people were doing what Lillian Rubin calls the "Big It."[2] Norms would start catching up to behaviors and greater numbers of ordinary citizens would feel that "it's OK for me to do it." Janet Boles said that the U.S. Religious Right as a social and political force was first conceived out of reaction to the Kinsey reports.[3] She added that it was not until the early 1970s that the Religious Right became an organized social movement in reaction to the proposed Equal Rights Amendment.

A Later Kinsey Institute Report

Kinsey was a zoologist studying the sex life of the gall wasp before he became interested in human sexuality. His successors at the Institute for Sex Research say that Kinsey's aim was to tell it like it is—to describe people's sexual behaviors.[4] Several years after his death, researchers from his Sex Institute did another survey of the adult population of the United States. Their chief aim was to examine norms and values about sex. They were interested in culture—what adults *believe* should and should not be done regarding both heterosexual and homosexual behaviors.

Their study is particularly significant because the researchers collected their information during the year 1970. During the 1960s, many researchers agree that the United States

and Canada experienced a sexual revolution (see Chapter 7). Thus, the study had a chance to find out if the tumultuous sixties had had any impact on what U.S. adults believed about sex. The 1970 Kinsey researchers began their report by asserting that the label "sexual revolution" was so vague and imprecise that they preferred to abandon it. Instead they wanted to find out if the 1960s had brought about any genuine changes in the *culture* of sexuality. Regardless of how they were actually behaving, what did adults believe was "right" and "wrong" about sex?[5] Were those beliefs different from what adults believed and said before the 1960s? Table 4-1 presents the results of their research with regard to extramarital sex, homosexuality, sex among heterosexual singles, masturbation, and prostitution.

Klassen and colleagues concluded that these numbers by themselves reveal that in 1970 the majority of U.S. adults held "conservative" or "traditional" views regarding sex. Furthermore, when the respondents were asked if they had "always felt the same way" about premarital and extramarital sex, 66 percent answered yes. And 82 percent said yes, about homosexual acts. Finally, 73 percent answered yes about maturbation.[6]

In sum, in 1970 a large majority of American adults perceived themselves as not ever having changed their views about sex, especially homosexuality and masturbation. Not only were they conservative after the 1960s, they'd been conservative before the sexual revolution. Interestingly, the authors added that most citizens believed that their own views were *more* conservative than the views of the majority of other citizens, that most other persons were more "permissive" than they were. Furthermore, many believed that the sexual behaviors they disapproved of should be kept illegal, and that " 'violators' [should be] 'cured' . . . or threatened with jail."[7] As expected, citizens felt most strongly about punishing homosexual violators.

TABLE 4-1
Beliefs about Sexuality Based on a 1970 National Sample of U.S. Residents

	Always wrong	Wrong*	Not wrong at all
Extramarital sex	72%[†]	25%	2%
Homosexuality—persons in love	71	16	12
Homosexuality—casual sex	78	16	6
Teenage girl—casual sex	68	26	6
Teenage boy—casual sex	53	37	9
Sex for teenage boy—loves girl	37	40	23
Sex for teenage girl—loves boy	46	35	19
Adult single man—casual sex	50	33	17
Adult single woman—casual sex	55	31	14
Adult single man—loves woman	33	33	33
Adult single woman—loves man	36	32	31
Masturbation	27	51	19
Female prostitution	57	31	11

* Includes "almost always wrong" and "only sometimes wrong."
[†] Percentages do not consistently total 100%
Source: Klassen et al., 1989.

The Respondents' Own Premarital Sexual Behaviors The chief reason these adults were more tolerant of heterosexual nonconformity was that 79 percent of the men and 41 percent of the women had had a premarital sexual experience. "Experience" was defined for respondents as heterosexual activity resulting in either the respondent, or her or his partner, having an orgasm. Respondents might, for instance, have been "technical virgins" (defined in Chapter 7). Nevertheless, the authors said that when respondents reported a sexual experience, they very likely meant actual intercourse.

Belief–Behavior Gap Importantly, when we compare the numbers regarding actual sexual behaviors with the numbers regarding sexual beliefs and norms, we come to the not too surprising conclusion that the majority of U.S. citizens believe and say one thing about sex but actually do the opposite. The respondents felt that premarital sexual activity was wrong, but they had done "It" anyhow. And doing "It" didn't change their minds—as adults they still believed it was wrong. Alongside the finding

that men were more likely than women to have had premarital sexual experience, the researchers reported that blacks, younger persons, urban persons, college-educated persons, and persons with nonreligious parents were also more likely to have had sexual experience than whites, older persons, rural persons, those with less education, and persons with religious parents.[8] Furthermore, when the researchers asked how frequently respondents had had premarital sexual experiences, precisely the same differences held: Men had sexual experiences more frequently than women, blacks more frequently than whites, younger persons more frequently than older persons, urban persons more frequently than rural persons, the better educated more frequently than the less educated, and the less religious more frequently than the more religious.

The researchers also discussed homosexuality, to reinforce their argument that in spite of the tumultuous sixties, most persons in 1970 still held conservative sexual attitudes. For example, they found that most adults believed that homosexuals are "that way" because they've been harmed by parents and/or other homosexuals.[9] Furthermore, the adults believed that homosexuals could be "cured" if they genuinely wished to be. And indeed, they believed that homosexuals should *want* to be cured. The researchers stated that most citizens hold "fear and revulsion" toward homosexuals chiefly because they perceive them as trying to "corrupt" children as well as other adults.[10] To stave off corruption, 59 percent of the sample felt that "any kind of homosexual act should be against the law."[11] And from two-thirds to three-fourths of the sample felt that a homosexual should not be allowed to work as a court judge, school teacher, minister, physician, or government official. Recently, fears about working with homosexuals have been expressed most vigorously in connection with military service. Opponents to gays in the military have argued that their presence undermines order and discipline. In short, homosexuals are still perceived as a "corrupting" influence. Not surprisingly, the researchers discovered that citizens who believed that *heterosexual* freedoms are wrong were also the ones likely to feel most negatively about *homosexual* behviors. Such persons were the most consistently conservative adults. They were the adults who'd had no premarital sexual experiences of their own, who'd grown up in rural areas, and whose parents were less educated, strict, and religiously devout.

Explaining Views on Sexuality

Why did some adults hold more conservative views about sexuality (both hetero and homo) than other adults? Klassen and co-workers identified three reasons.

Sexual Restraint as a Moral Virtue   First in importance was religious devoutness. Although in 1970 the Religious Right was not yet the potent political force it is today, persons who held conservative religious beliefs, whether Protestant, Catholic, or Jewish, also held conventional views about premarital and extramarital sex, homosexuality, masturbation, and prostitution. The authors pointed out that for many centuries the Judeo-Christian tradition has taught that the central feature of sexuality is *restraint.* Especially in the United States, "sexual restraint [is] seen as an index of social worth."[12]

The idea that persons who practice sexual restraint are morally superior to persons who don't is an important cultural belief. In recent years, for instance, the sexual lives of politicians have become front-page headlines and the stuff of TV talk shows. Senators Ted Kennedy and Gary Hart, among others, were considered morally unworthy to be president because of their nonconventional sexual behaviors: "Would you want Senator X's fingers on the nuclear trigger when he can't keep them off women's bodies?," cries the talk show host. Although the press knew about the extramarital relationships of previous presidents such as Franklin Roosevelt and John Kennedy, and those of officials such as General Dwight Eisenhower when he commanded Allied troops during World War II, the press concealed that information from the public. Reporters did so because they felt that public confidence in the worth and competence of those officials would be eroded if their lack of sexual restraint became known. The press reasoned it was in the national interest to hush up the facts. Today, by contrast, the press is eager to document the "smoking bed," that is, clear evidence that a candidate has violated sexual norms.[13] For example, during the 1992 presidential campaign, Bill Clinton was forced to answer charges about his alleged marital infidelity. Had he been unable to counter those charges successfully, it's unlikely he would even have been nominated, much less elected, as President. A sexual harassment lawsuit brought against him after becoming President kept alive nagging doubts about his "moral fitness" for the office.

If "worthy" people practice sexual restraint, is there ever a time when one can set aside restraint, and still be a good person? Obviously yes—during marriage. In traditional religious teaching, masturbation as well as premarital sex are wrong because they show lack of restraint—failure to wait until marriage to fulfill sexual urges. But even within marriage, sexual restraint (passionless sex) was once considered a virtue. Married couples were suspect and should feel shame (women in particular) if during intercourse they got swept away and became too passionate.[14] In current official Roman Catholic doctrine (and previously in Protestant as well), artificial contraceptive techniques are sinful because they interfere with God's will regarding reproduction. Hence a married couple that is morally worthy but does not want to have children just now will refrain from intercourse except during the woman's "safe" days. Couples who insist on using contraceptives are not practicing restraint, say some theologians; they are engaging merely in mutual masturbation.

Abstinence versus Safe Sex The belief that restraint is a superior moral virtue is much in the news today under the label of "abstinence" (vs. "safe sex"). When in 1991 Magic Johnson disclosed that he'd contracted the AIDS virus, he said he would devote much of his time and energy crusading for safe sex. *Safe sex* means using condoms when having sex. The main premise underlying the safe sex theme is that although restraint may be more desirable, persons who aren't restrained should protect themselves. But some critics disagree with the safe sex theme. Accordingly, they have gently chastised Johnson.[15] They say that if Johnson had been abstinent, he wouldn't be infected in the first place. Instead of a safe sex theme, some critics argue, abstinence (i.e., restraint) should be official public policy. Some citizens, for instance, oppose distribution of condoms in high schools and clinics because they be-lieve it sends the wrong message to adolescents and adults, namely, that sexual restraint until marriage may not be such a binding rule after all. Some citizens also use the restraint theme as one part of their reasoning to oppose abortion choices for unmarried persons.[16] They argue that if unmarried persons were abstinent, they'd never have an unwanted pregnancy in the first place. Having abandoned restraint and indulged themselves, persons have no right to abort the fetus.

Whether priests and nuns should marry is yet another current controversy arising from the belief that sexual restraint is a morally superior virtue. For many centuries the Roman Catholic Church has taught that being called by God to a life of celibacy is a special vocation. Men and women who are able to resist sexual urges are believed to operate at a higher moral level than persons who indulge themselves sexually, even within marriage. During recent years, many priests and nuns have in vain petitioned the Church to allow married clergy. Frustrated with the Church's refusal to budge, some have violated their vows and experienced both heterosexual and homosexual activity.[17] A number of them have abandoned their vocation in order to marry.[18] Some priests marry secretly and try to conceal their relationship from Church officials as well as their parishioners.[19] Because the Church continues to insist on the virtue of celibacy, it has recently had difficulty recruiting younger persons to become nuns and priests.

Klassen and colleagues assert that within the Judeo-Christian tradition homosexuality is viewed with total repugnance because it represents the ultimate in lack of restraint, as well as utter self-indulgence and debauchery.[20] Not only is this type of self-indulgence "sinful" in and of itself, it is also viewed as a threat to marriage, the one place where sexual indulgence is permitted. Many believe that if homosexuality became decriminalized, many people would ignore marriage and children, thus undermining the future of society. Table 4-1 shows that in 1970 extramarital sex was perceived as being just about as repugnant as homosexuality. It too is believed to be a potential threat to marriage and society, and also is seen as a classic example of self-indulgence rather than self-restraint. Nevertheless, for centuries most married men have engaged in extramarital sex (see Chapters 6 and 7). Under the cultural norm known as the "double standard," men's behavior was winked at so long as it was discreet and did not shame their families. "Wise men" obeyed the eleventh commandment: "Thou shalt not be found out."

Age and Views about Sex Although traditional religion is the most important factor accounting for conservative sexual views, Klassen and co-workers concluded that there are two additional factors as well. One of these is *age*. The researchers consistently found that older persons were more opposed to all forms of sexual nonconformity than were younger persons.[21] Many older persons interviewed in 1970 were likely to have experienced intercourse during the engagement period of their marriage. However, they held tenaciously to the norm that premarital sex is wrong (or at least not right). It takes many decades of consecutive cohorts of younger persons having nonmarital sex to seriously challenge older ideas and to insert newer ideas into the prevailing cultural climate.

Gender and Views about Sex Following age, *gender* was also significant in accounting for conservative sexual views. Klassen and colleagues' percentages showed that in 1970, fewer women than men had experienced premarital sex, and women had experienced it less frequently. Not surprisingly, these researchers reported that women were more conservative about sexual norms than men.[22] In other words, women were more likely than

men to believe that premarital sex, extramarital sex, homosexuality, masturbation, and prostitution, were wrong. The possible reasons for this gender difference included the fact that women are more likely than men to be religious, and that the double standard made it harder for women to ignore sexual norms. Moreover, the specter of pregnancy loomed as a constant deterrent to women's sexual deviance in ways that it could not for men.

Furthermore, younger women who were part of the 1960s' sexual revolution were often troubled about some of its implications[23] (see Chapter 7). In particular, some women felt that the revolution was causing them to lose control over their own sexuality. A number of men believed that sexual liberation meant that women had lost the right to say no. Thus, by 1970 some women might indeed have objected to certain sexual behaviors, but not on the grounds that the behaviors were right or wrong in and of themselves. Rather, the women may have objected because they felt that certain behaviors might contribute to women's continued exploitation.

TRENDS IN SEXUAL BEHAVIORS AMONG ADOLESCENTS AND YOUTH

The picture we've just painted about people's beliefs about sexuality is drawn largely from studies done some years ago. Nevertheless, when it comes to what people *say* they believe about sexuality, there's no indication that they have changed very much during the past several decades.[24] People's norms tend to be much more conventional than their behaviors. Arland Thornton, for example, recently compared a number of U.S. national surveys that were done between 1972 and 1986.[25] The surveys asked people their views about premarital sexuality. For the most part, the evidence showed that the majority of citizens (those in the middle and in the fixed-philosophy category of Figure 1-1) remain quite conventional in what they *say* about that subject. And numerous other studies show that citizens' views on homosexuality, extramarital sex, and so on continue to be quite conventional as well.[26] Nevertheless, there is firm evidence that the changes in sexual *behaviors*—especially women's sexual behaviors—that have been going on since the 1920s are continuing unabated. Robert Walsh, for example, says that research from the past two decades permits us to "draw fairly solid conclusions" about the following trends in the sexual behaviors of high-school and post-high-school youth[27]:

1. Since 1970 the percentage of youth who report having experienced premarital intercourse, or coitus, has increased substantially.
2. Since 1970 the rate of increase in reported coitus has been much higher among women than among men.
3. Owing in part to 2., women are catching up with men as far as degree of participation in coitus is concerned. The substantial differences in coital experience between the genders that Kinsey found during the 1930s and 1940s are rapidly shrinking.
4. The ages at which youth are having their initial sexual experiences are steadily dropping. Growing numbers of younger adolescents are experiencing "technical virginity" as well as actual intercourse.
5. Black youth tend to be more sexually active than white youth.

Sexual Behaviors among Adolescents

These five trends are borne out dramatically by the results of a recent government investigation. During 1990, the U.S. Centers for Disease Control did a comprehensive national study that was representative of students in grades 9 through 12 throughout the United States, Puerto Rico, and the Virgin Islands.[28] Labeled as a study of adolescent health, the students were questioned about, among other things, sexual intercourse and contraception.

Contemporary dancing and popular music represent people's actual sexual behaviors much more vividly than do cultural values and beliefs about sex.

TABLE 4-2

Percentage of U.S. High-School Students Reporting That They Have *Ever* Had Sexual Intercourse, by Sex, Race/Ethnicity, and Grade, 1990

	Female	Male	Total
Race/ethnicity:			
White	47.0	56.4	51.6
Black	60.0	87.8	72.3
Hispanic	45.0	63.0	53.4
Grade:			
9th	31.9	48.7	39.6
10th	42.9	52.5	47.6
11th	52.7	62.6	57.3
12th	66.6	76.3	71.9
Total	48.0	60.8	54.2

Note: Total number of students: 11,631.
Source: U.S. Centers for Disease Control, January 3, 1992.

Table 4-2 shows that the five trends just listed are not leveling off. Each is continuing into the 1990s. Increasing proportions of youth are sexually active, and the differences in coital experience between females and males continue to shrink, especially among eleventh and twelfth graders. In terms of the fourth trend—adolescents experiencing intercourse at increasingly younger ages—virtually a third of ninth-grade girls and half of ninth-grade boys are sexually active. Finally, blacks continue to be more sexually active than either whites or Hispanics.

Table 4-3 shows the percentages of high-school youth who said they had coitus during the three months before being interviewed. Once again, these numbers reinforce the same five trends.

However, Freya Somenstein and colleagues caution that we should not think of adoles-

TABLE 4-3

Percentage of U.S. High-School Students Reporting That They Have Had Sexual Intercourse During the 3 Months Preceding the Survey, 1990

	Female	Male	Total
Race/ethnicity:			
White	37.1	39.0	38.0
Black	42.3	68.1	53.9
Hispanic	31.4	44.6	37.5
Grade:			
9th	20.8	29.1	24.7
10th	32.4	36.4	34.3
11th	41.3	45.1	43.1
12th	52.7	56.9	55.0
Total	36.4	42.5	39.4

Note: Total number of students: 11,631.
Source: U.S. Centers for Disease Control, January 3, 1992.

cents as "sexual adventurers."[29] During 1988 they did a national study of adolescent boys in the United States. One of their findings was that boys who were sexually experienced had averaged just under two partners during the twelve months before the survey. Second, during the previous four weeks, the average number of times that the boys had had intercourse was slightly under three. A third finding was that during the previous twelve months, sexually experienced boys spent an average of six months with no sexual partner at all. Finally, a fourth finding was that during the prior twelve months only 21 percent of sexually active boys had more than one partner in any one month. Although Somenstein and co-workers did not interview girls, we can be confident that if they had done so the numbers would not be any higher. Instead, the numbers would probably have been lower.

This study suggests that although large numbers of adolescents have been and are sexually active, they do not seem to be promiscuous about it. That is, adolescents are not having frequent sexual encounters with numerous persons within a short span of time. It appears that intercourse generally occurs within the context of an ongoing relationship that is relatively monogamous. If the relationship "breaks up" the teenagers apparently wait a while before establishing another sexually active, monogamous relationship. In short, erotic friendships seem to be becoming increasingly common among adolescents, just as they are among adults.

Contraceptive Usage There has been a vast amount of publicity about adolescent pregnancies, teenage parenthood, and AIDS in recent years. Table 4-4 shows that in 1990 a substantial proportion of sexually active youth used some kind of contraceptive method at the time of their last intercourse. Indeed, during the past twenty years there have been considerable increases in adolescent contraceptive usage. In 1971, for example, Melvin Zelnick and colleagues found that among sexually active females aged 15 to 19, only 48 percent of whites and 44 percent of blacks used any contraceptive method at last intercourse. By 1976, those figures had risen to 66 and 58 percent, respectively.[30] And by 1990 the percentages, as shown in Table 4-4, had risen to 81 for whites and 71 for blacks. However, no contraceptive method is ever completely foolproof. And since many adolescents use methods carelessly, they get pregnant anyhow. In addition, Table 4-5 shows that among youth using some type of contraceptive, only about one-third to one-half used condoms either alone or in conjunction with some other method. Failure to use condoms placed them at considerable risk of contracting a variety of socially transmitted

TABLE 4-4

Percentage of U.S. High-School Students Sexually Active During 3 Months Before the Survey and Report They Used a Contraceptive Method at Last Sexual Intercourse, 1990

	Female	Male	Total
Race/ethnicity:			
White	81.1	80.1	80.6
Black	71.4	76.3	74.3
Hispanic	62.6	69.1	66.2
Total	77.7	77.8	77.7

Note: Total number of students: 11,631.
Source: U.S. Centers for Disease Control, January 3, 1992

TABLE 4-5
Percentage of U.S. High-School Students Sexually Active During 3 Months Before the Survey and Used a *Condom* at Last Sexual Intercourse, 1990

	Female	Male	Total
Race/ethnicity:			
White	4.71	50.0	45.9
Black	36.7	54.5	47.1
Hispanic	28.1	46.8	38.4
Total	40.0	49.4	44.9

Note: Total number of students: 11,631.
Source: U.S. Centers for Disease Control, January 3, 1992.

diseases (STDs), including the HIV virus, and thus AIDS.

Sexual Behaviors among Persons in Their Twenties

The numbers in Tables 4-2 and 4-3, although quite high, apply merely to high schoolers. Once persons leave high school they increase their levels of sexual activity.[31] The actual levels at which persons throughout their 20s engage in coitus are revealed in a national survey taken during the mid-1980s. This is the same decade in which large numbers of younger persons were saying that coitus is wrong.[32] In 1983, Koray Tanfer and Marjorie Horn investigated never-married 20- to 29-year-old women living in dormitories, sororities, and households throughout the forty-eight contiguous states.[33] They found that 80 percent of the white women and 90 percent of the black women had had sexual intercourse. It seems safe to say that the percentages for never-married men in their twenties are probably higher.

A Sexual Revolution?

Has there been a sexual revolution since the roaring twenties? Clearly, in terms of actual sexual behaviors among younger, never-married persons, there's been an almost 180-degree change, particularly among women. For many younger persons marriage (and its precursor, engagement) was once the social co-

coon safely surrounding sexual intercourse. It happened there and almost nowhere else. That is absolutely no longer the case.

However, we cannot say that the sexual revolution implies that most people have changed their basic beliefs about sex. Most citizens continue to believe that people who are sexually restrained are somehow more worthy or morally superior than those who indulge outside of marriage. In spite of the fact that more than 80 percent of them indulge, only half of persons in their 20s are willing to venture that premarital sex is not wrong. Among older persons, the proportion willing to say it is not wrong is even less. Avoiding sex carries the same mystique as jogging—people who avoid sex, or who jog, are more "virtuous" than those who engage in sex, or who fail to jog. The connection between sex and aerobics is not accidental. Elizabeth and J. H. Pleck report that most coaches once believed that male athletes expending sperm suffered a loss in physical prowess.[34]

Rewording the Question

In social science, question wording is everything. Right now, most researchers merely ask, "Is premarital sex wrong?" But suppose we add the word "responsible" and change "wrong" to "right." The question now might create a very different image in the respondent's mind: "Is responsible nonmarital sex always right, (or) almost always right, (or) right only sometimes, (or) not right at all?" The thinking behind the older wording (is sex wrong?) is the conventional belief that sexual restraint is good, but under certain conditions such as "love" or "engagement" indulgence might be discreetly tolerated. But when the words "responsible" and "right" are inserted, the focus necessarily shifts from "restraint" to "responsible indulgence." Ira Reiss says that persons are sexually responsible, first by negotiating their sexual behaviors on the basis of an honest and explicit statement of precisely what each person does and does not want.[35] Such negotiation rules out force or verbal coercion as a means for men (or women) to gain sexual favors (see Chapter 11). Second, Reiss adds that sexual responsibility demands that each party takes effective steps to guard against unwanted pregnancies and STDs. Consequently, the question becomes, "Can nonmarried persons ever be *responsibly indulgent* when it comes to sex? Never? Always? Almost always? Sometimes? Nevertheless, regardless of their own behaviors, when faced with admitting out loud that sexual indulgence is actually right, many persons are likely to hesitate. Even in the 1990s, it seems unlikely that many persons are prepared to affirm that indulgence is after all a good thing. It's much safer to continue to believe and say that restraint is better, even if one is not restrained.

The Next Phase of the Revolution Reiss suggests that the next phase of the sexual revolution would, on the part of a majority of Americans, be based on believing something very different from what they do now. They would have to believe and to say that sexual responsibility is more important than sexual restraint. Their beliefs would have to catch up with their behaviors. Or, put another way, citizens would have to be willing to assert that nonmarital sex is indeed a good thing, if it is *responsible.* By the same token, they would have

to assert that marital sex is a bad thing, if it is irresponsible.

EXTRAMARITAL INTERCOURSE— NORMS AND BEHAVIORS

Senator Gary Hart began his presidential campaign in February 1987. Three months later the strong frontrunner suddenly withdrew from the campaign because of a "smoking bed"— evidence that he'd had what G. C. Sponaugle calls EMC—extramarital coitus.[36] If any gap exists between what U.S. citizens say and do about nonmarital intercourse, there appears to be a much wider gap, some might say a chasm, between beliefs and behaviors about EMC. For example, during 1985 among U.S. women age 30 and under, 70 percent said EMC was always wrong, 18 percent said it was almost always wrong, 11 percent said it was wrong only sometimes, and only 1 percent said not wrong at all.[37] The 1985 numbers for EMC had hardly changed at all from what women age 30 and under had said they believed in 1973. Nor were the 1985 numbers for younger women much different than those for younger men. The cultural stereotype, of course, is that men are more likely than women to approve of EMC, and a few studies point in that direction.[38]

Given that over 90 percent of Americans of both genders, and of all ages, say that to one degree or another EMC is wrong, may we assume that 90 percent of them don't do It? Not according to Sponaugle. There are many fewer studies of EMC than of premarital sex, and the ones that exist tend to be flawed.[39] Nonetheless, EMC researchers estimate conservatively that at least 50 percent of ever-married men and 30 percent of ever-married women have had EMC *at least once* while married. Using those percentages, Sponaugle calculates that during the mid-1980s, at least 52 million Americans age 18 and over had EMC at least once while married. Those numbers don't take into account the large numbers of currently single persons having intercourse with married persons.[40] Sponaugle also says that if we add a third category—persons indirectly affected by extramarital relationships (spouses, children, friends, sibs, co-workers, and so on)—it's likely that all three categories make up a "majority of the population."[41] However, a 1992 survey of 3,442 randomly selected U.S. adults age 18 to 59 presents a more conservative picture of the extent of EMC. Among those currently married, 75 percent of men and 85 percent of women say that they have sex only with their spouse.[41a] The researchers admit they have no way to be sure their respondents are telling the truth.

The term *fornicator* (seldom heard anymore) was about the most disparaging label ever applied to single persons having coitus. EMC continues to be described by any number of terms that are both extremely negative and emotionally forceful: cheating, deceiving, betraying, being unfaithful, infidelity, breaking vows, adultery, and so on. In the Judeo-Christian tradition (as well as in other world religions such as Islam), adultery, especially by a woman, was and is considered a much more serious offense than fornication. Interestingly enough, most U.S. states retain nineteenth-century laws prohibiting fornication and adultery, as well as sodomy. A 1987 attempt in Minnesota to repeal all three laws failed in the legislature. In that state, as in most others, adultery is a crime punishable by a fine of up to 3000 dollars and/or up to a year in jail. Nevertheless, in spite of the laws and all the unflattering things said about persons having EMC, at the very least a quarter of husbands and 15 percent of wives admit to it. It would seem that EMC, like premarital coitus, is a pointed example of a gap between beliefs and behaviors.

Regardless of its actual numbers, the puzzlement over EMC is that in spite of being roundly condemned by both genders and all ages and races, "people are absolutely fascinated by the topic."[42] To back up his claim of fascination, Sponaugle demonstrates how frequently EMC appears in the arts and entertainment. Hawthorne's *The Scarlet Letter,* D. H. Lawrence's *Lady Chatterly's Lover,* as well as later works by John Updike, Margaret Atwood, and many others, represent serious efforts to consider EMC. Commercial and paperback fiction, of course, thrives on adulterous romances. Biographies of well-known persons (e.g., Franklin Roosevelt, Babe Ruth, Frank Sinatra, Billie Jean King, Jennie Churchill, John F. Kennedy, Joseph P. Kennedy, Martin Luther King, Jr.) focus on their affairs. And the supermarket tabloids sensationalize the infidelities of current celebrities—women and men alike. Among the most widely publicized recent celebrities were religious leaders Jimmy Baker and Jimmy Swaggart. Newspapers feature columns such as "Dear Abby" and "Ann Landers" in which EMC is a constant reader concern. Mall bookstores contain shelves of self-help books telling people how to "save your marriage from adultery," or how to survive it, or even, "how to have an affair." On TV, a main staple of the daytime soaps is EMC, and it's also a frequent prime-time theme. The list of commercial movies as well as serious films that portray EMC is endless. Among the most popular of 1991–1992 movies was *Prince of Tides,* based on Pat Conroy's novel. The entire movie dwells on the erotic friendship between Barbra Streisand and Nick Nolte, each of whom is married to someone else. In addition, infidelities are a common subject of music, including grand opera, blues, country, and rock. Finally, EMC is a favorite topic of stand-up comics, cartoons, and humorous skits on popular shows such as *Saturday Night Live.*

Americans' fascination with EMC in the arts and entertainment reinforces the idea of a wide gap between people's disapproval and their actual behaviors. On the one hand, better than 70 percent of the total population say EMC is always wrong, another 20 percent say it's almost always wrong, some 5 percent say wrong only sometimes, and only 5 percent say not wrong at all.[43] But on the other hand, sizable numbers of persons (currently married and single) have actually participated in EMC at one time or another. Furthermore, the vast majority of the population appears to participate vicariously in EMC via the mass media as well as through serious writing, films, and plays.

Explaining Disapproval of EMC

A number of studies have tried to explain why some persons disapprove of EMC more strongly than other persons. For example, why do some people say it's wrong always, while others say almost always, and sometimes, and a few say not wrong at all? Sponaugle summarizes the studies and reports that there are at least eighteen variables, or factors, that help to explain the degree to which persons disapprove of EMC.[44] For example, persons who approve of or who have ever experienced *pre*marital coitus are more likely to approve of EMC, as are persons who are better educated, who live in larger sized communities, who are single, and who are not parents. Approval is less likely among the religiously devout and those who are older. Persons who are less satisfied with their current marriages are more likely to approve of EMC. And so are persons who are less satisfied with the quality of the sex experienced in their marriages. Men appear more likely to approve of EMC, as do persons who believe in the goal of gender equality.

Sponaugle concludes, however, that there is no clear explanation why some people approve of EMC more strongly than others. Indeed, the fact that so many people disapprove of it and yet actually do it anyhow suggests that degree of approval is not a valid predictor of extramarital sexual behavior. It's like living in an area that's been flooding due to heavy rains and disapproving of the rains. The TV weather person ignores people's disapproval when forecasting the probability of rain. It seems clear that the great bulk of North American heterosexuals (and many homosexuals)

are to one degree or another uncomfortable with the idea of having sexual intercourse with someone other than their erotic friend, whether it occurs in a marital, cohabiting, or dating context. Nevertheless, many of them do it anyhow. (See Chapter 5 for a discussion of reasons.)

Comarital Sex: Swinging

A major reason people often give for disapproving of EMC is that it almost always implies secrecy.[45] The secrecy in turn gives rise to charges of "cheating." In the wake of the 1960s' sexual revolution, a number of persons during the 1970s were calling for more openness and honesty about sexual feelings and behaviors. *Open marriage* was the term coined by the married couple Nena and George O'Neill to describe marriages where the partners explicitly agree that sexual experiences (including coitus) with others are permissible.[46] As a result, the O'Neills became one of the most widely celebrated media sensations since Kinsey, although their reception was decidedly warmer than his. Jay and Mae Ziskin also drew media attention with their call for the extramarital sex contract.[47] They argued that if married persons could freely negotiate their "outside sex," it might help them achieve two things: avoid being in a "rut" and "find the kind of joy in marriage that we have."

Another type of open marriage was described by James and Lynn Smith as *comarital sex*, or what the popular press called "swinging."[48] Richard Jenks defines swinging as the "consensual exchange of marital partners for sexual purposes.[49] Most often, swingers exchange spouses in the context of a party, thus ensuring that each spouse knows what the other is doing. Many swingers maintain local and national networks, facilitated by magazines and conventions. Jenks collected some of the data used in his report at one of those conventions. He says that swingers who attend conventions are "out of the closet." But some swingers, he notes, have not gone public. "Hidden" swingers are couples that restrict their sexual exchanges to a select and closed group of persons. "Closed couples" are sometimes described as having group marriages.

Jenks found that the swingers he studied in 1982 were not much different from swingers studied during the late 1960s and early 1970s.[50] To be sure, the earlier labels of "wife-swapping" and "mate-swapping" have in recent years been dropped for obvious reasons. Otherwise, swingers still tend to be younger, white, well educated, and relatively affluent. Interestingly enough, two-thirds of Jenks's respondents had some religious affiliation, though not likely evangelical. Nonetheless, as David Denfeld and Michael Gordon put it, swingers tend to be "conservative and very straight." However, conservative is not at all how swingers were viewed by a sample of *non*swingers that Jenks also studied. His sample of nonswingers perceived (incorrectly) that swingers are very liberal on political and social issues, and are heavy drug and alcohol users. According to Jenks, nonswingers also believed that swingers are "sick," and thus require counseling to help them overcome their unhealthy behaviors.

Swinging, Honesty, and Jealousy   The actual percentages of persons who are now or have ever been swingers are not known. What is significant about swinging and other forms of comarital sex is that they represent an effort to practice responsible sexual indulgence within the context of formal marriage. Earlier we said that responsible *non*marital sex requires honesty regarding what each partner does and does not want. Accordingly, swinging's proponent's argue that they too are attempting to get beyond the double standard. They say they want to do away with the acrimonious charges of dishonesty and cheating that are leveled against the "guilty party" when he or she is "found out." Implicit in their reasoning is the idea that the emotions of jealousy and the

norms of exclusivity can to a large degree be overcome by being open and honest about sleeping with someone else. (See Chapter 5 for a detailed discussion of jealousy.)

HOMOSEXUALITIES

Homosexuality represents the third major social context of sexuality that we're considering in this chapter. The first context was younger, never-married heterosexuality, and the second was married heterosexuality. In the first two settings we paid special attention to differences between cultural norms and actual behaviors. Homosexuality too is an example of some persons behaving contrary to intensely felt prohibitions. Klassen and colleagues said that of all three types of sexual "deviance," most Americans feel most unfavorably toward homosexuality because they perceive it to be a corrupting influence on society, on families, and especially on children.

Explaining Homosexuality

The Essentialist Approach   Given widespread discrimination in jobs and housing against gay persons, along with the verbal abuse and physical violence (gay bashing) they must endure, why would anyone want to behave "that way?" Barbara Risman and Pepper Schwartz say that researchers have offered two major explanations for homosexual behavior.[51] They call one explanation the *essentialist* approach. This simply means that some researchers believe that homosexuality is the result either of biology and/or "unfortunate" psychological experiences. Researchers who hold the essentialist approach believe that homosexuals are the way they are owing to circumstances beyond their control. They are *predetermined* to be homosexuals either by biological or psychological factors, or perhaps by some combination of the two.

During 1991, two separate studies from

major universities saying that biological factors play a major role in causing homosexuality received considerable national press.[52] One study claimed that the cluster of brain cells guiding sex drive is twice as large in heterosexual men as in homosexual men. Another study compared identical male twins with fraternal male twins, and also with brothers who'd been adopted. The researchers found that 52 percent of identical twins were both gay, compared with 22 percent of fraternal twins and only 11 percent of adopted brothers. These results, they claim, suggest strongly that genetic factors are operating to cause homosexual behavior. However, Risman and Schwartz criticize studies alleging biological causes of homosexuality, saying they have many serious and glaring weaknesses. Also suspect, say these authors, are studies alleging homosexuality is predetermined by psychological causes, including childhood experiences such as a "strong" mother and a "weak" father. Hence, they reject the idea that homosexuals are emotionally sick or unstable. In a similar vein, the Society for the Psychological Study of Social Issues collected all of the recent information on homosexuality and concluded that "Homosexuality is as biologically natural as heterosexuality. [It] . . . is not a biological error or aberration. . . . [It] is not related to mental illness . . . neither is there a gay or lesbian personality structure."[53]

The Constructionist Approach   Having rejected the idea that homosexuality is predetermined either by biological or psychological factors, Risman and Schwartz turn to the second major explanation for homosexual behaviors. It's called the *constructionist* approach. Researchers in the constructionist camp never ask, "What makes a homosexual?" They don't agree that homosexuality is biologically or socially determined. Instead researchers in this camp believe that over time certain persons, as a result of their social circumstances, "come to identify themselves and label themselves as

gay men or lesbians."[54] But Risman and Schwartz find fault with this approach too and conclude that, as of right now, scientists have no clear and compelling explanations for homosexual behaviors.

However, Risman and Schwartz do argue that understanding homosexuality begins by rejecting the idea that a sharp dichotomy exists between gays and straights. Kinsey was probably the first to say that sexuality exists on a continuum.[55] At one extreme are persons who could only ever do heterosexual behaviors. At the other extreme are persons who could only do homosexual behaviors. As one moves away from either extreme, it becomes increasingly possible for some persons to engage in either kind of behaviors, depending on social circumstances. Recall that Chapter 2 showed how women prisoners who'd behaved in a heterosexual manner when they were free chose to do homosexual behaviors in prison under a totally different set of social conditions. Other researchers have found the same patterns among men denied access to women, such as in prisons, the military, monasteries, and boys' boarding schools.[56] The women prisoners, and also men in analogous situations, fully expected to return to their heterosexual behaviors after being released.

Defining Homosexuality

If social circumstances can influence people to behave sexually in ways they've never behaved before, does it become impossible to distinguish a heterosexual from a homosexual person? James Weinrich and Walter Williams suggest that persons can be defined as homosexual even if they don't do any homosexual behaviors, and even if they despise the gay community as well as their own homosexual feelings. Pesons are homosexual if they "experience romantic and/or sexual arousal repeatedly and consistently in the presence of some members of their own sex, but not with members of the other sex."[57] Using that approach, it's clear that some persons along Kinsey's continuum can and do think of themselves as homosexual, while others clearly think of themselves as heterosexual. Nevertheless, G. Dorsey Green and Frederick Bozett identify persons who think of themselves as homosexual (or at least suspect it) but do heterosexual behaviors because they want the esteem and respect for doing so.[58] For instance, Green and Bozett point out that a number of homosexuals marry, and some stay married, for reasons of respectability. Marriage shields them from the suspicion and rejection—the *stigma*—that accompanies being labeled as gay: "Oh," someone says, "he (or she) can't be gay—he (or she) is married!" Or, "They're just housemates." Sometimes married persons who are homosexual come to the point where they no longer wish to be involved in an ongoing heterosexual relationship such as marriage. As a result, they separate and then divorce.

Bisexuality

Sometimes, however, they prefer to remain married and experience homosexual behaviors "on the side," much like some married heterosexuals who have "side action" with other heterosexuals. Persons who can do both heterosexual and homosexual behaviors for an extended period are generally located somewhere in the middle of Kinsey's continuum. They are usually known as *bisexuals*. Most practicing bisexuals appear to be men, and a number of them are married.[59] Married male bisexuals often *cruise* bars and street corners to find homosexual partners, in the same ways that heterosexual men cruise to find female sexual partners. *Hustling* male prostitutes, however, is becoming increasingly risky because of the growing likelihood of contracting the HIV virus from either male or female partners who are promiscuous. Since bisexuals are usually secretive about their homosexual behaviors, they run the added risk of passing on the AIDS virus to women with whom they're

having casual or committed sex. If the relationship is a committed one (i.e., an erotic friendship), the unsuspecting woman is less likely to be on her guard against STDs because she believes her relationship is monogamous.

Not all bisexuals are secretive about their behaviors. Like the married heterosexuals discussed above, some bisexuals (and homosexuals) attempt to negotiate open and honest agreements about what they want. For example, when Patricia Ireland became the president-elect of NOW (National Organization for Women), she created a media stir when she revealed that she has two ongoing erotic friendships. Alongside the man in Miami to whom she has been maried for twenty-five years, she also lives in Washington D.C. with a female companion. Ireland asserted that "I have never been anything but honest about who I am and how I live my life."[60]

Comparing Gay and Straight Couples and Parents

The idea that homosexual and heterosexual behaviors exist on a continuum was also a recent conclusion of the Society for the Psychological Study of Social Issues. The evidence gathered by the Society pointed toward "the striking degree to which homosexuals and heterosexuals are alike."[61] They are remarkably alike in the ways in which they maintain their erotic friendships. For example, whether gay or straight, once couples take on the pains and pleasures of committed relationships, the matter of sexual preference fades when compared with issues such as power and negotiation[62] (see also Chapter 11). The alikeness is especially evident when couples share the same household and have to deal daily with mundane matters of housework, repairs, paying bills, and so on.[63]

Alikeness also appears when it comes to parenting. Most lesbian and gay parents became biological parents through previous heterosexual marriages.[64] Some homosexuals be-

The evidence shows that homosexual parents are neither more nor less effective than heterosexual parents.

come social parents because they've become an erotic friend of, and are often living with, someone who has children. Currently there are no accurate counts of the numbers of gay and lesbian parents. However, on the basis of the usual estimates that 10 percent of the male population is gay and 6 to 7 percent of the female population is lesbian, Green and Bozett calculate that the number of gay fathers in the United States is over 2 million and the number of lesbian mothers is between 1.5 and 3.3 million.[65] And in spite of cultural beliefs that homosexuals corrupt children, there is no sound evidence that homosexual parents are any worse, or any better, than straight parents.[66] Whether straight or gay, parents in any modern society face similar kinds of struggles and opportunities in dealing with their children.

Spectrum of Sexualities

Weinrich and Williams use the term *spectrum of sexualities* to capture the same idea as Kinsey's continuum.[67] They compared the United States with many other cultures, some from the ancient past such as the pre-Christian Greeks. They also compared the United States and the modern West with some of today's nonmodern societies, such as those guided by Islamic teachings. Weinrich and Williams conclude that what they call homosexualities are found in all societies at all times in history. They say that in the past, most societies simply defined homosexual behaviors as one more "natural kind of sexuality."[68] However, in the United States more than in any other Western society, homosexual behaviors are perceived as a threat to society's well-being. Consequently, say the authors, such behaviors are *taboo*—forbidden!

John Gagnon and William Simon found that one reason Americans have difficulty grasping the idea that all sexual behaviors exist along some sort of natural spectrum is because of our imagery of sexuality: "Our sense of normalcy derives from organs being placed in legitimate orifices."[69] Penises placed in vaginas make up the "normal" category of sex. Other kinds of connections between varied body parts are thought to be abnormal. "How do lesbians do It?," demanded a male member of the audience of a talk-show panel of homosexual women. Weinrich and Williams observe that particular body parts and the "missionary position" are not what sexuality is all about. Instead, sexuality is about underlying feelings. It's also about the social relationship between the persons who are being sexual with each other. If sexuality is thought of in those terms, instead of normal/abnormal unions of the "right" body parts, the idea of a spectrum of sexualities is much less difficult to comprehend. The idea of the erotic friendship (described in Chapter 5) is one way to capture the similarities, as well as the differences, between heterosexual and homosexual relationships.

"Coming out" and Affirming Responsibility

Heterosexuals are supposed to be sexually restrained except within marriage. Homosexuals are supposed to be restrained, *period*. Over a century ago, gays organized bars and clubs where they could secretly indulge (see Chapter 6). But before the 1960s, few homosexuals overtly challenged the cultural norm that they should be restrained and not do homosexual behaviors. One of the outcomes of the sexual revolution is the emergence into open society of the politically active gay community based on ideas such as "gay pride."[70] Homosexuals who have "come out of the closet" are symbolically rejecting the norm of sexual restraint,

even if they don't actually say they are. By "going public" they are making a symbolic statement that it's a good thing for homosexuals to be sexually indulgent. Importantly, gay leaders stress that inherent in the symbolism of going public is the notion of sexual responsibility, especially in light of the AIDS epidemic.[71]

POLITICAL STRUGGLES OVER SEXUALITY

The political muscle of certain conservative religious groups was flexed when in 1989 they succeeded in lobbying a U.S. House Appropriations Committee to delete 11 million dollars for a national study of the sexual behaviors and norms of 20,000 respondents.[72] Although the study was endorsed by a panel of social scientists, a coalition of conservative religious groups persuaded the Committee that asking people about their heterosexual and homosexual behaviors and norms would not be in the national interest. Their muscle was confirmed in 1991 when they lobbied Dr. Louis Sullivan, Secretary of Health and Human Services, to block a scientifically approved 18-million-dollar study of adolescent life, including sexual behaviors and norms.[73] In an effort to reinforce Sullivan, some U.S. House members tried to pass an amendment preventing the government "from conducting or supporting any 'national survey of human sexual behavior,' "[74] arguing that "this study was all part of a 'liberal,' homosexual plot." They added that "the decline of the Judeo-Christian ethic is responsible for the increase in teenage pregnancies and STDs, and that a study isn't needed to understand this. The problem is . . . that the words 'sin' and 'evil' are not in the vocabulary of the liberal philosophers that have wreaked such havoc upon the social sciences."[75] Although the conservatives' amendment didn't pass either, Sullivan's action nevertheless stymied the research in question. The House then passed a separate amendment directing Sullivan to carry out some kind of national survey of adolescent health. But Sullivan was unlikely to pay much attention to that amendment. And if he did, the survey would likely omit "sensitive" questions regarding either heterosexuality or homosexuality. Political struggles over sex research are not limited to the United States. In 1989, Britain's conservative Prime Minister Margaret Thatcher canceled a scientifically approved 1.2-million-dollar sex survey that would have interviewed 20,000 respondents throughout the United Kingdom.[76]

Sex research seems just as politically explosive now as it was when Kinsey first published his findings five decades ago. Indeed, had conservative religious groups been as politically powerful then as they are now, it seems unlikely that Kinsey would ever have been allowed to do his research. The House debate shows that certain groups effectively use the Judeo-Christian ideal of sexual restraint to put others on the moral defensive. Politically speaking, it's very difficult to argue against sexual restraint. Because many Americans continue to believe that sexual restraint indicates a person's worth, it's very uncomfortable for politicians to advocate instead for responsible sexual behaviors. As a result, those seeking to justify sex research resort to the theme of health—AIDS prevention in particular. That strategy, however, has not yet generated much emotional excitement (and thus political support) among the majority of citizens. Even though they themselves are by no means sexually restrained, most citizens seem to go along with the prevailing cultural belief that the best way to stay healthy is to be sexually abstinent—except, of course, within marriage.[77]

CONCLUSION—SEXUALITY IN THREE SETTINGS

This chapter began by describing erotic friendships, and it closes in much the same way. In between, it discussed three different kinds of social settings for sexuality. We learned that persons can behave responsibly or irresponsibly in each of them. The first setting included younger, never-married persons. Long-term trends demonstrate that these singles have become increasingly sexually active. Almost all of them are doing *It*. Nevertheless, cultural approval lags far behind their behaviors. Even among citizens who do not practice sexual restraint, the belief remains that restraint is better than sexual responsibility.

The second setting targeted married persons. Here, cultural norms overwhelmingly condemn extramarital coitus (EMC). Nevertheless, married men have been doing It since recorded history began. And today, throughout Western societies, substantial numbers of women and men engage in EMC. In the United States, at least, most of them try to conceal this behavior from their partners. Some advocates urge couples to be "responsible" about it, that is, negotiate agreements regarding sexual openness. So far, however, such advocates are not taken very seriously. Sexual restraint remains the only "proper" norm that involved couples are permitted to hold toward outside persons. However, analogous to singles, believing in restraint is one thing, being indulgent is quite another.

The final setting included homosexual persons. Homosexual behaviors are condemned much more strongly than either EMC or premarital sex. One reason is the widespread belief that homosexuals "corrupt" children and thus society. However, some researchers say that heterosexuals and homosexuals are much more alike than different. They talk about a continuum, or spectrum, of sexual behavior on which both heterosexuals and homosexuals are located. Although homosexuals are strongly expected to be restrained, in recent years a number of them have "come out." Their public declaration of gayness symbolizes a rejection of the notion that homosexuals should be sexually restrained. Most gay leaders hope it also represents an affirmation of responsible sexual indulgence.

NOTES

1. Kinsey, Pomeroy, and Martin, 1948; Kinsey et al., 1953; Pomeroy, 1982.
2. Rubin, 1990.
3. Boles, 1979.
4. Klassen, Williams, and Levitt, 1989, page xxii.
5. Klassen et al., pp. 9–10.
6. Ibid., pp. 18ff.
7. Ibid.
8. Ibid., p. 19.
9. Ibid., p. 46.
10. Ibid., p. 138.
11. Ibid., p. 139.
12. Ibid., pp. 268, 271.
13. *Atlantic Monthly*, December 1991, p. 131.
14. Cott, 1979b. Most evangelicals no longer hold this view. See Lewis and Brissett, 1986; Stacey, 1990; Stellway, 1990.
15. Bauer, 1991; Family Research Council, 1992.
16. Bauer, 1986.
17. Sipe, 1990.
18. Ebaugh, 1988.
19. Marciano, 1990.
20. Klassen et al., pp. 270, 274.
21. Ibid., p. 272.
22. Ibid., p. 273.
23. Rubin.
24. Reiss, 1990. Tanfer and Schoorl (1992), however, claim that sexual attitudes among teen and young adult women may be shifting in a less conventional direction.
25. Thornton, 1989.
26. Ibid.; Reiss.
27. Walsh, 1989, p. 176. For additional details regarding these long-term trends, see Luckey and Nass, 1969; Zelnick and Kantner, 1980; Zelnik, Kantner, and Ford, 1981; Kallen and Stephenson, 1982; Robinson and Jedlicka, 1982; Darling, Kallen, and VanDusen, 1984.
28. U.S. Centers for Disease Control, 1992.
29. Somenstein, Pleck, and Ku, 1991, p. 162.
30. Zelnik et al., 1981, p. 103.
31. Walsh.
32. Thornton.
33. Tanfer and Horn, 1985.
34. Pleck and Pleck, 1980.
35. Reiss, p. 219.
36. Sponaugle, 1989.
37. Thornton.
38. Sponaugle.
39. Scanzoni and Marsiglio, 1992.
40. Sponaugle, p. 188.
41. Ibid., p. 189.
41a. Laumann et al., 1994.
42. Sponaugle, p. 205.
43. Thornton.
44. Sponaugle, p. 205.
45. Richardson, 1988.
46. Nena and George O'Neill, 1970, 1972.
47. Jay and Mae Ziskin, 1973.
48. Smith and Smith, 1970.
49. Jenks, 1987, p. 145.
50. Denfeld and Gordon, 1971.
51. Risman and Schwartz, 1988.
52. Brenda C. Coleman, 1991. *The Gainesville, Florida, Sun*, December 15, p. 5a.
53. Gonsiorek, 1991, p. 246.
54. Risman and Schwartz, p. 130.
55. Kinsey et al., 1953.
56. Money, 1988.
57. Weinrich and Williams, 1991, p. 57.
58. Green and Bozett, 1991.
59. Kohn and Matusow, 1980; Money; Estep, Waldorff, and Marotta, 1992; Beth Schneider, 1992.
60. Eleanor Clift, 1991. "Patricia Ireland: What NOW?" *Newsweek*, December 16, p. 30.
61. Gonsiorek, p. 245.
62. Risman and Schwartz, p. 135.
63. Peplau, 1991.
64. Green and Bozett.
65. Ibid., p. 198.
66. Ibid.
67. Weinrich and Williams, p. 58.
68. Ibid., p. 59.
69. Gagnon and Simon, 1973, p. 5.
70. Risman and Schwartz, p. 137.
71. Ibid.
72. Marsiglio and Scanzoni.
73. American Sociological Association, 1991.
74. Ibid., p. 12.
75. Ibid.
76. Marsiglio and Scanzoni.
77. Katrine Ames and Marcus Mabry, 1992. "Practicing the safest sex of all." *Newsweek*, January 20, p. 52.

CHAPTER 5

INVENTING EROTIC FRIENDSHIPS

Chapters 2 and 3 talked about reinventing families in the broader sense of groups of persons helping each other out. We learned that obligations, and thus responsibility, are pivotal to what families are all about. Chapter 4 shifted our focus to two-person groups (i.e., dyads) in which sex is a central element. We learned that sexual behaviors, especially among women, have been changing dramatically throughout recent decades—much faster than people's beliefs about sex. Changes in sexual behaviors worry a lot of citizens. They're concerned that the changes are moving too far too fast. They worry that the changes mean that persons are behaving irresponsibly when it comes to sex. The fear is that they're hurting themselves, their children, and the larger society.

This chapter describes how contemporary persons are reinventing sexual dyads, or what we call the "erotic friendship." A key question is, when are erotic friendships responsible? When are they irresponsible? If there's been anything worthy of the title "sexual revolution," it's the emergence of the erotic friendship. Except for nineteenth-century free-love advocates and some 1960s' zealots, no one ever seriously believed that sexual promiscuity and hedonism would become widespread ways of living in North America or anywhere else.[1] And Chapter 4 showed that, in spite of increasing sexual activity, today's U.S. adolescents are not "sexual adventurers."

Neither is there any evidence suggesting that many adults make sexual adventurism a preferred and ongoing way of life. To be sure, many persons coming of age since the sixties do the "adventure bit" at one point or another throughout their life course. Indeed, most men have always "played around," but it was called "sowing wild oats." Since men had to get *It* out of their systems before marriage, everyone winked at It and acknowledged It by a sly grin. Now the big difference is that women can be adventurers too. But as heady as it may feel to be a sexual adventurer, after a while most persons, whether heterosexual or homosexual, seem to want something more.[2] After a time most people gravitate toward some sort of permanent relationship. This chapter explores what that's all about. And although we focus mainly on heterosexuals, the notion of erotic friendships applies just as accurately to homosexual couples as well.

HELGA'S STORY

The label "erotic friendship" was coined by the German sociologist Lerke Gravenhorst.[3] She came up with it while reporting her research on working-class German families. Specifically, Gravenhorst was talking about 27-year-old Helga. Helga told Gravenhorst that as an adolescent her parents kept her from developing "her own independent life."[4] They first insisted that she take care of her younger siblings, and then forced her into menial employment. In so doing, her parents failed to consider "her possible interests and ideas." When she finished vocational school at age 17, she wanted to "free herself from her parents" so she "escaped" to the metropolis of Munich and found a job as a waitress that paid well and that she enjoyed.

However, Helga wanted more education so she could get a job that was "important and recognized by society." As she was taking steps in that direction, she became pregnant—something she'd not planned for. She hardly knew the father and refused to have him in her life. Her pregnancy made her feel "overpowered, deserted and in despair." So did she have an abortion? No, she actually "fought for her child." Why? Because it gave her something that was "completely her own." Motherhood gave her the status and recognition that she craved. Nevertheless, it prevented her from going on with the "conscious shaping of her life." Instead of returning to school, she was forced to juggle the demands of employment and solo parenthood. Soon Helga had to put her child in temporary foster care until she earned enough money to take him back.

Enter Hans   At that point in her life Helga met Hans. Hans did two things for her. First, he listened to all her problems. Helga self-disclosed everything about her life and found it did her a lot of good simply to talk. She and Hans were developing *intimacy.* Hans became a source of strong emotional support. Although we're not told whether he self-disclosed to Helga, they began to think of each other as friends. Second, Hans began to help out Helga with her child. He provided services such as babysitting and transportation to the doctor. He also bought little extras for the child.

Social Exchanges   Intimacy is something that comes from inside a person. It is an *intrinsic,* or internal, benefit that persons give to, and get from, one another. Helga and Hans were sharing it, at least to some degree. Items such as services, goods, and money happen outside a person. And Helga and Hans were helping each other in those *external* ways too. Their giving and getting were similar to the social exchanges described in Chapters 2 and 3.

While Hans and Helga were exchanging both intrinsic and extrinsic benefits, they added yet a third interdependence—they became sexual partners. For a time they'd been just-friends. Now they were something different: *erotic* friends. Why didn't they stay just-friends? Why add the sexual dimension? Was it simply because of the pleasure involved? When we talk about erotic friendships, we are not focusing on the pleasurable aspects of sexuality, as crucial as those are. Instead we zero in on the social definitions of sexuality. It is those shared social and cultural definitions that make sexuality extraordinarily significant quite apart from its physiological sensations.[5]

We-ness as a Social Bond

Chapters 2 and 3 showed that certain shared definitions, not biology, describe what family is all about. Similarly, shared perceptions describe an erotic friendship. And just as family is a primary group bound by a sense of we-ness, an erotic friendship is also a primary group, or primary relationship, consisting (usually) of two persons—a dyad. The two persons define themselves as an in-group belonging to one another in a unique and special way: "I matter and I'm important to my partner; she/he matters and is important to me." Belonging supplies a sense of identity ("who I am"), and security ("who I am has a degree of continuity"). The Japanese word for we-ness and belonging is *uchi*.[6] Everyone else is they. The perceptions of *we* and *they* construct social boundaries letting us and everyone else know who is in and who is out. A sense of we-ness is often referred to as a kind of social bond, or social glue.[7] In effect, we-ness is the social glue that holds people together.

Throughout Western societies, a sexual partnership distinguishes we from they. Gravenhorst reports that when Hans and Helga shifted from being just-friends to being erotic friends, Helga's entire outlook on life changed. In her own eyes Helga had become a different person. But not in her eyes only: She gained social "recognition through the relationship with a man." Her family and friends now thought of her as different. Hence, having an erotic friendship adds to a person's status and prestige. All you have to do is listen to pop music to verify what it is and does. From rhythm and blues in the 1920s to today's rock, the themes have been the same: "I don't feel good about myself 'cause I'm not in a relationship. I'm empty, sad, lonely, depressed, and gloomy. What's more, I'd like to have an erotic friendship as soon as possible." Or, "Since I've been in a relationship, I feel fulfilled and happy. It's wonderful to belong to you and have you belong to me. What's more, I want us to last, I don't want us to end."

A large part of Helga's redefinition of herself and her grand new life centered around her child. She saw Hans as a "a solution to the problem that took the form of a personal miracle." Not only could she have friendship and

sexual pleasures with Hans, he could also help out with her material needs. Since a big chunk of those needs went for the child, Hans became a *social father* to the 1 1/2-year-old boy. Simultaneously, Hans parented him by intrinsic, that is, affectionate and loving, ways. With Hans, Helga believed she now had everything she'd ever wanted both for herself and her child.

But things never stand still. Persons as well as the circumstances and events surrounding them are continually changing. For example, we've seen Helga and Hans's relationship develop from being just-friends to being erotic friends. Since they were in control of those changes they felt comfortable with them. Suddenly, external factors began once again to crowd in on Helga. Up to now, her son had remained in foster care and Hans and Helga had each been living in separate residences. However, they regularly fetched the child from foster care to spend time with him on weekends and evenings. Helga and Hans were trying to save money for their own apartment, and they'd casually discussed the possibility of marriage. Suddenly, without warning, the foster mother gave back the child.

Helga could have chosen another foster home, but instead she wanted something else. She wanted to feel "grown up." She had moved to Munich in the first place to work, go to school, and eventually get a good job that would give her social recognition. Now, with those things seemingly out of her grasp, she reached for something else that would supply the recognition she craved: marriage. Just as they believed that having an erotic friendship was better than not having one, Helga and her friends and family strongly felt that being married was much more desirable than being merely a girlfriend. Marriage brings with it unique social approval and prestige that can be achieved in no other way. Marriage is a signal that the couple is seriously committed to their relationship: They intend to make it work and be together for life. That was especially important to Helga, because she believed that marriage assured her that Hans would be there over the long haul to help out with her son. She believed that marrying was the most responsible thing she could do for herself and her son.

Gravenhorst next observes that, "Opportunities to take charge of her own life resulted again and again in existential bottlenecks."[8] The first bottleneck Helga faced was that after marriage the only housing she and Hans could afford was a crowded and undesirable apartment. Helga was very distressed by the fact that the apartment's site kept her from meeting her neighbors and forming mutual help patterns with them. Even more distressing was the change in Hans's behavior since they'd become a "legal family." Previous to their marriage, Hans had been a good listener and had helped out with her son. But he "failed her now." Among other things, living together (whether married or not) imposes the dull and tedious routines of housework, and Hans wouldn't do them. Furthermore, he gradually eased out of communicating with her, and he began to get drunk every evening. When he encountered disciplinary problems at work he began drinking heavier than before. Meanwhile, he and Helga had their own baby together, and then another baby. Although both were employed, they were in constant need of money. The eldest of their three children developed an emotional problem because of previous foster-home neglect. On top of all this, Helga's divorced mother became ill and Helga felt obliged to care for her even though they detested one another and battled continually.

For the Time Being   "For the time being," remarks Gravenhorst, "Helga's life is limited to her family." She becomes totally absorbed in supplying the intrinsic and extrinsic needs of her children, as well as the extrinsic needs of her mother. It "makes me very, very happy . . . [to] know that I am needed," says Helga. But

what about her erotic friendship with Hans— her other primary group? How does she feel about having a partner who no longer talks with her? How does she feel now that their emotional closeness has evaporated? And how does she feel about being caught up in circumstances that prevent her from her earlier goals of achieving status and self-esteem by means of a job outside of her family? The answer seems to be that as long as Helga perceives herself at the center of an in-group (her blood family) providing such intense feelings of belonging, she's willing to tolerate a very low sense of we-ness, or belonging, in her relationship with Hans. *For the time being,* she's too busy gaining a sense of fulfillment serving her mother and her children to worry about cultivating her erotic friendship. As long as her mother and children are dependent on her, her perceived obligations to them take precedence over gratifications she might want to exchange with Hans.

Sources of Change   Helga's story illustrates a number of important ideas about erotic friendships. Perhaps the most important is that they are always subject to change. One source of change stems from the broader social environment surrounding an erotic friendship. Economic, political, and social conditions in the larger society are always in flux, always shifting. During the 1990s, for example, in the United States, defense industries are closing down and many other companies are downsizing, forcing the layoffs of thousands of skilled workers and technicians. Furthermore, new technologies, such as pills that permit morning-after abortions, are constantly being introduced.[9] During the 1920s, new inventions such as the car, radio, and phonograph had an enormous impact on relationships between the genders (see Chapter 6). Economic upheavals and technological changes are bound to affect how women and men relate to each other.

Changes in erotic friendships are also

caused by the partners themselves. Over time, partners tend to shift their behaviors. They also alter their beliefs, values, norms, goals, hopes, and so on. In recent years, adult change, or development, has been studied by researchers from history, psychology, and sociology (see Chapter 14). Although researchers have long studied *child* development, *adult* development has been neglected. Ann Swidler says the reason for the neglect was that up through the 1960s the prevailing image of adulthood was constancy and stability, not change and upheaval.[10] Everyone knew that persons developed until marriage. But when they got married and finally settled down they were supposed to quit changing. Men then spent their lives providing, and women spent theirs caring, for their families. Women did not pursue employment in serious fashion, and few couples divorced. Today, however, throughout their life course both women and men engage in many different kinds of behaviors, both primary and occupational. Laurel Richardson remarks that "contemporary women see that their lives can change over and over again."[11] And as partners change, their erotic friendships are likely to change as well.

Changes in the social environment, changes in partners, and changes in erotic friendships are closely connected with and often impact on each other. For instance, during 1991–1992, North America was in severe economic recession. White men (to say nothing of blacks) who believed they had secure jobs unexpectedly found themselves waiting in unemployment lines. The economic environment changed many of those men. They realized they'd have to get additional training to find different and better jobs than they'd had before.

Germany was also in recession at that time, and although Helga told her story to Gravenhorst in 1979 when she was only 27, let's do a fast-forward to 1991–1992. Let's imagine Helga and Hans twelve years later when

Helga is aged 39. Let's say that her mother has died, and only the youngest of her three children, now an adolescent, still lives with her and Hans. Although Hans has continued to drink heavily over the years, he's been able to hold on to his job. But the recession now puts him out of work. Instead of taking this event as an opportunity to get retrained for a better-paying job, he chooses to do nothing until he can get his former job back. The economic environment does not change him. He resists personal change, preferring rather to stay the same as he's always been.

Helga's Life-Course

But the recession has changed Helga. For more than twelve years, her sense of we-ness with— of belonging to—Hans has been slowly but steadily declining. However, she's been too busy fulfilling her obligations to her other primary groups (her mother and children) to fret over her feelings about Hans. But Gravenhorst remarks that most women experience a "life-long 'struggle for recognition.'"[12] Helga feels that her recognition is declining because her children don't need her as much as they once did. She also realizes that if she had a good job, she and Hans wouldn't be hit as hard by economic downturns. As a result, she rekindles her premarital dreams of going to school and getting a "middle-class" job, a job that will give her status and recognition in the wider society beyond her relationships with her children and with Hans. She urges Hans to get retrained for a better job too, but he refuses. In brief, the social environment is changing, and Helga is changing her own life goals. And both of those changes begin to alter Helga and Hans's relationship. First, Helga tells Hans she wants to quit her current menial job so she can attend school. They can reduce their standard of living, she says, and live off their unemployment checks till he gets his job back and/or she gets a good job. Furthermore, since she'll be studying a lot, he'll have to do housework for the first time since they married.

Decline of We-ness

Helga, in short, wants to make some significant changes in the extrinsic part of their relationship—money and housework, as well as in her educational and occupational levels. But Hans resists all of these changes and tells Helga she can't quit her job or go to school. Helga is profoundly distressed by Hans's refusal to cooperate with her "struggle for recognition." Since a sense of we-ness is stimulated by feelings that "I matter and I'm important to my partner," Helga begins to wonder how much she matters to Hans after all: "How important can I be to Hans if he won't share in what I wish to become?" As a result, her minimal feelings of belonging to Hans erode still further. In spite of Hans's opposition, Helga quits her job, enrolls in school, and simply lets much of the housework go. Sometimes she's late with his supper, and occasionally misses fixing it altogether. At those times he becomes violent and slaps and hits her. She considers moving out, but she can't live solely off her unemployment check. So she chooses to continue living with Hans even though its physically punishing, and they're emotionally distant, and they never go anywhere together, and they rarely have sexual intercourse. She convinces herself that she can't leave until she completes her schooling and gets a good job. Helga's current situation has been described as one of "quiet desperation."[13] Japanese women have a word for it too—*gaman*.[14] It means patiently enduring the pains of marriage.

Keep in mind, however, that Helga and Hans still perceive themselves as legitimate sexual partners. So do their friends and families. Even though they rarely have sex anymore, they remain legally married and living together. They still define each other as "my sexual partner." In that sense they remain erotic friends. Hans and Helga would each be-

come jealous and possessive if the other had coitus with someone else. There remains, in short, a clear boundary around their erotic friendship. Even though a great deal of the friendship has gone out of their relationship, there yet remains a clear *we* as distinct from *they*. Hans in particular feels extremely possessive of Helga. Fearing she might have an affair, he harangues her constantly about her school friends. But Helga has developed a number of platonic friends of both genders. She feels pleased about being accepted by her friendship network because they, like her, are older students struggling with different kinds of life-course issues than younger students. Among these friends is Kurt, with whom she talks often at the college snack bar.

After a while Helga begins to perceive Kurt in a way she's never viewed any man since before she met Hans. She begins to think of him as potentially an erotic friend. Kurt becomes a *prospect* for a "relationship." Simultaneously, he begins to think of her in the same way. Each begins to perceive that, potentially, they could add sexual interdependence to the intrinsic exchanges they already share. Kurt is somewhat younger than Helga, and divorced. After his divorce he cohabited with a woman for several years, but recently moved into a house with two other men. Kurt has told Helga his relationship with his former cohabitor woman is over. He says they're no longer erotic friends, simply just-friends.

Helga's Second Erotic Friendship More time passes, and Helga and Kurt become more than merely prospects—they become sexual partners. Although one or two of Helga and Kurt's friends know it, no one else does, including Hans. Helga thus finds herself in two erotic friendships at the same time, which at first she thinks she can handle. She discovers, however, that before very long her minimal sense of we-ness with Hans vanishes entirely. Helga knows the bonding is gone because she no longer feels sexually jealous or possessive toward Hans. Alongside not caring if he has coitus with someone else, she herself no longer wishes to have intercourse with him. For them to have coitus now, he has to force himself on her. In short, Helga no longer defines herself as having an erotic friendship with Hans. Hans, however, still perceives that they have one. Indeed, Hans has little grasp of any of Helga's actual feelings about him and their erotic friendship. Focusing instead on the facts that they have a formal tie of marriage and the extrinsic ties of shared household and money, he believes he has every right to have sex with Helga. If asked, he would deny he's forcing himself sexually on her. And although she defines intercourse with him as being against her will, she believes she has no other choice. Helga has become, in effect, a victim of what's called "marital rape" (see Chapter 12).

THE PHASES OF EROTIC FRIENDSHIPS

The Formation Phase—Assessing Prospects

Helga's story shows how the social environment (the recession; attending school; having friends that are hers, not theirs; and so on) first changed Helga and next changed her relationship with Hans. In particular, her story illustrates the fundamental idea that relationships are seldom static. To one degree or another erotic friendships are always in motion. The puzzle is, how can we describe their motion? Jessie Bernard says that before the 1970s it was sufficient to ask people whether they were single, married, or divorced.[15] Knowing this fact revealed vital things about people. But knowing that Helga and Hans are married (or that Kurt is divorced) tells us little of importance about them. As a result, Bernard suggested that it's now much more informative to ask persons how they feel about their relationships. Persons' feelings of we-ness and bonding tell us a lot more about them than whether

Formation (prospects)	Maintenance and change (MC) (partners)	Dissolution

FIGURE 5-1 **The Development Phases of an Erotic Friendship**
Each phase contains numerous subphases. Borders between the phases are not rigid; they are fluid and shifting. Partners in the maintenance and change phases may choose to add co-residence and/or legal status. They may remain indefinitely in the MC phase or in the dissolution phase. See Chapter 11 for ways in which negotiation and problem-solving impact on the development of erotic friendships.

they're married, divorced, or single, as we can plainly see from Helga's story.

Consequently, to describe the motion of erotic friendships we must concentrate on something more than formal ties, such as being married or not. Figure 5-1 shows that the motion of an erotic friendship begins with an initial phase called *formation*.[16] As Pamela Kalbfleisch puts it, during a formation phase persons are seeking both a friend and a lover.[17] Formation is characterized by the sorts of feelings Helga and Kurt had for each other: They were already just-friends. And they perceived themselves as prospects for becoming sexual partners. Having a sexual partner is *not* the same as participating in casual sex. A sexual partner is a person with whom one shares a commitment (whether verbal or tacit) to be exclusive with each other, a mutual pledge of monogamy.

Helga had, of course, passed through a similar formation phase with Hans some years before. Kurt too had experienced formation phases with other women. Viewing someone as a prospect is not the same as merely being attracted to or sexually aroused by that person. It is not even the same as having a one-night stand with that person. To be sure, attraction and arousal, as well as casual or even frequent sexual encounters, can eventually lead to imagining someone as a prospective partner, even if one never intended it that way.[18] But they are not the same thing. Being attracted to, or even having intercourse with, someone is not equal to defining that person as someone special—someone with whom one could have an exclusive and ongoing relationship. By defining each other as special, Helga and Kurt felt they might be able to develop a mutual sense of belonging and bonding, in other words, we-ness.

Although her study focused on single professional women having affairs with married men. Richardson captured the key elements inherent in any formation phase regardless of the person's marital status.[19] Lynne Atwater studied married women's affairs, and there is considerable similarity in formation phases between those two situations.[20] Moreover, both situations are similar to the formation phases passed through by persons not currently in an erotic friendship.[21]

Availability   Richardson suggested that one thing making the several kinds of situations comparable is that today all persons are *available* for an erotic friendship whether or not they currently have one.[22] During the 1950s, people would have said that Helga is unavailable because she's married. Bernard Farber was the first sociologist to assert that in Western societies, all persons are available for a fresh relationship regardless of their current relationship or lack thereof.[23] Before the sixties, said Farber, being married was a virtual guarantee that one would remain so till death. But in contemporary times, certainty about erotic friendships (including marriage) has all but vanished. Certainty has been replaced by the potential, or possibility (however small), that a change of partners (whether one is married or not) could at some future point occur. Farber's ideas were ignored for thirty years because they seemed farfetched, perhaps even

Today, growing numbers of women and men are co-workers in settings previously closed to women.

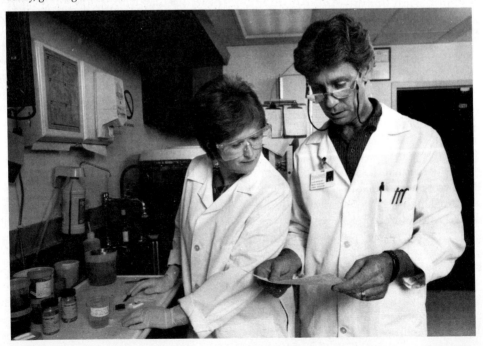

frightening and radical. Today their time has come.

Nevertheless, to be "available" by no means implies that one is necessarily "looking." Hans was potentially available but interested in no one save Helga. Helga, although also available (even though still married to Hans), was interested in no one but Kurt. A profound social change surrounding today's relationships is the growing number of women in paid labor. From police to surgeons to pilots, women and men work closely together in ways undreamed of in the past. And after work, men and women work out together at co-ed health clubs. Given that the genders mix in ways once bordering on the scandalous, every person

must learn the skill of managing her or his "erotic antennae."[24] According to Richardson, erotic antennae send and receive subtle, hardly perceptible, cues and clues regarding the presence of sexual attraction, ranging from none to high. If there is some degree of attraction, erotic antennae also send and receive an additional message, namely, that that one is or is not potentially interested in sexual interaction of one type or another.[25] All of us are well aware that persons occasionally sense a certain degree of mutual attraction, but have not the slightest interest in any kind of sexual interaction. They're not going to act on the attraction.

Nevertheless, given the subtlety of these kinds of clues and cues, there is plenty of room

Close working relationships between women and men sometimes give rise to garbled sexual signals.

for misperception.[26] Men in particular tend to misread women's signals. As a result, men often assume that women are sexually attracted to them when in fact they are not. Second, some men assume that women to whom they feel an attraction are interested in sexual interaction, when in fact they are not. In addition to garbling or ignoring the woman's message, some of those men make unwanted sexual advances. And that sometimes leads to the harassment and assaults of which all of us are becoming increasingly aware (see Chapter 12). On the other hand, many men (and women) interpret a "not interested" message at face value and look elsewhere.

Physical and Sexual Attractiveness   Farber argued that part of the evidence for his availability idea is the cultural emphasis on physical and sexual attractiveness throughout Western societies. Regardless of their current relationship (including marriage) women, and increasingly men, now dress in ways that before the sixties were interpreted to signify sexual looseness. The wearing of sexually evocative clothing styles were once thought to convey the message. "I'm interested." In today's cultural climate, however, physical attractiveness in general (a healthy, trim, well-toned body), and sexual attractiveness in particular, transmit a very different message. Randall Collins says those things are *resources*, like education and a good job.[27] Antonia Abbey adds that physical and sexual attractiveness, just like education and a good job, supply self-esteem along with prestige and status.[28] Abbey adds that women (and men) wear the kinds of clothing that will help them "look their best"— they're trying to "keep up with the latest fashion trends." At the same time, for someone not currently in an erotic friendship, any and all of those resources can be used to obtain the kind of partner (friend and lover) that she or he wants. For persons currently in an erotic friendship, she or he can use attractiveness, along with education and employment, to ne-

gotiate in ways that help make the relationship more fair and caring. And importantly, those varied resources imply that should the relationship not go well, one could employ them to find a new relationship.

Hence, the status symbols of physical and sexual attractiveness, along with education and employment, are foundational to the idea of availability. Those resources make it possible for persons, especially women, to be autonomous and to have choices. In today's cultural climate, the resources give women considerable control over their erotic friendships. They make it possible for persons to avoid being trapped in unsatisfying or punishing relationships. Additionally, they make it possible to consider alternatives to a current relationship. If two persons shift from transmitting signals indicating that, "I'm free to make choices about anyone, but I choose not to be interested in you," to signals indicating "I'm attracted to you, and I'm interested in you as a prospect," then we say that those persons have passed into a formation phase of an erotic friendship.

Gender and the Meanings of Friendships
We just learned that many researchers believe that women and men differ markedly in the meanings they attach to today's subtle sexual signals. Men are often more interested in the *erotic*, whereas women are aiming at the *friendship* that includes much more than mere companionship.[29] Women tend to view men as prospects for partnerships on the basis of emotional intimacy surrounded by sexual boundaries. And within the boundaries they share intimacy—"being vulnerable, open, self-disclosing, and emotionally supportive."[30] It also includes "the sharing of secrets, the feeling that one is a valuable, good person."[31] Being emotionally supportive includes something women have traditionally done for men—nurture them in their lifelong quest for affirmation and recognition.

Many men, on the other hand, appear more

willing to be sexual apart from emotional intimacy. Men are also more likely than women to have casual (i.e., uncommitted) sex with more than one person at a time.[32] Some women too engage in casual sex, but if the casual sex with a particular man continues for any length of time, women are likely to begin to perceive him as a prospective partner. In several studies, women reported that although at first they enjoyed casual sex with no strings attached, it wasn't long before they began to think about some strings.[33] The desire for strings is a search for ties that bind—ties that indicate a sense of bonding, belonging and we-ness.

In his classic novel, *Dubliners,* made into a 1980s' film, James Joyce complained that "Love between man and man is impossible because there must not be sexual intercourse, and friendship between man and woman is impossible because there must be sexual intercourse."[34] And in the popular 1989 movie, *When Harry Met Sally,* Billy Crystal declares to Meg Ryan that "Men and women can't be friends because the sex part always gets in the way." When she objects, saying she has several men friends with whom she "doesn't want to have sex," he retorts that "since men do, the sex thing is already out there and the friendship is ultimately doomed." Ryan's character represents women's complaints that men's inability to be emotionally close with women has led to men's "impoverishment."[35] And that inability has led some women to feel deprived about their relationships with men.[36]

Male Companionship Furthermore, men not only lack intimacy with women, they tend to lack it with one another. Graham Allan reports that most studies of friendship reveal that men have many more companions ("buddies," "mates") than women.[37] But it's primarily the activity that brings men together, not any particular person. Buddies gather to bowl, golf, hunt, fish, or play tennis or softball. The same buddies may or may not show up every time. Who is there is not as important as the fact that

there are enough buddies to do the activity. Consequently, men can be very friendly without actually being close.[38] Indeed, the social context of "mateship" tends to prohibit potentially embarrassing self-disclosure. As the beer commercials so vividly communicate, buddies banter with one another, and they needle and kid each other. But buddies rarely reveal or share their inner feelings.[39] The bantering effectively inhibits any emotional sharing that might possibly surface. Moreover, sharing feelings is most often a dyadic, not a group, experience. The award-winning TV program, *Cheers,* took place in the setting of a bar in which wit and cleverness were served up as endlessly as the beer. However, if one of the participants sensed that his buddy had been hurt by the needling, the two retired from the group to be alone together to soothe the pain. But that kind of one-on-one nurturing does not appear in the beer commercials. As the men lounge around the campfire at night with beer coolers full, agreeing that, "It doesn't get any better than this," it's not likely they're talking about how comforting it feels to bare their innermost fears and feelings. Hence, P. H. Wright describes men's friendships as existing *side-by-side.*[40]

Face-to-Face Closeness By contrast, says Wright, women's friendships tend to be *face-to-face.* Instead of doing something together, women enjoy simply being together—talking, sharing themselves. Women are less likely than men to require a particular social situation to be friends, they merely require one another. Allan reports that although women have far fewer friends than men, the level of closeness shared by women friends tends to be much greater than that existing among men.[41] Allan says that studies in Britain and North America show that one major reason for these gender differences is socialization. And by that he means the distinctive experiences that girls and boys have from birth onward. Both explicitly and implicitly, boys are encouraged to paris the cultivation of *face-to-face closeness* and the we-ness that springs from it.

The Maintenance and Change Phase— Cultivating a Partnership

One of the major motions, or changes, in an erotic friendship is the transition from formation to the next phase. Figure 5-1 describes it as the *maintenance and change, or* MC, phase. Being in MC meant that Helga, for instance, no longer defined Kurt as being merely a prospect. We saw that they moved from being prospects to being actual sexual partners— they became a couple. They perceived their sexual interdependence as special and unique. We say that they *made a transition from a formation phase into a maintenance and change phase.*

It turns out that Helga came to that perception quicker than Kurt. Before sleeping with Helga, Kurt was occasionally having what he defined as casual sex with Karyn. That casual relationship continued even after he and Helga became lovers. Although he never viewed Karyn as a prospect for an exclusive partnership (as far as he was concerned, they were never in a formation phase), Kurt never told Helga about her either. One night, however, he happened to let Karyn know about Helga, and Karyn immediately ended their sexual involvement. Surprised by her abruptness, Kurt asked Karyn why, and discovered that she (unlike him) had defined them as already having an erotic friendship—a sexually exclusive and committed relationship. When she learned her perceptions were not shared, she no longer wanted to have intercourse with him. That experience unnerved Kurt and sped him to the same view of things as Helga— these two became unique sexual partners. In his perception (as well as hers), they were erotic friends who were committed solely to each other. Symbolic of that commitment was their sexual exclusivity. Kurt and Helga never explicitly negotiated their monogamy; it grew

Emotional intimacy between female friends is a lifelong experience.

ticipate in activities with other boys. They learn to become what some researchers call task oriented—to focus on the goals of group-based activities. Girls, on the other hand, learn to become person oriented. Girls are encouraged to focus on the nature of their relationships with other girls—to communicate by disclosing information about themselves, and by cultivating a sensitivity to how other persons are feeling. Nevertheless, many of today's women and some men want to overcome their socialization and reinvent their friendships to include intimacy. Although some share intimacy without being sexual, the erotic friendship includes both. Its boundary is the perception of sexual exclusivity. But its driving force out of a tacit understanding, a silent bargain between them. Some researchers describe this process as a "turning point in romantic relationships." They view it as a shift from "passion" by itself to "commitment."[42]

The Goal of Permanence Just as the formation phase is marked by the hope of developing a we-group, the maintenance and change phase is marked by the sense that one has passed from hope to reality—one is now in an erotic friendship. And because one has gotten into something that's quite valuable and important, a second hope surfaces, namely, that this "good thing" will last. However, hoping it will last does not necessarily mean "last forever." Helga, for example, does not currently define her relationship with Kurt quite that way: "He's not necessarily the man I expect to spend the rest of my life with." In view of her painful experiences with Hans, she doubts she can be that certain about any man. Nevertheless, for the time being, Helga thoroughly savors her erotic friendship with Kurt, and she wants it to continue indefinitely into the future.

Cultivating an Erotic Friendship Struggling to make the relationship last—keeping the good things flowing that got you into the relationship in the first place—is what the MC phase is all about. The MC phase is like cultivating an apple tree. To keep the tree alive and flourishing you must do several things. First, you must maintain the tree by giving it water and fertilizer. In doing so, you allow the tree to grow and sprout new shoots and branches. As it grows, the tree changes; it never remains the same from year to year. Hence, to maintain your tree is inevitably to change it. Maintaining a living thing like a tree is very different from maintaining a car. Car maintenance keeps the car performing well, but doesn't make it bigger or add a door that wasn't there before. Maintaining living things always

makes them different. The act of keeping them alive is an act of change.

Second, to keep the tree bearing fruit you must alter it through ways that are more active and intentional than merely giving it water and fertilizer. *Intentional change* comes about in at least two ways. First, you prune, or cut away, certain (usually dead) branches. You get rid of parts you believe are hindering the tree's further growth. Next, you graft a new bud onto the existing tree. Grafting is like transplant surgery—you actually cut into the tree and attach a living bud to it. Something different is now a structural part of the tree that wasn't there before. Moreover, that new bud didn't sprout from the tree by chance. You've intentionally stepped in and actively changed your tree, hoping the new bud will develop into a healthy branch and make for a much more productive tree.

If your apple tree stops growing and changing, you assume it's dead. It's the same with a relationship. Once a commitment has been made to become exclusive sexual partners, the challenge is to keep both the relationship and the partners growing. The sign that both are growing is a continuing increase in the sense of *we-ness*—the mattering and bonding—that the partners feel for one another.

Love and We-ness Researchers often avoid defining *love* because it's like trying to capture the universe. But Richardson says that however we define love, it contains the core elements of a primary relationship—bonding and belonging.[43] Hence, when an MC phase begins, the partners tend to feel a relatively moderate sense of we-ness for one another. To be sure, Helga and Kurt feel a greater sense of we-ness now than before when they'd been just-friends. And as they moved from formation to MC, that sense of being special and unique increased because of their commitment to be monogamous sexual partners. In their case, the commitment was tacit—they didn't discuss it. Nevertheless, that commitment to exclusivity strongly reinforced the boundaries around their relationship: *we* versus *they*. Both Helga and Kurt, however, feel their sense of we-ness is nowhere as strong as they wish it to be. To keep their bonding growing, they're aware that they've got to maintain their relationship through "feeding and watering." Second, to keep that sense of we-ness growing they also have to keep changing their relationship through "pruning and grafting."

Personal Growth and Me-ness   Part of the feeding and watering occurs when each partner contributes to the other's personal growth. Helga in particular has been searching for the recognition, identity, and self-esteem that's eluded her most of her life. One reason her sense of we-ness with Hans eroded was that after a while he was unable and/or unwilling to provide the emotional supports she needed while she returned to school in preparation for a good job. A major reason she values Kurt is that he provides the supports she needs to grow as a person. Kurt enhances her sense of *me*-ness at the same time he cultivates their *we*-ness. Since they became friends, he's been a good listener as she self-disclosed. And she does the same for him. As each helps the other to grow, their sense of we-ness and belonging becomes stronger as well.

"Me-ness" is often described as individualism and self-fulfillment. Ann Swidler says that throughout Western societies the idea of personal growth, or me-ness, contains at least two ideas.[44] One is the idea of meaningful work. It's what Helga's been searching for. When she completes school, she wants a job that not only provides money but also self-fulfillment, plus esteem from others. Earlier in her life course, meaningful work meant taking care of her mother and children. Now she defines meaningful work the same way she did before she got pregnant the first time—prestigious paid

employment. And since Kurt is helping her achieve that goal he's stimulating her growth in the realm of work.

Second, Swidler says that persons also grow by experiencing meaningful love. Swidler is talking about the sort of emotional intimacy and self-disclosure shared by Helga and Kurt. Intimacy is a satisfying experience in and of itself. However, researchers tell us that the capacity to experience intimacy has to be nurtured and developed.[45] It doesn't simply bubble up magically from nowhere. Kurt feels that Helga is increasing his own capacity to be intimate. Both partners are helping each other to grow in this crucial realm. Consequently, as Helga and Kurt move through the initial period of their MC phase, each is helping the other to experience personal growth, or me-ness. They're expanding their capacities for intimacy and also for work. As each grows, their sense of we-ness, of bonding, is enhanced accordingly. After several months of being in MC, their shared sense of we-ness is considerably stronger than it was when they first became erotic friends.

Jealousy and We-ness   In Western cultures, the sense of we-ness that characterizes erotic friends is usually indicated by an agreement, unspoken or not, to be sexually monogamous. Violating that agreement often stirs up feelings of jealousy. Hence, jealousy is a basic element in fully understanding the MC phase. Many people limit the idea of jealousy to marriage. But there's plenty of evidence demonstrating that people don't have to be married to be sexually jealous.[46] Chapter 2 showed that women prisoners forming erotic friendships held strong feelings of sexual jealously and possessiveness, as well as norms of exclusivity and monogamy. During the early decades of the twentieth century, Emma Goldman became known as an international spokesperson for radical political and social causes. Among these many causes were free love and escape from sexual jealously. And although Goldman wrote extensively and gave public lectures throughout North America and Europe saying it is petty and small-minded to be jealous, she herself was ravaged by it for many years.[47] She had an erotic friend whom she loved deeply, and although he said he loved her, he also told her he simply could not resist sleeping with other women. As a result, Goldman found herself fiercely torn between the ideas she believed and preached and the feelings of intense jealousy she was never able to shake.

On reflection, Kurt sensed that Karyn ended their involvement because she was *jealous* of Helga. And he never told Helga about Karyn because he sensed that Helga too would be jealous. Jealousy is a powerful and intense emotion. Gordon Clanton defines it as a "protective reaction to a perceived threat to a valued relationship or to its quality."[48] If persons sense that their erotic friendship—their we-group—is threatened, they often react with jealousy. Clanton adds that in response to the perceived threat, jealous persons try to protect themselves and/or their relationship by thoughts, feelings, or actions. In the 1987 movie, *Fatal Attraction,* Glenn Close became so insanely jealous of the married life of her lover, Michael Douglas, that she boiled his child's pet bunny, and then tried to murder him in his own house. Clanton says that although jealousy may sometimes bring about damage, that's seldom what jealous persons actually mean to do. Instead, persons reacting out of jealousy believe they're protecting either their relationship (we-group) and/or the "ego of the threatened partner." Karyn terminated her erotic friendship with Kurt to protect her own ego—her own feelings of integrity, dignity, and self-esteem. Kurt feared that Helga might react the same way if she found out about Karyn. Both women felt that sharing their sexual partner with another woman was demean-

ing. Not only would it lower their own sense of self-worth, but if friends and families uncovered it their worth, status, and dignity would be debased still further.

Culture and Jealousy   Clanton reminds us that jealousy is an emotion that is shaped by a person's culture, it is not biologically determined. The chief evidence for that conclusion is, first, that the definition of what makes people feel jealous changes within a society over time. For example, in ancient Japan married men and women alike had additional ongoing sexual partnerships acknowledged publicly by all interested parties.[49] There was no indication of sexual possessiveness or jealousy by either gender. However, beginning with the Middle Ages and persisting through the early part of this century, wives were gradually prohibited from having lovers, but men could have concubines (a word that didn't exist in Japan prior to the fourteenth century). Hence, for the last few centuries, Japanese men felt they could be jealous and sexually possessive of their wives, but wives were culturally prohibited from being sexually jealous of their husbands.

Contemporary Japan has continued to change. Today, extramarital intercourse is formally prohibited for both genders. Nevertheless, a double standard permits husbands one type of socially controlled extramarital sex of which wives are not supposed to be jealous. Kittredge Cherry reports that Japanese businessmen spend many hours a day at work developing a strong sense of we-ness with their male colleagues.[50] After work, this social family goes out eating and drinking together, and the group sometimes visits prostitutes. Typically, Japanese wives react to those kinds of sexual behaviors on the part of their husbands with "benign neglect." Cherry adds that it is not unheard of for wives to add condoms to their husbands' luggage as they travel on business. Sex with prostitutes is defined as harmless by the wife because he "pays for it with money, not love."[51] Japanese wives have learned not to be jealous of their husbands having casual sex because it is not perceived as a threat to their marriage.

A Japanese wife becomes very jealous, however, if her husband keeps a mistress. The word for it is *nigo-san,* meaning wife number two, or sweetheart.[52] Since it is not uncommon for a well-to-do man to keep a mistress (often with a second set of his children), and since Japanese wives become jealous of *nigo-san,* how do wives protect themselves against this threat? Relatively few Japanese married women are employed, and thus they lack the economic and personal resources to do very much. To protect their sense of self-worth, wives can only gather and gossip together about their husbands' *nigo-san,* and malign the mistresses as being morally inferior to themselves. Indeed, a popular Japanese wedding custom is aimed at controlling the wife's expected postmarital jealousy over her husband's mistress. The bride wears a hat called a "horn-hider" to "show she will curb this fault."[53] The horns are said to grow as a result of the wife's jealousy over the *nigo-san* her husband is likely to have sometime after their marriage.

The fact that Japanese wives are not jealous when their husbands have sex with prostitutes, but are jealous when they keep mistresses, illustrates a second point regarding the cultural foundations of jealousy: Within the same society, identical behaviors (the husband having intercourse with other women) sometimes stimulate feelings of jealousy and sometimes do not. Japanese wives have learned to be jealous of mistresses and not jealous of prostitutes.

Those particular Japanese behavior patterns also illustrate a third point about jealousy being shaped by culture: Identical behaviors that do not stimulate jealousy in one society *do*

generate jealousy in a different society. Most if not all North American women, for example, would feel jealous if their erotic friend were to visit a prostitute, especially if he did so repeatedly and in the same city where they both live. Furthermore, most North American women would react very differently from Japanese wives to an erotic friend keeping a mistress. Instead of merely tolerating it, they would likely force the man to choose between themselves and the mistress. But although Japanese and North American women may be equally jealous of mistresses, only the latter have the economic options to react and the cultural support to their threatened dignity to force the man to choose partners.

Changing Definitions of Jealousy in North America   Not surprisingly, the cultural definitions of jealousy have not stood still in North America any more than they have in Japan. Peter Stearns describes jealousy as an emotion that's been evolving in the United States for the last 200 years.[54] Clanton agrees with Stearns, and adds that even in the relatively short span since 1945 there have been significant changes in how jealousy is culturally defined. To support that conclusion, Clanton examined major articles on jealousy appearing in popular magazines between 1945 and 1985. He claims that those kinds of magazines reflect shifts in prevailing cultural views. For example, Clanton found that from 1945 to 1965 Americans defined jealousy as a *proof of love.* "Normal" jealousy was distinguished from "pathological" jealousy. David R. Mace (a marital advice giver of the time) said that "normal jealousy is the instinct that flashes a warning when [marital] exclusiveness . . . is threatened. . . . [It] is a protective instinct that has saved many a marriage."[55] However, Mace never told his readers how to identify the difference between "abnormal" and "normal" jealousy. In any case, Clanton said the old view of jealousy, namely, that it's a natural proof of love and good for marriage, disappeared from popular magazines (and thus from most of U.S. culture) after 1970.

During the 1970s a new view took its place, namely, the perception of jealousy as a *personal defect*. This change in the prevailing social definition of jealousy was one of the outcomes of the 1960s' sexual revolution. For the first time, some people began to feel guilt or shame about feeling jealous. Clanton reports that the magazine articles he studied (as well as the TV talk shows) began to assert that people who've been "liberated" from sexual repression should not "stoop" to jealousy. Low self-esteem and the inability to trust were said to be jealousy's root causes. Persons with those "defects" were instructed to seek cures from a therapist. Jealousy was no longer defined as good but as unhealthy both for relationships and for persons' own freedom and growth. Popular articles suggested that people in open and honest situations (e.g., the swinging and the open marriages described in Chapter 4) had learned to escape from the crippling effects of jealousy. Clanton acknowledges that this new view of jealousy was held most strongly by persons living in urban rather than rural areas, and by better-educated and affluent persons. He might also have added that religiously devout persons were not likely to be converts away from the old view.

Commitment and Freedom   Finally, Clanton reports that during the 1980s the social definitions of jealousy changed yet again. This time they got much more complex than either the old view or the new view by itself. The complexity arises, he says, from the tension of trying to strike a balance between *commitment* to one's erotic friendship (whether girlfriend/ boyfriend, cohabitor, spouse) and *freedom* for oneself. To demonstrate the idea that such a balance is not easy to achieve, Clanton counted the numbers of articles devoted to jealousy.

From the late 1940s until the early 1960s, he found that one or two articles a year appeared on the topic. Between 1966 and 1972, however, almost no articles were published about jealousy. In 1973, articles began to appear again, but since 1978 the numbers of articles on jealousy have increased to five per year. Clanton says that growing interest in the topic of jealousy demonstrates that people are struggling with the commitment and freedom balance. Kurt's behavior in sleeping with two women at once reveals an emphasis on his own sexual freedom and a downgrade of his commitment to either woman. Losing the sexual part of his relationship with Karyn, however, jarred him into realizing how much he valued Helga. Hence, he gave up a certain degree of freedom (sleeping with Karyn) and established a firm commitment to his erotic friendship with Helga.

Clanton remarks that "jealousy protects whatever kinds of relationships cultures teach people to value.[56] Throughout Western societies, erotic friendships are defined as very important and highly valued relationships. For the vast majority of persons, this kind of dyadic relationship is unique and extraordinarily special. Persons learn to define intercourse as symbolic of that uniqueness. Sexual partnership sets the boundary around their relationship, distinguishing *we* from *they*. Most persons believe that sharing their partner sexually with someone else is a threat to that relationship and/or themselves, and they've learned various ways to meet the threat. Karyn, for instance, ended her sexual exchanges with Kurt in order to protect herself and her dignity.

Freedom and Trust   Clanton observes that the big debate today is not over intercourse itself. Most persons agree that jealousy is indeed appropriate if one's partner secretly sleeps with someone else. Given that consensus, the debate has moved in a more uncertain direction: How much freedom and trust should one accord one's partner for situations that have the potential for boundary violation? For example, when the only business travelers were men, wives trusted their husbands neither to keep mistresses nor to visit prostitutes. Arthur Miller's 1948 classic play, *Death of a Salesman,* was about the tragic consequences flowing from Willy Loman's betrayal of his wife's trust while working out of town. She preferred to ignore her suspicions of his betrayal because she wanted to avoid the jealous reactions that she knew would accompany her finding out. Today, women business and professional travelers are everywhere. Both genders often work together into the evenings or on weekends, perhaps away from home. Moreover, the social climate is infinitely more conducive to sexual experimentation than it was in Willy Loman's time. Even back then one reason given for keeping women out of the labor force was men's fear that, given some freedom, women might prove as untrustworthy as men when it comes to sex.[57]

However, today's cultural definitions have shifted markedly. People now learn that liberation from the double standard means that neither gender is supposed to be jealous over their partner's business travels, as long as they're *just* business. Nor are persons supposed to be jealous of their partners' local unmonitored work demands that have the potential for betrayal, as long as the demands are innocent. Instead of jealousy, persons in erotic friendships are supposed to learn to trust one another in order to allow partners, especially women, the freedom to pursue their own educational and occupational goals. For example, back in the 1950s, if a man and woman had a weekday lunch together, their spouses would very likely feel threatened and thus jealous. But today, the definition of weekday lunches, whether for business purposes or because the

persons are just-friends, has changed. Today lunches are almost always defined as innocent and not an acceptable basis for feeling threatened or being jealous.

But what about week*end* lunches? Or dinners at any time? Dinners were once almost always defined as a very serious threat. They are no longer perceived that way if the diners are on legitimate business, whether in or out of town. If, however, business hasn't brought Sally and Kevin together, their respective partners might indeed feel threatened, especially if the dinners occur on weekends. And after dinner? Would Sally's partner, as well as Kevin's partner, feel threatened if Kevin invites Sally to his hotel room or apartment for an after-dinner liqueur? What if Sally and Kevin insist afterward to their partners that "everything was innocent, nothing happened, we're just-friends?" What if they declare that "even though we share deep, emotional ties, we're nonsexual?" Does the fact of Sally and Kevin's emotional intimacy increase their partners' sense of insecurity? In Eco's novel, *Foucault's Pendulum,* the central couple are trying to figure out when outsiders should or should not be perceived as a threat to their relationship. When is it legitimate for a modern couple to be jealous? Finally, he comes up with a solution by telling her that he would be "jealous of anyone who makes a light bulb flash on in your head."[58]

Contemporary struggles to balance freedom with commitment spring in large part from women's increasing participation in paid labor. Economic resources give women the autonomy to make choices about their behaviors (innocent and otherwise) with men that their mothers and grandmothers simply never had. Autonomy also means that, compared with previous generations of women (such as Mrs. Willy Loman), and compared with today's Japanese women, Western women can take decisive steps to protect themselves upon perceiving threats to their erotic friendships.

Reevaluating Permanence   One of the ways to "protect oneself" is to terminate the erotic friendship, as Karyn did whe she found out about Helga. But how does the freedom to terminate relationships square with the goal of permanence? Up to recently, permanence was valued much more highly than it is today. That was especially true if a couple's erotic friendship was "legal." Everyone around them expected that their marriage would be stable— only death should be allowed to part them. Increasingly, however, the idea that permanence is a good thing *in and of itself* is being called into question. Many citizens wonder how healthy permanence is for either the adults or their children, apart from a strong sense of we-ness and bonding.[59]

The Dissolution Phase—The Winding Down of We-ness

Often the realization that we-ness is declining surfaces very slowly, as it did in Helga's case. "Runners," was the badge that the single women in Richardson's study often pinned to their married male partners.[60] The women were mindful that these men made a virtual career of moving from one extramarital relationship to another. If pressed, the men made no secret of the fact that they were unlikely to leave their wives. But in today's complex societies, many men and women who have multiple erotic friendships cannot necessarily be classified as runners. Remember that for a short time, Kurt had a relationship with Karyn as well as Helga. But Kurt had never been a runner, and once his commitment to Helga became firm, his erotic antennae began signaling his lack of interest in the women around him.

Helga's case was more complicated. During the time she and Kurt developed their relationship, she was married to and living with Hans, and was economically interdependent

with him. They were also parenting children together. Nonetheless, by this time Helga no longer perceived Hans as a legitimate sexual partner. She did not define herself as having an erotic friendship with him—she felt no sense at all of bonding with him. She knew she wouldn't feel jealous and threatened if Hans became sexually involved with another woman. But she hadn't told her husband she had an ongoing erotic friendship with another man, and she was well aware that Hans defined her as his legitimate sexual partner. Was Helga deceiving her spouse? Was she cheating on him in the same ways that Richardson's runners were betraying their spouses' trust?

Transitions   Unlike runners, neither Helga not Kurt had a life history of keeping multiple sexual relationships going simultaneously and indefinitely. Consequently, instead of calling Helga and Kurt runners, it makes more sense to think of them as persons in *transition*. Researchers report that several times throughout their life courses many persons in today's modern societies move from one erotic friendship to another.[61] As a result, it's becoming increasingly common for persons to experience transitions between relationships in ways that were unknown to prior generations. Before the sixties, persons were much more likely to experience lifelong marital stability rather than several life-course transitions into and out of erotic friendships. Richardson shows that in today's world, personal and education/job transitions often occur around the same time; many of the women she studied were experiencing one or both of those kinds of transitions when they first met their married men (see Chapter 15). Helga is an example of someone going through a transition into higher education and a better job at the same time she's experiencing crucial personal transitions. She intends, for instance, to move out of the house she now shares with Hans as soon as she's financially capable of renting her own apartment.

Priests and Transitions   Teresa Marciano's recent study of Roman Catholic priests is an intriguing example of persons being in transition as well as runners.[62] It is well known that many priests are leaving the Church to marry. What is less well known, says Richard Sipe, is that at any given time some 20 percent of priests are having affairs—maintaining hidden ongoing relationships (MC phase)—with women.[63] Another 8 to 10 percent are in a formation phase: exploring heterosexual activities with women, including casual sex. And, according to Sipe, another 20 percent are either engaged in homosexual activity or are struggling with their sexual identity.

Marciano's study examines the complex processes of transition through which many priests pass. She agrees with Sipe that many priests perceive themselves to be in the dissolution phase (Figure 5-1) of their primary relationship (their "marriage") with the Church. Their sense of we-ness and bonding with the Church is in sharp decline. Their feelings of erosion may go on for many years, during which the priest may have a series of ongoing illicit and adulterous erotic friendships, both heterosexual and homosexual. He must conceal his behavior, even though some parishioners are aware of and tolerate it. Some priests continue as runners throughout their religious careers. Other priests, however, maintain one erotic friendship (male or female) all their lives alongside their first love, the Church. Some of the priests in Marciano's study eventually added the formal tie of marriage to their covert erotic friendship. Nonetheless, they kept their marriage vows secret, enabling them to fulfill their earlier (and contradictory) vows as a celibate priest. Keeping their relationships secret was, however, extremely difficult in those cases where children were born. Other priests who married came out of the closet immediately, and severed their priestly ties with the Church. Some priests who at first kept their marriage secret also eventually went public.

Boundaries Between Phases   It should be quite clear by now that the distinctions between the three phases displayed in Figure 5-1 (formation, MC, dissolution) are amorphous and highly fluid. We're not talking about the sharp boundary line that divides North Dakota from South Dakota. At any time you can step either way across that border and know precisely which state you're in. By contrast, the boundaries between the three relationship phases are more like those waters where the Gulf of Mexico joins the Caribbean Sea, or the Caribbean melds into the Atlantic Ocean. A map gives us a neat picture of how to divide those three bodies of water from one another. But if you're on a boat there are no markers conveniently indicating you've passed from one into the other.

We learned that the distinction between formation and MC is the difference between *prospect* and *partner*. Persons in formation are sorting out a number of persons with whom they might consider having a relationship. Persons in MC perceive they've already established an exclusive sexual partnership. But what is the distinction between MC and dissolution? Marciano's study suggests that although persons in transition are different from runners in many respects, they appear to share one major characteristic: They are both likely to be found in the dissolution phase of an erotic friendship. Recall that an MC phase is marked by gradual enhancement of the person's sense of we-ness. As time passes, the feelings of special belonging may fluctuate up and down, or may plateau for a while. But over the long haul, the trajectory, or pattern, of we-feelings is at least level and perhaps upward. As long as feelings of bonding display this kind of pattern, we can say that the persons are in MC, and this phase could continue indefinitely.

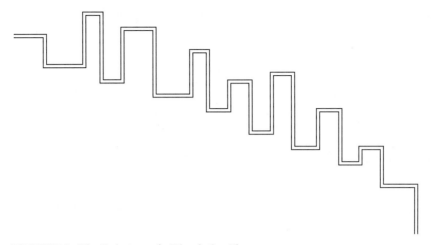

FIGURE 5-2   The Trajectory of a Dissolution Phase
Fluctuations shown reflect the sense of we-ness, bonding, and belonging.

But we all know that among many couples (girl/boyfriend, cohabitors, spouses) in modern societies, MC does not persist indefinitely. Instead, the sense of we-ness, or feelings of bonding, begin to erode. The pattern, though fluctuating up and down, may now reveal a long-term downward trend (Figure 5-2). Thus, the chief distinction between the MC phase and the dissolution phase is that in MC the trajectory is level or upward, but in dissolution the trajectory is downward. A dissolution phase is like a rollercoaster. After the initial pull upward to the highest point, the cars rise and fall, but the trajectory is inevitably downward.

Unlike a rollercoaster, however, a couple can reverse the downward trend. One might compare this with the reversal of a "bear" market (downward trend in the stock market) to a "bull" market (upward trend). A couple could change from dissolution to MC once again. The more Hans realizes his relationship with Helga is eroding, the more he might want to change back to what it was: "I still love you!," he cries. But Helga wants neither to go back, nor to go on, with Hans. She loves Kurt and values their erotic friendship. The more Hans

pleads for her love, the more she realizes she must signal some intent to him, let him know what she plans to do.

Unlike runners, persons in transition such as Helga have no intention of remaining indefinitely in a dissolution phase while cultivating an MC phase with someone else. Although for the time being Helga does have more than one relationship, her strong preference is to maintain just one at a time. When Helga feels that she's finally ready to cut her financial ties with Hans and move out, she tries to tell him. But she loses courage—she's afraid to hurt him more than she has already. So one morning after Hans leaves for work, a friend comes over to help pack her personal belongings and a few furniture items. Hans returns home that night to discover that Helga (along with their third child) has suddenly moved into a house shared by a number of her women friends. Hans and Helga are now separated.

Reactions to the Decline in We-ness

Explore and Exit   Helga's behavior is one example of how some persons behave when their sense of we-ness drops low enough. They begin to explore alternative relationships (in Helga's case, Kurt). Eventually they exit from the relationship they had been in before their explorations.[64]

Explore Alternatives, but Stay   A second reaction is found in the behavior of runners. Although they consistently explore alternative relationships, they have no serious intention to exit from their prior relationship. The married men told the single women in Richardson's study that their relationships with their wives were terribly empty, not only sexually, but emotionally as well.[65] Were the men lying simply to get the women into bed? Apart from asking the men, there's no way to be sure. But the men were well-to-do businessmen and professionals. Like their Japanese counterparts they could buy sex anytime they wanted it, especially since they were away from home a great deal of the time. Richardson remarks that very often their relationships came "full circle." That is, they started out as just-friends and their erotic friendships ended by the couple becoming just-friends once again. In short, the men appear to have been looking for more than merely sexual pleasure once they got into an MC phase with the women. They also wanted the gratifications of a special we-group—including intrinsic satisfactions—that evidently they were not receiving from their wives. Their sense of belonging to, and feeling special with, their wives is probably like the trend displayed in Figure 5-2. Their sense of bonding was on a downward, instead of a level or an upward, trajectory.

Atwater's study of married women having affairs points in a similar direction. The wives were definitely not out for casual sex, although sometimes they got just that. Rather, their aim was a friendship into which sex might or might not be woven. Most of the wives (like Richardson's husbands) reported that they were in "unhappy marriages."[66] There was no

hint they had an ongoing MC phase with their spouses and were looking around simply for the thrill of adding a second MC phase. Rather, they appeared to be in a dissolution phase. Atwater reports that those wives went through the same sorts of experiences as did the single women in Richardson's study. First, they became just-friends. Next, they entered a formation phase of an erotic friendship. Being in MC with someone other than their spouse filled a perceived void in their lives. Like the men in Richardson's study, they had no serious intentions to exit from their current marriages.

In sum, the few available studies seem to suggest that whether they stay or eventually exit, persons actively exploring alternatives to an ongoing relationship are likely to be in a dissolution phase.[67] To be sure, persons in an MC phase might occasionally have casual sex with outsiders. However, that is vastly different from maintaining a second ongoing erotic friendship, that is, having *two insiders*, one of whom (the second) is kept secret from the first.

Ignore Alternatives   A third reaction to a long-term decline in we-ness is simply to do nothing. Earlier in the chapter we said that resources include a person's perception of her or his physical and sexual attractiveness, along with education and a good job. Helga was attractive, and was working hard to get the other two resources. Her resources (actual and potential) helped make her willing to take certain risks. By contrast, although Hans had sensed for some time that his bonding with Helga was declining, he felt he lacked the resources necessary to seek alternative relationships. Because Hans saw himself as unattractive, and had few extrinsic assets, he never had casual sex nor did he seek prospects while he and Helga were living together. As far as Hans was concerned, he was willing to go on living with Helga forever even though he sensed they were in a long-term dissolution phase. That option seemed less painful to Hans than losing Helga altogether and then having to run the frightening risk of trying to find an alternative relationship.

What about the wives of the men who were having affairs with the women in Richardson's study? Did the wives perceive themselves as being in an MC phase? Or did they feel that their sense of we-ness was on a steady downward trajectory? Richardson reports that the wives tended to share their husbands's perceptions that they had "terrible marriages."[68] In many cases the wives sensed that their husbands were having affairs. One single woman reported that she went on vacations with her man and his wife during which the wife would "conveniently disappear." The woman and man took those opportunities to sleep together, and the woman sensed the wife knew all about it. Another woman said she worked with both her man and his wife and was certain the wife knew. Moreover, she was terrified the wife would one day confront her at work and publicly humiliate her.

Weren't those wives jealous of the women? Why didn't the wives react to protect themselves and their relationships? Were they perhaps having affairs of their own? Apart from asking the wives, we don't know for sure. But let's assume they were jealous, and that their sense of bonding with their husbands was being further eroded by what the wives probably defined as cheating. Why did they tacitly agree to their husbands' behavior? Why did they go on living with a steady decline in their level of we-ness? The answers lie in part with matters of resources and alternatives. Keep in mind that their husbands had the physical and material resources necessary to seek and maintain alternative relationships. For centuries, wives have had little choice but to tolerate their husbands' other women (i.e., kept women or "mistresses"). Today's Japanese wives still face that ancient situation. And in

North America, some wives apparently feel that even if they become jealous over their husbands' affairs (or casual sex), the best way to protect themselves and their marriages is to say and do nothing. Being silent and playing dumb protects against loss of a husband, including the loss of his economic support and of the social respectability that accompanies being married.

That wall of protection is especially relevant for nonemployed wives of upper-middle-class and upper-class men. For example, it was an open secret that President John Kennedy, his brother Attorney General Robert Kennedy, and their father Joseph Kennedy, who had been ambassador to Great Britain, frequently had ongoing affairs as well as casual sex.[69] And although their wives were well aware of the men's extramarital activities, they evidently chose to look the other way. Among privileged women of that era, that often seemed the easiest thing to do. Even today, some wives feel they lack the resources—attractiveness as well as tangible resources—to *re*enter the world of singleness (described in Chapter 8). Many of them also feel inadequate to compete effectively in the marketplace. Better, they feel, to endure the pains of gradually declining we-ness than face the risks of once again being on their own.

But things never stand still. If we follow Richardson's wives over time, it seems likely that some of them will eventually come to perceive that the protection of their marriage is occurring at too high a price when weighed against the damage to their own self-worth and dignity. At that point, they might do a number of things. They might, for instance, have their own affairs, as did the wives that Atwater studied. Or they might confront their husband and/or simply end their relationship. Richardson reports that a number of the husbands did indeed experience separation and/or divorce from their wives. In some of those cases at least, it seems likely that the wives' transitions were the result of their realizing full well what was going on and then acting to protect *themselves* instead of their marriages.

Before the 1960s it was apparently much more common than now for persons to live out a large portion of their marital lives in dissolution without exploring any alternatives (Goode's "quiet desperation"). A recent study found that now only 7 percent of the women and men in a national U.S. sample of married persons could be characterized as living indefinitely in a dissolution phase.[70] A chief reason contemporary Western persons aren't required to endure lifetime dissolution is the greater availability of alternatives, both economic and personal. Both genders have much greater access than ever before to persons whom they could define as prospects if they chose to do so. If someone has resources and alternatives, why would that person opt to remain in a dissolution phase indefinitely? Someone without the necessary resources may have no choice but to endure. Endure, that is, until he or she gets some resources.

If persons in a dissolution phase have resources enabling them to exit if they wish, why did the well-off husbands in Richardson's study stay indefinitely with their wives while having a series of affairs? As we saw in the cases of Helga and of Kurt, exercising options and seeking alternatives always imply some degree of risk and possible cost.[71] It may be that some of the husbands did not wish to risk the economic penalties of a divorce. Some husbands explicitly told the women they did not want to give up living with their children. Given the full range of potential costs and benefits involved in either leaving or staying, it apparently made sense to the husbands to remain married (although in a dissolution phase) but be in an MC phase with another woman. Nevertheless, not all of the runners stayed that way forever. Some of the men did

eventually leave their wives. Richardson reports, however, that seldom did these men form committed relationships with the women they'd been involved with while married. Instead, the men tended to find different women to be committed to, cohabit with, and perhaps marry. The women with whom the men had been involved had helped them realize how unpleasant it was to continue in dissolution. But once they made up their minds to separate from their wives, the men also ended their erotic friendships with the women as well. Richardson remarks that as painful as that was, most of the women actually preferred it that way. The women were not too anxious to enter committed relationships with the men for a number of reasons, one of which is quite obvious: Since they'd been runners with their wives, how could the women be sure the men would not do the same thing with them?

Exit Without Exploration   A fourth reaction to a continued decline in we-ness is simply to exit without searching for prospects and/or maintaining alternative erotic friendships. During his marriage Kurt had exerienced a steady erosion of his sense of belonging to, and bonding with, his spouse. For several years, however, he simply ignored the erosion. Finally, Kurt became so depressed and anxious, and so overcome by feelings of listlessness and boredom, that he and his wife sought marital counseling. The counseling sessions made it clear to both that their most prudent course of action was to separate and divorce. And they did so without either one ever seeking—much less having—an additional, secret erotic friendship.

CONCLUSION—REINVENTING RESPONSIBLE SEXUAL DYADS

The label "erotic friendship" is a convenient way to talk about today's relationships between women and men, as well as between persons of the same sex (lesbian/gay). It's an umbrella that covers boyfriends/girlfriends and cohabitors as well as married spouses. First of all, when we say "erotic" we're *not* focusing on the pleasurable aspects of sexuality, as important as they are. Instead, we're talking about the boundary of the relationship. What makes the erotic couple different from just-friends is that they perceive one another, and are perceived by outsiders, as sexual partners: "*We* have sex only with each other; *They* (everyone else) does not have sex with either of us." Second, when we say "friendship," we're talking about much more than mere companionship, that is, doing things together during leisure time. We're also targeting emotional intimacy in all of its many and varied aspects.

The erotic friendship indicates *social reinvention* in several ways. First is its growing public acceptance. Before the 1960s, couples who might be having sex did all they could to conceal it. Even engaged couples were expected to wait until their wedding night to do It. Today, most citizens (everyone except those in the fixed-philosophy category of Figure 1-1) are rather blasé about the fact that a couple may be doing It. What friends and families are more concerned about is what might come next. What about pregnancy risks? And risks of STDs, including the AIDS virus? Are they thinking about living together? Is marriage a possibility?

Second, the erotic friendship indicates reinvention because it transforms *responsibility* into something exceedingly complex. Until recently, being a responsible woman or man was a fairly simple and straightforward matter—get married and stay married in order to take care of one's children and one's spouse. For husbands, "care" meant providing material resources; for wives "care" meant looking after all the needs of everyone in the household as well as kin outside it. However, we're becoming increasingly aware of the reality that stable-marriage persons are not necessarily responsible persons. They may do damage to their spouses, their children, and themselves.[72]

Hence the requirement for responsibility has led to a redefinition of caring.[73] Today, caring means that persons seek to carry out all of the varied demands of the erotic friendship in ways that benefit, instead of hurt, others. Whether one is in a formation phase, or a maintenance and change phase, or a dissolution phase, one seeks to avoid exploiting potential and actual partners, as well as children. That is an excruciatingly difficult thing to try to do, however, as we learn from the lives of Helga, Hans, and Kurt and from the research described in this and later chapters. It is difficult because, among other things, there is no culturally established formula that is comparable to "get married and stay married." Next, it is difficult because conditions in the larger society, especially economic, are constantly shifting. Finally, it is difficult because persons themselves don't stand still: Their growth and development often have significant impacts on the adults and children in their lives.

Nevertheless, in spite of the difficulties and our frequent failures to be responsible, people are by no means giving up on erotic friendships. Belonging to and cultivating a primary relationship of this kind appears to be what some social scientists call a "cultural universal." The profound desire to belong to one other person in a special way that includes sexual partnership, along with other important elements, seems to show up in virtually all societies. To be sure, the behavioral expressions of that sort of unique we-group vary greatly across societies and within the same society over time. And that fact leads us to the third way in which erotic friendships indicate reinvention: In the West, formal (i.e., legal) heterosexual marriage is losing some of its unique social significance. It was once the only socially approved setting for erotic friendships and for parenting. Now, especially in the Scandinavian lands but also in North America, persons are creating a variety of social settings in which to publicly express their erotic friendships as well as their desire to parent (see later chapters, especially Chapters 8 through 10).

Does that mean that formal marriages will disappear any time soon? Not al all. But it does require that we place legal marriage under the scrutiny of a very different light than we did before. That light is visually displayed by Figure 5-1. And it shows us that there are far more socially significant questions to ask than merely. "Are you married, single, divorced?" The more fundamental questions are, "Do you have an erotic friendship?" If yes, "What phase are you in?" And, "Do you have more than one erotic friendship?" Or, "If you don't have an erotic friendship, are you 'prospecting' for one?" Or, "Are you 'prospecting' even if you're currently in an erotic friendship?" To be sure, we must also find out if people are cohabiting, or are formally married, and whether children live with them, and so on. But those pieces of information are useful chiefly because they fit into, and help us make sense of, the broader puzzle of the erotic friendship. Before the 1960s, marriage was the unique and all-encompassing umbrella under which everything else (sex, sharing the same household, parenting, friendship, etc.) was tucked in a very neat and tidy fashion. And now? The erotic friendship has become the umbrella under which we try, in a responsible fashion, to fit everything else, including marriages. The problem is that it's neither neat nor tidy nor simple. And that complexity is explored throughout the following chapters.

NOTES

1. Sears, 1977; Gitlin, 1987; John Spurlock, 1988.
2. Weeks, 1985.
3. Gravenhorst, 1988, p. 89.
4. Ibid., pp. 87ff.
5. Scanzoni et al., 1989.
6. Kondo, 1990.
7. Faris, 1937.
8. Gravenhorst, p. 90.
9. Edwards, 1991.
10. Swidler, 1980.
11. Richardson, 1985, p. 17; and see Jones, Marsden, and Tepperman, 1990.
12. Gravenhorst, p. 84.
13. Goode, 1963.
14. Condon, 1985, pp. 45, 48, 49.
15. Bernard, 1972, p. 101.
16. Scanzoni et al., 1989; Scanzoni and Marsiglio, 1993.
17. Kalbfleisch, 1993.
18. Richardson.
19. Ibid.; Koeppel et al., 1993.
20. Atwater, 1982.
21. Sprecher, 1989; Koeppel et al.
22. Richardson, p. 15.
23. Farber, 1964.
24. Koeppel et al.
25. Richardson, p. 16.
26. Koeppel et al.
27. Collins, 1975.
28. Abbey, 1991, pp. 100–101
29. Ibid.; Rubin, 1990; Koeppel et al.
30. Richardson, p. 23.
31. Ibid., p. 67.
32. Sprecher.
33. Atwater; Richardson; Rubin.
34. Joyce, 1914.
35. Reid and Fine, 1992.
36. Pleck, 1980; Swain, 1992.
37. Allan, 1989, p. 70.
38. Ibid.
39. Nardi, 1992.
40. Wright, 1982.
41. Allan, pp. 74ff.
42. Bullis, Clark, and Sline, 1993.
43. Richardson, p. 67.
44. Swidler, 1980.
45. Perlman and Fehr, 1987.
46. Clanton, 1989; Guerrero et al., 1993.
47. Falk, 1984.
48. Clanton, p. 179.
49. Cherry, 1987, p. 113.
50. Ibid., p. 114.

51. Ibid., p. 113.
52. Ibid., p. 114.
53. Ibid.
54. Stearns, 1989.
55. Clanton, p. 182.
56. Ibid., p. 187.
57. Pitts, 1964.
58. Eco, 1988, p. 151.
59. Swidler, 1980; Scanzoni, 1987.
60. Richardson, p. 41.
61. Furstenburg and Spanier, 1984; Duncan and Morgan, 1985; Owen, 1993.
62. Marciano, 1990.
63. Sipe, 1990.
64. Rusbult, 1987.
65. Richardson, p. 144.
66. Atwater, pp. 82ff.
67. Meyering and Epling-McWherter, 1986; Owen, 1993.
68. Richardson, pp. 89ff.
69. Koskoff, 1974; Martin, 1983; Brown, 1988.
70. Heaton and Albrecht, 1991.
71. Levinger and Huston, 1990.
72. Weil, 1990.
73. Thompson, 1993.

PART TWO

HISTORICAL PERSPECTIVES

point out that friendship tends to precede the formation of social families. Intrinsic as well as extrinsic exchanges occurring simultaneously are the basic elements giving rise to a sense that "I belong to my special we-group—my social family." Among both formal and social family members, the moral obligation "to share without reckoning" involves *universal reciprocity*. That is, everyone in the family is expected to exchange with everyone else in the family, at least to the extent that she or he is able. There are no notions of quid pro quo, or tit-for-tat. No calculations are made regarding "how much you've done for me in the past," or "how much I expect from you in the future."

Chapters 4 and 5 examined two-person "families" called *erotic friendships*. The unique tie that binds couples, or dyads, is sexual interdependence. Increasingly, women in these relationships want to share emotional intimacy with their men. Erotic friends may or may not share the same household. They may or may not be formally married, and they may or may not be parenting children. Erotic friends may include homosexual as well as heterosexual couples.

Although these are the several basic ties that bind families, people can arrange the ties—and then rearrange them in different ways—in order to keep on reinventing varied and complex kinds of families. Later chapters delve further into both the variety and the complexity of today's families. To help us get a better grasp on today's *re*inventions, we must first fathom the inventions of the recent past. Hence, Chapters 6 and 7 tell a story covering the last 200 years. Importantly, the story unfolds in the context of profound transitions in the broader economic and political spheres. Western societies have changed dramatically since the end of the eighteenth century, and families have followed suit. The idea of reinventing families is not a new one; people have been doing it for some time.

COLONIAL EXPERIENCES—THE 1700s

According to Elizabeth and J. H. Pleck, reinvention can be seen by the meanings that some men attached to friendship during the late eighteenth century. These authors report the language used in letters between men who together became officers in George Washington's army.[1] For three years Alexander Hamilton and John Laurens wrote long and passionate letters to one another while both were in their early twenties. At the time, Laurens was married and Hamilton was engaged. They exchanged letters frequently, using expression such as "my dear," and "I love you," an "I am a jealous lover," and "the other officers send their love." Pleck and Pleck added that we will never know for certain whether these men were sexual lovers. We do know, however, that they made no attempt to conceal their relationship from their fellow officers. We also know that although all sex outside of marriage was legally prohibited, sodomy was deemed the most reprehensible act of all, and was punishable by death. Consequently, it seems safe to conclude that higher status men of that era used words of love with each other without any homosexual overtones. Donald Hansen's historical research reveals that the same patterns may also have been common among some working-class men of that era.[2]

Pleck and Pleck concluded that "love between men was acceptable as long as it did not lead to sexual contact."[3] In short, it seems that men of that era could be more than buddies or mates—they could also be close *intimates*—friends who shared their innermost selves by disclosing their fears, anxieties, joys, and aspirations. Who could be more of an honorable and strong man during that era than an army officer? To "be a man" was not considered antithetical to close feelings—masculinity and intimacy were evidently not divorced. And evidently they were united among both the privileged and the working classes.

Patriarchy and Intimacy

One significant reason Colonial men may have sought intimacy from each other is that emotional intimacy was not considered a vital part of their relationships with women, including their wives. On the one hand, there can be no doubt that some wives and husbands of that era formed "deep and warm attachments."[4] On the other hand, both Howard Gadlin and Pleck and Pleck concluded that the broader social conditions of the Colonial era limited the degree of love and affection spouses had for one another. Pleck and Pleck labeled those conditions *agricultural patriarchy*. Gadlin defined them as a "severe . . . authoritarianism, a basic misogyny [hatred of women], and a fundamentalist Christian distrust of uncontrolled earthly pleasures and human passion."[5]

Pleck and Pleck described how the whole of Colonial society was built one social layer on top of the other. Few white men ever moved above the layer into which they were born. African slaves of both genders were the very bottom layer. At the top were the wealthy white male landowners who had a view of society derived from England. The king was commissioned by God and thus ruled everybody else. Under the king, white men likewise had a mandate from God to rule those below them—specifically their women, their children, their workers, and their slaves, if any. And God would hold white men accountable for their stewardship. Needless to say, women had no voting rights and no access to education, nor could they hold property if they had a father, husband, or adult son. Wives were considered the property of their husbands.[6]

How did that patriarchal society influence relationships between husbands and wives? First, Gadlin reported that Colonial leaders and opinion-makers (preachers, theologicans, politicans) worried about an absence of affection within families.[7] As a result, they were constantly exhorting wives and husbands to love each other, to be warm and affectionate within their families. Gadlin added that there was a public reason for these exhortations to be loving in private. The leaders believed that the family was the foundation of the whole of Colonial life. If peace and harmony did not exist within the family, Colonials believed the stability of the entire society would be threatened.

Unlike today, however, the dangers were not perceived as stemming from widespread divorce, since at the time it was virtually nonexistent. Instead, what was feared was that families were cauldrons of physical and verbal abuse between spouses, prisons from which there was no legitimate escape.[8] Gadlin says that one significant reason violence was so explosive in Colonial families was the constructed physical spaces in which people lived. Houses were small, rooms were few and multipurpose, walls were paper-thin, and large numbers of persons lived together. Furthermore, since there were few public inns, families often sold bed and breakfast to travelers. Beds were commonly multiply occupied by unmarried persons, and court records show that illicit sex often took place.[9] In short, there was no idea of privacy or a space of one's own to which one could retreat. Everyone was continually under everyone else's scrutiny. For persons who perceived themselves trapped by abusive and punishing conditions, desertion frequently became the solution of choice. According to Pleck and Pleck, more women than men opted for this means of escape from intractable life circumstances.[10]

In any case, it was conditions like this within families that worried many Colonial leaders. If peace, goodwill, harmony, and affection did not reign within the family, they reasoned that these conditions would not be able to exist within other institutions of society. Because they wanted social harmony, Colonial leaders, especially preachers, "commanded" citizens to show affection.[11] Persons were told it was their duty to God and society to love their spouses, they had a divine obligation to be affectionate and not to be abusive.

Whenever spouses had disagreements they couldn't resolve, they were told that God wanted wives to "give in" to their husbands.[12] Husbands were accorded ultimate authority over their wives (and children) because that's the way God had established order in the family. Colonials believed that patriarchy would have benign consequences. They held that if wives would submit to their husbands, affection would abound, abuse would diminish, and desertions would become less common. And the result of that domestic felicity would be an orderly society. Recent studies reveal that at least some of those eighteenth-century ideas persist today among religiously conservative families.[13] However, these studies add that today's evangelical couples have softened the apparent harshness of the older ideologies by incorporating many insights from contemporary psychological counseling. These include the learning of communication skills through participation in church-sponsored marriage-enrichment seminars.

Equality and Intimacy

But whether harsh or soft, what is the connection between patriarchy and intimacy? Graham Allan reminds us that at its core, intimacy demands *equality*.[14] Intimacy requires that persons self-disclose, and that they share the core of their beings with one another. To do that as fully as possible, persons must treat each other as equals. If persons occupy the same social category to begin with, it's much simpler to achieve intimacy eventually. The three major categories Allan discusses are race, gender, and social class. Recall that Alexander Hamilton and John Laurens were both upper-status white men. Since it was socially acceptable for eighteenth-century men to be close, they had all three things going for them in their quest

for intimacy. It's terrifying enough to make oneself emotionally vulnerable when one feels socially equal. When persons are not social equals, they are likely to have a very difficult time in becoming intimate friends. Nevertheless, history and literature provide examples of persons of unequal status who attempted to transcend formal barriers to friendship. For instance, when actress Elizabeth Taylor wed her eighth husband, a blue-collar construction worker, *Newsweek* commented that after previous marriages to celebrities and a politician, she "is scaling down her taste."[15]

Although no one did surveys in Colonial America asking wives and husbands whether they felt their spouse was their equal, most persons believed that men and women were not social equals—they willingly accepted the ideology of patriarchy.[16] Objectively, there is no doubt whatsoever about gender inequality—men had greater social, economic, and political privileges than women. And since men had higher social status, Gadlin says that it was very difficult to prevent male authority from contaminating intimacy between the genders. Close friends do not impose solutions to their disagreements. Yet that is precisely what Colonial men had the right to do. And, as far as we know, that's what they did to their wives most of the time. Some couples, such as Abigail and John Adams (second U.S. president), whose closeness is well documented in their extensive correspondence, were evidently exceptions to the rule and thus proved the rule.[17]

The Sexual Double Standard   Although women and men did not look to one another for intimacy, they were supposed to look solely to each other for sex.[18] At least that was the official line. Pleck and Pleck report that the double standard allowed men substantial leeway to seek nonmarital sex, particularly from prostitutes. Men were, of course, expected to be discreet and not disgrace their families through public scandals. Since the means of transportation were primitive, men who traveled on business tended to be away from their wives for long periods. The fact that they were enduring hardships to earn money for their families helped justify illicit sexual activity. The wives left behind did not have the same freedom. Since wives were the property of their husbands, Colonials believed that if another man had sex with a wife, the value of that property became "immeasurably diminished."[19]

Perhaps because women were men's property, and their social inferiors, the Colonials made no connections at all between sexuality and emotional closeness. Gadlin reports that they viewed sex solely in its lusty, raw, and raunchy senses.[20] Because they perceived it to be an explosive force, sex was officially limited to marriage so as not to cause social disorder. But even married persons were cautioned to "take care" lest their passions become so wild as to distract their minds and spirits from their religious obligations. Married couples were advised not to become obsessed or preoccupied with sex. Furthermore, women were thought to be the "spiritual daughters of Eve."[21] Eve, the Bible implies, was morally inferior to Adam, and thus succumbed first to the Devil's temptations. Eve then cleverly tricked Adam into (sexual) sin. Accordingly, women of the Colonial era were believed to be more prone than men to lose control of themselves, thus giving way to lustful passions and, in the process, drawing men with them into moral corruption.[22]

Children and Child Rearing

The idea that people reinvent families applies not only to relationships between adults. Reinvention applies with equal force to the relationships that adults have with children. And there is a close connection between the two. Critics charge that many choices made by today's adults are irresponsible because they

hurt children. Nevertheless, historians Steven Mintz and Susan Kellogg say that during the early Colonial period, "childhood was a much less secure and shorter stage of life than it is today."[23] Because of harsh and primitive living conditions, rates of death among infants and young children were extremely high. And if a child survived, she or he often experienced the death of siblings or of the mother, frequently in childbirth. The rearing of children was founded on the premise that every child was infected by a "sinful nature." Hence, after age 2 children were beaten severely and frequently in order to fashion the type of pliable and humble creature endorsed and valued by the churches of that time.[24] Patriarchal reasoning applied to children just as it did to wives: Husbands ruled their wives and children, and mothers ruled children.

By age 7, children were very much a part of the economic life of the household. They performed numerous gender-linked chores. Girls "were taught 'housewifery' or spinning . . . sewing, and knitting."[25] Boys began to do tasks outside the house, first in the vegetable gardens, later in the barns repairing harnesses, wagons, and so on. By age 14, most children were not living with their parents or sibs. To learn a trade, boys were apprenticed to and were living with blacksmiths, tavernkeepers, and others. Girls became maids, servants, and assistant cooks in larger households. Some children (usually boys) from economically advantaged households were away at boarding schools.

But as the 1700s were drawing to a close, people in New England were already reinventing their views of children and child rearing. What was especially startling was that "children were increasingly viewed as special creatures with unique needs."[26] Children were no longer perceived as miniature adults who as soon as possible had to be hammered into God-fearing persons. Mintz and Kellogg attribute these changes to social conditions in the form of growing prosperity. Parents needed to depend less and less on their children's labor for the economic survival of the household. As a result, parents "began to show greater concern for child development."[27] An indicator of this fresh concern was the "proliferation of books and games and toys aimed specifically at children."[28] Hence, as agriculture was giving way to the industrial era, children were increasingly seen as individuals with potential that adults could either cultivate or squash.

JACKSONIAN AMERICA—THE EARLY 1800s

Industrialization and the Gospel of Success

According to Pleck and Pleck, the "gospel of success" permeated the whole of American culture during the years between the American Revolution and the Civil War (1776–1865). Based on the rags-to-riches legend surrounding Andrew Jackson—the popular hero of the War of 1812 and later president—the New Gospel held that any *white* man, regardless of how poor or humble his beginnings, could through hard work, persistence, and diligent effort achieve success and wealth. This success theme was rooted, of course, in the industrialization and urbanization that was beginning to transform North America, as it had England. Because of the growth of factories, businesses, and commerce, large numbers of persons began to forsake the agricultural lifestyle of their ancestors. The countryside entered gradual decline, and cities began to expand rapidly.

The Industrial Revolution created jobs that had never existed before. It also allowed many more white men than at any time in history to participate in the quest for success and wealth. Before this era only white men who owned large tracts of land and then passed it on to their sons could ever expect to achieve economic success. Suddenly, for the first time, there were seemingly countless opportunities for landless white men. Horatio Alger wrote many popular storybooks for poor young boys, inculcating them with the rags-to-riches theme. Every white boy was told that he could aspire to enter the newly emerging middle class.

How did people respond to these profound and monumental social upheavals? How did they reconstruct relationships across and within gender?

Separate-but-Equal

Patriarchy—the notion that men had a divine right to rule over women—was gradually replaced by a more secular view called *separate but equal* spheres.[29] People believed that men's biology and personality—their masculinity—suited them for the cold, cruel, crass, and calculating world of business and commerce. Hence, as families moved to the cities, men were thrust out into the uncertain seas of economic competition. Conversely, people believed that middle-class women were far too delicate and fragile for such ruthless pursuits. Their feminine nature required them to remain at home. Their gentle femininity had been designed to nurture their men. Men could retreat to the haven of The Family and there have their wives bind up the wounds suffered in daily economic combat. Likewise, women, as mothers, could prepare their daughters for proper feminine pursuits and be a "civilizing influence" on their sons, balancing their surging masculinity with charm, grace, and good manners. (The separate-but-equal ideology is debated most vigorously today in terms of whether women should participate in military combat. Opponents argue that women lack the requisite masculine characteristics, especially the killer instinct, to be effective. Proponents point to women's stellar performances during the 1990–1991 Persian Gulf War, and argue that women should be given more chances to show what they can do.[30]) Thus, people began to believe that women were just as important as men in contributing to an orderly and healthy society. Women became more fully responsible for families than ever before. Up to this time, children had been under men's authority, as seen by the fact that fathers were always given custody in divorce or desertion cases no matter who was at fault. Now for the first time children began to pass to the authority of women. Although men might create the wealth that fueled an expanding economic base, women created the families that produced the men that turned out the wealth. People believed that "the hand that rocks the cradle rules the world."

Religion shifted in concert with these profound economic and social changes. Although the churches had endorsed patriarchy during the eighteenth century, during the Jacksonian era they began to embrace separate-but-equal ideas.[31] In their view, the divine plan now called for husbands to provide diligently for their families and for wives to nurture husbands and socialize children in Christian ways. Many of the churches of that era endorsed the *Protestant ethic*—the idea that material success is a sign of God's blessing.

Although the genders' separate endeavors were considered equally important for the good of society, women and men had no choice regarding which sphere to pursue. Women were expected to conform to the divine plan to be attentive mothers and obedient wives. And as before, when couples could not agree on something, it was the wife's duty to God to submit to God's representative for social order, her husband.

The Economically Disadvantaged But regardless of the Horatio Alger ideology and its religious endorsement, many men were simply unable to achieve economic success. Economic gaps between the successful white middle class and the less advantaged white working and lower classes were becoming wider than ever before.[32] Industrialization and urbanization brought with them rising rates of crime, delinquency, poverty, and illnesses both physical and mental. People believed that inadequate families were a major source of these new social problems, just as families had been blamed for eighteenth-century societal ills. Families were "inadequate" if fathers did not provide well enough for them, and/or if mothers did not train their daughters and sons to perform effectively in their socially assigned spheres. The inabilities of their husbands to provide forced many women into paid labor for the sake of family survival. And survival often demanded that the children themselves enter the labor market.

The Charles Dickens' novels describing the sordid consequences of vast urban poverty throughout industrial England were appropriate for North America as well. Gadlin reports that large numbers of families lived in a "gloomy situation."[33] The violence and abuse of Colonial times were carried on by Jacksonian men frustrated in their attempts to "make it." Desertion, which in the eighteenth century had been more common for wives than husbands, now became the husband's exit from the frustration of being unable to fulfill what Jessie Bernard calls *good-provider* expectations.[34] Trying to be a good provider was frustrating for men because there was no fixed idea of how much money they had to earn to be "good." No matter how much was earned, someone could always expect or desire more. Male desertion rates became so high that for the first time many states were forced to enact special legislation addressing the needs of abandoned wives.[35]

New Views on Gender and Friendship

Alongside these continuing changes, and probably because of them, something genuinely fresh surfaced in American culture: the mass media. For the first time, theme magazines and self-help books appeared aimed at a specific audience—the new families of the new middle class. Not only were such publications novel, but so was their theme: They encouraged wives and husbands to establish emotional bonds with one another.[36] Married couples were told that closeness was important for themselves, their children, and indeed all of society. Recall that during the eighteenth century couples were "commanded" to be affectionate. Nevertheless, Colonial wives and husbands did not consider each other their prime source of intimacy. Most men looked to men for friendship, most women to other women. Now, married couples were being encouraged to do something different from what their parents and grandparents had done. They were being urged to make one another their *prime source of friendship*.

Gadlin suggests several reasons for this fresh perspective on emotional intimacy. One is that as people moved from countryside to city, they sacrificed the daily contacts that many rural persons have with kin and long-time friends. Women and men had to face the anonymity and impersonality of city life without either the companionship or the emotional closeness they and their forebears had experienced for generations. Consequently, spouses needed one another in ways their parents' generations had not. Lacking the stable social networks of rural communities, wives and husbands were told by opinion-makers that they now had to look to each other for friendship. Before this, the home had not been considered a retreat from anything. Now opinion-makers portrayed it as a "haven" from the storms of the cruel, heartless urban and industrial society.[37]

Opinion-makers also noticed that something was happening to men and to the cultural definition of masculinity. To succeed in this new kind of society, a new kind of relationship surfaced in the commercial world of men. Since every white man was perceived as being in competition with every other white man, every man had to be cautious of other men.[38] Cautious in what way? Cautious that he did not share so much of himself with, and thus become vulnerable to, another man that the latter might somehow gain economic advantage over him. This fear was particularly relevant among men who were co-workers. During the eighteenth century, intimacy had evidently been part of the common experience of men. But gradually it was being undermined by the demands of commercial success. As it became less common for men to experience intimacy with other men, the new media encouraged couples to seek intimacy from one another. Couples were now expected to go beyond the mere affection and respect that might have characterized the marriages of their parents and grandparents.

Nevertheless, Gadlin reports that many men of the new commercial era found it extremely difficult to be intimate with their wives. Men discovered that it was not easy to be instrumental and task oriented all day at work, shift gears to become expressive and person oriented at home, and then shift once again the next day. Thus, couples were faced with contradictory pressures, a sort of *catch 22*. They were encouraged to be close friends because modern life is so anonymous and male commercial life so impersonal. But the demands of commercial success were redefining the meaning of masculinity, thereby making it difficult for men to cultivate intimacy with women.

Added to these problems was the issue already discussed—the significance of equality in order to have friendship. Even though the popular belief was that men's and women's social spheres were equal, and even though state legislatures were removing many of the gross injustices imposed on Colonial women, the objective realities remained much the same as they'd been before. Economically, politically, and in terms of social prestige, white men continued to be much more advantaged than white women. And African slaves remained at the bottom of the socioeconomic ladder. Free blacks were barely a notch above them. The upshot was that men and women trying to cultivate intimacy had to overcome powerful socially induced barriers. Although they might believe they were equal in the sight of God, and also in terms of popular culture, they were forced to cope with a contradictory theme: In a society in which achievement was the measure of a human's worth, women were excluded from achieving. Where then was the source of their worth? Women's natural virtues and motherhood were lavishly praised, but not rewarded with social status, power, money, or even the right to vote. Thus, the question that inevitably arose for both genders was: Are women actually as worthy as men? "How close can I be to someone of lesser, or greater, 'worth' than I—to someone who is not my social equal? Someone who lives in a totally different world from mine?"

The Emergence of Feminism

It is no accident that these kinds of questions were at the core of the feminist movement that emerged during this same era.[39] Many early-nineteenth-century feminists and their male allies had strong religious convictions. It is all well and good, they said, to assert that the genders are equal in the sight of God. But how can that equality be translated into greater control by women over their own lives? Equality demands autonomy, they said. It became apparent to feminists that if women were truly equal then they should be able to make choices, beginning with choices about elected officials. As the nineteenth century wore on, some feminists began to extend the idea of choice to which sphere of society (economic or domestic) women could enter. Feminists also pon-

Courageous suffragette of pre–World War I speaking to an almost all-male crowd.

dered the consequences of women's autonomy for husbands and children. Some signers of the 1848 Seneca Falls Declaration, for instance, questioned men's right to wifely obedience, and depicted wives as victims of "domestic slavery."[40]

Sex without Passion

But the immediate problem facing the opinion-makers of that era was how to foster intimacy between husbands and wives given the powerful social conditions operating against it. The solution that emerged was to de-eroticize sex.[41] What is labeled "Victorian sexual morality" first became popular during the early nineteenth century. Recall that the Colonials viewed sex as raw, lusty, and raunchy—an explosive force requiring social control. But in Jacksonian America, a new brand of evangelicalism was spawned through a series of religious revivals known as the *Second Great Awakening*. Among its by-products was a revised view of sexuality. Since natural biological sexual impulses, including masturbation, were at best suspect and at worst inherently evil, they had to be repressed even in marriage.[42] Sylvester Graham (originator of the Graham cracker) argued in the most vivid and dramatic language possible how male orgasms damage the human body and spirit. Even "sexual radicals" of the day, people who rejected monogamy and advocated free love, taught that while having intercourse men should remain motionless and not experience orgasm unless they intended conception.[43]

During the Colonial era, women and men were believed to be equally lusty and passionate. But now in keeping with the notion of women's gentle femininity, religious leaders began to say for the first time that women were, in fact passionless.[44] Their essential natures were thought to be purer and higher than those of men. Wives were, after all, entrusted with the care and nurture not only of their husbands, but of innocent children as well—the next generation. Not only were wives beyond the base level of carnal orgasms, they had the added responsibility of restraining men's lustful natures: The more capable wives were of reigning in men's wild passions, the more successful the couple would be in pursuing lofty and spiritual goals. And that in fact was the point of sex without *eros*. Passionless sex was believed to be the chief means whereby husbands and wives could achieve true love and spiritual intimacy.[45] In the gentle and tender embraces of an intercourse freed from the distractions of passion, lust, orgasm, and reckless abandon, husbands and wives could attain the grandest human feelings ever imaginable.

These spiritual feelings not only honored God, said evangelicals, they also bound the couple together forever in eternal bliss and harmony. By contrast, physical sex was something that prostitutes offered men straying from the God-given restraints and spiritual intimacy they could experience with their wives. Nevertheless, the secular double standard permitted men, if they wished, to stray (discreetly, of course) into the sinful realm of lusty sex offered by prostitutes.

In short, the idea that emotional intimacy might somehow be a dimension separate from sexuality was lost on most Jacksonians. Deep closeness, whether between or within gender, requires constant cultivation and struggle, as at least some persons of that era must have been aware. Women and men trying to achieve intimacy, and yet having to overcome their separate worlds of objective social inequality, found it to be hard work. It was much easier to work at being passionless and try to feel close that way, especially if it made one a more spiritual Christian.

There were several other reasons why marital passionlessness made sense to Jacksonians. First, it was believed that sexual purity achieved by resisting orgasms made a man much more effective in the world of work. By preserving his semen, he developed his character and built up his mental and physical powers.[46] Second, the emerging middle class recognized that fertility control was essential to enhancing their economic status. Since contraceptives were unreliable, passionlessness (along with "pulling out," should the man get carried away) was touted as a help in reducing the numbers of children. Third, some feminists used the image of the woman as asexual innocent as a means to exert control over men.[47] Since men were perceived as hapless victims of their lust and wild passions, they often forced their spiritually minded wives into unwanted sexual submission and excessive childbearing. Urging husbands away from loss of self-control and into spiritual intimacy was a way for wives to gain some bit of control over their own lives. Finally, women had other women in whom they could confide, close friends with whom they could experience emotional intimacy.[48] Much like their mothers and grandmothers, and in spite of urgings by opinion-makers, they did not actually expect that their husbands would be friends in the sense of confidantes or intimates. Nor did men expect intimacy from women, nor, for that matter, from men.

During this new era, men's companionship networks expanded far beyond what their fathers and grandfathers had ever known. Whereas their ancestors' social networks were limited to a relatively few men in the nearby town and countryside, persons from families who had known each other for generations, men now encountered large and ever-shifting numbers of other men at work, through commercial contacts, in varied neighborhoods, and so on. Pleck and Pleck add that during this time period "male camaraderie" found expression not only in "jovial drinking bouts in taverns" and in group "visits to prostitutes," but also in the founding of clubs.[49] These all-male enclaves, based most often on social class and/or on religious views, provided places where men could be legitimately absent from their wives and children. Here they could relax with their friends (or more accurately, buddies). Available historical evidence suggests that intimacy was not the purpose of these gatherings—companionship was.

Children and Child Rearing

Rejecting the early Colonial notion that children must be beaten into submission, Jacksonians *reinvented* child rearing to mean "the internalization of moral prohibitions, behavioral standards, and a capacity for self-government that would prepare a child for the outside world."[50] The media instructed parents to achieve those goals via some of the same techniques in vogue today: provoke guilt in children, confine them to their rooms, withhold love and privileges, and express disapproval. Although boys and girls had indeed been trained differently during the Colonial era, those differences now took on decidely sharper edges.

Parents must take care to make sure their boys became *achievers*. For boys to become good providers, parents had an obligation to prepare boys to compete successfully in the newly emerging commercial and industrial era. And parents had an equally compelling obligation to prepare their daughters to become successful wives and mothers—namely, women who in their turn nurtured their own successful husbands and children.

During the Colonial era, fathers were defined as having equal, if not greater, responsiblity for proper child rearing. But Jacksonians created the notion that "child rearing was a task for which women were uniquely suited."[51] Because of their allegedly gentler natures, Jacksonians believed that mothers could lovingly persuade children to choose the right paths.

Owing to their allegedly rougher natures, fathers had a tendency to try to compel children's obedience, a strategy the Jacksonians believed to be futile. In any case, by the mid-1800s, middle-class childhood and adolescence had been reinvented "in terms recognizable today. . . . Adulthood and childhood had been differentiated into two radically separate times of life."[52]

THE PROGRESSIVE ERA—1860s TO THE 1920s

The third phase in our examination of how, during the recent past, people were reinventing families ranges from the mid-1860s through the 1920s, approximately from the closing of the War Between the States to the onset of the Great Depression. This was (except for the World War I years, 1914–1918) a period of unbounded optimism about the future of humankind. Many opinion-makers believed that Western societies were progressing into a kind of second Renaissance.[53] Figure 1-1 used the label "process-oriented" to describe persons who question former ways of doing things in favor of new ways. They are also known as "progressives"—a label that first became popular during this era. Progressives were continually trying to reinvent ways of doing almost everything, including education, business, government, urban planning, and religion.

The Ideal Man

During the Progressive Era, women and men continued to live in separate worlds, but their dominant cultural images took somewhat different twists. The cultural ideals for men, invented earlier during the Jacksonian era, became sharper and ever more intense.[54] The "real man" was married, had children, and was a good provider for his family. At the same time, he "liked women" and was not above an occasional discreet dalliance. As evidence for that, Pleck and Pleck point to the large numbers of brothels and high rates of venereal diseases that characterized the Victorian period both in the United States and Europe. The real man also loved the strenuous life, whether challenging the wilderness or fighting in wars against the Indians or wars in Hawaii, Panama, the Philippines, Cuba, or Mexico. If he couldn't fight in forests or fields, he could fight in the marketplace. To help him in all his battles, opinion-makers urged him, among other things, to engage in bodybuilding and muscular development.[55]

Organized Sports

"Manly competition" in the form of organized athletics first emerged during the latter years of the nineteenth century. While Ivy League football games attracted highly educated men, professional baseball games and organized prizefights became the passions of most other men. Over time, organized athletics in general "accepted the style of male aggression common to the lower classes."[56] Around the turn of the century, the Boy Scouts was founded as a place where boys could learn all sorts of manly ideals, including *male bonding*. The founder of the Scouts was a man named Ernest Thomas Seton. He feared that American boys were in

Boy Scouts—at the service of other people at all times.

danger of developing "flabby muscles and weak character" because women had become responsible for their upbringing. Seton asserted, "I do not know that I have met a boy that would not rather be John L. Sullivan [heavyweight boxing champion] than Darwin or Tolstoi."[57] Getting a boy involved in the outdoors and in competitive sports was seen as the best means to rescue him from being effeminate. (Among other things, being effeminate meant enjoying the company of girls and women.[58]) The Scouts also provided a prestigious outlet for men—as scoutmasters—to affirm their manhood.

During this period, homosexual males both rejected and imitated the male heterosexual world.[59] They rejected the heterosexual world by retreating from it and constructing their own subcultures in large cities (New York, Chicago, Boston, Philadelphia, Denver). They imitated the heterosexual world by establishing bars, dance halls, baths, and Turkish cafes where they could feel safe from the threats of the larger society. Although in many respects these all-male enclaves were comparable to heterosexual settings, the major difference was of course that they permitted sexual activity. Police harrassment was not uncommon, but the authorities generally preferred to segregate homosexual behaviors to those bars rather than allow gays to be public and open.

New Choices for Women

As the 1900s dawned, clubs, union halls, fraternal lodges, and saloons had multiplied in every city. They provided male companionship ensconced within safe havens cloistered from women and children. But the home was supposed to be a man's haven from work. *Why then a haven from the haven?* Unlike the cultural norms surrounding maleness that were getting more sharply defined, the popular images of women were getting fuzzier, they were inching away from what they'd been throughout the Jacksonian era. What men found

alarming was that some women were breaking out of the old separate but equal sphere and beginning to experiment with things that belonged "properly" to males. By the 1890s, for example, some women began to ride bicycles, loosen their corsets and wear pantaloons (men's wide breeches extending from waist to ankle), and seek paid work before marriage. Hence, in comparison with the threats posed by fast-moving women's behaviors, the company of other men seemed safe, predictable, and comforting.[60]

If equality implies autonomy and thus choices, some ordinary, middle-class women of this era began embarking on a road from which there was no turning back. These unassuming women could not be maligned as radical feminist agitators set to destroy family and society. During the attempted August 1991 coup by right-wing hard-liners against the Soviet government, the world discovered that the genie of Russian democracy could not be shoved back in the bottle. Similarly, during the later years of the nineteenth and the early years of the twentieth centuries, women began escaping from the bottle of patriarchy, and there wasn't any way to force them back. Some women were constructing a new and fresh cultural image of women, one that allowed women to do some previously all-male things. To be sure, employment before marriage, less stifling clothing styles, and so on were not terribly earth shaking. Nevertheless, most men and some women denounced these innovative behaviors with the term *manliness*.[61] "Manliness," or "manly women," was a negative term meaning that the women involved were degrading themselves and hurting the family and society. But the die was cast. Although they may not have claimed it, some ordinary women were in effect asserting independence. Ordinary citizens were beginning to chip away at gender inequality, thus poking holes in the barriers to intimacy between men and women.

To be sure, conditions in the larger society were ripe for those kinds of social reinventions. The Progressive Era was the grand "Age of Confidence."[62] Around the turn of the century people throughout Western societies were extremely optimistic about the course of history. They believed that Western societies were moving upward and onward in unique ways. Part of believing that modern life was becoming more progressive was the feeling that social justice was spreading everywhere, including into relationships between women and men. Thus when some women chose to do nonconventional things, they could point to the society around them for justification and say, "Hey, it's OK, everything's changing!"

The Roaring Twenties

Nonconventionality reached a previously unknown peak during the 1920s. As one historian put it, those were the "first years of our own time."[63] World War I had just ended, and the initial sketch of society as we know it today became clear. The white middle class enjoyed unprecedented prosperity, and consumerism prompted by aggressive advertising began to be the American Way of Life. Automobiles became available for everyone, as did radios, phonographs, and numerous household gadgets. Silent movies, followed by talkies, became part of everyone's life. Women's hairstyles and clothing changed dramatically, for the first time publicly unveiling flesh previously covered in modesty. Mixed bathing at public beaches also became part of the fresh unveiling. The new popular music was jazz and rhythm and blues. Created by and for African-Americans, these strange and haunting sounds now made their way into white society. The tunes and words suggested lifestyles that in the past whites only whispered about. According to John Frohnmayer, social critics of the time said that pregnant women listening to jazz would bear deformed children.[64] Jazz was described as decadent jungle music and the Devil's music. Alongside jazz, social drinking

became an increasingly accepted part of middle-class lifestyles. Drinking was "in," in spite of a constitutional amendment (Prohibition) ordering it "out." And like drinking, smoking cigarettes became a symbol of chic, especially for "daring" women.

The Reinvention of Eroticism   New and sexually evocative dance crazes swept the United States and Europe. The new moves, along with fresh music and clothing styles, were important symbols: They symbolized the beginning of the end of women's passionlessness invented a century earlier. Gadlin reports that during the first three decades of the twentieth century Sigmund Freud and his disciples preached against Victorian sexual ideals. They argued that repression of sexual impulses is bad. The Victorian ideal of passionless sex was believed to be particularly unhealthy for women because of the double standard. Their husbands had options for lusty sex but they did not. As a result of women's sexual frustrations, said the Freudians, women, men, children, families, and society would suffer.

Freudians and other progressive thinkers of that time argued that the pleasures of erotic sex should be part of married women's (and married men's) self-fulfillment.[65] If they were having trouble being earthy and passionate, wives and husbands should undergo psychoanalysis to discover what was standing in the way of going with the flow of their normal and natural biological impulses. Husband impotence and wife frigidity, obstacles to total sexual fulfillment, became cocktail party chitchat. Chapter 4 noted that during the 1960s North America experienced a sexual revolution; Chapter 7 describes it more fully. But most researchers agree that its cultural foundation was laid during the 1920s' sexual *mini*-revolution.[66] The mini-upheaval consisted of a simple but potentially upsetting idea—namely, that women too had choices when it came to sexuality.

Chicago's bathing beauties disobeying a recent edict banning abbreviated bathing suits on the beach, talking to policewomen, July 10, 1922, Balboa Beach, California.

They were no longer inevitably locked into sex without eros.

More Choices and Reinventions Alongside sexuality, some women also began to question long-standing traditions about companionship and intimacy with husbands.[67] Husbands and wives had been sharing some leisure activities together at least since the turn of the century. However, spending leisure time with his wife meant a man had less time to spend with his buddies. "Why would a real man forsake male companionship for the company of women?," his buddies might ask. The answer was plain if the man was never-married. A single man had to spend time with women in

order to find a wife, and his buddies could understand and accept that fact. Indeed, dating was created during the 1920s; it legitimated the idea of companionship between *single* men and women (see Chapter 7). But why would a married man want to spend time with his wife when he could be with his buddies? One answer, of course, is that the wife wanted his companionship. She wanted it because she wanted to keep on doing the fun things they'd done while dating, and to do them with the man she'd married.

Furthermore, a wife desiring to achieve greater emotional intimacy with her husband believed that companionship was a social setting within which she might be able to get him to talk about himself. Doing things together might help him overcome his difficulties with self-disclosure. The wife hoped that companionship might lead to something more—emotional closeness. That this goal was achieved very often remains much in doubt.[68] Among the reasons closeness was so difficult to come by is the point made earlier—that intimacy requires that persons be social equals, or at least define themselves that way. Although much discussed in the 1920s' media, gender inequality remained a fact of life: Men had many more economic and political resources than women, and they had greater social status and prestige. Wives and husbands wanting to be intimates had first to struggle with and overcome those kinds of social realities. In addition, although it had become less fashionable to say out loud that men should be the heads of their households, in reality that was the case. Men continued to exercise considerably more influence and control over women than women did over men.[69]

Consequently, some feminists and psychologists became convinced that the surest way for women to get what they wanted by way of intimacy was for men to change. Thus, during the 1920s those advocates used the media to launch a direct challenge on the prevailing cultural images of the ideal man—strong and silent. Their strategy was to argue that men were suffering as much as women from men's incapacity to cultivate emotional intimacy. It was in men's own self-interest, they said, for men to get close to women. Their efforts, however, were not very successful. By and large, most men simply ignored the idea that getting close to their wives was a vital dimension of marriage.[70]

Women's Self-actualization Following the Civil War and continuing into the 1920s, divorce rates in the United States were rising noticeably. Some observers say that part of the reason for the steady increases were wives'

growing expectations about what they wanted from their husbands.[71] They began to want more than merely a good provider. As a result, women became more willing to divorce their husbands if they didn't get fulfilment in the forms of companionship and intimacy. A fresh buzzword entered the magazines and books read by 1920s' middle-class women. Gadlin reports that *"self-actualization* became a legitimate aspiration."[72] To be sure, there was strong opposition to this expression of women's individualism from what O'Neill calls conservatives. They claimed that women who divorced their husbands for such "trivial" reasons were being selfish and irresponsible—their behavior was damaging to children and society alike. Nonetheless, the 1920s was the first time that women's self-fulfillment became vigorously debated in the media and in public forums (as it is to this day).

Employment and Women's Self-actualization Significantly, some feminists also tried to steer women's self-fulfillment in another unheard-of direction. Most white women believed that being a wise consumer and an effective homemaker and mother were by far the chief sources of their fulfillment. Although some nineteenth-century feminists had talked about employment as one source of women's self-fulfillment, during the twenties what Gadlin calls "radical feminists" took a quantum leap further.[73] They asserted that being a homemaker and mother, although good, was not sufficient for women. To experience the highest levels of personal growth possible, women also required meaningful employment.

Since the turn of the century increasing numbers of white, middle-class, never-married women had in fact been entering paid labor. By contrast, black women had gotten active in paid labor much earlier, the late 1860s. Whether married or not, black women (middle and working class) had little choice but to earn money to support their families, chiefly because of severe discrimination against black men.[74] Unlike black women, most unmarried white women viewed their jobs as temporary stations on the track to marriage, after which they expected never to be employed again.[75] Popular magazines and movies conveyed the idea that employment was a place to meet men who were "good catches"—men who would be good providers for them and their children. In spite of the media hype over employment as a source of fulfillment, the vast majority of married white women believed that the degree of self-actualization they got from being a mother and homemaker far exceeded anything they could get from paid work.

Children and Child Rearing Progressives believed intensely that the scientific method would transform every sphere of life to which it was applied. They advocated, for instance, that childbirth should no longer take place in homes watched over by midwives as it had been since time began. Hence, by the end of the 1920s most citizens had redefined childbirth as something that should occur in hospital attended by a physician.[76] Similarly, progressives held that scientific principles should be applied with equal force to the rearing of children. By 1900 the ideal of "scientific mothering" based on the new disciplines of child development and child psychology had replaced the "traditional emphasis on character formation."[77] By the 1920s it was redefined still more. Parents were warned away from preoccupation with the future success of the child. They learned they had the responsibility for the "personality formation" of the child right here and now.[78] Being a healthy, happy child today was viewed as the best guarantee of the child's happiness tomorrow. Science includes prediction, and parents also learned that if they paid attention to the results of empirical research they could rest assured that their children would turn out just like they wanted them to.[79] To be sure, not all "experts" agreed

that parents had that much control over their children's destiny. What is plain, however, is that by the third decade of the twentieth century, children and child rearing had been reinvented in terms that were drastically different from those of the early 1700s. Instead of miniature adults who must have the devil beaten out of them, children were perceived as persons capable of exploring their full potential—but only if parents did it "right."

CONCLUSION—BALANCING ME-NESS WITH WE-NESS

Chapter 1 said that changes in families are linked with modernization. The urbanization and industrialization occurring during the Jacksonian era are foundational to what is meant by saying a society is "modern." If you visited Saudi Arabia you would see clear evidence for both patterns. You would see at least one large city—Riyadh, the capital—to which citizens from rural areas as well as foreign workers are migrating in large numbers. You would find evidence of industrialization—oil refineries, related industries and factories, banks, and worldwide commercial enterprises of all sorts. But we have also said that Saudi Arabia is not a modern society. Why not? Because modernization also embodies the idea of *individualism*, namely, self-fulfillment. During the Jacksonian era, North America started on the road to becoming modern because, among other things, self-actualization began to matter a great deal to ordinary citizens.

During the 1970s, Saudi Arabia's neighbor Iran was well on the road to modernity because it had a Western-educated middle class saying that self-fulfillment came via the successes of individuals—men and women. At the same time, Iran's middle class was experiencing drastic changes in public behaviors very much like those of the United States and Western Europe during the 1920s. In the 1970s, for example, it was not uncommon in the capital,

Tehran, to see the "modern" and the "traditional" strolling on the same downtown block. The modern women displayed the latest Western fashions in chic clothing and hairstyle, and was probably smoking. The traditional woman was sheathed in loosely fitting black garments that covered her from head to toe except for her eyes. But the 1979 fundamentalist Islamic Revolution jarred Iran back to its premodern ways.

Although self-fulfillment is indeed a central feature of modern societies, no one can have it all. Persons are inevitably forced to choose between many different options. Recall that during the Jacksonian era, when families left rural areas for cities in search of economic self-fulfillment they left their public lifestyle behind them. In small towns during Colonial times, persons felt they belonged not only to their kin, but also to their friends and townspeople in general. Jacksonian persons who moved to the cities could no longer belong to families, friends, and communities in quite the same ways their forebears had. That kind of wrenching experience was painful, and it remains painful for persons undergoing it today. For example, let us say that Angela's parents, kin, and friends live in Atlanta and she accepts a job offer in San Francisco. Her sister Michele, however, turns down all job offers outside the Atlanta metro area. As a result of their contrasting choices, the kinds of belonging the sisters experience with their family are likely to be quite different. Angela's choice may leave her with a sense of personal loss. Michele's choice may leave her with an equally painful sense of professional loss; having chosen to be geographically proximate to her family may cost her in terms of the degree of occupational self-actualization that might have been hers.

Remember too that the price paid by many nineteenth-century white men from their economic self-fulfillment was emotional impoverishment. They were *free men* in ways their fathers and grandfathers had never been. But their freedom made the potential for the sort of male intimacy experienced by eighteenth-century men like Hamilton and Laurens extremely remote. In addition, their economic freedom cut them off emotionally from women. Men had autonomy and self-fulfillment through achievement, but not belonging in terms of intimacy. They did, however, enjoy belonging to their buddies in a setting of shared activites.

The problem is that freedom and belonging are two essences of what it means to be fully human. Freedom to choose and to reinvent one's own destiny is a large part of being *Me*. The sense that one belongs, and matters, to significant others is a large part of being *We*. The painful dilemma is that it is extremely difficult to have both freedom and belonging at the same time. And this dilemma can be traced back to the early Jacksonian era. Remember too, we said that one of the reasons divorce rates began to climb during the Progressive Era was wives' growing concern for self-fulfillment. If wives didn't get the kinds of self-fulfillments they wanted, some were leaving their husbands. They were giving up the valued sense of belonging that comes from being married. Why go through that painful and costly experience? To try to get the freedom they wanted somewhere else. Until recently, that almost always meant another marriage.

At this point you may be feeling like many of the critics of self-actualization described in Chapter 1.[80] "What about the issue of responsibility?," they ask. "Don't people in modern societies ever do things for other people? Do they think solely about themselves? Don't they ever make sacrifices? Don't persons feel obligations to their partners or spouses? Where is the role of duty to their children? To their parents? To other kin? To friends? To the community, as well as the broader society?" These are complex questions, and the obvious response is that most persons in modern societies seek to reinvent families in a responsible manner. They strive for a perpetual balancing act between self-fulfillment and obligation—between me and we.[81] They're constantly walking a tightrope between what they *want* to do and what they *should* do. Chapter 6 has described some of the contradictions that were part of that balancing act during the recent past. And as Chapter 7 carries us to the nineties, we'll see the tensions even more clearly.

NOTES

1. Pleck and Pleck, 1980, p. 13.
2. Donald Hansen, 1992.
3. Pleck and Pleck, p. 13.
4. Edmund Morgan, 1966.
5. Gadlin, 1977, p. 36.
6. Scanzoni, 1982.
7. Gadlin, p. 37.
8. Ibid.
9. Ibid., p. 36.
10. Pleck and Pleck, p. 9.
11. Gadlin, p. 38.
12. Ibid., p. 40.
13. Bellah et al., 1985; Stacey, 1990; Stellway, 1990.
14. Allan, 1989, p. 20.
15. *Newsweek*, August 5, 1991, p. 35.
16. Edmund Morgan, 1966.
17. Butterfield, Friedlander, and Kline, 1975.
18. Gadlin, p. 39; Pleck and Pleck, p. 9.
19. Keith Thomas, 1959, p. 210.
20. Gadlin, p. 39.
21. Pleck and Pleck, p. 8.
22. Cott, 1979a.
23. Mintz and Kellogg, 1988, p. 14.
24. Ibid., p. 15.
25. Ibid., p. 16.
26. Ibid., p. 21.
27. Ibid., p. 23.
28. Ibid., p. 21.
29. Pleck and Pleck, p. 14.
30. In April 1993, the U.S. government ordered the armed services to let women fly aircraft and be stationed on surface warships during combat: See *The Gainesville, Florida, Sun*, April 28, 1993, p. A1 (from *The New York Times*). Less than a year later, the government took an additional step toward gender equity by allowing women to participate in ground combat support units (engineering, maintenance, etc.) that had formerly been considered too risky for women. See *The New York Times*, January 14, 1994, p. A10.
31. Cott, 1979b.
32. Pleck and Pleck, p. 19.
33. Gadlin, p. 45.
34. Bernard, 1981.
35. Gadlin, pp. 44–45.
36. Ibid., pp. 43–44.
37. Lasch, 1977.
38. Pleck and Pleck, p. 20.
39. William O'Neill, 1969.
40. Pleck and Pleck, p. 18.
41. Gadlin, p. 47; Cott, 1979b; Seidman, 1991b.
42. Gadlin, p. 49.
43. Ibid.
44. Cott, 1979b.
45. Gadlin, p. 49.
46. Pleck and Pleck, p. 16.
47. Gadlin, pp. 55–56.
48. Cott, 1977.
49. Pleck and Pleck, p. 20.
50. Mintz and Kellogg, p. 58.
51. Ibid., p. 59.
52. Ibid., p. 60.
53. William O'Neill, 1967.
54. Pleck and Pleck, pp. 21ff.
55. Ibid., p. 24.
56. Ibid., p. 25.
57. Nash, 1971, p. 23.
58. Pleck and Pleck, p. 25.
59. Ibid., p. 27; Seidman.
60. Pleck and Pleck, p. 22.
61. Ibid.
62. O'Neill, p. 88.
63. May, 1959.
64. Frohnmayer, 1991, p. 8.
65. Gadlin, pp. 57–59.
66. Reiss, 1990.
67. Pleck and Pleck.
68. Ibid.
69. Ibid., and see Waller, 1938.

70. Pleck and Pleck.
71. O'Neill; Mintz and Kellogg.
72. Gadlin, p. 59. Italics added.
73. Ibid., pp. 60–61.
74. Noble, 1966.
75. Nye, 1979.
76. Mintz and Kellogg, p. 120.
77. Ibid., p. 121.
78. Ibid., p. 123.
79. Ibid.
80. Lasch, 1977; Hewlett, 1991.
81. Bell, 1990.

FROM THE MODERN FAMILY TO THE INVENTION OF POSTMODERN FAMILIES— THE 1920s THROUGH THE 1960s

Chapter 6 and 7 give us historical perspectives on today's families. Chapter 6 began with the Colonial period and carried us through the Jacksonian and Progressive eras. Chapter 7 takes up the 1920s where Chapter 6 left off. The 1920s through the 1950s became the pinnacle of what's been called the Modern Family.[1] Earlier chapters called it the Benchmark Family. But during the 1960s, some people began to invent what have been called "postmodern" families.[2] Chapter 7 describes some changes in families occurring between the twenties and the sixties. It helps us better understand how people are continuing to reinvent today's families, as described in subsequent chapters.

INVENTING THE DATING GAME

For several decades before the 1920s, men had "courted" women. Courting often consisted of strolls after church and buggy rides in broad daylight.[3] Fortunate indeed was the couple who could finesse moments alone, whether in the parlor or on the front-porch swing. Ehrmann reports that that sort of "sanctioned privacy" was made available solely to mature youth who had serious intentions, namely, to get married. During their times alone, couples were allowed the privilege of what Ehrmann calls *spooning*, defined as gentle kisses and tender caresses of face, hands, and perhaps arms. Spooning was definitely not supposed to be erotic. It was not a way to stir the couple's passions. It was expected to be sweet and tender, almost platonic. Consequently, spooning reinforced the passionlessness that was supposed to characterize moral and high-minded persons both before and after marriage.

In the 1920s younger persons began to impose several fresh twists on these courting customs. One innovation was the creation of a youthful peer culture. Within this subculture, new music, dancing, and dress, as well as drinking and smoking, were endorsed and spread. Cabarets became popular places "to meet people." By contrast to the all-male clubs and lounges of an earlier era, in the cabarets women were welcomed. It was acceptable also for women to enter without a male escort, and they usually attended with one or more other

119

women. These mixed bars, along with sporting events, were favorite places to go on a "date." Schools, churches, and work sites were also places to meet people and get dates.

The 1920s and 1930s youth devised an extremely complex set of rules, or social codes, to govern their Dating Game.[4] As with any game, this game too had an ultimate objective or aim: to walk the aisle (get married). The ultimate purpose of the time invested in the company of the opposite sex—whether in schools, work, the cabarets, or actual dating—was to find a spouse. Underlying the process of sorting among prospects to unearth Mr. Right or Miss Right was a new idea that made dating very different from courting. It gradually became culturally acceptable for unchaperoned women and men to do activities together during leisure time.

The rules involved in eventually "walking the aisle" were intricate and subtle (as much so as any NFL team's game plan) when compared with the unambiguous courting norms that

Hollywood films, such as the 1940 *Philadelphia Story* with Cary Grant and Katherine Hepburn, reinforced popular myths and stereotypes about the Dating Game.

previous generations had lived under. The Game's chief commandment, however, was about as subtle as the rule that only the team with the ball can score. The commandment was, "Thou shalt not abandon thyself to lust."[5] Its axioms were: "If a girl, thou shalt not 'get in trouble'," "If a boy, thou shalt not 'get a girl in trouble.'" "In trouble" meant, of course, pregnancy, and there were several reasons why couples wanted to avoid it. The most obvious was that pregnancy was public evidence that sexual intercourse (coitus) had occurred. And the reason women in particular were not keen on revealing coitus was tied to another fundamental rule of the Game: that coitus was something respectable single women simply did not do.[6] If perchance it somehow did happen, it should happen only in exchange for a promise of marriage, usually after a public engagement and very close to the wedding day.[7]

Chapter 6 said that one reason married women were not supposed to have nonmarital coitus was the belief that they were men's property, and such coitus would reduce the value of that property. A subtle version of this notion crept into the Dating Game. Female virginity was defined as a highly valued commodity.[8] A nonvirginal woman was tarnished goods. "Why would you buy used stuff when you can buy new?," was a common rhetorical question. Men wanted the prestige of marrying a virgin. They wanted the social esteem and respect that accompanied being the first man to "deflower" their wives—the first to "use" their pure and unsullied commodity. Incidentally, that way of looking at women's virginity, although softened somewhat, is still prevalent in certain conservative religious groups. It is part of the rationale used to motivate the young women to remain virginal.[9] At the 1993 Southern Baptist Convention in Houston, hundreds of teenagers signed a pledge of sexual purity and abstinence.[10] The program is called "True Love Waits," and is aimed at providing a network of social support for the ideal of virginity until marriage. "'It's positive peer pressure,'" said one adolescent as she signed the pledge.

Women's Dilemma

The sharp dilemma facing women during the days of the Game was to supply enough sexual allure and enticement to keep men coming back for more, but not give so much that the women lost their market value. A woman could not afford to be reputed as "easy." She had to be sure she kept her reputation unsullied so she could catch the best possible man. "Best" generally meant a handsome man and what Chapter 6 called a good provider. The bases of men's market value were mostly money and companionship, and to a lesser degree handsomeness. The "marriage market" of that period was based on a social exchange of a woman's commodities (virginity, along with promise of being a good wife, mother, and companion) with a man's commodities. Since husbands were preoccupied with being good providers, wives did not expect that the husband would get involved in daily household routines, including the care and discipline of children.[11]

Underlying the Game was another cultural holdover from the nineteenth century—the assumption that men were more lusty than women.[12] This idea complicated the Game because it was believed that men dated women in order to get "It" without having to make a promise of marriage. In his classic study of dating on a college campus, Willard Waller observed that the largely middle-class male students would frequently go "slumming."[13] That meant visiting-off campus bars for the express purpose of meeting, and getting sexual satisfactions from, working- and lower-class women. Unlike the case with prostitutes, the students could have sex with these women without paying for it. They never publicly dated the women because that would tarnish

their reputations, which were based on being able to date, and be seen with, the most beautiful *eligible* (i.e., middle-class) women on campus.

Eligible Players

In any game, certain persons are declared eligible to play, others are not. To be eligible to play the Dating Game with middle-class men, women had to be seen as potential good wives. And part of women's eligibility was their family background. Not only must a middle-class man marry a virgin to achieve social respect, he must also choose a woman of his own class, or even better, a woman with higher social status than his. "Picking up" a woman of lesser status meant he could get sexual satisfactions (perhaps even coitus) without playing the Game and making any marriage promises. This behavior was winked at by others. They believed it was a means for respectable men to discharge their enormous sexual urges (sow their wild oats) without messing up their lives and careers by marrying someone of lesser status.[14] But middle-class women had to confront those allegedly uncontrollable male urges and protect their own market value. Hence, they had the responsibility of putting the brakes on men's sexual behaviors. Men, it was thought, would go all the way to coitus with every woman they dated if the women didn't stop them.

Passion without Intercourse

Although a quaint expression today, "going all the way" was fraught with meanings for pre-1960s' daters. The commandment not to abandon oneself to lust was peculiarly a woman's commandment. Abandoning to lust meant losing control of oneself and succumbing to coitus. Once aroused, a man might not be able to curb his animal passions. Hence, it was the less lusty woman's obligation to keep his passions in check. That goal was by no means a simple task given the intricate character of pre-sixties sexual behaviors.

The behaviors that had replaced spooning were known as *petting* (stroking anatomy below the waist—thighs, genitals, buttocks) and its variant, *necking* (stroking anatomy above the waist, specifically, the woman's breasts). Petting and necking are what most daters did most of the time until the 1960s. In today's sex manuals, petting and necking are captured by labels such as *foreplay*—behaviors inherently linked with coitus aimed at enhancing its pleasures. But when daters played the Game, those behaviors were rarely defined as a prelude to coitus; they were erotic satisfactions defined to be an end in and of themselves. Unlike spooning, men's and women's passions were supposed to be aroused, but never consummated in coitus. This paradox of "passion without coitus" was managed by another rule of the Game—the invisible, yet ever-shifting, *Line*.[15] Most men worked at pushing the Line as far as they could toward intercourse. Women struggled to hold the Line back as much as possible.

Struggle over the Line, though carried out in private by daters, was nonetheless publicly influenced. Ehrmann reports that women and men belonged to groups or cliques of friends. Those friends supplied informal norms to its members regarding how they should manage their struggles over the Line. Moreover, the friends monitored how well the members complied with those norms. For example, a woman might be warned by her friends, "Don't kiss until the third date." Anna's friends realize, as does she, that this is only her first date with Herbert. She's keenly aware she must stoutly resist all of Herbert's efforts to kiss her because her friends will quiz her about her date and she doesn't want to lie. The kissing maxim does three things for Anna. First, it tells her what she musn't do ("Don't kiss until . . ."). Second, it tells her what she should do

("Do kiss on . . ."). Third, it provides a justification for her behaviors ("I'm sorry I can't, Herbert, because this is only our first/second date"). The maxim also justifies turning Herbert down for a third date although he's taken her out twice. The reason? He's not a kissable candidate. But what should Anna allow on the first two dates? Should she let Herbert hold her hand? Put his arms around her? Anna knows that Herbert will try those behaviors for two reasons. One, they are the first steps toward arousing more passionate feelings. Two, he will be able to report these modest successes to his buddies. But Anna also knows that she must report what went on to her friends.

If Anna does consent to go out a third time with Herbert, she is obliged to let him kiss her. To do otherwise is to break the Game's rules. In Waller's terms, she would be perceived by her and his friends as exploiting him, since he is paying money for the dates but she is not paying him with kisses. As her exploitative behavior becomes public, she is likely to be stigmatized as a tease.[16] Anna's friends would then probably pressure her to stop dating him, and his mates would tell him to forget her.

Following the third date, the sexual norms of the Dating Game got more muddy. Anna's and Herbert's friends will keep on monitoring the pair's sexual behaviors, but with differing objectives. Anna's friends hope she is able to manage the couple's sexual behaviors so that eventually Anna will get publicly engaged and then married. Herbert's buddies, on the other hand, hope that he is able to "get as much as he can" without having to give up his buddies and his carefree bachelorhood.

Measuring the Line

During the era under discussion, researchers became quite interested in studying this Line of permissible sexual behaviors.[17] Over time the Line appeared to be continually shifting in both directions. For any given couple the woman might at one point allow greater permissiveness, but later she might reduce the degree of permissiveness. To try to measure that fluid Line, researchers asked respondents about their sexual attitudes and behaviors. For example, respondents were asked about their attitudes toward hand holding and allowing the boy to put his arm around the girl's shoulder: "Are those behaviors acceptable or not? If 'yes,' under what conditions? First, second, or third, or later dates?" Respondents were also asked whether they actually did those two things. If yes, on which date did they start? The same logic regarding attitudes and behaviors was followed while trying to measure aspects of necking/petting. For example, respondents were asked about kissing—"ordinary" and/or "French." Did they believe in such things? Did they do them? If so, when did they start? When did they stop?

Next, they were asked about necking and petting. How much clothing should the woman and man retain, or actually did retain, while groping was taking place? How much touching should or did occur through the protection of blouses, shirts, skirts, and pants? Should they merely keep on their underwear? Did they actually keep it on? Was wearing nothing ever acceptable? If it was, at what point in their relationship? Was it ever acceptable to pet to orgasm? When, if ever, did they do it? Respondents were also asked about oral and/or anal sex. Persons who experienced either of those behaviors but reported no vaginal penetration were labeled *technical virgins*.[18] Since the woman's hymen presumably remained undisturbed, her market value continued intact. Furthermore, technical virgins believed they needn't fear pregnancy, and thus did not need to worry about contraceptives. Nor did they think they were susceptible to the two most frightening venereal, or socially transmitted, diseases (STDs), of their day, syphilis and gonorrhea.

Sexual Bargaining

In any situation lacking clear and explicit rules, persons tend to make up norms as they go along. When two or more persons are involved, the process of figuring out what to do is often called *negotiation*.[19] Since the Dating Game supplied few guidelines regarding what to do or not do after the first few dates, the issue of where to draw the Line between hand holding, kissing, necking, petting, technical virginity, and coitus became a matter of what Waller called *bargaining*. The negotiations were largely implicit, that is, nonverbal and tacit.

However, simply because they were not being verbal does not mean the woman and man were not striking deals. Through implicit negotiation the pair was constructing the moves of the Game. For instance, in a movie theater the man might first put his arm around the woman's shoulders. If she accepted this, and if it was the third or later date, he might *without asking her* gradually lower his hand onto her blouse over her breast and thus feel her breast. If she pushed his hand away and by her looks and other body language indicated displeasure, he knew he'd gone too far. But if she allowed his hand to remain on her blouse, he would be encouraged to go further, either on this or a subsequent date. These behavioral arrangements regarding where to draw the Line were worked out silently. There was no rule book to consult. Nevertheless, the silent arrangements were no less significant for the pair or for the friends that monitored them than if negotiations had been verbal. The closest thing to dating education came via experienced peers. Men who had dated a great deal would pass tips on to other men on how to increase their successes. Experienced women would coach other women on how to manage situations so as to protect their reputations and still be popular.

Absence of a rule book in no way meant the woman lacked rationale for deciding where to draw, and then redraw, the Line. Remember that the ultimate goal of this Game was marriage. Whereas women acknowledged this goal, men protested it claiming they didn't want to get tied down, or trapped. They said they didn't wish to relinquish the fun they were having "dating around." Men also alleged they didn't want to give up their bachelor buddies for marriage. But Swidler observes that at some point it was expected that a man would settle down—he had to quit sowing wild oats and find a Good Wife.[20] Otherwise the esteem and social respectability attached to being a good provider and "family man" would be denied him. His buddies could understand because they all faced the same thing. Hence, the seemingly private negotiations between daters and courters regarding drawing and redrawing the Line were governed by public considerations. If the man failed to show that their dating relationship was headed toward the public events of going steady, engagement, and finally marriage, the woman was not very likely to keep on redrawing the Line in his favor.

During their nonverbal communication and negotiation, she would monitor the level of sexual liberties permitted with these public goals in mind. If she didn't want him to cross a certain point, she would make it clear (nonverbally) what that point was and *why*—his lack of commitment to her public agenda. Remember that her friends and his buddies were (along with both sets of parents) part of the public context of their dating. Her friends and parents were reinforcing the maxim that she shouldn't be giving too much away without some sort of commitment on his part. To get him to go steady or get engaged did not necessarily require talking to him about it. She could move the Line ahead and at the same time nonverbally communicate the idea that if he didn't want the Line moved back, or if he wanted it moved ahead still further, he had to provide her a public commitment of some sort. Hence,

shortly after Anna moved the Line ahead, Herbert might slip his class ring on Anna's finger without saying a word. Her eyes and facial expression reveal her pleasure; she responds by providing him additional "appropriate" pleasures (redrawing the Line in his favor).

Rings were one of the social markers suggesting how close the couple might be to marriage. These markers had labels such as "going steady," "engaged to be engaged," "engagement," and so on.[21] Part of becoming public was to announce the establishment of exclusivity: "This is my boyfriend/girlfriend, and he/she is no longer on the dating market." A powerful social boundary line was thus drawn around the pair. Rituals, such as the exchanges of photos, class rings, pendants, and lockets, and wearing of his sweater or jacket, often accompanied the social markers. Upon engagement, besides giving of the ring, celebrations and parties often took place as well.

However, the implicit negotiation style sometimes failed. Ehrmann, building on Waller's research, talks about the "frustrated and often·irate male, and the girl walking home in disgust as her defense against [his] unwanted advances."[22] Even darker is the image of what Chapter 12 calls "date rape" or "acquaintance rape." Only in recent years has that issue become a subject of empirical investigation and public discussion. We have no way of knowing how frequently men of that earlier era forced women they were dating to cross a Line they did not wish to cross. Aside from Waller, few researchers of the period supplied any clue that some men might indeed be forcing unwanted sexual advances on the women they dated.

The Place of Love

Burchinal reports that feelings of love, and of being in love, were inherent to the Dating Game. When persons told researchers how much necking and petting were permissible, they connected it to degrees of affection and love. Reiss even used the phrase, "permissiveness with affection" to capture the drawing and redrawing of the sexual Line.[23] Persons who were going steady reported they had feelings of liking and deep affection for their partner. Those feelings, alongside the fact they were going steady, justified the degree of necking and/or petting allowed by the woman. Additionally, the more in love persons got with one another, the more progressively permissive she got in redrawing the Line. Hence, the three elements of deeper love, greater sexual permissiveness, and steady progression along the public path of going steady, being engaged to be engaged, engagement, and actual marriage, tended to be correlated.

Feelings of affection and love helped to justify breaking the cultural rule that sexual passion, and especially coitus, should be reserved for marriage. Although (as Chapter 4 said) everyone formally agreed that the right thing was to wait till marriage, adults winked at the necking, petting, and coital behaviors of youth because after all, "Anna and Herbert love each other." Reiss and others compared the newly emerging standard—permissiveness with affection—with the ancient double standard described in Chapter 6. Under the latter, men's promiscuity was quietly winked at and thought to be inevitable. Under the newer standard, men's *and women's* premarital sexual activity, in a context of love and affection (particularly engagement), was believed to be equally inevitable and thus was also winked at.

These two standards differed drastically in several respects. For instance, public announcements of going steady, being engaged, and so on were understood to mean that the couple's relationship was monogamous and exclusive. Public declarations of exclusivity, along with feelings of love, reinforced the idea that the emerging sexual revolution was decidedly *not* a license for promiscuity.[24] Younger

persons were not creating situations in which everyone was doing It with everyone else. Love meant that a person cared for someone else in a special way. As a result, necking or petting (or eventually having coitus with one's fiance) became justified. Nevertheless, Waller and other researchers pointed out that the rule of exclusivity was more binding on women than on men, especially if the pair were not yet engaged. Appealing terms such as "rake," "ladies man," "gay bachelor" were applied to single men able to obtain sexual favors from several women at a time.[25] Those clever men often earned the admiration of other men: "How does he do it?" was the common rhetorical question. But women seeking to behave in similar fashion were labeled by both genders with the much less appealing term "slut." According to Rubin, even the sexual revolution of the sixties did not completely do away with the less flattering labels attached to nonsexually exclusive women.

Dating Concluded and Virginity Relinquished

Upon becoming engaged, the couple defined itself, and was perceived by families and friends, as having concluded the dating phase. The label "courtship" was redefined to mean the period when couples were engaged to be engaged, as well as the engagement itself.[26] After engagement and as part of courtship, petting got very heavy, with the likelihood increasing of the partners becoming technical virgins. As the Big (wedding) Day loomed into view, the woman might even be willing (perhaps reluctantly) to relinquish her virginity. Having preserved her market value this long, there seemed little doubt she was finally going to cash in. Pregnancy was an important consideration to women of that era because of the difficulties in obtaining (often illegal and ineffective) contraceptives. Even though they were soon to be married, it was still considered morally wrong to have intercourse. Thus the couple didn't want to advertise it by letting other people know they were trying to get contraceptives.

Hence, if the woman were going to allow coitus, she had to try to manage it close enough to the wedding day so that if she did get pregnant she wouldn't show too much through her dress. Research carried out from the 1920s to the 1960s revealed gradual but steady increases in the percentages of women experiencing premarital intercourse.[27] The upward trend in the likelihood of women's premarital coital activity was unmistakable. Nevertheless, the studies showed that the vast majority of the women were engaged to the men they were having intercourse with.[28]

The Kinsey Reports

Chapter 4 referred briefly to Alfred C. Kinsey and his pioneering studies of the sexual behaviors of U.S. women and men.[29] Kinsey and his colleagues collected their data in the late 1930s and the 1940s—during the era of the Dating Game. They published their findings in two massive books that created media sensations.[30] Even today some religiously conservative advocates continue to label Kinsey a charlatan.[31] Among the most startling of Kinsey's findings was that among women born between 1900 and 1910, nearly 50 percent had had sexual intercourse before marriage. By comparison, only 25 percent of women born before 1900 experienced premarital intercourse. In short, one brief decade witnessed a doubling of the incidence of women's premarital sex. Women born after 1900 who came of age during the roaring twenties were much more likely to have experienced premarital intercourse than women who'd matured earlier.

Nor is it surprising that 1920s women were making those kinds of choices. The social climate of the twenties described in Chapter 6— daring clothing styles, sensuous music, movies, drinking, unchaperoned cars, and so

on—enhanced and facilitated the nonconforming, or "deviant," sexual behaviors of single women and men. At the same time, in view of the double standard and widespread prostitution, it should have come as no surprise that their year of birth made no difference at all in men's premarital sexual activity. Kinsey and his associates found that 98 percent of men with a grade-school education had premarital intercourse. Among men with a high-school education the figure was 85 percent; for men with some college it dropped to 68 percent.

The Great Depression and Sex during Engagement

According to John Modell, the Great Depression was one of the major societal reasons rates of premarital intercourse took a sharp blip upward during the 1930s. The thirties marked a unique interval in North American life, and indeed, life in the entire Western world. For one thing, white men couldn't find jobs. Black men and women, who'd always faced job scarcity, found the Depression even more devastating than whites. For example, although the white unemployment rate rose to 25 percent at the Depression's peak, the black unemployment rate was 50 percent.[32] To make the pain worse, the crushing realization of severe economic deprivation followed on the heels of the roaring twenties, a decade of unprecedented prosperity. Essential to the Dating Game was men's generous spending on women.[33] Suddenly, men no longer had much, if any, money. Expectations about dating had to be scaled down.

But what about men who were courting— men who were engaged and planned soon to be married? How could they be good providers if they couldn't find a job? Modell says that during the 1920s, young persons had established the norm of a relatively brief engagement period—perhaps six months to a year. The major reason given by opinion-makers, along with the popular and religious media, was that waiting any longer would make the sexual tensions of engagement too difficult to bear. Hence, to avoid crossing the taboo Line of sexual intercourse, couples who believed that this person would be their spouse for life should marry as soon as possible. However, the dilemma they now faced was that the man must have a job, or at least reasonable prospects, to marry, and during the 1930s the vast majority of men had neither job nor prospects. At best they might sometimes depend on *relief* (social welfare), or on temporary public construction projects. The result was that since men couldn't provide, many couples weren't able to marry when they wanted to.[34] Engagement periods became longer than they'd been in the 1920s, and much longer than most couples desired.

The result, claims Modell, was a fundamental change in the character of engaged couples' implicit negotiating over intercourse.[35] Even though it was still culturally prohibited, women became more willing than ever before to indulge their fiances. The longer the engagement dragged on, and the heavier petting became, the more difficult it was for her to keep on communicating (nonverbally or verbally), "let's save it for marriage." It follows that during the 1930s, rates of premarital intercourse became higher than they had been in the 1920s. Even after the Great Depression ended and brief engagements resumed because of World War II pressures and postwar prosperity, engaged couples did not return to premarital chastity. Youth increasingly came to define engagement as a time when coitus was a live option, even though in terms of broader cultural norms it remained prohibited.[36] And, as Carol Darling and colleagues report, rates of premarital intercourse continued to climb steadily throughout the 1940s and 1950s.

AFTER THE GAME—THE MODERN FAMILY

To play the Dating Game well demanded that players learn and hone the intricate skills of nonverbal communication. Everything about the Game muted the idea that the couple should self-disclose or in other ways make themselves vulnerable to one another. Cultural ideals lauded the coquettish woman and the strong, silent man.[37] Women and men had spent years learning how to deal with each other in a tacit, coy, demure, and subtle fashion. Not only had they never needed to learn how to negotiate explicitly, the rules of the Game decreed this to be crass and uncouth. After the wedding, then, the couple was thrust into a situation totally different from any they'd previously encountered. The only skills they carried with them were the ones that had worked before. Would they work now? In one sense, it didn't matter, because married couples played roles strictly governed by cultural scripts.[38] A good wife knew precisely what she must do both in and out of the household; and a good provider knew exactly what he must do. If differences of opinion arose between them, the same norms applied that we first encountered in the Colonial era: To keep peace and harmony in The Family, and for the good of children and society, the women must defer to the man.

Managing Men

Nevertheless, in spite of wives' surface deference, the media of the day (movies, radio programs, cartoons, comics), as well as social critics writing in newspapers and magazines, gradually became aware that wives were putting the subtle skills learned during the Dating Game to their own purposes.[39] Middle-class wives were doing something their mothers and grandmothers had not done (at least to the same degree). Having made their way through the minefields of the Game, they had become highly effective in covertly "managing" men. This tacit management had previously involved keeping a man's passions in line with their own agenda and nudging him gently along the road toward marriage. Now

A typical 1941 strip showing Dagwood the oaf and Blondie the bemused and superior onlooker.

the woman's agenda shifted to focus on household matters including finances, the care and nurture of the children, and leisure companionship. Many wives simply applied their premarital skills to quietly orchestrating these household matters. The result was that wives got a great deal of what they wanted without overt conflict and explicit negotiation.[40] As one wife from that era was overheard to say, "Frank wants to go to the mountains for our vacation, and he thinks the family's going with him. But we're actually going to the seashore, although he doesn't know it yet."

Some alarmed critics called this the *Blondie and Dagwood* pattern.[41] In that comic strip and on certain radio comedies, the husband was portrayed formally as the unquestioned family head, with the cultural right to make all final decisions. Because the wife and children were seldom able to negotiate with him explicitly, they formed coalitions and finessed situations to get what they wanted by making him believe he was actually the final decision-maker. Needless to say, men in those situations appeared as hapless dupes. They were Dagwoods, bumbling about striving vainly to stave off the wiles of the much cleverer Blondies. During the early years of TV, this same comedic theme was repeated, most notably in the *I Love Lucy* show. In this show a twist was added by explaining that part of Desi's ineptness was his foreign (Cuban) heritage. Interestingly enough, when the innova-

tive comedy, *All in the Family*, appeared in the early 1970s, Edith and the adult children seldom tried to finesse Archie in the Blondie or Lucy manner. Instead, open conflict, struggle, and hostility were routinely displayed, and there were times when Edith overtly forced Archie to back away from his stated goals.

Sexuality and Contraception for Married Couples

Steven Mintz and Susan Kellogg report that during the 1920s and 1930s some physicians and counselors were encouraging married couples to break out of the cocoon of women's passionlessness.[42] (See also Chapter 6.) A major problem, however, was that women were virtually ignorant about sex. Although men's experiences with prostitutes had taught them something about women's sexual responses, including orgasms, it was emotionally difficult for men to transfer that knowledge to intercourse with their fiances and wives. Men of that era had to struggle to believe their wives could conjure up the same carnal and lusty behaviors as prostitutes. Even though the first modern manuals had appeared as early as 1909 admonishing husbands to awaken their wives to the pleasure of sex, it woud not be until the 1950s that large numbers of North American wives began to demand sexual enjoyment as their right.[43]

A second problem that married couples

faced in experiencing sexual fulfillment was contraception, and it had two heads. First, the contraceptive technology of the period was, by today's standards, exceedingly primitive. Existing condoms, pessaries, and diaphragms often failed, as did withdrawal, which meant that wives frequently got pregnant when they didn't want to. Recall that in the nineteenth century, nonorgasmic sex as well as avoidance of sex were means women had to gain some control over their lives and childbearing. The rediscovery of orgasmic and relatively frequent sex in the context of primitive contraceptives meant they were at risk of losing that control. Next, a series of stringent federal and state laws made it very difficult indeed for ordinary citizens to get those contraceptives. In terms of the prevailing cultural norms, it was definitely *not* okay for married persons (and certainly not for anyone else) to use contraceptives. They were condemned as sinful by virtually all Protestant church bodies, as well as the Roman Catholic Church. President Theodore Roosevelt warned that contraceptive use would lead to "race suicide"; some opinion-makers called condoms "rubber articles for immoral use."

But the issue of contraception is a dramatic and striking example of people ignoring both the law and powerful cultural norms. Over time people created a new set of norms and justified them in two ways. First, they said contraception was socially responsible because it kept them from having more children than they could afford. Second, they said it enhanced their sexual pleasure because they didn't have to fret about pregnancies. In the years immediately preceding the 1920s, Margaret Sanger, the founder of the modern birth control movement, spent time in jail and suffered much public scorn for establishing birth control clinics and freely distributing contraceptives. During the 1920s, the U.S. government prohibited imports of the particularly effective Mensinga diaphragm from Germany.

In response, Sanger smuggled large numbers of the devices into the country via Canada. Because Sanger was influencing married couples' behaviors, another type of gap between beliefs and behaviors came into being. Uninhibited, or carnal, sex requires freedom from as many fears as possible. To reduce the fear of unwanted pregnancy meant using effective contraceptives even though prevailing cultural norms proscribed them. But several more decades had to pass before cultural norms approving and endorsing married-couple contraception finally caught up with behaviors. Still today there is no equivalent cultural approval for the contraceptive behaviors of singles, adolescents in particular.

Gender (In)Equality

Companionship Chapter 6 said that during the Jacksonian period, married couples were declared to be equals, even though economically and politically women remained as subordinate to men as they'd ever been. Between the 1920s and 1960s the idea that wives and husbands were equals was revived with fresh vigor. In large part that happened because of the increasing centrality of husband-wife companionship during leisure time. Since they'd spent so much time together during dating, it seemed natural they'd continue those "fun" activities during marriage. Those activities, besides being fun, were also supposed to be settings in which friendship could be nurtured. In other words, a "companionate marriage" of that era was marked not only by shared leisure activities but also by friendship. But what kind of friendship? While playing the Game, women and men had never learned to be what Chapter 5 called *inti*mates, but neither had they learned to be buddies. Instead they'd become what Robert Klemer called "sex-appropriate" friends.[44] The woman was supposed to be a woman-friend to the man; she was not expected to behave like a man-friend, a buddy.

What was a woman-friend? Essentially, it was an updated version of the home-as-haven-from-work idea of the Jacksonian era. The man was portrayed as struggling to be a good provider in a cruel and heartless world. He comes home exhausted to his wife and expects her to be his *friend*. Meaning what? That she will place the "meeting of his basic emotional needs for recognition, response, security, and new experience" *above meeting her own needs*.[45] She will listen to him vent the frustrations he's encountered during his daily struggle to provide, and make him feel good about himself no matter how much his daily work experiences might shake his self-esteem.

The "Emotional Hub"   A good wife became what sociologists of that era called the *expressive,* or *socioemotional,* or *nurturant,* hub of her family.[46] She was the pivotal one that her husband (and children) turned to for emotional massaging, comfort, and security. She was obliged to be as successful in her role as expressive hub as her husband was in his role as provider, or instrumental hub. Those two highly specialized roles lay at the core of the Modern Family, or what Chapter 1 called the Benchmark Family. If both spouses were successful in their respective roles, The Family would be happy and stable. It was in this sense that the spouses were said to be equal. Each spouse was equally responsible for family well-being and stability. For The Family to be a viable unit, each spouse was said to be equally necessary. Neither could go it alone.

Consequently, couples of that era were taking a half-step toward emotional intimacy. The media (magazines, self-help books, newspaper columns) informed couples that a crucial dimension of the modern companionate family was *verbal* communication.[47] Specifically, women had prime responsibility to be "good listeners." The man who'd been strong and silent before marriage suddenly had to be encouraged to talk about the difficulties of his life in the world of work. If she could get him to talk about *his* problems, she might be able to get him to listen to the problems she was having with the household and children. The result of their communication would be resolution of conflicts arising over household matters.[48] Even if she couldn't get him to listen to her, she could not give up listening to him. No matter what, she must function as the expressive hub of The Family for the family to be happy and stable.

The Economic and Political Realm   A big problem with making the wife chief nurturing agent and then calling her the husband's equal was that it failed to redress her social inequalities in the economic and political realms. Howard Gadlin says he can't believe that "satisfying, passionate, and loving relations . . . are possible between people who are not free to be equals."[49] Women of that era did not have the same access to economic and political participation that men had. Although the percentage of white employed wives (living with husbands) had increased from around 5 percent in 1895 to around 30 percent by 1960, employment held vastly different gender meanings. For men, employment was both a duty and a right. For married women, it was a *prohibition*.[50] Paid work was something they weren't supposed to do except under unusual circumstances (e.g., the husband was not able to provide enough money for the children's needs). Married women's employment is yet another example of a gap between beliefs and behaviors—people creating new behavior patterns long before they're accepted as normative. The point to keep in mind is that even though some white wives of that era were employed some of the time during their marriage, such employment did not enable them to be "free to be equals."

Anna and Herbert's Modern Marriage
Anna and Herbert, for example, boasted they had a modern or companionate marriage. The 1991 film, *Mr. Bridge and Mrs. Bridge* (with Paul

Newman and JoAnne Woodward), will give you a feel for the ideal 1930s and 1940s marriage, a marriage like that of Anna and Herbert. Anna had overcome their premarital game playing by learning to be a good listener. Herbert felt he could talk to Anna about his work problems. Although he spent time with his buddies, he didn't open up to them as freely as he did to Anna. Anna had been responsible for achieving success in dating, namely, to get married. She was now responsible for achieving the success of the marriage, namely, to stay married. A modern marriage was *successful* if it turned out to be *stable*. And its success rested on husbands being good providers and wives being able to please their husbands.[51] Since Anna and Herbert each scored high on what they were expected to do within the family, they felt they had a successful marriage and that they contributed equally to its success. This was so even though Anna was not judged to be Herbert's equal in the social, economic, and political spheres.

What about the idea that emotional intimacy is most intense when persons are genuine equals? It probably would never have occurred to either Anna or Herbert to worry about whether they were equals in the larger society. If pressed on the question by a researcher, they would admit they operated in totally different spheres. They would also acknowledge that Herbert's economic and political activities commanded greater status, prestige, power, and money than Anna's domestic activities. But "So what?," they might ask, and, "Who cares?" Today, many process-oriented advocates (see Figure 1-1) would say that their quest for intimacy was hindered by the objective social restraints placed on Anna. However, our image of Anna and Herbert is inevitably colored by our 1990s' vantage point. Many of today's women (and educated men) hold far stronger expectations for intimacy than did women of Anna's day.[52]

Husbands of Anna's era felt little responsibility to cultivate intimacy. Wives rarely ex-

pected husbands to be able to draw them out in the same ways wives drew out husbands. Nor did husbands believe in working very hard at intimacy; they had enough difficulty being good providers. Studies from Anna's era suggest that women had considerable difficulty getting their husbands to open up about ther own lives, much less listen to the wife's problems.[53] Although working-class wives had more difficulty than middle-class wives, in neither category did shared intimacy appear to be a major dimension of interaction between women and men. The primary source of women's emotional satisfactions continued to be other women, as they had been since the Colonial era.

Difficulties in achieving intimacy were not due solely to men's emotional incapacities. The fact that women and men lived in two contrasting social worlds and that the man's world was more prestigious reinforced the long-standing cultural definition of women and men as basically distinct creatures.[54] Even though Anna was a good listener, she'd never been where Herbert was—her capability to empathize with the stresses and strains of trying to be a good provider was necessarily limited.[55] Herbert, like most men, hadn't the slightest idea of what it felt like to maintain children and household day after endless day, and he could not genuinely empathize with his wife's situation.

Another question colored by our vantage point in time is why wives stayed in marriages if they weren't sharing much intimacy with their husbands. Part of the answer is that since women of that day didn't expect much intimacy, they weren't disappointed. A second and major part of the answer lies with their objective economic inequality: Most wives could not support themselves and their children in the ways their husbands could. Compared with men, women had few choices. A white man of that era could usually earn enough money to support himself and others. A woman usually could not. Thus, even if wives were disappointed with intimacy, or with companionship, sex, or even the dollars the husband supplied, the alternatives of separation and/or divorce loomed as considerably more threatening than what they currently had. In describing marriages of that era, one sociologist concluded that most couples lived in a state of "quiet desperation."[56] A study by John Cuber and Peggy Harroff from that same era concluded that although a minority of marriages could be described as either "vital" or "total," the majority seemed to be "conflict-habituated," "devitalized," or "passive-congenial."[57]

World War II and Modern Marriage

During the years (1941–1945) the United States was in World War II, large numbers of women were recruited to work in aircraft plants, shipyards, vehicle plants (tanks, armored vehicles, trucks), munitions factories, and the businesses and offices that supported those industries. Rosie the Riveter became a popular symbol of women happily doing unfeminine dirty work to help the war effort. While replacing the boys defending liberty overseas, the women earned higher wages than most women had ever gotten. Infant and child-care facilities were placed directly on the work site so that mothers had no excuse not to pitch in.[58] As the boys came back from the war, however, the women were ordered to exit those good jobs. Now their patriotic duty was to go home and be good wives and mothers to their returning good providers.

Hence, although it might have seemed that the war had opened a window of opportunity for woman, in fact it merely solidified relationships between the genders.[59] Many of the fathers of men serving in World War II had been unable to be good providers because of the Depression. But men who'd been in the war had access to the G.I. Bill of Rights, which gave them generously subsidized college educa-

tions and home mortgages. They were thus strongly encouraged to believe they could be good providers, which made them eager to get married. And they did! The 1950 census revealed that veterans aged 25 to 29 years were much more likely to be married than were men of that same age category in 1940.[60] Furthermore, among men of all ages in 1950, veterans were much more likely to be married than were nonveterans.

Soldiers and the Double Standard   Although the popularity of modern marriage was soaring, the double-standard remained largely intact. During 1945, the U.S. Army surveyed soldiers overseas and asked them how often, if at all, they'd had heterosexual intercourse during the last three months. The men were also asked if they were married. If not married, were they engaged? The general conclusion of those Army studies was that for the majority of soldiers, being married or engaged in no way prevented them from having sexual intercourse with other women.[61] Furthermore, that conclusion held more strongly for black men than for white men.

Postwar Family Togetherness

Intriguingly, once the veterans were home and married, one of the casualties of the modern marriage was the gradual erosion of some of the extensive buddy patterns that men had experienced for many decades. Especially in the middle class, leisure-time activities became increasingly *couple* centered.[62] Many middle-class men were involved in careers demanding travel as well as evening and weekend work. The spread of suburbs required greater commuting time. As part of the broader cultural image of husband-wife equality, it became normative that whatever nonwork time was left over belonged to The Family. The exception to that rule was the golf/tennis game with the boss or other colleagues who might help the

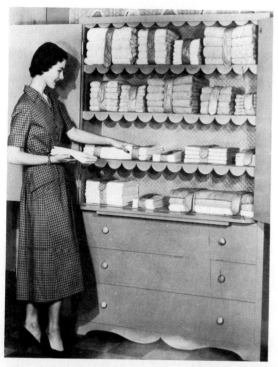

Wives of the fifties devoted themselves entirely to the challenges of housekeeping and mothering.

man get ahead. In the working and lower classes, men's work demands were generally restricted to the forty-hour week. Since they had more time than middle-class men to hang out with buddies at the local tavern or bowling alley, they were more likely to maintain the mateship culture of their fathers and grandfathers.[63] Nevertheless, among both working and middle classes the idea of leisure *togetherness* became increasingly popular: "The family that plays (and/or prays) together stays together," said the media.

1950s' Adolescents and the Dating Game

Before World War II, researchers focused most of their attention on post-high-school youth because it was they who were creating the new norms and behaviors known as dating. But during the 1950s adolescents began to construct their own unique subcultures.[64] Parents, teachers, and religious leaders placed great pressures on high-school students of that era, especially boys, to graduate from high school and then attend vocational school or college. The examples being set by unprecedented numbers of working-class and lower-middle-class veterans attending college and becoming economically successful became widely endorsed cultural role models. The Horatio Alger myths of the Jacksonian era were updated to emphasize that education was the way to success for every male, white or black. But at the same time that high-school graduation and college became increasingly important for boys, the notion of sexual permissiveness with affection was becoming ever more widespread and accepted by adolescents. Parents and opinion-makers were becoming alarmed that growing numbers of teens were behaving sexually (necking and heavy petting), and doing so at younger ages than before.

Adults believed that adolescents were emotionally immature. Hence, with heavy petting, girls would be unable to keep boys from crossing the Line to coitus. And if girls got in trouble, boys would have to marry them, thus ruining their chances for completing high school and attending college. Going steady became a particularly severe bone of contention between parents and adolescents.[65] Parents worried that spending a great deal of time alone with one person would increase the likelihood of intense levels of sexual experimentation, leading eventually to intercourse and pregnancy. Conversely, adolescents felt that going steady supplied more security than dating around. Going steady meant that one could be sure of having someone to go with to the next dance, or game, or party. Moreover, going steady with a popular person meant sharing some of her or his popularity vicariously. Indeed, being able to go steady became a badge of prestige. And the greatest prestige accrued to persons who were able to change steadies frequently, especially if each new steady was more popular than the one before.[66] If that side of the coin seemed too crass, adolescents reported that another important reason for going steady was that it provided a setting in which they could become friends—they could perhaps get to know each other unhindered by the constraints of dating around.

Teenage Marriages   Being friends was something married persons were supposed to be. Thus it should come as no surprise that researchers discovered that frequency of adolescent dating, and especially frequency of going steady, predicted the likelihood of an early marriage. More than ever before, growing numbers of couples still in their teens were getting married.[67] Going steady with a number of different partners provided a steady diet of sexual gratifications, though not necessarily intercourse. More likely were the behaviors described earlier in this chapter, including the technical virginity option. Going steady also supplied a taste of the satisfactions that come with having a man-friend and a woman-friend. The male could vent to the female, and she could hone her skills at emotional massaging. Consequently, the sharp distinctions between engagement and merely going steady that had prevailed before the war became fuzzier. Adolescents were practicing marital roles in ways that earlier high-school youth had not. And since marriage commanded much greater popularity and prestige than singleness, "Why not get married?" Adolescents who were highly popular in high school kept on being popular by remaining single as short a time as possible.

Adults were deeply pessimistic about teenage marriages because they were very likely to end in divorce.[68] Nevertheless, adults found it difficult to argue against such marriages. After all, adolescents were being totally conventional by seeking the same type of modern marriage their parents had. The fifties were years of unprecedented prosperity, and jobs were plentiful. Fresh out of high school, the 18-year-old youth could reasonably assure his and his wife-to-be's parents that "I will work hard and be a good provider for my family."

Children and Child Rearing

Mintz and Kellogg describe the 1950s as the *Golden Age* of the Modern Family. Between the 1920s' era of "scientific child rearing" and the golden fifties, children had been exposed to the Great Depression and World War II. The Depression made life difficult for children because the vast majority of families were poor, near-poor, or in danger of becoming poor. During the war, adults worried about children because so many fathers were away in the military and so many mothers were laboring in factories and businesses. As things began "settling down" during the Golden Age of the 1950s, child-rearing philosophies moved in a fresh direction—"relaxed methods of child discipline."[69] The most popular advocate of "taking it easy" with children was Dr. Benjamin Spock, who sold millions of his paperback guides to child rearing. Instead of urging anxious patients to seek expert scientific advice, Spock soothed them by saying, "You know more than you think you do." Spock encouraged parents to pick up their babies and enjoy them.[70] Although his critics said otherwise, Spock believed in firm child discipline. However, discipline should be balanced, he argued, by parental love, especially the mother's love. The mother who devoted her life to meeting "her children's needs for love, attention, and maternal care . . . in turn would find fulfillment."[71]

Mintz and Kellogg report that in spite of Spock's comforting words, many 1950s' parents, especially mothers, were extremely anxious and uneasy about the "right" way to rear children. The chief reason for this unease was that mothers—who were with their children all day long—were told that their children's destinies were completely in their hands. If they were "good" mothers, their children would turn out to be good citizens. If they "failed" as mothers, their children would falter as well. Perhaps as never before, children were viewed as passive creatures, clay that could be molded at the parent's will. Discounting the child's inputs into the shaping of her or his own destiny placed enormous burdens and responsibilities on the shoulders of parents, especially mothers. This view of children has remained unchallenged until recently. But Chapter 16 shows that some of today's researchers are asking fresh questions. They want to know about children's own choices regarding their destinies. Today's question is, how much do children actually participate with adults in shaping and controlling the course of their own lives? To what extent do children, like adults, invent their lives?

INVENTING POSTMODERN FAMILIES

David Cheal called it the "big bang." He borrowed the label from astronomers claiming that billions of years ago the universe exploded into existence with some sort of big bang. Cheal claims that during the late 1960s and early 1970s, the Modern Family experienced its own big bang transformation, it saw the explosion of diversities described throughout this book. Instead of there being merely one kind of family, many kinds of families began to emerge onto the social scene. Other researchers agree with Cheal that the 1960s and 1970s were at least as important in the shaping of families as were the 1920s—and probably more significant.[72]

Gary Bauer also agrees that the sixties—the big bang era—was the time when The Family began to shift markedly away from its Golden Age. However, he labels the changes "family decline."[73] Bauer is an influential Washington, D.C. spokesperson for what is known as the Religious Right—a coalition of politically active organizations that lobby congress for their viewpoints. (See Chapter 4.) Bauer (who has appeared on the popular news program, *Nightline*) often reflects the opinions of that 20 percent of the population located within the fixed-philosophy category of Figure 1-1. People in this category believe that the sixties marked a radical and negative departure from the Modern Family that had been developing in North America since the Jacksonian era. Bauer says that since the 1960s, we've had decades of "abrasive liberal experiments" when it comes to families.

Before the 1960s, the Modern Family had achieved predominance over the North American scene. It was unquestioned and appeared unquestionable. During the late fifties and early sixties, most sociologists and virtually all ordinary citizens believed that the Benchmark Family represented the *ultimate* family.[74] Almost everyone believed that it worked for adults, children, and society—that it provided the best possible fit between the demands of modern industrial societies and the emotional and economic needs of persons. For that reason, it was often explicitly called the *modern family*.[75] No one could imagine any other single type of family that could replace it in the same way that it had replaced earlier kinds of families. And indeed, no other type has replaced it. Nor is there any single type on the horizon that could possibly do so.

Today, however, we're living in what some observers call a "postmodern" era.[76] What's the difference between this and what earlier chapters called "modern" societies? Much of what we said about modern societies also applies to postmodern societies. For example, at the close of Chapter 6 we talked about struggling to balance *we-ness* with *me-ness*, and about conflicts over gender equality, and so on.

Those kinds of tensions are very much a part of postmodern societies. Indeed, it is those very tensions that contribute to the many diversities that we see all around us. The label "postmodern" appeared first in the field of architecture. Postmodern architects say there is no single type of building that represents the ideal form of building. Unlike architectural "modernists," they gave up looking for the *ideal* building style to replace Gothic, or Colonial, or Victorian architectural styles. Postmodern architects say that any number of new designs could be as valid, or as good, as any other.

Accordingly, researchers such as Cheal and Stacey and Skolnick call this the era of "postmodern families."[77] People are behaving in many different ways while constructing their families, and it's impossible to conclude which behaviors necessarily work the best. "Postmodern" celebrates ideas such as pluralism and diversity. It seems that throughout many parts of society, the notion that there is one best anything is being replaced. It's being replaced by a quest for solutions that work within the social context in which people find themselves. For example, Jerald Hage and C. H. Powers use the following language to describe today's and tomorrow's (postmodern) workplace. And what they say about paid work applies just as strongly to the inventing of families—today's primary relationships: "Work tasks . . . [are] defined in terms of information gathering, problem solving, the production of creative ideas, and the ability to respond flexibly to new situations or adjust flexibly when interacting with others."[78]

The Modern Family (like yesterday's workplace) was all about *conformity*—"doing what you're supposed to do." Postmodern families (like the emerging workplace) are all about *creativity*—"What works?" and "What makes life better?" But how did we get from there to here? What was it about the sixties that led us from conformity to creativity? How did we drift so far from the Benchmark Family?

Social Movements of the 1960s

The sixties were marked by several social movements that received extraordinary media publicity. Although very different in specifics, the movements shared one major feature: They launched explicit challenges against established ways of believing and of doing things. Those overt challenges to the establishment lie at the core of what the sixties were all about.

The Student Movement   One of the earliest of these movements was known as the *student movement*. It got media attention because its leaders demanded free speech for students to complain about the varied injustices they perceived on college campuses. At first they merely held public rallies asking for greater student participation in the governing of universities. Later on, as other movements became popular, students pressed their demands more vigorously by boycotting classes, picketing college buildings, and staging sit-ins, not only on campus, but off campus as well. During campus sit-ins, students would sometimes physically invade an administration building, preventing business as usual and demanding that administrators accede to their demands. Often they had to be carried away by police and were charged with trespassing. The two causes generating the fiercest passions and unruliest student demonstrations were the anti-Vietnam war movement and the black civil rights (later black power) movement. Both of these causes represented severe challenges to the established order and reflected deep divisions within U.S. society. Todd Gitlin shows how these and other activist movements of the decade were in turn captured by the label, the "New Left."

The Counterculture   An added and important twist was the emergence of the *counter-culture*. It was made up largely of college students and others in their 20s. Neither a movement

A love-in during a 1960s counterculture gathering.

nor an organization in its own right, it represented a particular lifestyle shared by many persons from among the several movements. The essence of that lifestyle was *nonconformity*, symbolized by a number of things such as bizarre kinds of dress, beards, and hairstyles; rock and roll and folk protest music; and drug use, especially marijuana and LSD. The challenge of the counterculture to the larger society sprang largely from its threatening symbols. Its clearest agenda for social change centered around the decriminalization of drugs.

Persons from the several movements just mentioned (who were often part of the counterculture) had a wide range of specific demands for social change, as did two remaining social movements of the decade: women's liberation, and gay liberation. Recall that Chapter 6 described feminism as a social movement appearing early in the Jacksonian era. Its overriding goal was to get voting rights for women. By 1920, that goal was achieved through an amendment to the Constitution. William O'Neill says that with that success, the U.S. feminist movement relaxed and stopped pressing for additional political and economic changes.[79] By contrast, in most European countries feminism continued as an active social movement. By the late 1950s, U.S. feminism was no longer the organized and active social movement it had been during the nineteenth century.

Feminism Revived   During the 1960s, feminism was revived for a number of connected reasons. In 1963 Betty Friedan published a book called *The Feminine Mystique*. The book became a popular best-seller and captured a great deal of media attention. Among other things, Friedan said severe discontents were simmering beneath the surface of middle-class women's apparent contentedness with the Modern Family. Picking up on a theme made by some 1920s' feminists, Friedan believed that being a housewife and mother was simply not enough to satisfy the personal and intellectual needs of intelligent, well-educated women. She asserted that, among other things, women needed to become more active in paid labor to fulfill their full human potential. Other women thinkers and activists of the sixties reminded their audiences that some nineteenth-century pioneer feminists were considered "radical" because they too said that getting the vote was merely the beginning.[80] Those early pioneers had advocated the liberation of women from what they believed were injustices throughout all of society—economic, political, and religious as well as familial. A number of the pioneers noted that, ironically, the federal government paid much more attention to guaranteeing the political rights of freed slaves than to addressing the political and economic rights of women, even though women had vigorously supported the abolition of slavery. Feminists of the 1960s argued that the time had finally arrived for government to pay attention to women's rights.

As revived feminism spread throughout college campuses during the 1960s, its more activist wing became labeled the *women's liberation movement*. Its avowed aim was to achieve justice for women in all areas of social life. As had been the case a century before, the 1960s' women's movement identified strongly with the black movement in seeking to redress perceived racial as well as gender injustices. And many women's activists were simultaneously very much a part of the anti-Vietnam war movement. Nevertheless, in spite of many overlapping goals across these several movements, there were also sharp differences among them. Some black men, for instance, were suspicious of white and black women's demands for greater economic opportunities. Having been threatened for centuries by white men, some black men felt that women's liberation was yet one more major threat.[81]

Furthermore, some middle-class counterculture white men voiced severe criticisms of the Horatio Alger legend—the ethic of work and success that had been drummed into boys for well over a century. They believed the fifties had been poisoned by excessive materialism and consumerism, destroying the capabilities of persons to be caring and considerate. In short, counterculture white male students were saying that work, achievement, and success should count for *less* in society at the same time that feminists were arguing that they should count for *more* in women's lives. Furthermore, privileged white males were saying that work should count for less while educated black men were demanding greater access to work opportunities. Neither did working-class white or black men (hard hats) take kindly to the sons of the privileged preaching that persons should "light up, tune in, and drop out."

A crucial point to remember is that the numbers of activists in all of these movements made up a small fraction of the total U.S. population. The great majority of citizens, including college students, were for the most part pursuing business as usual. However, like that of today's New Religious Right, the social influence of the 1960s movements far exceeded their numbers. Perhaps their most obvious influence was their continual pressure on the government's pursuit of the Vietnam war. Antiwar demonstrations reached a plateau after the highly publicized student slayings by the National Guard at Kent State University in 1970.

Choice and Control   One of the most lasting effects of the 1960s was the reinforcement and expansion of something that had been part of North American culture since the early Jacksonian years—the idea of personal choice and control over one's destiny. Starting with the end of the Colonial era, we've seen that the range of options open to persons, especially men, was steadily expanding. By the 1920s self-fulfillment became something people no longer had to be ashamed of. It became okay, for instance, to talk about self-actualization, especially for men pursuing material success. Cultural norms finally caught up with what men had been doing for a century. And the sixties became for women what the twenties had been for men. The upheavals of the 1960s began to make women's self-fulfillment okay, something they didn't have to be ashamed of (at least not as much as before). As a result, gender relationships and families were never quite the same again.[82]

During the 1880s and 1890s conservative critics had blamed increasing rates of divorce and delinquency, as well as other social problems, on women's desires for self-fulfillment.[83] Because women were the guardians of the family, and thus of society, conservatives believed women could not be allowed the luxury of self-fulfillment that might in any way threaten social order. Although some women had been ignoring the cultural ideal of self-denial for many decades, the 1960s saw a significant closing of the gap between women's behaviors and cultural norms.

Some North Americans came to believe that self-fulfillment belonged as much to women as it did to men. A centerpiece of the Modern Family had been women's emotional massaging of men. Suddenly, women no longer had to be ashamed of nurturing themselves as well.

Transition from the Dating Game   Nevertheless, reports Rubin, 1960s women did not find the transition to self-nurturing an easy one: "A lifetime of training to put the needs of others before those of self made it difficult suddenly to make decisions in their own behalf."[84] A major problem that women faced stemmed from what Gadlin calls the 1960s "liberation" of sexuality from marriage.[85] Before that time, few persons were willing to say that nonmarital sex was a legitimate option. Engaged couples having sex justified it by thinking and saying, "We're soon to be married anyhow. What difference does It make?" Their sexual activity was definitely connected with marriage. But the sixties made the words of Frank Sinatra's 1950s' hit song sound hilariously quaint and naive: "love and marriage go together like a horse and carriage." For many younger persons sexuality was no longer viewed as having any necessary or inherent connection with marriage. The sixties marked the beginning of the end of the Dating Game that had been around since the twenties.

Painful Dilemmas   Devising new rules meant painful dilemmas. Although many younger persons embraced the idea of sexual freedom, there was considerable disagreement over what that meant in everyday life. Some persons (more men than women) believed it meant that anyone could have sex with anyone else whenever he or she wanted to.[86] Several of the women in Rubin's study commented that although the Dating Game was discredited, some men were amending it solely to get women into bed. Instead of a man saying to his fiance, "Since we'll be married in a month, why not now?," the pitch to *any* woman became, "Since it's cool to believe in sexual freedom, why not have sex with me?"

One side of the dilemma women faced in responding to that pitch was that they genuinely and passionately believed in the new freedom they were grasping. Rather than sex being a secret shame for them, women were creating situations in which sex was publicly and openly celebrated. They were exercising choice and control over their sexuality—and thus over their lives—in ways never before open to them. This was indeed an authentic sexual revolution! But the other side of the dilemma was, how much control had they actually gained? Rubin points out that although they now had enough control over their lives to say yes, many men and some women felt that women had relinquished the right to say no. How could a woman claim she was sexually liberated, but yet refuse sex?

Implicit Bargaining   Complicating the new sexual situation further was another holdover from the Dating Game. Rubin reports that the sexual experimentation of sixties' youth was not characterized by explicit negotiation.[87] The new experimentation seemed to rest on the same sort of covert bargaining that had characterized the old Game. Instead of explicitly negotiating guidelines to manage their newly unstructured sexual situations, many women and men were continuing to be as tacit about sex as their parents had been. Hence, men seldom actually said, "If you're sexually free, you'll have sex"; women rarely used the words "yes" or "no."

The Beginnings of Erotic Friendships One additional factor complicated women's dilemma, or perhaps it's the reason their dilemma existed in the first place. Rubin describes it as the differing goals that women and men bring to their sexual experiences, and indeed to their relationships in general. These divergent goals are also a holdover from the Dating Game. During the Game, men wanted what Rubin calls the "Big It," but women wanted marriage. Now that they were freed from insisting on marriage, what did women want alongside lusty, carnal, and orgasmic sex? One woman in Rubin's study described it as an "emotional *something*."[88] Striving for that "something" has resulted in what earlier chapters called the erotic friendship. As younger persons "liberated" sex from marriage they were also inventing a unique relationship that, although not excluding the idea of legal marriage, did not require it.

Men's Liberation   Although the sixties brought about a revolution in women's sexual behaviors, there was no comparable revolution in men's emotional capacities.[89] In spite of the fact that a men's movement was launched during the 1960s to assist men in becoming emotionally sensitive and competent, it was not as prominent or successful as the women's movement.[90] Gadlin observed that the 1920s had launched the notion of women as sex objects into popular culture. In advertising and elsewhere, it became publicly acceptable to image women primarily as *things* to be *had* sexually, instead of as human persons. The woman-as-sex-object motif expanded with the popularity of World War II pinup girls, followed by the introduction of *Playboy* magazine during the 1950s. And, says Rubin, one of the effects of the sixties' removal of most public sexual restraints was a huge expansion of the same motif.[91] The 1991 film, *Switch*, protrays vividly how the woman-as-sex-object motif thoroughly pervades men's perceptions of women.

Why didn't 1960s men make intimacy with women a major goal? Why weren't men able to move beyond believing that emotional massaging is a one-way street? A major theme of the time was *equality*—between the races, between poor and rich, between women and men. Despite new sexual possibilities, however, the everyday lives of sixties' men and women were pervaded by ancient economic and political inequalities that could not be swept away by mere fiat. Objective inequality continued to be a barrier to intimacy, just as it had been for the Jacksonians, for Progressives, and for parents of sixties' youth.

Indeed, Rubin's respondents suggest, and some feminists observed, that the new sexual freedoms, in the context of continuing social inequalities, made some women more vulnerable than before to sexual exploitation. Many women were not getting what they wanted, emotional closeness, in exchange for the sex that seemed to be flowing so freely.[92] If their mothers allowed coitus, they got marriage in exchange. Recall that Anna was able to get what she viewed as a series of fair deals from Herbert through effectively managing their sexual behaviors. But by the 1960s the old Game had largely evaporated. Karin is pleased that it has. But she's not at all pleased with what she's getting from Andy. She doesn't think it's fair that although she's sleeping with him, he's not relating to her in an emotionally close and intimate way. Andy, however, doesn't see their relationship as unfair at all, he doesn't understand what Karin wants. What is Karin to do?

Women's Alternatives   It turns out that Karin is in a much stronger negotiating position than Anna could ever have dreamed of. Late sixties' feminists were reviving the 1920s' idea that women should view labor force participation as their *right*, not merely as an option. Karin is developing a resource that Anna never had, the idea that she could take care of herself economically. She does not require a man to support her.[93] Because she doesn't view Andy as an eventual "meal ticket" (good provider), Andy has much less leverage than Herbert had. Since Karin has the choice, or option, of not having to trade sex for marriage, she can

afford to be more choosy about men. Consequently, after trying unsuccessfully to get Andy even to understand what she's after, she ends their relationship.

Andy, like many other 1960s' men, failed to genuinely define women as his economic and political equals. He, and they, continued to perceive women as uniquely alien, for any number of reasons. Most men of that era felt that because of certain biological and psychological characteristics, women were not able to participate as effectively as men in the economic and political spheres.[94] Believing that women were drastically different established a built-in separateness, a formidable barrier to emotional closeness. An ongoing major feminist goal, besides that of challenging legal and formal gender inequities in the economic and political spheres, is to demonstrate that there are no inherent biological or psychological reasons why women cannot perform effectively in those spheres. Women's demands to serve in military combat are a vivid example. Andy's generation of men was the first to face women's demands for large-scale changes not solely in the public arena but in the private realm as well.[95]

Women's Autonomy   In both the public and private realms, what 1960s' women wanted most of all was *autonomy*, that is, personal choice and control over their own destiny.[96] Autonomy included being able to take care of themselves, particularly in economic terms.[97] The women in Rubin's study who were most autonomous reported that sexual freedom is a myth if the woman was in some way or another doing *It* for the man. That merely repeats ancient history. However, if "you're doing it for yourself, then you can say you're sexually free."[98]

Karin viewed herself as an autonomous person. After splitting from Andy and going out with other men, she chose when to say no as well as yes. Furthermore, she sometimes chose to initiate sex, thereby placing men in women's historic reactor position. As the women in her study reflected back on the sixties, Rubin asked them how much control they felt they'd actually had over sex. To what degree were they still at the mercy of men's whims? Women who perceived themselves as autonomous were less likely to have allowed men to sexually exploit or "use" them. By contrast, women who saw themselves as less autonomous were more likely to have felt exploited by men.

One of Rubin's respondents used the term *transition generation* to capture what happened to young people during the 1960s. When the rigid sexual restraints of the past were first challenged, some persons floundered in the absence of guidelines regarding who sleeps with whom and when. Gradually, by the decade's end, a few well-educated women began to resist sexual exploitation through asserting their own autonomy—their right of personal choice and control. That shift from coercion to choice, from conformity to creativity, was a major essence of the transition generation.

The "Big Change"—Women's Employment Revolution

The 1960s saw a revolution not solely in women's sexual behaviors, but also in their employment behaviors. And postmodern families emerged from both of those dramatic shifts. Charles Jones and colleagues are Canadian sociologists who use the label "Big Change" to describe, first, the gradual shifts in women's employment patterns that were occurring throughout the twentieth century.[99] The Big Change also describes the jolt that women's employment patterns got during the sixties. Basic to the Big Change, say Jones and co-workers, is the idea of women's autonomy. We learned that for Karin and other sixties'

women, economic autonomy meant the capability to support themselves. They no longer wished to have to depend on a good provider. Added to the sexual revolution, this meant that relationships between women and men could never be quite the same again.

Contraceptive Technologies Jones and colleagues call the 1960s a "watershed" in the lives of North American women (and men), for the following reasons.[100] First, the decade witnessed the introduction and widespread dissemination of oral contraception (the Pill), the intrauterine device (IUD), and improved diaphragms. Because these technologies (the Pill in particular) were so effective in reducing pregnancy risk, they played a major role in the demise of the Dating Game and the emergence of the new sexual patterns just described. But the changes in contraceptive effectiveness also played a major role in changes in women's employment patterns. The new technologies made it much more possible for women to control their child-bearing behaviors: how many children to have (if any), when to get pregnant, and how much spacing between pregnancies. Greater efficiency in planning for children made planning their employment choices that much simpler.[101] As a result, the new technologies expanded women's sense of autonomy.[102] Throughout North America and all of Western society, the pace of women's entry into paid labor picked up markedly during the late 1960s. It continues to increase steadily, as discussed further in Chapter 15.

Employment and Divorce Chapter 13 talks about the many changes in divorce laws passed during the sixties in both Canada and the United States. One result of those changes was that North American divorce rates began to rise steeply. Before then, wives in the Benchmark Family were expected either to live lives of quiet desperation or to improve their situation by subtly manipulating their husbands.

The loosening of divorce laws corresponded with the growing access of women to paid employment. Recall that part of the reason Karin ended her relationship with Andy was that she realized she had an alternative to being supported by a man—she could support herself. That *economic* alternative helped lead her to seek a *relationship* alternative.

Paid work provides two kinds of resources, material and nonmaterial. Nonmaterial resources include feeling good about oneself. In one study, working-class and middle-class women alike made comments such as: "You are more powerful if you work. You can support yourself—more independence—no matter what your husband does"; "Work is fulfilling and keeps you in touch with other people."[103] Increased feelings of self-esteem, self-worth, and self-respect encouraged many sixties' and seventies' wives to try to negotiate explicitly with their husbands about things they wanted in their relationships.[104] If wives felt their negotiations were ineffective, that is, if the negotiations failed to achieve fair and equitable outcomes, wives could draw on the second resource jobs provide, namely, money. According to Jones and colleagues, independent incomes, in the context of flexible divorce laws, supplied many wives of the 1960s, 1970s, and 1980s with the courage to leave their husbands and try to make it on their own.

The Ancient History of Women's Labors Of course, women have always worked. From tiny girls to grandmothers, women participated fully in the rigors faced by pre-industrial households barely eking out a living. Economic survival for most families required women's (and children's) labor, whether on farms or in towns, villages, and cities. Only upper-class wives (a small fraction of the total population) were exempted from the labor of the masses of people: Their husbands could afford servants and/or slaves for domestic work and child care. In the Jacksonian era middle-class wives began to be freed from the necessity of laboring to survive economically, but most of them still did their own housework and child care. However, working- and lower-class households required the paid labor of women and children to survive.

The Societal Context of Women's Employment Thus far we've discussed the issue of employment choices in conjunction with women's sense of control and autonomy. On the other side of the coin is the broader societal context that enhanced women's employment choices. This context consisted of significant shifts in the structure of large-scale occupational systems throughout Western societies. Chief among the shifts was a greatly expanded range of occupations from which women might choose. For example, women's nursing opportunities sprouted during the Civil War (1861–1865); elementary school teaching became increasingly available to all North American women during the 1880s and 1890s. In the twentieth century came clerical and office work of all kinds, opportunities in library science, occupational therapy, rehabilitation medicine, social work, and so on. As women gradually became more numerous than men in certain kinds of occupations, the jobs were described as having been "feminized," or as having become women dominated.[105]

A second important twentieth-century shift consisted of union contracts and legislation aimed at undercutting economic discrimination against women by employers. Canada and most West European countries have established many more extensive and elaborate protections against gender discrimination than has the United States. This distinction is seen most vividly in the U.S. failure to adopt the Equal Rights Amendment. Nevertheless, the United States has moved in the direction of redressing discrimination beginning with the 1964 Civil Rights Act, which prohibits discrimination not solely on the basis of race but also of sex. This Act was followed by a series of more concrete legislative and judicial efforts (i.e., "affirmative action") aimed at achieving greater economic and political equity between the genders. As a result of antidiscrimination legislation, and in conjunction with the goal of women's autonomy, 1960s' feminists began to advocate that women break out of stereotypically feminine jobs. Consequently, the decades since the sixties have seen a third type of shift. Chapter 15 shows how ever-increasing numbers of women are entering "male-dominated" occupations, for example, medicine, pharmacy, law, dentistry, journalism, university faculties, politics, the military and law enforcement, space exploration, engineering, and so forth. In 1993, for example, women accounted for 42 percent of all medical school applicants.[106] In addition, some women in business and industry have moved beyond clerical levels into professional sales, management, and executive positions. Virtually all of these occupations are prestigious, requiring brains, not brawn. Ever since the end of World War II, and especially since the 1970s, they've been expanding at the same time that heavy manufacturing jobs ("men's jobs") demanding great physical strength have declined.

CONCLUSION—DESCRIBING POST-MODERN LIVES AND FAMILIES

One of the many concepts captured by the label "postmodern" is the spread of *diversity*, or differences. Jones and colleagues identify two major ways in which the lives of today's women express considerable diversity. First, at any given point in time their lives may be very much unlike the lives of women who are approximately the same age. Before the sixties, women who were located in comparable age categories experienced very similar life circumstances in terms of singleness, marriage, divorce, child bearing, employment, and so on. Today the trend is for growing numbers of

same-aged women to be found in many diverse kinds of life circumstances.

Second, the life courses of today's women are becoming increasingly unpredictable compared with those of their mothers. Before the 1960s, a woman such as Anna could predict her life with reasonable certainty. Although she might be employed in clerical work or some other "feminine occupation" before marrying Herbert, she would get pregnant soon afterward, quit her job, and look forward to staying home with several children at least until the last was through high school. Besides parenting, being a good wife primarily meant emotionally massaging Herbert and supporting his good provider efforts. At different points in time, Anna might expect to get a part- (or full-) time job if the family had financial needs or simply wanted extras, or to help send children to college. She would, however, expect a zigzag employment pattern: She would enter paid labor if there were needs, but would exit when the needs were met or if her paid work interfered with being a parent or good wife.

Most of all, she could look forward to being with Herbert until one of them died. She could count on him to be her constant companion and good provider through old age. To be sure, Anna was aware that accident or illness could remove Herbert before the children reached maturity, but wasn't that why they had life insurance? Anna would never imagine that throughout her life course she needed to be an economically autonomous person in the same way Herbert was. She would never seriously consider that she should be able to support herself and any children she might have. Chapter 14 explains how today's women and men are able to predict their life courses with much less certainty than pre-sixties' persons. Although men may retain somewhat greater predictability than women, today, both men and women face futures that are much less clearly mapped out than those of their parents.

Longer periods of never-married singleness, parenting and sex outside of marriage, cohabiting arrangements, marriage, divorce, resingleness, remarriage, and so forth, may occur and reoccur at any age and in virtually any sequence. Furthermore, changes in these kinds of behaviors are closely connected with shifts in education and employment behaviors.

The uncertainties and ambiguities attached to predicting the futures of relationships and of employment help us understand what is meant by the idea of *post*modern families. The lives of today's men and women—and thus of their families—are marked by variety and fluidity. The sexual and employment revolutions have made choice and control central to women's lives. Since choice and control had always been central to men's lives, the result is that men and women are becoming more like each other than ever before in history. Ironically, the outcome of this growing similarity is greater diversity in relationships and families than ever before. During the 1950s, the lives of women and men contrasted much more than today in terms of employment patterns, sexuality, and shared intimacy. At the same time, family patterns were much more uniform than they are today. The Benchmark Family was built not on gender similarity but on gender divergence—on *gender role specialization*. That specialization resulted in family uniformity, sameness, and predictability. Those were the hallmarks of the Modern Family.

Part of what makes today's and tomorrow's families postmodern is the slow but irreversible convergence between the genders in the amounts of choice and control that they have. Chapter 6 closed by saying that a major dilemma facing today's families is how to balance the need for *freedom* with the need for *belonging*. In the past, that balance was achieved largely by placing clearly defined cultural limits on women's choices. Those limits helped to account for the high levels of uniformity and stability experienced by pre-1960s modern families. As the limits decline in strength, family uniformity and stability become less common; diversity and unpredictability become more frequent. Nevertheless, postmodern families face precisely the same dilemma of how to balance the needs of freedom and belonging. Today that task is more difficult than it's ever been before.

NOTES

1. Bell and Vogel, 1960.
2. Cheal, 1991.
3. Ehrmann, 1964, p. 593; Rothman, 1984.
4. Ehrmann, p. 594.
5. Ibid.
6. Modell, 1989, p. 147.
7. Kirkendall, 1961.
8. Rubin, 1990, p. 94.
9. Durfield, 1990.
10. *The New York Times*, June 21, 1993, p. A7.
11. Mintz and Kellogg, 1988, pp. 116–117.
12. Ehrmann.
13. Waller, 1938.
14. Ehrmann.
15. Ibid., pp. 594–595.
16. Ibid., p. 595.
17. Burchinal, 1964, p. 636.
18. Reiss, 1960.
19. Scanzoni et al., 1989.
20. Swidler, 1980.
21. Ehrmann, p. 603.
22. Ibid., p. 595; Burchinal, p. 627.
23. Reiss, 1967.
24. Ehrmann, p. 597.
25. Swidler.
26. Modell, p. 145.
27. Darling, Kallen, and Van Dusen, 1984.
28. Ehrmann.
29. Pomeroy, 1982.
30. Kinsey, Pomeroy, and Martin, 1948; Kinsey et al., 1953.
31. Reisman and Eichel, 1990.
32. Jewell, 1988, p. 22.
33. Modell, p. 131.
34. Ibid., p. 151.
35. Ibid., p. 143.
36. Ibid.

37. Swidler.
38. Douvan, 1977; Long-Laws and Schwartz, 1977.
39. Demos, 1982.
40. Seeley, Sim, and Loosley, 1956.
41. Ibid.
42. Mintz and Kellogg, pp. 115–117.
43. Pleck and Pleck, 1980, p. 31.
44. Klemer, 1959, p. 12.
45. Ibid., p. 189.
46. Bell and Vogel; and see Kingsbury and Scanzoni, 1993.
47. Ehrmann, p. 595.
48. Spiegel, 1960.
49. Gadlin, 1977, p. 70.
50. Nye, 1979, p. 11.
51. Scanzoni, 1970.
52. Pleck, 1980; Nardi, 1992.
53. Seeley et al., 1956; Rainwater and Weinstein, 1960.
54. Bernard, 1972.
55. Pleck and Pleck, p. 31.
56. Goode, 1963, p. 380. The 1991 film, *Mr. Bridge and Mrs. Bridge*, conveys poignantly this sense of quiet desperation.
57. Cuber and Harroff, 1965.
58. Karen Anderson, 1981.
59. Modell, pp. 162–165.
60. Ibid., p. 162.
61. Ibid., pp. 173–174.
62. Ibid., p. 208.
63. Pleck and Pleck, p. 35; Babchuck, 1965.
64. Modell, pp. 227ff; James Coleman, 1961.
65. Modell, pp. 233ff.
66. Ibid., p. 235.
67. Bayer, 1968.
68. Ibid.
69. Mintz and Kellogg, p. 187.
70. Ibid.
71. Ibid., p. 188.
72. Gadlin, 1977; Pleck and Pleck, 1980; Mintz and Kellogg, 1988.
73. Bauer, 1986.
74. Goode.
75. Bell and Vogel.

76. Gitlin, 1987.
77. Cheal; Stacey, 1990, 1993; Skolnick, 1991.
78. Hage and Powers, 1992, pp. 11–12.
79. O'Neill, 1969.
80. Dahlerup, 1986.
81. Gitlin.
82. Ibid.
83. Mintz and Kellogg.
84. Rubin, p. 94.
85. Gadlin, pp. 65–66.
86. Rubin, p. 94.
87. Ibid., p. 103.
88. Ibid., p. 102.
89. Pleck, 1980.
90. Ibid. See also Jerry Adler et al., "Drums, Sweat and Tears," *Newsweek*, June 24, 1991, pp. 46–53.
91. Rubin, p. 96.
92. Ibid., p. 111.
93. Vance, 1984.
94. Pitts, 1964.
95. Valverde, 1989. Also, in April 1993, the U.S. government ordered the armed services to let women fly aircraft and be stationed on surface warships during combat: See *The Gainesville, Florida Sun*, April 28, 1993, p. A1 (from *The New York Times*). Less than a year later, the government took an additional step toward gender equity by allowing women to participate in ground combat support units (engineering, maintenance, etc.) that had formerly been considered "too risky" for women: See *The New York Times*, January 14, 1994, p. A10.
96. Kraditor, 1968.
97. Rubin, p. 114.
98. Ibid.
99. Jones, Marsden, and Tepperman, 1990, pp. 36, 49.
100. Ibid., p. 7.
101. Scanzoni, 1975.
102. Jones et al., pp. 12–17, 31.
103. Ibid., p. 26.
104. Scanzoni, 1978.
105. Jones et al., p. 40.
106. *The New York Times*, May 18, 1993, p. A1.

PART THREE

EXAMPLES OF TODAY'S REINVENTIONS

CHAPTER 8

SOME QUESTIONS ABOUT SINGLENESS

Chapters 2 and 3 talked about families as networks of households helping each other out, especially with regard to tangible and material needs. Sometimes the households are linked by blood and are known as formal families. At other times the households are not blood linked and are known as social families. In either case, we learned that people construct or reinvent families in response to certain needs that they feel, and also in response to the social conditions in which they're located. Chapters 4 and 5 showed how persons have been reinventing the social patterns surrounding sexual behaviors. In particular, we talked about the erotic friendship and how it acts like an umbrella that covers girlfriends/boyfriends, cohabitors, and spouses. Chapters 6 and 7 described the ways in which people have been reinventing families between the late 1700s and the 1960s and 1970s.

As we examined the ways people have been and are reinventing families and relationships, we've also pursued a difficult question: Are people making these many and profound changes in a responsible manner? Or are they being *irresponsible* about their reinventions? As we struggled with that question, we noticed that there were some things about past families that were not especially responsible. How responsible, for instance, was the old Dating Game? How responsible was it to create gender relationships that cut men off from the benefits of emotional intimacy? How responsible was it to cut women off from making contributions to the larger society in terms of its educational, artistic, scientific, economic, and political life? Certainly one of the reasons people are trying to reinvent families is precisely because old families were, in some respects, irresponsible. Nevertheless, while trying to improve on the old, are today's people being more or less responsible than their parents and grandparents? To try to answer this question, Chapters 8 through 17 present some specific examples of today's reinventions, along with the ways in which people may or may not be struggling with issues of responsibility. And we begin with *singleness*, which was and still is very much tied to the matter of responsibility.

DISCRIMINATION AGAINST SINGLES

Harold Saltzman complains in the national press that he's discriminated against because he's *single.* Married persons, he says, are invited to weddings as a couple. But single persons are not allowed to bring a friend unless the wedding planners define their relationship as "ongoing and serious." To qualify, the relationship must be "monogamous," and also "moving swiftly" in the direction of marriage. If the relationship is merely a platonic friendship, if the single person has an erotic friendship that his or her friends perceive is headed nowhere, or if the single person has a gay or lesbian partner, "well that's too bad. . . . [None of these is] a real relationship in the eyes of the about-to-be-married."[1] In her classic study, *Single Blessedness,* Margaret Adams described the plight of 1970s' singles in words that are remarkably similar to Saltzman's 1990s' complaint. She said that singles are in the "perpetual poor-relation role, always waiting to be included in social activities . . . and depending on the charitable interest of their more socially established married friends."[2]

Whatever Saltzman's pain, it's got to be less than that of the woman accused of being a witch because she happened to be a single woman living several hundred years ago in Europe or North America. The historian Erik Midelfort tells us that witch trials of that era often resulted in the woman being hanged or burned at the stake. The severe sentence "served to register society's fear and intolerance of single women—a group that lived 'without family and without patriarchal control.' "[3] Those clusters of unmarried women were often the forerunners of today's physicians. They used herbs to promote healing, and/or they were midwives. But because of their special skills, they were accused of being accomplices of the devil.[4] If merely one woman was doing something idiosyncratic, others could dismiss her as a harmless eccentric. But if a group of unmarried women was doing something unusual, citizens were more likely to take notice. In their view, large numbers of single women constituted a threat to estab-lished values and patterns, and the society took extreme measures to quash the deviance. Arthur Miller's play, *The Crucible,* portrayed such a group in seventeenth-century Salem, Massachusetts, and their trials for witchcraft. Bram Buunk and Barry van Driel point out that throughout U.S. history, "attitudes toward singlehood have been quite negative."[5]

Singleness as Deviant

Chapter 7 said that today we're living in an era of postmodern families. This simply means that we're living in a time of growing diversity. Throughout the course of their lives, increasing numbers of persons are choosing (or are forced into) many different kinds of families and family experiences. Being single (i.e., not legally married) is part of the emerging diversity, but it continues to be viewed with considerable ambivalence. Although Western societies have come a long way from burning witches to allowing singles' bars, it seems clear that in all of them, being single still has less prestige than being married. Married persons continue to command higher esteem, respect, and status than single persons.

The U.S. Census Bureau counts singles, but not because it believes singleness is improtant in and of itself. Researchers are interested in the "notness" of singleness. They want to know how many people are *not* ever-married, or have been but are *not now* married, or do *not* have the legitimate right to bear children, and so on. Collecting numbers on singleness is justified because the numbers shed light on things that are considered vital to the health of society—marriage, divorce, and children. The label "deviance" can be applied to any sort of straying from established and legitimate cultural and social patterns. "Straying" means failure to conform to what others expect. Legal/formal marriage is what most citizens expect of other citizens. Since marriage is central to the Benchmark Family, unmarried

In this Western singles' bar the woman might be pursued—unimpressed and in control. By comparison, the Japanese couple utilizing the "marriage center" is in a vastly different situation. Here the woman has much less control than her Western sister.

adults are, by definition, straying. Consequently, say observers such as Adams, and Leonard Cargan and Matthew Melko, single persons become labeled as "deviant."[6] That is especially true the longer they remain single (e.g., past their late-20s). And because staying single is perceived as deviant, it also smacks of being irresponsible.

Feelings of Stress   Like all other social patterns that diverge from that of the Benchmark Family, singleness "lacks institutional definition and support."[7] Because no social norms have existed recognizing singleness as a valid way to live on a permanent basis, the single person asks, Who am I? Where do I belong? What's my role in life? During the past, aside from entering a monastery or nunnery, there were no culturally approved answers. As a result, says Adams, single persons felt a great deal of "ambivalence [and] identity confusion."[8] These negative feelings are often connected with symptoms of anxiety, stress, and depression. Stress can come from many sources. One source is the anxiety that stems

from *not* having a legitimate and respected place in life—for example, being single. Studies show that a major way persons can reduce stress is to take control of situations that produce anxiety and confusion.[9] Saltzman, for example, took charge of his potentially stressful situation by "staying home on the wedding day. . . . Having to ask [to bring a guest] is demeaning," he asserted.

Trends in Attitudes toward Singleness

During the Colonial era single persons were taxed because lawmakers believed there was a great need for lots of children to perform the arduous tasks necessary to maintain an agrarian society.[10] Since marriage was considered the only legitimate place to produce children, that tax put pressure on deviant single persons to conform by getting married for the good of society. Although by the 1950s the tax had long been abandoned, Daniel Yankelovich reports that as recently as mid century some 80 percent of Americans agreed with the statement that "a woman must be sick, neurotic, or immoral" to remain unmarried.[11] By 1978 attitudes had changed; that year only a quarter of Americans agreed with the statement.[12] In short, while North Americans are less likely now than before the sixties to view singles as "deviant, immature, and sexually disturbed," the status of being single is hardly an envied one. At best it is viewed with considerable ambivalence. There are no cultural or social pressures on persons to "get single," compared with the enormous pressures on persons to "get married." Nevertheless, according to Cargan and Melko, the 1960s and 1970s represented a significant turning point in the history of U.S. singleness. Some things began to change during that era. However, they quickly add that many things about singleness remained the same.

DEFINING SINGLENESS

Before we examine things about singleness that have and haven't changed, we first need to sharpen our definitions of singleness. However, trying to define "single" in a precise way is not simple. All of us have an intuitive feeling what it means, but when we express that feeling it often turns out to be ambiguous. For instance, if you stand on a busy downtown street corner in a large city and ask every third person who goes by what "single" means, almost all will probably respond, "someone who's not married." But suppose you pursue them down the block and ask if they think that being single means the same thing for persons who've never been married, as it does for persons who are no longer married. And suppose you continue to chase after them and ask, "What if they're married but have been separated for five years: Are those persons *single*?" What response would you get if you pressed them further by asking about cohabiting couples, straight or gay, who've been living together for ten years: "Are they single, or not?"

Trends among Never-Married Persons

The U.S. Census Bureau generally collects numbers about "families and household living arrangements" in March of each year. Table 8-1 shows the trends between 1960 and 1988 in the percentage of persons who had never been legally married on the day the census taker contacted them. If we look at the second row in the table—persons under 40 years of age—we see a clear trend upward for both women and men. In 1960 only 28 percent of women under age 40 had never been married, compared with 40 percent in 1988 (figures are rounded to the nearest whole number). Among men the increase is from 40 percent to 51 percent. This same trend continues when we drop down to row 7—persons 20 to 24 years old. In 1960 only 28 percent of women that age had never married, whereas by 1988, 61 percent were in that category. The pattern is comparable but not as dramatic for 20- to 24-year-old men—53 percent to 78 percent. In short, the proportion of never-married women aged 20 to 24 more than doubled in less than thirty years. Among men, the proportion increased some 46 percent.

Furthermore, if we glance downward over the Table 8-1 columns, we learn, as expected, that for both genders the percentage that had never married declines with age. What is striking, however, are the differences *across* time, especially for women. In 1960 only 11 percent of women aged 25 to 29 had never married; but by 1988 the proportion had risen to 30 percent. For both men and women aged 30 to 34 years, the percentages that *never* married more than doubled between 1960 and 1988.

Age at First Marriage

The trends toward increased numbers of younger persons who have never been married do not mean that most persons do not eventually marry at least once. Although

TABLE 8-1

Percent Single (Never Married), by Age and Sex: 1988, 1980, 1970, and 1960

Age	Women				Men			
	1988	**1980**	**1970**	**1960**	**1988**	**1980**	**1970**	**1960**
Total 15 years and over	22.9	22.5	22.1	17.3	29.9	29.6	28.1	23.2
Under 40 years	40.4	38.8	38.5	28.1	51.1	48.8	47.7	39.6
40 years and over	5.1	5.1	6.2	7.5	5.5	5.7	7.4	7.6
15–17 years	97.7	97.0	97.3	93.2	99.3	99.4	99.4	98.8
18 years	92.4	88.0	82.0	75.6	98.0	97.4	95.1	94.6
19 years	86.0	77.6	68.8	59.7	95.1	90.9	89.9	87.1
20–24 years	61.1	50.2	35.8	28.4	77.7	68.8	54.7	53.1
20 years	78.7	66.5	56.9	46.0	88.5	86.0	78.3	75.8
21 years	71.6	59.7	43.9	34.6	88.7	77.2	66.2	63.4
22 years	58.9	48.3	33.5	25.6	80.4	69.9	52.3	51.6
23 years	56.0	41.7	22.4	19.4	72.7	59.1	42.1	40.5
24 years	43.7	33.5	17.9	15.7	61.2	50.0	33.2	33.4
25–29 years	29.5	20.9	10.5	10.5	43.3	33.1	19.1	20.8
25 years	39.0	28.6	14.0	13.1	56.6	44.3	26.6	27.9
26 years	32.6	22.7	12.2	11.4	49.5	36.5	20.9	23.5
27 years	27.4	22.2	9.1	10.2	44.5	31.5	16.5	19.8
28 years	26.3	16.0	8.9	9.2	33.2	26.8	17.0	17.5
29 years	22.2	14.6	8.0	8.7	31.9	24.0	13.8	16.0
30–34 years	16.1	9.5	6.2	6.9	25.0	15.9	9.4	11.9
35–39	9.0	6.2	5.4	6.1	14.0	7.8	7.2	8.8
40–44	6.2	4.8	4.9	6.1	7.5	7.1	6.3	7.3
45–54	5.1	4.7	4.9	7.0	5.6	6.1	7.5	7.4
55–64	4.0	4.5	6.8	8.0	4.9	5.3	8.0	8.0
55 years and over	5.3	5.9	7.7	8.5	4.6	4.9	7.5	7.7

Note: Figures for 1970 include persons 14 years of age.
Source: U.S. Bureau of the Census, *Current Population Reports,* P-20, #433, March 1988.

Chapter 10 explores legal marriage in depth, it makes sense to look now at the numbers in Table 8-2. These numbers are the logical complement of Table 8-1. Since 1960, the median age at first marriage has been rising steadily for both genders. There is an obvious connection between staying never-married for a longer period and marrying when one is older. Thus far, at least for most persons in the United States, staying never-married tends to postpone, but not eliminate, eventual first marriage.

Demographers are fond of pointing out a very interesting fact about Table 8-2: The trends toward increased age at first marriage that began in 1960 represent a *reversal* of the trend that had been occurring during the seventy years since 1890. From 1890 to 1955, age at first marriage had been steadily declining for both genders. Jay Teachman and colleagues note that "a particularly steep decline [in age at first marriage] occurred during the 1940s and 1950s."[13] Chapter 7 described the 1950s as the Golden Age of the Modern Family. It

TABLE 8-2
Median Age of Men and Women at First Marriage, 1890 to 1988

Year	Men	Women
1988	25.9	23.6
1985	25.5	23.3
1980	24.7	22.0
1975	23.5	21.1
1970	23.2	20.8
1965	22.8	20.6
1960	22.8	20.3
1955	22.6	20.2
1950	22.8	20.3
1940	24.3	21.5
1930	24.3	21.3
1920	24.6	21.2
1910	25.1	21.6
1900	25.9	21.9
1890	26.1	22.0

Note: A standard error of 0.2 years is appropriate to measure sampling variability for any of the above median ages at first marriage, based on current population survey data. *Source:* U.S. Bureau of the Census, *Current Population Reports*, P-20, #433, March 1988.

TABLE 8-3
Percentages of Persons Never Married in the United States, 15 Years of Age and Over, by Gender and Ethnic Category, March 1988

	White	Hispanic	Black
Both genders	24.4	32.1	39.4
Men	28.1	36.9	42.5
Women	20.9	27.3	36.9

Source: U.S. Bureau of the Census, *Current Population Reports*, P-20, #433, March 1988.

seemed that everyone, including adolescents, could hardly wait to get married. After the fifties, however, growing numbers of persons began to postpone their first marriage. The result was that a demographic trend that had gone on for decades was suddenly halted. That reversal is part of what Cargan and Melko meant when they said that some things began to change during the sixties and seventies.

Racial and Ethnic Patterns

Table 8-3 compares never-marrieds among whites, blacks, and Hispanics. It shows that in 1988, among persons 15 years and older blacks were most likely to have never been married, followed by Hispanics and finally by whites. Moreover, in each of these three ethnic categories men were more likely to be never-married than women, with black men least likely to have *ever* been married. Later in the chapter

we look at educated black singles. But for the time being we can say that in spite of some differences between these three categories, they are quite comparable: Throughout the past three decades, the demographic trend has been toward increases in the proportions of younger aged persons who have never been married.

Cross-National Patterns

This trend toward increases in the proportions of younger never-married persons has also been occurring in most other Western societies, including Canada, Sweden, the United Kingdom, West Germany, and France.[14] According to Dutch sociologists Buunk and van Driel, most Europeans evaluate the idea of having never been married in a much more positive light than do most North Americans.[15] For example, they report that in the Netherlands, "virtually all adults approve of women living as singles." By comparison, we learned earlier that a quarter of Americans still withhold that sort of social approval.

Trends among Divorced Persons

As we learned earlier, figuring precisely what single means is not a simple task. Besides the never-married, "single" also includes divorced persons. Table 8-4 compares the number of divorced persons against clusters of

TABLE 8-4
Divorced Persons per 1,000 Married Persons with Spouse Present by Age, Sex, and Race,* 1988, 1980, 1970, and 1960

	Total	Race		
		White	Black	Hispanic
Both sexes:				
1988	133	124	263	137
1980	100	92	203	98
1970	47	44	83	61
1960	35	33	62	NA
Male:				
1988	110	102	216	106
1980	79	74	149	64
1970	35	32	62	40
1960	28	27	45	NA
Female:				
1988	156	146	311	167
1980	120	110	258	132
1970	60	56	104	81
1960	42	38	78	NA

NA, not available.
*Persons of Hispanic origin may be of any race.
Source: 1970 Hispanic data: *1970 Census of Population,* Vol. II, 1C, Persons of Spanish Origin; 1960 black data: *1960 Census of Population,* Vol. II, 1C, Nonwhite Population by Race; 1980s' data: U.S. Bureau of the Census, *Current Population Reports,* P-20, #433, March 1988.

one-thousand married persons living with their spouses. On the basis of that criterion, column 1 and row 4 of Table 8-4 reveals that in 1960, among all races and genders, for every thousand marrieds there were only thirty-five divorced persons. By 1988 (row 1) that number had increased almost fourfold, to 133. If we compare the three ethnic categories in columns 2, 3, and 4, we learn that in 1988 there were more than twice as many black divorced persons as white or Hispanic. Overall, Table 8-4 shows that among women and men, whether white, black, or Hispanic, there have been steady increases in this type of singleness between 1960 and 1988. The result is that in the United States, there are many more divorced singles now than there were three decades ago. Thus, when we think about increases in the

numbers of singles since 1960, we must keep in mind both the never-marrieds and the formerly-marrieds.

Singles within the Total Population

Table 8-5 shows the increases in both categories of singles between 1960 and 1988, based on the total population. It reports what the Census Bureau calls "marital status." Marital status is calculated on the entire population of Americans. By March 1988, 26 percent of Americans 15 years old and over had never been married, and 7 percent were divorced. (This figure does not include divorced persons who had remarried.) Those two numbers add up to 33 percent. If we add the percentage (7%) who were widowed in 1988, the total goes up

TABLE 8-5
Marital Status Distributions of All Persons in the United States Aged 15 Years and Over by Gender, March 1960 and March 1988   (In Percent)

	1988			1960		
	Both genders	Men	Women	Both genders	Men	Women
Never-married	26.3	29.9	22.9	22.0	25.3	19.0
Married/spouse:						
Present	55.8	58.3	53.6	63.1	65.7	61.1
Absent	3.3	2.9	3.7	4.8	3.9	5.7
Separated	2.4	2.0	2.7	1.7	1.4	2.0
Other	0.9	0.9	0.8	3.1	2.5	3.7
Widowed	7.2	2.5	11.4	8.1	3.5	12.1
Divorced	7.4	6.4	8.4	2.2	1.8	2.1

Source: U.S. Bureau of the Census, *Current Population Reports,* P-20, #105, 1960; P-20, #433, March 1988.

to 40 percent (almost 41% if unrounded percentages are added). This is the percentage of singles in the 1988 U.S. population as measured formally—by current legal status. Table 8-5 also reveals that all of these figures have increased since 1960 except for persons currently widowed.

What about the 2 percent of persons in Table 8-5 who in 1988 were separated from their legal spouses? Were they single or not? Strictly speaking, they were not single. But in the minds of many people, the term "separated," like the term "single," usually conveys the idea of someone living alone.

Living Arrangements

Trends in Informal Co-residence To what extent do single people, whether never-married, divorced, or widowed, live alone? During the 1950s, when separation and divorce were much rarer than today, most separated persons did indeed live alone.[16] But today? It's far less certain that this will be the case. Although separated from their legal spouse, they may be co-

residing with someone else (Chapter 9 explores *informal marriage*). Table 8-6 shows the increases since 1960 in the numbers of what the Census Bureau calls "unmarried couple households." Such a household is "composed of two unrelated adults of the opposite sex . . . who share a housing unit."[17] Hence, one or both members of a *cohabiting couple* could simultaneously be married to, but separated from, their legal spouse. Indeed, the cohabiting couple may consist of any combination of married and separated, never-married, divorced, or widowed persons.

What is especially striking about Table 8-6 is that it shows that over a thirty-year period, the total number of U.S. cohabitor households has increased almost six times, from 439,000 to 2,588,000. And interestingly, 31 percent of that figure includes households with children under 15 years of age.

Trends in Lone Living Even though we just said that being single does not necessarily mean living alone, the overall picture can be complicated. For example, let's examine per-

TABLE 8-6
**Unmarried-Couple Households, by Presence of Children, 1960 to 1988
(Numbers in Thousands)**

Year	Total	Without children under 15 years	With children under 15 years
1988	2,588	1,786	802
1980	1,589	1,159	431
1970	523	327	196
1960	439	242	197

Source: 1960 and 1970 data: U.S. Bureau of the Census, *1960 Census of Population,* PC(2)-4B, Persons by Family Characteristics, table 15; *1970 Census of Population,* PC(2)-4B, table 11; 1980s' data: U.S. Bureau of the Census, *Current Population Reports,* P-20, #433, March 1988.

sons who are not cohabiting and do indeed reside alone. The Census Bureau uses the technical label "nonfamily householder" to describe such persons.[18] In prior years their technical label was "primary individual." These kinds of householders may currently be never-married, divorced, married and separated, or widowed. Paul Glick said that the "rate of increase in lone living has been far and away the greatest among adults in their twenties and thirties."[19] Table 8-7 shows that between 1960 and 1980 among women and men 18 to 24 years old, there were indeed substantial increases in the percentages of them genuinely living alone. Although by 1988 the percentages had leveled off and even dropped slightly, the thirty-year trend seemed clear enough.

A number of sociologists speculate about the reason for the recent leveling off in the popularity of "lone living."[20] In light of Table 8-6, as well as the broader discussion in Chapter 9, it seems that growing numbers of younger persons are opting for something else. Increasing numbers are choosing to cohabit. In looking back at the sixties and seventies, we can say that one of the first kinds of diversity that became popular during those decades was singleness in the form of delaying marriage and living alone. A second expression of diversity has now become popular. That is to delay marriage, but not to live alone.

Table 8-7 shows that among slightly older women and men (aged 25–34 years) there was also a leveling off in lone living by 1988, but

TABLE 8-7
Percentages of Nonfamily Householders, by Gender, 1988, 1980, 1970, 1960

	1988	1980	1970	1960
Ages 18–24 years:				
Both genders	8.7	9.5	4.8	2.4
Men	9.8	11.1	5.4	2.7
Women	7.7	8.1	4.2	2.2
Ages 25–34 years:				
Both genders	12.6	12.0	4.9	2.9
Men	16.0	15.3	6.5	3.7
Women	10.0	8.8	3.5	2.1

Source: U.S. Bureau of the Census, *Current Population Reports,* P-20, #433, March 1988.

there was no decline. Over a thirty-year period, the proportion of men in this age bracket living alone went up almost four and one-half times (3.7% to 16%), and among women it went up almost five times (2.1% to 10%). In both age categories, men are more likely than women to be doing the lone living.

Young Adults Living with Parents: The Boomerang Generation   According to George Masnick and Mary Jo Bane, the trends in lone living shown in Table 8-7 represented a dramatic departure from the past because "traditionally, adults have lived in households with other adults."[21] Cohabitation is one mechanism that is reducing the amount of lone living. Living with parents is another. The media have nicknamed adults returning to the parental home as the "boomerang generation."[22] Just when parents believe they have finally gotten rid of their adult children, and can now have a life of their own, the offspring surprise them and move back in. The U.S. Census Bureau reports that "between 1960 and 1990, the proportion of persons 18–24 years old who lived in the home of their parents in 1990 increased from 43 percent to 53 percent."[23] Furthermore, the trend among persons 25 to 34 years old was in the same direction: The number increased from 9 percent in 1960 to 12 percent in 1990. Of 18- to 24-year-olds living with parents in 1990, 97 percent had never been married. The figure was 80 percent for 25- to 34-year-olds. One frequently voiced explanation for this particular trend is the shrinking job market facing many of today's young adults, making them unable to support themselves on their own.[24]

Couples Living in Separate Households Let's complicate things even further by focusing on another set of well-known behavior patterns. Chapters 4 and 5 talked about girlfriends/boyfriends. Although they are erotic friends, each partner retains her or his own

household. Because they keep their own household, they are not census-defined cohabitors. Some are classified as living alone; others have children living with them. A crucial point about these kinds of couples is that they spend considerable amounts of time sharing the same physical space, whether in her or his household.[25] They may also share a great deal of time together outside of either household, including whole days or nights or whole weeks together. These persons are technically "single" (except for those who are separated), but they are clearly not *alone*.

Furthermore, the behavior of the couples is virtually indistinguishable from that of married or cohabiting couples. This is especially true if one or both partners are living with children. These couples are part of the diversity of families we've been talking about since Chapter 1. Up through the fifties, "dating" indicated a very different way of living from, say, engagement or marriage. Today, however, any distinctions in the ways that girlfriends/boyfriends, cohabitors, and marrieds live on a day-to-day basis have gotten increasingly blurred. If you went to a park on a Sunday afternoon and watched two couples strolling (each with two children), you'd be hard pressed to distinguish between couple *A* (divorced man and separated woman who even though they have their own households spend five nights per week together) and couple *B* (legally married, but he's out of town on business several nights per week, while she's an emergency-room physician who must work odd shifts).

Unfortunately, since the Census Bureau doesn't collect information on dual-household couples, we cannot document, say, trends in numbers of partial nights (she makes him leave at 5:30 a.m. before her child and/or the neighbors wake up) shared together. Nor can we document trends in whole nights, entire weekends, or entire vacation periods, that these couples might share together. Nevertheless, it seems safe to assert that the numbers of such couples, as well as their proportions of the whole population, are not likely to diminish any time soon.

FOUR OUTLOOKS ON SINGLENESS

In spite of how complicated singleness is becoming in modern societies, most of us still want to simplify things by slicing the world in two parts—single and married. The reason is not hard to figure out. Chapters 9 and 10 show that marriage rituals of any kind (even if done in the county jail basement by a magistrate in the presence of one witness) separate the washed from the unwashed. Formal marriage is taken as a sign of social seriousness, and married persons are blessed with public approval. Thus far we've seen that singleness consists of many different outward statuses (divorced, etc.). In addition, singleness gets complicated because of the different ways that single persons view themselves and their lives.

Voluntary and Resolved

For example, among the women in Adams' study "there was an almost universal emphasis on personal independence as the most valuable feature of being single."[26] What Adams calls the "blessedness" of being single arises from the degrees of freedom, autonomy, and self-determination that it allows. Peter Stein and also Arthur Shostak label the kinds of singles that Adams studied as "voluntary" and "resolved" singles.[27] According to Stein and Shostak, those kinds of singles consciously prefer *not* to be married. They choose to remain single regardless of whether they are currently never-married, divorced, widowed, or perhaps cohabiting. But since the label "single" conveys the *absence* of something, namely, marriage, Adams would prefer to give singleness a more positive connotation. For instance, years ago the Census Bureau used the term "nonwhite" to describe blacks. African-Americans insisted that instead of nonwhite the Census should use "black," to indicate the positive features of being black, rather than the absence of something. Adams talks about "single pride" in the same ways that African-Americans refer to black pride. Adams argues that there's something special (blessed) about being a resolved and voluntary single, and that specialness is a high degree of freedom and autonomy.

Another label for these particular kinds of singles is *freepersons*. Adams says that resolved and voluntary singles have their own unique and highly satisfying lifestyle. This lifestyle is different from that of marrieds, and should not be judged by marriage standards. Adams also says that freepersons, like blacks, are a distinct *minority category* who suffer discrimination because they are judged as deviant and irresponsible by the larger society.[28] Adams does not want freepersons to view themselves as unworthy anymore than black leaders want blacks to see themselves this way. Adams believes that freepersons should think of themselves as unique: They possess the freedom to control their own lives and destinies in ways that are totally beyond married persons.

Voluntary and Ambivalent

Three other categories of singles stand in sharp contrast with the lifestyle of freepersons.[29] One is called "voluntary and ambivalent." These are persons (never-married, divorced, or widowed, perhaps cohabiting) who are definitely not searching for a spouse—they tend to be oblivious to the idea of marriage. They have, however, not explicitly rejected the idea of perhaps eventually getting married. Other things are currently more important to them—education, occupational achievement, travel, dependent children, and so on. Although their current focus is on their independence and freedom, they might consider negotiating away some of that autonomy if an exceptionally suitable person appeared on the horizon.

Involuntary Wishfuls

"Involuntary wishfuls" is another category of singles. These are persons who definitely and explicitly believe in marriage.[30] They are currently and actively seeking a spouse. Furthermore, they would like to have one as soon as possible. They do not prefer being single, nor do they consider autonomy as great a blessing as that of having their loneliness relieved. Relief, they believe, would come with their spouse, along with a sense of identity and the escape from a lesser (deviant) status.

Involuntary Regretfuls

The final category of singles is called "involuntary regretfuls." Just like the wishfuls, they would prefer to be married. But unlike the wishfuls, the regretfuls have given up the quest for the holy grail and have resigned themselves to fate's decree that they accept singleness as a "life sentence."[31] According to Shostak, the regretful status is likely to be common among women over age 30 who are well educated and in high-status occupations. One reason is that since men tend to marry women younger than themselves, the pool of eligible spouses—men who are also well educated and high status—shrinks for these women. Draining the pool still further is the fact that it's far more common in the United States for a higher status man to marry a woman with less education and status than it is for a higher status woman to do same thing.[32]

SINGLENESS AMONG EDUCATED AFRICAN-AMERICANS

Staples reports that educated black women have faced the reality of a tiny pool of eligible men much longer than educated white women.[33] This reality took root in the rural South during the decades following the Civil War. Young black men, it was thought, could earn money by participating in the then dominant farming economy of the South. Consequently, education was not a priority for these men. In sharp contrast, blacks thought the only way their daughters could earn money was through education. Hence, women became elementary and secondary school teachers, and later on nurses, librarians, and social workers. Although these black women worked in segregated facilities, they were becoming a part of the newly emerging professional middle class.

As African-Americans moved to the urban North throughout the twentieth century, black women continued to enter higher education. Urban black men began to pursue higher education as well, but at a lower rate than black women. In 1956, some 62 percent of all the college degrees earned by blacks went to women.[34] The gap in numbers of educated black women and men began to close during the sixties and seventies. Nevertheless, as late as 1977 there were 84,000 more black women enrolled in U.S. colleges than black men.[35] In contrast, 672,000 more white men than white women were enrolled in colleges during that same year. And in 1988, for African-Americans the "same pattern exists today."[36] Black women continue to enroll in and to graduate from college in greater numbers than black men.

In short, for historic reasons that seem to persist to the present, educated black women have always faced a disproportionately smaller pool of eligible spouses than educated white women. Robert Staples adds an additional factor that further reduces the numbers of educated black men available to black women. Black men are three times more likely than black women to marry "outside their race."[37] And the men most likely to do that, says Staples, are blacks who are well educated. (Clarence Thomas, the black man appointed to the U.S. Supreme Court in 1991, is a well-known example.) Consequently, cross-racial marriages further drain the short supply of eligible men available to higher-status black women.

UNSETTLED QUESTIONS

Well-Being, Loneliness, and Suicide

Earlier we said that because singleness is considered less than ideal, nonsingles often have negative feelings about singles, and many singles have negative feelings about themselves. To try to measure these negative feelings, researchers ask questions about what they call "well-being." And they also ask questions about loneliness. Well-being is often measured by asking persons how happy they are with their lives in general, and/or with some specific aspect of it such as their occupation, or being single, or being married. Up to now, most studies have revealed that singles tend to report less happiness than marrieds, and to be less satisfied with their lives.[38] Well-being can also be measured by asking persons about their symptoms of stress. For example, Cargan and Melko report that compared with marrieds, the singles they studied were more likely to feel: anxious, guilty, despondent, and worthless.[39] Interestingly enough, however, marrieds were more likely than singles to have headaches, insomnia, or ulcers.

But on another dimension of well-being—reports of contemplated or attempted suicide—singles ranked higher than marrieds: 55 percent to 35 percent.[40] A hundred years ago, the pioneer and influential sociologist Émile Durkheim was the first researcher to discover empirical connections between singleness and actual suicide.[41] On the basis of numbers from late nineteenth-century census reports for France and several other Central European societies, he found that singles were more likely than marrieds to have committed suicide. Given the apparent connections between singleness and suicide, it should come as no surprise that many studies have found that singles tend to report greater loneliness than marrieds.[42] Cargan and Melko found the same thing. They add that compared with marrieds, singles are more likely to report they have no one with whom they can share things, or talk to, about life's everyday happenings. Singles are also more likely to feel depressed when, in their homes, they enter an empty room or eat alone.

Freedom and Belonging

How can we square these findings—that singles tend to have less well-being and greater loneliness—with Adams saying that singleness is blessed? And equally puzzling, if singleness is so unpleasant, why are growing numbers of persons in postmodern societies spending increasing years of their lives being single? Why are they spending more time than ever before as never-married, separated, divorced, or widowed? We begin to answer those questions by reminding ourselves that Adams labeled only one category of singles as blessed, namely, the voluntary and resolved, or what we called freepersons. Shostak says it's a serious error to compare the well-being of singles with nonsingles without first taking into account precisely which category of singles we're talking about. For example, suppose we compared only freepersons and marrieds of the same race and gender, who are well educated and aged 30 to 45 years. If we compared these two categories, we might expect to find no differences at all in their levels of well-being or loneliness? Why not?

The main reason goes back to some things already said. Remember that research shows that stress is lower, and feelings of well-being are higher, when persons feel they're in control of their lives. Freepersons are quite likely to feel they're in control because control (freedom, independence, autonomy) is the fundamental reason they choose to be nonmarried in the first place. Freepersons tend to be quite suspicious of marriage precisely because they believe it will limit their freedom to be and do the things they strongly wish to be and do. Unlike those in the other three categories of singles, freepersons have no desire whatsoever to "graduate" into marriage. The other three categories of singles define their lifestyles as *temporary*, but freepersons define theirs as *permanent*.

It would seem that persons who view their lifestyles as permanent feel in control—they're currently achieving what they wish to achieve. By contrast, persons who view an important aspect of their lives as temporary are not achieving what they wish. They want to be something other than what they are. It should not be at all surprising that many of these singles experience stress and loneliness. But the reason for their stress and loneliness *is not singleness in and of itself*. The basic reason is that they do not currently have what they want—they lack the sense of control of their lives that most voluntary resolveds have most of the time.

A Special We-Group   It's extremely vital that we keep in mind some other things about freepersons. Earlier chapters said that a primary group is a place where a person feels a unique and special sense of we-ness with the other person, or persons, in the group. A we-group supplies a sense of belonging, identity, meaning, and security. There are several kinds of relationships a freeperson can cultivate to gain that sense of belonging, of "being special." Besides possibly having children in the household, Adams makes it clear that freepersons may have a "special person" in their life. They may have an erotic friendship in which they maintain separate households but share a good deal of physical proximity. Or they may share the same household with their partner (cohabit). They may have a significant nonerotic (platonic) friendship with a person

of the same or opposite gender. They may simultaneously have both a platonic and an erotic, friendship with different persons. In addition, they may belong to a closely knit friendship network and/or to a social family, as described in Chapters 2 and 3.

Each of us knows that being married is no guarantee of feeling that "I belong in a special way to my special person who belongs to me in the same way." When we compare freepersons and marrieds, we thus want to find out how strongly both sets of women feel that sense of we-ness. Some married women may possess merely tepid feelings of we-ness, or bonding, with their spouse and be in what Chapter 5 called a dissolution phase of their erotic friendship. Those wives are likely to have less sense of well-being, and to experience greater loneliness, than freepersons who feel a keen sense of we-ness with their special person.

One reason increasing numbers of people today are choosing singleness is because of social conditions in the larger society. Postmodern societies allow persons to have two highly valued dimensions of what it means to be fully human: They can be autonomous and can simultaneously belong to an erotic friendship that is defined as permanent. That is not to say, however, that cetain degrees of autonomy and freedom are not relinquished in an erotic friendship. The only freeperson who doesn't have to negotiate constantly with her or his erotic friend is the one with no partner! Later chapters (especially Chapter 11) show that negotiation indicates a willingness to share power, control, and influence over one's own destiny.[43] Negotiation lies at the core of contemporary relationships because it is the prime means of balancing the often contradictory demands for both autonomy *and* belonging.

Modern media and contemporary literature, as well as their own personal experiences and their observations of kin and friends, have led many persons to recognize that being married can produce the bitterest kind of loneliness. Growing numbers of persons have become aware that they can enjoy much of what they want outside of and apart from marriage. Chapters 9 and 10 show, however, that one thing they *cannot* have outside of marriage (at least in the United States) is the social approval, prestige, and esteem that come simply with marriage. Consequently, most singles are not resolved and voluntary—they wish themselves on the road to "something better." Today's never-married persons do, however, postpone marriage as long as they can in hopes that when they eventually do marry, they will experience that special sense of belonging, of we-ness. Many formerly married persons eventually remarry for precisely the same reason.

Changes in Outlooks

Persons, and their primary relationships, are continually changing in one way or another. And those ongoing changes are occurring in the context of societies that are also in constant flux. Consequently, we must bear in mind that no matter which of the four outlooks on singleness a person currently holds, she or he can eventually adapt a different one.[44] Over time a freeperson (voluntary and resolved) can shift into being voluntary and ambivalent, or vice versa, and so on for the other categories. For example, a woman who at age 18 graduates from high school and begins clerking at K-Mart is likely to be an involuntary wishful. She marries but soon discovers that she is lonelier than she was before. At age 23 she divorces and gains custody of her child. She's employed but also enrolls part-time at her local community college. Her outlook on singleness shifts into being voluntary ambivalent—she's concentrating on her job, her child, and getting her degree. Since her complicated life demands maximum flexibility, she has neither time for nor interest in marriage. But she never

rules it out entirely. And later on? She may retain her current outlook on singleness or adapt a different one.

Singleness is but one example of the many ways in which people in today's postmodern societies are creating new ways of organizing their lives. During the 1970s, Adams urged singles to "set up their own standards and initiate their own life patterns."[45] Because U.S. mortality rates have been declining and citizens are living longer than ever before, they have the potential to spend many more years of their lives as married persons and as resident parents than did their own parents or any of their forebears. But instead of doing that, Susan Watkins and co-workers found that today's adults are spending fewer years as spouses and as resident parents than their forebears, even though they are living longer.[46]

What are they doing with those extra years of life? Throughout their life courses they are being single in the many different ways we have defined that term in this chapter. Furthermore, they are being single in the senses urged by Adams—they're creating new and different ways of life. John Modell calls it being "modern in a new way."[47] He says it represents the "emergence of a new phase of life for Americans." Americans have "taken control of the construction" of their "emotional relationships," and they've done so in a kind of ad lib (unplanned) fashion. This recent innovative behavior by Americans, Modell says, has been part of European societies for some time.[48]

Being Temporary   Another way that Europeans and North Americans differ is that here many innovations tend—so far at least—to be viewed as temporary. Chapter 9 shows that after a cohabiting couple have been together for a certain amount of time, they begin to sense certain vibrations from friends and families. Through subtle messages, relatives, friends, and co-workers begin to enforce the idea that the couple should get serious or get out. Paul Glick and Graham Spanier concluded that cohabitation is perceived as merely a temporary situation.[49] They added that it is defined as temporary to keep the couple from having children. As he described lone living, Glick said it had become socially "acceptable, especially if it turned out to be temporary.[50] Why this fear that singles' innovations should be anything but temporary and child-free? The response, of course, is that since the Benchmark Family is defined as the cultural ideal, any other *public* arrangements that possess both permanence and children might be perceived as undermining the ideal. Permanence and children add a considerable degree of cultural legitimacy to a relationship, and inevitably raise the serious question as to how this relationship might in fact differ from the Benchmark.

Compared to the 1950s, singleness today has many different meanings—including that of being an unmarried woman with two children living in a shelter for the homeless.

In several European cultures, single persons having children is no longer a strong prohibition.[51] If anything, it could be argued that in those cultures, parenting is becoming defined as the *right* of every responsible adult regardless of marital status.[52] In U.S. society, however, a great deal of ambivalence persists regarding single parenting. On the one hand it is increasingly accepted (grudgingly) as an unwelcome but inevitable fact of modern life. On the other hand there are enormous social pressures on single parents to make the status *temporary*—to get out of that status as quickly as possible and get (re)married.[53]

The fact is that during the last several decades throughout all Western societies there have been steady increases in singles residing with children, and this represents significant social change. In describing U.S. trends in "mother-led families," Kenneth Fox shows that their numbers have been growing very rapidly among whites.[54] He adds that instead of indicating "family disintegration," these trends in single women with children might be part of women's "struggles to escape dependence on marriage for economic support." Modell, too, reminds us that women's struggles for greater control of their own economic and personal destinies lie at the core of all the changes we have examined in the lives of singles.[55]

Women and Innovation   In her book, Adams describes a particular kind of single woman that she says was quite common to her native Britain from the 1920s to the early 1960s. Since World War I (1914–1918) had decimated the population of young males, many women of that era had no choice but to remain never-married. Of these a goodly number became educated professionals and filled jobs for which, because of the war, there were no available men. The women were earnest, dedicated, highly competent, and single-minded professionals. Jessie Bernard, in her book, *Academic Women*, shows that such women could be found during the 1950s at American universities as well.[56] However, both Adams and Bernard make it clear that these single professional women were not innovators in the senses described here: They did not maintain public erotic friendships. Neither were they cohabiters or solo parents, as described in Chapter 16.

By contrast, what is novel about many of today's women is that they are not willing to compete with men merely for equal economic opportunities.[57] They also want the same choices regarding sexuality, relationships, and parenting. Women's desires for autonomy in both the economic and personal realms go hand in glove. Women's interest in occupational involvement makes it possible for them to bring about changes in the ways single women *and* men live. These changes simply would not happen without women's occupational involvement. Changes in the occupational world inevitably bring about changes in the personal realm. Having tasted relative freedom in the occupational world, most of today's women also seek it in the personal realm. Most of the professional women described by Adams and Bernard not only denied themselves erotic friendships (or for that matter even casual sex, since "immorality" would have threatened their livelihoods) and solo parenting, they'd also made up their minds they would not marry even if the opportunity presented itself. Although marriage would have supplied them sex, it would have ended or crippled their careers in ways far more devastating than anything imaginable today. Dorothy Sayers, the well-known British writer of *The Lord Wimsey* detective stories, was a striking exception to the prevailing pattern among well-educated professional women of the 1920s and 1930s. Not only was she an eminent university professor who never married, she was also a single parent.

CONCLUSION—BEING SINGLE AND RESPONSIBLE

Through the 1950s, being a *responsible adult* meant not being single any longer than one had to. It meant settling down, getting married, having children, and then staying married for the sake of the children. But in recent decades, many persons have squarely faced what they always knew: Being a stably married parent by no means guarantees social responsibility. "Responsible" is something that people choose to be whatever their social circumstances: married or single, with or without an erotic friendship, with or without children. Moreover, during recent decades social conditions have been changing, making it possible for adults, women in particular, to have a greater range of choices than ever before. Some adults exercise those choices responsibly, and some do not. Being single or married has virtually nothing to do with it.

It's useless to ask if men would have pressed for the changes described throughout this and other chapters if women had not. The facts are that women are pressing, that men are relatively less eager for change, and that significant changes are happening throughout Western societies. Moreover, it seems improbable that in the foreseeable future these kinds of changes will go away. Instead, they seem likely to increase in both frequency and tempo. Understanding the changes, as well as the continuities, regarding singleness helps us better understand the other shifts, as well as the sameness, described in this book.

NOTES

1. Harold Saltzman, "No kick from the Champagne," *Newsweek*, June 24, 1991, p. 8.
2. Adams, 1976, p. 50.
3. Middlefort, 1972, p. 196; cited in Lips, 1991, p. 23.
4. Ibid., p. 22.

5. Buunk and van Driel, 1989, p. 25.
6. Adams, p. 5; Cargan and Melko, 1982, pp. 203–205.
7. Adams, p. 50.
8. Ibid.
9. Rodin, 1990.
10. Murstein, 1974.
11. Yankelovich, 1981.
12. Ibid.
13. Teachman, Polonko, and Scanzoni, 1987, p. 5.
14. Buunk, 1983; Bernardes, 1986; Popenoe, 1988; Moen, 1989; Jones, Marsden, and Tepperman, 1990.
15. Buunk and van Driel, p. 26.
16. Goode, 1956.
17. U.S. Bureau of the Census, *Current Population Reports,* P-20, No. 433, March 1988, p. 67.
18. Ibid.
19. Glick, 1988, p. 867.
20. Bumpass and Sweet, 1989; Bumpass, 1990; Bumpass, Sweet, and Cherlin, 1991.
21. Masnick and Bane, 1980, p. 19.
22. Melynda Dovel Cox, "Life with the 'Boomerang Generation,' " *The Gainesville, Florida, Sun,* January 6, 1993, p. 1D (from *Kiplinger's Personal Finance Magazine*).
23. U.S. Bureau of the Census, *Current Population Reports,* P-20, No. 450, May 1991, p. 10.
24. Buchmann, 1989; Aquilino, 1990; Ward and Spitze, 1992.
25. Trost, 1979; Macklin, 1983.
26. Adams, p. 205.
27. Stein, 1981; Shostak, 1987.
28. Adams, pp. 14, 15.
29. Stein; Shostak.
30. Stein, p. 11.
31. Shostak, p. 357.
32. Doudna and McBride, 1981, p. 23.
33. Staples, 1981a, b.
34. Staples, 1981b, p. 43.
35. Ibid.
36. Jewell, 1988, p. 75.
37. Staples, 1981b, p. 43.
38. Cargan and Melko, pp. 197–198; Shostak, pp. 358–359.
39. Cargan and Melko, p. 198.
40. Ibid., p. 199.
41. Durkheim, 1951, p. 176.
42. Shostak, p. 357; Cargan and Melko, p. 210.
43. See Scanzoni & Godwin, 1990.
44. Shostak, p. 356.
45. Adams, p. 50.
46. Watkins, Menkin, and Bongaarts, 1987.
47. Modell, 1989, p. 324.
48. Ibid., p. 324.
49. Glick and Spanier, 1981, p. 196.
50. Glick, 1988, p. 867.
51. Buunk.
52. Popenoe; Manniche, 1985.
53. Thompson and Gongla, 1983.
54. Fox, 1986, p. 237.
55. Modell, p. 328.
56. Bernard, 1964.
57. Jeanne Spurlock, 1990.

CHAPTER 9

COHABITATION—THE SPREAD OF INFORMAL MARRIAGES

Chapter 8 talked about singleness as a prime example of the ways in which people are reinventing today's families. We learned that one of the chief reasons singleness has gotten to be so complicated is because of the ever-increasing popularity of cohabitation. That's what this chapter is all about.

DOMESTIC PARTNERSHIP ORDINANCES

"Your federal tax dollars ... will pay for ... unhealthy lifestyles." So said *Washington Watch*, the publication of a Religious Right political organization that successfully lobbied Congress to defeat a domestic partnership bill proposed for the District of Columbia.[1] Previously, the D.C. city council had unanimously passed an ordinance allowing city workers to enroll the person with whom they were living in the insurance plan (medical, life, disability, etc.) provided by the city. Married persons had enjoyed that fringe benefit for a long time. The bill would have expanded it to just about anyone sharing a household "including siblings or platonic friends."[2] A number of cities through-

out the United States have recently passed domestic partnership (DP) ordinances, but unlike D.C. they do not count sibs or just-friends as domestic partners. The other ordinances are "exclusively limited to [adult] cohabitants who have a stable, intimate relationship and are financially interdependent."[3]

Not all of those cities grant fringe benefits in their DP statutes. In some places, the DP ordinance simply lets people "declare [publicly] that they have an intimate relationship, that they have lived together at least six months and that they will be jointly responsible for living expenses."[4] In other places, DP ordinances require hospitals and jails to allow domestic partners visiting rights that are usually restricted to spouse and blood kin. San Francisco, West Hollywood, Santa Cruz, and Berkeley, California; Madison, Wisconsin; Tacoma Park, Maryland; Ithaca, New York; Seattle, Washington; and Ann Arbor, Michigan have various kinds of DP ordinances. Recently, Cambridge, Massachusetts, and New York City also began to permit couples to formally register what Chapter 5 called their erotic friendship.[5] A number of additional cities are considering DP ordinances as well. Furthermore, several private firms have allowed employees to enroll their domestic partners in their fringe benefit programs. With 23,000 workers, Levi Strauss is so far the largest of these companies. Others include Lotus Development Corporation, Ben & Jerry's Homemade Ice Cream, Inc., and Apple Computer Company.

Religious Reactions to DP Codes

When Apple first proposed to build a new plant that would create more than 1,500 high-tech jobs for a Texas town, civic leaders were ecstatic. However, after conservative religious groups discovered that Apple has a DP policy, they pressured the city council to back out of the deal. Only after intense lobbying from community business leaders did the council reverse itself to approve the deal by one vote.[6] Groups opposing Apple said they feared its domestic partnership policy would help legitimate homosexual lifestyles. Among other things, the groups claimed that those lifestyles spread AIDS, for which taxpayers end up paying huge bills. The groups were also keenly aware that DP ordinances help legitimate the lifestyles of heterosexual cohabitors. Among cities and companies that have DP ordinances, heterosexuals make up anywhere from 70 to 84 percent of the couples taking advantage of them.[7] Because there are millions more of them in the population, heterosexuals stand to benefit to a much larger degree than homosexuals from DP legislation.

But whether for gays/lesbians or straights, conservative religious groups vigorously oppose DP policies because they believe that the policies undermine the Benchmark Family. At the very core of The Family, they argue, is *legal heterosexual marriage.* They, along with other citizens located in the center of Figure 1-1, believe that legal marriage is socially and morally superior to any other arrangement. Their position is based on two major reasons,

each comprising a number of important facets. These two reasons can be gleaned from the statements of Ms. Ellen Graham who, along with her husband Charles, filed a lawsuit seeking to overturn the DP statute passed by Ann Arbor.

First, said Ms. Graham, "'[The statute] really implies a sexual relationship among unmarried couples.'"[8] Chapter 4 reported that throughout North America a yawning chasm exists between what people say about sex and how they actually behave. On one hand, people tend to say that, ideally, sex should be saved for a formal marriage that lasts a lifetime, that is, *abstinence* followed by monogamy is the best policy. On the other hand, people admit that they behave in less than ideal fashion—most nonmarried people have sex, and some married people have sex with persons beside their spouse. In justifying either type of behavior, people often say, "Well, it just happened—I didn't plan it." Or, "We love each other." Few persons will openly affirm that they believe in what Chapter 4 calls *responsible indulgence,* that is, that sex is right and good in and of itself as long as it is done responsibly. For many citizens, only marital sex exists under the tent of social legitimacy, and thus respectability.

However, as Ms. Graham correctly observed, DP ordinances convey an aura of legitimacy and respectability to nonmarital sex that simply wasn't there before. In most places in North America, the police generally ignore unmarried couples who live together even though fornication is against the law. Cities with DP ordinances not only officially recognize those couples, however, they sometimes accord them privileges once reserved exclusively for marrieds. Instead of being punished for breaking state laws prohibiting fornication, they are now rewarded for "openly living in sin." DP statutes indeed help close the gap between what people say they believe about sex and how they actually behave. Domestic partnership laws are passed as a response to the ways in which ordinary people are already carrying on their everyday lives. When heterosexual cohabitation first came to the public's attention during the early seventies, many citizens reacted with fear and outrage.[9] Certain employers would not hire cohabitors, and fired employees who were found out. Some landlords would not knowingly rent to cohabitors and would evict them if they were discovered. Now, however, the degree of public toleration for heterosexual cohabitators has grown to the point that few of them report problems with either employers or landlords. In many cities, however, homosexual cohabitors continue to face discrimination from both sources.

Informal Marriages and Social Families

DP ordinances reinforce the idea of the erotic friendship as a broad umbrella sheltering the three kinds of ways people express an ongoing committed relationship. Among heterosexuals, this social umbrella covers girlfriends/boyfriends, cohabitors, and spouses. Among homosexuals the erotic friendship covers *non*-co-resident couples as well as cohabitors. Most homosexuals have no access to the social equivalent of marriage. But, in San Francisco, a number of clergy will solemnize, and thus provide the church's blessing on, homosexual as well as heterosexual *informal* marriages.[10] The term *informal marriage* simply means that the co-residing couple has not obtained a formal marriage license.

Later in the chapter we show that a co-residing couple may have an informal marriage even if it doesn't have the Church's blessing, or even if the couple fails to register as domestic partners. In addition, if the couple has children living with them, we say that they have an *informal family*. The label "social family" is reserved for what Chapters 2 and 3 described as a number of households linked through patterns of giving and receiving.[11] Recall that the Census Bureau defines cohabitors as "unmarried couple households": An unmarried couple household is "composed of two unrelated adults of the opposite sex . . . who share a housing unit." Although the census limits informal marriages to heterosexuals, this book does not, because of evidence showing that erotic friends sharing the same household are far more alike than unlike, regardless of sexual preference (see Chapters 5 and 11 as well as this chapter).

A gay couple hug under a shower of bird seed confetti after exchanging vows in a wedding ceremony.

What about Children? Besides its according nonmarital sex a much greater degree of social acceptance, Ms. Graham complained against the Ann Arbor DP ordinance for a second reason: " 'What do you do when children are involved?' "[12] In addition to believing that The Family is the *only* place for sex, many citizens located in the middle of the Figure 1-1 continuum believe that it is the *best* place for children. Nevertheless, when those citizens themselves were children, a large number of them probably lived at least part of their lives in other varieties of families. In addition, many are now living part of their adult lives in informal families with children that are not biologically their own. Census figures show that increasing numbers of North American children live with adults (heterosexual or homosexual) who are cohabiting.[13] Many other children live with an adult (solo parent) who has a girlfriend/boyfriend. Chapter 8 showed that even though that erotic friend maintains an apartment, she or he may sleep over at the partner's house several nights per week. A number of these couples may eventually decide it makes more sense to share the same household rather than maintain separate dwellings. If they live in a city with a DP ordinance, or work for a company with DP privileges, these informal families could stand to benefit accordingly.

Hence, domestic partnership ordinances communicate a certain message to both children and adults, whether they're ever part of one or not. The message is that because some governments and employers have legitimated their arrangements, it's okay. Their informal family has become socially acceptable. This is happening at the same time that most citizens still believe that anything besides The Family is less than ideal. They are afraid that children suffer growing up in informal families. They also worry that if children grow up thinking that informal families are okay, they'll be more likely to live in informal families themselves when they're adults.[14] As growing numbers of children and adults live in such families, if even for a few years of their lives, society will suffer irreversible decay and corrosion. During the sixties, fears about family disorganization and social chaos were restricted to black families.[15] Now that informal families are becoming increasingly common among whites as well, those kinds of fears have become societywide.

The idea that informal families contribute to social chaos received enormous media attention in the wake of the 1992 Los Angeles riots. Vice President Dan Quayle as well as other prominent spokespersons claimed that the looting, burning, and violence that rattled LA could be blamed in large part on the breakdown of The Family.[16] By "breakdown" the advocates were describing people who were behaving in ways other than those allowed by the formal family blueprint. And domestic partner ordinances reinforce precisely the kinds of informal family behaviors that, in the view of some, undermine the fabric of society.

Social Markers of Seriousness and Commitment. Most persons involved in an erotic friendship do what they can to assure themselves, as well as their friends and families, that they're in a serious and committed relationship. For example, the commitment to be sexually monogamous—to be coupled in an MC phase—is not something most couples keep to themselves. It's a very important social marker that they publicly and proudly share with their friends and families: "This is my boyfriend; this is my girlfriend." The boundaries they've established around their erotic friendship become public knowledge. If their families and friends join them in supporting their relationship, the couple is likely to feel better about it (and about themselves) than if friends and families are not supportive.

Cohabitation versus Marriage

Chapter 8 showed that increasing numbers of today's girlfriends/boyfriends *cohabit*, that is, establish informal marriages within a single household. When couples (straight or gay) move in together they send an important social signal. Cohabitation is a much stronger public marker of their seriousness and commitment than remaining merely as girlfriend/boyfriend. All of us have noticed that cohabitors often have difficulty introducing their special (cohabiting) friend.

They grope for an adequate label because they wish to publicly convey the idea that their special person is someone more meaningful than a mere boyfriend/girlfriend, and that their co-residence signifies a greater degree of seriousness and commitment than that of couples *not* living together. But whether girlfriend/boyfriend or cohabitors, heterosexual couples who stay together long enough will inevitably hear the question, "When are you getting serious?" Homosexuals are likely to hear the same question if their blood kin are unaware of their homosexuality and believe that the person they've been sharing a household with for some years is just a housemate.

Throughout North America, seriousness and commitment are publicly indicated in the strongest way possible by marriage. Marriage remains a powerful social marker in a symbolic sense. Marriage is the ultimate indicator that the couple has finally "settled down" and has committed itself to a lifelong relationship. Bumpass is correct in asserting that rarely do marriages any longer signify the actual beginnings of a relationship.[17] Nevertheless, marriage remains a unique way of formally announcing we-ness, belonging, mattering. In our culture there is as yet no more compelling way of doing so.

Part of the evidence for the uniqueness of marriage is what happens when a couple marries: People warmly congratulate them, given them presents, have parties for them, and most of all, share lavish public celebrations known as weddings. And on every wedding anniversary they get cards or gifts. By contrast, people who simply move in together are seldom congratulated; neither do they get gifts or much public attention. (Interestingly, Ames and colleagues report that when one of the couples they interviewed went downtown and got their official domestic partnership certificate, people at work "hung up streamers and put a JUST DOMESTICATED sign over the door."[18]) And who remembers a couple's cohabitation anniversary? Even less public note is paid to girlfriends/boyfriends announcing. "We're now a couple—we've made a mutual commit-

"Women would take their husbands' name, there were no domestic partners—It was a lot easier when everyone was Mr. and Mrs."

ment to be sexually monogamous, and are thus in the MC phase of our erotic friendship." Who celebrates that event on a yearly basis?

Indeed, the reason few persons celebrate these events is that most persons don't expect their situation to be permanent. Instead, the situation is perceived as a stepping stone to Something Else. The "something else" is either marriage or exit from the erotic friendship. Chapter 8 reminded us that, technically speaking, a cohabitor remains a single person. Since singleness is defined as less desirable than marriage, marriage remains the goal.

Fading Social Markers—Marriage and Divorce Larry Bumpass reminds us that not too many years ago marriage and divorce were like clocks: They were unambiguous *social markers*. Just as a clock marks the beginning and ending of, say, a basketball game or a class period or an eight-hour workday, marriage marked the beginning of a unique relationship and divorce marked its termination. Now, says Bumpass, that's no longer the case.[19] Throughout modern societies, marriage and divorce are being stripped of their marker capabilities. People experience sexual intercourse, have children, and live together, quite independent of whether they're married or not. Growing numbers of persons devise their own clocks regarding when relationships begin and end. Chapter 5 showed that erotic friendships begin before a formal marriage takes place (if it does at all). And Chapters 5, 11, and 13 show that erotic friendships may end long before a divorce occurs. Or friendly relationships may continue after a divorce.[20] Hence, formal and official chalk lines such as marriage and divorce are slowly, almost imperceptibly, becoming less significant than the lines drawn by people themselves.

Helga and the other characters studied in Chapter 5 make that point quite clearly. When we say people are drawing their own lines we mean they are fashioning erotic friendships, including their several phases—formation, maintenance and change (MC), and dissolution. What matters most to people is the sense of we-ness (belonging, bonding, importance, mattering) that erotic friendships are all about. Perceiving the potential for bonding means that persons are in a formation phase. Keeping that bonding going and helping it to grow indicates that persons are in an MC phase. But if bonding winds down, we say that persons are in a dissolution phase. The lines that indicate the development into, and through, and perhaps out of, these phases of an erotic friendship are not indelibly marked by some referee. The persons themselves draw them, so they tend to be subtle and easily overlooked by outsiders.

PREVALENCE OF AND DURATION OF COHABITATION

A 1988 national study representative of all U.S. women aged 15 to 44 years found that 5.2 percent of the sample were cohabiting at the time of the survey.[21] A 1983 study representative of never-married women aged 20 to 29 years reported that 12.2 percent were currently cohab-

iting.[22] These percentages do not seem very large. But the figures have been growing rapidly since 1970. Recent U.S. government data, for instance, show that during the 1980s the percentage of unmarried couple households grew by 80 percent.[23] The number of couples cohabiting at any one time went from 1.6 million to 2.9 million. Double that figure and you can see that as the nineties began, close to 6 million persons were cohabiting at any one time.

Even more significant, however, is the percentage of persons who have *ever* cohabited during their lives. During 1987 to 1988, Larry Bumpass and James Sweet did a national sample survey of 682 cohabiting couples.[24] They found that approximately half of the persons in their early thirties had cohabited at one time or another, usually before their first marriage. They also report that about half of all persons recently married in the United States had cohabited at some time. To grasp how common cohabitation has become in this country, we must focus on what Bumpass and Sweet call the *experience* of cohabitation. That "experience" gives us a much different view of things than merely knowing how many are doing it right now. The trend toward persons ever experiencing cohabitation at some point in their lives is moving rapidly in an upward direction. One reason that the percentage of persons currently cohabiting is much lower than the percentage who have ever cohabited is because the duration of cohabitations tends to be relatively brief. Bumpass and Sweet say that during the 1980s, the median duration was 1.3 years.

Nonpermanence

Ever since researchers began to study cohabitations, they have remarked about their relative nonpermanence. Swedish sociologist Jan Trost, working in the 1970s, was one of the first "doing scientific work in the field of cohabitation and marriage." Because the 1960s' Swedish marriage rate started going down and the cohabitation rate started going up, Trost "tried to find out what was going on." In 1974 he interviewed 101 newly married couples and 111 unmarried cohabiting couples. In 1978 he found that twice as many of the cohabs as the marrieds had separated. He explained the cohabitors' greater instability this way: Cohabitation was happening during the later stages of the going steady and engagement periods. The last two time frames were essentially "trial" periods to help the couple determine whether they should marry. Before the 1970s, lots of persons who went steady or who were engaged but not living together broke off their relationships. During the 1970s, many boyfriends/girlfriends began to live together. But just like earlier couples who had not co-resided, they too eventually broke off their relationships.[25]

In summarizing the North American cohabitation research done during the 1970s, Eleanor Macklin cautions that most of it was done on college students.[26] She also reports that North American research verified Trost's conclusions that cohabitations tend to be short-lived compared with marriages. To get away from sole reliance on college-student information, researchers have begun to study national samples that represent persons of varied ages and with varied levels of education and job status. For example, Jay Teachman and co-workers studied the relationship histories of persons between their 1972 graduation from high school and the year 1986.[27] They found strong evidence that during that fourteen-year period cohabiting couples were much more likely to split from their "co-residential unions" than were married couples.

Bumpass and Sweet studied a different national sample of U.S. households.[28] They too found that cohabitations, when compared with marriages, tend to be nonpermanent. Bumpass and Sweet studied the relationship histories of persons who had cohabited during the period 1975–1984. They focused on the person's first cohabitation experience. They found that after one year of nonlegally co-residing, 59 percent of the persons were still doing so. By the end of the second year the number was only 33 percent. At the end of three years, 21 percent were cohabiting; four years, 14 percent were cohabiting; five years, 9 percent cohabiting; and at the end of ten years only 2 percent were still nonlegally co-residing.

Marry or Split? What happens, of course, is that throughout North America most cohabitors eventually either marry or split. (A few choose the third option: remain together indefinitely without marriage.) Over the ten-year period, 60 percent of the cohabitors Bumpass and Sweet studied got married, but not necessarily to each other. Those who married did so soon after they began their first cohabition: "One quarter marry within a year [of having begun to cohabit], and half have married within 3 years, representing 42 and 80 percent, respectively, of those who eventually marry."[29]

Many cohabiting couples are probably in what Figure 5-1 describes as a maintenance and change phase of an erotic friendship. Their relationship supplies them with a certain degree of we-ness. Nevertheless, most of them don't seem to be content with the level of commitment and seriousness signaled to themselves and to others by mere co-residence. That discontent may exist alongside considerable satisfaction with their levels of emotional intimacy, companionship, sexual pleasures, economic and household task sharing, and even parenting. Satisfaction with their current giving and receiving, however, is not sufficient to motivate them to keep on cultivating their MC phase. They feel strongly that they must eventually graft marriage onto their erotic friendship. Marriage is their eventual goal, and pressure from friends and families to "get serious" reinforces that objective.

Dotti, for example, perceives her current co-habiting partner (Rudi) as someone she would like to marry, and she tells him what she wants. If Rudi agrees they should marry (whether immediately or when they're ready), their feelings of we-ness are enhanced and they continue their nonlegal co-residence for a short while longer. When they finally marry, their sixteen-month nonlegal co-residence is ended, but of course they're still co-residing. The major difference is that from this point forward, it's legal (i.e., formal). If Rudi is not interested in marrying Dotti, her feelings of we-ness and bonding are likely to shift to a downward trajectory. Eventually they're likely to drop so low that she finds herself in a dissolution phase (Figure 5-2). The decline occurs even though otherwise she has no complaints abut Rudi. He's a good listener and a good lover, and they have fun doing things together. He's an affectionate parent to her small child, and their joint incomes make for a reasonable lifestyle. Nonetheless, her sense of we-ness erodes because he's not interested in marrying her. While in the dissolution phase with Rudi, Dotti meets Sherman and, unknown to Rudi, enters first a formation and next an MC phase with Sherman. She then splits from Rudi. Although Dotti and Sherman don't actually co-habit, they spend many nights together at her apartment. Chapter 8 called their arrangement "physical proximity." Soon Dotti and Sherman decide to add marriage to their relationship. For the first time they actually co-reside and share a single dwelling. Let's assume, however, that Dotti wasn't interested in marrying anyone, including Rudi. If that were the case, she might have continued co-residing with Rudi. Since they both agreed (usually tacitly) that for now they weren't interested in marrying one another, their sense of bonding was not undermined. Because both were getting what they wanted, they continued in their MC phase.

COHABITATION AND THE INSTABILITY OF MARRIAGES

It's not a puzzle why most cohabitations in North America tend to be brief compared with most marriages. What is puzzling, however, is the association between cohabitation and marital instability, defined as separation and/or divorce. What Macklin said during the late 1970s remains true today: "For many social critics, the crucial question [regarding cohabitation] is: What effect does living together before marriage have on the later marriage relationship?"[30] Researchers and citizens alike are preoccupied with whether cohabitation is *good* or *bad* for marriage. *Good* is defined as something that helps to avoid divorce; *bad* means something that aids divorce. When cohabitation first came to public attention during the seventies, many of its defenders alleged that it was actually good for marriages.[31] They described it as an opportunity to sort out partners within the realistic context of humdrum, everyday co-residence. If the partners didn't like what they found, they could split before they became serious and got married. Consequently, in the long run cohabitation would be good for marriage because it would cut back on the soaring divorce rate.

Many of its detractors say that cohabitation is bad for what Chapter 1 called the *institution* of marriage. By "institution" they mean the sets of cultural norms prescribing what people should and should not do regarding sex and parenting. What people should do is considered good for an orderly society; what they shouldn't do results in social disorder and chaos. Jeffrey Alexander remarks that very often people hold the mistaken idea that the norms that make up an institution have a life of their own."[32] People (e.g., Ms. Graham) believe that somehow those norms exist outside of the heads of the people who carry and share them with one another.

Likewise, persons who think of The Family as a social institution tend to view it as a real thing, as if it is outside of, and free from, human beings. They believe that people who conform to the institution's demands are contributing positively to the larger society. (Marriage is but one social institution; some others are the educational, political, economic, and religious systems.) Conforming to an institution's demands means accepting something that is outside of, bigger than, and ultimately more important than any single individual. If there is conformity, both children and the larger society benefit. Since cohabitation is definitely not conformity, some observers label it a *deviant* behavior.[33] John Modell, on the other hand, says that people who cohabit are actually creating behavior patterns that they believe will make their own lives better.[34]

Who is correct? Is cohabitation merely deviant or is it creative? If it contributes to marital stability, some might say, "Yes, indeed, it's a creative response to a rapidly changing society." If it does not, its detractors could say, "See? It *is* deviant because it hurts children and thus the society." Answering these kinds of questions speaks to the theme of reinvention that we've been talking about since Chapter 1. We've learned that people have been reinventing marriages at least since the 1700s. Today this continues, with informal marriages. The basic issue is, are people being responsible? In reinventing today's marriages, are people concerned for their partner's well-being? For the well-being of children who might be involved? What are the consequences of their actions for their community and the larger society?[35]

The Corrosive Effects of Time

A number of recent studies suggest that in the United States there is a strong and pervasive connection between premarital cohabitation and marital instability. Among married couples, those who did cohabit before marriage seem more likely than those who did not cohabit to experience separation and/or divorce.[36] On the basis of those studies, cohabitation's detractors have an edge. They can claim that cohabitation does have negative consequences for society.

Some investigators, however, are not so sure that the linkage between cohabitation and marital instability is as simple as it appears on the surface. Jay Teachman and Karen Polonko, for instance, say that once we take into account the *duration* of any erotic friendship, the link between cohabitation and instability tends to disappear.[37] Recall that Dotti and Sherman did not live in the same household before their marriage in January. Let's assume that we interview them sixty months after their marriage to discover whether they've divorced. Let's also assume that Rudi and Angela began to cohabit the same January that Dotti & Sherman were married. Twelve months later, Rudi and Angela marry. Forty-eight months later we try to find out whether Rudi & Angela have divorced. Keep in mind that both couples have been co-residing for sixty months, one couple legally the entire period, the other couple non-legally for twelve months and legally forty-eight months. We might be tempted to predict that after sixty months Rudi and Angela, because they cohabited before marriage, are more likely to have split than Dotti & Sherman, who did not cohabit.

But according to Teachman and Polonko when we actually compare large numbers of couples who have co-resided for the same number of months, some married for the entire time, some who cohabited and then got married, we find no differences at all between the two sets of married couples! Those who were married the entire time are just as likely to have split as couples who cohabited. Why don't we discover any difference? Because of the time spent actually sharing a household.

Co-residence—being with someone on a day-to-day basis—imposes routine demands, raises conflicts, and dulls romantic excitement in ways that simply don't happen when couples maintain separate households. For six decades, studies have shown that the longer a marriage endures, the less satisfied the spouses are with its intrinsic, compassionate, and sexual components.[38] Time tends to erode feelings of bonding and belonging. The longer any erotic friendship persists (whether formal or informal), the more likely it is to edge into a dissolution phase. Furthermore, argue Teachman and Polonko, time does not discriminate on the basis of marital status. It takes its toll equally from cohabitors and marrieds alike. Thus, instead of saying that premarital cohabitation is negative for marriage, they claim that the longer *any* couple co-resides, legally or nonlegally, the more likely it is they will find themselves in a dissolution phase that could eventually result in the termination of their erotic friendship.

Elizabeth Thomson and Ugo Colella's study came up with similar findings.[39] They looked at couples who'd been married fewer then ten years, some of whom had premaritally cohabited and some who had not. Those who had done so had cohabited only with their current spouse. Thomson and Colella asked the couples (all of whom were married) what they thought the chances were that they and their spouse would eventually separate or divorce. They discovered that persons who had cohabited perceived greater chances of marital breakup than those who had not. They also found that the longer the couples had been co-residing, the more likely they were to perceive instability. In short, time was taking its toll. The number of months the couple had actually been co-residing was more influential in making them dissatisfied with their relationships than the mere fact of having premaritally cohabited or not. Like Teachman and Polonko, Thomson and Colella argue that time, not mar-

ital status, influences the sense of we-ness felt by persons in erotic friendships.

However, reporting on their own study, Alfred DeMaris and Vaninadha Rao say that even when they took into account the number of months couples had co-resided, married couples who had cohabited were more likely to get divorced than married couples who had not.[40] DeMaris and Rao explain the connection between cohabitation and instability using an argument made by a number of sociologists. This argument is that cohabitors are *unconventional* people or they would never have cohabited in the first place. Presumably, unconventional persons have a weak commitment to the institution of formal marriage. They tend to be what earlier chapters called individualistic: to be obsessed with me-ness at the expense of we-ness. According to this argument, persons who are individualistic reject the idea that the marriage license is meaningful in and of itself, or that it helps to make life better. Finally, the argument states that individualistic persons deny that cohabitation or divorce are necessarily and inevitably harmful for adults, children, or society.

Unconventionality and Pressures to Marry

However, the unconventionality argument makes us wonder: If the partners were so unconventional, why did they bother to get married at all? Why didn't they simply remain cohabitors? What pushed them into domestic conformity? Although being unconventional might have played some part in their marital instability, perhaps another equally compelling reason was the social pressures they felt from families and friends to get married. For instance, it may be that after a period of nonlegal co-residing, Tanya and Ken feel uneasy about continuing their relationship. They may even be in a dissolution phase. However, because they're uncertain, and because their families and friends pressure them to marry, they opt for what at the time seems like the least painful thing to do—get married. "Who know?" they perhaps reason, "It might just work out after all."

Nevertheless, getting married and thus becoming legal does nothing to reverse their declining sense of we-ness. So after a while, Tanya and Ken decide to separate, and later to divorce. They may regret that, in their own view, they caved in to social pressures to prove their commitment by getting married. In short, although unconventionality might have gotten them into cohabitation in the first place, pressures to marry undermined their better judgment about the future of their relationship. The fact that they did divorce was much more the result of those social pressures than it was of being unconventional.

Trends among Younger Persons

Evidence that both unconventionality and pressures to marry may be playing less of a role in relationship permanence than they once did comes from Robert Schoen's recent study.[41] To examine the connection between cohabitation and marital instability, Schoen studied "birth cohorts," persons born during clusters of years. The clusters he studied were 1928–1932, 1933–1937, 1938–1942, 1948–1952, and 1953–1957. Schoen compared persons born within each cluster in order to come up with several probabilities: (1) The probability that their cohabitations and their marriages would be terminated; (2) the probability that they would cohabit before marriage, and (3) the probability that premarital cohabitors would experience instability. While making these comparisons, Schoen also took *time* into account. He calculated the total number of months that couples had been co-residing, both informally and formally.

Schoen found that, compared with older cohorts, (1) people in the youngest cohorts (1948–1952 and 1953–1957) had higher proba-

bilities of terminating both their cohabitations and their marriages; (2) people in the youngest cohorts had higher probabilities of being cohabitors; and (3) totally unexpected and surprising, married persons in the youngest cohorts who had cohabited had *lower* probabili- ties of experiencing instability than comparable persons from the older cohorts. "As the prevalence of cohabitation rises sharply, the instability of marriages preceded by a cohabitation drops markedly."[42] Strange as it seems, as more and more citizens cohabit, the chances of cohabitation being connected with even-tual divorce go down. Why is that? What's happening?

The reason, says Schoen, is that today's "cohabitors are less likely to be a select group." It is becoming increasingly common for younger persons to be part of two major trends that are pervasive throughout Western societies: (1) to live together informally and (2) to terminate unsatisfying erotic friendships irrespective of whether they are informal or formal. If growing numbers of citizens are participating in those two major trends, then cohabitors can hardly be a select or special category. They're just like everybody else.

During the 1970s it may have made sense to suggest that cohabitors were unconventional people who sneered at the rules and thumbed their noses at the accepted wisdom of their day. The upheavals of the 1960s may indeed have emboldened some in the 1970s to disdain what they perceived as the shackles of marriage. Cohabitation may once have been a "big deal," just as earlier chapters showed that premarital sex was once a big deal.

Today, however, neither seems to be much of a big deal. Cohabitation appears to be becoming about as commonplace as premarital sex is among girlfriends/boyfriends. If cohabitors choose eventually to marry, it may be less the result of feeling pushed into it by family and friends and more the result of wanting to do it. Whether the couple stays together after marriage depends less on their alleged unconventionality and more on their patterns of negotiation and problem-solving as described in Chapter 11.

The Economics of Cohabitation

Another important reason to question the unconventionality argument is the linkage between social status and cohabitation. The 1970s' image that cohabitors were unconventional was based on the assumption that they were well-educated white elites who were thumbing their noses at the unwashed masses. By contrast, a number of studies report that throughout the general population, the *more* years of schooling and the more income persons have, the *less* likely they are to cohabit.[43] Linda Jacobsen and Fred Pampel suggest that very often cohabitation may simply be a pragmatic response to economic need.[44] In particular, the growing numbers of lone mothers in the U.S. population means ever-expanding numbers of economically strained households. One obvious way to relieve economic strain is to pool two incomes within the scope of one household. Until recently, that pattern for economic well-being was quite common among African-Americans. Lately, however, cohabitation has become so widespread among whites that its current rate actually exceeds the rate among blacks.[45]

Macklin attributes a certain proportion of college student cohabitation to economic constraints. Unable to pay bills by living alone or with roommates, the sharing of household expenses with someone who's already an erotic friend becomes perceived as a highly attractive option. Since cohabitation no longer raises eyebrows, the costs of social disapproval have declined substantially. If we add to that fact the perception that "lots of my friends are doing it," there seem to be few apparent downside risks to the option of nonlegal co-residence among students. Fewer dollars, and lower risk of social disapproval, contribute to the

Bumpass and Sweet finding that more than a quarter of college graduates cohabited prior to marriage. These authors use that 25 percent figure to argue that cohabitation is becoming increasingly common throughout all levels of society. However, keep in mind that up to now college people have been less likely to cohabit than persons who never graduated from high school. Disadvantaged persons do not fit the image of unconventionality. Income, not ideology, drives their behavior.

LONG-TERM COHABITATIONS— UNCONVENTIONAL

Recall that one of the options Dotti and Rudi had was to keep on cohabiting indefinitely without adding marriage to their erotic friendship. Gertrude Wiersma is one of the few researchers who have studied long-term cohabitations.[46] In comparing long-term cohabitors and married, both in the United States and the Netherlands, she could find virtually no differences between them. The major point of Wiersma's study is that if the notion of unconventionality has anything at all to do with cohabitation, then it applies mostly to co-residing couples who choose to defy the accepted convention: marry or split. Schoen's suggestion is that the experience of cohabitation is becoming commonplace. But in North America, it is still a big deal to remain together forever, especially if the couple has a child together. If this is true, then the authentically unconventional thing would be for Dotti and Rudi to become long-term cohabitors.

If they do remain informally married, we would want to discover how they feel about domestic partnership ordinances. Do they live in a community or work for an employer that has DP codes? If so, have they taken advantage of those codes? If not, why not? If they don't live or work under DP codes, do they wish they did? In short, even though they choose not to marry in the conventional sense, do they wish for the limited degree of social approval and legal rights accruing to them from a DP status? Another area of investigation would be their future: If they've never done so, do they expect to bear children together? If so, why? If not, why not? Next, do they ever expect to marry formally? If so, why? If not, why not? It would also be interesting to compare marrieds with long-term cohabitors in terms of their stability. A Swedish study, for instance, found that after both sets of couples had been together for at least eight years, cohabitors were no more likely to split than were marrieds.[47]

COHABITATION AND MARRIAGE RATES

Just as 1970s' social critics were worried that cohabitation might make marriages more unstable, they were also anxious that it would make younger persons less motivated to marry.[48] Nevertheless, during the 1970s U.S. marriage rates remained steady. More recently, however, the rates have indeed begun to follow the declining marriage rates of most European countries. One way to calculate a marriage rate is to compare birth clusters (cohorts), as we just did. Only this time we will look at women born in 1945 and in 1965 to discover how many of them were married at least once when they were 20 to 25 years old. Using this technique, Bumpass and colleagues found that over time there has been a steady decline in first marriage rates: "Marriage before age 25 was 24 percent lower among the most recent cohort [women born in 1965] than among those reaching this age around 1970 [women born in 1945]."[49]

Nonetheless, these investigators are quick to point out that the decline in U.S. marriage rates among persons under age 25 does not mean that, compared with yesterday's women and men, today's youth prefer to live alone. Quite the contrary. Bumpass and colleagues report that the slack in *legal* co-residence has largely been taken up by the marked increases in *nonlegal* co-residence. In short, younger persons already in an ongoing erotic friendship appear just as eager as ever to experience the pleasures and pains of co-residence. What has changed is their greater willingness to graft co-residence onto their relationship in an informal manner, alongside their corresponding *un*willingness to be formal about it. As they get older, Larry Bumpass says that 90 percent of them will probably marry at least once.[50] The point here is that what used to be considered the prime marrying ages (under 25 years) are gradually ceasing to be defined that way both in Europe and North America.

The reason some people worry about declines in marriage rates goes back to their view of The Family as an institution that exists "out there"—outside of the control of citizens. Institutions are something to which people conform, not something that they continually reinvent. And because the norms of the institution prescribe that people should get married, declines in marriage rates mean that growing numbers of younger persons are ignoring those norms. Ignoring the norms is perceived as bad for the institution. Critics worry that fewer marriages, as well as marriages delayed until people are in their late 20s or early 30s, will result in fewer children being born. Worse yet, critics fear that fewer and/or delayed marriages mean greater numbers of children living within informal marriages and families. Fewer children, say the critics, puts the survival of the society in jeopardy. And we've already discussed the fear that lots of children growing up in informal settings such as cohabitations and lone parenthood leads eventually to societal decay.

Comparing Informal Marriages with Other Relationships

With Formal Marriages As cohabitations seeped into the public's consciousness during the 1970s, another big question that arose was, "How different are they from marriages?" Do nonlegal co-residers treat each other differently than legal co-residers? In Sweden, Trost found virtually no behavioral differences between married and cohabitors in the ways they acted toward one another. After reviewing studies done in North America during the 1970s, Macklin came to a similar conclusion. Take, for instance, performance of routine household chores. Although cohabitors believed more strongly than marrieds that men and women should share those chores equally, Macklin said that no differences could be found in their actual behaviors. In both settings, women did more of those chores than men.[51] Studies done during the 1980s came to the same conclusions.[52] Cohabitors (especially men) did a lot more talking than acting when it came to equity in everyday task sharing. In her review, Macklin also found no differences in amount of interpersonal communication, satisfaction with the relationship, and self-disclosure.[53]

On a third matter, however, differences did turn up. Married couples reported higher levels of commitment than cohabitors.[54] Because commitment was defined as a person's perceived determination to stay with the relationship, Macklin says this difference is not surprising. We've already seen that the decision to marry sends a social message that the partners are serious. Marriage symbolizes their commitment to spend the rest of their lives together. Linda Budd reports that during the early 1970s, few if any cohabitors had come to the point of making that sort of serious commitment.[55] If they had, they would have gotten married.

Edward Markowski and co-workers compared cohabitors with marrieds in terms of their sexual histories as well as their current sexual patterns.[56] They found that although the two categories of couples did not differ in terms of current sexual attitudes and behaviors, they were quite distinct in terms of their prerelationship (pre-MC phase) history. Compared with marrieds, cohabitors had experi-

enced a wider variety of sexual partners, had been less satisfied with those experiences, had been more likely to engage in group sex, and had been younger at the time of their first intercourse. Nevertheless, no matter how unconventional their prerelationship sexual behavior may have been even for the 1970s, it does not appear to have made them any more or less sexually conventional than married once they started co-residing.

With Gay and Lesbian Couples   During the mid-1970s, Philip Blumstein and Pepper Schwartz compared four sets of couples living in the same household: married, gay, lesbian, and nonlegal heterosexual.[57] Although they found certain specific differences among the sets in terms of sex, work, and money (e.g., married are more likely to pool their money than cohabitors), there was one overriding theme common to all—gender. The theme of *gender* seemed more important than any specific differences.[58] Heterosexual men shared many things in common with homosexual men. Heterosexual women shared much in common with homosexual women. The most significant areas that persons within each gender shared in common stem from things we've talked about in earlier chapters. Since recorded history began, women have lived in a subordinate social position to men. Men have had greater access to money, power, and prestige. Women and men carry those social status differences into their erotic friendships regardless of their sexual preference.

One impact of those gender-based social status differences emerges from Peter Carter's 1992 study comparing cohabitors—gay, lesbian, and nonlegal heterosexual.[59] Carter found that gay couples were least able to negotiate effectively. Chapter 11 shows that "effective" means that both partners are able to influence their discussions and disagreements so as to arrive at mutually acceptable, or win-win, agreements. Lesbian couples, said Carter, were the most effective negotiators, and heterosexuals were in the middle. Both Blumstein and Schwartz, and Carter, say that gay men have difficulty negotiating with one another not because they're gay, but because they're men. Similarly, lesbian women are highly effective negotiators not because they're homosexual, but because they're women. Since women negotiate with one another from within a shared *subordinate* status, they tend to be quite sensitive to their partner's interests. They also tend to be flexible in what they're willing to settle for. By contrast, because men approach one another from within a shared *dominant* status, they tend to be less sensitive to their partner's interests, and also less flexible. That is so whether their partner is female or male. Thus, heterosexual couples fall in the middle because the women are more sensitive and flexible than gays, but the men are less flexible and sensitive than lesbians.

The upshot of these and many other studies comparing types of relationships is that the behaviors of coupled partners toward one another are not substantially influenced by whether they are legal or informal, or whether they are straight or gay.[60] What is far more significant is, first, their gender. Second is the phase of their erotic friendship. If a couple is in an MC phase, whether married or not, and whether straight or gay, then Chapter 11 reports that they're negotiating in ways that enhance their feelings of bonding and belonging. But if they're in a dissolution phase, their negotiations have gotten less effective, and their sense of we-ness and bonding is declining. Consequently, knowing whether a co-residing couple is gay or straight, or legal or not, tells us much less about them than their current relationship phase. To be sure, if they're both male, their negotiations will be marked by a much higher level of struggle and uncertainty about outcomes than if they're both women. Nevertheless, some gay couples do persist indefinitely in an MC phase, and some lesbian couples drift into dissolution and eventually split. Straight couples can and do go in either direction, and largely for the same reason—the ways in which they negotiate issues of importance.

With Girlfriends/Boyfriends During the 1970s and 1980s researchers also became interested in comparing heterosexual cohabitors and marrieds with couples who were not co-residing: How different are girlfriend/boyfriend couples from couples who co-reside? If a couple decides to graft co-residence onto the MC phase of their erotic friendship, what difference does that important change make? Do cohabitors treat each other differently than girlfriends/boyfriends?

One recent study, for example, compared marrieds, cohabitors, and also girlfriends/boyfriends who were not living together.[61] The researchers found that the three sets of couples differed a great deal in terms of social status. As expected, marrieds had higher levels of education and income than the two other sets of couples. They also differed in how long they had been together as a "special couple" (being special meant having an understanding that they shared a sexually exclusive relationship), in other words, the length of time they'd been in an MC phase.

On the basis of that criterion, the marrieds had been together many more years than the cohabitors, and the cohabitors in turn had been together longer than the girlfriends/boyfriends. However, the three kinds of couples were similar when it came to feelings of satisfaction with their partners, their sense of psychological well-being, and, interestingly enough, their level of commitment. Given these latter similarities, the authors did a second study to try to find out why the persons might either feel good or not so good about their partners and about themselves.[62] They found that two things were more important than whether they were married or not, and whether they cohabited or not, in affecting how satisfied persons were with their partners and how committed they were to them.

In addition, those same two things contributed more than anything else toward a positive sense of psychological well-being. The two things were their intimacy levels and their conflict resolution tactics. Couples who shared higher levels of emotional closeness and self-disclosure, and who also aimed at negotiating win-win solutions to their disagreements, were more likely to feel good about themselves and also about their relationships.

These two studies reinforce an earlier conclusion based solely on comparisons of co-residing couples. And that is that the key to understanding erotic friendships of any kind lies with how much the partners care about each other, and how effectively they negotiate with one another. The objective facts that couples are or are not married, or that they are or are not co-residing (or that they're straight or gay), are not by themselves very interesting. What is much more interesting and important is what Chapter 5 called the cultivation of the MC phase, including its pruning and grafting. Chapter 11 describes in detail how couples in any erotic friendship treat one another, and how that's connected to how much they care for each other, and also how they feel about themselves and their relationship.

Physical Aggression among Nonmarrieds

Chapter 12 describes studies indicating that cohabitors as well as girlfriends/boyfriends tend to report more violence than marrieds. Jan Stets says that part of the reason may be that compared with marrieds, cohabitors are more socially *isolated*, that is, less connected to groups, clubs, churches, neighborhood organizations, and so forth.[63] He also found that many cohabitors are "youthful and black," and may be subject to "depression and alcohol problems." Other studies describe the realities

of violence and abuse among both gay and lesbian couples (some cohabiting, some not).[64]

Chapter 12 shows that the privacy factor may be one reason erotic friendships in general (including marrieds) experience as much violence as they do. If cohabitors (both straight and gay) are even more isolated than marrieds from groups that might exercise some control over their violence, then their greater privacy might indeed be one factor explaining their greater violence. If cohabitation continues to become increasingly commonplace throughout all parts of society, it will be important to find out if abuse continues to be associated with these informal relationships. The fact is that persons who are socially and economically better off (including well-off cohabitors) are less likely to be isolated. Hence, it may be that in the future the current differences in violence between formal and informal marriages would gradually diminish.

INVENTING CUSTOMS AND LAWS

Earlier we said that domestic partnership policies demonstrate efforts by governments and companies to respond to the ways in which growing numbers of ordinary persons are carrying on their day-to-day lives. Mary Ann Glendon remarks that in the past "traditional family law rigorously policed the boundaries of the legitimate family."[65] Until recently, laws throughout Western societies were based on the belief that The Family is an institution, a real thing that tells people how they're supposed to live. Central to those beliefs, said Chapter 3, is the idea that The Family is restricted to ties of blood or marriage. People bound in those two ways were covered by family laws. People not linked by blood or marriage were considered outside the boundaries of The Family: " 'There is no family in law but the legitimate family.' "[66] The laws ignored people, says Glendon, even if they behaved in familylike ways. For example, when African-Americans created the social families described in Chapters 2 and 3, white authorities paid them no heed and offered no support. White social scientists noticed them, but labeled them deviant.

Common-Law Marriages

Furthermore, for several hundred years, in some parts of Europe, in Puerto Rico and other Caribbean islands, and in a number of southern states, some couples (usually poor) have publicly co-resided without license or religious blessing.[67] Almost always they had children. At first the laws preferred to ignore them and regarded them as "legal strangers to each other."[68] After a while, however, people living in familylike ways could no longer be ignored for two major reasons: Laws had to be written to protect both the *property* and the *children* of persons in what were often called *common-law marriages*. Pedro Silva-Ruiz says that in Puerto Rico they are de facto, or informal, marriages.[69]

H. Jay Folberg traces the creation of more recent U.S. domestic partnership laws to precisely the same two conditions.[70] During the 1970s, the courts left no doubt that cohabitation was both immoral and illegal. Nevertheless the courts also recognized that when people share the same residence, they inevitably become "partners in the acquisition of the amenities of life."[71] They gradually begin to share what earlier chapters called *extrinsic* interdependence. They tend to pay jointly for rent, mortgage, gasoline, utilities, repairs, food, waterbeds, stereos, TVs, VCRs, CD players, children's clothes, leisure activities and vacations, and so on, and on. They also pool their labor in routine household chores and the care of children. If after a while the couples split, and if they're able to distribute their material amenities equitably, the law can safely ignore them. However, since many cohabiting (like

married) persons dispute what their partner wants to do about their shared amenities, the courts must become involved. Folberg says the courts reason that these couples—like business partnerships—possess material things that must be distributed fairly when they split. But since the partnerships are situated in households, the partnerships are called *domestic*.

Likewise, until recently, children living in informal families were largely ignored. Children not born to a legally married couple were labeled *illegitimate* (bastards) and had no claims on the father, either to be supported by, or inherit anything from, him. Recently, however, the courts in Western societies have paid greater attention to the rights of children whether couples are legal or informal, and whether or not couples split. Child support, for example, is being demanded from children's biological fathers, even if they never married the mother.[72] If children are cared for and their rights are protected, the courts stay out of the picture. But if children's interests are threatened—either in a stable relationship or from one that is splitting—then the courts intervene. Glendon notes that Western societies are moving away from illegitimacy laws that focused on matters of wealth and status. Increasingly, today's laws reflect "concern for the children themselves."[73] For example, the trend in Western societies is for the children of unwed parents to be given the same legal rights of care, support, and inheritance as married parents' children.

In spite of that trend, Glendon says that laws guaranteeing equal rights for all children are much stronger in European countries such as Sweden than they are in the United States or Canada. Ironically, she notes that "child-guarantee" laws are in fact much less required in Sweden because the majority of children born outside of marriage are born to informal *couples*. By contrast, Chapters 13 and 16 show that among the majority of U.S. children born to an unwed mother, no informal partner is present. And since most of these noncohabiting mothers are poor and unable to get much if any material support from the equally poor (nonresident) father, the child often faces severe economic deprivation.

Erosion of Legal Marriage

Glendon observes that "the . . . central position of legal marriage in family law has been extensively eroded everywhere."[74] By "everywhere" she means in Western societies. By "eroded" she means that people in informal marriages and families are increasingly being given the same legal rights, privileges, protections, and responsibilities as people in formal settings. From a legal standpoint, marriage is slowly losing its uniqueness. By contrast, informal marriages are absorbing the things (protection of each adult's rights as well as children's rights) that used to make legal marriages special and qualitatively distinct. Legal versus informal marriages are no longer as different in kind as they once were. Domestic partnership codes by governments and businesses are a striking example of that point.

The Situation in Sweden This long-term trend toward the blurring of distinctions between formal and informal marriages is much further along in Sweden that it is in North America. For one thing, the incidence of informal marriages is much higher in Sweden.[75] In Sweden during the mid-1980s, some 20 percent of all co-resident couples were unmarried.[76] For Denmark during the same period, the figure was almost as high—18 percent.[77] Earlier we learned that during that period some 5 percent of U.S. women aged 15 to 44 were cohabiting.

Second—and very important—there appear to be many more *long-term* cohabitations in Sweden than there are in most other societies.[78] At the same time, marriage rates are much lower in Sweden than they are in North America. As a result, during 1986 almost half of all Swedish children were born to unwed mothers.[79] We just learned, however, that at the time of birth most of those mothers were co-residing with the child's natural father or with some other man. Moreover, says Glendon, there has been a long Swedish tradition among "country folk," and among the urban working class, for a sexually active couple to defer formal marriage until they conceived a child.

Finally, Glendon adds that Swedish "feminists and socialists" had been subjecting marriage to severe critiques since the early 1900s.[80] The upshot of these several threads is that throughout Swedish culture there is much more acceptance and greater social approval of informal marriage than anywhere else except perhaps other Scandinavian societies. A few pages ago, we noted that informal marriage is much less of a big deal in North America than it's ever been before. Nevertheless, when compared with cohabitation in Sweden, cohabitation in North America remains at least a moderate deal.

A useful way to contrast Sweden with the United States is to say that in Sweden, not only is cohabitation *not* a big deal, but marriage itself is much *less* of a big deal than it used to be.[81] In the United States, cohabitation is indeed much less of a big deal than it used to be. But marriage remains a *very big deal!* Chapter 10 shows that in this country marriage remains the unique social symbol of serious commitment. Couples desiring optimum approval and affirmation by families and friends obtain it via marriage. In Sweden, on the other hand, marriage appears to have lost many of the symbolic meanings that were once attached to it.[82] Because marriage in and of itself no longer signifies serious commitment for the Swedes, it cannot achieve for couples the levels of social respectability and legitimacy that it still does in North America.

Nevertheless, co-residing Swedes place

high value on cultivating the maintenance and change phases of their erotic friendships. Studies show that like all Westerners, they place the utmost significance on long-term relationships that provide love, caring, and mutual support of every kind.[83] Erotic friendships that supply a sense of belonging and bonding are as vital to them as they are to all other human beings. If children are present, the adults feel just as much responsibility as other Westerners to love and care for them in optimal fashion. Unlike North Americans, however, the Swedes are much less likely to perceive that legal marriage adds much of anything to an already existing commitment, or that being married will by itself benefit children. In contemporary Swedish culture, marriage simply does not carry the same sort of symbolic meanings and weight that it once did.

A major reason Swedish law has made cohabitation virtually indistinguishable from legal marriage is that over the years Swedes have become less and less persuaded that marriage is culturally and socially unique. In other words, the blurred *cultural* definitions have resulted in pressures to blur the *legal* distinctions. A striking example of this comes from recent Swedish legislation mandating additional legal protections for cohabitors. Not only does the legislation apply to heterosexuals, it also applies explicitly to "persons who live together 'in a homosexual relationship.' "[84] In a similar but separate legislative move, the "European Parliament in Strasbourg offered support for the idea of homosexuals' marrying and having children."[85]

These and additional efforts at blurring the social and legal distinctions between cohabitation (heterosexual and homosexual) and marriage lead some European scholars to wonder how useful the label "marriage" is from a legal standpoint: "It may be that in the future marriage will become both an unnecessary and an inconvenient legal concept in various European countries."[86] The larger context of E. M.

Clive's remarks is the gradual movement of many European countries toward eventual political union. Since the label "marriage" does not appear to designate anything unique either socially or legally, Clive wonders how much sense it makes to retain the label within the laws of a newly United Europe.

Comparing Sweden, North America, and Japan Whatever the Europeans eventually decide, there seems little doubt that at this point in North America's history the label "marriage" continues to carry significant cultural symbolism. That label is fraught with powerful emotional meanings and thus maintains considerable social weight. At the same time, many legal distinctions between informal and formal marriages are gradually eroding. How much North America will in the future eventually come to resemble Europe is as uncertain, and as intriguing, as the question of how much Japan will eventually come to resemble North America.

Earlier chapters described the gap between what people say they believe is right and proper about sex versus how they actually behave. Figure 9-1 compares Japan, North America, and Sweden in terms of a belief-behavior gap regarding formal and informal marriages. The left-hand side of the figure shows that Japan is currently experiencing very little discrepancy in this regard. In spite of the fact that since 1945 they have changed enormously to become a worldwide economic and industrial giant, the Japanese people continue to perceive that formal marriage and family are culturally unique and special compared with informal marriages and families.[87] The 1993 marriage of the Japanese crown prince to a Harvard-educated Japanese woman, viewed everywhere via CNN, imprinted that point most vividly on the world's consciousness. Furthermore, Japanese legal codes are pretty much in line with their cultural beliefs. There has been little

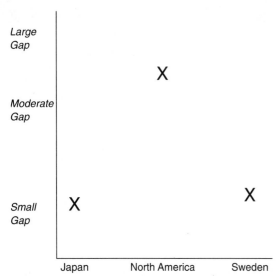

FIGURE 9-1 Comparison between Japan, North America, and Sweden over the degree of gap between behaviors on the one side and culture and legal statutes on the other with regard to marriages and families.

official movement to blur the legal distinctions between formal and informal marriages.

Likewise, in terms of premarital behaviors, it appears that the Japanese are still adhering to customs that were common in the United States during the late 1940s and the 1950s.[83] First, for example, cohabitation as it's practiced in the West is virtually unknown. Second, boyfriends/girlfriends maintaining publicly tolerated erotic friendships are exceedingly rare. Instead, what is quite common is the Japanese version of what Chapters 6 and 7 called the Dating Game. And after the Japanese marry, the model that most of them generally follow are the modern family patterns described in Chapter 7.[89]

At the same time, the right side of Figure 9-1 shows that Sweden, too, currently experiences relatively little discrepancy between what people say is proper and how they actually behave. Unlike the Japanese, however, their small gap is not the result of keeping people's behaviors in line with tradition. Rather, the Swedes maintain a small gap because

they're in the process of changing both laws and culture to bring them into line with how people are actually behaving. Although the Swedes maintain some legal distinctions between formal and informal marriages, those differences have become very few and miniscule indeed.[90] Unlike both Japan and North America, the Swedish government is officially engaged in a long-term process of inventing fresh approaches to adult relationships. They are also trying to construct fresh approaches to relationships between adults and children.

As far as relative gaps are concerned, Figure 9-1 suggests that North America lies somewhere between Japan and Sweden. When it comes to actual everyday behaviors regarding erotic friendships, as well as to informal marriages and families, North Americans resemble the Swedes. When it comes to legal codes, they are again slowly moving in the Swedish direction. Recently, for example, the Hawaiian supreme court ruled that denying formal marriage to homosexuals may violate the state constitution's ban against gender discrimination.[91] If homosexuals are permitted to marry formally in Hawaii, other states might have a difficult time denying similar rights to their homosexual residents. In general, however, most North American legal codes maintain obvious distinctions between formal and informal relationships. In that regard, Americans remain somewhat closer to the Japanese than to the Swedes. North Americans are also removed from the Swedes in terms of cultural beliefs about formal marriages. There remains, in North America, the persistent belief that formal marriage is in and of itself different from informal marriage.

Although North Americans are comparable to the Swedes in terms of everyday behaviors within informal marriages and families, there are also some crucial differences between them. Among the clearest of those distinctions is the tendency for North Americans, so far at least, to ignore the notion of long-term informal marriages. They still favor the "marry or split" option. Nevertheless, North American and Swedish citizens do share a fundamental likeness at the unofficial behavioral level. And that likeness marks them as being very different from the Japanese. The likeness is that Swedish and North American citizens are engaged in a long-term construction, or reinvention, process. They are creating informal marriagelike arrangements that, in terms of actual behaviors, are virtually indistinguishable from the formal arrangements.

CONCLUSION—INFORMAL YET RESPONSIBLE

For a number of decades, nonlegal co-residence has been becoming increasingly common in the West, most prominently in the Scandinavian countries, especially Sweden. It has been marked by impermanence and, among cohabitors who subsequently marry, instability. Its rise has been accompanied by a decline in the legal distinctiveness of formal marriage. Valued prizes once reserved exclusively for persons conforming to formal ties are increasingly available to couples creating informal bonds. Alongside the blurring of legal distinctions, behavioral differences among formal and informal unions are becoming harder to identify (other than differences attributable to gender, rather than legal status, or to sexual preference). Nevertheless, *cultural distinctions* remain tenacious, particularly throughout North America. The belief that marriage signifies a unique status, marked by greater seriousness and more intense commitment than cohabitation, is a major factor accounting for the relative impermanence of the latter.

"Do all roads lead to Sweden?," asks Glendon. Moen calls Sweden a *prototype*—a model for families that may influence other Western nations. Although increasing numbers of North Americans are in fact experiencing co-habitation at one or more points throughout their life course, it is unclear just how closely informal marriage patterns will eventually come to resemble those in Scandinavia. Indeed, no one is certain just how much the Scandinavian patterns themselves will continue to develop in their current direction. Thus far, Scandinavian societies appear to have been reinventing informal marriages in a responsible manner—a manner that takes into account the well-being of adults and children as well as the good of the community and larger society. To the extent that North American reinvention proceeds along the Scandinavian road, the hope is that we would be at least as responsible as Scandinavians have been.

What does seem apparent is the truism that certain basic characteristics of human beings remain everywhere constant. Only their social and cultural expressions vary. In the West, persons (women, men, gay, straight) desire what is known as the erotic friendship. Bounded by sexual commitment and guarded by jealousy, this unique type of primary relationship provides a much sought after and highly valued sense of we-ness, mattering, bonding, and belonging. Possibilities for numerous benefits are subsumed beneath its canopy. Among these are companionship, emotional intimacy, and economic sharing. Very often, the erotic friendship evolves to include a common residence and, sometimes, children. In other cases, one or both partners bring children to the relationship. There is considerable variation across cultures in the degree to which people believe that erotic friends who also co-reside require, in addition, official religious blessing and formal legitimation. In today's Japanese society, there is virtually no socially approved deviation from the requirement to get formal. But in Scandinavia there is so much deviation that many observers wonder how much, if any, actual significance is left to formal marriage. Between those extremes lies North America. Here the cultural significance of formal marriage endures, alongside increasingly wide-spread participation in the everyday experience of the informal.

NOTES

1. Family Research Council, *Washington Watch*, June 1992, Vol. 3, p. 2. Washington D.C.
2. Katrine Ames, Christopher Sulavik, Nadine Joseph, Lucille Beachy, and Todd Park, "Domesticated Bliss," *Newsweek*, March 23, 1992, pp. 62–63. See also Wisensale and Heckhart, 1993.
3. Ibid., p. 62.
4. *Tampa, Florida, Tribune*, February 15, 1991, p. A1.
5. Jonathon P. Hicks, *The New York Times*, March 2, 1993, p. A13; *The Gainesville, Florida, Sun*, November 17, 1992, p. 4A.
6. Sam Howe Verhovek, *The New York Times*, December 8, 1993, p. A10.
7. Ames et al., 1992.
8. Ibid., p. 63.
9. Macklin, 1983.
10. Woodworth, 1989.
11. It's also possible to have several generations living in one household. The generations could be blood based, or they could be what Chapter 3 called "social generations." In the latter case, we would have a "social family" living in one household. A second option is for a social family made up only of persons within the same age range to share the same household. Some studies show, for instance, that a growing number of senior citizens are forming these kinds of social families. This pattern is labeled "co-housing" (Streib, Gordon F., Edward Folts, and Mary Ann Hilker, 1984. *Old Homes, New Families: Shared Living for the Elderly*. New York: Columbia University Press).
12. Ames et al., p. 63.
13. London, 1991.
14. Thornton, 1991.
15. Moynihan, 1965.
16. W. V. Robinson, *The Boston Globe*, June 11, 1992, p. 1.
17. Bumpass, 1990.
18. Ames et al., p. 62.
19. Bumpass, 1990, p. 487.
20. Behrman, 1985; Masheter and Harris, 1986.
21. London, 1991.
22. Tanfer, 1987.
23. U.S. Bureau of the Census, *Current Population Reports*, P-20, #450, May 1991, p. 14.
24. Bumpass and Sweet, 1989.
25. Trost, 1979.
26. Macklin, 1983.
27. Teachman, Thomas, and Paasch, 1991.
28. Bumpass and Sweet.
29. Ibid., p. 621.
30. Macklin, p. 65.
31. Ibid.
32. Alexander, 1988.
33. Gupta and Cox, 1987.
34. Modell, 1988.
35. Etzioni, 1991; Avineri and DeShalit, 1992.
36. Booth and Johnson, 1988. Teachman et al.; Bumpass and Sweet.
37. Teachman and Polonko, 1990.
38. Dizard and Gadlin, 1990.
39. Thomson and Colella, 1992.
40. DeMaris and Rao, 1992.
41. Schoen, 1992.
42. Ibid., p. 283.
43. Tanfer; Bumpass and Sweet.
44. Jacobsen and Pampel, 1989.
45. Bumpass and Sweet.
46. Wiersma, 1983.
47. Bennett, Blanc, and Bloom, 1988.
48. Macklin, p. 69.
49. Bumpass, Sweet, and Cherlin, 1991, p. 916.
50. Bumpass, p. 488.
51. Macklin, pp. 61–62.
52. Denmark, Shaw, and Ciali, 1985.
53. Macklin, pp. 62–63.
54. Ibid., pp. 60–61.
55. Budd, 1976.
56. Markowski, Croake, and Keller, 1978.
57. Blumstein and Schwartz, 1983.
58. Ibid., p. 324.
59. Carter, 1992.
60. Howard, Blumstein, and Schwartz, 1986; Kurdek and Schmitt, 1986a, 1987; Byers and Heinlein, 1989; Berger, 1990; Reilly and Lynch, 1990.
61. Scanzoni, Godwin, and Donnelly, 1993.
62. Godwin and Scanzoni, in preparation.
63. Stets, 1991.

64. Island and Letellier, 1991; Renzetti, 1992.
65. Glendon, 1989, p. 231.
66. Ibid., p. 264.
67. Landale and Fennelly, 1992.
68. Glendon, p. 231.
69. Silva-Ruiz, 1992.
70. Folberg, 1980, p. 350.
71. Ibid., p. 353.
72. Kahn and Kamerman, 1988.
73. Glendon, p. 283.
74. Ibid., p. 282.
75. Mozny and Rabusic, 1992.
76. Ibid., p. 273.
77. Manniche, 1985.
78. Moen, 1989.

79. Trost, 1990.
80. Glendon, p. 274.
81. Ibid.; Trost, 1990.
82. Popenoe, 1988.
83. Lewin, 1982; Intons-Peterson, 1988; Moen.
84. Glendon, p. 275.
85. Alan Cowell, *The New York Times*, February 23, 1994, p. A5.
86. Clive, 1980, p. 78.
87. Condon, 1985; Kondo, 1990.
88. Bornoff, 1991.
89. Condon.
90. Glendon.
91. *The Gainesville, Florida, Sun,* May 7, 1993, p. 4a (from *The New York Times*).

CHAPTER 10

EXPLORING FORMAL MARRIAGES AND REMARRIAGES

They seem to think the family is an arbitrary arrangement of people who decide to live under the same roof, that fathers are dispensable, and that parents need not be married or even of opposite sexes. They are wrong.
—DAN QUAYLE, Quoted in the *Boston Globe*, June 11, 1992, p. 29.

Chapter 7 talked about the old Dating Game and showed that since the 1960s the Game has been overhauled significantly. Nevertheless, Chapters 8 and 9 said that for many North Americans, the ultimate goal of the new game remains the same as that of the old Game— marriage. We've seen that in the United States, being married is still defined culturally as more desirable than not being married. Even if someone has an erotic friendship, the person is perceived as single. Previous chapters also said a great deal about the importance of people's own views, or perceptions, of things. We learned that if some people define a group of persons—themselves or others—to be "family," then that group *is* family. But is it a *real* family? If people aren't joined by blood, or if they're not legally married, is it as the Coke ad says, the real thing?

What constitutes the real family is a major political issue in the United States. During the 1992 presidential campaign, then Vice President Quayle made international headlines by his attack on the popular TV sitcom, *Murphy Brown*. He complained about an episode in

which the unmarried star of the show (a professional woman played by Candace Bergen) decided to have a baby. Quayle said that because she purposely wanted to become a mother outside of marriage, *Murphy Brown* was a horrible role model for American's youth. But because many citizens felt that his attack was inappropriate, he later defended himself in a speech to the 1992 Southern Baptist Convention. The gist of his speech is captured by the opening quote. His argument was that the only *real* family is one that is anchored in a legal, heterosexual marriage. For Quayle and other citizens, especially those in the fixed category of Figure 1-1, the 1950s' Benchmark Family is not merely one ideal among several. It's the only *real* family; every other kind is *un*real.

7-Up proudly advertises itself as the *un*cola. It wants everyone to know that 7-Up is absolutely different from colas. What's more, 7-Up is not simply unique it's *better*, says the ad. Real diamonds are better than fakes, real flowers are better than artificial ones. The Real Family, claim certain advocates, is clearly better for adults, for children, and for society in general. They believe that solo-parent lifestyles such as *Murphy Brown's*, or the invented cohabitations of Chapter 9 (whether heterosexual or homosexual), or the social families of Chapters 2 and 3, are pale imitations—they're fakes.

WHAT'S REAL?

Since time began philosophers have fought over what's real and what's not. Soft drinks, water, gasoline, flowers, and diamonds are real in a physical or chemical sense. They possess what's called *material* reality: They can be felt, seen, heard, tasted, or smelled. Material reality also means that the objects exist apart from human beings. The neutron bomb is a weapon that destroys people but leaves buildings intact. If neutron bombs killed everyone in New York City, the buildings, bridges, and streets would still be there. But not the city government. The government is known as *nonmaterial* reality. You can't touch it; and if people and politicians disappear, so will the government. Government is people feeling, thinking, and behaving in certain ways. It does not exist outside of people's emotions and minds and their shared interactions. The pioneer sociologist, W. I. Thomas, said that governments are real because of what they do to and for us.[1] Children grow up under a government that influences how they feel, what they think, and how they behave. North American children learn to love democracy and hate dictatorships. Government policies affect the quality of their schools. When they become adults, government taxes them and provides benefits. Moreover, governments can and do compel people into the military and allow them to be killed.

Hence, when we say that governments are real in a nonmaterial sense, we're talking about how they impact the lives of people. Second, we mean that nonmaterial things, such as governments, are created by people. People don't create water, diamonds, trees, or flowers. Those things have material reality—they're simply *there*. People do invent nonmaterial reality such as governments. The United States wasn't *there* until it was created in part out of a violent revolution that displaced the British monarchy. During the late 1980s, citizens throughout Eastern Europe and the Soviet Union dramatically displaced their communist governments and constructed fledgling democracies.

Marriage is like government because it's real solely in a nonmaterial sense. Marriage is people feeling, thinking, and behaving in certain ways. It's not simply *there*. Social scientists use the term *reify*, or *reification*, to describe an error common to many people. To reify a government, a college, or a marriage is to stumble into the pitfall of thinking about cultural beliefs and social patterns as if they are real in a material sense. You can't touch or see or smell a marriage because it's not real in any sort of physical or chemical or biological way. Although everyone knows that to be true, people still refer to "my marriage" or "their marriage" as if marriage actually had independent existence, an existence separated from the ways that people feel, think, believe, and behave. Many of us carry an image in our heads of some sort of free-floating black box that we think of as "marriage." Unless we're cautious, we're likely to think of that box as being as physically real as a candy box or a flower vase.

Even though marriage is not a material reality, it is an extraordinarily powerful *social* reality. The social and cultural patterns that make up marriages affect us deeply. They significantly influence how we feel, think, and behave. At the same time, we too can affect marriage—influence is a two-way street. And that's precisely why it's so important not to reify marriage. If we think of marriage as having some existence outside of and apart from our own control, then we feel helpless to change it in any significant ways. But because a marriage, or a cohabitation, or any kind of social relationship is a set of cultural and social patterns, then, if we wish, we can try to change, or reinvent, those patterns.

THE INVENTION OF FORMAL MARRIAGES

The chief reason people can change social patterns is because people created them in the first place. No one is completely certain about the historical origins of marriage. What is clear is that all of the world's ancient civilizations (e.g., Babylonian, Egyptian, Hebrew) had legal codes that included the notion of formal marriage. Some scholars have argued that among societies existing before recorded history there were no formal, or legal, rules regarding female/male unions. They claim that there was no formal regulation of sex or of exchanges of money, goods, or services, nor were there rules about co-residence and children.[2] But gradually people began to write rules and laws setting forth the responsibilities and rights of husbands and wives. Actually, it was men much more than women who wrote the laws, including marriage laws. Rarely did men allow women to participate in the construction of formal marriage, family, or government, or for that matter, anything else.[3]

Wives as Property

As men throughout history wrote, and rewrote, laws about marriages and families, they created very different roles for themselves as husbands than they did for their wives. Wives were designated the *property* of their husbands, who in effect were their *owners*.[4] Men's responsibilities consisted largely of providing for the economic needs of their wives and children. Their authority over every aspect of their wives' existence knew virtually no limits. Husbands even had the right to be physically violent with their wives in the interests of social order (see Chapter 12). About all men couldn't do was murder their wives. One reason sometimes given for tolerating a husband's violence toward his wife is the wife's flirting with another man, or worse yet, actually sleeping with him. By contrast, one of the most significant rights that husbands had was the right to extramarital sex. Although few if any societies ever formalized the right of a man to have sex with someone other than his wife (or wives), the *double standard* was a powerful informal social custom.

Earlier chapters showed how people winked at men's sexual adventures but severely condemned women who dared deviate from formal rules against nonmarital sex. *Cuckold* was a term of derision and disdain applied to husbands who weren't able to control their wives sufficiently to keep them out of some other man's bed. No comparable term was ever applied to wives, because they weren't expected to control their husbands in any fashion. Least of all could wives curb men's overwhelming sexual needs, even if that meant occasional discreet dalliances or, perhaps, keeping of a mistress.

Many societies punished a wife's adultery by death, or at least by divorce. An adulterous wife also lost her rights to her husband's support and access to her children. The term *adulterate* means to taint, or to make impure and inferior. Since women were men's property, a wife's adultery meant making his property less valuable, not only in his eyes but in the eyes of everyone who knew about it. A husband's sexual adventures were never viewed in that light because, after all, men were the owners, not the property. In the Bible, for example, Old Testament law said that the wife taken in adultery could be stoned to death. But a husband having sex with another man's wife was usually required merely to say "I'm sorry," and to pay a sum of money to the husband whose property he'd devalued. Besides his wife, the husband's property included whatever material goods, land, and capital the family might possess. In many cases, even assets the wife might have gotten from her father before her marriage had to be turned over to her husband's control. She was seldom allowed to own any goods or property. Once married, wives were not allowed any independent authority over financial and material matters except the choices "graciously" accorded them by their husbands.

Patriarchal Norms

Until very recently in the world's history, the construction of marriage was largely a male affair. Women began to participate in the *recon*-struction of marriages only during the past two-hundred years, largely as a result of the nineteenth-century feminist movement, along with the upheavals of industrialization. Nonetheless, Chapters 6 and 7 show that before the 1960s, women's capabilities for reinvention were relatively minimal because they were excluded from full participation in the labor force.

Furthermore, the re-creation of marriages is limited chiefly to Western societies, as illustrated in connection with Figure 9-1. Throughout the remainder of the world, including highly industrialized places such as Japan, Taiwan, and South Korea, the formal norms and rules governing marriage continue to be based on what feminists call a *patriarchal* view of society. From that view, the best interests of society and children are served by conformity to long-standing traditional norms about marriage. And among these norms is the idea that women are men's property. In practical everyday terms, a patriarchal view (whether in Japan or North America) means leaving things pretty much as they've always been. By contrast, earlier chapters showed that growing numbers of women and men in the West are paying increasing attention to inventing new norms regarding marriage. In particular, they're unhappy about the fact that in the past men have done most of the creating while women have done most of the conforming.

THE STRUGGLE TO MAKE LIFE BETTER

Since Chapter 1 we've referred repeatedly to the most serious and stinging charge made by critics against the many changes that people have wrought in marriages and families since the sixties—that people are being irresponsible. The critics complain that many of today's women and men think about nothing but themselves—"*me first!*" Critics say that during the 1970s and 1980s individualism ran amok.[5] But today, they add, some people have finally come to realize that the costs of their individualism (me-ness) have been enormous for society, and especially for children.[6] Does that mean that the reconstruction of marriages and families is subsiding? Has someone pushed the pause button when it comes to reinventing social families and erotic friendships? Are we now going to rewind to the old rules written almost exclusively by men?

To answer these questions we must first ask ourselves why, for so many thousands of years, men wrote the kinds of rules and laws that they did. Some feminists have charged that men invented marriage with the specific intention of exploiting women. Men acted, says the charge, in basically selfish ways designed totally to benefit their own interests—*me first!* Men subordinated women and kept them as property with no concern at all for the best interests of women.

But was that actually the case? Does such a cynical and sinister view oversimplify what actually went on during the distant (and not so distant) past? Steven Seidman seems to think so, and says that recently other feminists have begun to think so too.[7] It appears that in the past many men sincerely believed that by inventing marriages as they did they were making life better than it was before they wrote the rules. To be sure, the outcome was to make wives the property of their husbands and to deny them many basic rights and privileges.

But most men believed they were doing the right thing, and historically they justified their rules by appeals to their religion (e.g., Judaism, Christianity, Islam).

Even today, fundamentalists within all three world religions justify women's continued subordination by asserting, *"Women's place is God's will!"* They don't, of course, describe women's place as subordination. Fundamentalist women (married and single) believe just as fiercely as men that God told men what to write in the first place. Consequently, rules from the Bible and the Koran telling wives what they should and shouldn't do simply spell out the natural order, indeed the *divine* order, of things.

Chapter 7 said that during the nineteenth century the prevailing view in the United States among both genders was that wives were equal to husbands. "Equal," of course, meant that each gender stayed in its "place," its own unique and "appropriate" sphere of life. Today's fundamentalists (whether Protestant, Catholic, Jewish) hold pretty much the same view.[8] They acknowledge, however, that patriarchal rules may sometimes lead to excesses such as the violence against women described in Chapter 12. Although they condemn the violence, they refuse to blame it on the rules. Instead, they say, if husbands sufficiently loved their wives they wouldn't beat up on them. Following traditional rules, they claim, is the only genuine way to make life better.

Interestingly enough, most of today's women and men trying to reinvent primary relationships, including marriage, hold the precisely the same goal. Remember Helga from Chapter 5. For several decades people like her have been struggling to make life better than they'd experienced it before they started making their changes. Indeed, why would they ignore the old rules if they didn't believe that life would get better by trying something different? Chapters 4 and 5 showed that relatively few women had premarital intercourse before the 1920s and 1930s in large part because the rule said, *Thou shalt not.* But because the Great Depression forced engaged couples to postpone marriage, some began to ignore the rule in order to have sex. Did they think of themselves as wildly daring, as selfish and narcissistic? Hardly. More likely they felt deep pangs of anxiety and guilt over breaking the rule. Nonetheless, they reasoned, "What difference does it make? Since we're going to marry anyhow, the rule makes little sense. Meanwhile, we'll be better off if we do It than if we don't."

Injustices and Excesses

Nevertheless, at least for some of them, life didn't get better after all. Some men promised their fiances marriage in exchange for sex and then disappeared if they got bored or she got pregnant. Furthermore, Chapter 7 showed that people in the sixties began to disconnect sex from engagement and marriage—also in hopes of making life better. Nevertheless, many women felt pressured into sex against their will because many men believed women had lost the right to say no. And today some critics assert that the AIDS epidemic is justified retribution for the irresponsible sexual choices persons have been making for many decades.[9]

Figure 1-1 shows that the vast majority of citizens belong neither to the fixed nor to the process camps. The Silent Majority doesn't go about explicitly advocating new ways for women and men to reinvent either their erotic friendships or their social families. When pollsters ask them what they believe, they sound much more like they belong in the fixed rather than the process camp. Nevertheless, their behaviors, such as the informal marriages described in Chapter 9, are more likely to match those of people in the process camp. Why? Because in their everyday struggles to make life better, they discover the traditional rules (e.g., the ban on premarital sex, or the rule against living together without a license) simply don't work for them. The result is that in terms of sexual patterns and informal and formal marriages, as well as many other things described throughout this book, the great majority of North Americans are making up new rules for their primary relationships as they go along.

Not that today's couples ignore past norms entirely. Most married women, for example, still follow the traditional custom of taking their husband's surname. But a few choose to keep their own surname. What is sharply different from pre-sixties days is the pervasiveness of choices. Before the 1960s, aside from movie stars or other entertainers, women never dreamed of having the option of choosing a married name. It was an ironclad expectation that they'd assume their husband's name. Today's women, however, have a choice: Should they follow long-standing social (and legal) custom, or try something different? Invariably, choices carry many excesses and injustices. Alongside unintentional hurt, a few adults do make choices designed intentionally to harm their partner. An extreme case of that can be seen in the 1991 movie, *The War of the Roses*, in which a divorcing couple stop at nothing, including murderous violence, to inflict damage on one another. And in 1993, a husband was convicted of lacing Tylenol capsules with poison in order to murder his wife and collect a large sum of insurance money.

However, most adults have no intention of making choices that harm either their partners or their children. If harm occurs, it's purely unintentional and regretted. Ronald Rindfuss remarks that researchers, and the social critics who read their reports, are the ones who complain the most, for instance, about the alleged negative effects on children of the various choices being made by today's adults. Interestingly, he adds that those "negative effects . . . may not be as self-evident" to the adults or the children themselves.[10] In any case, say advocates in the process camp, don't blame excesses on the reinvention being done by today's women and men. They shouldn't be blamed, they say, any more than men should be blamed for the excesses that inevitably occurred when they alone made the rules. Once upon a time most men thought they were doing the right thing, even though today many people understand that patriarchy inflicted a great deal of suffering and injustice on women and children.

The Case in Japan

Today, women are gradually joining with men in inventing the rules. It seems a flight of fancy that men will ever again be able to exclude Western women from participating in the ongoing construction of every kind of primary relationship, including formal marriages. Even in Japan, some researchers report that a few well-educated women are becoming increasingly discontent with patriarchal rules, and especially with the huge difficulties encountered in trying to change them.[11] Because of that discontent, can the Japanese expect as many excesses—and perhaps pain—as we experience in the West? More than likely the answer is yes. Kay Itoi and Bill Powell report that a great deal of male bashing occurs already in Japan, just as it did in North America during the sixties and seventies.[12] They add that well-educated men find it increasingly difficult to find the kind of traditional wife their fathers had, even though they yearn to do so. In July 1992, two female TV personalities announced they were members of the Reverend Sun Myung Moon's (patriarchal) Unification Church, and that they were going to marry total strangers selected by Rev. Moon in a mass wedding ceremony: "Within minutes the Unification Church was swamped by calls from Japanese men seeking information about the church."[13]

Until recently, a married Japanese woman was prohibited by law from using her premarriage surname in any social setting. After years

Some well-educated Japanese women who are married are struggling to "make it" in a patriarchal corporate world.

of pressing for change, however, a number of married women professionals have finally obtained the right to use their own surname—but only on the job: They eventually "convinced executives that such freedom wouldn't cause serious disruption."[14] Although IBM-Japan and several other multinational corporations reluctantly approved this concession, married women are still required to use their husband's name for taxes, insurance and other matters. And no matter how successful she might be within the company based on her own merits, outside of it a married woman remains "respectfully yours, *Mrs. ———.*" While describing the overwhelming obstacles Japanese women executives encountered in trying to make this seemingly modest change, Schlesinger, remarks that their struggle "underscores the tremendous difference between Japan and the U.S. *While Americans have virtually unlimited freedom unless a specific act is prohibited, Japanese often can only do what is specifically permitted.*"[15]

He adds that today's rules about Japanese families and households were written (by men) originally in the sixth century, and were "recrafted" (once again by men) some 120 years ago.

No Perfect Society Whether in the West or in Asian cultures, women and men struggling for changes in gender relations of any sort, including marriage, can never look forward to utopia. Bryce Christensen, a conservative spokesperson, charges that some advocates in the process camp hold out the dream of *utopia:* a perfect society if women and men keep on reinventing new ways of organizing marriages and families.[16] The reality, however, is that no set of social arrangements is ever pain-free or perfect. As long as men's rule-making powers went unchallenged, women and children bore most of the pain. Now that Western (and a few Asian) women are challenging men, the pain is being spread around more. Elizabeth and

Joseph Pleck say that, even under the previous system, men also paid a heavy price.[17] Chapters 6 and 7 showed how boys and men were denied opportunities for emotional intimacy either with other males or with women. Men's preoccupation with work and achievement, and their subsequent emotional distance from their wives and children, have been criticized in the West at least since the 1950s.[18] Recently, similar male "shortcomings" have become topics for research and media attention in Japan. As in the West, the charge is made that Japanese men, utterly preoccupied with success, are cut off from emotional closeness with their wives and children.

Nevertheless, as she ends her book criticizing the changes in marriages that have been happening throughout the United States, Sylvia Ann Hewlett applauds "The Japanese Model" in near-utopian terms: "The economic miracle of postwar Japan has hinged on the family." In particular, the miracle was due, she claims, to the " 'education mama.' "[19] Hewlett praises those "mamas" for their selfless devotion to their *sons'* success in school, which in turn makes them successful businessmen. Hewlett says that because Japanese family life revolves around the needs and interests of children, the adults don't have time to worry about "individualistic" things such as mothers' employment or divorce. Hence, Hewlett congratulates the Japanese for having such a strong family life, which she asserts is amply demonstrated by their low divorce rate.

However, Jane Condon's in-depth interviews with a sample of Japanese women re-

A Japanese family enjoying their new baby.

veal some significant oversights in Hewlett's portrayal of a near-perfect fit between traditional marriage patterns and national economic success. Condon reports that the stability of Japanese married couples "would be the envy of any American. The country has been enormously successful economically. *But at what price for the women?*"[20] The price, her study reveals, is that up through the early eighties, few married women pursued any interests of their own. Their sole objective in life was the educational and occupational success of their sons. Condon reports that Japanese women who questioned that pattern were asked by other women (and men), "Why tinker with success?"

"Tinkering" (i.e., reinventing marriage) is extraordinarily difficult in Japan. It is infinitely harder even than Japanese women trying to get permission to use their own surname on the job. Condon says there are at least three reasons why Japanese marriages are so change resistant. The first is traceable to the Japanese term *wa*. That term means that the Japanese value quiet harmony over explicit confrontation. To "rock the boat" has not been part of Japanese culture in general, much less a part of marriage. A good Japanese wife covets a placid, not a participatory, relationship with her husband.

The second reason relates to *meiwaku*—the importance of not bothering others. Japanese wives feel that because their husbands have so much on their minds worrying about their careers, they have neither the interest nor the energy to worry about their wives' needs. The only exception is when a wife is pleading her child's need. In that case the husband might listen—if he has time. The third reason is because of strong adherence to *amae*—dependence of the individual on the group. In the wife's case, her dependence is much more than economic. To be sure, because most Japanese wives are not employed their economic dependence is extremely significant. But most of all,

a Japanese woman is dependent on her husband for her validation as a full-fledged member of society.

At the core of Japanese culture lies the belief that a woman has no meaningful adult status unless she is married and subsequently has children. Moreover, children must *follow* the wedding—never precede it. A *Murphy Brown* scenario for a professional Japanese woman is unimaginable. A mature, never-married, childless woman in today's Japan is viewed in an extraordinarily negative light, a view strikingly similar to that of mature, single women in North America and Britain before the 1960s. Chapter 8 showed that they were pitied and often derided as spinsters or old maids until such time as they got "lucky enough" to find a man.

Condon says that for these three reasons (*wa, meiwaku, amae*), the "urge to maintain the status quo [in Japan] is stronger than in most societies."[21] Interestingly enough, however, research done in North America during the 1950s found those same three dimensions among both working- and middle-class wives.[22] For the same three reasons most Canadian and U.S. wives for that era were just as reluctant to openly challenge their husbands as most Japanese wives are today. Hence, when Condon reports that a few Japanese wives are now beginning to "tinker," that might be a harbinger of a lot more tinkering to come. She found evidence of a "small but widening gap between what [Japanese] men want—a wife in the kitchen—and what [their] women want—a chance to experience life in the outside world."[23]

One result of women wanting a more balanced life, reports Condon, is a slow but steady increase in Japanese divorce rates. Rates are rising for the same reasons they've risen in the West since the late 1800s—educational and occupational opportunities provide women with alternatives to what Chapter 5 called *gaman*. *Gaman* describes the patient acceptance of the sufferings of marriage by a woman (or man) caught indefinitely in a dissolution phase. Besides divorce as a means to solve *gaman*, some Japanese wives choose desertion, which Condon observes is more frequent in Japan than in the West.[24] In addition, Condon reports that increasing numbers of Japanese wives, feeling unable either to divorce or desert, choose suicide rather than continued *gaman*.[25]

MARRIAGE AND THE PRESSURE TO PARENT

In North America formal marriage is perceived, said earlier chapters, as the ultimate symbol of serious commitment. Kate and Marshall (now in their late 30s) had been cohabiting for over a dozen years. But not until they finally obtained a license did they convince their families and friends that they genuinely intended to spend the rest of their lives together. Moreover, a second and equally significant message that marriage sends is that the couple now has "social permission" to parent.[26] Because unmarried couples have no legal right to bear children, it's the license that transforms their situation and formally allows them to do so. Indeed, not only are Kate and Marshall now permitted to bear children, they're expected to do so. During the first few years of their cohabitation, the question they heard repeatedly was, "When are you getting serious?" A bit more time went by and a second question got mixed in with the first: "When are you going to have children? Since you're not getting any younger, you'd better soon get married so you can have kids." Kate's mother (Emma) was fond of quoting a rhyme to Kate that a friend had inscribed in her own high-school yearbook: "First comes love, then comes marriage, then comes Emma with a baby-carriage."

Kate got the subtle message from Emma and everyone else that she should be married before having a child. At the heart of the famous *Murphy Brown* uproar was this very issue: Should an unmarried woman have a child? Kate at least had a co-resident partner—Brown did not. Up to now Kate and Marshall had resisted pressures to marry in order merely to please their families. Although Kate felt it was okay in general for an unmarried woman to bear a child, it was not her personal choice. Precisely because she wanted to parent, she indicated her feelings to Marshall that it was indeed time to marry. He too was strongly in favor of adding parenting to their erotic friendship, but he was not keen about adding marriage. Nonetheless, because Kate wanted it, he agreed. Their families were so elated with their decision that they proposed paying for an elaborate wedding and a lavish reception. But Kate and Marshall schemed to resist their pressure. One evening they secretly slipped away to a nearby town where they had the local sheriff perform the ceremony witnessed solely by her two deputies.

Armed with their license, they told everyone they were now going to "work hard" at getting Kate pregnant. When they finally announced a positive pregnancy test, their families were exultant. The next question was, "What are you going to name him [or as an afterthought, her]?" What their families were curious about was the child's first, not last, name. Even though Kate, a businesswoman, had kept her own surname after marriage, everyone assumed they would surely assign the child Marshall's surname. Instead, however, the couple discussed assigning Kate's surname. They also wondered about assigning a hyphenated surname, for example, Smith-Brown. Or they could even create a new name, as did their local clergy couple when faced with the same issue. The surname the clergy couple gave their infant was derived from the (Greek) New Testament term for "peace." Kate and Marshall liked that idea so much that they created a fresh surname for their child derived from the New Testament term for "tender love."

Kate and Marshall's story illustrates the

point that throughout North American culture, marriage is inherently linked with having children. A person is not considered socially complete until he or she (especially) is married. Nor is their marriage complete until a child is born. Furthermore, the dual signals that marriage sends—serious commitment and permission for children—are also themselves inherently linked. The whole point of getting serious—of spending a lifetime together—is to supply the children with a stable environment in which to grow up. Hence, when a couple marries they're signaling to families, friends, and everyone else that their seriousness extends not only to one another but also with equal force to children. At the present time in North American culture, these ideas cannot be separated. Before, during, and after the 1992 national elections, politicians used the phrase *family values* repeatedly. Although no one bothered to define it very carefully, the bottom line seemed to be this: "The best way for Americans to live is to get married, have children, and stay together forever."

But because growing numbers of parents do not stay together, some critics finger easy divorce as a major culprit in what they believe to be the decline of family values. In particular, they're worried about increasing numbers of children growing up in lone-parent households. Chapter 13 shows that a number of adults become lone parents because of divorce. Consequently, some conservative advocates want to remove the *no-fault* divorce laws that are currently on the books in most states and to reimpose laws that make it virtually impossible for parents with minor children (aged 18 and under) to obtain a divorce. Joanne Schrof characterizes those stricter laws as "wedding bands made of steel."[27]

Thou Shalt Love Thy Neighbor
as Thyself

A chief reason persons in the fixed category of Figure 1-1 wish to make divorce next to im-

possible to obtain is because they believe that many Americans, especially women, no longer consider children the most important thing in their lives. Hewlett praises Japanese women for being education mamas, and worries that feminism teaches American women that "'self-development is a higher duty than self-sacrifice' "[28] Conservatives charge that because many women place their own interests ahead of their children's concerns, both the children and society suffer. In fact, however, few Progressives ever simplemindedly asserted that women should think of themselves *before* they think of their children or their men. Rather, Carol Gilligan suggests that feminism "enabled women to consider it moral to care not only for others but also for themselves."[29] Similarly, the biblical idea is that one should love one's neighbor as *much* as—neither *more* nor *less* than—oneself.

It's fair to say, however, that during the past, North American wives/mothers loved their husbands and children *more* than they loved themselves. Like that of today's Japanese wives, their existence centered in the things that mattered most to the other people in the family. For a woman to love her family more than herself required a lot of courage and self-sacrifice Her self-sacrifice was a simple solution to the problem of "making life better." Whenever a wife/mother had to choose between something her child or husband wanted and something she might want, she knew what her choice had to be. That is perhaps the major reason the pre-sixties Benchmark Family worked as well as it did. The woman's heart told her what "family values" meant.

A Logical Contradiction However, the belief that a person should care for herself/himself as much as others is also an important family value, and it did not begin with feminism. According to pioneer sociologists such as Simmel and Weber, that idea's been part of Western culture at least since the time of Jesus.[30] Jesus taught that the individual's duty to God, and thus to his or her own spiritual integrity, may sometimes conflict with duty to family. Western culture has always contained these two contradictory values: On the one hand, the individual is told to love others and sacrifice for the group (e.g., family, government). The group is said to be much more important that any individual person. On the other hand, schoolchildren learn with equal force that in our culture the individual matters supremely. She or he has dignity and rights that the Declaration of Independence proclaims as inalienable.

It's impossible to reconcile these two values in any logical fashion. So people simply do what they've always done—by trial and error they figure out what works to make life better, and they do it. Before the 1960s, for instance, men put their jobs ahead of emotional closeness to wife and children. They pursued economic success far more than they sought emotional intimacy. But simultaneously, a husband could also say that he used the money he earned to take care of his wife and children instead of spending it on himself. Rather than buy the fishing boat or bowling ball he feverishly coveted, he bought food and clothing for his family. In that sense, he was sacrificing for them.

Hence, even though it seems logically contradictory, husbands had it both ways. On the one side they could be *individualistic* by striving for their own achievement and economic success. On the other side they could be *altruistic* because they were sacrificing for something bigger than themselves—The Family. That arrangement worked very well as long as wives were allowed to go only one way, the altruistic route. What the sixties and seventies did was permit women's lives to become as contradictory as men's had always been. For probably the first time in history, women, like men, were finally allowed to draw on both sets of contradictory family values—individualism and altruism.

Moral Obligations Desmond Ellis observed that altruism and individualism are both moral obligations.[31] Chapter 3 said that a moral obligation is something that is distinctively ethical and elevated, that is inherently right in and of itself. A moral obligation is an inescapable duty: You can't get out of doing it, and when you do it, you'll feel good. Paying taxes, for example, is an obligation that citizens can't easily escape. Politicians tell us that when we pay our fair share we'll have the satisfaction of knowing that we contributed to something bigger than our own self-interest. Caring for one's erotic friend (spouse or partner) and children is a moral obligation. And doing it feels good. You're doing something you're *supposed* to do and yet something you *want* to do, both at the same time.

By the same token, in Western culture men have felt the same kind of moral obligation for their own personal development. Chapter 6 showed that beginning with the Jacksonian era, achievement and success became moral obligations for all American men. Boys learned that they could not flee from striving for achievement. What is more, they were assured they'd feel good about themselves if they succeeded. Girls, however, were not morally obliged to be individualistic. They did not have to achieve in the marketplace. Just as men had no cultural option to choose *not* to be individualistic, women had no cultural option to choose to be. Family values were applied selectively, by gender. However, in Western culture it's becoming increasingly difficult to exclude women from the mix of individualism and altruism. Growing numbers of women are forming erotic friendships in which they feel they are inalienably entitled to that curious mixture.

Rapoport's Dilemma

The resulting dilemma, say Rhona Rapaport and colleagues, arises from trying to *balance* the often clashing interests of children, women, and men.[32] The challenge is to figure out how to shift away from the Modern (1950s') Family, which had as standard equipment a built-in chauffeur (Mom) for Freddie's Little League games and Suzy's dancing lessons, to varieties of postmodern families that are much less fixed and more unpredictable. Growing numbers of couples are grappling with Rapoport's dilemma.[33] On the one side are wives and mothers slowly gaining what husbands and fathers have always had. On the other side are the implications this has for the permanence of relationships, and thus the well-being of children. Earlier chapters described this dilemma as the struggle between we-ness and me-ness.

Some citizens want to solve the dilemma by making it go away. They prefer returning to the time when women had access solely to the altruistic route.[34] During the 1992 national elections, President Bush was fond of saying that he wanted a country based on the *Walton's* family rather than the *Simpson's*. But the first is nostalgia, the second is a parody, and neither is realistic for the future. Rapoport's dilemma is not going to go away. Growing numbers of couples are going to have to face it for both ideological and structural reasons.

Ideology—Equal Means Interchangeable

The 1950s' Modern Family was based on the nineteenth-century notion that wives and husbands could be equal even though they lived in separate spheres of life—she at home, he in the workplace. For two centuries, however, feminists argued against the "separate-but-equal" viewpoint. Feminists said instead that husbands should lift their altruism to balance their individualism, and that wives should raise their individualism to balance their altruism. Feminists meant that the genders should be *interchangeable*—they should have the same rights and responsibilities both in the marketplace and the home place.[35] Now, finally, femi-

nists and their allies in the process segment of Figure 1-1 have been vindicated. From a cultural, or ideological, standpoint it's become embarrassing to argue that men should be able to be both individualistic and altruistic but that women should merely be altruistic.

Recent studies suggest that the majority of North Americans now *say* that they agree with the emerging cultural ideal of gender interchangeability.[36] When asked about their beliefs, most citizens reject the old separate-but-equal ideology. They pay lip service to the ideal that the genders should be interchangeable both at home and in the marketplace. (See discussion about interchangeability in Chapter 12.) For example, the majority of citizens believe that women should get the same pay as men for the same job, wives and husbands should have equal household authority, husbands should do as much child care and housework as wives, and so forth. Furthermore, studies show that, on the basis of those kinds of questions, larger percentages of citizens today say they believe in gender equality than there were thirty years ago.

But by no means does merely believing in gender equality imply that women are in fact the equals of men either inside families or throughout the larger society. Earlier chapters showed, for example, that there are large gaps between what people say they believe about sex and how they actually behave. And Chapter 15 reveals that a huge gap exists between people's beliefs and behaviors about gender. There are still major distinctions between what people say, and how they actually behave, when it comes to matters of women's education and employment, child care, and housework. Nevertheless, to assert that women and men *should* be equal, or interchangeable, is very much a socially desirable, or "politically correct," thing to say. It is just as correct as saying that "blacks and whites should be equal." Few if any politicians would ever publicly say anything else about either gender or race. Gender equality, like racial equality, is a cultural ideal whose time has finally come. Even politicians or other opinion-makers who might dismiss those ideals in private rarely if ever do so in public.

Structure—Shifting Character of Labor Markets Spreading beliefs about gender equality is one reason Rapoport's dilemma is not going to disappear. A second reason it's going to stick around is what sociologists call *structural*. A structural factor is a powerful force happening in the larger society that may either limit or increase people's choices, or perhaps do both. Chapter 7 said that the Great Depression limited people's choices for marriage but also expanded their choices to have sexual intercourse during engagement. During the 1990s, the economies of the United States and Canada, as well as of other Western societies, seem relatively sluggish. In the United States, there is great concern that our school systems are inferior and are failing to produce the kinds of citizens that will make us competitive in what Chapter 15 calls the "global economy." Demographically, the proportion of white men in the population is shrinking relative to the proportions of minorities and women.

And as all that is happening, many good jobs (i.e., well paying and interesting) are simply disappearing from the labor market.[37] The most obvious example is found in the defense industry. As the Cold War ends, thousands of well-paying blue-collar and white-collar jobs are vanishing. Many other businesses and industries are "downsizing," that is, eliminating jobs. Chapter 15 shows that many of the lost jobs were located in male-dominated occupations such as machinist, tool and die maker, and so forth.

All of these and many other factors suggest that during the years ahead there will be a big push to make the United States as competitive in the world economy as it is in the Olympic Games. National leaders are talking seriously about totally revamping our school systems. One of the aims is to identify bright and talented children and to encourage them to push themselves to their full potential. Charlotte, North Carolina, in cooperation with Davidson College, already has a pilot program of this sort in place for black high school students. The TV ad for black colleges stating, "A mind is a terrible thing to waste," applies to women of all races as well as to blacks. In future, the demand for talented and skilled persons, regardless of gender or race, is likely to expand in an effort to make the United States more competitive on the world scene. The demands will probably be backed up with generous incentives, financial and otherwise, to lure that talent into the marketplace. Growing numbers of women (white and black) are likely to experience increasing opportunities for participation in the labor force. Expanding opportunities mean that couples will face a greater range of choices and options than ever before. In turn, those choices and options will impact on their erotic friendships in general, as well as on their marriages, both formal and informal.

Hence, if we think that Rapoport's dilemma—the struggle between we-ness and me-ness—seems painfully sharp now, it's likely to become even more painful for greater numbers of couples during the years ahead. As women encounter the kinds of structural features that appear to lie before us, they're likely to become highly motivated to raise their levels of individualism to seize fresh opportunities. But where are the incentives for men to raise their levels of altruism? And what are the implications for the permanence of marriages, both formal and informal? What about the thorniest question of all—the well-being of children? At this time it's impossible to predict how couples during the years ahead will be reconstructing marriages (formal and informal) to manage the Rapoport dilemma. What does seem plain is that reinvention *in and of itself* will become even more of a permanent and pervasive feature of marriages than it is right now.

TYPES OF MARRIAGE REINVENTIONS

Head-Complement Marriages

Although both the tempo and the significance of future reconstruction are likely to pick up, marital reconstruction is not new to the twentieth century. We learned that in the West wives were the legal property of husbands until the early part of the nineteenth century. Chapter 6 described the Jacksonian and Progressive eras during which North America became highly industrialized and urbanized. During those periods, as a result of pressure from feminists, social reformers, and others, persons reconstructed marriages by rewriting laws and making changes in social customs. With the passage by many states of the Married Women's Property Acts during the mid-1800s, most of the legal restraints imposed on women were finally removed.[38] As a result, the role of the husband was changed from being his wife's *owner* to that of being the *head* of the household. And rather than being her husband's *property*, the wife became his *complement*. The Head-Complement marriage is simply another label to describe the Benchmark Family discussed in earlier chapters.

The husband was the Head for both cultural and economic reasons. Culturally, people believed that every family had to have an authority figure who could make final decisions in the midst of disagreement. People believed that kind of authority promoted family order and well-being. They also believed that the husband was the person best suited (by God and/or nature) to make tough decisions. Because he was most often the sole economic provider for the family, his wife and children depended on him totally for financial support.

Thus, the economic resources he supplied also earned him the right to make final decisions. That was particularly true if the decision was connected with his occupation. For example, he might come home one day and announce to his wife and children that they had to move to another city so he could take a better job. Although the family might disagree and resist moving, in the end they had little choice.

Simultaneously, the wife was her husband's Complement in the sense that he needed her for him to be "socially complete" (being a full-fledged and highly respected member of his church, community, and society). She took the money for which he worked so hard and wisely allocated it to household needs, thus creating a home that brought him prestige, esteem, and respect. Likewise, she brought up their children in ways that would be a credit to him and to their community.

Senior and Junior Partners

Chapter 7 described the Big Change in women's employment behaviors. About a hundred years ago, white married women began to make employment choices that have been impacting the reinvention of marriages ever since. Although most married black women had been forced to work outside the home since 1865 in order to help support their families, white married women did not do so until the 1890s and the early part of the twentieth century. Since that time they have been entering the paid labor force in increasing numbers.

Nevertheless, during most of the century there's been a big gap between women's actual employment behaviors and what people believed about "women's work." Prevailing cultural beliefs failed to endorse the idea of a married woman working outside the home, especially if she had small children. Quite the contrary, says Ivan Nye; until the 1940s such

A head-complement marriage of the 1950s.

behavior was culturally prohibited.[39] For over a hundred years, conservatives have been critical of married women's employment, chiefly because they believe that children will be neglected and thus harmed.[40] Nevertheless, beginning with the 1890s, many wives responded that their families needed the money and thus they had to take on paid jobs. It was not a matter of choice.

Husband as Chief Provider Besides having potentially negative consequences for children, another major reason wife employment was viewed suspiciously was because it was thought to reflect negatively on the husband. Being a good provider meant being the *sole*

provider—the wife did not have to work.[41] A man whose wife took a paid job lost respect in the eyes of others, and that meant a decline in his own self-respect as well.

To combat that threat, women and men gradually created the cultural definition that her paid work was not on the same plane as his. Her employment was perceived as not as important as his. He had a permanent, full-time job that gave him the right to be the final authority in his family. That cultural perception did not change. But another cultural definition did: The husband became redefined from being sole provider to being merely *chief* provider.

If he was chief provider, then she was the

secondary provider—the backup. Before the sixties women were urged to get as much education as possible so they could "step in and help out" with family finances if needed. Her work was perceived as temporary, and was often part-time. It was defined as a short-term, stop-gap measure to help out with extra family expenses. What is pivotal about the cultural redefinitions of married women's employment during the twentieth century is that they justified such employment solely on altruistic grounds. Over the years it gradually became okay for women to work in order to help out their children, or their husbands, or perhaps an ailing parent. Their employment was never justified on individualistic grounds, however. Unlike men, they were not simultaneously working for themselves—for their own respect, esteem, and prestige.

Hence, compared with men's employment, married women's employment was not viewed as a serious life interest. A married woman's chief interests were the home, children, and often voluntary organizations. In particular, the children had to come first. Outside employment was merely a burdensome and often intrusive necessity: It kept women from doing the things they really wanted to do. Given those sharply contrasting definitions of paid work, most twentieth-century husbands were viewed as the *senior* or chief providers for their family. Wives were imaged as *junior* or subordinate providers for their family.

In spite of the fact that junior partners have incomes, and complements do not, there seem to be many more similarities than differences in the two kinds of marriages. In both instances, the household revolves around the husband's occupation, and he is recognized as its chief provider. Whether the wife works part-time or full-time, and whether she's employed permanently or intermittently, are far less significant than how the couple perceives and defines *his* paid work versus *her* paid

work. The "family value" that binds couples in all of these situations is that both partners perceive that if and when she works, she does so primarily for altruistic reasons. During the late twentieth century the majority of North Americans gradually accepted the idea that it's okay for the Good Wife to be employed because she's doing good—she's helping out her family.

Equal Partners

As a result of the 1960s' and 1970s' Big Change described in Chapter 3, researchers began to identify certain married couples as "dual-career," "dual-achiever," "equal-partner," and so on." Not only were the husbands and wives in these couples well educated (a college degree or beyond), the wife had an occupation that both spouses perceived as a *career*. One major distinction between a career and a job is that a career implies a steady path of upward progress in terms of earnings, prestige, authority, and so on. The newspaper says that a baseball player is "at the peak of his career." Or, "she's shifting her career from player to coach." Whether it's sports, medicine, business, sales, management, teaching, politics, or whatever, a career implies that she or he never ceases working extremely hard in order to keep on achieving. Achieve what? Money? Partly, yes. But a career person also wants far more than money. She or he also wants to achieve ever-increasing amounts of intangible rewards such as prestige and esteem. A career person wants to be well thought of by her or his peers—she or he wants to have a strong and positive reputation. The goal of having a reputation includes peers living beyond one's particular work site. Career persons want to be well known throughout their state, the nation, and perhaps other nations as well.

Those are individualistic-type rewards that in the past were legitimate solely for men. *Equal-partner* marriages (whether formal or informal) are those in which both persons define their quest for individualistic gratifications to be as important as their altruistic responsibilities to their partner and (any) children. In short, each loves herself or himself as much as her or his neighbor. However, each person does not *have* to have a career to be an equal partner. For example, a working wife with a "job" might feel that her individualism is just as important to her as her altruism. And her husband might share that view. In this case we could classify them as equal partners. By the same token, each person does not *have* to be constantly employed for the couple to be equal partners. For example, Marshall might opt to take an unpaid one year leave of absence from his career in order to be the prime caregiver to his newborn infant. That doesn't mean that he and Kate are no longer equal partners. Even though he has no current income, they continue to share their commitment to the ideals of struggling to balance individualism with altruism.

The basic point is that the Rapoport dilemma previously described comes into its sharpest focus among equal-partner marriages, both formal and informal. The fact that the Rapoports were among the earliest researchers to study dual-career marriages meant they were among the first to uncover the importance of trying to negotiate the often competing interests of women, children, and men. The reason their dilemma became so apparent is that a career is an unrelenting master. One can never work hard enough. One can never get enough intangible rewards. There are always a few more gratifications just beyond reach. During the sixties, one researcher described this as a sense of "boundlessness."[43] At that time, however, it applied solely to men. Now growing numbers of well-educated women also find themselves pursuing careers and thus being afflicted with this same sense of boundlessness.

Hence, what makes equal partners distinc-tive from other couples (head-complement; senior-junior partner) is that the man's (husband or partner) occupation is not defined as more significant than hers, nor is he perceived as the chief provider. The "family value" that binds equal-partner arrangements is that women's individualism and altruism are viewed on the same plane as his. And just as equal partners do not expect women's altruism to exceed their individualism, they do not expect men's individualism to exceed their altruism. In practical terms, women expect their husbands/partners to be just as committed as they to their relationship, to child care, and to routine domestic chores. However, Chapter 15 reports that many career women (to say nothing of women who are complements and junior partners) tend to be more involved than their partners in both child care and routine chores.

Emotional Intimacy   Among many other things, being committed to a relationship includes the cultivation of emotional intimacy. Chapter 5 said that one of the major and lasting outcomes of the sixties is the notion that friendship between women and men ought to include more than shared leisure activities.[44] Educated women in particular seek to reinvent their erotic friendships with men by introducing them to such things as self-disclosure, baring one's innermost being, exposing anxieties and joys, and so on. Just as intensely, women such as Helga (Chapter 5) want men to start asking them, "Who are you? How can I find out what you're really like?" Women also want men to start being models of emotional intimacy to children, especially to boys. In sum, on the one hand loving *oneself* means fulfilling the moral obligation to develop one's skills, talents, and abilities to the fullest extent possible. On the other hand, among erotic friends loving one's *neighbor* means fulfilling the moral obligation to care for that person's emotional needs as well as his or her material needs. Hence, it should come as no surprise that equal partners face a greater, more complex, and often more painful range of contradictions than do head-complements and senior-junior partners.

Nevertheless, growing numbers of head-complements and senior-juniors are probably facing at least some of these contradictions. That's especially true if one partner or the other is changing her or his definitions of what their relationship should be like. For example, a wife who hasn't been employed during fifteen years of marriage may wish to enter the labor force over her husband's objections. Or a wife who's had a job during ten years of marriage gets the opportunity to enter a career and wants to take it, even though her husband objects. A husband who's had a dual-career marriage for six years becomes gradually aware that he and his wife are unable to nurture the profound mutual intimacy he desires. As he sees it, the main reason they can't is because most of the time she's away traveling on business. Issues such as these, as well as many others, tend to generate the conflicts and negotiations described in Chapter 11.

OTHER REINVENTIONS SURROUNDING MARRIAGE

Married Women's Name Change

"What's in a name? That which we call a rose by any other name would smell as sweet." During the 1992 national elections, the question that Shakespeare's Juliet posed was a mini-issue that became symbolic of a much bigger question. After Hillary Rodham married Bill Clinton during the early 1970s, she kept her own surname. Hillary, like Bill, had a career as an attorney. After a few years, however, the fact that Hillary was using her own surname became perceived as a serious liability to Clinton's political career. Hence she started using her husband's surname instead of her own.[45] And from her birth, their daughter Chelsea was also

First lady Hillary Rodham Clinton gestures while testifying on Capitol Hill, Thursday, September 30, 1993, before the Senate Finance Committee, which was holding hearings on health care reform.

named Clinton. Whether Hillary should keep her own name or not was part of the bigger issue of citizens' feelings about a political couple being perceived as genuine equal partners. Early in the campaign Hillary said: "If you elect Bill, you get me."[46] Two more of her widely reported, and highly criticized, comments were, first, "I'm not some little woman standing by her man like Tammy Wynette." Second, "I suppose I could have stayed home and baked cookies and had teas. But what I decided to do was fulfill my profession."

Could a man be president and have a wife who was something more than either his complement (e.g., Barbara Bush) or at the most his junior partner (e.g., Marilyn Quayle)? Former President Richard Nixon made some comments about Hillary and Bill that most political analysts believed reflected the views of many Americans in the center and fixed categories of Figure 1-1: "If the wife comes through as being too strong and too intelligent, it makes the husband look like a wimp."[47] Apparently, Clinton strategists took Nixon's comments seriously, because the longer the 1992 campaign wore on the less Hillary said, and the less she was perceived as in any way acting independently of Bill. It's likely that if Hillary had chosen to keep her own name, Clinton critics would have used that as evidence that Clinton was a "weak" man and thus not worthy to be U.S. president. After the election, however, Hillary struck a compromise by letting it be known that she now wanted to be identified as Hillary *Rodham* Clinton. That shift corresponded with her leadership role in seeking to reorganize the nation's health care system.

Among most English-speaking countries, the custom of a married woman assuming her husband's surname can be traced back as far as the thirteenth century.[48] Shirley Weitz says that her name change is symbolic of the passing of the woman from the authority of one man (her father) to that of another man (her husband).[49] By the seventeenth century it became customary to insert the term Mrs. ahead of her name, and so she was known as Mrs. *Jane* Smith.[50] But by the early 1800s (around the start of the Jacksonian era), married women had given up their own first names as well: The new custom became to address them as Mrs. *John* Smith. Consequently, nineteenth-century feminist leaders made name change one of their major issues.[51] They believed that one's name is intimately connected with one's identity and sense of self. When a woman gives up her name, they reasoned, she gives up some part of the essence of who she is. Hence, the 1848 Seneca Falls Convention (the first ever on women's rights) advocated the policy that married women should keep at least their own first name. At that time, feminist leader Elizabeth Cady Stanton said that when a woman took her husband's first name, it was like a slave taking his or her master's name: In both cases, they suffered a loss of identity. When slaves got freedom the first thing they did, argued Stanton, was to select a name for themselves.[52]

Another feminist leader got even more dar-

ing. Lucy Stone married Henry B. Blackwell in 1855. She was the first American woman known to retain her own surname after marriage. Stone said, "My name is the symbol of my identity and must not be lost."[53] However, few women followed Stanton's moderate example, much less Stone's more radical departure from accepted custom. No state except Hawaii actually ever compelled a wife by law to assume her husband's surname. Nevertheless, whenever the courts were called on to settle a dispute involving the wife's name, women lost out: "By the 1930s, it was accepted as 'law' that women lost their maiden names at marriage."[54] Although a number of 1960s' feminists revived the issue of women's name change, it does not appear to have generated much more interest during the past three decades than it did during the previous century. The vast majority of North American women seem willing to take their husband's surname, at least the first time they marry formally.[55]

However, if in future the numbers of equal-partner couples increase, it may be that the proportions of women choosing to keep their own names will expand as well. For instance, a 1990 study of college students found that women who expected to have nontraditional work roles after the birth of their first child were less likely than other women to want to change their last name to that of their spouse.[56] The connection between equal-partner status and refusal to take the husband's name is plain: The woman believes that married women and men should exercise comparable levels of individualism and altruism. When a woman uses her spouse's name we can't be certain precisely how she feels about the balance of altruism and individualism. She may believe that the two obligations should be balanced, but simply doesn't want to make a big deal of keeping her own name. Or, she may genuinely feel that she ought to pay more attention to altruism than individualism.

Weddings as Rituals

According to Pamela Freese, name change is but one part of the broader transformation that North American culture prescribes for women at marriage. Freese recently studied fifty American weddings.[57] She started with the idea that weddings are *rituals*. Anthropologists have long observed that every culture has rituals of all kinds. The rituals symbolize changes in the persons who pass through them. Circumcision, for instance, symbolizes the change from being merely male to being a Jewish male. Similarly, among Roman Catholics, infant baptism also symbolizes change: before baptism, the child had "original sin"; baptism removes the sin and brings the child into God's family.

If we look for them, we find rituals everywhere. The diploma being handed from principal to student at Commencement symbolizes the student's passage from being merely a student to being a graduate. The army's "swearing-in" ceremony changes a person instantaneously from a civilian to a soldier in everyone's perception. Rituals remind people of what's important in their culture, and thus help celebrate values they believe are important and must be respected. Most sporting events in the United States are preceded by the singing of the "Star-Spangled Banner." In Britain it's "God Save the Queen." Singing the national anthem is a ritual that many people define as a celebration of the greatness of the country. Doing anything during the ritual that indicates disrespect to the nation is viewed negatively. Many Americans were extremely put out at Roseanne Barr's allegedly obscene gestures during her singing of the national anthem before a 1991 nationally televised baseball game.[58] Her behavior, they felt, demeaned the dignity of the United States. However, the players did the very same thing during the game, and they weren't perceived negatively. What made the behavior bad was

when it was done—during the singing of the anthem.

By saying that weddings are rituals Freese means two things: (1) They symbolize women's social transformation, and (2) they celebrate important cultural values. Freese reports that things such as the flowers, the parties and receptions, the ceremony itself, the bridal dress, and the name change, symbolize the dramatic transformation that women undergo as a result of getting married. The chief transformation is that suddenly she belongs to someone other than her father—she now belongs to her husband. As much as any other symbol, says Freese, her wedding dress signals her new allegiance. Her white dress is meant to symbolize the virginity and purity that come from never having had sexual intercourse: She is thus a "fit bride" for her husband. Freese adds that the honeymoon is also symbolic of her change from being a virgin to being a wife and potential mother. And motherhood, reports Freese, is an extraordinarily important cultural value symbolized and celebrated by weddings. The bride is now expected to have children and to raise them so as to promote their well-being and thus an orderly society.

Freese states that most contemporary wedding customs symbolize what Chapters 6 and 10 call a *patriarchal* view of marriage, that is, the idea that children and society are best served by conformity to traditional norms about women and men. Hence, most wedding rituals tend to symbolize a Head-Complement or Senior Junior type of marriage. Freese says that so far very few wedding customs have been invented to signal the couple's preference for an equal partner kind of marriage. Even among couples who definitely intend to be equal partners, the feeling often prevails that it's no big deal to follow most of the traditional (i.e., patriarchal) wedding customs, especially if doing so pleases their families. Nevertheless, Freese notes that some couples reject certain customs. For instance, in those cases where the woman plans to keep her own name, the couple deletes the practice of being introduced as Mr. and Mrs. Fred Brown.

Postponing the First Formal Marriage

Chapters 8 and 9 showed some numbers revealing long-term trends about marriages. A major conclusion from those numbers is that during the past several decades there have been steady increases in the percentage of younger persons (aged 20–29) who have never been legally married. However, there are two things those numbers do *not* seem to mean. First, they do not imply that most younger single persons are content to live alone. To be sure, some are indeed living alone, or with parents, or with housemates. A much more significant trend, however, is that expanding numbers of young persons are choosing to form *co-resident* erotic friendships. Larry Bumpass and colleagues say that there are just about as many younger persons today as there were in prior decades who "set up housekeeping" together.[59] The major difference between them is that many of today's joint "housekeepers" are not legal. Second, so far as sociologists can tell, the trends do not suggest that the vast majority of North American youth will never formally marry. It seems more reasonable to say that many younger persons are reinventing their life course. They're simply postponing formal marriage until they are older. Some wait until their mid to late 20s. Others wait until they are in their 30s.

Disinventing Teenage Marriages

Chapter 7 noted that during the 1950s, social critics worried about teenage marriages. The frequency of teen marriages was higher during the fifties than at any other time in the twentieth century.[60] The critics' major fear was that because young, poorly educated bridegrooms would be unable to support their wives and

children, they would end up getting divorced. It seemed apparent that most of those adolescents were getting married either because they wanted to have sexual intercourse or because they'd already crossed the Line and she was pregnant. However, Chapters 4, 5, and 7 showed that the 1960s sexual "revolution" began to disconnect sex from marriage. As a result, the unease of 1950s' critics about teenage marriages have been set aside and forgotten.

Today, critics express instead their profound anxieties over the high rates of never-married teens having sexual intercourse and bearing children. After all, by getting married and then having a child, fifties' adolescents were in fact conforming to powerful cultural expectations. Nat King Cole could reassure 1950s' parents by singing: "They tried to tell us we're too young, too young to really be in love, . . . As the years go by they will recall, we were not too young at all."

In spite of the fact that nonmarital sex remains culturally prohibited, Chapter 4 showed how common it is becoming among today's adolescents. Added to its growing prevalence is the availability of legal abortion since 1973, which supplies an alternative to "shotgun marriages." The result of both factors is that "Teenage marriage has declined an average of 50%" since the 1950s.[61] Bumpass and colleagues add that, "Among males, blacks, and the college-educated, teenage marriages have declined by two-thirds to three-quarters, and have nearly disappeared." The declines in marriage rates among adolescents have been much sharper than they've been even among persons in their 20s, which as we learned are sharp indeed. Nevertheless, Bumpass and co-workers suspect that many of today's adolescents are merely postponing marriage until they reach their 20s.

In short, better-educated persons who during the fifties tended to marry in their early 20s, appear to be delaying their first formal marriage until their late 20s or, very often, their thirties. And persons with average education who tended to marry in their late teens seem to be postponing formal marriage until their 20s. Because the general idea of postponing legal marriage seems to be catching on in North American culture, and because increasing numbers of persons are in fact postponing it, it seems safe to say that *formal* adolescent marriage will probably become an increasingly rare event—it's becoming *disinvented*.

REMARRIAGES

Chapter 13 shows that since the 1960s growing numbers of persons have been getting divorced. As a result, researchers have wanted to know, "Do divorced people get *remarried* or not?" Some 1960s' and 1970s' critics charged that high divorce rates demonstrated that "people were 'giving up' on marriage, and that it would soon disappear." But its defenders responded that "it wasn't marriage itself that people were rejecting, merely 'bad' relationships." And to prove their argument, defenders pointed to the large numbers of divorced persons who were getting remarried "in hopes of working out a good relationship the second time around." Indeed, as the numbers of divorces rapidly piled up between 1970 and 1983, the numbers of people remarrying shot up accordingly. During those thirteen years, the numbers of people remarrying increased by 82 percent.[62] Marilyn Coleman and Lawrence Ganong remark that the United States "has the highest remarriage rate in the world; over 40% of [all] marriages are remarriages for one or both partners."[63]

Barbara Wilson adds that "divorced men and women marry at higher rates than do single men or women." In addition, among divorced persons over age 25, "divorced men remarry at higher rates than do single or widowed men and [all] women."[64] However, the older a person becomes, the *less* likely she or he is to remarry: "Women divorced after 40 have little likelihood of remarrying." Moreover, the effects of social status (education or income) on remarriage are precisely opposite for women and men. The more status a man has, the *more* likely he is to remarry. But the more social status a woman has, the *less* likely she is to remarry. In particular, divorced women with a graduate degree have a very slim likelihood of remarriage, especially if they're black.[65] Moreover, according to Coleman and Ganong, black persons in general are less likely to remarry than whites, and Hispanics are less likely to remarry than either whites or blacks. The effects of children on the probability of remarriage vary by the woman's age: If she's under 25 and has children, she's less likely to remarry than if she's childless. However, among women over 35, childless women are less likely to remarry than women with children.[66]

Its not at all surprising that remarriage has become such a commonplace occurrence in U.S. society. We have repeatedly made the point that throughout North American culture the status of being married is defined as much more desirable than that of not being married—of being single. The pressures from families and friends to marry a second or third or fourth time are no less intense than the pressures to marry the first time. In addition, Chapter 13 reports that throughout North American culture, divorce is defined as *failure*. We often hear that someone we know, or a celebrity, has experienced a "failed marriage." Many divorced persons are keenly sensitive to the perceptions of others that they did not have a successful, that is, *stable* marriage. Many of them are thus eager to *remarry* to prove to their significant others that they are indeed able to achieve a marriage that "works"—one that is stable and thus successful.

Divorce among Remarriages

Ironically, in spite of that strong desire for "success," some evidence suggests that remarriages have a higher probability of divorce than first marriages.[67] For example, approximately one-half of all current first marriages are expected to end in divorce. For remarried men in their 30s, the expected *re*-divorce rate is 61 percent, and for remarried women in their 30s the expected rate is 54 percent.[68] However, a different set of researchers suggest that when we take into account how much education the parties have, remarriages may not necessarily be more divorce prone than first marriages.[69]

Declines in Remarriage Rates

Next, although it may seem paradoxical, remarriage rates have actually been going *down* at the same time that the numbers of persons who remarry have been going *up*. The chief reason that the numbers of people remarrying have been going up is that there are so many divorced people around. Given this large pool of eligibles and the strong cultural pressures to be formally married, it follows that numbers of remarriages are bound to increase.

Rates, however, are computed over some kind of base such as every 1,000 previously divorced women. We use that base to make comparisons over time to get an accurate picture of whether a certain behavior is in fact increasing or decreasing. For example, Wilson reports that in 1970 the remarriage rate for every 1,000 previously divorced women was 123.3. By 1983 that rate had dropped to 91.6, a decline of 26 percent. Furthermore, "The remarriage rate for previously divorced men was 142.1 per 1,000 in 1983. That figure is 31 percent lower than in 1970 when it was 204.5."[70] Another way to describe the declines in remarriage rates is to say that in 1970, 12 percent of divorced women and 20 percent of divorced men remarried. But by 1983, only 9 percent of divorced women and 14 percent of divorced men remarried.

Since 1983, remarriage rates have continued to fall rapidly. Consequently, Bumpass and co-workers wondered what's been happening to all those divorced persons who used to remarry formally. First, recall from Chapter 9 that these investigators showed us that recent declines in *first* marriage rates are being offset by cohabitations: Some 50 percent of never-married persons had at one time or other cohabited before their first formal union. In short, never-married persons in their 20s who used to marry legally are now entering informal marriages with increasing frequency. The result is that the overall proportion of younger (never-married) couples engaged in joint housekeeping is about the same as it was several decades ago.

Cohabitation among the Divorced

Second, Bumpass and colleagues add that "cohabitation is even more common among separated and divorced persons [than it is among the never-married]."[71] Sixty percent of formerly marrieds cohabited at one time or other after separation and/or divorce. In view of the finding that cohabitation is so common among formerly marrieds, do we then discover the same result for them as we did among the never-marrieds? *Yes*, according to Bumpass and co-workers: "Cohabitation has compensated fully for the fall in remarriage [rates]."

In short, today's major trend is not for separated or divorced persons to live alone (although some do), any more than it is for never-married persons to live alone. Growing numbers of separated and divorced persons are choosing to add co-residence to their ongoing erotic friendships. The result is that the proportion of divorced persons who are establishing new households (joint housekeeping) is about the same now as it was several decades ago. The major difference is that their new marriages are informal rather than formal.

Declines in Total Numbers of Years Formally Married

Thomas Espenshade captures the significance of the several interconnected trends described in Chapters 8, 9, and 10 by saying that *"the total time white females spend married (including first marriage and remarriage) has been declining."*[72] Such trends, he adds, have been occurring among black women throughout the twentieth century. They have become quite noticeable among white women only since 1960.

Emma (Kate's mother) graduated from high school on Friday night and got married on Saturday afternoon. She and Ezra never spent a single night apart until his death at age 84, a total of sixty-six years. By contrast, Kate postponed her first formal marriage until she was 38, twenty years later than Emma. In view of the overall probability that at least 50 percent of first marriages will result in divorce, Kate faces a far less predictable future with Marshall than Emma did with Ezra. By the time she's in her 80s, Kate (whose life expectancy is greater than Emma's) will have lived far fewer years in a formal marriage (either first or second) than Emma. According to Espenshade, the same trend toward spending fewer years in a formal marriage or remarriage holds also for men.[73] The fact that Marshall lived for such a long time in an informal marriage means that he will spend far fewer years in a formal one than his father. London adds that "both men and women can now expect to spend more than half their lives [formally] *un*married."[74]

Before the 1960s, in North America as well as in other Western societies, most women and men spent the great bulk of their adult years legally married, or else remarried mostly as a result of spousal death or the occasional divorce. That many people spending that much time married contributed not only to the pervasiveness of the married state but also to its uniqueness. Because the trend now and into the foreseeable future is for more persons to spend far fewer years in a formal marriage or remarriage, the distinctiveness of marriage is being eroded. The plain reason that growing numbers of people are spending fewer years in a formal status is they can get what they want and need from informal marriages, an option not readily available to Emma and Ezra. As a result, says Espenshade, the *"institution of marriage may be declining."*[75] His assertion means that it's becoming harder and harder to argue that formal marriage is a unique social arrangement. Over time, increasing numbers of persons are constructing informal marriage-like arrangements that for most practical purposes seem to meet their needs, wishes, and obligations.

CONCLUSION

Formal marriages and remarriages were invented by people, and people have been reconstructing them ever since. Although marriage is not a real thing in any material sense, people commonly make the error of reifying it. They treat marriage as if it is a thing—as if it has some actual physical existence outside of and apart from the shared behaviors and beliefs of persons. Marriage is real solely in a social sense because it influences how people think, feel, and act. And because marriage is a social reality, people can and do change it to fit their interests, goals, and responsibilities. People keep on reinventing marriages because they believe, rightly or wrongly, that doing so will make life better for them and their children. They at least hope that they are reinventing in a responsible manner.

During the past several decades the pace of marriage reconstruction has picked up markedly throughout the West. Foundational to this increased tempo is the shifting balance between individualism and altruism. In the past, husbands had two loves. The first love was paid work and the individualism it gratified. The second love was their family, which gratified their need to be altruistic.[76] However, wives had but one love—their family and the sense of altruism it supplied. For at least two-hundred years, that distribution of loves worked fairly well if one judges by one indicator, the stability of marriages. Recently, women have sought (or economic conditions have forced them to seek) the second love of paid work. And they have tried to somehow balance that with their first love—family. At the same time, women have wanted men to increase their altruism so that the genders would move toward some sort of parity in terms of both individualism and altruism.

"Ah, there's the rub," as Shakespeare put it. When wives and husbands each have two loves, their marriages become exceedingly complicated. People today have discovered that they can have erotic friendships that contain sexuality, emotional intimacy, and children, as well as co-residence. As a result, increasing numbers of persons are postponing the point at which they might eventually add a legal tie. Some hope that by living together informally they will gain experience in dealing more effectively with the complications of a subsequent formal marriage. Many informally married persons discover, however, that the complexities of each co-resident partner trying to have two loves are no less real in an informal than in a formal marriage, particularly if children are present. The result is that for many younger persons (aged 20–29), both informal and formal marriages tend to be highly unstable, in the sense of couples eventually splitting.

A number of critics worry that widespread divorce has harmful consequences for children and thus for society. They view individualism as the underlying virus and easy divorce as its outgrowth. Their cure is to get persons to mute

their individualism by making divorce harder to get. Some progressives, however, respond that the critics' chief target is women's, not men's, individualism. In any case, one thing is quite clear—there are no easy answers to the dilemma that springs from loving oneself as much as one's neighbor. One way to help us understand the dilemma further is to explore how couples in an erotic friendship (whether formally or informally married, whether co-residing, whether straight or gay) try to negotiate their everyday discussions and disagreements. That's what Chapter 11 is all about.

NOTES

1. Thomas, 1918–1920.
2. Davis, 1949.
3. Tong, 1984.
4. Scanzoni, 1982.
5. Aldous, 1987.
6. Hewlett, 1991.
7. Seidman, 1991a.
8. Dobson, 1992a.
9. Dobson, 1992b.
10. Rindfuss, 1991, p. 508. See also Fox, 1986, for the same point.
11. Condon, 1985.
12. Kay Itoi and Bill Powell, *Newsweek*, August 10, 1992, pp. 38–40.
13. Ibid., p. 39.
14. Jacob M. Schlesinger, *Wall Street Journal*, July 2, 1992, B6.
15. Ibid., p. B6. Italics added.
16. Christensen, 1990a,b.
17. Pleck and Pleck, 1980.
18. Seeley, Sim, and Loosley, 1956.
19. Hewlett, p. 273.
20. Condon, p. 17. Italics added.
21. Ibid.
22. Seeley et al., 1956; Rainwater, Coleman, and Handel, 1959; Rainwater and Weinstein, 1960.
23. Condon, p. 57.
24. Ibid., p. 58.
25. Ibid.; see also Lehmann, 1990; Steve Stack, 1992.
26. Davis.
27. Joanne M. Schrof, "Wedding Bands Made of

Steel," *US News & World Report,* April 6, 1992, pp. 62–63.

28. Hewlett, p. 280, based allegedly on Gilligan, 1982, p. 129.
29. Gilligan, p. 149.
30. Gerth and Mills, 1958.
31. Ellis, 1971.
32. Rapoport et al., 1977; see also Scanzoni, 1991.
33. Dizard and Gadlin, 1990; Stacey, 1990.
34. Bauer, 1986.
35. Mill, 1869.
36. Yankelovich, 1981; Bellah et al., 1985; Thornton, 1989.
37. Buchmann, 1989. Another pattern that seems to be emerging is that when companies need help, they hire workers on a temporary basis. These "temporaries" are then laid off when company demand slackens. See Janice Castro, "Disposable Workers," *Time,* March 29, 1993, pp. 42–50.
38. Weitzman, 1974.
39. Nye, 1979.
40. Mintz and Kellogg, 1988.
41. Bernard, 1981.
42. Fogarty, Rapoport, and Rapoport, 1971; Hertz, 1986; Smith and Reid, 1986; Gutek and Larwood, 1987; Rose and Larwood, 1988.
43. Mizruchi, 1964.
44. Gitlin, 1987; Rubin, 1990.
45. Ginny Carroll, Eleanor Clift, Howard Fineman, and Tom Morganthau, *Newsweek,* March 30, 1992, pp. 30–31.
46. Ibid.
47. Alice Mundow, *The Boston Globe,* March 22, 1992, p. 36.
48. Stannard, 1977.
49. Weitz, 1977.
50. Donnelly, 1991.
51. Stannard.
52. Ibid.
53. Donnelly, p. 5.
54. Weitzman, 1981.
55. Dralle and Mackiewicz, 1981; Intons-Peterson and Crawford, 1985; Schroeder, 1986.
56. Scheuble and Johnson, 1993, p. 747.
57. Freese, 1991; see also Leonard, 1990.
58. The gesture consisted of moving her hand over her crotch area—something that many male athletes on the field or court do repeatedly.
59. Bumpass, Sweet, and Cherlin, 1991.
60. Ibid., p. 916.
61. Ibid.
62. Barbara Wilson, 1989, p. 2.
63. Coleman and Ganong, 1990, p. 926.
64. Wilson, p. 2.
65. Coleman and Ganong, p. 926.
66. Ibid.
67. Ibid.
68. Ihinger-Tallman and Pasley, 1987, p. 12.
69. Martin and Bumpass, 1989, p. 48; Wilson and S. C. Clarke, 1992.
70. Wilson.
71. Bumpass et al., p. 918.
72. Espenshade, 1985, p. 199. Italics added.
73. Ibid., p. 203.
74. London, 1991, p. 1. Italics added.
75. Espenshade, p. 194. Italics added.
76. To say that persons have two loves does not ignore the fact that many people dislike and may even hate their paid employment. The latter may be an extremely jealous and possessive master, imposing unrelenting pain on its victim. This reality does not change the point of the argument: that postmodern persons face two very powerful and often conflicting sets of demands. In future it seems likely that these countervailing pressures are likely to become more intense for growing numbers of persons.

CHAPTER 11

CONFLICT, NEGOTIATION, AND PROBLEM-SOLVING

This third section of the book is considering examples of people reinventing families and relationships. Thus far we've examined singleness, informal marriages, and formal marriages and remarriages. Chapter 11 turns us to the ways in which people in relationships and families discuss, argue, fight, and try to negotiate. Earlier chapters showed that if men have the final authority in deciding things, there isn't a whole lot to talk about. Instead, through sly and subtle means women try to finesse what they need or want for themselves and their children. But as the position of Western women gradually changes, chiefly as a result of paid employment, they seem more likely to challenge men directly and openly. Overt confrontations between the genders require that their rules of decision-making be reinvented. That's what this chapter is all about. The chapter focuses on decision-making across three kinds of erotic friendships: heterosexual, lesbian, and gay.

UNHAPPILY EVER AFTER

"Unhappily Ever After" proclaimed the 1-inch headline describing the goings-on between Woody Allen and Mia Farrow.[1] For weeks the media were filled with stories about the public breakup of their decade-long erotic friendship. Both Farrow and Allen were making charges and countercharges against one another, and each was threatening court action. An enormous amount of publicity was showered on the 56-year-old filmmaker's new erotic friend—Farrow' 19-year-old adopted Korean daughter. Through all the confusion one thing became clear: Any future dealings Allen and Farrow might have would be marked by enormous amounts of bitter, hostile, and painful struggles. It also seemed clear that no matter how the courts might decide for or against either of them, the cankerous residue of their conflicts would persist for a long, long time.

Allen's life appeared to be imitating his film

released in the fall of 1992, just after the storm of publicity. In *Husbands and Wives*, Allen and Farrow portray a married couple who bicker constantly with each other and finally divorce. As the two wind down their filmed dissolution phase, he becomes emotionally involved with a woman 30 years his junior, and Farrow falls in love with an office colleague. Allen's films differ vastly from 1950s' Hollywood movies that often ended with the words, *"And they lived happily ever after,"* flashing across the screen. Those older movies reinforced children's fairy tales about the princess and prince struggling against, and finally triumphing over, every obstacle placed in the path of their love. Once married, the fairy-tale couple, like the 1950s' couple, left their struggles behind to bask forever in the sublimity of their pure and pristine love. The focus of the fairy tales, as well as the movies, was how to fish for and land a husband or wife. During that same era, sociologists did research on how to select a mate and on how to predict marital "success."[2] They studied "marital adjustment" because they believed that well-adjusted couples were more likely to be successful, that is, to have stable marriages. How could they tell if a couple was well adjusted? Among other things, well-adjusted couples shared common values, liked the same activities, and had few disagreements.

Love and Conflict

Perhaps more than anything else, having a well-adjusted marriage meant the absence of conflict. After all, people wondered, how could couples who were constantly fighting be well-adjusted? How could they love each other? Advice columns, counselors, and researchers alike promoted the idea that conflicts were symptoms of underlying marriage problems. Just as a temperature warns you that your body is suffering some ill health, conflicts were said to be symptomatic of marital ill

health. Couples were advised to try to avoid conflicts as much as possible. "Discussions" were certainly permissible, even encouraged. The assumption was that couples who knew how to "discuss" their problems could solve them long before they ever got to be "disagreements," much less "conflicts." Robert Klemer's advice to young women on how to find and keep a man was typical of that era. Klemer urged wives to think of their husband first—to place his needs and interests ahead of their own.[3]

This foolproof recipe for conflict avoidance sprang from *love*, as described in earlier chapters. Recall that the husband had the moral obligations to love both himself *and* his wife and children. She, on the other hand, had the moral obligation to love *only* her husband and children. Hence the chief responsibility to keep the peace and not rock the boat was hers. It was her duty to see that order, harmony, and tranquility prevailed throughout the matrimonial vessel. She settled disputes among the children. And she interceded on behalf of any complaints the children might have against the father, and vice versa. Above all, she made sure her husband had no complaints against her regarding her several roles as mother, housekeeper, wise consumer, and companion. It was obvious to everyone that if the husband had no complaints, the couple couldn't be having any disagreements, much less conflicts.

Chapter 7 showed how Willard Waller was perhaps the first sociologist to question that idyllic view of relations between women and men.[4] He is best remembered for his vivid descriptions of the ways in which the genders struggled with one another as they pursued the old Dating Game. But he also made two very important points about conflicts after the wedding, conflicts within marriage itself.

Constructive versus Destructive Conflicts
First, Waller challenged the accepted wisdom that all conflicts are bad, negative, and un-

healthy for relationships. Not only were some conflicts not *un*healthy, he asserted that some could actually be *healthy*. Although some conflicts might eventually undermine a relationship, others might actually be constructive. Sometimes, he said, conflicts help to rebuild, renew, revitalize, and strengthen relationships. He added that conflicts can often accomplish the sorts of positive things for relationships that nothing else can. Since Waller's time, many other sociologists have shown how conflict often has positive consequences for all of social life, not just for gender relations.[5]

Conflicts Are Pervasive A second point made by Waller and many other sociologists is that conflict cannot be avoided—it permeates all parts of social life, including gender relations. When we say something is pervasive, we mean that it's always with us. When you're in a desert, sand permeates your water, food, and clothing. Armies waging desert wars are constantly plagued by sand getting into and disrupting their equipment. When you're sailing in the ocean, saltwater is equally pervasive, sticking to food, clothing, and skin. Sand and saltwater are woven into the fabric of certain experiences—they're always and inevitably *there*. Likewise, conflict is woven into the fabric of social life—it is always and inevitably *there*. Sometimes it's positive and healthy for both relationships and persons; sometimes it's negative and unhealthy.

Making the points that social conflicts may be healthy or unhealthy, and that they pervade social life, raises certain objections in people's minds. Ingrid, for instance, responds that, "My spouse Albert and I never fight. How can you say conflict is pervasive?" Ingrid adds that before she formally married Albert she'd spent several years in two different informal marriages: "I fought all the time with each guy. The main reason we broke up was because of all the disagreements we had. How can you say conflict could be healthy?"

Struggles between the Genders

In responding to these and other similar objections, we fast-forward for a moment. Chapter 12 examines violence, sexual harassment, and assault. There we learn that until researchers started probing these kinds of behaviors, no one paid them much attention. Although pervasive to relations between women and men, violence was largely ignored. For example, when 1930s' researchers began studying marital adjustment, they seldom if ever talked about woman abuse and assault. One reason abuse was ignored is the cultural myth we hold about gender relations. No one wanted to believe that violence could exist within the atmosphere of love that supposedly pervades marriage. On the job we like to believe that men respect women's dignity enough to treat them the way they'd like to be treated. Nevertheless, although those are the cultural ideals, we've become painfully aware that violence, as well as sexual assault and harassment, pervade life between the genders, including life on college campuses.

Violence and assault are connected with the idea of conflict. Indeed, on hearing the term *conflict* many people immediately conjure up images of men beating up or raping women, and women trying to shove men away. However, conflict is an idea that is far broader than physical force and harassing words. It is also broader than what some researchers call emotional violence. Conflict is about struggle, and struggle is not always violent. During the 1990s, the United States is engaged in a very serious struggle with Japan and also Germany over imports and exports. When politicians say they're worried about trade wars among those nations, they don't mean a repetition of the shooting and bombing of World War II. They mean that the economic struggles among them could escalate to the point where each nation does extreme, yet nonviolent, things. For example, if the United States prohibited

Japanese car imports, Japan might retaliate by keeping out American machinery. Those are "extreme" activities because they would severely strain the overall relationship between the United States and Japan. The strain would arise out of the pain and suffering that both economies would suffer as a result of those sorts of struggles.

When Chapter 12 talks about the "ancient battle of the sexes," the idea is that since the beginning of recorded history men have written laws and constructed social customs in rather consistent ways. Those ways have resulted in women being placed in a social category subordinate to men. For the past two-hundred years, some women have struggled against being dumped into a subordinate status. Their struggle is a prime example of a serious social conflict that has been largely nonviolent. Nevertheless, the image of women struggling with men has never become a popular cultural ideal. As with woman abuse and assault, no one has wanted to believe that it's *there*—that (nonviolent) conflict is a pervasive element of gender relations. Instead, the cultural ideal has been and continues to be that women and men who are dating, cohabiting, or married share mutual respect, dignity, and love. Moreover, the cultural belief is that because of those types of shared feelings, couples should be able to work out their differences via peaceful discussions. The cultural ideals presume that women and men operate on a level playing field. Unfortunately, the playing field is not level. Our cultural ideals fail to recognize that men hold a socially superior, and women a subordinate, status.

In comparable fashion, many whites have trouble accepting the idea that today's African-Americans exist in a social category subordinate to whites—that most blacks remain second-class citizens. To show that blacks are making it, whites point to wealthy black athletes such as Michael Jordan. They also point to the growing numbers of blacks in management positions, the professions, and the media and government. Nevertheless, researchers show how even successful middle-class blacks continue to live in a subordinate social position compared with whites.[6] Similarly, as they see women becoming increasingly visible in the media, sports, space exploration, politics, business, and professions, many men (and some women) have trouble grasping the notion that the genders do not yet operate on a level playing field. Chapter 15 shows how women still lag behind men in key areas such as educational attainment, job opportunities, and income. It's still a big deal for a woman to be an astronaut or a U.S. senator, because there are so few overall. And many military women do not yet have the same freedom of choice that men do regarding combat.[7]

To say that struggle between the genders is pervasive does not necessarily contradict Ingrid's claim that "Albert and I never fight." If in fact they don't struggle, the puzzle is, why not? He, being male, has greater prestige, authority, and probably income, than she does. He very likely also has a greater range of life choices and opportunities. She probably does more of the housework and child care than Albert, even though they're both employed full time. Hence, it's very surprising she's not trying to change various parts of their relationship. It's remarkable that they never have disagreements.

CONFLICT—THE *NORMAL* THING

If a researcher came across Ingrid and Albert, she would try to figure out why they weren't "normal." The researcher could very well ask, "Why aren't Ingrid and Albert having conflicts?" To be sure, many citizens and some researchers prefer to believe that the absence rather than the presence of conflict is normal. When researchers have purposely set out to discover what actually is normal, however, they discover that most of the time, and among most couples, disagreements are pervasive and frequent (i.e., normal). For example, during the 1950s—the peak period of the Modern Family—a group of researchers studied a white, Canadian upper-middle-class suburb. They fully expected to find that normal families were marked by "agreement, consensus, and integration."[8] What they found instead among the great majority of the families was "confusion, internal contradiction, and incompatibility."

During the same decade other researchers interviewed white working-class wives in the United States and discovered a similar pattern.[9] They found that although the wives had many complaints about their husbands, and

disagreed with them on a number of things, they never said a word to their husbands about how they felt. They were afraid that if they tried to negotiate, their husbands would become angry and perhaps get violent. The men might even "take a walk," that is, leave them to try to support their children on their own. In any case, the husbands were not about to change their behaviors simply because the wives wanted them to do so. And since the wives kept their feelings to themselves, the couples in fact had no overt disagreements or conflicts. What is more, they had successful (stable) marriages. The wives were managing to hold their marriages together.

By the 1970s, Lillian Rubin's study of white

Virtually all couples struggle over money—how to make it; how to use it.

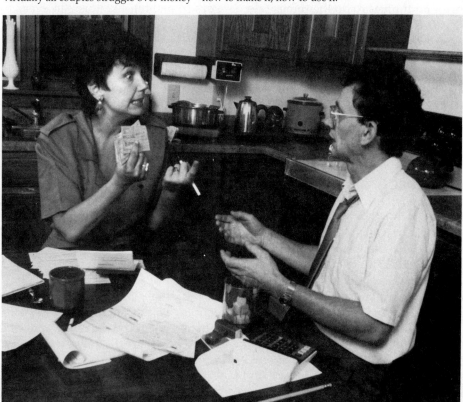

working-class wives revealed that it had now become culturally permissible for a wife to "say her piece".[10] It became common for working-class couples to have a "battle to [try to] reconcile differences"—a battle that was marked by a great deal of "heat and smoke." Nevertheless, Rubin reports that although 1970s' wives were more likely to voice disagreements than 1950s' wives, "almost always, it is the man who decides . . . it is he who holds the final veto power."[11] Rubin adds that the cost of the wife's compliance is high. What cost? After all, their marriages were stable and thus successful. In addition, for their entire eighteen years the children had grown up in households with both parents present. The price for the "success," according to Rubin, is that the wives felt extremely frustrated and dissatisfied with marriages that allowed them few if any opportunities to do the things they wanted to do, both for their children and for themselves. Because their husbands allowed them little freedom, flexibility, or independence, they felt they lacked control over their own lives. Rubin adds that although they'd experienced more freedom and control than their mothers, and thus felt better off, they fervently prayed that their daughters would be much better off than they. Mothers urged daughters to get lots of education and a good job. In particular, they urged their daughters to marry as late in life as possible.

During the early 1980s, some researchers studied a sample of white middle-class American families. Like the previous 1950s' researchers, they fully expected that the families would be "normal"—marked by agreement, consensus, and harmony. They anticipated finding that the husbands and wives would be unified in coping with the many problems and difficulties that are imposed on families from outside their households. What they discovered instead was "surprising . . . [especially] the little agreement between husbands and wives over major family variables."[12] They found even less agreement between adoles-

cents and their parents. As a result, these researchers add that when we image families in our minds, we must not draw a picture based chiefly on harmony, agreement, consensus, and integration. The picture we draw should *assume disagreement* and lack of congruence among family members."[13]

In other words, conflict seems to be a normal (i.e., common, everyday, usual), thing throughout most North American families. The absence of conflict is *not* normal; it is unusual and uncommon. As Mary Anne Fitzpatrick puts it, "Marriage [or any erotic friendship] can be conceived of as a continuous confrontation between participants with conflicting . . . interests."[14]

The same conclusion emerges from a number of studies done over several decades in which respondents were asked a question that goes something like this: "In every marriage, couples have disagreements about many things. What is the one thing that you and your spouse disagree about most frequently?" In virtually all of the studies, some 80 to 85 percent of the respondents acknowledged at least one disagreement. And many reported more than one.[15] Only 15 to 20 percent were like Ingrid who claimed that "we never disagree about anything." Finally, researchers using hidden video cameras to observe married couples in a laboratory came to similar conclusions. When those couples were asked to portray a topic of frequent argument, almost all of them got into an actual quarrel.[16]

Conflict and the Quest for Equality

In her study, Fitzpatrick compared married couples who'd had open conflicts with couples who'd tended to avoid open confrontation and thus (like Ingrid) could declare, "We don't have disagreements." She found that what Chapter 12 calls "gender role traditional" couples were the ones most likely to avoid confrontation and direct negotiation.[17] On the other side, couples who were less traditional (what Chapter 10 calls equal partners) were more likely to engage in open and direct confrontation. Chapters 10 and 12 make the point that "nontraditional" couples believe that gender equality is a desirable goal, that women and men should have the same kinds of responsibilities and opportunities both in the workplace and the home.

Change and Conflict Because nontraditional couples hold to gender equality, they are constantly seeking to tinker with (i.e., reinvent) their erotic friendship: "The roles, rules, and norms . . . [are continually] redefined and renegotiated. . . . Attempts . . . to establish new role patterns . . . bring . . . conflict, stress, and tension to the relationship."[18] Compared with traditional couples, nontraditional couples are more likely to engage in struggle because they are more interested in *change*. But not merely for its own sake. They believe that the new patterns they wish to create in their erotic friendships will bring them a little closer to gender equality. After all, most of today's couples, even the ones who by today's standards are comparatively traditional, are much less traditional than couples of the 1950s.[19] Hence the normal thing for most of today's couples (women in particular) is to want their erotic friendships to be as equal as possible.

However, what couples perceived to be a fair and equal relationship last year may not be defined the same way this year. Last year, Ingird did almost all the housework and believed that was fair since she had fewer work demands than Albert. This year, however, she got a promotion and now has less time for housework and child care. She has tried to discuss this with Albert but he flatly refuses to do any more housework. For the first time ever, they have a disagreement, a conflict. And the conflict springs from her desire for change— change that in her view would make their relationship more balanced, or equal.

Change and conflict are closely connected. "Change" is simply another term for *reinven-*

tion. If persons such as Ingrid (or Helga in Chapter 5) weren't seeking changes of one sort or another in their erotic friendships, the chances for conflict would go down considerably. Albert, for example, isn't interested in reinventing their housework patterns—he's perfectly content the way things are. "The way things are" is called the *status quo*. People who prefer the status quo tend to believe that reinvention would cause them to lose more than they gain. People who are discontent with the status quo perceive that they stand to gain rather than lose from change. The changes they favor, however, very often result in conflict. In the realm of erotic friendships, women are more likely than men to perceive the status quo as no longer appealing. Women are thus more likely than men to reinvent the status quo.

Areas of Conflict This is not to say that men are forever content with the status quo mode. Men can and do initiate changes in their relationships. However, the areas in which men are likely to press for change tend to differ from those pursued by women.[20] Women tend to be concerned chiefly for three broad and overlapping areas of change. First, like their mothers before them, they are interested in changes that will benefit any children they might have. For decades, an area of frequent disagreement was the amount of time husbands spent with the children. And when wives disagreed with their husbands over spending money, it was often because the wives thought the men spent too much on themselves and not enough on the children. If wives tried to get their husbands to switch jobs and earn more money, it was so they'd have more for the kids.

A second and more recent area in which women seek reinvention is the quest for greater quality and autonomy. One 1970s' wife described her struggle with her husband over greater autonomy in these terms: "I cannot be the way I was ten years ago. . . . He can't un-

Preoccupation with sports versus the "quest for intimacy."

derstand some of the things I do. . . . I have to be an individual, a person as well as his wife. . . . I want to maybe go to college. I want to walk *with* him and not *behind* him. . . . I don't want to destroy his ego so I have to handle this with grace. The problem is I am no longer completely dependent on him and he can't seem to understand this. . . . This is a changing world . . . and I have to lead a different life than I did before."[21]

Women's quest for autonomy is not removed from children's interests. Women often seek employment because their husbands' earnings will not meet the children's needs. Hence, Ingrid's wanting her husband to participate more fully in child care and housework is connected to her children's interests, as well as to her own autonomy.

The third area in which women seek reinvention is something we've been describing throughout the book: The area of friendship and intimacy.[22] One part of this struggle is for companionship. Since the 1920s (and perhaps even earlier), wives have tried to get their husbands to spend less time with their buddies and more time with them. The second part of the struggle is more recent in origin: Women want emotional closeness, openness, and self-disclosure. Judith Stacey points out that unlike yesterday's working-class women, today's women (both working and middle class) demand shared intimacy from their men. Failing to get it can be a source of severe conflict.

By contrast with women, men tend to initiate conflicts over money because they feel their wives spend too much (not too little) on the children or the household.[23] Husbands also argue with their wives over how the wives are raising the children (not good enough). In addition, men initiate conflicts over frequency of

A couple discussing and solving a problem.

sexual intercourse (too low), their wives' housekeeping (not good enough), visiting relatives (too often), and their wives alleged flirtations. Chapter 12 shows that flirtation, as well as actually sleeping with another man, is a behavior that citizens of both genders seem most willing to tolerate as a reason for a man to physically assault his erotic partner.

Seldom, however, does intercourse with someone besides one's partner ever become an explicit and ongoing conflict issue in the ways that money, children, or companionship do. Recall from Chapter 5 that even when wives intuited their husbands were "playing around," they rarely confronted him with it. Wives were not likely to make it an up-front conflict issue. Instead, Stacey reports that when a certain wife suspected her husband was having an affair, she expressed her anxiety in a highly oblique fashion by inquiring, "Do you love me?" If he told her he "didn't know,"

her intuition was strongly reinforced. Even in Japan where the custom of a well-to-do man having a *nigo-san* (a mistress with his second set of children) remains a cultural option, *wife number-one* seldom makes that an explicit conflict issue unless he becomes remiss in supporting her children.[24]

Nonnegotiable Matters

The reason extrapartner intercourse is seldom a legitimate conflict issue is that in North American culture it's defined as *nonnegotiable*. A nonnegotiable matter is one that the parties, as well as their audience of families and friends, perceive to be settled and not open to any changes whatsoever. The chief reason Woody Allen's erotic friendship with Mia Farrow's adopted daughter caused so much furor was that his behavior was widely perceived as incest, which is both legally and culturally prohibited. Incest, as well as sex with a minor, is a nonnegotiable matter.

In spite of strong prohibitions, some issues once defined as nonnegotiable can later be *reinvented*. They can be redefined as negotiable after all. Chapter 9, for instance, described domestic partnership ordinances making it possible for informally married couples to receive a greater degree of public approval than ever before. Recall that Sweden has moved beyond North America in the degree to which it officially recognizes the legitimacy of certain kinds of homosexual unions. Chapter 9 also reported that Hawaii may likewise be moving toward granting marital status to homosexuals.

Chapters 4 and 5 showed that during the early seventies, some advocates tried to shift extrapartner coitus away from the sphere of the nonnegotiable into the negotiable. The advocates argued that because extrapartner coitus (EPC) is perceived as nonnegotiable, persons who do it anyhow are fearful of talking about it with their partners. One solution to getting rid of secrecy and deceit was *open marriage*, which simply meant that couples would agree at least to talk about EPC.[25] Couples could try to negotiate the conditions under which EPC might or might not be permissible. Another set of advocates tried to shift EPC into the sphere of the negotiable through what they called *swinging*. Once couples accepted the idea that swinging was legitimate, they tried to negotiate the concrete circumstances under which one or both partners are, or are not, allowed to swing.

However, we learned that a major block to open negotiations over extrapartner coitus of any kind is jealousy. Jealousy is a powerful emotion that marks off the boundaries of sexual property: "This is mine, so stay away." Gordon Clanton showed that sixties and seventies persons who tried to make EPC a negotiable issue found it very difficult to prevent jealousy from bubbling up into their decision-making.[26] The reality of that intense emotion tended to make conflicts over EPC destructive. Hence, as far as researchers can tell, most persons in erotic friendships (formal or informal) today do not wish to make EPC a negotiable issue.[27] This is so even among persons who actually engage secretly in EPC. Recall from Chapter 5 that although Helga was living with and married to Hans, she gradually began sleeping with Kurt. But she did not tell Hans about it nor try to negotiate the matter. For a brief time Kurt was sleeping with both Helga and someone else, but never sought to negotiate it with Helga.

External Forces The importance of cultural values in sorting out what is or is not "proper" for couples to negotiate underscores a crucial point made throughout this book: What goes on within persons' primary relationships is strongly influenced by what's going on in the larger society. Women's employment is a striking example of a matter that once was nonnegotiable but now has become probably the central conflict issue among today's erotic friendships.[28] F. Ivan Nye shows that before World War II there was no discussing the belief that "a mother's place is in the home."[29] Everyone accepted a woman's domesticity as a nonnegotiable issue. As recently as the 1970s, although increasing numbers of women began to make their employment a conflict issue, many men resisted even talking about it.[30]

Chapter 10 describes two powerful external forces that have made it impossible for men to maintain women's employment as nonnegotiable. One is economic: Rising inflation coupled with expanding consumer aspirations make it very difficult for households to get by on the man's income alone. Recently, unforeseen layoffs of skilled and professional (white) men who believed their jobs were secure is an additional external reality pressing in on both partners. In many cases, the wives never expected and never wanted to enter paid labor.

When husbands, reinforced by social critics, censure wives for working and thus "neglecting" their families, ordinary citizens respond by saying, "But we need two incomes merely to survive."

The second external force is *ideological*. Western cultural values strongly endorse the idea that individuals have the moral obligation to love themselves, and thus to grow and develop to the fullest extent possible. For men, a large part of this growth has meant labor force participation. But as Charles Jones and co-workers say, a "Big Change" during the past thirty years is the realization that employment is now as much a vehicle for women's personal development as it has been for men's.[31]

Conflict issues inevitably get tangled up with one another. If a couple is struggling over her employment, invariably they also begin struggling over household chores, child care, time for companionship, and so on.[32] Matters once defined as being just as nonnegotiable as wife employment have now been transformed into critical conflict issues. Couples never used to fight over who would swob the toilets, sweep the floors, or take care of the kids. Women seldom dared ask their men to do those sorts of things; it was already established that those chores were "women's work." But Chapter 15 shows that what was once perceived as women's work has now become the focus of numerous and often bitter disputes between women and men.

Impacts on the Broader Social Fabric

Influences between the larger society and families go both ways. Not only do cultural values and structural elements (e.g., inflation) impact on the negotiations of erotic friendships, the latter significantly influence the course of the larger society. And that reciprocal influence has become a major political and social issue. Earlier chapters reported how some social crit-

ics censure what they believe to be the alleged individualism and narcissism (the me first attitude) of today's citizens. They fear that the growing trend for women to love themselves as much as their husbands and children is harming the larger society.[33] In particular, they worry about children. Are children mere pawns in the complex chess game known as gender negotiations? Are children being sacrificed as women and men experiment with self-fulfillment? If children are being harmed, is the well-being of North American society suffering in turn?

Earlier chapters reported that citizens in the fixed category of Figure 1-1 allege that as a result of peoples' choices regarding sex, abortion, divorce, cohabitation, women's employment, and so on, adults have been harming the social fabric of society since the 1960s. Chapter 10, however, showed that the situation is much more subtle and intricate than most critics allow. The complexity stems from the fact that the dual obligation to love one's neighbor as much as oneself is a logical contradiction. And it is precisely that contradiction that makes social responsibility such an elusive goal: How can a woman balance what she needs to do to take care of herself with what she needs to do to take care of her man?[34] How can a man balance what he needs to do to take care of himself with what he needs to do to take care of his woman? And how can a woman and a man, together or alone, balance their own needs with the needs of any children they might have? (Chapter 16 raises the question of children's participation in reinventing their own lives. Hence the matter of their responsibility toward adults and others in their lives becomes a live issue as well.) How do adults balance their obligations to themselves with their obligations to something outside of, and bigger than, themselves? In short, how do adults fulfill obligations to: their partners? their children? their families? their community? their society? How can they be *responsible* adults?

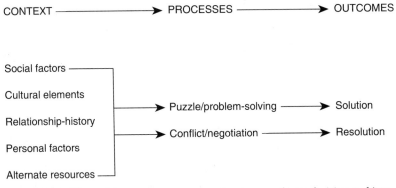

FIGURE 11-1 The social context, processes, and outcomes of joint decision-making in contemporary erotic friendships.

JOINT DECISION-MAKING

Unfortunately, there are no easy solutions to these questions. There is, however, one place to start searching for answers. That place is portrayed in Figure 11-1 as the joint decision-making that occurs between women and men (as well as between erotic partners of the same gender) regarding the many areas of potential conflict between them. Joint decision-making is a process of arriving at choices that affect each partner, and that may affect certain other adults (e.g., an aged mother), children, or the community and society. The decision-making processes can be carried on either responsibly or irresponsibly. Recall from Chapter 7 that during the old Dating Game partners often tended to bargain in an irresponsible (i.e., exploitative and unfair) manner. And although that Game has been replaced by today's more complex sexual scenes, there is lots of room for irresponsible decision-making.

Sondra, for instance, is 17 years old and has recently started sleeping with Len. Every time they have intercourse she asks him to use a condom to protect her against pregnancy, as well against diseases such as herpes and especially AIDS. But he sweet talks her out of it, saying it's too much trouble and no fun. Thus, they continually experience a decision-making

process marked by conflict. Its outcome is that he keeps on getting what he wants (sex and freedom from condoms) and she is denied protection. After several months, Sondra finds herself pregnant, something she definitely didn't want. Len urges her to get an abortion, but she can't bring herself to do it. Over that struggle she gets her way, because she asserts that she will carry the fetus to term.

Len merely shrugs off her intention. And since he figures condoms no longer matter, he expects to keep on having sex with her for as long as possible without their use. But suddenly she begins to insist on condoms because now she's panicked that she and her baby might get AIDS. He continues to refuse, and she stops having sex with him. She ends their erotic friendship, hoping they can be just-friends. Sondra badly needs a friend to help her through her pregnancy. She lives with her mother, who is distracted trying to take care of several younger children of her own. Since the mother doesn't have medical insurance, Sondra can't get prenatal care. But Len tires of being merely a platonic friend. He starts sleeping with someone else, and after a while he and Sondra stop hanging out together. After five months of pregnancy she begins to feel agonizing labor pains and she's rushed to the hospital emergency room. The baby is delivered and is placed in premature infant care, requiring elaborate and expensive life-sustaining equipment to survive.

To what extent have Len and Sondra fulfilled their obligations to one another, to their baby, and to their community and society? How responsible have they been? Although Len took care of himself, he didn't seem to care very much about anything outside himself. He ignored Sondra's preferences regarding condoms, and he forgot about her when she needed him most. He heard about the birth of his baby several weeks afterward, but never bothered to visit. Since he didn't have a job, and because Sondra couldn't afford day care, she had to quit waitressing and go on public assistance. Public funds had also covered the enormously high costs of keeping the infant on life-sustaining equipment for some months. The baby was weak and sickly, and Public Assistance paid for the medical care he needed once he got home. How responsible has Sondra been? How well has she taken care of herself? As a result of her decision-making with Len, she now has a sickly infant and no way to support him. How responsible has she been to that child? And how responsible have she and Len been to their community? Other members of the society are fulfilling their moral obligations to take care of persons in need. In this case, that includes the high medical costs of infant delivery, life-support, and subsequent sickliness.

Chapter 16 reports that there are growing numbers of adolescent women and men in situations like Sondra's and Len's.[35] Their private decision-making behaviors have public political impacts. They can even influence presidential campaigns. (Recall former Vice President Quayle and *Murphy Brown* in Chapter 10.) A number of critics charge that persons like Sondra and Len are irresponsible—they have no sense of moral obligations either to the children that are born or to the taxpayers who must foot the bill for their choices. Some critics

also add that they're failing to take care of themselves. And because so many taxpaying voters agree, President Clinton and other influential politicians support the viewpoint that persons like Len and Sondra are not carefully weighing their responsibilities to society. The accepted viewpoint of both major political parties is that Len and Sondra must think about something bigger than themselves, that is, the larger social fabric. Consequently, persons like Len and Sondra are being told they must change their behaviors and begin behaving in a socially responsible fashion. The "carrots" encouraging them to do so are promises of expanded day care and job-training programs, as well as good jobs. The "stick" is the threat of reductions in welfare benefits. In October 1992, for example, New Jersey became the first state to "freeze income benefits for women who have additional children while on welfare."[36]

The Social Context of Joint Decision-Making

Growing numbers of citizens in the process category (i.e., progressives) of Figure 1-1 concur with citizens in the fixed category. They agree that persons like Len and Sondra are failing to fulfill their moral obligations to each other, to their children, to society, and to themselves. At the same time, progressives assert that Len & Sondra's decision-making does not occur in a social vacuum. Like 1930s' couples making decisions about engagement sex in the context of the Great Depression, today's couples making decisions like Len's and Sondra's are influenced by powerful social forces. For example, most couples making decisions like theirs tend to be relatively disadvantaged. Len's and Sandra's parents had minimal education, low-status jobs from which they were often laid off, and low incomes. Len and Sondra attended inner-city schools that did not inspire them to work to their capacities. Neither had any hope of ever fulfilling the American

Dream and doing better than their parents. And because she'd learned traditional gender roles—North American cultural ideals—Sondra believed that a woman's chief mission in life centered in home and family. She was never presented with the idea that whatever else a woman does with her life, she must become economically autonomous (capable of independently supporting herself and any children she might have).

Past History   Put another way, people who fulfill moral obligations and act responsibly tend to perceive that society has treated them well. But Len and Sondra don't define society as having been particularly good to them during their lives. They don't feel that society has woven them into its own larger social fabric. Hence, their motivation to make decisions that will benefit both themselves and society is undercut. Occasionally, disadvantaged persons who don't feel part of the social fabric have faith nonetheless. They believe that if they start behaving responsibly, society, in the form of teachers, employers, and so on, will start being good to them, even if society hasn't done so in the past. However, Len and Sondra lack that faith, and accordingly lack the desire to fulfill the moral obligations that faith inspires.

Plainly, the history of how one has been treated in the past is an important context factor that affects current decision-making. The idea of history moreover applies not just to perceptions of how society in general has treated a person. History also applies to perceptions of how she or he has been treated by specific persons.[37] For example, a year after their child's birth, Len called Sondra and said he wanted to see her and their baby. But she had grown quite bitter about the way he'd treated her, so she hung up while he was still talking. His previous behavior influenced her to decide to have nothing more to do with him.

Additional Context Factors   Besides history and status factors (education, occupation, in-

come), and alongside gender, race, age, gender-role preferences, and also inflation and number of job opportunities, there's an almost endless array of factors that could become part of the context of a couple's joint decision-making. Earlier chapters, for instance, talked about the sexual identity of the partners: Is one or both gay, or lesbian or heterosexual? If heterosexual, are they girlfriend and boyfriend, or co-residing? Do they have a formal or informal marriage? Other context factors include region of the country (Deep South vs. San Francisco), rural or urban residence (Gnawbone, Indiana vs. New York City), number of previous marriages (both informal and formal), and personality factors such as self-esteem.

Additional context elements include religious conservatism or liberalism, aspirations for the future (does one hope to go (back) to school, get a (better) paying job, have a child, and so on?), and the culture in which one lives. The broader culture includes beliefs about gender equality. Figure 9-1, for instance, implies that Swedish couples negotiate very differently from Japanese couples, and both negotiate differently from North American couples. And increasingly, advances in biotechnology and genetic engineering present a vast range of options (e.g., altering fetal development) never before imagined.[38]

The Social Processes of Joint Decision-Making

"If I could be a fly on the wall," someone says. The speaker wishes she could have been in a certain place to find out what *really* went on. What place? Any place where two or more persons are deciding what to do about something important. Since the place is exclusive, outsiders are not welcome. The things insiders say to each other are classified. Anything they reveal to outsiders about what went on is merely what they choose to reveal. While they were making decisions there were no nosy outsiders (such as sociologists) snooping, observing, and recording what went on between them.

The place could be a jury room. Let's say the jury is deciding whether several white police officers are guilty of wrongfully assaulting a black motorist, Rodney King. After some days they reveal their verdict—not guilty. The jury does not have to explain to the judge or anyone else how they arrived at this verdict. Only the fly on the wall could disclose who said what to whom, who had the most persuasive arguments, who started shouting, who kept interrupting, who never opened his mouth, who pounded her fist on the table, who started crying, who came up with clever and creative solutions to others' objections, who held out to the end for conviction, who refused to budge from his viewpoint, and so on. Because no one knows what went on among the all-white jurors, some black citizens assume they agreed to free the officers simply because the motorist was black. The result is the April 1992 Los Angeles riots.

Politicians, and business, union, and university officials operate the same way. A boundary is drawn around who's in on the discussions or negotiations, and who's out. The insiders talk only with each other. Later on, if outsiders are told anything at all (if information is "leaked"), it's merely each insider's perceptions of what went on. Some state governments have sunshine laws, laws requiring officials to deliberate publicly so that reporters and citizens can watch the actual give-and-take of the negotiations. But officials prefer privacy to the fishbowl. Hence they talk informally among themselves before the public meeting. They learn one another's viewpoints and what solutions are or are not possible. Thus, the only people surprised during the public meeting are the observers.

The Black Box—Decision-Making and Privacy   Some researchers describe the mystery of negotiation dynamics as a *black box*.[39] Since insiders prefer to exclude outsiders, it's very

difficult for researchers to study any kinds of decision-making. The erotic friendship is a set of insiders—a we-group—which is almost always a dyad. There is a social boundary around the couple based on sexual interdependence. Unlike persons having casual sex, they have agreed, either tacitly or explicitly, to be sexually exclusive: They have a commitment to monogamy. Because they perceive themselves and are viewed by others as a special we-group, they prefer to be alone while they're engaging in decision-making. Afterward they might tell their friends, families, or a counselor what went on between them, but interestingly enough, their reports seldom mesh: They each have their own perception.[40]

Couples did not always have the luxury of keeping their fights secret. Chapter 6 reported that during the Colonial era almost all citizens were poor, and shoddily constructed housing often consisted of several apartments between which the walls were paper thin. A family in one apartment knew literally everything that went on across the wall. Along with that reality was the cultural belief that persons *should* know what went on in other persons' families to guard against excessive physical violence and incest. Privacy did not become an important cultural value, said Chapter 6, until the nineteenth century. At that time, a middle class emerged that could afford single-family housing and sturdily walled apartments. Privacy became built in to the life of North American families. One outcome of our passion for privacy is the cloak that continues to shroud woman and child abuse. Physical violence, like nonviolent arguments, is protected by the cultural maxim that, "It's nobody's business but their own."

Privacy and Image   Why do couples almost always prefer to be alone while having nonviolent conflicts and negotiations? The chief reason is the cultural ideal that erotic friends (formal or informal) are not supposed to have conflicts. Most persons continue to view conflict between erotic partners as a bad, not a normal or healthy, thing. Hence, if they fight secretly, they feel that outsiders will presume they're conflict-free. In spite of the fact that everyone knows that's a myth, most citizens wish to maintain a conflict-free image.

Style and Substance—Being Considerate and Cooperative Sometimes, however, couples will sheepishly acknowledge that they fight occasionally. But they also claim to be considerate and cooperative. A *considerate* person pays close attention to the other person as a person. A considerate person asks, "Is my partner comfortable, at ease, tense, pessimistic, nervous, upset, anxious, upbeat, and so forth?" A considerate person likes to think that during conflicts, "I never yell or lose my temper; I'm sensitive to my partner. Even if I disagree with my partner, I communicate with her or him in a civilized manner."

A *cooperative* person pays close attention to the disagreements themselves. She or he likes to think, "I'm always willing to be flexible, to compromise. Whenever possible, I go along with my partner's viewpoint." Nevertheless, since people often find it difficult to be civil—to be considerate and cooperative toward their partners during conflicts—they don't want their image tarnished by outsiders finding out about their failings. Hence they desire secrecy.

Recall from Chapter 5 that when Helga first met Hans she was gratified to discover he was a good listener. As the years went by, however, Helga became disappointed to find out that Hans was a very poor talker. Not that he didn't tell her about events that happened on his job, or to chat about sports, politics, news events, and so on. But he didn't talk, that is, *communicate at a deep level*, about his feelings and reactions to the problems he was having at work. He didn't share what he wanted out of life in general, and from her in particular. Because intimacy involves sharing as well as listening, after a while Helga too gave up shar-

Conflict is the *normal* thing!

ing. Nevertheless, for a long time they had a marriage that fulfilled cultural ideals of being conflict-free and, needless to say, stable.

That's why Hans was shocked when after several years she began to suggest that he should get job retraining, and that she should attend school to prepare for the type of job that would give her the social recognition she'd wanted all her life. He suddenly found out what really mattered to her. Although outsiders assumed Hans and Helga had a "quality" marriage, Helga had nonetheless been undergoing a gradual metamorphosis. And just as a caterpillar weaves a cocoon that shields its metamorphosis, Helga had shielded hers from Hans. When she finally emerged from her cocoon by telling him what she wanted, his reactions was both negative and adamant: "No, I won't, and, no you can't." She concluded that her life-long dreams didn't seem to matter to him at all.

Moreover, when she tried to negotiate with him about specific changes in housework, child care, and so on, he began to attack her personally. He accused her of being "selfish" and of "trying to rise above her raisings." Plainly, he felt threatened by the thought of her becoming upwardly mobile. They began to experience screaming and shouting sessions that left them emotionally drained and incredibly upset. But because they shared the cultural ideal that couples should be civil in dealing with one another, they did everything they could to conceal those volatile episodes from outsiders. In short, even though they'd once had a considerate communication style while dealing with each other, they'd now become anything but considerate. While trying to figure out what to do about their disagreements, their communication *style* (words and body language, including facial expressions) had become hostile, bitter, coercive, and rejecting.

Even though they had once viewed each other as cooperative and flexible, each now perceived the other as uncooperative and inflexible over the *substance* of their conflicts. "Substance" simply refers to specific patterns of behavior regarding child care, housework, and so on. Helga perceived Hans as inflexible because he wouldn't budge from the behaviors he'd been doing for some years. She felt he was uncooperative because he wasn't trying to experiment with new behavior patterns. But Hans felt Helga was too rigid about the kinds of behavioral changes she wanted him to make—she was uncooperative about the substance of what she wanted.

Discussion and Negotiation as Risk-Taking

Helga's struggles with Hans illustrate another reason why negotiators (whether erotic partners, jurors, or politicians) prefer privacy. "Working things out" is to one degree or another always risky because the partners are trying to figure out something different, and thus new, for them. Helga is risking a lot to suggest things to Hans that none of their friends or families have ever done. She knows that if her ideas for changes in their relationship seem farfetched and wild to Hans, they would appear astonishingly bizarre to others. If Helga and Hans were forced to negotiate publicly, she would feel constrained from describing all the things she wants. She needs to be free to say precisely what's on her mind, even if it seems outrageous at first. Effective discussion and negotiation tends to be a creative process during which partners make up, that is, *invent*, new ideas as they go along. At first Helga could bear the thought of Hans laughing at her ideas, and even severely censuring her. She could do so because of their history. She trusted him enough to make herself vulnerable to him. Conversely, she did not trust outsiders enough to make herself vulnerable to them and possibly have them laughing at her.

Decision-Making and the Maintenance and Change Phase

Chapter 5 said that maintaining a relationship comes about by nurturing the behavior patterns—the substance—that's currently in place. During their years together, Hans believed he was nurturing, and thus maintaining, their erotic friendship by trying to do everything Helga expected from him and avoiding what she didn't want. But because he wasn't talking with her, he was failing to nurture her in that vital respect. An additional result of not talking was that he did not know the metamorphosis she was experiencing. Hans forgot that to nourish living things does not mean just keeping them alive. Living things by their very nature constantly change, and thus require appropriate reactions. Hans wasn't on the lookout for changes in Helga, and in spite of the fact that he valued their relationship, he wasn't alert to certain kinds of reactions he should have been making.

Discussions and Problem-Solving   If he'd noted subtle changes, Hans could have reacted by *discussing* them with Helga. Discussions are different from negotiations because discussions are neither preceded by, nor linked with, disagreements.[41] Instead, discussions are linked with what some call *problem-solving*. The pitfall in using the word *problem* is that when we hear it we assume something is wrong or broken. Someone says, for instance, "My car has a problem—it won't start. Something is wrong, it's broken." By contrast, in this book we use the term *problem* differently. We mean something like a math problem. In that case, nothing is wrong or broken, but the problem must be addressed and solved. Discussions consist of erotic friends talking about a problem, or puzzle, that requires attention and a solution, although nothing is wrong or broken.

Hans wasn't sensitive to Helga's changes, and so he didn't perceive any problems or puzzles requiring solutions. Nevertheless, when Helga first began sharing her aspirations for education and a good job, and her desire for Hans to do more housework, he could have perceived those matters the same way she did. She defined the matters as merely a problem requiring a solution. Instead of opposing her, he could have discussed the problem with her and together they could have found a solution.

Discussions emerge when the partners engage in a mutual give and take of ideas and suggestions regarding a solution to a puzzle. Like two students wrestling jointly with a math problem, the partners are free to be as creative, wide ranging, imaginative, and innovative as they can in searching for a solution.

Discussions are marked by a considerate back-and-forth communication style between the partners, that is, each partner is sensitive to the other's needs for him or her to be warm, conciliatory, sympathetic, affirming, upbeat, and so forth. Discussions are also marked by a high degree of cooperativeness and flexibility

regarding the substance of the problem. The partners are sensitive to the goal of fashioning and inventing new sets of behavior patterns that, as fully as possible, take into account the wishes, desires, and interests of both persons.

However, unlike a math puzzle, there is never only one correct solution to problems faced by partners. How do the partners know which of several solutions is best? The answer is that the partners themselves become persuaded that their new behavior patterns represent the best, or sometimes the least negative, solution. Because their discussions have been both considerate and cooperative, the best solution generally tends to flow rather naturally and obviously from their discussions. But by no means is that solution necessarily either painless or pleasant. It may be both painful and unpleasant.

The preceding scenario describes how Helga and Hans could have solved the problems Helga posed. They could have discussed the problems at length and invented solutions that consisted of new sets of behaviors regarding: shared housework activities; how many hours per day she would spend in classes and studying; how they would pay for the schooling; which job retraining courses he would enroll in; how to reorganize their leisure time to allow for companionship; and so on.

Problem-Solving and a Sense of We-ness   If Helga and Hans had actually behaved in that manner, not only would they be maintaining their relationship, they would simultaneously be changing it. Recall that Chapter 5 compared relationship change to the pruning and grafting that an apple farmer does to her tree. Pruning means cutting away the branches that are no longer productive. Grafting means organically inserting new buds that will increase the tree's productivity. The preceding scenario depicts Hans and Helga as pruning and grafting—cutting away former ideas and behaviors regarding housework, education, and employment and inserting new ideas and fresh behavior patterns in all three areas.

Chapter 5 also said that erotic friends who both maintain (nurture and pay attention to) their relationships and change (prune, graft) them are likely to feel good about them. They are likely to feel a strong sense of *we-ness*, or bonding, with their partner. We now have a clearer idea of why that is so. We-ness is based on the feelings of *belonging* to someone and of *mattering* to him or her. It's plain to see that processes of discussion and problem-solving have a major impact on those feelings of bonding.[42] A communication style that is highly considerate promotes a sense of belonging and mattering. A style that is *inconsiderate* undermines those feelings. If Hans and Helga had each used a considerate style while trying to solve the puzzle she raised, each would have thought, "Yes, I really do belong, I genuinely do matter, to her/him."

At the same time, the substance of problem-solving affects a sense of we-ness in similar fashion. Working out new behavior patterns that are mutually acceptable to both partners is a highly gratifying experience. Being able to change things in her relationship was very important to Helga. If she and Hans had together been able to arrive at a good solution to her problem, she would have felt very positively about him indeed. Her sense of belonging with him and mattering to him would have been strengthened.

THE OUTCOMES OF JOINT DECISION-MAKING

Another way to describe what Helga and Hans might have done is to say they could have engaged in shared or joint decision-making. Figure 11-1 calls the solution they could have achieved the *outcome* of decision-making. The back-and-forth discussions they might have had with each other are called the *processes* of decision-making. And we're already familiar

with the *context* of their decision-making. This includes variables such as their education, job status, and income, along with their ages, number of children, number of years they've been together, aspirations for the future, and so on. The context also includes things such as inflation, plant closings, unemployment trends, availability and costs of quality day care, and expanding or declining job opportunities.

Problem-solving is one way for erotic friends to carry on their shared decision-making. The partners operate out of a certain social *context*. They engage one another in give-and-take processes that are both considerate and cooperative. Finally, they arrive at an outcome representing a satisfactory solution to their problem. Moreover, their decision-making helps them feel good about their partner, themselves, and their relationship.

Dialectic Tension

As neat and tidy as that may sound, decision-making among today's erotic friends is inevitably characterized by what researchers call a "dialectic tension."[43] In plain English, that means that things never stand still. No matter how carefully couples may craft a solution to their problem, the solution is always subject to reconsideration: Yesterday's solution may become today's problem. Or as everyday folk wisdom has it: "Solve one problem, create two more."

Assume, for example, that Hans and Helga had been able to solve their puzzle and work out a fresh set of behaviors regarding housework, education, and employment. During subsequent months, that outcome became part of the revised social context of their relationship. Hans, for instance, now goes to his job retraining program in the mornings, and works part-time in the afternoons. After a while the program's instructor recognizes that Hans has considerable talent for doing the kind of job that the program is all about. The instructor offers Hans that kind of job in a factory of which she's a part owner. But the factory is located 250 miles away. Suddenly, Hans and Helga have a new problem that sprang directly out of the solution they'd so carefully devised to solve an earlier one. The problem is that if Hans moves, should Helga move with him? To move to the other city where there's no college would mean she'd have to drop out of school. But the fact that Helga's going to school to prepare for a good job is the bedrock foundation on which rests all the changes they've recently made. Hence she tells Hans she doesn't believe that dropping out of school is a good step toward solving their new problem. At this point, they can begin again to brainstorm. They can again go back and forth with each other, exchanging creative ideas aimed at coming up with a solution to their new painful dilemma.

The Emergence of a Conflict Mode

The Pause Button   But they can also shift in a different direction. Let's say that after a good deal of brainstorming, using a considerate communication style, they run out of ideas that they both believe are acceptable. Helga, for instance, suggests they start a *commuting* relationship.[44] She would live here and go to school, he would live there and work; they'd get together on most weekends and holidays. Hans doesn't like that idea, and he also very much wants that job. Each of them is stymied about what else to suggest to solve their puzzle. Occasionally it's possible for a couple to push the "pause" button on their problem-solving. They agree to do nothing until they can figure out a solution they can both live with. Very often, however, that's difficult to do, especially if there's a deadline in the picture. Obviously, Len and Sondra couldn't wait indefinitely to decide whether she should have an abortion. In Hans's case, his potential employer has given him two more weeks to make up his mind. If he can't make up his mind by then, she'll offer the job to someone else.

A Subtle Shift   Because he wants the job very much, Hans subtly begins to shift from a problem-solving mode to a conflict mode. This kind of shift is never easy to detect. There is no clearly marked black and white boundary between problem-solving and conflict. The ground between them is more like varying shades of gray blending into one another. One crucial difference between the two is that in a conflict mode the search for new ideas has been replaced by efforts to insist on one particular solution. The search for alternative solutions fades slowly into the background. In this case, Hans tries, gently at first, to persuade Helga that she should move with him and postpone going to school for a couple of years. She resists Hans's solution. However, she, like him, doesn't come up with any new solutions. And again, just like him, she continues to insist on her earlier idea that he didn't like. She keeps on saying, "Let this job offer pass by; another will come up by the time you finish your retraining."

At this point the fly on the wall would say they're in a conflict mode. Each partner has a goal—a certain behavior—that each would like to achieve: He wants her to move with him. She wants him to stay put with her. In effect, they have a conflict. Moreover, because of the employer's deadline Hans refuses to put their disagreement on pause: He keeps bringing it up every day. It seems apparent they have opposing goals in mind, and that each is resisting the other's aims.

In view of their mutual opposition and resistance—their conflict mode—the fly on the wall pays close attention both to their substance and their style. Substance, we learned, refers to the behaviors that each is proposing to the other on a give-and-take basis. Are they engaging in the type of back-and-forth process in which each person merely keeps on repeating the same old thing to his or her partner? Or is one or both partners trying to modify their suggestions, perhaps even coming up with new ones? Creative modifications are not limited to a problem-solving mode. In spite of being in an opposition and conflict mode, partners may still be able to make innovative suggestions. These may be quite different from merely repeating the same old thing.

Negotiations

When couples in a conflict mode are making back-and-forth proposals, they're *negotiating*.[45] Negotiations differ from discussions because of the opposition between the partners. Their awareness of their mutual opposition generates a distinctive atmosphere. It's not simply a matter of coming up with a solution they can both accept. Instead, negotiators must first overcome their differences—the feelings of resistance that each holds toward the other's suggestions. That's why Figure 11-1 shows that whereas discussions probe merely for solutions, negotiations search for *resolution*. Negotiating partners must resolve differences at the same time they're making fresh suggestions. When a couple is in a conflict mode both are essential if they're somehow to invent new arrangements.

Another thing that makes negotiation very different from discussion is that during an opposition mode it's very difficult to come up with modifications without falling into an *inconsiderate* communication style. Figure 11-1 shows that context factors influence give-and-take processes, and that both context and processes influence outcomes. The obligation to love one's partner discussed in Chapter 10 is part of the social context of a couple's decision-making. Before the sixties and seventies, part of loving her husband meant that even if she disagreed with him, a Good Wife was not supposed to verbalize her opposition. If for some reason she felt she had to disagree, she must above all employ a considerate style.[46] If we think about it, the characteristics we've used to describe "considerate" are the same characteristics that in the past were used to define *"feminine."*[47] Even if a wife argued with her hus-

band, she had to be careful lest she sacrifice her essential femininity.

But today's woman, said Chapter 10, is now obliged to love herself as much as her partner. Women now have the option to verbalize their opposition to their partners just as men do. In addition, women are escaping the taboo on being inconsiderate during negotiations—a taboo men never faced. Just as men have always been granted the option to yell, use profanity and obscenity, and become verbally nasty, women are gradually gaining that same option. It is precisely because of that symmetry in communication style, as well as in substance, that present-day negotiations between women and men have become more excruciating than ever they were in the past. Chapter 10 stated that the obligation to love oneself and one's partner equally is a logical contradiction. One reason it is a contradiction is that loving oneself invariably triggers disagreements and strenuous negotiations. Life was much easier for men when women loved their husbands more than they loved themselves!

Acceptable Outcomes After all, says Paul Gulliver, the goal of negotiations is to be successful or *effective*. Effective means that an outcome is "discovered that each party can accept."[48] As long as wives were not obliged to love themselves as much as their husbands, they tended not to launch overt opposition against them. On the infrequent occasions when women felt bold enough to oppose their husbands overtly (e.g., on behalf of their children's interests), their style was carefully monitored so as not to offend their man unduly. Furthermore, when wives and husbands were unable to resolve their differences in ways that wives could accept (which was most of the time), wives had to live with the unresolved conflicts.[49]

Consensus Recall that since the 1950s researchers have found that conflicts are far more common than consensus between wives and husbands. The researchers are not merely saying that couples have disagreements. They're also asserting that most couples are unable to resolve many of their disagreements. Consensus means that the couple has negotiated their disagreement and arrived at an acceptable outcome—the conflict has been resolved.[50] If Hans and Helga could have negotiated their disagreement over his job offer and where they should live in ways that were acceptable to each of them, they would have achieved consensus. But since they seem unable to resolve it, they simply live with it. Hans feels the pain of it more sharply than Helga, because the deadline passed and with it his job. In the past, however, the picture would more likely have been reversed. Helga would have had to move with Hans and sacrifice her own educational and job aspirations. Thus, she would have felt more keenly than he the discomfort and pain of unresolved conflict.

Fairness and a Sense of We-ness   When they hear the term *outcome*, most people do not think about feelings. Instead they focus on the outward behaviors that have or have not been negotiated. For example: Did Helga and Hans keep their old arrangements by not moving? Or did they make new arrangements by moving? Nevertheless, people's feelings about and reactions to the arrangements are actually more significant than the arrangements themselves. The reason that feelings and reactions are more significant is because of the dialectic tension described previously. Feelings about unresolved conflicts have a way of leading to new conflicts.

For instance, if Hans feels that Helga has been unfair in "making" him forgo his job offer, he's also likely to wonder how much she actually cares for him, how much he matters to her. Thus, his sense of we-ness, or bonding, with Helga is diminished to a certain degree. If he doesn't feel she's been what John Mirowsky and Catherine Ross call "fair and caring," in

the future he'll be eager to challenge their arrangements whenever and wherever he can.[51]

One way to challenge them, for example, is to stop doing the housework he'd so recently agreed to start doing. Or he could do the housework in a sloppy and halfhearted manner. Additionally, he might begin to oppose her over the amount of money her education is costing them. Helga tries to negotiate with Hans on both matters. She tries to get him to start doing the housework again and to do it carefully. She also argues that she can't go to school for any less money: "I don't set the fees and the cost of books." But they're not able to resolve these two recent conflicts any more satisfactorily than the earlier ones. Now Helga believes that Hans is being unfair and uncaring on all these matters, and, her feelings of belonging and mattering—her sense of bonding with Hans—is being undermined as much as his.

Another important element that affects a person's feelings of we-ness is the *style* his or her partner uses as they're negotiating. When Helga and Hans were negotiating solely over his job and their move, each used a relatively considerate communication style. However, as they gradually escalated into the housework and money issues, their styles began to alter.[52] Each of them became increasingly inconsiderate. And the more they argued over the several interconnected matters without being able to resolve them, the more inconsiderate they both became. In the past, some sociologists believed that an inconsiderate style showed that a marriage was not well-adjusted.[53] To shout and scream and raise one's voice was not only considered bad form, impolite, and uncouth, it also "damaged" the marriage. Remember, of course, that it was women more than men who were not supposed to negotiate in an inconsiderate (i.e., unfeminine) style.

Today, however, differences between the genders in negotiating style appear to be diminishing. Hence, the longer a couple dredges a conflict back and forth using inconsiderate styles, the more likely it is that those styles will impact negatively on their feelings of we-ness. That's what's happening with Helga and Hans. The relentless bickering between them is becoming increasingly tense and unproductive. Their language and overall communication style are growing more hostile and bitter all the time. It is easy to see why each partner's sense of bonding with the other keeps on declining.

By contrast, recall that Ingrid and Albert had a similar kind of conflict. At first Ingrid tried to negotiate using a highly considerate communication style. But that didn't work: She couldn't get Albert to budge from his insistence that housework "is not for me." That made Ingrid extremely angry, and so her style became anything but considerate. She began to shout at him, and to fling invectives and obscenities. She also displayed a body language that clearly communicated she was furious with Albert for refusing to negotiate in a cooperative manner, and for refusing to make some changes in his behavior.

Her negative style grabbed Albert's attention, and he was forced to consider carefully what she was trying to say. Consequently, he was jarred into negotiating via a cooperative manner. And because he did so, her style shifted once again to being considerate. They were then able to resolve their differences in ways that both partners felt were fair and thus acceptable. In addition, each felt a stronger sense of we-ness and bonding, in part because of the new arrangements (the substance) they'd worked out. Moreover, their feelings of belonging and mattering were enhanced because of the considerate style that each had used once they finally got serious about figuring out what to do.

Thus, an inconsiderate style can sometimes strengthen a sense of we-ness, but sometimes it can surely undermine it. A major difference

between these two couples lies with the *context* of their negotiations, as in Figure 11-1. Albert and Ingrid had a history of profound intimacy that included a great deal of self-disclosure and openness regarding their deepest feelings. By contrast, Hans and Helga lacked a trail of intimacy. When Ingrid began to get negative, Albert's experience of that intimacy triggered something inside him. Intimacy is a rich and satisfying experience, and he felt it being threatened by what was suddenly going on between him and Ingrid. He felt moved to end the threat by negotiating seriously with her. Indeed, the fact they were able to share themselves so fully became woven (as it had many times before) into the considerate style they both began to adopt. Ingrid shared how much her promotion at work alleviated her own insecure view of herself. Albert shared how his father calls men who do housework "pansies."

This incident dramatically changed Ingrid's view of conflict and health. Recall that she used to believe that healthy relationship were conflict-free, which helped make them stable. Instead, she found that although they could indeed have avoided the conflict if she'd not opposed Albert, that would have been unhealthy both for her and her relationship with him. They would have had a stable marriage, but one that would have been extremely painful for her to bear. That pain in turn would have had negative consequences for Albert as well as their children. By resisting and struggling with him, her own health, as well as the health of her partner and children, was enhanced.

OTHER FACTORS THAT AFFECT DECISION-MAKING

Besides a history of intimacy, many other context factors influence how erotic friends make decisions—whether they do it by discussion and problem-solving, or by negotiation and conflict resolution. Chapter 5 said that today's couples have access to a wide array of resources from outside their relationship that simply weren't there for pre-sixties' couples. Women in particular benefit from the recent expansion of educational and occupational opportunities. After all, the chief cause of the serious conflicts between Hans and Helga, as well as between Ingrid and Albert, is each woman's desire for the esteem and respect that Western culture attaches to paid work in general. Neither woman, however, is content with merely any paid job. Each wants the prestige attached to what Chapter 10 described as a *career*. Ingrid is already on a career track. Helga wants to be.

The fact that Ingrid has a well-paying career is a context factor affecting every segment of her discussions and negotiations with Albert. Her career reinforces their shared perception that they're what Chapter 10 called *equal* partners. Each recognizes that they come from different backgrounds: He belongs to the dominant social category; she belongs to the subordinate category.

Economic Autonomy

Nevertheless, Ingrid and Albert are trying to overcome that social difference in their relationship by establishing a level playing field for their decision-making. They carry on their decision-making by rejecting the cultural perception of her as a subordinate. Their shared definition of Ingrid as being equal to Albert is strongly reinforced by her actual career and by the fact that she is as much a household provider as he. Both of them know she's what Chapters 5 and 12 call an "economically autonomous" person: If she had to go it alone, she could support herself and their children to the same degree he could if he were alone.

Inevitably, being economically autonomous means that she discusses and negotiates much differently with Albert than her mother did with her father. She is much freer in making suggestions and devising creative solutions.

She's also much more assertive during negotiations, being willing even to communicate with an inconsiderate style if need be. Although her mother often wished she could behave in those ways, she was fearful of doing so lest she offered her husband and lose her marriage. Ingrid knows, and so does Albert, that if he ever became offended to the extent of giving up their relationship, she would be okay economically. Her lifestyle might be cut back, but she would not be threatened by the specter of economic deprivation, and perhaps poverty, faced by many solo mothers in the United States.

However, it would be a mistake to assume that Albert feels threatened by her economic autonomy. He doesn't negotiate with her out of fear that, if he doesn't, she'll pack up and leave. He respects her because she's achieving so much in her career. He also respects her as his equal. Howard Gadlin claims that because they perceive themselves as equals, their intimacy is enhanced.[54] The satisfactions supplied by their shared intimacy enhance Albert's perception that they care about and love each other. He feels they share a sense of belonging and mattering, that is, we-ness. In short, he negotiates because both she and their relationship mean a great deal to him. And Ingrid negotiates because both he and their relationship mean a great deal to her.

Availability

Besides economic factors, *personal availability* is a second context variable that, according to Chapters 5 and 12, represents an alternative to one's current relationship. It too affects how couples discuss and negotiate. Today's men, and especially women, do not define themselves as locked into any erotic friendship in quite the same ways their forebears did. They perceive themselves as potentially available to pursue another relationship, if they so choose. Neither Ingrid nor Albert defines herself or himself as *currently* available. Nor do they expect they will ever want to be available. Nevertheless, Chapter 5 showed that regardless of a person's current relationship, physical and sexual attractiveness are significant to both genders for several reasons. One reason is that attractiveness is a source of pride, esteem, and prestige. Another reason is that, "It helps, just in case. . . ."

Ingrid and Albert both realize that the other remains a physically attractive person. But neither perceives the other's attractiveness as a "stick" forcing them to negotiate, because if they don't, she or he could always find someone else. Nevertheless, as with economic factors, having that particular resource stimulates their mutual freedom to be creative, persistent, and assertive during their back-and-forth, give-and-take processes of discussion and negotiation. Women in particular benefit from personal availability, especially when it's connected with economic autonomy. However, if women lacked economic autonomy, their personal availability would by itself have far less impact on their joint decision-making—especially as they age and physical beauty declines.

Autonomy, Power, and Well-being

Back in the sixties, when people asked feminists what they wanted, their answer was straightforward—autonomy.[55] Women wanted, and want, the same degree of control over their lives that men have. For men, being economically autonomous is the basis for whatever degree of control they have over their lives in general. It's hard to imagine a man who is not economically autonomous feeling in control of his life. Growing numbers of women are striving for that same feeling and for the reality beneath it.

Researchers have paid a lot of attention to the *power* that husbands and wives have during their decision-making processes.[56] Power means the capability to shape or influence the course of give and take during discussions and negotiations regarding specific situations.[57] For example, during the course of their conflict over housework and child care, Ingrid had many more ideas and suggestions than Albert for changes in their behavior patterns. In responding to Ingrid, Albert eventually went along with all of her proposals, and offered only one modest suggestion for changes in her behavior. When we compare how much she was able to change his behavior with how little he changed her behavior, we conclude that in this specific situation, Ingrid exercised more power, or control, than did Albert.[58]

That does not mean that Ingrid "wears the pants" in their relationship. Before this time, during their discussions over numerous other specific matters, Albert had consistently offered many more suggestions and ideas than Ingrid. Hence, most of the time in most situations, he had exercised considerably more power (control, influence) than she. That was fine with her. She didn't mind that he'd shaped most realms throughout their erotic friendship. The solutions he'd devised to the specific problems they'd faced had not undermined her overall sense of autonomy.[59] On the contrary, she felt that his solutions contributed to her sense that she was in control of her life. In her view, he was taking care of the "ordinary" things of life so that she could concentrate on the things that mattered most to her—her career and their children. As long as she was free to shape and control those two realms, she felt in control of her life in general. It was not until Albert refused to discuss or negotiate the changes she proposed in those two realms (plus housework) that she felt her overall, or *global*, sense of autonomy being threatened.

After those particular situational conflicts were satisfactorily resolved, Ingrid's feelings of a strong global sense of autonomy was restored. She once again felt in charge of her life, largely because she was now fully able to pursue her career. One way to describe global autonomy is by the term *me-ness*. According to Chapter 5, me-ness describes the degree to which a person feels he or she is in control, or in charge, of his or her own life. Part of the obligation to love oneself discussed in Chapter 10 lies with seeing to it that one has as strong a sense of me-ness as possible. A major reason why me-ness is so critical is because of its connections with mental and emotional health.

In recent years, researchers have paid increasing attention to what they call *well-being*. Well-being can be a very slippery term, but what they appear to mean by it is the absence of *stress* symptoms.[60] For example, respondents are asked questions such as, How are you feeling in general? Have you been bothered by nerves? Do you have sweaty palms, or a sour or upset stomach, or sleeplessness, or rashes and hives, or sudden twitching? Do you feel depressed or sad or hopeless? Do you feel you're losing your mind, or that everything's going wrong? Have you recently been anxious, worried, tense, depressed, or blue? And so on.

Researchers have found that the stronger a person's sense of global control or autonomy (me-ness), the fewer of those (and other) kinds of stress symptoms a person has.[61] Not only do persons with great autonomy have fewer symptoms, but when the symptoms occur they're less severe and don't last as long. Hence, feeling in charge of one's life and having a strong sense of autonomy help to promote mental and emotional health. Some researchers believe that control contributes to better physical health as well[62] (see also Chapter 14).

When Betty Friedan published *The Feminine Mystique* in 1963, thus helping to revive feminism in North America, she noted a peculiar thing. On the one hand, the 1950s had been the Golden Age of The American Family. Divorce was extremely rare, mothers took care of their own children at home, and family together-

ness seemed part and parcel of the American Dream. On the other hand, Friedan and other feminists noted that in spite of all this outward happiness and harmony, housewives and mothers paid many more visits to their physicians then men. They were afflicted, says Friedan, with "the problem that has no name." The problem consisted of the sorts of stress symptoms just described. The strategy (besides aspirin) used most commonly by their (mostly male) physicians to treat the women was to urge them to become better adjusted to their biologically ordained roles as wives and mothers.

Those gender roles were quite rigid, offering little to women in the way of autonomy and a sense of control over their lives. Hence the roles themselves were a major reason for their stress symptoms. Urging women to conform more strictly to those roles was likely to increase, not decrease, their stress. By contrast, feminists, believing that lack of control resulting from role conformity was at the root of women's "problem," urged women to invent fresh ways to relate to men and to children.

Inventing anything (from sand castles to lives) gives a sense of control. With control comes well-being—emotional and mental health. When Ingrid negotiated with Albert (and Helga with Hans), what each woman wanted ultimately was a sense of autonomy and the well-being that accompanies it. Todd Gitlin remarks that although most of the objectives of the 1960s' counterculture were never attained, one that was was women's individual rights.[63] Today's women (Helga, Ingrid) have gained the right to strive for autonomy and the emotional well-being that springs from it. Explicit conflicts and overt negotiations, virtually unknown to husbands and wives of the fifties, have become melded into the core of the contemporary erotic friendship, whether among girlfriends/boyfriends, cohabitors, or marrieds.

Me-ness, We-ness, and Commitment The rub comes when me-ness clashes with we-ness. We learned in Chapter 10 that the obligation to love oneself invariably clashes with the obligation to love one's partner and (any) children. Chapter 5 talked about the commitment that erotic friends make to one another as they enter their maintenance and change phase. Commitment means a number of different, but connected, things. First, it means that partners pledge (explicitly or implicitly) to be sexually exclusive with each other. Second, they pledge to work at their relationship. Among the many things that's included by "working" on an erotic friendship is the pledge to participate seriously and actively in problem solving, as well as conflict resolution, with one's partner.[64] Third, commitment means the intention to stay with one's partner at least indefinitely and perhaps forever.

It is during the complex and intricate processes of decision-making, whether done as discussion or negotiation, that all three dimensions of commitment are eventually either enhanced or undermined. Recall from Chapter 5 that because they could not resolve their conflicts in acceptable ways, Helga's commitment to Hans gradually diminished over all three dimensions. First, she began to consider Kurt a potential prospect for a relationship, and then became his sexual partner although she also remained Hans's sexual partner. Next, she gave up negotiating with Hans in any serious manner because she had finally made up her mind to separate from him, although she lacked the courage to tell him so.

Commitment and the Dissolution Phase Commitment is tied to a person's sense of we-ness. The longer that Helga and Hans were unable to resolve their conflicts in acceptable fashion, the more her sense of we-ness (belonging and mattering) with him declined. As one's sense of bonding drops, so does one's commitment, including one's intention to be exclusive, to negotiate, and to stay. If we-ness and commitment continue tilting in a downward direction apart from significant upward blips, then, according to Chapter 5, the couple is in a dissolution phase. Helga and Hans got into their downward spiral because they were unable to negotiate effectively over Helga's me-mess—her desires for autonomy and the emotional health it supplies.

Conversely, Ingrid and Albert were able to negotiate effectively over her me-ness. One of the outcomes of their conflict resolution was an enhanced sense of belonging, mattering, and bonding—we-ness. Ingrid and Albert continued to live in the maintenance and change phase. Thomas Scheff and Suzanne Retzinger observe that social bonds, or a sense of belonging and mattering, are continually "being built, maintained, repaired, or damaged."[65]

CONCLUSION—DECISION-MAKING AND THE QUEST FOR RESPONSIBILITY

The theme of this book is that throughout today's Western societies people keep on inventing and reinventing their primary relationships—their families. The erotic friendship is a highly significant primary relationship. By its very nature, an erotic friendships does not remain static. It exists in a dialectic tension. One or both partners are continually changing (if ever so slightly) the relationship. At the same time, the partners themselves do not stand still. One or both is changing in conjunction with changes in the relationship. Sometimes the partners cause changes in their relationship. And sometimes the relationship causes changes in the partners.

Moreover, previous solutions to old problems can cause new problems and conflicts. Sometimes partners and their relationships change as a result of powerful forces in the larger society. These include inflation, plant closings and unemployment, plant openings, fresh educational and job opportunities, and shifts in government policies. The forces also include demographic trends in divorce, women's employment, cohabitation, and so forth. Very often, erotic friendships change the character of the larger society—they influence the broader social fabric.

In one way or another, changes within erotic friendships are often connected to one or more aspects of joint decision-making. Whether by problem-solving and/or by conflict resolution, partners seek to bring about or to resist changes in their relationships. Before the 1960s marital decision-making was largely implicit and covert, with wives using subterfuges of every sort to wangle and finesse things from their husbands that would benefit their children first of all. More recently, decision-making has shifted from the hidden periphery of marriages to the very core of the erotic friendship. It has become overt and explicit. The ancient struggle between the genders is now being played out on the center stages of erotic friendships.

Although on-stage dynamics generally remain hidden from public view, their consequences for the broader social fabric are open for everyone to see. People's refashioning or erotic friendships, as well as their construction of today's social families (Chapters 2 and 3), represent significant shifts away from our old image of The Modern Family. Daniel Bell remarks that, "The reigning fear of the right is the destruction of the family."[66] As growing numbers of persons re-create relationships and families in response to individual rights (me-ness, autonomy, the obligation to love oneself), where, asks Bell, is people's concern for what he calls the "public household?" In particular, as women and men keep on reinventing adult relationships, is the well-being of children somehow being overlooked and forgotten? As adults carry on their problem-solving and con-

flict resolution, do they care about being responsible for anything besides themselves?

There are no simple answers to these recurrent themes, and we keep on addressing them throughout the book. But one thing seems evident: A couple's decision-making is a prime site for the struggle between freedom, rights, creativity, justice, me-ness, and individualism on the one hand, versus commitment, bonding, restraint, conformity, order, we-ness, and responsibility on the other. It follows that in seeking to achieve ever-shifting balances between individual interests and the public household, growing numbers of persons will have to become increasingly adept at mastering the complex skills of joint decision-making. Couples will have to figure out how their shared decision-making may or may not contribute to the building of the public household. They will have to consider what consequences their reinventions of relationships and families might have for the ongoing reinvention of the larger society.

NOTES

1. Jerry Alder, Lucille Beachy, Jean Seligmann, Patrick Rogers, Vera Azar, Daniel McGinn, and Jeanne Gordon. "Unhappily Ever After," *Newsweek*, August 31, 1992, pp. 52–59.
2. Burgess, Locke, and Thomes, 1963, p. 294; Locke, 1968, p. 45.
3. Klemer, 1959.
4. Waller, 1938.
5. For example, Coser, 1956; Alexander, 1988; Scheff and Retzinger, 1991.
6. Vera and Feagin, in preparation.
7. In April 1993, the U.S. government ordered the armed services to let women fly aircraft and be stationed on surface warships during combat: See *The Gainesville, Florida, Sun*, April 28, p. A1 (from *The New York Times*). Less than a year later, the government took an additional step toward gender equity by allowing women to participate in ground combat support units (engineering, maintenance, etc.) that had formerly been

considered "too risky" for women: See *The New York Times*, January 14, 1994, p. A10.

8. Seeley, Sim, and Loosley, 1956, p. 395.
9. Rainwater, Coleman, and Handel, 1959.
10. Rubin, 1976, p. 112.
11. Ibid., p. 113.
12. Olson and McCubbin, 1983, p. 235.
13. Ibid. Italics in original.
14. Fitzpatrick, 1988a, p. 149.
15. Scanzoni, 1978; Scanzoni and Szinovacz, 1980; Godwin and Scanzoni, 1989b.
16. Scheff and Retzinger, p. 69.
17. Fitzpatrick, 1988a; Scanzoni and Fox, 1980.
18. Fitzpatrick, p. 172.
19. Thornton, 1989; Stacey, 1990.
20. Godwin & Scanzoni, 1989a.
21. Scanzoni, pp. 18–19.
22. By "intimacy" we mean the full range of issues captured by terms such as marital "quality," marital "satisfaction," marital "communication," and so forth. See Noller and Fitzpatrick, 1990.
23. Godwin and Scanzoni, 1989b.
24. Cherry, 1987.
25. Reiss, 1990.
26. Clanton, 1989.
27. Bringle and Buunk, 1991.
28. Gerson, 1985; Stacey.
29. Nye, 1979, p. 11.
30. Rubin; Scanzoni.
31. Jones, Marsden, and Tepperman, 1990.
32. Millman, 1991.
33. Dizard and Gadlin, 1990; Bellah et al., 1991; Hewlett, 1991; Skolnick, 1991.
34. Scanzoni, 1991.
35. See Nathanson, 1992.
36. Lucia Mouat, *The Christian Science Monitor*, October 2, 1992, p. 2.
37. Godwin and Scanzoni, 1989b.

38. Edwards, 1991.
39. Hicks, Hansen, and Christie, 1983, p. 174. Also see parts of Knapp and Miller, 1985; Baxter, 1988; Fitzpatrick, 1988a, 1988b; Schaap, Buunk, and Kerkstra, 1988; and Levinger and Huston, 1990.
40. Tannen, 1990.
41. Scanzoni & Szinovacz; Donald Hansen, 1988; Tallman and Gray, 1990; Baxter et al., 1993.
42. Scanzoni, 1989b; Scanzoni and Marsiglio, 1993.
43. Raush, 1977; Kingsbury and Scanzoni, 1993.
44. Gerstel and Gross, 1984; Winfield, 1985.
45. Godwin and Scanzoni, 1989b; Jonathon Turner, 1988.
46. Spiegel, 1960.
47. Pleck, 1980.
48. Gulliver, 1979: xiii.
49. Seeley et al.; Rubin.
50. Hill and Scanzoni, 1982; Scanzoni and Godwin, 1991.
51. Mirowsky and Ross, 1989.
52. Gottman and Levenson, 1988.
53. Bernard, 1969.
54. Gadlin, 1977.
55. Kraditor, 1968.
56. See Godwin and Scanzoni, 1989b, for a review of the "marital/family power" literature.
57. Zartman, 1978; see also Canary and Stafford, 1993.
58. Godwin and Scanzoni, 1989b.
59. Scanzoni and Arnett, 1987.
60. See McDowell and Newell, 1987.
61. Mirowsky and Ross; Syme, 1990; Ross, 1991.
62. Rodin, 1990.
63. Gitlin, 1987, p. 432.
64. Raush, 1977.
65. Scheff and Retzinger, p. 97.
66. Bell, 1990, p. 69.

CHAPTER 12

AGGRESSION AGAINST WOMEN

Chapter 11 focused on conflict and nonviolent decision-making. This chapter shifts the focus to a phenomenon quite ancient—male violence against women.

Previous chapters said a lot about the expansion of women's choices in postmodern societies. Those choices are both economic and sexual, and include the freedom to publicly maintain erotic friendships. However, there's a dark side to relationships between women and men that most of us would rather ignore. The dark side consists of the aggression that men inflict on women—sexual assault, sexual harassment, and physical force. Throughout history men have used their greater physical strength to limit women's choices. Male aggression continues to coerce and constrain women even today.

Many women and some men are trying to reinvent male violence by stopping it. The Liz Claiborne company sponsors big-city billboards urging, "STOP domestic violence: Don't die for love."[1] The billboards also convey some chilling statistics: "Every 12 seconds a woman is beaten in the U.S.; 25% of the violent crime in America is wife assault; 4 women are killed every day by their husbands or partners; 60% of battered women are beaten while they are pregnant."

SEXUAL EXPLOITATION

Early in 1992, heavyweight boxing superstar Mike Tyson was convicted of raping Desiree Washington, a contestant in the 1991 Miss Black America beauty pageant. In his defense he claimed she'd willingly gone with him to the hotel room, that they were having a good time, and that he didn't hurt her. He stated he was out to hurt boxers, not women. Washington claimed that Tyson had forced her to have sexual intercourse with him. She also alleged that leaders of a large African-American religious denomination (to whom Tyson had previously promised generous donations) had offered her lots of money to drop the charges.

According to novelist Joyce Carol Oates, Washington was a heroine in the stand against sexual abuse.[2] Oates adds that press reports indicate some citizens (white and black) were sorry Tyson was convicted. A few black citizens remarked that they didn't care for the spectacle of a black woman accusing a black man of the crime that whites stereotypically attach to all black men. Other citizens wondered aloud where to place the blame for Tyson's action: A sex-saturated culture? Men's macho self-image and their view of women as sex objects? Oates cites an earlier biography of Tyson in which he himself vehemently rejected the labels of "poor guy" and "victim" that have trailed him all his professional life: "No one is to blame," concludes Oates, except Tyson.

A few months earlier, another rape trial drew as much if not more national attention. William Kennedy Smith (nephew of Senator Ted Kennedy) was acquitted of raping a white woman. They met at a chic Palm Beach, Florida, nightspot, danced and had a few drinks, and she returned with him to his family estate. She claimed that once there he forced her to have sexual intercourse against her will. His story was that she willingly consented. The jury took his word over hers. Once again press reports showed that citizens were divided: "Why did she go home with him if she didn't want It?" asked some. Other citizens believed he did it but the high-priced lawyer bought with Kennedy money "saved his neck."

These and similar media events have focused attention on a matter that until recently no one thought very much about—sexual assault in the form of *acquaintance rape*. During the early 1990s, popular TV series such as *Designing Women, L.A. Law, A Different World,* and *Civil Wars* devoted several episodes to it.[3] In the late eighties and early nineties, "date rape" became a live issue on college campuses because for the first time officials were trying to cope with date-rape lawsuits.[4] The women claimed that universities were not taking their charges of rape seriously and thus not punishing alleged offenders. One person who rejected the arguments of activist women was

University of California Professor Neil Gilbert. On the major talk-show circuit and in the national media, Gilbert asserted that "rape" was an incorrect label for what some men did on dates. Men might be "insensitive," he acknowledged, "but you can't call that rape."[5]

Alongside this mountain of attention from the media, numerous researchers have begun to focus on the topic of acquaintance rape. Does this newfound interest mean that acquaintance rape is a new thing? That it didn't happen before the 1980s? Laurie Bechhofer and Andrea Parrot cite an Old Testament Bible story showing that acquaintance rape has been around for at least 2,500 years.[6] Amnon talked his unwilling half-sister Tamar into bed, and after he pleasured himself he threw her out of his house. When she reported the incident to her full brother Absalom, he responded, "Don't worry about it, it's no big deal." It was not until the 1950s that Kanin presented the first social science evidence for sexual aggression.[7] Yet recall from Chapter 7 that Willard Waller figured a lot more sexual aggression went on among 1930s' daters than anyone realized. He based his suspicion on the essence of the Dating Game: Women were supposed to sexually titillate men enough to keep them interested, but not so much as to ruin their own reputation.

Although North Americans have been edging away from the Game since the 1960s, there's a lot of disagreement on what the new rules should be. Lillian Rubin points out that the sexual freedoms of recent decades may actually leave some women more vulnerable to sexual aggression than ever before. In the old Game, "nice girls" never said yes. In today's world, liberated women can't say no—or so many men (and some women) seem to believe.[8] Researchers will probably never know for sure if there's more or less acquaintance rape today than there was during the 1930s or 1950s, or the 1700s, or in ancient Israel. But for the first time in history it's become a live issue and will remain so for many years. The reason it's become a live issue is clear. Before the sixties, women's personal and economic choices were very narrow, so narrow indeed that they were wrapped up in the same man. Women had the freedom to marry the man they loved, but once married they were "taken." The married woman had given up the personal freedom to consider any other man. And the only economic choice she had was to hope that the man she loved could support her and their children.

Economic Autonomy

The Big Bang was about choices that today's women have more of than ever before. Chapter 15 shows that although women continue to face marketplace discrimination, increasing numbers of them are achieving economic autonomy, and many others want to. Economic autonomy simply means being able to support oneself, and any children, at a *reasonable* level ("reasonable" is defined by the person). Economic autonomy is what men have expected for themselves since the start of the Jacksonian era. To be sure, inflation, unemployment, a shrinking job market, and poor education make it difficult for any person to be autonomous. But according to Charles Jones and co-workers, the Big Change is that growing numbers of women prefer economic autonomy to having no option other than dependence on a man.[9]

Availability

Alongside, and indeed because of, economic choices, women (and men) also have greater personal choices than ever before. Chapter 5 said that *availability* means that every adult always retains the choice to select prospects and/or partners regardless of any relationship (including formal marriage) he or she may currently have. Today, not many persons need

to be locked forever within the "quiet desperation" of the pre-sixties era. Nevertheless, to be available does not imply that one is *interested*. Neither Helga nor Kurt (Chapter 5) is interested in anyone else even though each retains that option. And after Karyn ends her relationship with Kurt she wants nothing to do with any man for a long time. Having a good job gives Karyn that choice.

Having that much control over their economic and personal lives is something new for women. It's a feature of postmodern societies. The difficulty comes in translating their newfound control into their relationships with men. Since ancient times, men have had far more economic and political resources, and thus greater control over their own lives, than women. One result has been that men have thought of themselves as pursuers, or hunters, and women as their prize, or prey. It was quite common for men such as Amnon to get the sexual pleasures they wanted from women without giving women what they wanted. Taking something from someone without giving that person what he or she wants in exchange was how Waller defined *exploitation*.[10]

It seems evident that men have sexually exploited women since time began. The rules of the Dating Game, as well as the rules of the Victorian courting era that preceded it, were designed to try to protect women from exploitation.[11] What women needed and wanted was marriage; an honorable gentleman was supposed to promise it to his lady in exchange for sex. At the least (as in today's Japan) he should provide for the needs of his mistress and any children ("bastards") he might sire. Prostitutes have always been exceptions to the rules. And today's women now lack the protection of the rules as well. Many of today's women thus seem more vulnerable than before to sexual exploitation. The ancient exchange between sex and marriage has evaporated. Apart from religious conservatives, few people in modern societies view sex as something reserved for marriage. The rub is that many men still see themselves as hunters and women as their rightful prey.[12] Another way to describe this is to say that some men hold "macho attitudes" toward women. Kanin used the term "sexually predatory."[13] One result of how some men perceive women is acquaintance rape.

DEFINING RAPE AND SEXUAL ASSAULT

Although rape laws vary across the fifty states, Bechhofer and Parrot have identified three conditions that are fundamental to a legal definition of rape. These three conditions provide the narrowest possible definition of rape. First, penile penetration of the vagina must occur, "be it ever so slight."[14] Second, that penetration must be against the woman's will and without her consent. Third, there must be coercion, whether actual or threatened. A few states have dropped the narrower term *rape* and replaced it with a more general label, *sexual assault*. In these states sexual assault occurs when the man's penis penetrates the woman's vagina, anus, or mouth. Furthermore, since any unwanted penetration is a punishable crime, this definition includes men committing sexual assaults against other men both anally and orally. Most states, however, retain the narrower definition of rape. They prefer to place other kinds of nonconsensual sex under the *sodomy* and *sexual abuse* categories of crimes.

Sexual Assault among Acquaintances

The matter of acquaintance rape has become a public controversy both legally and socially. Citizen reaction to the Tyson and Kennedy trials shows that many people hold widely varying ideas and feelings about what rape is and

is not. Feminists and other researchers carry on very active rape research programs. In addition, they vigorously advocate for changes in rape laws and in public attitudes towards it. Their objective is to broaden the definition of rape. The advocates wanted citizens and the courts to label certain behaviors as rape that in the past were not viewed as rape. And the advocates want those behaviors severely punished. The idea of a broad-based citizen movement against rape began in earnest with the publication of Susan Browmiller's book, *Against Our Will*. Bechhofer and Parrot consider themselves part of that movement. To help us understand what acquaintance rape is, they compare and contrast it with three other kinds of situations.

Stranger Rape   What do most people think of when they hear the word *rape*? A woman is walking along minding her own business. Suddenly a knife-wielding man she's never seen before jumps her and drags her into an alley while she tries to fight back. The stranger batters and bruises her into submission and then rapes her. Stunned and bewildered, she wanders to a hospital emergency room; she's treated for her wounds; the police are called; and a search is begun for her unknown assailant.

Ronald Holmes divides stranger rape into two categories: attempted rapes and completed rapes. An attempted rape occurs typically during daylight hours on a street or playground or in a parking lot or garage.[15] In an actual example, a 29-year-old man accosted a 65-year-old woman at 1:45 p.m. in a city's busy downtown area. He began to pull up her dress and wrestle her to the ground.[16] Astonished onlookers rushed to the woman's assistance, chasing the man for several blocks before they trapped him in the lobby of the public library. A completed rape usually occurs in the victim's home from 6:00 p.m. to midnight. According to Holmes, fewer than 10 percent of all stranger rapes of either type are ever reported to police. In spite of the underreporting, Bechhofer and Parrot say that the vast majority of rapes are not done by strangers, but rather by men previously known to the women.

Anonymous Sex   Although the 1963 movie, *Love with the Proper Stranger,* doesn't convey exactly what Bechhofer and Parrot mean by "consensual sex with a stranger," it points in that general direction. The 1986 film describing the pre-AIDS singles' scene, *About Last Night . . . ,* is more on target. For Bechhofer and Parrot the term *anonymous sex* means that sometimes a man and a woman (or two same-sex persons) who are total strangers meet and their erotic antennae tell them both, "Let's do It." The woman in particular defines this as something she wants and agrees to. Incidentally, the William Kennedy Smith trial was about two strangers meeting for the first time. Smith maintained that he had the woman's consent; she denied it. Before the AIDS epidemic, consensual sex with a stranger was a much more common occurrence among gay males than among either heterosexuals or lesbians.[17]

Lovemaking   Consensual sex between acquaintances is what Bechhofer and Parrot call their third situation. For them, "acquaintance" means any man who is not a stranger. If he was *not* previously unknown to the woman, he is by definition an acquaintance. Being an acquaintance does not imply that the couple know each other on merely a casual basis. The man could be a neighbor, co-worker, friend, husband, cohabitor, sibling, cousin, or whatever. The woman may have known him for a few days, weeks, months, or years. How long she knew him doesn't matter at all. What does matter are two things: (1) She does not define him as a "stranger," as a person previously unknown to her. (2) She sleeps with him because

she wants to. She perceives herself as willingly consenting to sexual intercourse with someone she knows.

How Widespread Is Acquaintance Rape?

The *National Crime Survey* (NCS) carried out annually by the U.S. Justice Department reports that in 1982 some 52 percent of "completed rapes . . . were perpetrated by someone who was known to the victim." But Christine Gidycz and Mary Koss believe that the NCS figures are much too low.[18] Their own national studies lead them to the conclusion that the majority of women who are assaulted by an acquaintance tend *not* to define their experience as rape, even though someone they knew coerced them into sex against their will. If a woman doesn't perceive her own experience as rape, she won't report it as such to the NCS interviewer. If all women who were actually coerced into unwanted sex could somehow be included in the NCS survey, the total percentage of completed rapes would be much higher than slightly over one-half.

The Issue of the Woman's Consent

In contrast to stranger rape, acquaintance rape means two things: first, the woman knows who the man is, she does not define him as a stranger, and second, she does not *willingly consent* to intercourse. Bechhofer and Parrot readily acknowledge that in real life distinctions among anonymous sex, lovemaking, and acquaintance rape are often blurred. Nonetheless, the central issue remains—*the woman's own perception of her consent.* Does she define herself as having coitus willingly or unwillingly? If it is unwilling, it violates her freedom of choice, and thus it is rape.

Chapters 2, 3, and 5 show that being in family or being in an erotic friendship rests ultimately on the person's own definitions of what's going on. His or her special relationship does not rely chiefly on something outward, or objective, such as a blood tie, or a marriage license. In similar fashion, whether a woman is giving her sexual consent is a matter of her own perception of what's going on. It does not depend on something outward, or physically "real"—something that can be seen and judged by outsiders.

Date Rape   "Date rape" is merely one form of acquaintance rape. Date rape means that the rape occurred between persons who had known each other and were "out together." But we just learned that acquaintance rape is a much broader term that includes many other situations besides being out together at a party or bar.

Marital Rape   Until recently, the social and legal definitions of rape in fact rested on outward or physically real things. For example, one physical thing defining rape was the marriage license itself. A husband could never be accused of raping his wife. Indeed, say David Finkelhor and Kersti Yllo, a married man had a "license to rape."[19] The license in and of itself transformed something that was previously wrong into something that after the wedding suddenly became right. Carol Bohmer reports that the "marriage exemption" made it legal for a man to demand sexual "services" from his wife anytime he pleased. His demands were justified on the basis of his economic support.[20] As a result of major efforts by feminists and other reformers, most states have now removed the marital exemption. As a result, a wife in one of those states who feels she is not giving sexual consent can charge her husband with rape.

On the other hand, not only have some states retained the marriage exemption, they have even broadened it: They now apply the same exemption to cohabiting couples.[21] In those states neither wives nor cohabiting women can charge their partners with rape.

Marrying and/or moving in with a man is thought to be consent enough. Those outward facts give the man permission to demand and receive sex quite apart from the woman's consent.

When it comes to sentencing husbands convicted of wife rape, at least one state applies lesser penalties to them than it does to men convicted of raping "nonwives."[22] The 1993 North Carolina legislature agreed to allow up to fifteen years in prison for husbands convicted of raping wives. By contrast, men raping "other" women could get up to life in prison. Chapter 5 described Helga as a victim of marital rape because, in her view, her husband was sexually forcing himself on her. Helga and Hans are an example of what Finkelhor and Yllo describe as *force-only* marital rape.[23] In those situations the husband uses only a minimal amount of coercion—no more than necessary—to get his wife to submit sexually. The coercion may include physical force such as pushing or shoving, but not necessarily so. These authors report that many husbands force their wives into having sex via constant verbal badgerings.

Finkelhor and Yllo contrast those situations with what they call *battering* rape. Here the husband beats his wife to a far greater degree than would be necessary simply to get her to submit sexually. The husband rapes her at the same time that he hits, punches, slaps, and in other ways hurts her. Perhaps the best-known example of battering rape is the John and Lorena Bobbitt case. She alleged that because her husband regularly beat her into having sex, she became "temporarily insane" and cut off his penis while he slept. A jury believed her and acquitted her of all criminal charges.[24] Finally, Finkelhor and Yllo identify a third type of marital rape as *obsessive* rape. In this situation the husband adds "strange and perverse" activities to his rape and violence.[25] Those activities include painful bondage and torture, such as burning the woman's breasts, but-

Lorena Bobbitt leaves the courthouse in Manassas, Virginia, after testifying in the 1994 marital sexual assault trial against her husband, John Wayne Bobbitt. Lorena testified that she cut off her husband's penis with a knife after he sexually assaulted her.

tocks, and genitals with cigarettes. He may also use foreign objects such as sticks or bottles to penetrate the woman sexually.

Consent and the Woman's Reputation and Demeanor Besides the marriage license and/or co-residence, a second set of outward, or physically real, things that some people look for to judge whether a rape has been committed is the woman's reputation and demeanor. If the woman's behaviors are judged to be "sexually provocative," then she "got what she deserved," and rape cannot be proven.[26] In the 1991 film, *Thelma & Louise*, Louise was at a bar drinking heavily and dancing uninhibitively with a stranger that a waitress had warned her was of questionable re-

pute. The pair then went outside where he roughed up Louise and attempted to rape her against her obvious resistance. After Thelma discovered them and shot the man to death, Louise wanted to go to the police. But Thelma refused saying, "A hundred people saw you dancing 'that way' with him. Are they going to believe us? Wake up to the real world." Thelma was convinced that witnesses would testify that Louise had been "provocative"— that she had "asked for it." So how could you blame the man? Louise had "led him on."

Bohmer reports that very often, "provocative" behaviors or dress on the part of the woman are taken as proof, or as valid indicators, of her consent, no matter how strongly she protests to the man. A 1989 Florida case drew national attention when a man charged with rape was acquitted because the woman was wearing a tank top, a white lace miniskirt, and no underwear. The jury foreman stated, "We all feel she asked for it for the way she was dressed; her clothing was too enticing."[27] The prevailing idea in North American culture has been that ordinary citizens can intuitively figure out whether it was rape because of something *outward,* no matter what the woman says. Outward evidence includes a woman's provocative clothing or lack of clothing and/or her overall demeanor. If she didn't behave like a "lady" (or if she was a wife or cohabitor), then there was no way to prove rape.

Additional outward circumstances making it very difficult for a woman to prove rape include her reputation. Someone known to be a "loose woman" is fair game for assault, say Bechhofer and Parrot. So is a woman who is either asleep or drunk.[28] In one incident a woman and her boyfriend had been drinking together with his male friend. She fell asleep, but then woke up with the male friend cutting her face with a knife and trying to rape her.[29]

Consent—Saying *Yes* and Not Saying *No*
Bechhofer and Parrot state that the cultural assumption—held over from the Dating Game, has been that unless a woman explicitly says no, then she's saying yes. The consent issue enters what Bechhofer and Parrot call the "gray zone" if the couple have in fact been "making out."[30] At some point she may say enough, but he may feel she has tacitly given her consent to intercourse by participating in passionate foreplay. He thinks she has no right to tease him by stopping short of intercourse, and that she is now obliged to complete the act. Nevertheless, Bechhofer and Parrot say that legally and morally, consent requires that she (or he) must first, say yes, and second, not say no. Making out cannot by itself be taken as evidence for consent if the woman does not define it that way.

Bechhofer and Parrot add yet another crucial point about consent. They believe that Tuesday's consent can never be assumed because of Sunday's agreement. Because a woman sleeps with man today does not mean she's obliged to do so again the next day, next week, or whenever. That point is particularly relevant for couples in an ongoing erotic friendship. The woman (man) is free at any time to say no regardless of how often she (he) has said yes in the past. On a recent (April 29, 1992) national TV news special called *The New Rules of Love,* ABC devoted twenty minutes to the subject of a woman's sexual consent. In one of the scenes a group of college men were asserting their conviction that a woman's *no* actually means *keep on trying.* Furthermore, the men rejected the idea that a woman who sleeps with a man regularly has the right to say no whenever she wishes. One male quipped that on a "couple's golden wedding anniversary the man surely has a right to a 'piece.' "

Rape Myths

According to Martha Burt, a *rape myth* is something many people use to distinguish a real rape from a nonrape.[31] A *real* rape is limited to the stranger category described previously. Anything else cannot be rape. Burt says there are at least four types of cultural stereotypes, or rape myths, in North America. All of the myths apply to acquaintances. And they all boil down to this: If the woman knew the man, and if he didn't slap, punch, or hit her, or use a weapon—and thus by physical pain force her to comply—then it can't be rape. In addition, all four myths ignore the idea of consent and its legal and moral definition: She does say yes *and* she doesn't say no.

One myth is that nothing actually happened. In this stereotype women are said to accuse men of sexual assault even though it isn't true. The woman wants to get revenge on the man because, as the belief goes, he's no longer interested in her and wants to end their relationship. Or she makes up the accusations simply to convince herself she's sexually desirable. A second myth is that no harm was done. That was the gist of Absalom's remark to his sister Tamar—"no big deal." In this stereotype, unless a woman was a virgin or married to somebody else, what difference does it make? Burt adds that a corollary of the no harm myth is that only bad girls get raped. Since they're defined as loose women anyhow, what difference can it possibly make if some guy "has fun" with her? A third myth is that she wanted it. Underlying this stereotype is the idea that even when a woman says no she in fact means yes. Saying no is merely her way of being coy and playing hard to get. In the words of a 1950s' popular song, "Your lips tell me no-no, but there's yes-yes in your eyes." Burt says this myth applies particularly to a woman who's been doing consensual necking or petting with a man. If somehow she doesn't want It, she should walk away even if he gets violent. Burt adds that a dark corollary of this third myth is the belief that some women get turned on by being beaten up and raped. A final myth is that she deserved It. Examples of this would be Louise (in *Thelma and Louise*), and also the Florida woman with the white lace miniskirt *sans* underwear.

Negotiation and Rape

Since consensual lovemaking requires that she say yes *and* not say no, how does a woman let a man know what she wants and doesn't want? Must she be verbal about her wishes? Is it possible to communicate her wishes nonverbally? Throughout North American society, persons tend not to be straightforward and explicit about sex. Most people rely chiefly on subtle, nonverbal cues and clues—the erotic antennae described in Chapter 5. By contrast, Bohmer reminds us that in some cultures persons are quite direct about sexual invitations,

and do not hesitate at all to be explicit.[32] She tells of a male friend attending a party in Iceland approached by a woman speaking Icelandic, which he did not understand. On translation, he learned that she'd asked, "Do you want to screw?" Being that forthright about sex, although very much a part of Icelandic society, is virtually unknown in North America.

Two Views of Sexuality To a large degree, the matter of being verbally explicit about sex is connected to the two views of sexuality described in Chapter 4. The traditional view is that abstinence till marriage is morally superior. Since nonmarital sex is defined ahead of time as bad, illicit, and less than virtuous, nonmarried persons holding that view are understandably hesitant to openly discuss sex, contraception, and sexually transmitted diseases with a potential sexual partner. Furthermore, even persons who don't hold the traditional view are often uncomfortable about telling a potential sexual partner how they feel. They fear that the person will somehow view them as bad or immoral.

But Chapter 4 said that a second view of sexuality is called responsible indulgence. In this view, as the influential and widely respected columnist Ellen Goodman puts it, sex is defined as good *in and of itself* regardless of marital status. Although its pleasures are fully acknowledged, its inherent responsibilities are emphasized just as strongly.[33] One of its chief responsibilities is that a person must never coerce his or her partner into having sex. It follows that avoiding coercion applies as much to married as to nonmarried persons—responsibility overrides the license. Furthermore, being responsible and avoiding coercion generally means being verbally explicit—it means talking about what one does and does not want.

Verbal Coercion But merely talking about whether or not to have coitus does not guarantee that sexual coercion is avoided. We just

women should have access to any kind of training or education they want, from brain surgeon to bricklayer to bouncer. They also believe that women should have the same access as men to being hired, to wage increases, and to promotion. In addition, persons toward the left side of Figure 12-1 believe that men should participate fully with women in the routine chores of maintaining a household. And if the couple chooses parenting, men should participate fully in its burdens and joys. Advocates of gender equality believe that the more fully men participate in home work, the more fully women are able to participate in paid work.

Since the 1960s there have been steady increases in the numbers of citizens who (regardless of their actual beliefs) will *say* they believe in gender equality.[41] For example, if we compare 1960 with 1990 we find that during 1990 more persons were toward the middle and left of Figure 12-1 than were located there during 1960. Similarly, fewer persons were on the right side of Figure 12-1 than were located there during 1960. There has been a gradual but steady movement of citizens from right to center to left along the continuum of Figure 12-1. Regardless of their actual beliefs, fewer citizens today than ever before will admit that they believe in traditional behaviors for women and men.

Nevertheless, citizens located toward the right side of the figure do believe in traditional gender behaviors. They prefer that men specialize in paid work and women specialize in domestic work. In particular, they believe the woman should be the children's chief nurturer and caretaker. They hold that there are significant differences between the genders—biological, psychological, spiritual, and physical. Gender differences make it impractical and unworkable for women and men to be interchangeable. They don't agree that men can fit into the demands of parenting and do it as well as women. They are also doubtful that women can fit into the demands of certain kinds of

paid work and do it as well as men. Earlier chapters showed that one of the most controversial examples of this belief in gender specialization is the belief that women can't do combat as effectively as men. During World War II, some 2,000 women officers flew the identical fighter and bomber planes that men flew, but only in the United States. The women ferried the planes from factories to bases, where men then flew them overseas. The belief was that women were simply not interchangeable with men when it came to the rigors and dangers of actual combat.

It should come as no surprise that for decades almost every study of preferences about gender equality reveals that women believe more strongly in equality than do men.[42] Men tend to be more gender-role traditional than women. And recent research reveals that the more traditional a man is, the more likely he is to believe that acquaintance rape is permissible. For example, 35 percent of college men admitted they would be likely to rape a woman if they believed they would not be caught.[43] Robin Warshaw and Andrea Parrot report that men who feel that way tend to do so because of gender.

Some women too believe in highly specialized roles for men and women, based on cultural norms learned as children and reinforced as adults. And many women are in the middle of the continuum shown in Figure 12-1: They mix elements of traditionalism with elements of freedom, choice, and control.

Accepting the Old Script   The fact that women vary among themselves regarding how gender traditional they are is connected specifically with acquaintance rape. First, for example, Warshaw and Parrot report that the more gender traditional a woman, the more likely she is to accept the "stereotypic sexual script."[44] Chapter 7 called that script the rules of the old Dating Game. The whole point of the Game was that men should get as much as they can from women. Warshaw and Parrot add that this idea is built into the "macho sex role." Being macho also means that the man should ignore what the woman says—when she says no she's merely playing the Game. Everyone senses that she's supposed to say no even though she wants It as much as he does. His goal as a "real man" is to overcome her token resistance and give her what they both want.

The more gender-role traditional a man is, the more likely he is to accept the macho sex role.[45] Several researchers such as Thomas Beneke argue that "rape is a man's problem . . . men solve it."[46] He and other rape awareness advocates assert that if men regularly met in support groups for consciousness raising, they would eventually learn to accept the idea that it's *not* unmanly for a man to accept a woman's no as final. Very likely, the more strongly a man prefers gender equality, the easier it is for him to accept fresh views regarding a woman's protests and sexual intentions.

Abstinence versus Responsible Indulgence Second, say Warshaw and Parrot, the more gender traditional a woman, the more torn she is between abstinence and responsible indulgence.[47] Because she's not sure that sex is a good thing (nice girls can't do sex), she's nervous about talking openly, freely, and honestly about it. And because she's anxious about the morality of sex, she's also hesitant to negotiate explicitly with the man in a situation that has the potential for intercourse.

The Stroking Norm Third, the more gender traditional a woman, the more likely she is to accept the "stroking norm."[48] That's the old idea that women are supposed to put the needs of others, including men, ahead of their own. Chapter 7 said that in North American culture women are expected to nurture men and to take care of their emotional needs, but men are not equally responsible for women's emotional needs. Consequently, if the man

persists in wanting sex, a woman who believes in stroking is more likely, even if reluctantly, to acquiesce, because "after all, he'll feel better if I give in."

Controlling the Sexually Charged Situation
Thus far we've learned that men who are more gender-role traditional are more likely to think it's no big deal to coerce (verbally and/or physically) a woman into having sex. In addition, women who are more gender-role traditional tend to be caught between the old Game and the new. Not being sure which Game is right, they're more vulnerable to sexual exploitation. They seem less willing and/or able to negotiate for control over sexually charged situations. Researchers report that the sexually charged situation or setting is a critical element in understanding acquaintance rape. Jacquelyn White and John Humphrey say that the situation is built around, first, a location—a party, a car, or a dwelling with no one else around, and second, a situation that includes heavy use of alcohol and/or drugs.[49] Finally, the situation may include previous intimacies (heavy petting, coitus), amount of money spent by the man, the woman's type of dress, the man's and woman's reputations, and so on.

Clarise, for instance, dresses for a party (where alcohol is freely flowing) in a way that makes her extraordinarily sexually attractive. She defines the way she looks as a status symbol, not as a signal that she wants sex. She simply wants to have fun and enjoy herself. But some men at the party define her way of dressing as a signal of her sexual interest. According to White and Humphrey, Clarise finds herself in a sexually *charged* situation. A number of studies suggest that women who are less gender-role traditional tend to be more aware of and alert to the realities of that kind of situation.[50] Clarise adheres strongly to gender equality. She is determined to try to control the sexually charged situation. There is no guarantee she will be successful. It is quite possible

Women karate students pair off in an adult extension self-defense class at a Brockton, Massachusetts, community college.

that a man, because of his superior physical strength, will overwhelm her and force her into unwanted sex. Nevertheless, Clarise is wending her way through the minefields of a very different game than the one described in Chapter 7. By contrast, women who are more gender-role traditional appear less willing to face the intricacies of the contemporary sexually charged situation. They tend to be more sentimental about men and more trusting of them than someone like Clarise.

Controlling the War between the Genders
According to Warshaw and Parrot, a large part of facing reality is recognizing that women and men have been locked in the battle of the genders since time first began. Women are *less* gender-role traditional are *more* likely to accept that bottom-line reality. Instead of being senti-

mental abut the old Dating Game and its leftovers, those women readily acknowledge that the Game was but one example of that ancient battle. Women who prefer gender equality are also keenly aware of the ambiguities of today's fluid sexual scene. The old rules of battle are flaking away, and there are few new rules regarding what constitutes a fair fight between the genders.

Furthermore, women who are less gender-role traditional agree with Warshaw and Parrot that "in any battle, the outcome usually depends on which side has better fighting skills.[51] Chapter 11 showed that "fighting skills" means, among several other things, the capability to negotiate effectively—to exercise control. Recall that while negotiating on previous occasions with her friend Horace, Clarise was able to achieve a win-win situation. Because each party got something of what they wanted, they each shared some degree of control. Clarise, however, is quite prepared to impose a *win-lose* situation on Russ, an acquaintance she runs into at the party, if that's what it takes for her to have control over her own body. When he gets too pushy and ignores her explicit no, Clarise warns him off using spicy profanity. When he continues to badger her, she threatens to scream, kick, run, or make a scene. According to Pauline Bart and P. H. O'Brien, those particular strategies are highly effective in thwarting acquaintance rape.[52] Russ finally backs off—Clarise has won, Russ has lost.

SEXUAL HARASSMENT

For several days during October 1991, millions of Americans sat glued to their TV sets watching the Senate confirmation hearings of Clarence Thomas for the U.S. Supreme Court. What transfixed everyone was the testimony of Anita Hill. She charged that when she worked for Thomas some years earlier, he had *sexually harassed* her. Her testimony brought the issue of harassment onto the center stage of American consciousness. Before that media event, many Americans, men especially, had only a vague idea of what sexual harassment is all about. Hill described Thomas as "a boss who pestered her for dates and spoke graphically about pornography, bestiality, rape and his skills as a lover."[53] Hill further alleged that Thomas "talked about pornographic materials depicting individuals with large penises or large breasts involved in various sex acts."

In commenting on the Hill/Thomas incident, A. Press and colleagues observe that harassment "may be as subtle as a leer and a series of off-color jokes, or as direct as grabbing a woman's breast. It can be found in typing pools and factories, Army barracks and legislative suites, city rooms and college lecture halls. It is

Oklahoma law professor Anita Hill testifies in 1991 before the Senate Judiciary Committee. Hill claimed she was sexually harassed by then Supreme Court nominee Clarence Thomas when he was her boss at the Equal Employment Opportunity Commission in the early 1980s. Thomas denied the charges.

. . . an exercise of power almost analogous to rape, for which women pay with their jobs. . . . Sexual harassment, the boss's dirty little fringe benefit, has been dragged out of the closet."[54]

Although those kinds of behaviors have been around probably as long as acquaintance rape, the label "sexual harassment" wasn't coined until 1975.[55] As soon as it appeared, the popular women's magazine, *Redbook,* did a 1976 survey of 9,000 readers to find out how many of them had ever experienced harassment. Eighty-eight percent of the women reported they had indeed experienced it; 92 percent believed it was a serious problem on the job.[56] Rosemarie Tong asserts that sexual harassment has several components[57]: (1) It usually occurs in a formal setting, such as the workplace, school, religious meeting place, and so on. (2) Within this formal setting, a person or persons (usually but not always men) say or do things in a woman's presence that she perceives as having sexual overtones. (3) Because she defines the man's words and actions as annoying, unwelcome, and an imposition, she rejects his overtures, his unwanted behaviors.

Harassment from Superiors

The consequences of rejecting the man's unwanted overtures are significantly affected by the differing amount of authority that he has compared with what she has. If he is her superior, for example, her boss (as Clarence Thomas was to Anita Hill) or her teacher, then he's in a position to reward or penalize her in a number of ways. In situations where the man has an authority position over the woman, harassment includes the woman's perception that she'll be penalized if she rejects the unwanted behaviors but rewarded if she goes along with them. In the case of a woman employee, she perceives she'll be promoted or get a higher salary if she goes along with the harassment. If she doesn't put up with it she might get neither promotion nor money, and she might even lose her job. If she's a student, the rewards for going along might be better grades or financial assistance of some sort.

When Hill was asked why she didn't report Thomas at the time of the alleged harassment, she responded that she was afraid that she might lose her job and her entire career would be put in jeopardy. Before the Hill/Thomas case, women employees who felt they were being harassed were seldom encouraged to initiate grievance procedures or complain to management or personnel directors.[58] If a woman did complain, she'd likely be perceived as a troublemaker and eventually be fired. And troublemakers have a tough time finding another job. Since the Hill/Thomas confrontation, however, *The Wall Street Journal* reports that American business has begun to shift in the direction of taking women's harassment complaints more seriously.[59] Many businesses now encourage women to come forward with those kinds of complaints. And even before Hill/Thomas, *Business Week* asserted that companies were getting the message that they must seek to end sexual harassment.[60]

The Wall Street Journal adds that a major reason businesses, as well as schools and universities, are scrambling to respond to women's complaints is recent court decisions awarding money to harassed women. "The Supreme Court ruled that students who claim they were sexually harassed and sue schools or school officials under federal law may seek money damages in addition to other damages."[61] Before that ruling, businesses and schools were not required to pay money damages to women proving harassment. In the particular case on which the Supreme Court ruled, a high-school student claimed that a teacher "made unwelcome verbal advances [and] forcibly kissed her on the mouth." Months later his unwanted behaviors drifted beyond harassment into actual acquaintance rape: "On three occasions [he] pressured her into having sexual intercourse in a private office."

Harassment versus Acquaintance Rape
Legally, acquaintance rape differs from harassment because during harassment there is no

actual rape, as defined previously. The harasser may, however, desire intercourse with the woman, and his harassing behaviors may be the prelude for coercing her into having nonconsensual sex. Under current U.S. law, a woman does not have to suffer actual assault to prove harassment and collect money damages. Interestingly enough, the same principle holds in Japan, a culture that is considered much more gender traditional than the United States. A 34-year-old woman claimed that although her boss never touched her, he had sexually harassed her in a verbal manner.[62] He had also spread unfounded rumors that she was a sexually promiscuous woman. She was forced to quit her job. The Japanese courts ruled that he had sexually harassed her and ordered the man's company to pay her monetary damages.

By no means, however, is it a simple matter for a woman to prove harassment in a court of law even if a man touches her but no actual sexual assault takes place: "Touching a woman's breast without permission isn't a crime in Arkansas if no force or threats are used," ruled a local judge in dismissing a suit by a 16-year-old girl against her teacher.[63] She claimed that he'd invited her into his office to counsel her, and then began to ask questions about her sex life. Next, she says, he "touched her left breast, then moved his hand down toward her belt." At that point she got scared and left his office. The teacher denied her charges, but the school board suspended him with pay until they decided what to do next.

Harassment by Women Although it is rare, the courts have occasionally ruled in favor of a man, charging that his female supervisor sexually harassed him. In a 1993 decision, a California jury awarded more than $1 million in damages to a man who claimed that his boss had sexually harassed him daily for six years.[64] He said that she would enter his office and close the door, then embrace and kiss him.

Sometimes, he added, she would "fondle my genitals."

Harassment from Peers

Thus far we've been looking at sexual harassment from superiors. Superiors can give rewards to women (or male) employees or students in exchange for going along with their harassment. And they can punish subordinates for not cooperating. We've also drawn a distinction between harassment and acquaintance rape. Not all men who harass women wish to have sexual intercourse with them. In the man's own perception, he believes that by his comments and behaviors he's "just having a little fun" with the woman. Because he doesn't intend to coerce her into sex, he doesn't see anything wrong with what he's doing. He doesn't perceive himself as intruding on the woman's privacy, eroding her dignity, or limiting her freedom.

Besides superiors, women are also subject to considerable sexual harassment from peers—men who have no formal authority over them, having neither rewards to give nor penalties to mete out.[65] Since the women are with these male peers in an employment or school setting, it's difficult for the women to escape the harassment.

The Tailhook Scandal In a much publicized example of peer harassment, the U.S. Navy investigated complaints by women officers and civilians who in 1991 had attended a convention of naval aviators in Las Vegas (the Tailhook Scandal). The women said that when they attempted to return to their hotel rooms, the male officers forced them to "run the gauntlet." The men blocked their way and not only made sexually degrading and insulting remarks about them, but also attempted to pull down their underwear. The men "groped and grabbed parts of their anatomy including breasts and buttocks." Moreover, this kind of harassment had been an annual event at those conventions for six years, and higher-ups knew about it.[66]

The Navy Brass who investigated admitted that all the charges were true, but at first refused to discipline the men involved. Instead the Brass said that in the future they would " 'teach our people . . . the difference between acceptable and unacceptable behavior.' " The subsequent media outcry became so great, however, that Congress compelled the Pentagon to discipline the male officers involved in the harassment. Navy Secretary Lawrence Garrett was forced to resign in 1992 because of his failure to take the women's charges seriously in the first place, and to investigate them thoroughly. By 1993, the Pentagon reported that some 175 officers would face serious "disciplinary action" as a result of their involvement in *Tailhook*.[67] In reality, not a single one of those officers was ever court martialed. Moreover, the admiral in charge of all naval operations was accused of undermining the entire *Tailhook* investigation; his only "reprimand" was an agreement to take early retirement.[68]

In a separate 1992 example of peer harassment, some girls in a Florida middle school complained about the boys' graphic sexual remarks aimed at them.[69] They also complained to the principal about the boys' touching, patting, slapping, and grabbing them on their buttocks and breasts. Even though the remarks and grabbing occurred in school corridors as well as in class, the girls claimed that teachers ignored the boys' behaviors. When asked about it, the principal said, " 'There's a lot of what I call love taps. Its childish behavior, where they're showing their affection in some ways toward each other.' " The guidance counselor commented that although "consensual sex play among adolescents does occur, that is not the same as unwanted touching. If the girls tell me they feel uncomfortable and didn't want it to happen, I respect that. Un-

wanted touching can constitute criminal sexual abuse." One 14-year-old girl said that the boys "slap girls on the butt because they think it's funny and because they think that's how they're supposed to act. But now I won't take it from them. I told a boy who slapped me on the butt that if you ever do that again, I'm going to the guidance counselor and have you kicked out of school. They leave me alone now that they know I won't take it . . . I have my life . . . and I won't let anything get in the way." This same girl added that many other girls "don't know what to do. So they act like it's not really happening." She also added that most girls don't report harassment because they'll be marked as troublemakers: "Oh, you're the girl who got that boy in trouble."

These girls' experiences are borne out by a 1993 national study of 1,632 students in grades 8 through 11 conducted by pollster Lou Harris that was commissioned by the American Association of University Women (AAUW).[70] The AAUW study describes "school hallways as a gauntlet of sexual taunts." Among other things, the researchers report more than 75 percent of girls and 56 percent of boys say they have been the "target of unwanted sexual comments, jokes, gestures or looks, while two-thirds of girls and 42 percent of boys have been touched, grabbed or pinched." These and comparable findings lead AAUW officials to conclude that the climate of sexual harassment that pervades today's public schools undermines the learning process, especially for girls. For example, 70 percent of the girls said they were "very" or "somewhat upset" by the harassment, compared with only 24 percent of the boys.

Whether at work or school, many girls and women find themselves with male peers who sexually harass them by words and sometimes by actions. And since girls and women must share those social situations and physical spaces with those boys and men, they find themselves constrained. Women's freedoms are thus limited in ways that men's freedoms are not. Sexual harassment from peers places women in situations that are oppressive and painful, yet difficult to escape.

Explaining Harassment

Whether by superiors or peers, why is sexual harassment as widespread as many women and some men believe it to be? Nancy DiTomaso argues that harassment is an expression of gender discrimination. Simply by being in the workplace women become competitors with men for scarce economic rewards as well as for prestige. Attending the same schools also makes women competitors with men for grades, prestige, and sometimes financial aid. DiTomaso notes that harassment stems from the "fears that men have about losing their privileged place in the labor force."[71] She adds that when women are competing with male peers for the same jobs, those peers tend to be more hostile than are the men who are the women's superiors. To give vent to their hostility and resentment toward their women competitors, many men behave in a sexually harassing manner. DiTomaso observes that most men themselves do not view their harassment as an expression of hostility. They view it just like the middle-school boys or male naval officers—"we're merely enjoying a bit of innocent fun."

DiTomaso concludes that whatever the complex explanations for male harassment, it is very real. And its reality has a profoundly negative effect on women's "access to good jobs, good training, and sufficient rewards." For example, the middle-school girl cited above sensed that the boys' harassment was getting in the way of what she wanted to do with her life, and she simply wouldn't tolerate it. And the AAUW study agreed that sexual harassment is detrimental to girls' school performance and thus to their chances for future success in college and/or the work force.

Harassment expresses gender discrimination because it's a problem that men face much less frequently than women. Every person (regardless of gender) confronts the stiff demands that are built into being a good student or a good employee in today's highly competitive world economy. However, women must in addition face the painful demands inherent in coping with harassment. Their options are to fight it head on or try to act as if nothing's happening. In either case the energies required to cope with something men rarely face means that women have fewer energies left over to compete in the marketplace. Disbursing energies in this fashion may be one reason that men continue to enjoy the labor market advantages over women discussed more fully in Chapter 15.

PHYSICAL FORCE

So far this chapter has considered constraints on women's choices in two realms—rape and sexual harassment. A third way of intruding on women's personhood and limiting their choices is use of physical force. As is the case with rape and harassment, it's difficult for researchers to know for sure whether there is more or less physical force against women today than there was years ago. Douglas Besharov concludes that its growing.[72] He asserts that, "Each year hundreds of thousands of wives are abused by their husbands."

Social researchers didn't pay much attention to violence within families until the late 1960s and early 1970s. Murray Straus was among the first to study it in a comprehensive manner.[73] He said that although counselors had long been aware of wife beating, researchers had neglected it for several reasons. One reason was that everyone wanted to believe that the Modern (pre-sixties) Family was a place of sweetness and light, grace and harmony. It was socially defined as a *nonviolent* place. Since "everyone knows" that The Family is nonviolent, peaceful, and tranquil, researchers didn't bother to investigate whether what everyone knows was actually true or not.

Second, adds Straus, because most persons defined The Family as a nonviolent place, no one labeled acts of physical force in families as real violence. The 1960s had been marked by many incidents of horrific and unspeakable violence, including the assassinations of John Kennedy, Martin Luther King, Jr., and Robert Kennedy. In addition, for several years there had been numerous riots and unruly civil disturbances in cities and on college campuses throughout the nation. People could watch those happenings on TV and plainly see they were *real* violence. They also watched the first TV war—Vietnam—and daily saw acts of brutality on both sides.

But just as some people have difficulty imagining acquaintance rape as *real* rape, or grasping that sexual harassment is bitterly painful, many people—during the sixties and still today—have difficulty thinking of physical force in families as *real* violence. Straus says that many citizens impose a "perceptual blackout" on physical force in families, that is, whenever physical force is used, the persons who use the force and those on the receiving end don't generally define it as real violence. This tendency holds whether the force is used by husbands against wives or by wives on husbands, by parents on children or by siblings against one another (Chapter 17). Rather, most people believe that real violence is what they see on TV news, not what happens at home, and surely not within their own four walls.

The Social Acceptability of Physical Force

In short, the use of physical force, like most things we've talked about in this book, is socially defined. Like a blood tie, or a marriage license, or sexual intercourse, the thing is not "real" in and of itself. The thing becomes meaningful and thus real based on how we perceive it—how we define it. Acquaintance rape, sexual harassment, and physical force have a great deal in common. One of the major elements they share is the variable of *social legitimacy*. That simply means the degree to which people conceive of those three kinds of behaviors as socially acceptable or not. In the past, most people tended to think of all three as relatively acceptable social behaviors. To be sure, the behaviors were seen as unfortunate, but nonetheless inevitable. The rape myths discussed earlier showed that most people felt that if the woman knew the man, the act could not be defined as rape. Similarly, acts of "naughty fun" at women's expense were just that—*fun*, with no harm intended. Certainly few people defined the naughtiness as intrusive. And when it came to physical force between husbands and wives, many people accepted it as *simply there*—as an unfortunate part of life—like sometimes going hungry or getting evicted, or losing a limb, or becoming seriously ill. Not that anyone liked any of these things. "But," thought most people, "What can you do? That's life."

The degree of social acceptance, or legitimacy, of domestic force, was and is ratcheted upward many notches when it comes to children. Chapters 16 and 17 report that some citizens hold that God requires that they physically discipline their children. A few even believe that severe beatings are necessary to "drive the devil" out of the children and make them spiritual.[74] On the other side, there is a minority of Christians who do not believe in physical force of any kind. Called *pacifists*, they are best known for the ways they perceive war. They do not define war as an inevitable part of life. Nor do they believe that acts of military force are justified simply because the government says they're okay. Among other things, they refuse to serve in the military.

The matter of governments stating that cer-

Pittsburgh Action Against Rape holds a Take Back the Night rally.

tain physical force is okay while other force is not okay is much in the news these days regarding both capital punishment and abortion. Until the 1960s, most states believed they had the right to execute people. But during the 1970s and 1980s, a number of states said, "no, we don't have the right to execute people after all." More recently the U.S. pendulum has swung the other way, and state governments (along with the federal government) are once again saying that it's socially acceptable to execute. In contrast, most European countries continue to define capital punishment as unacceptable. Before the 1970s most state governments said that abortion was an unacceptable act of physical force against the fetus. Then the U.S. Supreme Court decided it was okay. Some observers believe the Court may change its mind yet again and say that it's up to the states to figure out when abortion is or is not okay.

Interestingly enough, it turns out that many people who believe that capital punishment is *not* okay feel that abortion is okay, and vice versa.

Physical Force within Primary Groups

Just as citizens and their governments can change their minds regarding whether or not physical acts of force such as capital punishment and abortion are legitimate, they can also shift their definitions regarding physical force among persons within primary groups. Recall from previous chapters that primary groups are special we-groups. They include platonic friendships, erotic friendships, blood families, and social families. Testifying before a U.S. congressional committee, Straus drew a sharp distinction between primary groups and what some sociologists call *secondary* situations.[75]

Secondary situations include people who work or share a class together, shop in the same store, ride the same elevator, share a hallway or sidewalk, sit together at a library or ball game, live in the same dorm or neighborhood, and so forth. One thing all these situations have in common is that it is never socially acceptable for co-workers, fellow students, neighbors, shoppers, and so on to punch, hit, kick, slap, pummel, stab, or strike one another with a blunt object. Nor is it ever acceptable to push, shove, or in any other ways beat up on one another.

Sometimes violence happens in those kinds of situations anyhow. But if it does, no one would ever dream of saying, "Well, it's OK, the slapping was just work related." Or, "Since they're dorm mates or neighbors, it's no big deal if they beat up on each other." A person who uses physical force in any of those secondary situations is liable to be arrested and charged with criminal assault. Arrest is especially likely if the violence happens more than once, or if the attack leaves obvious marks such as bruises or abrasions, to say nothing of broken bones. By contrast, Straus reminded the congressional committee that in the United States a certain level of physical force is tolerated between erotic friends (spouses, cohabitors, girlfriends/boyfriends). He reported that if they slap, push, shove, or "mildly hit" one another, those types of physical force are culturally defined as *ordinary*—no big deal. People seem to expect it and don't get very excited about it. The other kinds of force listed above, such as striking with a blunt object or stabbing, are placed in a second and separate category and culturally perceived as *extra*ordinary. In contrast to ordinary force, Straus says that most citizens seem shocked and surprised by extraordinary force within families and believe that something should be done about it.

Nevertheless, research carried out during the past twenty years concludes that many husbands and some wives use a certain degree of extraordinary force, and many more use a large amount of ordinary force, on one another. To demonstrate that physical force is far more common inside than outside of families, Straus reports that a man is twenty times more likely to experience violence of some kind at the hands of a family member than from an outsider.[76] And a woman is 200 times more likely to experience violence of some kind from a family insider than from a stranger. Straus also reports that in the United States, 25 percent of all homicides are done by someone who was linked to the victim either by blood or marriage. In Canada, he says, the figure is 50 percent.

Measuring Force between Adult Partners
Straus and his colleagues surveyed national samples of U.S. households during 1975 and again in 1985. They measured violence between co-residing adults using what they called the Conflict Tactics Scale, or CTS. The CTS questionnaire is divided into two parts, the first of which is called "minor violence." Under minor (ordinary) violence they asked their respondents if during that year they had ever pushed, grabbed, shoved, threw something at, or slapped their partner.

Under the second part of their questionnaire ("severe," or extraordinary, violence that might cause injuries requiring medical attention) they asked their respondents if during that year they had ever kicked, bitten, punched, beaten up, choked, or burned their partner, or else threatened her or him with a knife or gun or actually used those weapons. In 1985, 161 of every 1,000 married or cohabiting couples reported either minor or severe violence.[77] That translates into an estimated 8.7 million U.S. couples (16%) who experienced some kind of violence that year. The number of couples who said they experienced severe violence was 63 of 1,000, or 3.4 million couples.

Straus and his colleagues also compared the amounts of violence done by husbands and male cohabitors against their female partners with the amounts of violence done by women to their male partners. They found that 116 couples of 1,000 reported male violence that was either minor or severe. And 34 of 1,000 reported severe male violence. Straus reserves the label "wife beating" for this latter category.

At the same time, 124 couples of every 1,000 marrieds and cohabitors reported that the women did either minor or severe violence to their male partners. Finally, 48 of every 1,000 couples said that the woman did severe violence to her male partner. If we compare this 48 figure with the comparable 34 figure for men, and if we also compare the 124 figure for women with the comparable 116 figure for men, we come to a surprising and unexpected conclusion: Women seem to be more violent than their male partners! However, what seems to be is actually an illusion, as we shall see throughout the next few pages.

Straus acknowledges that a number of feminists, as well as other researchers, have been highly critical of the investigations of domestic violence that he and his colleagues have done.[78] For one thing, he himself notes that all of the foregoing numbers are probably understated. That is, both spouses and cohabitors are almost certainly being less than truthful in telling the interviewer about the violent acts they do to their partners. They are also being less than candid about violent acts their partners do to them. Straus adds that instead of concluding that 16 percent of all couples experience some sort of violence in any given year, the figure is probably closer to a third.[79]

Historic Roots of Male Force But there's something far more fundamental at stake than the question of how much U.S. couples underreport domestic violence. The more basic issue is an understanding of what's actually happening during partner violence. By way of illustration, hearing the final score of a baseball game gives us very little sense of the dynamics

of that particular game. To figure out what went on we have to know the back-and-forth processes (hitting, pitching, running, fielding) that took place between the two teams throughout the nine innings. To learn about those dynamics, we must either watch the game or read a play-by-play account written by someone who did. Few if any researchers, however, have ever watched adult men and women slapping, hitting, pushing, biting, kicking, choking, or knifing or shooting one another.

To help us understand what's going on in situations of domestic violence, Russell and Emerson Dobash say we must first get a "vision of what our ancestors were like and what forgotten social baggage they left us."[80] Their research reveals that throughout recorded history many women, wives in particular, have been the victims of male violence. Just as the Old Testament story of Amnon and Tamar reveals that acquaintance rape has been around for quite a while, Dobash and Dobash show that husband violence against wives has been with us just as long.

Let's say that a police officer orders a citizen to submit to arrest. If the citizen submits peacefully, the officer is prohibited from using physical force on the citizen. If the citizen resists, the officer is permitted to use "reasonable" force, including hitting him or her with a club or even using a gun if need be. The cultural rules surrounding the arrest scenario say that the person with legitimate *authority* (the officer) should avoid using force, if possible, but if the person decides force is necessary, he or she may use it in restrained measure. Everyone agrees it's much more desirable for police not to use force. But in U.S. society, force by police officers is defined as sometimes requisite to maintain law and order.

Dobash and Dobash say that during the early Roman period a similar logic applied to husbands' use of force on their wives. Cultural rules gave the husband the responsibility and authority to maintain *order* over his entire household. If husbands failed to maintain order within their four walls, the Romans believed society would collapse. If a wife submitted to whatever the husband asked her to do in the pursuit of order, the Romans believed he should not use physical force on her. If, however, she opposed him and he decided that the use of force was necessary, force was "condoned and even praised for its beneficial effects on domestic order."[81] Violence was considered unfortunate and excesses were condemned; a few Romans even rejected the use of violence to control women. Nevertheless, in the interests of social order, the vast majority of Roman citizens (the men, anyhow) accepted husband violence as legitimate for male (patriarchal) control of women.

During the 1600s and 1700s, most Christian churches in the New World mixed beliefs inherited from the Romans, as well as from British common law, with religious views regarding the subordination of women to men.[82] Christian theologians of the day taught not only that God had ordained Africans to be slaves to white men, but that God also expected wives to be obedient to their husbands. If wives were obedient, men had no right to use force on them. But if a husband, who after all had the responsibility to God to maintain family order, decided that violence against his wife was necessary for order's sake, then he had the authority, indeed the obligation, to use it.

The Notion of Family Privacy By the 1800s (what Chapter 6 called the *Jacksonian* period), men were legally permitted to "chastise" their wives without any fear of charges of assault and battery. Wives were told to " 'kiss the rod that beat them' " because it rescued them from their waywardness.[83] Additionally, during the Jacksonian and Progressive eras, the family household (husband, wife, dependent children) became more private than it had ever

been before. Not only could a rapidly expanding and prosperous middle class afford the type of sturdy housing that effectively shut out nosy neighbors and relatives, it became part of North American culture for outsiders to keep away from the family's "own business." The implications of the powerful cultural norm of family privacy for husband violence are quite obvious. Before that era, if a husband used excessive force on his wife (or children) the neighbors were very likely to know about it and to try to stop it. But as families became enclosed within solidly built walls and became ever more culturally private, community and neighborhood control over husband violence became virtually nonexistent.

In recent years, the idea of community control over police violence has gained widespread acceptance. By contrast, the concept of community control over male, as well as parental, violence within households remains foreign to most U.S. citizens. Moreover, conservative religious groups vigorously oppose that concept. A 1980 bill introduced in Congress would, for example, have provided federally funded local community shelters for women and children seeking "safe haven"— places where women could flee their physically abusive men. Successfully opposing those shelters, the conservatives argued they would become "antifamily indoctrination centers."[84]

The conservatives' fear was and is that official places of this type would legitimate the idea that the government can interfere in the sacred, and thus private, interactions that occur between husbands and wives. They believe that government interference would undermine the divinely given authority of the husband over his wife. It is not that they necessarily condone a husband using force on his wife. But if, in their view, a husband is unfortunately driven to that extreme, the matter is between God, him, and his wife. Outsiders, particularly the secular authorities, have no role whatsoever in the matter. An even stronger reason for their political opposition is that the shelters would also house the mothers' children. Because they believe that God commands them to use physical force on their children, the idea of the State keeping children sheltered from their fathers simply cannot be tolerated.

Gender and Physical Force

This historical background opens the way for us to better understand violence among couples who are erotic friends—who claim they *love* each other. It also gives us a clue about explaining the numbers that imply women are more violent than men. First, according to Dobash and Dobash, this background tells us that the label "marital violence," along with labels such as "family violence" and "spouse abuse," miss the mark—they are inaccurate.[85] These labels "neutralize, sanitize, and provide euphemisms for wife abuse." Dobash and Dobash claim that the reasons those labels are inaccurate is that they're "gender blind": They ignore the historical reality that although men have for centuries had official permission to use force on their wives, *women never have had nor do they now have permission to use force on their husbands.*

In addition, labels such as "marital violence" ignore the physiological reality that men are bigger and stronger than women. For instance, do the labels "spouse abuse" or "marital violence" create the same images in the mind when the average woman hits, slaps, kicks, or punches a man as when the average man does those same things to a woman? As we think about it, we're likely to conclude that the numbers describing U.S. women as being more violent than men are extraordinarily misleading. They're misleading because women's hits don't mean the same thing as men's hits. Even if a woman punches a man ten times, it's not likely to hurt as much, or cause as many

bruises, abrasions, or broken bones, as when he punches her even once.[86] If she kicks him on five separate occasions, the pain and suffering are likely to be considerably less than if he kicks her just once.

Woman Abuse

Given these historical and physiological realities, Dobash and Dobash assert that the only accurate label to describe what's going on in many contemporary households is the label *wife abuse*, not "marital" or "domestic" violence.[87] They say that instead of being gender blind, the label "wife abuse" is *gender aware.*

However, even the label wife abuse is much too narrow to capture the complete picture of male violence against women. In recent years a number of studies have shown that some male cohabitors and boyfriends also use force on their woman partners.[88] A few studies even suggest that violence may be somewhat more common among cohabitors than among marrieds or dating couples.[89]

Consequently, a more accurate label to describe what's happening is *woman abuse*. This label is plain, simple, and direct. It means that because of our cultural history and male muscle mass, many men use force of various kinds to control women with whom they share an erotic friendship. Men do not commonly use violence on co-workers or store clerks or librarians. Furthermore, men rarely if ever use force on women with whom they are just-friends.

The puzzle then is why many men use force on women they profess to love—women with whom they share a unique kind of primary relationship. Straus and others say that the marriage license is a license to *hit*. It gives the husband cultural permission to use force on his wife. But we just learned that men without licenses—male cohabitors and boyfriends—also use force on their female partners. Officially, there have been laws on the books for about a hundred years prohibiting woman abuse.[90] The laws are hardly ever enforced, however.

Dobash and Dobash say that the laws are overridden because whenever a man and woman form what they call a permanent relationship (erotic friendship), two things happen.[91] First, their social network (friends and families, i.e., outsiders) recognize them as having a unique bond—they belong to each other in a special way. Because they're enclosed within their own social boundary, outsiders tend to stay out of their business. Consequently, social network control of couple violence becomes minimal. Even if outsiders know that woman abuse is happening, they often try to ignore it.

The second and perhaps more crucial thing that happens is that men develop a sense of possession and rightful domination over "my woman." Underlying the idea that "she has become mine—my lover, my sexual property" is the notion that a man might sometimes need to use physical force of one kind or another on *my* woman. People seem to accept the idea that somehow, because of the exclusivity and monogamy inherent to erotic friendships, male violence, though unfortunate, "happens, and can't be avoided—after all, this ain't a perfect world."

Incidentally, the idea that sexual property helps to justify physical force within erotic friendships may in part explain partner violence among both lesbian and gay male couples.[92] Many of the things, gender differences in particular, that account for violence among heterosexual couples would not apply. But notions of property and feelings of jealousy could apply equally among heterosexual and homosexual couples.

Control via Physical Force   In any case, to label force as severe or minor based on how much physical damage the force does is highly misleading. The basic question is rather, to what degree does the woman feel that her partner controls her life via whatever level of force he applies? Studies show that many wives live in constant foreboding of their husbands' greater physical strength.[93] Whether he uses it or not, his strength is an ever-present potential resource for controlling her that she can never hope to equal. In contrast, few if any healthy men live in fear of their partners' physical strength even if their women hit, slap, kick, or punch them. Healthy men rarely if ever define their partner's violence as a means of potential or actual control over their own lives.

Intriguingly, Cathy Greenblatt reports that *if asked directly,* most of the respondents in her study did not perceive men's violence as a means of exercising control over women. Instead, most felt that men became violent because they "got out of control"—violence happens because men lose charge of their passions, arms, or legs. Her respondents felt that a man should *not* use physical force on women; they did not outrightly approve of it. Nevertheless they believed there might be valid reasons explaining *why* he lost control, for instance the woman's sexual behaviors such as flirting with another man or actually having an affair. Or the couple might be having an argument about something and he just "flew off and hit her even though he didn't mean to." Or he might be drunk or on drugs, and so forth. In short, Greenblatt's respondents felt the action is "deplorable, but the hitter cannot be held accountable for his behavior."[94] What about when women use force on men? Once again, most respondents disapproved of violence, but they were also willing to tolerate a woman's use of force because, "after all they are not likely to create physical injury."

Greenblatt's findings are complemented by a national study showing that some 20 percent of Americans believe it's okay to slap one's spouse on "appropriate occasions."[95] Although the authors didn't follow up by asking what occasions these might be, we can fill in the blanks from Greenblatt's study. Male slapping is tolerated if the woman "drives" him to it. Female slapping is tolerated since it's self-defense and she can't hurt him anyhow. Interestingly enough, 25 percent of college-educated persons approved of spousal slapping, compared with only 16 percent of those with eight years or less of schooling.

Gender Traditionalism and Woman Abuse

Greenblatt wondered why women and men alike tend to absolve men of responsibility for woman abuse by blaming the victim: Why is it okay to explain his behavior by saying he simply lost control? Why wouldn't that explanation be acceptable on the job? In a dorm or store? Greenblatt suggests that many citizens absolve men due to continuing beliefs in the gender traditionalism displayed by Figure 12-1. Many persons still believe that when partners disagree, men "have the right to the final say, and when they are thwarted . . . they have the right as well the power to use physical force."[96] Since their partners are physically weaker than they are, men have little to fear from them. Nor do men expect reprisals from the police, courts, neighbors, friends, or kin. Furthermore, because women are generally not as economically autonomous as men (it's more difficult for women to support themselves and children), most men have little fear their wives will leave them even when they use force.

Straus and Smith report that each of the many studies they have done over the past two decades reveals that "male-dominant marriages have the highest level of violence."[97] Hence they agree with Greenblatt that the more gender-role traditional men are the more likely they are to use force on their wives; and the more gender-role traditional women are the more likely they are to tolerate it. Believing the husband is the Head of The Family legitimates the man's physical force. If a man thinks of himself as the Head, then he's more likely to cave in to those primal urges to use force on his wife (or cohabitor or girlfriend) than if he

views her as an equal partner. If a woman defines him also as the Head, she's more likely to live with force even though she doesn't like it. Furthermore, research shows that the more strongly a person holds to fundamentalist religious beliefs the more likely she or he is to believe that the husband is indeed the Head of the wife.[98]

In short, the man has the privilege of flying off the handle and using force, even though his actions are judged as unfortunate. He remains the ultimate authority figure in families. The fact that he's excused for not controlling himself gives him effective control over his partner. Because she knows he might lash out at any time, she must mind her words and actions in ways that men simply never have to with women.

Men need only mind their words and actions with other men lest the men get violent with them. Even when men use life-threatening force on women, their partners still have a tendency to excuse them. One of the women in Greenblatt's study was choked several times by her husband. Nonetheless, she claimed, " 'it wasn't serious because he didn't really want to hurt me.' "

Defining Violence as a Means of Control

Those choking incidents also suggest that Straus's definition of violence is misleading. Violence, he says, is "an act carried out with the intention or perceived intention of causing physical pain or injury to another person."[99] In these reported choking incidents, neither the husband nor the wife believed that the husband intended to hurt her. As a result, Straus might not label the choking as violent. The more important point is that in choking her the man effectively controls his wife's behavior. Even if she thinks, "He loves me, he doesn't mean to hurt me," being choked is hardly a pleasant experience. In future she is likely to do all she can to avoid provoking an outburst. To keep the peace (and possibly her life), she will probably go along with his agenda.

Research evidence shows that few women are likely to initiate force against a healthy partner. The great bulk of women's acts of force are undoubtedly in "retaliation or self-defense."[100] Tiptoeing around her man doesn't always work. A little thing she does or says, something the kids do or say, something that happened at work, "ticks him off" and makes him violent. To protect herself, or the children if he's beating up on them, she might hit, slap, or kick him. Her aim is to resist his physical force and to gain some semblance of order within a highly volatile situation. Her attempted force might indeed shock him into ceasing his abuse. On the other hand, it might incite him to escalate the abuse. Some husbands go so far as to shoot their wives. National homicide statistics show that 76 percent of female homicide victims are murdered by their spouses, and 21 percent are murdered by strangers.[101] In spite of media attention to crime in the streets, women have much more reason to fear being murdered by their erotic friends than by strangers.

At the same time, a number of women abused by husbands or partners resort to knives or guns as a means of protection during a violent episode, or as a means to forestall future abuse. The Bobbitt incident described previously is probably the best known example of women reacting violently to an ongoing pattern of extreme partner abuse.[102] The actual degree to which women attempt to defend themselves can be surmised by comparing the numbers of murders women perpetrate *inside* their household with murders they perpetrate *outside*. For example, in considering murders of "strangers" in the United States, only 10 percent are done by women.[103] The finding that 90 percent of strangers are murdered by men shows that they are exceedingly more violent with strangers than women are.

By contrast, in considering the murders of spouses in the United States, 48 percent are done by women, and 48 percent by men. Why is there such a wide gap (10 percent versus 48 percent) between murders by women inside and outside their households? Simply put, women have little reason to murder strangers, but do have reason to murder their partners. Among the 132 women in the Chicago jail during 1976, 40 percent were held on charges of killing their male partners after the men had consistently abused them.[104]

Woman Abuse and the Law   Until recently, state laws treated wives much more harshly for murdering husbands than they treated husbands for murdering wives. The reason, says Tong, is rooted in English common law, which defined husband killing as a "crime against the state." Since God and the State had made the husband the wife's *lord*, killing him was a form of treason analogous to murdering the king. If on the other hand he killed her, that was an unfortunate by-product of his duty to curb her waywardness and thus almost certainly justified. In the United States, wives who murdered spouses were not allowed to plead self-defense, because in legal jargon self-defense means the murder was justified.[105] On the other hand, if a woman pled insanity (temporary or otherwise), she might perhaps be acquitted of the charge. The reason, says Tong, is that insanity excuses her behavior but does not justify it.

As part of a broad-based effort to reform its domestic laws, Florida passed a 1992 statute aimed at granting women greater latitude in making complaints of abuse against their partners. The wording of the law, however, described the issue as *spouse* abuse rather than *woman* abuse, unintentionally implying that women are on a level playing field with men when it comes to physical force. As a result, when an officer responds to an abuse complaint (almost always made by the woman), the officer is now required to evaluate the man's statements as fully as hers.[106] Ironically, the result of that well-intended legal effort to achieve equity has been a substantial increase in the numbers of *couples*—the woman as well as the man—being arrested. The man tells the officer that the woman has been just as violent as he and, "What's more she started it!" Unable to sort out who's telling the truth in the midst of a very stressful setting, the officer simply arrests them both. Hence a law designed to assist victims is turning out to place greater limitations on women than ever before. A number of advocates fear that as more abused women discover how liable they are to be arrested for complaining, they'll become even less likely to complain and will simply "take it."

African-Americans and Woman Abuse

Because of the severe economic discrimination faced by black men in the white-controlled marketplace, researchers have wondered whether black men are more abusive than white men toward their partners.[107] How likely is it that black men will take out their frustration with white discrimination and prejudice by abusing women they love? On the one hand, on the basis of the national studies of the U.S. population described above done in 1975 and 1985, Robert Hampton and co-workers found that black women were indeed more likely than white women to report that their male partners had been violent towards them.[108] However, the differences between black male violence and white male violence were less in 1985 than they had been during 1975. On the other hand, on the basis of a study done in 1982 in a major southeastern metropolitan city, Lettie Lockhart did not support the idea that black men are more abusive than white men toward their wives.[109] She compared African-American with European-American couples and found no significant differences in the proportions of women re-

porting that their husbands were violent toward them.

Tong says that whatever the level of abuse they face, "black women are even more prone than white women to excuse their husbands' violent behavior."[110] Because black women are keenly aware of the discrimination their men face, they are more likely to make greater allowances for them when they lose control. As one of the black women in Tong's study put it, " 'If he can't have things his way out in Whitey's world, at least he can have them his way at home.' " Tong adds that black women are also less likely than white women to report their man's violence to the police. One reason for their hesitancy is that, although the police are slow to respond to *white* women's requests for help against male violence, officers are even slower in their responses to such requests from black women. Aware of how long it takes to get official help, black women see little advantage in calling for it. A second reason black women are less likely to report their partner's violence is black distrust in general of the police. African-Americans perceive the police to be on their side in few if any social encounters. Even white women are uncertain whether the police will take their side in situations of male violence. Hence it should not be surprising that black women are much less likely to expect that the police will support them against their partners.

WOMAN ABUSE AROUND THE WORLD

Anthropologist David Levinson observes that woman abuse and parental violence against children are "a reality of daily life for many people around the world."[111] To illuminate his point he cites a love poem from India:

> Your abuse is the ring in my ear,
> Your blows are my toe-rings,

If you kick me, it is my pulse and rice,
The more you beat me with your shoes,
The more we are united.

Levinson wanted to find out whether some societies had more or less woman abuse than other societies. If they did, *why*? To satisfy his curiosity he compared ninety "small-scale and peasant" societies from North America, South America, Oceania, Africa, Asia, the Middle East, Europe, and the Soviet Union. He found that some of those societies had much less, and some much more, wife beating than other societies. Indeed, some societies had no wife beating at all, including a grouping of some 10 million people who live in Central Thailand. Levinson concluded that the more family life is "characterized by cooperation, commitment, sharing and equality," the less likely it is that wife abuse will occur.[112] Hence, looking again at Figure 12-1, we can say that the more strongly women and men prefer gender equality, the less likely it is that men will use physical force on their female partners and that women will tolerate it. These conclusions appear to be valid not only in a postmodern society such as the United States but also among developing societies around the world.

In his study of the Central Thai people of Bang Chan, where wife abuse is nonexistent, H. P. Phillips reported that women and men do identical kinds of work inside and outside the household.[113] Their lives are what Figure 12-1 describes as highly interchangeable. Both genders do plowing as well as paddling of river boats. Both genders also own and operate farms on an equal basis, share equitably in the inheritances from their families, and divide property equally in the event of divorce.

Phillips adds that individualism is central to the Bang Chan people, alongside a commitment to the idea of controlling aggression within families. *Individualism* to those people means that the rights and interests of women are just as important as those of men. The no-

tion that the husband/male possesses final authority or headship over the woman has never been, nor is it now, part of their culture. At the same time, they are keenly aware of the potential for physically stronger males to use force on women, and they consciously seek to avoid it. Unlike many persons in the United States, they simply do not accept the notion that male violence, though regrettable, is inevitable and unavoidable.

CONCLUSION—THE IRRESPONSIBILITY OF AGGRESSION

The last several decades have witnessed an expanding array of both economic and sexual options for women. Nevertheless, women, throughout their life courses, continue to be more severely coerced and constrained than men. Chapter 12 examines three forms of aggression by which men exercise constraints over women. The first is known as rape. "Consent" requires that the woman say yes and *not* say no to a man's sexual overtures. Many men (including husbands) ignore one or both of those conditions and force women whom they know into intercourse against their will, which is sexual assault, or rape.

The second example of aggression and coercion is called sexual harassment. Although sometimes connected with acquaintance rape, a great deal of harassment occurs quite apart from an actual sexual assault. Harassment involves subjecting women (and sometimes men) against their will to sexually tinged words or actions that the women find demeaning and offensive. Generally occurring in formal settings such as work or school, harassment takes on added significance when the harasser is in a position of authority over the woman. In such instances, her willingness to tolerate the harassment may result in certain rewards, but her unwillingness to do so may lead to penalties.

The final example of coercion is called

woman abuse. To one degree or another many men use physical aggression, or its threat, to control women. It is a curious fact that men use physical force most frequently on the woman they profess to love. Their shared sexual bond appears to create a feeling of possession that apparently legitimates the use of male force.

Around the world, as well as in North America, the more strongly men hold to ultimate male headship and authority, the more likely they are to use physical force on women. At the same time, the less women accept patriarchal ideas as a way to organize relations between the genders, the less likely they are to live with physical force. In other words, the *more* women strive for equality with men, the *less* willing they are to accept the one thing that perhaps more than any other signifies inequality and subordination—being subject to harassment and violence.

This book is about reinventing families in a responsible manner. As the Modern Family declines, how can persons create varieties of postmodern families that attend to the well-being of all their members as well as the largest society? One of the best kept secrets of the Modern Family is its pervasive physical and sexual aggression. Because it damages well-being, aggression within families is plainly irresponsible. Hence, constructing today's families requires figuring out ways to minimize aggression. It appears that one way to minimize it is to encourage the social and cultural conditions that promote equality between the genders.

NOTES

1. Shelley Donald Coolidge, *The Christian Science Monitor,* March 7, 1994, p. 9.
2. Joyce Carol Oates, "Rape and the Boxing Ring," *Newsweek,* February 24, 1992, pp. 60–61.
3. John J. O'Connor, *Gainsville, Florida, Sun,* April 12, 1992, p. B3 (New York Times News Service).
4. Keller, 1989.
5. Collison, 1992.
6. Bechhofer and Parrot, 1991, p. 15.
7. Kanin, 1957.
8. Rubin, 1990, p. 93.
9. Jones, Marsden, and Tepperman, 1990.
10. Waller, 1938.
11. Rothman, 1984.
12. D'Emilio and Freedman, 1988.
13. Kanin, 1984; D'Emilio and Freedman.
14. Bohmer, 1991, p. 318.
15. Holmes, 1989, p. 100.
16. *The Gainesville, Florida, Sun,* April 14, 1992, p. D4.
17. Gonsiorek and Shernoff, 1991.
18. Gidycz and Koss, 1991, p. 217.
19. Finkelhor and Yllo, 1985.
20. Bohmer, p. 327.
21. Ibid., p. 329.
22. *The Greensboro, North Carolina, News & Record,* June 26, 1993, p. A2.
23. Finkelhor and Yllo, p. 38.
24. *The Gainesville, Florida, Sun,* January 22, 1994, p. 1A (from *The New York Times*).
25. Ibid., pp. 50, 55.
26. Bohmer, pp. 320, 321.
27. James F. McCarty, *Miami Herald,* October 5, 1989, p. 1A.
28. Bechhofer and Parrot, p. 13.
29. *The Gainesville, Florida, Sun,* April 13, 1992, p. D1.
30. Bechhofer and Parrot, p. 13.
31. Burt, 1991.
32. Bohmer, p. 320.
33. Ellen Goodman, *The Gainesville, Florida, Sun,* March 3, 1992, p. A8 (from Boston Globe Newspaper Co.). See also Reiss, 1990.
34. Muehlenhard and Schrag, 1991, p. 122.
35. Koss, Gidycz, and Wisniewski, 1987.
36. Abbey, 1991.
37. Ibid., p. 97; Bernard, 1969.
38. Bechhofer and Parrot, p. 21.
39. Fitzpatrick, 1988a, b.
40. Scanzoni and Szinovacz, 1980; Scanzoni, 1983; Hatchett, 1991, pp. 88ff.
41. Thornton, 1989; see also Scanzoni, 1978.
42. Scanzoni, 1975; Thornton, 1989.
43. Malamuth, 1981.
44. Warshaw and Parrot, p. 75.
45. Ibid.

46. Beneke, 1982.
47. Peterson and Franzese, 1987.
48. Warshaw and Parrot, p. 75.
49. White and Humphrey, 1991, p. 46.
50. Ibid.
51. Warshaw and Parrot, p. 76.
52. Bart and O'Brien, 1985.
53. Taken from her congressional testimony and reprinted in Chrisman and Allen, 1992, pp. 15ff.
54. A. Press, et al., "Abusing Sex at the Office," *Newsweek,* March 10, 1980, p. 81.
55. Tong, 1984, p. 66.
56. Backhouse and Cohen, 1982, p. 34.
57. Tong, p. 67.
58. Backhouse and Cohen, p. 72.
59. Stephanie Strom, *The Wall Street Journal,* October 20, 1991, pp. 1, 15.
60. Michele Galen, *Business Week,* March 18, 1991, pp. 98–100.
61. Paul M. Barrett, *The Wall Street Journal,* February 27, 1992, p. B8.
62. "Office Lady," *Newsweek,* April 27, 1992, p. 38.
63. *The Gainesville, Florida, Sun,* April 26, 1992, p. 8A (from Associated Press News).
64. *The New York Times,* May 21, 1993, p. A12.
65. DiTomaso, 1989.
66. Eric Schmitt, *The New York Times,* September 23, 1992, p. 1A.
67. *The Gainesville, Florida, Sun,* April 24, 1993, p. 1A (from *The New York Times*).
68. Douglas Waller, *Newsweek,* February 28, 1994, p. 31.
69. *The Gainesville, Florida, Sun,* April 25, 1992, p. 1A.
70. Felicity Barringer, *The New York Times,* June 2, 1993, p. A12.
71. DiTomaso, p. 89.
72. Besharov, 1990, p. ix.
73. Straus, 1972.
74. Greven, 1991.
75. Straus, 1979, p. 15.
76. Straus, 1991, p. 18.
77. Ibid.
78. Straus, 1990, pp. 9ff.
79. Straus, 1991, p. 21.
80. Dobash and Dobash, 1990, p. 125.
81. Ibid.
82. Dobash and Dobash, 1983, p. 270.
83. Tong, p. 127.
84. Scanzoni, 1983, p. 202.
85. Dobash and Dobash, 1990, p. 110.
86. Stets and Straus, 1990b.
87. Dobash and Dobash, 1990, p. 127.
88. Makepeace, 1989; Alexander, Moore, and Alexander, 1991; Sugarman and Hotaling, 1991.
89. Stets and Straus, 1990a; Stets, 1991.
90. Greenblatt, 1983, p. 236.
91. Dobash and Dobash, 1990, p. 127.
92. Island and Letellier, 1991; Renzetti, 1992.
93. Ibid.
94. Greenblatt, p. 256.
95. Tong, p. 170.
96. Greenblatt, p. 258.
97. Straus and Smith, 1990a, p. 514.
98. Scanzoni, 1983.
99. Straus, 1991, p. 18.
100. Straus and Gelles, 1990, p. 98.
101. Ibid.
102. See note 24. See also David A. Kaplan, *Newsweek,* January 24, 1994, p. 52 ff.
103. Straus and Gelles, p. 8.
104. Tong, p. 145.
105. Ibid.
106. *The Gainesville, Florida, Sun,* April 18, 1992, p. 7A.
107. Staples, 1976.
108. Hampton, Gelles, and Harrop, 1991.
109. Lockhart, 1991, p. 171.
110. Tong, p. 170.
111. Levinson, 1989, p. 9. See also a recent U.S. State Department report on worldwide abuse of women: *The New York Times,* February 3, 1994, p. A1.
112. Ibid., p. 104. See also Kirk Williams, 1992.
113. Phillips, 1966, p. 82.

CHAPTER 13

DIVORCE AND ITS RESPONSIBILITIES

We've just seen that "responsibility" means reinventing *primary relationships* (blood and social families; and erotic friendships, including girlfriends/boyfriends, cohabitors, spouses) so that they are aggression-free zones. But to critics of postmodern families, perhaps nothing demonstrates greater irresponsibility than today's divorce patterns. Children, say the critics, suffer as a result of widespread adult desires to keep on switching partners. This chapter examines divorce patterns and tries to figure out what the critics have in mind, and whether it's even possible to have a "responsible" divorce. (Other chapters that have considered this question are chapters 1, 5, and 8 through 11.)

Jeffrey Knight was the fifth husband of Ms. J. Z. Knight, "perhaps the most popular of the New Age spirit-channelers."[1] Mr. Knight sued Ms. Knight on the grounds that in 1989 she'd "bullied" him into accepting a "meager" divorce settlement. She'd coerced him into the agreement, he said, through the voice of Ramtha, whom she asserts is a 35,000-year-old warrior spirit. In his suit Mr. Knight de-

manded a much larger share of the millions of dollars J. Z. made during the 1980s from thousands of ordinary citizens, as from celebrities such as Shirley MacLaine. J. Z. claims that for a fee Ramtha speaks through her, advising and commanding adherents how to live. Mr. Knight says that he helped transform J. Z. from a "mere housewife" into a "spiritual guru who lives in a $2 million ranch house." Consequently, he says he deserves a greater portion of the wealth than he'd gotten from their divorce settlement. Although he no longer believes in Ramtha, he still had faith while they were negotiating that agreement. And through J. Z., Ramtha commanded him to settle for only a few dollars.

Few court battles over divorce settlements are as bizarre as the struggles between Jeffrey and J. Z. Nevertheless, since the 1960s growing numbers of persons have passed through the formal divorce experience. In many cases they've had to negotiate legal agreements regarding money and property, or child custody, or both. Table 13-1 shows the numbers of divorces occurring annually from 1940 to 1991.

TABLE 13-1

Numbers and Rates of Divorces and Annulments: United States, 1940–1991

| | Divorces and annulments | Rate per 1,000 | | | Divorces and annulments | Rate per 1,000 | |
		Total population	Married women 15 years old and over			Total population	Married women 15 years old and over
1991	1,187,000	4.7	NA	1965	479,000	2.5	10.6
1990	1,175,000	4.7	NA	1964	450,000	2.4	10.0
1989	1,163,000	4.7	NA	1963	428,000	2.3	9.6
1988	1,167,000	4.7	20.7	1962	413,000	2.2	9.4
1987	1,166,000	4.8	20.8	1961	414,000	2.3	9.6
1986	1,178,000	4.9	21.2	1960	393,000	2.2	9.2
1985	1,190,000	5.0	21.7	1959	395,000	2.2	9.3
1984	1,169,000	5.0	21.5	1958	368,000	2.1	8.9
1983	1,158,000	4.9	21.3	1957	381,000	2.2	9.2
1982	1,170,000	5.0	21.7	1956	382,000	2.3	9.4
1981	1,213,000	5.3	22.6	1955	377,000	2.3	9.3
1980	1,189,000	5.2	22.6	1954	379,000	2.4	9.5
1979	1,181,000	5.3	22.8	1953	390,000	2.5	9.9
1978	1,130,000	5.1	21.9	1952	392,000	2.5	10.1
1977	1,091,000	5.0	21.1	1951	381,000	2.5	9.9
1976	1,083,000	5.0	21.1	1950	385,000	2.8	10.3
1975	1,036,000	4.8	20.3	1949	397,000	2.7	10.6
1974	977,000	4.6	19.3	1948	408,000	2.8	11.2
1973	915,000	4.3	18.2	1947	483,000	3.4	13.6
1972	845,000	4.0	17.0	1946	610,000	4.3	17.9
1971	773,000	3.7	15.8	1945	485,000	3.5	14.4
1970	708,000	3.5	14.9	1944	400,000	2.9	12.0
1969	639,000	3.2	13.4	1943	359,000	2.6	11.0
1968	584,000	2.9	12.5	1942	321,000	2.4	10.1
1967	523,000	2.6	11.2	1941	293,000	2.2	9.4
1966	499,000	2.5	10.9	1940	264,000	2.0	8.8

NA = not available.

Source: National Center for Health Statistics, U.S. Department of Health and Human Services, *Monthly Vital Statistics Reports,* Vol. 39, No. 12, Suppl. 2; Vol. 39, No. 13; Vol. 40, No. 13.

During those fifty years, the numbers grew from around one-fourth million to over 1,200,000.

More informative than the sheer numbers is the *crude divorce rate*—the number of divorces per 1,000 persons in the population. Table 3-1 shows that except for the "quickie" World War II marriages that ended in divorce during the mid to late forties, the crude divorce rate stayed below 2.5 until 1965. Then, as the effects of the *Big Bang* took hold, the crude rate dou-

bled in just ten years, to 5.0 by 1976. Generally speaking, it has stayed around this level ever since.

Table 13-1 also displays a third way to measure the frequency of divorces—the number of divorces for every 1,000 *married* women aged 15 and over. Since this rate is based solely on persons at risk of divorce, it is more refined than the crude rate, which includes many persons who are not formally married and thus not at risk of becoming formally divorced. The movement of the refined rate since 1940 closely resembles that of the crude rate.

Table 13-2 compares the United States with Canada, several European countries, and Japan in terms of the refined divorce rate. It is plain that the United States has the highest rate, and that the rate doubled between 1960 and 1988. The Canadian rate was seven times higher in 1988 than it was in 1960, while the French rate increased almost three times; West Germany's rate grew about two and a half times; Sweden's rate more than doubled; and the United Kingdom's rate went up more than six times. Even though Japan's divorce rate is much lower than the rate among Western nations, it too increased by a third during the same three decades.

The trend throughout most industrialized nations seems clear: During the past thirty years, more and more persons are experiencing the legal ending of their first formal marriage. (Chapter 10 showed that growing numbers of persons are experiencing the legal ending of their formal *re*marriages as well.) Among persons who got formally married for the first time during the 1980s, the chance is approximately one out of two (50%) that the marriage will become legally dissolved.[2] Teresa Martin and Larry Bumpass go a step further and estimate that the likelihood of a

formally married person experiencing a *disruption* (separation as well as divorce) has now reached as high as two out of three (66%).[3]

SOCIAL CATEGORIES AND THE LIKELIHOOD OF DIVORCE

Although overall divorce rates familiarize us with long-term trends in society as a whole, we also need to understand that up to now certain social categories of persons have been more likely than others to experience divorce.[4] One such category is persons who marry at a younger age. The younger a person is at the time of her or his first marriage, the more likely it is that the marriage will end in divorce. A second category is education. In general, the less education a person has the more likely it is that she or he will experience divorce. The major exception is among women holding a graduate degree: Women who have more than a college education are more likely to experience separation and divorce than women with less education.

A third category is women who begin their marriages with a child, especially when the husband is not the child's father.[5] A fourth category is race/ethnicity. African-Americans are more likely than either whites or Hispanics to experience divorce. The risk of separation or divorce is "more than twice as high for blacks as for whites among women who attended college and who neither married early nor had a premarital birth."[6]

In thinking about these four characteristics, it's necessary to keep in mind that they don't occur in isolation. We could say that the women most likely to experience divorce in the United States are black, have children before their marriage to a man who is not the children's father, marry young and are poorly educated. However, there is nothing about being black that in and of itself "causes" divorce. The root cause is that because blacks have fewer educational and occupational op-

T A B L E   1 3 - 2

Refined Divorce Rates from Selected Industrialized Nations
(Divorces per 1,000 Married Women)

Country	1960	1970	1980	1988
United States	9.2	14.9	22.6	20.7
Canada	1.8	6.3	10.8	12.6
France	2.9	3.3	6.3	8.4
Germany (western)	3.6	5.1	6.1	8.8
Japan	3.6	3.9	4.8	4.9
Sweden	5.0	6.8	4.9	11.4
United Kingdom	2.0	4.7	12.0	12.3

Source: U.S. Statistical Abstract, 1991.

portunities than whites, they are economically disadvantaged. People who are disadvantaged—whether white, Hispanic or black—often tend to behave in ways that multiply their economic and social disadvantages.

Economic Disadvantages and Families

Recall from Chapter 11 that Sondra and Len are white and poor. They did not feel themselves part of the larger, economically advantaged, mainstream society. After Sondra got pregnant, dropped out of school, quit waitressing, and went on public assistance, she found herself much worse off economically than she'd ever been before. Although at first she resisted Len's efforts to see her and their baby, he eventually got a job, which changed her mind, and they began going out again. Soon he told her he loved her and painted a wonderful vision of their married life together. She too believed it would be beautiful and so they married. It wasn't long afterwards, however, that Len began to run around on her. Each time he pleaded for forgiveness, but finally she got so disgusted she went back to living with her mother, and eventually divorced Len.

At age 19 and lonely, she met Cedric, who was in his early 20s and had a steady job as an unskilled worker in a local factory. She immediately perceived him as a prospect for an erotic friendship, and thus they entered a formation phase. Soon after they became sexual partners and found themselves in a maintenance and change phase. Cedric seemed to like and enjoy her baby boy, and sometimes bought toys and clothing for him. After a while he suggested she and the boy move in with him. Sondra loved Cedric, and she also realized that his earnings would result in a big improvement over the strained lifestyle she shared with her mother and younger siblings. So she agreed to cohabit and add informal marriage to their erotic friendship. About a year later, just after she turned 20, he offered to marry her formally and she accepted.

At the time of their wedding, Sondra's sense of bonding, of we-ness, with Cedric was extremely strong. She felt they belonged together and that they mattered to each other a great deal. After a time, however, she began to notice that instead of discussing their problems and coming up with solutions as they used to do, Cedric was adopting a conflict mode. He began to oppose and resist her ideas and suggestions. Not only did he become less cooperative, but his negotiating style became increasingly less considerate. It became more and more difficult for them to resolve their conflicts effectively and come up with acceptable outcomes. One result was that the bonding between them began to get frayed, like a string being rubbed against the edge of a table.

When Cedric was laid off at the plant, he became physically abusive to Sondra—behavior that surprised and shocked her. He also began to abuse her sexually by forcing her into unwanted intercourse, and also into sexual practices she wasn't comfortable with. Their fights usually started with his complaints that she was spending too much of his unemployment check on "her kid," as well as on the child they'd recently had together after several years of marriage. The longer Sondra lived under these conditions, the more significantly her sense of we-ness and bonding with Cedric declined. So much so, in fact, that she perceived herself as having evolved into a dissolution phase. Nevertheless, she was committed to staying with him because she had no alternative to his economic support. Since she was not economically autonomous, the only thing she could hope for was that he would soon find another job. "If he has a job," she thought, "he'll feel better and stop hurting us."

To help supplement their family income, Sondra went back to waitressing during the evenings. One night she returned home to discover that Cedric had badly beaten her boy. No longer a cuddly baby, the child had been "getting on his nerves" for a long time. Cedric's child abuse became another conflict issue between them, and her feelings of we-ness and bonding dropped further still. She still felt she had to stay with him out of economic necessity. One night, however, the abuse became so severe that she fled to Safe-Haven, a women's shelter.

Remarriage Instability   Sondra's separation eventually led to divorce, and so by her mid-20s Sondra became part of the numbers reported in Chapter 10 showing that *re*marriages are even more prone to divorce than first marriages. Sondra's story fits the explanation that some researchers offer for the greater instability of remarriages[7]: (1) People who marry while they're young make up a large proportion of those who get divorced after their first marriage. (2) Those persons tend to be poorly educated, and when they're employed they have low-paying jobs. (3) The women tend to have children living with them, while the men trying to support them tend to have children living elsewhere and are struggling (often unsuccessfully) to help out with their material needs. (4) The women perceive *re*marriage as the best means to lift them and their children out of economic deprivation, including poverty. Indeed, government data show that two-adult households tend to be much better off economically than households headed by women (see Table 13-6). (5) Finally, as a result of (4), the women tend to remarry. However, many of the same kinds of economic strains encountered during their first marriages surface once again. The economic strains become compounded if the couple feels (as they often do) that "we must now have *our own* love-child to cement our new marriage." In sum, the researchers suggest that events set in motion while these persons were adolescents or young adults maintain an exceedingly long reach. Like savings bank interest, early life circum-

Professional musician George Bohannon plays for his blended family, consisting of his spouse, his children and her children at their Los Angeles home.

stances have compounded effects. But unlike bank interest, over time the compounded effects become increasingly negative.

Sondra's Social Family   It would be misleading, however, to conclude that Sondra, Len, and Cedric are merely hapless and helpless victims of their cultural and social environments.[8] This book is about how persons invent and *re*invent their primary relationship—their families—throughout their lives. Recall from Chapter 5 that early in her life Helga had experiences comparable to Sondra's. Like Sondra, Helga felt out of control of her life for a number of years. And like Sondra, Helga's lack of autonomy resulted in her feeling psychologically and emotionally depressed and unhealthy. Helga's route toward taking charge of her life was to go back to school and prepare for a career that would give her the status, and eventually the autonomy, that she craved.

None of that was in Sondra's mind as she began her stay at Safe Haven. Like most wives in her situation, she first wondered when she'd be able to return to Cedric. Because she perceived no alternatives, she felt committed to living with and remaining married to him. Like Helga, however, she was eventually able to terminate her relationship with Cedric. But unlike Helga, an alternative relationship in the form of a different erotic friendship played no role at all in the development of Sondra's life course. A very different set of alternative relationships provided her with the options and choices required to leave a relationship deeply mired in a dissolution phase.

The major transitions in her life were triggered when Sondra began talking with other solo parents who waitressed at the same place she did. These and a few other women belonged to what Chapters 2 and 3 called a *social family*. From economic necessity, and because of their desperate needs for goods, money, favors, and services, especially child care, they had formed their own special *we-group*. What had begun merely as a network of friends gradually became much more than that. At first they got together to grumble about men and provide group therapy through sharing problems and feelings. But like the African-Americans described in earlier chapters, they became more than just-friends. The reason they did was because they established what Chapter 3 called "general exchanges" in which they kept on giving and receiving goods, services, and money. The result was that over time they developed a unique sense of social bonding out of which they perceived themselves as *family*. As Moncrief Cochran and co-workers put it, these mostly white solo mothers were *extending* the idea of family to encompass something besides blood ties.[9]

As Sondra gradually became part of the orbit of this socially constructed family, she was able to increase her job hours because of shared child-care arrangements. She also moved with her two children out of Safe Haven into her own apartment. For the first time ever she was now living by herself with no adults around. That fact plus her increased earnings gave her a greater sense of control over her life than she'd ever enjoyed before. As her feelings of depression diminished, her sense of well-being and emotional health improved accordingly.

Sondra now perceives herself as belonging to two families. She continues to feel obliged to her natural mother and sisters to be there for them should they ever need her. Her mother, after all, had been there for her throughout her life and especially so during the past several years. At the same time, she considers her commitment to her social family to be no less strong than her commitment to her blood family. The reason goes back to the Chapter 11 discussion of alternatives, control, and well-being. Sondra's social family is an alternative to her blood family. If she remains solely within the orbit of her blood family, she lacks the means—the alternatives—to achieve a sense of control and well-being. By comparison, her social family supplies something her blood family simply cannot offer—the means to take charge of her own life and thus feel better about herself. Besides the *extrinsic* benefits her family supplies, she likes her new "sisters" a great deal. The level of intimacy she shares with two of them in particular is more profound than anything she's ever experienced before. By contrast, she receives very little in the way of *intrinsic* benefits from her blood family.

Social families are no more conflict-free than blood families or erotic friendships. For example, Sondra's mother often feels jealous and hurt when Sondra places her obligations to her social sisters ahead of obligations to her mother. But when Sondra places obligations to her blood family ahead of obligations to her social family, her social sisters tend to feel jealous and perhaps betrayed. An ongoing dispute among the sisters in Sondra's social family stems from trying to balance the two sets of moral obligations! Obligations to their birth families versus obligations to the family they have created.

Furthermore, although several of the sisters maintain erotic friendships with men, they have in each case limited them to boyfriend status, which means that each girlfriend maintains her own household. Although some of the boyfriends have suggested moving in, the women have declined. The reason for their hesitancy is obvious. Each of the sisters has been through painful experiences similar to Sondra's. To become interdependent with a man to the extent of cohabiting with him (to say nothing of marriage) would put the women at risk of repeating their earlier painful and punishing experiences. If they had to endure that same kind of suffering and loss of control again, their children would suffer as well. Hence, out of strong concern for their children's well-being, as well as their own, they are at this point in their life courses opting to limit their involvements with men.

Such a choice would be much more difficult to make were it not for the existence of their social family. Currently the sisters supply one another with goods, financial help, and services (especially child care), as well as with companionship and intimacy. Due to those valuable benefits, the women feel less pressure and constraint than women who have to depend on an erotic friendship.

DIVORCE AND CHILDREN

The implications for children of Sondra's choices (as well as the choices of thousands of adults like Sondra and Len) have become a major political issue in the United States. Although the *Murphy Brown* incident described in Chapter 10 has faded from public view, the controversy underlying it will be with us for many years to come. Table 13-3 explains in part why this is so by comparing the kinds of households in which today's children live with the households they lived in during the pre–Big Bang era. The top panel of Table 13-3 shows that between 1960 and 1990 the percent-age of children of all races living with two parents dropped from 88 to 73 (numbers are rounded to nearest whole numbers). The percentage of children living with only one parent almost tripled, from 9 to 25. (In 1990, 88 percent of all children living with one parent lived with the mother, and that percentage has not changed since 1960. Then and now the great bulk of solo-parent households are headed by women.)

Comparing whites with blacks reveals striking differences and major similarities. Both racial categories have experienced similar trends *down*ward between 1960 and 1990 in the proportions of children living with both parents: Among whites the percentage dropped from 91 to 79, and among blacks from 67 to 38. Likewise, both racial categories experienced similar trends *up*ward in the proportions of children living only with their mother: Among whites the percentage increased from 6 to 16, and among blacks, it went up from 20 to 51. A major difference is that the proportion of white children living solely with their mothers (16%) is much less than it is for black children (51%). However, because there are so many more whites in the population as a whole, there are many more white children (8.3 million) than black children (5.1 million) living solely with their mothers.

Table 13-4 describes significant trends in the likelihood that a solo mother has *ever* been married or not. For example, between 1960 and 1990 the percentage of white solo mothers who had previously been divorced rose from 28 to 49, a slightly less than twofold increase. The percentage of white solo mothers who had *never* been married rose from 2 to 19, a slightly less than tenfold increase. By comparison, the percentage of black children living with never-married mothers in 1990 rose more than five times from what it had been in 1960: 10 to 52. Thus, on the one hand we learn that the *rate* of increase of white children living solely with never-married mothers (ten times vs. five

T A B L E   1 3 - 3

Living Arrangements of Children Under 18 Years Old: 1990, 1980, 1970, and 1960
(Excludes Those Maintaining Households or Family Groups)

Living arrangement for children under 18 years	Percent distribution			
	1990	1980	1970	1960
All races:				
Two parents	72.5	76.7	85.2	87.7
One parent	24.7	19.7	11.9	9.1
Mother only	21.6	18.0	10.8	8.0
Father only	3.1	1.7	1.1	1.1
Other relatives	2.2	3.1	2.2	2.5
Nonrelatives	0.5	0.6	0.7	0.7
White:				
Two parents	79.0	82.7	89.5	90.9
One parent	19.2	15.1	8.7	7.1
Mother only	16.2	13.5	7.8	6.1
Father only	3.0	1.6	0.9	1.0
Other relatives	1.4	1.7	1.2	1.4
Nonrelatives	0.4	0.5	0.6	0.5
Black:*				
Two parents	37.7	42.2	58.5	67.0
One parent	54.8	45.8	31.8	21.9
Mother only	51.2	43.9	29.5	19.9
Father only	3.5	1.9	2.3	2.0
Other relatives	6.5	10.7	8.7	9.6
Nonrelatives	1.0	1.3	1.0	1.5
Hispanic:†				
Two parents	66.8	75.4	77.7	NA
One parent	30.0	21.1	NA	NA
Mother only	27.1	19.6	NA	NA
Father only	2.9	1.5	NA	NA
Other relatives	2.5	3.4	NA	NA
Nonrelatives	0.8	0.1	NA	NA

NA=not available.
* Black and other races for 1960.
† Persons of Hispanic origin may be of any race.
Source: 1970 Hispanic origin date: U.S. Bureau of the Census, _1970 Census of Population,_ PC(2)-1C, Persons of Spanish Origin. 1960 data: U.S. Bureau of the Census, _1960 Census of Population,_ PC(2)-4B, Persons by Family Characteristics, tables 1, 2, and 19 (excludes inmates of institutions and military in barracks). U.S. Bureau of the Census, _Current Population Reports,_ P-20, No. 450, issued May 1991.

times) is much greater than it is for black children. On the other hand, we learn that in the United States more than half of all black children are born to never-married women but only a fifth of all white children are born to never-married women.

Table 13-5 puts the picture in perspective for the entire U.S. population. Between 1960 and 1990 the proportion of children living with a divorced solo parent went from 23 to 39 percent, an increase of 16 percent. But the proportion living with a never-married solo parent went from 4 to 31 percent, a 27 percent increase. If these trends continue, the percentage

TABLE 13-4
**Children Under 18 Years Old Living with One Parent, by Marital Status of Parent:
1960, 1970, 1980, and 1990**

Marital status of parents	Percentage distribution			
	1960	1970	1980	1990
All children:				
Divorced	23.0	30.2	42.4	38.6
Married, spouse absent	46.3	42.9	31.3	23.7
Separated	27.6	30.3	26.7	20.3
Other	18.7	12.6	4.6	3.4
Widowed	26.5	20.1	11.8	7.1
Never married	4.2	6.8	14.6	30.6
White children:				
Divorced	28.4	39.1	52.0	49.1
Married, spouse absent	41.1	35.7	28.4	23.9
Separated	19.6	21.7	23.0	20.1
Other	21.3	13.9	5.4	3.8
Widowed	29.0	22.7	12.7	7.8
Never married	1.6	2.6	7.0	19.2
Black children:*				
Divorced	11.9	14.6	25.1	20.4
Married, spouse absent	57.2	55.1	36.6	22.4
Separated	43.7	14.6	25.1	20.4
Other	13.5	10.3	2.6	2.3
Widowed	21.3	15.1	9.6	5.1
Never married	9.6	14.1	28.7	51.8
Hispanic children:†				
Divorced	NA	NA	30.6	26.6
Married, spouse absent	NA	NA	40.6	33.8
Separated	NA	NA	34.7	26.8
Other	NA	NA	5.9	7.0
Widowed	NA	NA	8.9	6.9
Never married	NA	NA	19.8	32.6

NA =not available.
*Nonwhite in 1960.
†Persons of Hispanic origin may be of any race.
Source: 1960 data: U.S. Bureau of the Census, *1960 Census of Population,* PC(2)-4B, Persons by Family Characteristics, tables 1 and 19. U.S. Bureau of the Census, *Current Population Reports,* P-20, No. 450, issued May 1991.

of children living with a never-married parent will catch up to, and eventually surpass, the percentage of children living with a divorced parent.

Recall that over time, Sondra was both a never-married and a divorced mother. After her first child was born, government data classified her as a never-married mother. By the time of her second child's birth she was in her second marriage. After her second divorce she is again reclassified—this time as a divorced solo mother residing with two children. Sondra's case underscores a crucial point about the numbers in Tables 13-3, 13-4, 13-5, and 13-6: they are like snapshots instead of a video. The snapshot captures an instant in time; the moments before and after it are unknown. The video, capturing minutes and hours, some-

TABLE 13-5
U.S. Proportion of Children in Single-Parent Situations: 1960, 1970, 1975, 1980–1990

	Children living with	
Year	Divorced parent	Never-married parent
1960	23.0	4.3
1970	30.2	6.8
1975	35.9	10.7
1980	42.4	14.6
1981	43.8	15.2
1982*	42.0	21.0
1983†	42.0	24.0
1984	41.9	24.0
1985	41.2	25.7
1986	41.6	26.6
1987	40.7	28.5
1988	38.3	30.5
1989	38.9	30.9
1990	38.6	30.6

*Partial implementation of processing change.
†Full implementation of processing change.
Source: U.S. Bureau of the Census, *Current Population Reports*, P-20, No. 450, issued May 1991.

times days, of action, tells a more whole and detailed story of what went on over time.

For example, in Tables 13-4 and 13-5 there are probably a substantial number of women like Sondra. Right now they're classified as divorced or separated solo mothers. But some years before they'd been classified as never-married mothers. Other women in the tables may have been married at the birth of their first child but are unmarried by the time of their second child. The interesting and important things about these women are the twists and turns of their life course. As with Sondra, the question is, what is the chain of events, or the story, describing how over time they moved in and out of erotic friendships, social and blood families, public assistance, pregnancy and parenting, employment, and so on?

In spite of the time-bound limitations of these tables, they provide useful information. Table 13-6, for example, compares solo parents

with dual parents and suggests the following conclusions. (1) Solo parents tend to be younger than dual parents. (2) Solo parents tend to have fewer years of schooling than dual parents. (3) Solo parents tend to have less money than dual parents. (4) Solo parents are currently less likely than dual parents to hold a paying job.

Feminization of Poverty

These four generalizations from Table 13-6 support the conclusion that many children of solo parents live in economically disadvantaged circumstances. In particular, 34 percent of white children, 50 percent of black children, and 48 percent of Hispanic children live with a solo parent (usually a woman) whose annual income is *less* than $10,000. Another 27 percent, 26 percent, and 26 percent of white, black, and Hispanic children, respectively, live with mothers whose annual income is between $10,000 and $19,999. The fact that such a large proportion of solo mothers and their children live in disadvantaged circumstances has been labeled the *feminization of poverty.* Lenore Weitzman concludes that "They have become the new poor."[10]

At the other end of the spectrum, Table 13-6 also suggests the *Murphy Brown* effect: Twenty-nine percent of white children living with a solo parent live with a parent (usually a woman) who has between one and four or more years of college. Among black children the figure is 22 percent, and among Hispanic children it is 15 percent. As far as income is concerned, 23 percent of these white children live with a solo parent earning $30,000 and above. Among blacks the figure is 12 percent and among Hispanics it is 14 percent. In other words, a minority of solo parents are well-educated and have "reasonable" family incomes.

Reasonable, however, depends on two main factors. First, how many children is the parent responsible for? Murphy Brown had only one.

TABLE 13-6

Percentages of Children Under 18 Years Old Living with One or Two* Parents, by Race and Hispanic Origin of Child and Characteristics of Parent: 1990

(Numbers in Thousands)

Characteristics of parent	All races Two parents	All races One parent	White Two parents	White One parent	Black Two parents	Black One parent	Hispanic† Two parents	Hispanic† One parent
Total children	46,503	15,867	40,593	9,870	3,781	5,485	4,789	2,154
Percent	100.0	100.0	100.0	100.0	100.0	100.0	100.0	100.0
Age of parent:								
Under 25 years	2.7	14.2	2.7	12.4	3.3	17.8	5.7	15.1
25–34 years	34.2	43.4	34.5	41.3	35.8	47.6	38.7	46.1
35–44 years	47.0	32.3	47.6	34.9	41.9	27.4	39.8	29.2
45 years and over	16.0	10.0	15.2	11.5	19.0	7.2	15.8	9.7
Education:								
Less than high school	16.1	30.1	15.5	27.4	20.8	33.8	51.6	55.4
High-school graduate	36.5	43.1	36.8	43.5	42.3	43.9	27.7	29.8
College: 1–3 years	20.3	18.3	20.1	18.6	22.3	17.8	12.8	11.7
4 or more years	27.1	8.5	27.7	10.5	14.5	4.4	7.8	3.0
Employment status:‡								
Employed	87.2	58.1	88.6	64.0	75.8	48.2	81.1	48.4
Unemployed or not in the labor force	10.5	41.7	9.5	35.8	18.6	51.7	17.1	53.5
Presence of adults:								
Parents only	83.5	58.2	84.7	57.4	77.6	60.3	71.8	51.9
Other relatives	15.5	28.1	14.3	26.4	21.2	30.4	25.8	35.9
Nonrelatives only	1.0	13.7	1.0	16.2	1.2	9.2	2.4	12.1
Family income:								
Less than $10,000	4.4	39.6	4.1	33.8	6.6	50.2	10.1	48.3
$10,000–$19,999	12.5	26.4	11.5	26.6	21.4	25.7	27.2	26.7
$20,000–$29,999	16.5	14.9	16.2	10.9	19.1	11.9	22.4	10.6
$30,000–$39,999	18.1	8.4	18.4	9.9	17.7	5.7	15.1	5.7
$40,000 or more	48.5	10.6	49.8	12.8	35.1	6.5	25.2	8.6
Tenure:§								
Owner	72.8	35.3	75.1	42.2	55.3	23.6	45.7	23.2
Renter	27.2	64.7	24.9	57.8	44.7	76.4	54.3	76.8

*Characteristics of the reference person are shown for children living with two parents.
†Persons of Hispanic origin may be of any race.
‡Persons in the Armed Forces are not included.
§Tenure refers to tenure of the householder (who may not be the child's parent).
Source: U.S. Bureau of the Census, *Current Population Reports,* P-20, No. 450, issued May 1991.

Chapter 16 shows that well-educated women like Brown generally have fewer children. Second, how much of her income flows from child support and/or alimony payments; and how much from her own earnings? Money from ex-spouses, even when the men are well paid, tends to be minimal and often difficult to col-

lect.[11] Hence, well-educated women who have fewer mouths to feed and who have their own earnings—in addition to whatever irregular payments might possibly accrue from ex-spouses—are the solo parents most likely to have "reasonable" family incomes.

Finally, Table 13-6 suggests another over-

Some poor solo mothers find themselves and their children among the nation's homeless population.

looked dimension regarding the lives of solo parents. Among all children living with a solo parent, 28 percent have an additional blood-relative adult sharing their household. Very often that adult is their grandmother or their mother's sister.[12] That was the case with Sondra after her first child: She was a solo parent living with her natural mother and sisters. Furthermore, Table 13-6 shows that 14 percent of children living only with their mothers also have a nonblood relative sharing their household. In most of those cases, the person is probably an adult male cohabiting with the mother in an informal marriage. Adding these two percentages together (28+14), we can say that more than two-fifths of children thought to be living with one parent actually have more than one. They also have a second, or what some researchers call a *social*, parent.[13]

Figure 13-1 shows the steady rise in the numbers of children living as part of informal marriages. Between 1960 and 1990 in the

United States, the numbers of cohabiting households with children under age 15 rose from 197,000 to 891,000.[14] Between 1980 and 1990 the proportion of informal marriages with children present rose from 27 to 31 percent.[15] In some of these informal marriages, the woman had been a never-married mother. In other cases, the woman had been a divorced mother. In either case, Figure 13-1 suggests that a recent trend is for growing numbers of informally married couples to have children living with them.

Furthermore, the 58 percent figure in Table 13-6 describing the proportion of U.S. children living with their mothers and no other adults masks some additional and important information. Recall that before Sondra moved in with Cedric he was quite supportive of both the material and emotional needs of her child. Thus, boyfriends of solo mothers may often help out with the children even though they don't co-reside. And many solo mothers get a

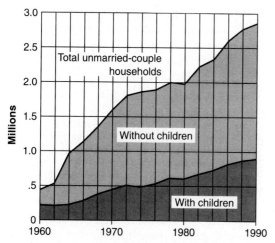

FIGURE 13-1   Unmarried-Couple Households
(*Source:* U.S. Bureau of the Census, *Current Population Reports,* P-20, No. 450, May 1991, p. 15.)

viously, qualified candidates such as the 1950s' democrat Adlai Stevenson and the 1960s' Republican Nelson Rockfeller had little chance for the presidency, in part because they bore the stigma of divorce. It is indeed ironic that the man under whose administration the Religious Right first came to national prominence and power was the first divorced and remarried president.[19] And it is doubly ironic when we realize that it was also he who signed the 1970 pioneer no-fault divorce reform law while he was governor of California.[20] The Right strongly opposes the concept of no-fault divorce and advocates drastic changes in divorce laws. Their goal is to make it impossible for persons who select what they call a "marriage of commitment" (as opposed to a "marriage of compatibility") to get a divorce if they reside with children under age 18.[21]

certain amount of help from blood kin living in separate households. Finally, a part of that 58 percent includes children like Sondra's who belong to, and receive material aid and companionship from, a social family.[16]

THE SHAME OF DIVORCE

Table 13-4 shows that in 1990, 69 percent of white children and 41 percent of black children living with solo parents got there because their parents were separated or divorced. Divorce laws have changed dramatically since 1970 when California put in place the first *no-fault* divorce law. By 1985, South Dakota became the last of the fifty states to allow no-fault divorce.[17] Before the late 1960s, only a relatively few persons were able to get divorces (Table 13-1). Those who managed it suffered the severe stigma of shame and reproach. Not only did people in stable marriages view divorced persons as shameful, but the divorced persons viewed themselves as "morally less worthy" or even as "inferior" persons.[18]

Ronald Reagan was the first U.S. President ever to have been divorced and remarried. Pre-

Adultery and Divorce

Before no-fault laws, the only category of persons culturally permitted to get divorced and remarried were movie stars such as Ronald Reagan. The public did not boycott the movies of divorced actors, in spite of their deviant behaviors that often included fornication, adultery, divorce, and remarriage. Before Reagan, however, politicians were not publicly allowed any of those deviant behaviors. During the 1930s, when Eleanor Roosevelt discovered that President Roosevelt was sleeping with her social secretary, she kept it secret. Although she could have gotten a divorce on the grounds of adultery, she refused to do so because she knew that the fact of the divorce itself, as much as the adultery, would forever ruin his political career.[22]

The reason divorce was so shameful was that in most people's minds negative feelings about adultery were transferred to the act of divorce. This happened because among states that allowed divorce, adultery was the chief, and often the *sole*, grounds for divorce. (A few

states refused divorce even for adultery.) Divorce and adultery were like inseparable Siamese twins; it was widely believed that anyone getting a divorce must also be an adulterer. People's revulsion over the betrayal and deceit of adultery became embodied into their aversion toward divorce and their hostility toward divorced persons.[23]

The Fault Concept

Formerly, to get a divorce one party had to prove that he or she was the "innocent party" and that the spouse was the "guilty party." The aggrieved person had to show in court that the spouse had violated their marriage contract. Anyone obtaining a marriage license at that time automatically signed a contract stipulating that each spouse could have sex only with each other, that *she* would take care of the children, and that *he* would provide for their economic needs.[24] In support of that contract, the Tennessee Supreme Court affirmed that " 'divorce is conceived as a remedy for the innocent against the guilty.' "[25] The innocent party is harmed because the guilty spouse has violated the contract. "Harm" almost always had to be defined as adultery. Seldom could a woman (as long as they lived together) get a divorce by saying he was harming her by not providing her enough money.

In charging the spouse with adultery, however, the innocent party was never allowed to come before the court with " 'dirty hands.' "[26] If it could be shown that the innocent spouse was also an adulterer, the court could deny the petition for divorce, because they were *both* at fault. If both spouses were indeed at fault but both wanted a divorce, they had a problem: They canceled each other out and couldn't get one. A couple had precisely the same problem if neither was at fault but both wanted a divorce anyhow. To try to solve the problem of how to get a divorce if either *both* or *neither* was at fault, many couples often lied to the judge.

Before going into court they secretly agreed which of them would plead guilty to being at fault. Even though that practice was known as collusion or fraud and could be severely punished as perjury, citizens and attorneys frequently did it anyway, and judges conveniently winked at it.[27]

Moreover, under the fault system, a person could be blocked from divorce as long as the spouse opposed it. For example, Henry admitted his guilt and wanted a divorce, but Harriet refused to go to court and give it to him. Such refusals were often based on the laws connecting money to guilt and innocence. Alimony, for instance, was a punishment that the guilty spouse paid to the innocent one. Thus, Harriet told Henry she wouldn't give him a divorce until he agreed to higher alimony payments. If, however, Harriet had been the guilty party, she would have gotten no alimony: " 'If a woman has been a tramp, why reward her?' "[28] Furthermore, if Harriet had indeed been guilty, Henry wouldn't have been able to collect alimony because Harriet (like most women of her day) had no independent income of her own. Since Henry pled guilty, Harriet's attorney advised her to hold out for as much alimony as possible. As one attorney put it, " 'It's the screwing he gets for the screwing he got.' "[29]

Like cash, property awards (residences, furnishings, cars) were used in precisely the same fashion—to get as much as possible in exchange for the divorce. The greater and "uglier" the husband's guilt, the greater the amount of property she could demand. Money and property were defined as a "reward for virtue and a punishment for sin."[30] Contested divorce proceedings often became media circuses, especially if the parties were celebrities. The idea was to be as lurid and salacious as the judge would allow in order to convince the jury to award generous settlements. If the woman was a movie star and had money, the husband's attempts to prove the enormity of her guilt became particularly juicy. Court ex-

Former model Ivana Trump reacts to reporters and cameras as she enters the New York divorce court in downtown Manhattan. Ivana and Donald Trump both appeared for a hearing, ending more than two years of haggling over the financial settlement of their 1991 divorce.

hibits that proved very effective were photos of the guilty party (woman or man) in bed with the interloper, taken surreptitiously by private detectives.

Even when the amounts of money and property were not large, court awards were always emotionally charged. They were perceived as symbolic of the moral virtue of the innocent party. Since it was almost always husbands who controlled money and property, for them divorce was frequently very costly. Weitzman argues that the fault concept *discouraged* divorce precisely because it was so costly to men. That was especially true for middle- and working-class men whose assets were generally limited to small equities in their home and car, their life insurance, and a modest savings account.

A Blocked Exit   In effect, the fault concept was a powerful external constraint on the couple's choices. Recall from Chapter 7 that the Great Depression kept engaged couples from getting married because they couldn't afford it. Similarly, fault laws kept married couples from getting divorced, once again because they couldn't afford it. Even though one or both of them perceived their erotic friendship to be in a long-term dissolution phase, they were blocked from terminating its *formal* aspect, that is, marriage. Most men lacked the economic resources to support two households—the old and the new. Women (whites, especially) were generally not employed. And those who were were seldom economically autonomous. Consequently, how could women support themselves and their children apart from generous alimony, property, and child payments?

Because divorces were so difficult to obtain, it was probably not uncommon for some marriages of that period to have ceased being erotic friendships. Although the couple remained married and co-residing, their dissolution phase persisted so long they may have stopped defining one another as exclusive sexual partners. They may no longer have perceived themselves as a special we-group. Emotional feelings of jealousy subsided to the point of being almost nil, and norms of monogamy and sexual exclusivity became virtually nonexistent. One or both may have been having casual sex and/or an external erotic friendship. Very likely each spouse knew about the other's sexual connections (if any). But they had silently negotiated an agreement to look the other way. That was the sort of arrangement worked out between Eleanor and President Roosevelt. After uncovering his sexual indiscretion, she never slept with him again, but lived with him until his death in 1945. That was, to be sure, an extreme resolution of their conflict. Very likely, most married couples in a long-term dissolution phase simply continued defining one another as sexual partners, even though they seldom actually had intercourse with each other, and even if one or both had outside sexual connections.

Many persons living in those situations of

long-term dissolution (wives in particular) were very likely to feel that "my life is out of my control; it's out of my hands." Chapter 11 said that one apparent result of women feeling out of control was what Betty Friedan called "the problem that has no name"—wives' depression and emotional ill-health. Few wives had Eleanor Roosevelt's option to take charge of her life by becoming an internationally recognized, independent political figure in her own right. The great majority had to be fortunate enough to have a relationship that gave them what they wanted, or they had to accept the relationship they had. Rigid divorce laws and women's economic dependence made leaving difficult. Women's economic dependence also made the option of staying but significantly changing the relationship (as Ingrid did in Chapter 11) both difficult and uncommon.

THE DIVORCE REVOLUTION

Many citizens (especially those from the left side of Figure 1-1) viewed those kinds of marital situations (including collusion, fraud, and perjury) as hypocritical and intolerable. Hence, during the 1960s they targeted the California legislature with the goal of removing the fault concept, thus reforming divorce laws.[31] Interestingly, the debate between progressives and conservatives over divorce reform started during the late 1880s and raged rather fiercely until 1914, when the United States turned its attention to World War I. The debate revived between 1920 and 1960. However, William O'Neill notes that during the years between the 1880s and the 1960s, much was said but very little was actually done in the way of basic divorce reform. About the only concessions that progressives were able to wrest from a few state legislatures during that period was the broadening of the grounds for fault. In particular, some ordinary citizens began to entertain the idea that cruelty might

be included under the fault concept. Cruelty was defined as physical, mental, and or emotional abuse.

Just as with adultery, however, the innocent party had to prove in court that the guilty party had been cruel. A woman who continued living with an abusive husband often undermined her case because the courts (white male judges) tended to ask "If it's that bad, why didn't you move out?" Of course if she did move out, she'd have no way to support herself and her children. An additional catch 22 tagged to the cruelty fault was that if he was being cruel to her, she was driving him to it. Recall from Chapter 12 that male violence sometimes tends to be excused on the grounds that she's partly to blame, often because of flirting with other men. Indeed, by the 1960s even the adultery of the guilty party began to be viewed in that same light. If, for example, she charged him in court with adultery, his attorney might retort that she was partly to blame because she was "frigid in bed. A good wife knows how to keep her husband in her own bed."

Ironically, Progressives had argued for decades that notions of innocence and fault are nothing but myths. Their goal, however, was never to condone either adultery or cruelty to women. They simply wished to undercut the myths. Nevertheless, by the sixties the idea that there is no such thing as an innocent party to a divorce became popularly accepted. But we have learned that if both were guilty, then both were blocked from divorce. This sort of impasse became yet another reason why there was little public outcry opposing divorce reform.

Legal Innovations

Weitzman asserts that the no-fault divorce law first passed by the California legislature, and later adopted by the remainder of the states, was a revolution because it introduced "six major innovations."[32] First, the new laws got rid of the idea of grounds, or reasons, for divorce. The notion that divorce must be justified on the basis of certain universally recognized moral criteria was dismissed. Second, the new laws did away with notions of innocence and guilt. No more was there an aggrieved plaintiff seeking to prove the spouse guilty of moral laxity of one kind or another, usually sexual. Hence the cultural idea that divorce is shameful was successfully undermined. Third, each spouse had the unilateral right to obtain a divorce quite apart from the consent of the other. The old image of one spouse giving the other his or her freedom was blanked out.

Fourth, because fault has vanished, there can be no connection between fault and finances. Since there were no more guilty parties, they couldn't be punished by being forced to reward innocent parties with money and property. Instead, the new standard for awarding money and property became each spouse's own financial resources and needs. Fifth, the new standards for awarding money and property stemmed from the ideology of gender equality, or at least gender neutrality. The old law was based on the belief that because the man is the provider he is economically responsible for the woman, who in turn is dependent on him. Inspired by the revived feminism of the 1960s, the reformers repudiated women's economic dependence. In its place they asserted that because women are the equals of men, they should no longer suffer the indignity of being supported by, and thus being dependent on, him.

A few reformers also wished to undermine the cultural stereotype that some husbands were being unjustly burdened by ex-wives lavishly "living it up" on their former husbands' earnings. In that same vein of gender equality, the reformers insisted that no longer should mothers automatically get child custody. The new standard became "the best

interests of the child." Joint custody was viewed as a prime means to serve the child's interests, and the new law made mothers equally responsible with fathers for child support.

Finally, the new law aimed at replacing the former adversarial, and often ugly, courtroom circuses with "civilized" discussions and negotiations. Since spouses didn't have to prove one another guilty of fault, they weren't forced to lie or collude or commit fraud. Weitzman compared studies of persons getting divorces under a fault system with persons getting divorces under a no-fault concept.[33] She reports that persons under the no-fault system were much more satisfied because they could be honest and straightforward: They felt they weren't being coerced into the hypocrisy, falsehood, and acrimony of the old system. For the first time ever, the notion of an amicable or friendly divorce seeped into the public consciousness. Previously, most people held that the very thought that divorced persons could be civil—perhaps even friendly—toward each other was an outrageous flight of fantasy. But today studies show that for some divorced persons, that fantasy has become reality.[34] Perhaps the best known example in recent years is the divorce but ongoing friendship and work partnership between William Masters and Virginia Johnson, the famed 1960s' sex researchers who were named the successors to Alfred Kinsey.

FROM MARITAL PERMANENCE *TO* PERMANENT AVAILABILITY

In 1971, about the same time that divorce reform was occurring in California, the United Kingdom (England, Scotland, and Wales) put into place its Divorce Reform Act. Between 1960 and 1980 divorce petitions in the United Kingdom went up almost six times, from 30,000 to 170,000.[35] One result of divorce reform there is the same as it has been in the

United States, Canada, and virtually all other Western nations: Reform helped contribute to sharp increases in divorce rates (Table 13-2). Persons marrying before the sixties expected they would stay together *forever* (or at least until death). Today the most that can be said is that one "hopes for the best."[36] Most persons entering their first formal marriage, thus signifying their commitment to spend the "rest of our lives together," fervently hope that will happen. Conservative religious couples are convinced it will. But many never legally married couples have already experienced one or more informal marriages. And whether they have or not, they're well aware that their first formal marriage may not be their last marriage, either formal or informal. British sociologist Ronald Fletcher describes this situation in strikingly dramatic terms: the "shaking of the foundations of family and society."

From Constraint to Choice

Whether today's situation actually ranks as being earth shaking, everyone agrees it's extremely significant. The change is important not merely because of the fact that today's couples can no longer expect the sort of stability that characterized the marriages of earlier generations. What is more important is what underlies that fact—*choice* rather than constraint. Even couples who firmly believe they will stay together feel that way because they're convinced they can make it work: They feel they can discuss and negotiate in ways that will achieve the balance of me-ness and we-ness described in Chapter 11. By contrast to earlier generations, their expected stability does not stem chiefly from beliefs such as, "once married, always married," or "divorce is a wrong and shameful act." Persons expecting stability today believe they will be choosing to stay committed: They will stay together because they *want* to, not because they *have* to.

Even today's religious conservatives no longer tolerate the idea of being caught for life in a painful dissolution phase. Although they reject divorce, they believe that troubled couples who earnestly seek help from a religious counselor can in fact resolve their difficulties.[37] Nevertheless, Judith Stacey reports that evangelicals endorsing the notion that they need not tolerate unhappiness (a declining sense of we-ness and me-ness) become divorce prone.[38] Just like the choices of everyone else in Western societies, evangelicals' choices are now enhanced by two external social forces—the legal divorce revolution and the women's employment revolution. Hence, even if one declares vehemently that "marriage is for life" because it's God's will or for other reasons, down deep she or he realizes that today it doesn't *have* to be for life. Everyone knows that if it gets *too* bad, the range of choices is much greater than the choices available a few decades ago.

Availability and Control

Powerful beliefs in the permanence of marriage as well as low divorce rates masked a great deal of 1950s' "quiet desperation," especially on the part of women. Chapters 5 and 11 showed that today most persons are shifting from the idea that permanence is a good thing in and of itself to a belief in what Bernard Farber called *permanent availability*.[39] Today, people believe that if the relationship is good, permanence becomes an inevitable result. If it's not good, many people ask, "Why stay together?" Each person is thought to be free at all times to choose to be, or *not* to be, available for an(other) erotic friendship. That choice is a constant feature coloring everything about today's erotic friendships. The prevailing belief is that most persons need not remain in an unsatisfying relationship unless (like Helga with Hans in Chapter 5) they choose to do so for the time being.

Possessing availability gives people a certain feeling of control over their erotic friendships rarely enjoyed by pre-sixties' persons.

That sense of control contributes potentially (along with other things such as a good job and good health) to a person's overall sense of well-being, as described in Chapter 11. Some persons today, of course, still feel caught by their marriages (formal or informal) and see no way out. Many other people leaving one web of relationships for another discover themselves more hemmed in and out of control than they were before![40] Nevertheless, the possibilities for change and thus control at least *seem* to be more real and salient to greater numbers of people now than they were during the 1950s.

UNFORESEEN NEGATIVE CONSEQUENCES OF DIVORCE REFORM

We just saw that many people today question the wisdom of remaining indefinitely in a dissolution phase. We also learned that the idea of people being coerced in that manner was a major issue for the divorce reform movement. Weitzman reports that in California the reformers originally proposed that a family court be made part of the changes.[41] Troubled couples would be required to obtain counseling that might restore them once again to a maintenance and change phase. Couples that either could not or would not resolve their differences would be assisted by a mediator in negotiating an amicable divorce settlement, particularly if children were involved. That mediation feature led some conservatives and many moderate citizens to support divorce reform. Weitzman says that even the Roman Catholic Church, which officially rejects divorce, did not oppose reform largely because of that family court feature. At the last minute, however, legislators were forced to compromise the court out of the bill. Lawyers lobbied against the court, says Weitzman, because they were fearful of nonlawyers (e.g., counselors, mediators) advising potential clients.

The failure of states to integrate family courts into their no-fault divorce systems is but one reason for what Weitzman and others call the unexpected negative outcomes of reform.[42] The negative outcomes cluster mostly around what happens to women and children after a contemporary divorce. Table 13-4 shows that although growing numbers of solo mothers have never been married, most solo mothers were married and then got divorced. The effect of a divorce today on many working- and lower-class mothers is to depress their standard of living so drastically that they become near-poor or actually poor.[43] The definition of "poor" is based on the government figure of how many dollars it takes for a family of four to survive in an urban environment. In 1989 that calculation was $12,675.[44] If you look again at Table 13-6, it's easy to see that the majority of solo mothers and their children live under or somewhat above (e.g., $13,000–$19,000) the poverty line.

Relative Deprivation

Simultaneously, the effect of divorce reform on many middle- and upper-middle-class wives was to create a sharp turn downward in their postdivorce standard of living. Weitzman uses the term *relative deprivation* to capture what happens to wives who had a comfortable life before divorce. Her argument is that the greater the husband's income before divorce the less well off the wife is after divorce compared with her husband. Weitzman found that among working-class couples whose *pre*divorce family income was under $20,000, the wife's *post*divorce income was $6,500; but the husband's was $11,950, a difference of $5,450.[45]

Next, Weitzman examined middle-class couples whose predivorce family income was $40,000 or more. The postdivorce income of the wives was $8,500; the husband's income was $28,640, a difference of $20,140. Placing that $20,140 alongside the $5,450, we can conclude that the middle-class wives are much worse off than working-class wives compared with their ex-husbands. And middle-class wives *perceive* themselves as worse off. Someone could say that the middle-class wives are better-off than the working-class wives because their annual income is $2,000 higher ($8,500 vs. $6,500). Indeed, Leslie Morgan points out that after divorce settlements, "Middle-class wives typically fare better [than other wives] in objective terms."[46] Nevertheless, compared with what their husbands are getting, middle-class wives *feel* they're a lot worse off. Working-class wives may be more likely to figure there isn't much of a difference between what they're getting and what their ex-husbands are getting. A sense of relative deprivation makes a person feel out of control, which increases stress symptoms and undermines feelings of emotional well-being.

Trying to maintain their earlier $40,000+ lifestyle on $8,500 is extraordinarily more difficult for middle-class women than it is for husbands trying to do the same thing on $28,640. Consequently, middle-class ex-wives are likely to feel even more out of control, and to have more severe stress symptoms, than their ex-husbands. They might even have more stress than working-class wives. However, we learned earlier that middle-class wives tend to have several advantages over working- and lower-class wives. One is fewer children, meaning that their resources don't have to be stretched quite as far.

Midlife Women and Changes in the Rules

Another 1970s' study showed that the postdivorce period can be extremely traumatic for upper-middle-class wives, quite apart from a sharp reduction in available dollars.[47] What seemed to be especially painful for the women in this study, those in midlife in particular, was that their identity as a person was wrapped up in a very comfortable, pleasant, and orderly way of life. Their suburban lifestyle often included heavy involvement in their community, for example voluntary organizations such as PTA, churches, charities, civic improvement

groups, and so on. The more intelligent, talented, and educated the ex-wives were, the more distressed they were likely to feel. Their postdivorce deprivation made them keenly aware that in order to be a Good Wife and mother, as well as a conscientious community volunteer, they'd had to set aside any ideas for "something of their own"—a job or career, for example, in which they might have done quite well. That pain became even greater if they perceived themselves to be more gifted and intelligent than their ex-husbands. After fifteen, twenty, or more years of failing to pursue seriously their own occupational interests, and living instead to please their husbands and children, many midlife ex-wives suddenly perceived themselves doing much worse off than their less talented ex-husbands.

Complements and Junior Partners Studies of the 1970s' and 1980s' divorce experiences of midlife women are very important.[48] Those women are historically unique because they got married under one set of rules but got divorced under a totally different set. For all its flaws, the fault system did serve to protect women's interests, and thereby the interests of their children.[49] Women's interests, however, were integrally connected with and inseparable from their roles either as *complement* or as *junior partner.* Chapter 10 described the complement as the wife who lived for, and to fulfill the needs of, her husband and children. She had no strong wish to be employed. Occasionally she entered the labor force on a temporary basis to help meet a particular family need. The junior partner was described as the wife who worked more or less on a continuous basis. However, neither she nor her spouse defined her occupation as important or as significant as his. He is the senior partner and chief provider; she is the secondary provider.

Equal Partners by Fiat As either complement or junior partner, the wife was dependent on the husband for economic support. If they divorced the rules were clear: He had to continue taking care of her. In contrast, the no-fault concept challenged women's dependence and by fiat declared women and men to be equal! However, declaring something to be true by executive order is one thing; making it a reality is quite something else again. The thirteen American colonies declared their independence from England in 1776. But it took seven years of bitter war for the declaration to become a reality.

The basic flaw with the no-fault concept is that by trying to make women equal overnight, its framers failed to figure out how to overcome centuries of gender inequality. Women who had been married in the 1950s and 1960s under the old rules as complements and junior partners suddenly found themselves divorcing during the 1970s and 1980s under the new rules asserting them to be what Chapter 10 called *equal partners*. In reality they weren't equal partners at all, because relatively few couples had (or have) the kinds of shared definitions under which that label makes sense. For example, one of the key definitions of equal partners is that the woman, like her partner, pursues the goal of economic autonomy. Somehow the designers of the no-fault system assumed that after the sixties most women had magically passed from being economically dependent to being economically autonomous. The fact is that most women were not autonomous, even if they were employed. Hence when they got divorced under the new laws abolishing alimony, they discovered that without their husbands earnings they were in serious economic straits. Their burdens were multiplied because of two additional unfulfilled ideals of the no-fault concept: Men would assume equal responsibility for child caretaking, including joint custody where possible, and the ex-spouse with the most economic resources would be financially responsible for the children. How did this work out? In 1990 there were 10 million women living with children under age 21

whose father was absent from the home.[50] Of those 10 million, merely half had been awarded child support, and thus were supposed to receive child-support payments during 1989. Among this half, only another half (2.5 million) received the full amount due. Of the others, some got nothing and others received only partial, often minimal and erratic, payments. In short, many solo mothers today lack the education and/or experience to compete effectively in the job market but often find themselves chiefly responsible for the day-to-day material (and emotional) needs of their children. It was this grim reality that catapulted Sondra into becoming part of her social family.

REFORMING THE REFORMS

Deborah Rhode and Martha Minnow offer a broad agenda for correcting the flaws of the no-fault system. Advocates are trying to make the reforms more *responsible*—more attuned to the interests of children and women, as well as men. We've already learned that the main reform offered by some conservatives is to enact laws making divorce by parents of dependent children virtually impossible to obtain.[51] Rhode and Minnow, along with most citizens, wonder if forcing couples to remain indefinitely in a dissolution phase is genuinely in the best interests of the child, to say nothing of the adults' interests. A connected point stems from Table 13-4. The number of solo parents who have never been married and divorced is increasing rapidly. Solutions aimed at addressing the needs of divorced solo mothers must be broad enough to encompass the needs of never-married solo mothers as well.

Furthermore, say Rhode and Minnow, reforming the reforms must take into account the termination of informal marriages. They state that growing numbers of informal couples are now sharing finances and property, as well as extensive child caretaking responsibilities. Consequently, when terminating, they, like formal couples, are forced to address matters of financial settlements and child custody.

Rhode and Minnow suggest that a fundamental reform is to place erotic friendships and families more in the context of what Chapter 11 called the "public household." Adults negotiating the financial settlements and child caretaking arrangements inherent to the termination of relationships need to be concerned for much more than their own interests. However, Rhode & Minnow are very much aware that concern for the broader social fabric is difficult enough even when couples do not hold deep hostilities and mistrust for one another. And when they're suspicious and hostile, as is often the case while they're negotiating termination settlements, socially responsible conflict resolution is highly elusive. To try to move in that direction, the State of Florida now requires that divorcing couples struggling to resolve conflicts over children and money must allow a mediator to assist them.

Because effective decision-making is elusive during termination struggles, women's autonomy becomes a pivotal matter. Whatever other fresh reforms are put in place, the broader issue of women's behaviors in the workplace, alongside men's behaviors in the home place (child care and housework), must be central to them. Chapter 11 said that women who are economically autonomous are more able to discuss and negotiate effectively, and thus achieve equitable outcomes, than women who are not autonomous. If that conclusion holds while erotic friends are discussing or negotiating during a maintenance and change phase, it would seem doubly true if they ever arrive at the point of having to negotiate the distribution of money and property, and the caretaking of children. The fact that gender equality is *implicit* in the no-fault system is by itself no flaw. Indeed, the great majority of Americans say they believe in gender equality.[52] Chapter 18 shows that the flaw stems from failing to invent public policies making gender equality an *explicit* issue with which women and men must struggle throughout their life courses.

DIVORCE—AN AMERICAN "TRADITION"

Social historian Glenda Riley labels divorce an American tradition.[53] She argues that there is nothing new in the idea of married women and men struggling with each other. Furthermore, at least since the eighteenth century (the Colonial era), evidence shows that many women and men have been deeply dissatisfied with their marriages. In an attempt to respond to that reality, the American colonies established divorce laws that were a bit more permissive than those in Anglican England or Roman Catholic Europe. At that time, except for the Lutheran and Calvinist parts of Europe, it was virtually impossible for ordinary citizens to obtain a divorce for *any* reason.[54] The American colonies, and later the states, were influenced a great deal by the comparatively permissive Calvinist approach to divorce based on the *fault* concept. Hence the American laws enacted in the eighteenth and nineteenth centuries made at least some divorces possible under that concept.

In addition, both Riley and Roderick Phillips add that even if fault couldn't be proven or one spouse wouldn't grant a divorce, strict laws were not a foolproof way of boxing people into a long-term dissolution phase. Until the early 1900s, North America was a vast and often uncharted frontier. The records suggest that many persons who felt frustrated at being unable to divorce, either because they couldn't afford it or were denied it, simply took off and disappeared into burgeoning urban centers or "out West." Because it was virtually impossible to trace those persons, they were often able to start new lives and create new families. It was not uncommon for newspapers to carry notices pleading for aid in uncovering the whereabouts of a wife or husband who had deserted her or his spouse and helpless children. Consequently, when Riley says divorce is an American "tradition," she means that long before the no-fault concept persons were figuring out ways (including desertion) to escape what the Japanese call the pains of *gaman*—an interminable dissolution phase. Others thought of it as escaping from the "empty shell" marriage.[55]

Another escape (described in Chapter 5) was to stay with the marriage but to form and maintain a second and secret erotic friendship. This choice involved enormous risks for wives. If husband found out he could severely beat the woman and receive tacit community support for doing it. The husband could also divorce the wife, leaving her penniless and childless. In spite of those risks, Riley suspects that many more wives made that choice than today's liberated persons might think. Riley adds that husbands—because of the double standard—had the additional option of easy (but discreet) access to a flourishing trade in prostitution.

Divorce as "Failure"

Although divorce, desertion, and extramarital sex may have been very much a part of North American society, they were never culturally sanctioned. Few things were more highly prized than a successful marriage. Having a successful marriage meant avoiding divorce. A stable marriage was a successful one. The couple was doing whatever they must to stay together. Couples who divorced had unstable (i.e., unsuccessful) marriages. Friends and kin whispered in hushed tones that "their marriage had *failed*." Quite apart from the adultery issue, stigma was attached to the inability of couples to "hang tough during tough times." People whose marriages failed were suspected of personality defects, or lack of moral fiber, or perhaps worse. On the other hand, couples with successful marriages were congratulated because of their obvious personal and moral superiority. They were accorded high levels of prestige, esteem, and respect.

Those powerful beliefs operated at cross-purposes with divorce as an American tradition. It seems likely that many persons wishing to leave their marriages were kept from doing so out of fear of being labeled a quitter. Even now, says Herma Kay, most North Americans do not accept divorce as normal social occurrence.[56] How can divorce be "normal" if it is still labeled as failure? Earlier chapters noted that the responsibility for marital success was not equally distributed between husband and wife. Wives were perceived as chiefly responsible for marital success; husbands were mainly responsible for occupational success. To be successful, wives were required to give in to, and placate, their husbands' wishes. Many marriage failures were thus avoided by wives placing their husband's interests ahead of their own. As (younger) women now become increasingly unwilling to behave in that subordinate fashion, it becomes ever more difficult for marriages (formal or informal) to remain stable on that account.

Family Disorganization and Breakdown

Alongside the idea that divorce represents failure is a second cultural belief. That is that divorce signifies family disorganization, breakdown, and disintegration. Disorganization happens, said William Goode in 1976, when wives and husbands cease doing their roles—the things they're supposed to do. What spouses were "supposed" to do was stay together and take care of their children—husbands by supporting them, wives by nurturing them. If adults don't fulfill their roles, the question was and is, who will take care of their children? The belief was, and still is for many people, that when adults fail to perform their roles properly, children suffer and thus the whole society is weakened. According to Sylvia Ann Hewlett (and others), the outcome of widespread family breakdown is chaos and social disorganization.[57]

Termination and Transition

As long as women had the moral obligation to love husbands and children more than themselves, it might have made some sense to label divorce as failure. But Chapters 10 and 11 said that things have gotten as complicated for today's women as they've always been for men. For centuries, men have had to figure out how to balance love for themselves with love for their neighbors (i.e., wives and children). If he had to be away from home for weeks, months, even years at a time, that was okay because he sent money to his family. If he never saw his children because he worked from before they got up until after they went to bed, that too was okay because he was doing it for them. Men achieved that balance of two loves because women were supposed to have only one love—their families. Now that growing numbers of women are assuming the obligation to love themselves as much as their neighbors, things have gotten extraordinarily more complex. Chapter 11 showed how difficult it is for women and men to negotiate their equally compelling obligations to one another, to their children, and to themselves.[58] Trying to do it represents a contradiction in logic. Nevertheless, increasing numbers of couples are trying to do it anyhow.

But remember that the ultimate ideal, or goal, is no longer marital permanence. Few of today's couples are striving for stability at any cost as their parents and grandparents did.[59] The famous football coach, Vince Lombardi, once said that winning is *everything*. But other coaches tell their players that winning is not as important as whether they play the game as well and as hard as they possibly can. Under the old rules, most married couples believed that winning was everything. Staying together was, of course, the definition of winning.

By contrast, today's erotic friends (whether in formal or informal settings) are inventing new rules, the objective of which is no longer winning (stability) at any cost. The objective now is to play as hard and as well as they can. Among other things, loving one's neighbor as much as oneself means to discuss and negotiate in as fair and as caring a way as possible. If at some point during their attempts to negotiate unresolved conflicts one or both adults perceive it would be better for them (and any children) to terminate the action (as Helga did in Chapter 5), then it makes no sense to call that a failure resulting in breakdown and disorganization. Instead many sociologists prefer to label the changes as *termination* resulting in *transition*.[60] Importantly, those labels are the same for informal as for formal marriages. And they apply to girlfriends/boyfriends as well.

The reason Helga believed that terminating her relationship with Hans was better than keeping it was because she became convinced he didn't love her as much as he loved himself. In her view, he no longer had the capacity to be fair and caring toward her. Just as important, she sensed she could no longer fulfill her obligation to love herself if she stayed with him. Under the new rules, Ann Swidler argues that at that point in their relationship Hans's response to Helga should have been: "I love you, therefore I want what's best for you, even if that means termination."[61] Instead, his response was governed by the *old* rules: "I love you, therefore you are mine forever." Even as Hans was refusing to let her go, however, Helga was taking steps to terminate their erotic friendship. Chapter 5 showed that although they remained married and co-residing, she was already in transition: First, she was getting the education that would make her economically independent from Hans (and any other man). Second, she was maintaining a covert erotic friendship with Kurt that would eventually become public when she separated from Hans and later moved in with Kurt.

Starting a New Life   If Helga herself is asked, she would respond that for her, termination and transition were positive events in her life course. She would not think of herself as experiencing failure or marital breakdown. Like the women Catherine Riessman interviewed for her study, she sees herself as starting a new life.[62] To be sure, Riessman's respondents also experienced a great deal of pain, suffering, and disappointment as they sensed themselves moving out of a maintenance and change phase and into a dissolution phase. As their dissolution phase continued to wind downward—as their feelings of we-ness became increasingly weaker—their stress and anxiety grew accordingly. Early in her dissolution phase, Helga felt very much out of control of her life. She sensed that Hans could or would not do for her what she wanted—they could not negotiate their conflicts. As time went by and she began to take control of her own life, her stress levels stopped getting worse. As her sense of me-ness increased she began to feel better about herself even though she was still living with Hans. Her new life was beginning long before she separated from, and later divorced, Hans: It began during the same time that her old life was winding down.

Helga was taking charge of her life to fulfill her moral obligation to love herself. Nevertheless, by passing through these transitions, she was causing Hans a lot of grief, anxiety, and stress. How does that fulfill her moral obligation to love him? Helga has no certain answer except to say that although in the short run it is painful, in the long run she believes it is best for both of them (and also for their resident child) to go their separate ways. Since she cannot love him in the ways he deserves to be loved, how can it be in his best interest for her to remain with him?

The upshot is that growing numbers of persons are beginning to define termination and transition as part of the creation and *re*invention of their erotic friendships in particular, and their life course in general.[63] For that reason, termination and transition are increasingly perceived as positive, that is, *good* things. They stand in sharp contrast to the negative cultural images attached to labeling divorce as failure, disorganization, or breakdown.

The paradox is that good things always come at a high price. In many cases, persons such as Hans perceive their own lives being diminished by their partners *re*-creation. In other cases, women and children suffer severe economic deprivation. (Chapter 16 examines the social and emotional consequences for children in connection with solo parenthood, divorce, remarriage, and so forth.) Such are the inevitable dilemmas inherent in seeking to balance obligations to love oneself with obligations to love one's partner and children. Chapter 18 suggests that growing awareness of that dilemma may spur public policies aimed at assisting couples to negotiate equitable financial and child caretaking arrangements. The solution proposed by some conservatives, namely to quash obligations to oneself, is a throwback to an earlier era.[64] It is not likely to gain many adherents.

THE DECLINING SIGNIFICANCE OF DIVORCE

Riesmann says that divorce is here to stay, and the numbers in Table 13-1 lead many people to agree with her. In view of those numbers, and in view of the "love dilemma" just discussed, is it not curiously odd to suggest that divorce could be losing its significance? In making that suggestion, we must distinguish between the event of a divorce decree and the long tradition Riley sees underlying it. The *tradition* is becoming widespread and promises to keep on growing in importance. The tradition trains our attention on the processes of relationship development described in Chapters 5 and 11. The tradition makes us focus on how people *feel* about their erotic friendships, and how they attempt to *re*construct them. The tradition helps us understand what it means to say that the event of divorce is not such a big deal after all, and every day it's becoming less and less significant.

Part of the reason the divorce event is declining in significance is because of divorce reform. The shame of adultery once connected with divorce has largely vanished. Furthermore, as people's attention becomes taken up with the processes of problem-solving and conflict resolution, it becomes increasingly apparent that divorce is not actually the end of a marriage. Recall from Chapter 9 that Larry Bumpass said that the markers of relationships are not as clearly discernible as they once were. The idea, for instance, that a formal wedding ceremony represents a unique beginning is being carefully scrutinized. Similarly, Helga's case reveals that a formal divorce decree may not represent unique endings after all. The diminishing significance of formal divorce is connected with the declining importance of formal marriage and also with the growing significance of informal marriage, as discussed in previous chapters. For example, Table 13-1 shows that for a number of years the divorce rate has been more or less on a plateau. Some observers claim the fact that divorce rates are no longer rising as steeply as they were during the 1970s is a sign that marriages are becoming more stable. They say that people have become less prone to take the easy way out.

Demographers, however, tell us the picture is not quite that simple.[65] We've already learned that first-marriage rates and remarriage rates are declining, whereas cohabitation rates are increasing and the median age at first marriage is rising. The result of all four trends is that at any given time, fewer people are living in a formal marriage than, say, during the

seventies. The fact that the pool of "legals" is down means there are fewer persons eligible for a formal divorce. If there are ten people in swimming pool A and fifty people in swimming pool B, and a chill breeze suddenly blows in, fewer persons are likely to jump out of A than out of B simply because there were fewer in A to begin with!

Chapters 9 and 10 reported that the slack in formal marriages and remarriages is being taken up by steady increases in informal marriages. Persons are not retreating from the idea of having relationships, that is, erotic friendships. The pool of couples maintaining erotic friendships is probably just as large now as it was during the 1970s. What is dramatically different today is people's caution in adding formal marriage to their erotic friendship. Fewer formal marriages mean fewer formal divorces. Nevertheless, Robert Schoen points out that among the youngest age categories he studied, termination was equally high among both marrieds and cohabitors.[66] For marrieds, termination was defined as divorce. For cohabitors, it was defined as moving out. Hence the tradition Riley says has been with us for more than two centuries is by no means diminishing: Persons whose sense of me-ness and we-ness declines significantly are not disposed to remain in erotic friendships indefinitely, regardless of whether they've been formalized.

THE HASSLES OF "GETTING-OUT"

The reality of the no-fault concept means that the hassle of getting out of a relationship is not necessarily greater for either marriage or cohabitation. As a result, the question of how difficult it is to get out is not answered by discovering whether or not the couple is formal. Instead, the basic question is, does the couple have shared money, property, and child caretaking responsibilities? So far, at least, formal couples in North America are much more likely than informal couples to share in those several ways. But remember that increasing numbers of North American informal couples have children residing with them. In addition, growing numbers of informal couples are becoming economically interdependent.

In view of those trends, a glance at the Scandinavian experience is helpful. First, the median length of informal marriages in Scandinavia tends to be longer than it is in North America.[67] Second, the longer those informal marriages persist, the more probable it is for partners to become interconnected both economically and in terms of child caretaking responsibilities. During the near future it's likely that growing numbers of North American informal marriages will also persist for longer periods, mostly because the partners (like Kate and Marshall in Chapter 10) simply postpone getting legal, or never get legal. If the partners eventually terminate, matters of finances and children may become just as relevant for them as they now are for many formal couples.

It's precisely for those kinds of reasons that Rhode and Minnow argue that safeguards must be applied to the endings of informal, as much as formal, marriages. The interests of all parties, but especially women and children, must be protected whether or not the couple is legal. Protection comes about in part via legal statutes addressing the equitable distribution of shared finances and child caretaking. Protection also comes about via public policies enhancing the economic autonomy of women as well as the domestic responsibilities of men.

In their 1993 movie, *Mrs. Doubtfire*, Robin Williams and Sally Fields portray a divorcing couple capturing the spirit of what it means to pay attention to children's interests at the same time that they're taking care of themselves. There is no hope that the couple could move on to a fresh maintenance and change phase: Instead, each must travel his or her own way. Nevertheless, they go to extraordinary lengths (e.g., Williams dresses in drag) to make sure that their three children (ages 5 to 15) are okay. The couple shows us that the old question, "Isn't divorce bad for children?" (considered further in Chapter 16), is the wrong question to ask. The more important questions are: How do couples try to keep their children from being harmed by their transition? How do they help their children to benefit and grow from the experience? In short, being a responsible parent does not mean hanging on to a relationship that is corrosive for both adults and children. But responsibility does require that every effort be made to ensure their children's well-being, as well as their own.

CONCLUSION

Divorce trends cannot be understood apart from trends showing declines in formal marriages and remarriages, as well as increases in cohabitations. Divorce trends must also be connected to increases over time in never-married childbearing. Wedding ceremonies and divorce decrees alike continue to be charged with powerful cultural meanings. Nevertheless, their significance *qua events* is diminishing relative to people's awareness that the states of being married or being divorced are not the bottom line. Persons are becoming increasingly persuaded that what is ultimately important are the patterns and processes that are central to what erotic friendships are all about. In short, how they play the game has become more vital than winning (stability) for its own sake.

Today's views on playing the game are based squarely on an historic American tradition of unwillingness to be boxed into a long-term dissolution phase. Nevertheless, divorce laws based on the fault concept once made it difficult for many persons to formally end their marriages. A positive feature of those laws, however, was their protection of wives and children. Because wives were defined as complements or junior partners, they were entitled to the husband's economic support both before and after divorce.

Although no-fault divorce reform declared wives to be equal partners, it never addressed the policies and laws that might help achieve the goal of women's economic autonomy. One result is that today large numbers of solo mothers and their children experience sharp declines in their post divorce living standards. The fact that many never-married solo mothers also lack economic autonomy means that they too are often caught in severe economic straits.

Another American cultural tradition is that divorce is a failure resulting in breakdown and social disorganization. One of the outcomes of no-fault reforms has been a gradual *redefinition* of changes occurring in the course of erotic friendships. Instead of failure, those changes are increasingly being labeled as termination and transition. People are recognizing that distress and anxiety stem from feeling out of control of one's relationship and/or one's life in general. Such feelings are likely to accompany the awareness that one's erotic friendship is sinking into a dissolution phase long before actual termination (e.g., separation or divorce) is ever contemplated. The fact that some persons feeling that way begin to take charge of their own lives is increasingly perceived as a good, that is, a *positive*, thing. It is viewed as positive because as people search for control, their stress levels are likely to diminish. The fact that searching for control sometimes means that one's partner and/or children are forced to encounter stressful challenges is perceived as unfortunate. However, the belief is that the partner and children would be worse off if the couple continued in an interminable dissolution phase. Hence it becomes critical that adults in transition behave in a responsible manner, namely, that they make every effort to place their children's interests on the same plane with their own.

The upshot is that the changes in erotic friendship known as termination and transition are increasingly being viewed as inevitable parts of the ongoing construction of the life course of most persons in modern societies. The stories of Helga and of Sondra help us to see that construction involves many things that tend to be closely interconnected. These include belonging to blood and/or social families, paid employment, domestic chores, childbearing, and child caretaking. What has been called divorce, that is, the legal decree ending a formal marriage, is but one part of the larger mosaic of one's life. And as the lives of modern persons, women in particular, become increasingly complicated, the social significance of the decree is likely to diminish further compared with the numerous other matters in which it is embedded.

NOTES

1. Timothy Egan, "Worldly and the Spiritual Clash in New Age Divorce," *The New York Times*, September 25, 1992, pp. A1, A11.
2. Lynn White, 1990.
3. Martin and Bumpass, 1989, p. 40.
4. Ibid.
5. Ibid., p. 43.
6. Ibid., p. 44.
7. Scheff and Retzinger, 1991, p. 97; Martin and Bumpass; Wilson and Clarke, 1992.
8. Fox, 1986; Michael Smith, 1989. Chapter 14 explores life-course changes in detail.
9. Lindsey, 1981; Cochran et al., 1990.
10. Weitzman, 1985, p. xiv. Also see Richard Peterson, 1989; and Holden and Smock, 1991.
11. Krause, 1990.
12. U.S. Bureau of the Census, *Current Population Reports*, P-20, No. 450, May 1991, pp. 7, 8.
13. Marsiglio, 1991.
14. U.S. Bureau of the Census, Table N.
15. Ibid.
16. Cochran et al.
17. Kay, 1990, p. 6.
18. Goode, 1956.
19. As governor of California, Mr. Reagan also signed a liberalized abortion statute (before the

U.S. Supreme Court *Roe v. Wade* decision) that set a pattern followed by many other states.

20. Weitzman, p. 18.
21. Joanie M. Schrof, "Wedding Bands Made of Steel," *US News & World Report*, April 6, 1992, pp. 62, 63.
22. Lash, 1971, pp. 302ff.
23. O'Neill, 1967.
24. Weitzman, 1981.
25. Weitzman, 1985, p. 10.
26. Ibid.
27. Ibid.
28. Ibid., p. 12.
29. Ibid.
30. Ibid., p. 13.
31. Weitzman, 1985, pp. 15ff.
32. Ibid., pp. 15, 16.
33. Ibid, pp. 37ff.
34. Berman, 1985; Masheter and Harris, 1986; Ambert, 1989.
35. Fletcher, 1988, p. 49.
36. Espenshade, 1985; Thornton, 1989; Schoen, 1992.
37. Bellah et al., 1985; Stellway, 1990.
38. Stacey, 1990.
39. Farber, 1964.
40. An example can be seen in the story of Sondra before she became part of a social family. Solo parents sometimes feel out of control, which is accompanied by high stress levels.
41. Weitzman, 1985, pp. 18ff.
42. See various chapters in Sugarman and Hill, 1990. For an international perspective on un-

foreseen negative consequences of divorce reform, see Weitzman and Maclean, 1992.

43. Garrison, 1990.
44. U.S. Bureau of the Census, *Current Population Reports*, P-23, No. 173, July 1991, p. 18.
45. Weitzman, 1985, p. 333.
46. Leslie Morgan, 1991, p. 144.
47. Wallerstein and Kelly, 1980.
48. For example, Halem, 1982; Morgan.
49. Rhode and Minnow, 1990, p. 193.
50. U.S. Bureau of the Census, *Current Population Reports*, P-23, No. 177, February 1992, p. 2.
51. See Note 21.
52. Thornton.
53. Glenda Riley, 1991.
54. Roderick Phillips, 1988.
55. Cuber and Harroff, 1965; Goode, 1976.
56. Kay, p. 28.
57. Hewlett, 1991.
58. Scanzoni, 1991.
59. Stacy.
60. Furstenberg and Spanier, 1984; Espenshade, 1985; Scanzoni et al., 1989; Bumpass, 1990.
61. Swidler, 1980.
62. Riessman, 1990, p. 161.
63. Ibid.; Halem; Furstenberg and Spanier; see also Chapter 14.
64. See Note 21.
65. Espenshade; Schoen et al., 1985; Schoen, 1987; Martin and Bumpass, 1989; Bumpass, 1990; Schoen, 1992.
66. Schoen, 1992.
67. Trost, 1990; Manniche, 1991.

AGING, THE FAMILY LIFE CYCLE, AND LIFE COURSES

Plainly, nonviolence is responsible, and so is looking out for children's interests. But what does it mean to *age* responsibly? Like most of the questions asked in this book, this one too has no simple answer. The idea that people age has always been intertwined with the idea that people live in families. Earlier chapters talked about the many ways people are making changes in families. Similarly, people are making changes in aging. Chapter 14 tries to show how the two kinds of changes are connected. Just as we've tried to figure out what responsibility means in terms of changing families, we'll now ponder what it means to *age* in a responsible manner.

"Hey," says Ned to Ted as they meet strolling their children in the park: "You have a good-looking kid! How old is he?" "He's 19 months old," replies Ted. *Old* at 19 months? How can a *child* be old? If Ted were wheeling his 98-year-old grandmother, we might agree that's old. But 19 months? The answer, of course, is that *old*, like *beauty*, lies in the eye of the beholder. Like all the labels used in this book, "old" can be perceived and defined in

many ways. Ted is aware, for example, that although his child hasn't been around very long, the process of aging has already set in. In fact, aging began as soon as the child was born.

But that isn't what Ted's talking about, nor what Ned understands. What Ted actually means, and what Ned understands, is that his child is 19 months *grown*. For a child, aging is viewed as a process of growth and development. *Old* means movement toward becoming an independent and competent adult. For the toddler, many important and highly significant years lie ahead. The very core of our understanding of childhood is that nothing is ever standing still.

As children age, they grow physically stronger and mentally more alert. With each passing year they extend their degree of control over their lives. "What are you going to be when you grow up?" reminds them that childhood and adolescence are not permanent statuses. Nor do the youths want them to be. They want to grow up. They perceive adulthood as a time when they can finally take charge of their own lives instead of being controlled by adults. The curious thing is that although every youth wants to age ("I want to be 16 so I can drive; 18 so I can vote; 21 so I can drink"), *no adult wants to keep on aging*. It's actually not so odd, because up to a point biological aging corresponds with an increase in the degree of control a person has over her or his life. The word "old" describes Ted's grandmother because, among other things, she has little control over her existence. She's at one polar extreme while her 24-year-old great-granddaughter, Monika, is at the other. Monika's just finished college and has taken a good job. She feels more in control of her life than she ever has before.

Already, however, Monika senses the paradox that with continued aging comes the threat of loss of control. She can't seem to do much, for instance, about the almost imperceptible decline she's recently noticed in her physical beauty. And although Monika's always managed to keep her weight under control, suddenly she finds herself 10 pounds above the charts and counting. Much grimmer is the news she's just received about her 30-year-old cousin, a professional dancer and dance instructor. He's been diagnosed with multiple sclerosis (MS). The incurable disease is gradually causing him to lose control of his legs. As that happens, he perceives his whole life becoming chaotic and pointless. Monika is shocked—it's bad enough to be 30, to say nothing of having one's life shattered by such an uncontrollable, and often fatal, illness.

Monika has a particular view of her past, present, and future life. Her view is probably shared by most persons of her age and education, especially if they've been fortunate enough to find a good job. She views her childhood and adolescence as having been a time of steadily increasing control of her life in every dimension—physical, mental, emotional, social, and financial. The present is seen as a kind of plateau during which her cousin's illness, along with many other things, impresses her with the fact that life can indeed spin out of

control. Nevertheless, Monika views the future with guarded optimism. She expects to be able to maintain full control of her life. To achieve that goal she intends to keep on growing mentally, emotionally, and socially, and she hopes to earn enough money to continue being economically autonomous. She intends to cope with her body's aging as best she can by staying fit via aerobic exercise and "eating right."

CONTROL AND RESPONSIBILITY

Arlene Skolnick describes Monika's view of her life as part of an emerging "life course revolution."[1] According to Skolnick, the *revolution* lies with the different ways today's persons are beginning to view the courses of their lives. Aging has always been an inevitable fact of being alive. The big question is, how do people respond to aging? Until the advent of modern medicine, sanitation, and nutrition, people passively accepted the idea that fate alone determined how long their lives would be. The science and technology of the twentieth century have brought about dramatic changes in how long people in industrial societies can expect to live. Now, instead of passively accepting fate, persons can actively take control to increase their longevity. The *quantity* of their years is expanded significantly through proper diet, sanitation, antibiotics and vaccines, laser surgery, and so on.

A growing number of researchers are saying that a similar kind of revolution is spreading in the social sciences such as sociology and psychology.[2] Here the revolution focuses on the *quality* of the increased number of years available to many persons. These researchers believe that life quality is achieved in much the same way as life quantity: Persons actively seek to take greater control over their lives. Consequently, researchers are beginning to study "human control" (also known as *human agency*) in contemporary societies.[3] Chapters 5 and 11 talked about the feelings of well-being that arise from perceiving that one is participating effectively in the control of one's erotic friendship. But a person's life consists of many realms. To feel good about herself in general, Monika needs to feel she has a reasonable amount of control not only over her erotic friendship but also over her health and her job.[4]

That's where responsibility enters the picture. Control over one's life course goes with the moral obligation to love oneself described in Chapter 10. In part, the life course revolution means that a moral person is obliged to take charge of her or his life course as fully as possible.[5] Loving oneself, and thus taking care of oneself implies that it's irresponsible to sit back passively and merely accept that "what will be will be." Taking over the management of one's life course is a topic to which sociologists have only recently turned their attention. Previously, sociologists were preoccupied with social control. The topic of social control is, "How does society get persons to do what they're supposed to do to achieve social order?" The answer? Socialization via The Family, church, and school. If people still don't conform, punish them via the legal system. Today, by contrast, sociologists are asking, "How can persons do what they must to achieve a sense of life-course control and thus experience the well-being that accompanies it?" The answer is explored in this chapter. As the reader will recognize, it is woven throughout the book.[6]

AGING AND THE FAMILY LIFE CYCLE

One of the most popular ideas that stemmed from the old views of socialization and social control was known as the family life cycle (FLC). It was popular because it blended important social behaviors with biological aging. The basic idea of FLC is simple indeed: As persons age biologically they behave in socially appropriate ways. The behaviors are "appropriate" because they promote the well-being of

Premarital stage (expected to be childless)

Marriage (expected to be first marriage)

Pre-first child stage (expected to be brief)

First-child stage

Second-child stage

Third-child stage (and so on, if additional children)

Stage of youngest child in elementary school

Stage of youngest child in middle school

Stage of youngest child in high school

Youngest child leaves home

Parental empty-nest stage

Death of one spouse

Death of other spouse

FIGURE 14.1   Family Life-Cycle Stages
This simplified presentation outlines the overall image of the life-cycle approach. More complex presentations are available (e.g., in James White, 1991).

The Family and also of society. By way of illustration, biology courses often display diagrams describing the life cycle of a plant. A plant grows to maturity and then develops seeds. The seeds drop off or blow away and fall into the soil. Meanwhile, the parent plant dies. The seeds sprout a new plant, which follows precisely the same cycle of growth, reproduction, and death as the parent plant.

Figure 14-1 shows how in similar fashion the life-cycle idea was applied to the pre-sixties' family.[7] A heterosexual couple—Lester and Amelia—married during their early 20s. Since neither had ever had children, they were placed in the *childless* stage of the family life cycle. Within a year they had their first child, and thus they shifted to the next stage, which was often called the *infant* stage. (The key to figuring out which stage a family is in is generally the age of the youngest child.[8]) When the second child came along two years later, Lester and Amelia's family remained chiefly in the infant stage, even though they were also partially located in the *toddler* stage. Two years later their third child was born and they now found themselves partly in three stages: *preschool*, toddler, and infant. Since most of their energies and efforts were presumably devoted to their youngest child, they remained chiefly in the infant stage. Finally Nan, the fourth child, was born and they were now partly in four stages: *early grade school*, preschool, toddler, but most of all, infant.

Figure 14-1 displays the subsequent stages in the cycle. By the time Nan entered first grade, the family was chiefly in the early grade-school stage, even though the ages of Nan's older siblings placed the family partially in later stages. As Nan and her sibs matured biologically, family stages shifted accordingly, until finally Nan entered her junior year in high school. The family was now in the *later high-school* stage, and Nan's sibs were no longer living at home. When Nan went off to college, Lester and Amelia's family was finally in the *empty-nest* stage. Although parent birds in the wild seldom stay around the nest or each other once their offspring are mature enough to leave, few researchers have pushed the nest metaphor that far. Lester and Amelia remained in the empty-nest stage and enjoyed being grandparents. After a time, Lester retired from his lifelong job as an engineer, and they lived comfortably until his death. Although Amelia was physically healthy, she found herself unable to cope with the emotional trauma of life without Lester. Hence, within a year of losing him, she too died. Amelia's reaction to her husband's death was very different, however, from that of her neighbor Harriet. Harriet said: "For fifty years I lived my husband's life. Now it's time to live my own life." And she proceeded to do just that for a dozen more years.

Meanwhile, Nan and her siblings were attempting to repeat the life cycle of their parents. They fully expected to marry, have their own children, and watch them grow. They then expected their children to "leave the nest," just as they had left Lester and Amelia. Thus the family life cycle would be repeated generation after generation.

Role Conformity and the Life-Cycle Approach

Most sociologists once believed that a predictable family life cycle was the bedrock of social control and social order. Before the events of the 1960s and what's been going on ever since, it was the most common way to describe the aging of most persons. Today, however, the foundations of the FLC approach have been severely rocked by the life-course revolution, to say nothing of the sexual and employment revolutions. To their credit, FLC researchers were trying to show that aging is a lifelong process of change that begins in childhood. Nevertheless, in trying to describe aging, FLC researchers made an assumption that has since been undercut by the three revolutions.[9] The assumption was that as people age, they conform to appropriate social roles. What FLC misses is that throughout their life courses, today's people are increasingly likely to keep on *reinventing* behaviors rather than merely conforming to existing roles.[10]

Sociologists once described social roles as if they were something physically real, like a suit of clothes. Chapter 10 said that marriage is often *reified:* People confuse it with a physical object that can be touched, smelled, heard, seen, or tasted. The same is true for a social role such as mother or husband. People often think of a role as if it's physically real and can be put on like jeans or a T-shirt. Instead, says Donald Hansen, we should think of a role merely as a *metaphor*—a figure of speech that helps us communicate important and often unique feelings, ideas, and behaviors. If a friend says, "I was walking on air," or, "I carried the weight of the world on my shoulders," we understand those words to be metaphors conveying joy or sadness. He wasn't really doing either thing. Similarly, when Nan says, "I've taken on the role of mother," we know it's not like putting on a dress, or a suit, or a robe. And it's certainly not like playing the role of Lady MacBeth in Shakespeare's play. While acting in a role like that, one generally follows the script telling one precisely what to say and do.

By way of contrast, Nan made changes in the script: She became a mother for several years and had two informal marriages before she ever got formally married. She did so even though the role of "mother" as scripted by the family life cycle simply doesn't allow for that kind of "deviant" behavior. Moreover, it was never part of Nan's own *anticipatory socialization* about the mother role: She never expected to behave that way. And she wasn't following any script because there are surely no cultural norms saying a woman should become a mother before a formal marriage.

Anticipatory Socialization Meliza is a high-school senior. She's never been anywhere near a college in her life. Nevertheless, she thinks she has a pretty good idea of what her classes and social life will be like once she enrolls next year as a freshman. She got her ideas about college life from her parents and teachers, the media, and talking to college students, as well as from books, magazines, and catalogs. Meliza has been experiencing "anticipatory socialization" about college life. She's learning what to expect and she's picturing herself in the role of university student. She's anticipating what she will and won't do in that role. Once Meliza actually gets to college, however, she discovers that a lot of what she'd learned must be modified, and some of it doesn't work at all. As a result, she has to keep on reinventing the role of university student in ways she never anticipated.

The same unexpected reinvention takes place when it comes to erotic friendships and

parenting throughout people's lives. FLC researchers, however, ignored the idea of re-creation. First, they assumed that as youth were growing up they would be socialized into traditional gender roles of husband and father and wife and mother, as in Figure 12-1. Second, they believed that having learned those roles, youth such as Nan would anticipate what the roles would be like. Third, they thought that the youth, on having taken on the roles, would fulfill them pretty much as they had anticipated they would. The assumption was that youth would in general behave in pretty much the same ways as their parents. Thus the family life cycle would repeat itself.

Family "Development" Some researchers have tried to bring the FLC approach up to date by, among other things, changing its name to family "development."[11] But one of the most recent discussions of family development continues to concentrate on role conformity rather than role creation. For example, James White says there are "timing norms" about when a newly married couple should have children.[12] The cultural norms state that a newly married couple can wait a couple of years to have children, but not ten or more years. Recall that Lester and Amelia conformed to that timing norm: two years after marriage they had a child. Consequently, their family "developed" from the childless to the infant stage. Lester and Amelia believed the cultural norm that "being an only child is not a good thing," and so two years later they had a second child. Having that child caused their family to "develop" further. They also believed that "a woman's most important task in life is taking care of children," and so they had a third and a fourth child. As a result, their family developed still further. Their family kept on developing because of the connections between certain cultural norms prescribing what they were supposed to do, and the actual birth and growth of their children.

Conformity versus Construction But according to White, Nan (or, from earlier chapters, Helga and Sondra) is labeled "deviant" because, among other things, she didn't conform to traditional norms saying that people are supposed to marry *before* having children.[13] The label "deviant" doesn't do much to satisfy our curiosity about what today's erotic friendships and families are all about, however. Rather than say they're deviant, it makes more sense to say that Nan and the others are making certain kinds of choices. Those choices are part of their efforts to control their lives, even though the results may turn out to make them feel more out of control than they felt before. (Recall that Helga's choice to carry her first pregnancy to term significantly undermined her sense of control and her well-being.) Furthermore, Chapter 11 showed how certain choices could be viewed as socially irresponsible.

Nevertheless, these women are constructing families with their choices. And at different times in their lives, they are likely to make quite different kinds of choices, resulting in different sorts of families. Thus, instead of our thinking of a role as something that is governed by a script, we can understand Nan's role as mother as a kind of metaphor. Her role describes particular behaviors and identifies unique feelings.[14] Although in some ways her mother-role behaviors will be similar to those of her own mother, in many other ways they will be markedly different. The greatest contrasts are that Nan is unmarried, is not living with a man, and is employed full-time. Nor does she ever want a second child. Additionally, the way Nan constructs her role of mother can be very different from the roles constructed by other women in her same age bracket and similar economic circumstances.

By contrast, when Amelia was a young mother, just about every woman in her neighborhood played the role of mother in pretty much the same way. At that time, prevailing cultural images defining the Good-Mother role were captured by the traditional side of Figure 12-1. Today Nan has the option of constructing gender roles that are less traditional and more flexible than ever before. Moreover, she can, if she wishes, change her gender-role behaviors throughout her life course. One result of that flexibility is that if Nan ever chooses to have a second child, she is free to construct the role of mother differently than she did the first time. Recall from Chapter 13 that Sondra's mother role was very different the second time around than it had been with her first child. And when she joined her social family, her mother role shifted even more dramatically.

The issue of conformity versus construction is vividly illustrated by White's definition of the family. He says that the family development approach requires a parent-child bond of some sort; a social group that is not intergenerational cannot be a family.[15] Hence, if an adult has no living relatives yet wishes to experience family, she or he has no choice except to have children either by natural or by social means, such as adoption or cohabiting with someone who has children (White mentions stepchildren as well). By White's reasoning, children are requisite to the idea of "family." The option described in Chapters 2 and 3 of inventing social families quite apart from the presence of children doesn't exist.

Hence the FLC approach fails to take sufficient account of the 1960s and the years since. Recent decades have ushered in fresh kinds of social conditions influencing women and men to respond very differently than before to the inevitability of lifelong aging. Rather than conforming to preexisting social roles that are supposedly appropriate for a particular chronological age, persons are instead recreating new roles—fresh ways of relating to one another and to children. Not only are people changing, but broader political and economic conditions are continuing to shift as well. Consequently, persons such as Monika know that it's extremely difficult to anticipate the specifics of one's life course. Although Monika hopes for satisfying primary relationships (whether they be erotic friendships, social families, or just friends), she can't be certain about either their sequencing over time or their actual content.

Monika also looks forward to meaningful occupational experiences, but here too their sequence and content are unclear. She's aware, for instance, that economic experts are predicting that throughout their life courses people of her age and education may be forced to switch occupations several times. Furthermore, she's unable to anticipate exactly how her occupational trajectory will influence her primary relationships, and vice versa. Chapter 13 showed that before the 1960s, people like Lester and Amelia who graduated from high school and waited until their 20s to marry could, with considerable certainty, predict a lifelong marriage and a stable life overall. Today most persons simply hope for the best both in their occupations and their primary relationships. Throughout postmodern societies, we've moved from the image of aging marked by a predictable family *life cycle* to the notion of a very fluid and highly uncertain *life course*.

AGING AND LIFE COURSES

Transitions

The term *transition* has already appeared in this book several times. In Chapter 5, people shifting from one phase of their erotic friendship to another were said to be in transition. Persons moving out of an erotic friendship or perhaps moving into another were also in transition. Chapter 13 showed that "termination and transition" is a better way to describe the official ending of a formal marriage than terms such as "divorce" or "disorganization." Now we say that the idea of transition is central also to the life-course revolution identified a few pages ago. Why is the idea of transition so central?

Recently a number of researchers from sociology, psychology, and history have gotten excited about studying "life courses." Life-course students distill the best ideas from the family development approach while avoiding its pitfalls; they also add many new ideas. In contrast to the term "cycle," the term "course" carries the sound of flexibility as well as the image of choice. Carrie wants to drive to Chicago. She's not in a hurry and there are many roads, or courses, she can follow. She also works as a recreation specialist. Part of her job is to design trails throughout the city park for people who want to walk, run, or do calisthenics. She's free to create those trails, or courses, in the ways she thinks are best. The freedom to choose *what seems best* is the sort of freedom college instructors have in designing their courses.

This is part of what Arlene Skolnick means by applying the label "revolution."[16] She believes that today people like Nan or Kurt (Chapter 5) have considerable freedom to do what they think is best. By comparison, what was best for Amelia and Lester was handed down to them as the *right* thing to do. The sole view of what was "right" and therefore "best" was prescribed by prevailing cultural norms. Today, the idea that there is only one prescription that works or works best is widely questioned. The freedom to keep on recreating new rules and roles throughout the course of one's life is, in Skolnick's view, a revolution. Nevertheless, let's not forget that people have always been creative in getting around established norms. Chapter 13 talked about desertion and extramarital sex as ways of coping with rules and laws against divorce. And Amelia and Lester were part of the Great Depression generation that began to invent engagement sex (see Chapter 3). Even though the cultural rules said, "Premarital sex is neither right nor good," Amelia and Lester (along with other 1930s' couples) felt it was for them. Did they believe it was the right thing to do? Almost certainly not! They probably felt exceedingly guilty. Chapter 4 added that even though today some 80 percent of the population does It, when they're asked, relatively few persons will actually assert that premarital sex is right.

The Faces of Transition Most people today make the transition from virgin to nonvirgin apart from marriage. Philip Cowan defines *transition* as a long-term process that reorganizes "both inner life and external behavior."[17] As they started having sex, Lester and Amelia definitely passed through a transition, for two reasons. First, from that time forward each viewed himself or herself differently from before. Amelia had a particularly difficult struggle with what Cowan calls her "inner world," that is, her *identity*. She had trouble thinking of herself as the same "nice girl" she'd been before. She was terribly anxious because if her parents found out, they'd call her a "fallen woman" unless she married Lester at once. Since the only means they used to prevent pregnancy was pulling out, she was deeply fearful that her parents would indeed discover the awful truth. Lester too felt guilty. Like Amelia, he felt he'd made a transition from one segment of his life to another. He became obsessed with the fear that if she got pregnant, he'd have to drop out of college and marry her even though there were no jobs. For both of them, having sex strongly increased their commitment eventually to marry. Although they couldn't marry just yet, they each knew beyond any doubt that their partner was the person with whom they would spend the rest of their life.

The second reason we say Amelia and Lester experienced a transition was the fact of their new behavior patterns. Before doing It for the first time, they'd only had heavy petting sessions in the front seat of his father's car. Now they were doing It as often as they could in the back seat. In short, for outward behavioral reasons and because of their new identities, becoming sexual partners was for Amelia and Lester a crucial life-course transition.

Life Markers Cowan draws a distinction between what he calls a "life marker" and a genuine life-course transition.[18] The classic illustration of passing a marker but not making a transition is that of the married professional or executive man working seventy to eighty hours per week whose wife gives birth to a child. She passes through an indisputable transition into parenthood: Her behaviors change drastically, her view of herself changes, and so does her perception of how others view her—she senses they view her much more positively than before. His behaviors change barely at all. If he's home on the weekends (and not out golfing), he tries to find time to play with the baby when it's awake. Second, his view of himself, his identity, doesn't alter in the slightest. He feels neither the need nor the responsibility to become connected with the child's life in any intrinsic sense. His wife sees herself as a different person, and thus she's experienced a life-course *transition*; he's merely passed a life *marker*.

Chapter 9 reported Larry Bumpass's reasoning that events such as marriage and divorce were losing their significance as life markers.[19] What he meant to say was that back in Lester and Amelia's time, most people experienced those two events as genuine transitions—marriage and divorce did indeed change people both inwardly and outwardly. But for growing numbers of persons today these events have lost that type of impact, and are often little more than markers. For instance, at the time of Nan's first formal marriage she'd already been living with her partner for two years. Legal marriage didn't change her outward behaviors in the slightest. Nor did she view herself much differently. Unlike her mother Amelia, she didn't have the transition to parenthood to look forward to—that was already long behind her! She had indeed experienced a vital transition a year earlier when she and her current partner entered the maintenance and change phase of their erotic friendship: Many of her behaviors changed, including setting aside casual sex in favor of monogamy. She decidedly saw herself differently than before, including, among other things, a strong desire to be a committed person: She hoped to stay with her partner indefinitely.

Markers, Transitions, and Stress   One reason it's important to be aware of the distinction between transitions and markers is that things have gotten much more complex than they appear on the surface. At one time marriage was a transition for just about everyone. Now it's not, except perhaps for religious evangelicals. For many people today marriage has become more of a life marker than a genuine transition.

A second reason the difference between transitions and markers is so important is because of their potential connection with stress symptoms. Chapter 11 described the things that can happen to people when they feel out of control, including stress symptoms such as sweaty palms, sleeplessness, extreme blushing, skin rashes, abdominal pains, anxiety and the blues, depression, and so forth.

According to Cowan, a life marker by itself is not likely to make a person feel out of control. Consequently, it's not likely to result in stress and its symptoms. If neither the executive becoming a parent nor Nan marrying her partner is changed either inwardly or outwardly, how could either feel out of control? Similarly, when Helga (Chapter 5) divorced Hans, she passed a marker, not experienced a transition, because the divorce changed nothing in her life. She felt neither out of control nor stressed. Helga had, however, experienced a transition several years earlier during her separation from Hans. That painful process changed her outward behaviors as well as her own view of herself. It was painful in part because it was so stressful. Some of the stress sprang from her secret erotic friendship with Kurt.

Helga's history of stress had actually begun much earlier when she experienced the gradual transition from the maintenance and change phase she'd enjoyed with Hans into a dissolution phase. Throughout most of the downward spiral of that dissolution phase, she felt out of control and experienced numerous stress symptoms. Once she finally moved out of the house—after that transition was fully accomplished—she felt she was finally in control, and her symptoms began to disappear.

Does Helga's experience with dissolution and separation tell us that transitions are inevitably accompanied by stress? Do transitions always pose a threat to a person's sense of well-being? Not necessarily, says Cowan.[20] He notes that some family life cycle and family development researchers did, and do, believe that getting married, having the first child, facing an empty nest, getting divorced, being a working mother, being a solo parent, changing jobs, going off to college, and so forth, are almost certainly going to be stressful events.[21] But Cowan responds that it's not the event in and of itself that tells us whether it's stressful or not. We just learned, for instance, that if the person defines the event merely as a marker, it's much less likely to create stress.

Cowan adds that even if the person perceives the event as an actual transition, the amount of stress, if any, that she or he experiences depends on the level of *control* the person has during the process of transition. At the onset of her dissolution process, for instance, Helga felt only slightly out of control, and, her stress symptoms were modest. The longer her dissolution phase wore on, however, the more out of control she felt, and the more intense the symptoms became. As it gradually dawned on her that leaving Hans was the only way to relieve her depression, gloom, and listlessness, she pondered plans to accomplish the separation. The mere fact of considering those plans meant that she was beginning to face choices and to exercise some control over her life. In fact, it was during that time that her feelings of well-being began to rise somewhat in anticipation of her actual separation.

For Hans the story was quite different. Cowan says that sometimes transitions simply *happen* to people. They neither want them nor have any control over them. Hans's experience of dissolution and separation was very painful and stressful on both counts: He didn't want either transition, and he felt absolutely out of control. The classic examples of *imposed* transitions stem from death or widowhood, natural disasters such as floods or hurricanes, terminal illness such as AIDS, physical or mental disabilities, war, and so on. Because persons rarely plan for such events and tend to feel utterly helpless during them, their sense of well-being drops dramatically.

CHILDHOOD, ADOLESCENCE, AND CONTROL

Cowan states that one major difference between the life courses of children and the adult life course is precisely that: Things always seem to be *happening* to children. Very little appears to be under the child's voluntary control.[22] Transitions such as toilet training; entering day care or first grade, or middle or high school; the onset of puberty; and so forth, all seem to be processes imposed on the child by the towering adult world. Take, for example, adolescence (a social invention of the last hundred years or so). In premodern societies, after someone made the transition from childhood to puberty she or he was defined as an adult woman or man. Hence the person was soon married and compelled to behave as a responsible adult.

Contemporary societies create a gap between childhood and adulthood—adolescence. Adolescents are expected to make a gradual transition to adulthood. According to prevailing cultural norms, youth make the transition most successfully by learning and conforming to "proper" adult roles: "You'll be treated like an adult when you learn to behave like one," they're told. How does one behave like an adult? For one thing, since prevailing cultural norms say that premarital sex is wrong, adolescents are told to say no to sex until they're married.[23] Alongside the inherent "rightness" of chastity, adolescents are told that by being chaste they will avoid the hassles of birth control and the threats of disease, pregnancy, and abortion, to say nothing of the burden of parenthood. At the same time, adolescents are exposed to intense anticipatory socialization regarding adulthood. They're learning that they should expect to get married, to have children, and to be a good husband/father or wife/mother. For both genders, being good means conforming to the traditional norms described in Figure 12-1.

But instead of conformity, adolescence is often characterized by severe conflict between youth and adults. Youth make many choices to which adults object, especially when it comes to sex. There's no mystery why adolescents prefer choice over conformity. Choice supplies a sense of control and well-being. For the first time in their short lives adolescents discover that they're able to take charge.[24] Although lots of things continue to happen to them, they also can now *make* things happen. Jack Katz says that what most outsiders call deviance is perceived instead as a heady experience for the person actually making the choice.[25] Sex, drugs, alcohol, fast cars, and so on are enormously exhilarating to many adolescents. The feelings of control and well-being come from violating the taboos against those things: The high comes from tasting the forbidden fruit.

Adolescence obviously qualifies as a major life-course transition: Not only do youth behave very differently from how they behaved as children; they also view themselves and one another very differently—their identities change. But earlier chapters revealed the perils of violating social control to exercise personal control. Choices inevitably have consequences. Exercising choice runs the risk that short-term exhilaration (immediate gratification) may be followed by longer term pain and depression because one's life has gotten more out of control than before. The most obvious example of that is spontaneous and unprotected sex resulting in infection with the HIV virus.

Gay and Lesbian Adolescents

That risks are often associated with transitions is clearly seen in a recent study of adolescent gays and lesbians living in a large metropolitan area. The authors claim that the United States has about 3 million homosexually inclined youth.[26] Their research shows that there are some significant similarities as well as differences between heterosexual and homosexual adolescents. Heterosexuals justify their "deviant" premarital sexual activity in part by saying it represents natural biological drives: "This is the way I'm made."[27] Adolescent gays/lesbians are following the lead of the adult same-sex community by making an identical argument. Just as heterosexual adolescents claim they have no choice regarding their sexual orientation, homosexuals say they don't either.

Both straight and gay adolescents do have a choice in the matter of sharing their transition from nonsexual to sexual being with their parents. Recall that Cowan claims that a transition is marked by two things: changes in behavior and changes in identity (i.e., one's image of oneself). We can add a third element that was implicit in Cowan's discussion—a person's perception of how others view him or her. For instance, after Helga moved out from Hans, she sensed that her friends thought of her very differently than they had before. She knew that she'd finally proved to them that she was serious about terminating her relationship with Hans. She sensed they no longer felt uneasy that she'd been sleeping with Kurt while living with Hans. In short, the affirmation and approval of friends and/or families often adds a sense of completion and legitimacy to the transition. Marlis Buchmann calls it a validation of a person's social identity.[28]

Andrew Boxer and co-workers report that gay adolescents are in a double bind when it comes to sharing their sexual identities and activities with parents and/or other significant adults.[29] On one side, all children and youth are taught to be honest with their parents. On the other side, all youth are told they must be celibate. Most straight adolescents resolve that dilemma by being dishonest with parents and other adults. Although their transition to sexual being is affirmed by their friends, very few parents openly acknowledge it. At most, some some adolescents sense their parents know, but a tacit agreement exists between the generations not to talk about it. One reason both sides tolerate that sort of duplicity is the comprehension that it's merely temporary. Later on the parents will fully accept their child's transition to sexual being, particularly in the context of marriage and parenthood.

By contrast, today's homosexual youth are keenly aware that their duplicity will not be resolved by subsequent conformity to parental expectations—by doing what their parents want. Adult same-sex persons report that in the past, many homosexual youth resigned themselves to the prospect of cross-sex marriage for a variety of reasons, not least of which was parental approval.[30] But Boxer and colleagues found that the gay youth they studied were not choosing that course. Today's gay youth wished to add a sense of completion to their transition by gaining parental affirmation of their homosexuality. Although their biology was same-sex, they had after all been exposed to years of socialization aimed at making them cross-sex persons. Moreover, as part of their own quest to ascertain whether they could possibly go cross-sex, Boxer and colleagues report that over 70 percent of them had sexually experimented with heterosexuals. Most discovered that those cross-sex behaviors were much less satisfying than their same-sex experiences.

In short, their behaviors were homosexual, and so was their own view of themselves. They had experienced a transition from a culturally imposed heterosexuality to being gay/lesbian. They had also "come out" to many of their friends, but not yet to their parents. But they wanted to. The risks of their coming out to their parents pivoted around rejection, including parental attempts to restrict their same-sex friendships. Nevertheless, 63 percent of the girls and 54 percent of the boys in the study had shared their sexual identities with their mothers. And 37 percent of the girls had told their fathers, as had 28 percent of the boys.[31] Interestingly enough, neither the girls nor the boys were consistently able to detect much negative reaction from their parents. Some reported that relationships with their parents actually improved somewhat because of their coming out.

It's likely that the youth who took the risks of coming out sensed ahead of time that their parents would not reject them and would at least be neutral toward them. Boys reported that neutrality was in fact the most common reaction they got from their fathers. Those who chose not to come out to their parents apparently felt that the goal of adding a sense of completion to their transition was not worth the risk of alienation from their parents, at least for now.

Economic Support and Parental Control

Plainly, adolescence represents a major bridge between childhood and young adulthood. Adolescents are struggling to take control of their lives: They want the sense of well-being that springs from being able to make choices. Whether straight or gay, their transitions involve major changes in behaviors, shifts in identity, and a quest for the approval of significant others. But adolescence is by definition temporary; legal statutes prescribe its end somewhere between ages 18 and 21. Adolescents neither expect nor desire to be supported indefinitely by their parents—parental dollars strongly reinforce the control over their lives that they resent. Hence, to get their own dollars, growing numbers of U.S. high-school students are taking part-time jobs. A recent University of Michigan study reports that 74 percent of Minneapolis teenagers were employed compared with 21 percent in the comparable Japanese city of Sendai.[32] The American youth worked almost sixteen hours per week, while the Japanese worked less than ten hours.

The outward reason growing numbers of adolescents hold jobs is to acquire the mass of consumer goods served up endlessly by the media. Nevertheless, the Minneapolis study reported that the most important thing adolescents buy with their money is greater independence from their parents. The study showed that because they had their own money they were treated, and actually felt, more like adults. The money was a means—a *resource*—for opening up choices, expanding their sense of control, and enlarging their feelings of well-being. Earning money is a chief mechanism of anticipatory socialization: It provides adolescents with keen insights into the worlds of adulthood.

AGING INTO YOUNG ADULTHOOD

Education is touted as the best means both to earn a "good living" and to contribute to society. Adolescents are urged to graduate from high school and then attend vocational school or go to college. Throughout contemporary societies, economic independence (i.e., autonomy) is the hallmark—the bottom line—of what an adult is. The transition from youth to adult pivots around the behavioral shift of earning enough to support oneself. Part-time jobs while in high school or college rarely achieve that goal. Persons capable of supporting themselves right out of high school are for the first time behaving as full-fledged adults. Furthermore, they view themselves as adults, and so do friends and families: They have made the transition to adulthood.[33] By contrast, college students depending partly or entirely on their parents for support have not made that transition. Parents and faculty often still refer to them as kids, a label rarely used to describe high-school graduates of the same age working in a local factory or office.

Buchmann, a German sociologist, studied what he calls the "passage" from youth to adulthood. He claims that youth in other Western societies are following the same types of passages as U.S. youth. He compared 1960 with 1980 high-school graduates from across the United States, collecting information about the first four years after their respective graduations. Buchmann was curious whether there were significant differences between the 1960 and 1980 graduates insofar as their "script of life" was concerned. We talked earlier about the script in connection with the family life cycle. The script consists of cultural rules telling youth what they should and shouldn't do to make their passage into adulthood as successful as possible. Buchmann's hunch was that 1960s' youth followed a much more standardized, or scripted, transition to young adulthood than did the 1980s' youth. His hunch was based in part on the Big Bang and Big Change described in Chapter 7. He reasoned that the many things occurring in the broader U.S. society during their childhood and adolescence would influence the 1980 graduates to choose a much more flexible life course—to interject it with considerable variety.

Structural Changes

Among the many things "happening out there" are certain structural changes in the nature of modern societies. Politicians and business leaders of the nineties are debating how to respond to the shifting global economy in which the United States and all industrial (and emerging) nations find themselves intermeshed. One of the most worrisome concerns is that the payoff from educational investments is growing ever more uncertain.[34] At the core of the American Dream is the belief that after a person (i.e., a male person) graduated from high school or college, he would be able to get and keep a good job all his life, and support his family in the bargain. Recently, however, many persons who finish school or college haven't been able to find and/or keep good jobs. A major reason they haven't, says Buchmann, is the steady decline in the sheer numbers of high-paying, highly skilled manufacturing jobs. Those blue-collar jobs (e.g., in the defense, steel, and auto industries), and many of the white-collar and management jobs connected with them, have simply vanished. A second reason is the microchip revolution. This "revolution" first generates a whole new range of computer-based technologies, and then makes them obsolete, all within the space of a few years. Most schools fail to prepare persons for those sorts of continually evolving technologies. For example, by the time a skilled tool-and-die maker replaced by last year's computer has finished learning fresh skills, those skills have in turn become outdated by still newer technologies.

Men's Life Courses   Buchmann describes the vast majority of the vanished manufacturing jobs, for example, tool-and-die maker, as male dominated. Since those kinds of occupations were made up almost entirely of males, they were defined as "men's work." One result of this enormous and far-reaching shift in the structure of male occupations is that today the course of many men's lives is much less stable and predictable than it once was. For example, two years after high-school graduation in

1970, Mal completed vocational college as a highly skilled machinist. Mal's father had worked as a master machinist all his life—fifteen years for one company, then thirty years for another. He was particularly proud of the fact that he'd earned such a good living that his wife never had to go to work. By the time he retired at age 65, Mal's father could look back on a comfortable life and ahead to an enjoyable retirement.

Mal wanted the identical thing for himself: He wanted to age within the context of the same sort of stable and predictable life course. Unfortunately for Mal, the 1970s, 1980s, and 1990s were marked by the structural changes just cited. After all the machinist jobs in his city were either automated or moved overseas, he was forced to attend evening classes to become a mainframe computer operator, earning much less than he did as a machinist. And after a couple of years, desktop computers replaced most mainframes and he was once again out of a job. He had to take an even lower paying job as a clerk in a local home-improvement store.

Women's Life Courses Those same structural changes pressured hundreds of thousands of women such as Mal's wife Brenda.[35] Unlike her mother-in-law, Brenda had to work to help pay the bills while Mal was experiencing his zigzag occupational course. Mal's continuing difficulties in holding a job, though not of his own making, resulted in conflicts Mal and Brenda were unable to resolve, and edged the couple into a dissolution phase. When Brenda refused to quit working even after Mal got his clerking job, they both sensed that separation and perhaps divorce were not far off. Comparing Mal and Brenda's life course with that of Mal's parents helps us understand why the label *revolution* makes a great deal of sense in describing today's life courses. Between the mid-1940s and the 1970s, both the economic and personal lives of adults proceeded in a relatively more-or-less predictable and stable

fashion. Now, however, structural upheavals "out there" influence persons to make certain *choices*. Those choices in turn often result in significant *changes* for both their erotic friendships and their families. Consequently, predictable and stable life courses are being increasingly replaced by unpredictable and fluctuating life courses.

Life-course fluctuation is further stimulated by the cultural changes "out there" described in Chapter 10: Growing numbers of women are coming to accept the moral obligation to love themselves as much as (not more than) they love their neighbor. Her mother-in-law (Joy) perceived that Brenda was beginning to love herself in that manner. Because Joy defined that kind of love as Brenda's "problem," she blamed Brenda for her son's divorce.

Rebending the Tree Buchmann says that women like Brenda, who come from blue-collar and lower-middleclass backgrounds, are the women most likely to be impacted by structural changes. They were socialized to love their husbands and children more than themselves. They learned to place their family's needs ahead of their own. The idea of becoming economically autonomous, and thus an equal partner, was never part of their anticipatory socialization. Nevertheless, structural changes pressured women such as Brenda to behave in economic and personal ways that they neither intended nor wanted: Brenda never wanted a job; and she surely never expected a divorce!

Judith Stacey's research shows that shifting economic conditions pressure even evangelical wives into behaviors that were never part of their youthful socialization.[36] She studied lower-middle-class families—many of whom were devout religious evangelicals—living in Silicon Valley, California, during the early 1980s. The numerous computer industries of Silicon Valley are classic illustrations of the sorts of structural changes just described.

Many of the thousands of jobs they offer are semiskilled; others are skilled or unskilled. Regardless of skill level, each new technological innovation renders many of the jobs obsolete. Men working at those jobs thus lose the economic means to support their family. After a period of unemployment, new technologies create new jobs for those men. No one knows, however, how long the new jobs will exist. The uncertainty of this economic seesaw makes it very difficult for the men to be their family's Head, as described in Chapter 10.

Wanting to be a good complement, the wife knows she should stoically accept their economic setback and weather the storm until the next wave of technology gets her husband a new job. Nevertheless, Stacey reports that many evangelical wives ignore what they learned to be "right," that is, stay home to care for their children and submit to their husbands. Wives now feel sharp economic pressure to do what seems "best," that is, get a paying job. However, the wives' new behavior generates serious conflicts with the husbands, resulting frequently in separation and divorce. When some of the women and men later get *re*married, they are taking another serious step away from their earlier religious socialization.

Perhaps the biggest question about childhood and adolescent socialization is how long it lasts: "As the twig is bent, so grows the tree," is a folk saying describing the widely held belief that how parents train children has enormous and lasting influence throughout their lives. The biblical promise that evangelicals learn is, "Train up a child in the way he should go, and when he is old he will not depart from it." Nonetheless, the question remains: How long does the bent twig influence the shape of the mature tree? The answer is that norms and beliefs learned as a child or adolescent last as long as they make sense for adults in the light of changing social conditions. In the case of women like Brenda, what they learned as youth failed to work during adulthood

because of new structural conditions. The more Brenda changed her behaviors to fit the conditions, the more she forgot about the ideas she learned as a youth. Gradually, new ideas took their place because they made more sense for her adult life. The main reason she wouldn't quit her job after Mal went back to work was because she was learning to be economically autonomous: She was beginning to feel that being an equal partner with her man is for her a good idea. On the basis of her study of women like Brenda, Myra Dinnerstein concludes that *"adults continue to develop new values, beliefs, and aspirations as they encounter changing historical and social circumstances."*[37]

Although Brenda didn't start absorbing those emerging cultural notions until she was thirtysomething, Buchmann notes that growing numbers of today's females learn them much earlier, as children and youth. Many of those females, he says, come from upper-middle-class backgrounds where one or both parents are college educated. Recall from Chapter 10 that Kate's mother (Emma) was quite traditional, in part because she'd never been to college. But Kate's father had graduated from college and insisted that Kate do the same. Throughout the years she was growing up, he socialized her to anticipate becoming autonomous as well as an equal partner. And as she moved into adulthood and became aware of rapidly shifting economic conditions, Kate felt that her father's ideas made sense for her. Hence she put them into action for all the relationships she had with men, including her current long-term erotic friendship with Marshall. By contrast with Brenda, the norms she'd learned in her youth had greater lasting effects. The reason they did persist is that they made sense for her as an adult within the context of broader structural and cultural conditions.

In short, as Kate was making her transition to adulthood, the inner world of her own identity was clear: "I am an economically autonomous person." Brenda's identity was just as sharp, but different: "I am a Good Wife and Good Mother." Although Kate experienced a number of other transitions during her 20s and 30s, her fundamental view of herself did not change. To be sure, it could have shifted in a more traditional direction. Kathleen Gerson, for example, reports that some women like Kate who begin adulthood wanting to be autonomous nonetheless experience a transition into accepting more traditional women's roles.[38] Brenda headed in the opposite direction: She'd experienced a dramatic transition both in terms of her behaviors and her identity. For the first time in her life she viewed herself as an autonomous person. Furthermore, she reasoned that over the long haul autonomy was the best way for her to become an effective mother as well as a good erotic partner.

Comparing 1960 with 1980—Complexity and Diversity

Buchmann's hunches regarding differences between 1960 and 1980 high-school graduates during their four-year transition to adulthood proved to be correct. Owing to the many changes occurring out there, today's youth are experiencing a much greater range and variety of life-course choices than youth of a generation ago. Buchmann agrees with John Modell that today's choices are captured by the terms "complexity and diversity."[39] By contrast, 1960 graduates were more likely to follow the scripted family life cycle path than were 1980 graduates. Furthermore, because the 1960 path was simpler and more uniform, those earlier graduates, says Buchmann, were more likely to make a socially recognized transition to adulthood much earlier than were the 1980 graduates.

Buchmann used three tests to find out whether a person had made a socially recognized transition: "Are you still in school?"

"Have you been married?" "Have you had a child?"[40] The percentages of youth in each cluster of students answering yes to all three questions were much higher in 1964 than they were in 1984. All three of those behaviors conform to the cultural definition of what it means to be an adult. Persons who had done all three things thought of themselves as adults, as did their families and friends. Persons who had not, or who had done merely one or two of them, had not yet made the transition to full-fledged adulthood. It was not that the 1980s' cultural scripts had been "officially" altered; youth were simply paying less attention to the old scripts. Moreover, that trend of indifference to the standard life-cycle scripts seems to be continuing into the nineties.

Given that today's youth are increasingly indifferent to the scripts, how do they actually behave? Among other things, says Buchmann, growing numbers of high-school graduates appear to be delaying their entry into college for a year or two or perhaps longer. When they enroll, they may do so for a while as part-time, but later as full-time, students. If they do enroll in college immediately after high school, they may "stop out" of college for a year or two. Meanwhile, they may intersperse part-time with full-time employment. They may also intersperse periods of casual sex with periods of erotic friendships. If the latter, they may be girlfriends/boyfriends who each week spend several overnights together, or they may actually cohabit for a while. Two things that most high-school graduates do *not* appear to be doing during this initial four-year period is to marry formally and then soon afterward have a child.[41] By comparison, the 1960 cluster of graduates moved along a much clearer, certain, and standard track: *As soon as possible,* they felt they had to do the three things that marked them as an adult: finish school, marry, and have children. After all, the 1960 cohort was one of the last to graduate from high school before the upheavals of the mid- to late-sixties. Two major "revolutions" emerged from those upheavals, which in turn contributed heavily to today's life-course revolution. Chapter 5 identified one as the emergence of the erotic friendship; Chapter 15 describes the second as women's employment patterns, or what Chapter 7 called the Big Change. Buchmann claims that because both of those revolutions profoundly affected women, the life courses of most women have changed more dramatically during recent decades than they have for most men. That is not to say that the male life course has not changed. It has, as in Mal's case. But by comparison, Brenda's changes were greater and more significant.

Variations on Themes John Gottman uses jazz to illustrate today's transitions from youth to adulthood.[42] The art of jazz is that, while acknowledging a theme tune, musicians strive to create as many variations on that theme as they possibly can: *improvisation*, it's called. Most of today's youth follow a general theme that includes the goals of education, a good job, and meaningful primary relationships with adults as well as children. But the specifics of the general theme are open to a great deal of improvisation. Not only during the first four post-high-school years, but throughout their early adulthood, growing numbers of persons are interjecting unpredictable and often unexpected "notes" as they go along. For instance, people such as Brenda, Helga and Kurt, Sondra, and Kate and Marshall are making choices about school, work, sex, partners, informal and formal marriage, social families, children, and so on, that are clearly recognizable as belonging to the larger themes. But the sequence as well as the contents of their choices are no longer standard, scripted, or scored.

Instead, persons make choices that seem to make sense at the time. Recall that Helga's choices made sense to her, first because of the ways in which she viewed her own complicated social situation, and second because of the ways in which she viewed her broader

structural and cultural environment. Even after she'd made up her mind to leave Hans, she put it off for a while: She felt she had to wait until the "time was right." In short, instead of worrying a great deal about doing what they're supposed to be doing as defined by prevailing cultural scripts, today's young adults appear to have a somewhat different agenda. To be sure, they're following certain general themes regarding the importance of work, relationships, and families. And, they seem concerned to exercise as much control as possible over those and other parts of their lives and, as a result, achieve a sense of well-being. Finally, the fact that they're often frustrated while attempting to invent their own life courses does not diminish their determination to keep on trying.

AGING INTO THE MIDDLE YEARS

Earlier we said that life-course transitions occur when people change behaviors, when they think of themselves as being different, and also when they perceive that significant others affirm their new behaviors and identity. Persons begin to define themselves as young adults if they believe they're developing control over both the economic and personal dimensions of their lives.[43] Hence a young adult is someone who defines himself or herself as becoming weaned from parental controls.

Settling Down

What then is a midlife adult? How can we describe the transition to midlife? Ann Swidler, and later Arlene Skolnick, observe that mid*life* is something that has only recently been "discovered."[44] Before the last couple of decades, persons were merely middle-*aged*. According to Swidler, the key phrase describing middle-aged persons was that they had settled down. Young adulthood was the time when men sowed their wild oats and played the old Dating Game; women merely played the Game. Men might also experiment with different occupations in search of their "life's work." But marriage and its aftermath symbolized settling down for both genders. Husbands and wives had committed themselves to a lifelong course of action centering around his occupation and her skills as wife and mother. Having put their hand to the plow, there was no turning back from either of those parallel rows. Thus, if a man's transition to adulthood was symbolized by a steady job, marriage, and children, his transition to middle-aged adult was symbolized by his own realization (acknowledged by others) that he had indeed *settled down*. He had given up the range of choices and options available to single young adults. Both he and his wife now had responsibilities; to fulfill them they had to conform to scripted roles.

Swidler notes that the contrasts between early and middle adulthood were once striking, indeed. Young adulthood was viewed as an escape from parental controls and a period of having considerable personal freedom regarding one's own life. By contrast, middle-age adulthood meant relinquishing a great deal of that hard-won freedom. Choices, says Swidler, were replaced by conformity to culturally approved gender roles. Accordingly, for some persons "middle age" may have begun when chronologically they were no more than age 25. If the husband kept on being a Good Provider, and if the couple was successful in having a stable marriage, then by the time they aged into their early to mid-30s they were culturally labeled as middle-aged. Their friends might tease the 30-year-olds by saying, "You're nothing but an old married couple." They were affectionately communicating that, "You've been together such a long time your lives aren't likely to change very much." The absence of change, the presence of predictability—those were the hallmarks of being middle-aged.

Interestingly enough, Skolnick notes that

this sort of life-cycle certainty was a relatively new thing, having come on the scene around the 1920s. The certainty enjoyed by Mal's parents, for instance, was made possible, first, by medical advances reducing the risk of sudden or early death due to serious illness. As a result, Mal's parents were part of a generation that could expect to live many more years than their forebears. Second, until the 1970s there was a largely uninterrupted expansion of heavy manufacturing, male-dominated jobs. Since neither of those factors was present to the same degree before the 1920s, the family life cycles of many couples back then were quite uncertain. Sudden death and/or male unemployment had devastating effects for many pre-1920s' families. Now, says Skolnick, after an interlude between the 1920s and the 1970s, the pendulum has once again swung in that same direction of life-course uncertainty. The luxury of looking forward to a predictable and stable middle-aged period of one's life is slowly evaporating.

Rediscovery of Choice

But if today's *midlife* couples don't settle down, what then do they do? Women like Helga or Brenda, or the women in Dinnerstein's study (born between 1936 and 1944), *rediscover* the choices they previously relinquished when they got married, had children, and became full-fledged young adults. A best-selling 1976 book brought the term *middle-age crisis* into everyone's vocabulary.[45] Gail Sheehy claimed that every middle-aged person goes through a radical transition in terms of both identity and behaviors. But Sheehy was writing about men and women both before recent structural and cultural changes in the larger society. Married under the old rules, midlife suddenly confronted them with new rules, or worse yet, no rules. Women and men who never expected to reenter school did so. Men who never expected to lose their jobs, and women who never intended to get serious about paid work, did. Persons who never expected to have "affairs," or be unwed parents, or cohabit, or get separated, divorced, and remarried, were surprised by their own behaviors—some pleasantly, others not.[46] But the biggest shock of all for people like Mal and Brenda was that they were back where they were before they got married: Their lives were once again filled with choice and uncertainty. Their hopes for "settling down" had been rudely dashed. Unwittingly, they had stumbled into the *rediscovery* of choice.

The Reaffirmation of Choice

We began this chapter by saying that Monika, a college graduate in her mid-20s with a good job, already expects that her life course will be characterized by unpredictable twists and turns. She neither is married nor has children, and she doesn't intend either anytime soon. Nonetheless, she perceives herself as a young adult because she's economically autonomous, and she hopes that will continue. What makes her strikingly different from Brenda (when Brenda was her age) is that she does not intend ever to relinquish choice and control over her life. Since Monika hasn't given it up, her transition into midlife cannot be the rediscovery of choice. Instead, she expects her chronological aging will be accompanied by an ongoing lifelong *reaffirmation* of choice.

Permanent Availability   Monika knows several women like Kate and she takes them as role models. Chapter 10 showed that Kate, a professional woman, and Marshall maintained a richly satisfying informal marriage for over a decade. As she approached age 40, they formalized it because of their desire for a child. But at no point did either Kate or Marshall ever view themselves as settling down. Although they were strongly committed to each

other and to developing a strong sense of we-ness, they were equally committed to the idea that each should nurture the other's sense of me-ness. Chapters 5, 11, and 13 said that *permanent availability* is the notion that a person is potentially a prospect for an erotic friendship regardless of whether she or he now has a partner. The fact that one may currently choose not to be a prospect in no way implies that one has given up that option in favor of settling down the way Mal and Brenda had done. Even if Kate or Marshall or Monika never expects to exercise that option, nonetheless each always retains it.

Permanent availability, along with commitment to the idea that each partner should be economically autonomous, means that the midlife courses of persons such as Monika, Kate and Marshall, and Kurt and Helga are likely to be quite unpredictable. But since their young adulthood was also unpredictable, that's nothing new. Furthermore, ongoing upheavals in the national and global economies increase the likelihood of midlife uncertainty. What does seem apparent is that the idea of a middle-age crisis will become increasingly irrelevant.[47] Persons like Brenda, Mal, and Hans had middle-age crises because they'd comfortably settled down. But as the goal of settling down becomes increasingly elusive for growing numbers of persons, it becomes replaced by the idea of learning to live with varying degrees of built-in uncertainty throughout one's life course.

In short, transitions into young adulthood are marked by an expanding range of choices and control over one's life. Slowly, a person begins to perceive of himself or herself as an adult. Throughout much of this century young adulthood merged into middle age as people made choices of marriage partners and (the men) employment and settled down. Other choices were severely limited by expected social roles. Today, by contrast, midlife choices and uncertainty have become expanded so

This 1992 photo of Judy Collins in performance suggests several things. For one, in no way does she define herself as "old." For another, she seems very much in control of her life.

that, apart from the ticking of the biological clock, young adulthood and midlife are becoming increasingly comparable.

AGING INTO THE LATER YEARS

"I must be getting old," was once a frequently heard folk saying. It contained a note of wry humor and also a sense of sad resignation to the inevitable. But that was before Jane Fonda, Paul McCartney, Barbara Streisand, Aretha Franklin, Bob Dylan, Frank Zappa, Paul Newman, Paul Simon, Art Garfunkel, Tom Hayden, Raquel Welch, and Robert Redford, along with other notables, turned 50 years of age. Now the predominant folk saying is, "You're as young as you feel." Fonda's trim and youthful body, clad in brightly colored tights, appears in video stores everywhere, convincing consumers that aerobic exercise is the new fountain of youth. The citizen's hope for continued youth is reinforced by reports from serious medical journals showing that exercise is a key

element in controlling obesity and cholesterol levels, which in turn reduces the risk of heart disease. Additionally, the federal government has now imposed strict standards on food packaging, giving the consumer fuller information about fat content. Researchers say that fat contributes to heart disease and perhaps some forms of cancer. Citizens are told that reducing their fat intake should make them healthier.

Throughout the twentieth century, medical and related technologies helped prolong people's lives dramatically. As the century closes, growing numbers of middle- and later-year persons are hoping that being a nonsmoker, along with exercising and "eating right," will lengthen their lives still more. But it's not merely the quantity of years that interests them. Good health, they hope, should also enhance the *quality* of those years. Being able to exercise like, and be as trim as, Jane Fonda vividly symbolizes control over one's life even though the biological clock ticks away. Although they're aware that death is inevitable, many older persons hope to postpone it as long as possible and "have fun" doing so.[48]

Many observers say that one way today's midlife and older persons try to have fun is to prolong indefinitely the enjoyment of sex. Before the 1960s, sexual pleasures were seen as perverse and decadent for older persons (i.e., those in their 40s and beyond). But Diana Harris and her colleagues claim that since the 1960s, the United States has experienced an "aging of sexual desire."[49] They studied *Playboy* centerfolds between 1954 and 1989 and report that over time there has been an increase in the average age of the models. They attribute that increase to shifting cultural definitions about sexual pleasure. Growing numbers of midlife and older men (and women) identify pleasurable sex with persons of their own age, not just with younger persons. Viewing older models in the media reinforces the connection between sexual pleasure and maturity.

Thus, say the researchers, "If we are to continue to have centerfolds, they should represent a broader array of womanhood than the adolescent angel of *Playboy's* youth."

Sliding Downhill versus the "New Aging"

Just as the transition to middle age was once marked by the perception that one had settled down, the transition to *old* age was once marked by the perception that one was "sliding downhill." Driving through steep mountainous areas, the motorist encounters signs warning of runaway vehicles. Due to faulty brakes or other causes, a vehicle may be unable to slow itself from disaster as it plunges downhill. "I must be getting old" conveys the idea that a person views himself or herself on a seemingly uncontrollable downhill path plunging toward death. But one seriously doubts that Fonda, Simon, or Redford would

ever use that folk saying. The reason they would not is that they, along with growing numbers of other persons, are redefining and reinventing their later years. Their transition to the later years is marked by keeping one eye on the biological clock while reaffirming the notions of choice and control that characterized their middle and early years. Skolnick labels their redefinition *"The New Aging."*[50]

We learned, for example, that Monika perceives that her middle years will be an extension of her younger years, a continued reaffirmation of choice and control. If asked, she perceives her later years in precisely the same mode. Skolnick contrasts Presidents George Bush and Franklin Roosevelt to illustrate the New Aging. Crippled by polio as a young man, Roosevelt had spent many years in a wheelchair unable to walk. He was also a heavy smoker and somewhat obese. In photos taken during 1945 at age 64 just before his death from coronary disease, he appeared to

Keeping fit is a lifelong, life-course enterprise!

be sliding downhill as fast as he could—he looked very old. But when Bush became president at age 64, he didn't seem old at all. A non-smoker, he was in excellent health and had a trim body caused in part, he claimed, by jogging and other forms of exercise. Furthermore, when he left office four years later Bush seemed hardly to have aged at all.

Bush was followed in office by the first baby boomer President, Bill Clinton, also an avid jogger. Matilda Riley is a leading expert on aging who at age 81 works full-time for the National Institute of Aging. She notes that the boomers (persons born during the dozen or so years after 1945), symbolized by public figures such as Clinton and Vice President Gore, represent the first generation to widely embrace the revised ideas known as the New Aging. The boomers are approaching their later years as "physically vigorous, intellectually strong adults who are in no mood for fading away and making room."[51]

Enforced Retirement as Social Control   By contrast, the generation of Mal's parents perceived no options other than for the husband to retire from his job in order to make room for younger men. Indeed, Mal's father worked for a company that required its employees to retire at age 65. Enforced retirement is a striking example of what this chapter earlier called *social control*. Once a certain chronological age is reached, certain norms kick in: "By the time a married woman reaches age 30, she should have a child." "When a man reaches age 65, he should retire." By contrast, *personal control* represents the idea that behaviors such as childbearing and labor force activity ought to be matters of choice, not constraint. Furthermore, prevailing cultural expectations also strongly influenced the older couple's years after the man exited from his job. Retirement became a unique lifestyle quite distinct from that of the husband's work years. As the couple lived out their "declining years"—sometimes in a retirement community—their lifestyle became

much less active and pressured, and much more leisurely.

But boomers such as Mal and Brenda have spent their middle years exercising choices (often painful), and attempting to control their lives (often ineffectively). Furthermore, young adults such as Monika will be spending their entire adult lives in a personal control rather than a social control mode. Consequently, argues Riley, it doesn't seem likely that persons who have spent many years learning both the pleasures and perils of choice will at age 65 suddenly, or easily, conform to conventional expectations regarding retirement. Instead, says Riley, they will favor "more choices and more varied roles for older people."[52] As a result of their preferences for varied rather than prescribed lifestyles, Riley believes that "the potential for increased intergenerational strife will be tremendous."

Choice versus Coping

Since the majority of persons currently in their late years were born before World War II, they're classified as preboomers. Recall that as Lester and Amelia entered retirement they could look back on a long and satisfying cycle of life safely governed by prevailing social customs. For them and for the majority of today's older persons, the view that their retirement years could be a continuation of an ongoing life course that they'd always been inventing and reinventing seems quite foreign indeed.

First, they believe that throughout their lives they've been conforming to life-cycle demands. They do not view themselves as having created innovative life courses. Second, they perceive retirement as being a sharp disjuncture from the past: They define themselves as having moved through a significant transition from preretirement to retirement. Preretirement was a time of "doing what other people (especially the boss) want." Retirement "gives me the opportunity of doing what I want." Thus, for many of today's older persons, retirement is not a continuation of a lifelong pattern of choice and control. Rather, it is defined as the first time since youth for them to *rediscover* choice and control.

Rather than *choice*, however, the label that applies more accurately to the retirement period of many of today's older citizens is *coping*.[53] More than anything else, Lester and Amelia spent their retirement worried about economics and health. As long as they had enough money, and as long as their health was good, they felt okay about themselves. But as Lester's health deteriorated due to Alzheimer's disease and the couple ran out of money, Amelia no longer felt able to cope with life and she got exceedingly depressed. Her daughter Nan stepped in and relieved Amelia of many of the burdens imposed by Lester's constant care. Nan's siblings helped out as well—not so much with Lester's physical care, but with needed financial aid. Emily Abel reports that in the United States the vast majority of needy and disabled older persons are cared for by their blood relatives. Most relatives provide this type of caregiving without any assistance from public or private agencies.[54]

Furthermore, the caregiving tends to be gender linked: the caregivers usually are women. They either do the caregiving themselves, like Nan, or they orchestrate it for other family members. If no daughter is available, daughters-in-law are often expected to be the chief caregivers.[55] A recent study, however, shows that a growing minority of men are also willing to behave as caregivers. Indeed, the researchers report that some men are currently deeply involved as caregivers to elderly parents.[56]

Bottom-Line Obligations

Why is Nan investing so much of her time and resources to help out her parents? For decades she's been quite distant from them not merely geographically, but emotionally as well. Lester and Amelia were extremely negative toward her because of her unconventional lifestyle; they never forgave her for it. All of Nan's sibs felt closer to their parents than she did. However, when their mother got to the end of her tether, each of those sibs came up with a good reason why he or she couldn't be the *chief* caregiver, although each agreed to contribute money. The sibs also agreed that Nan was the only one who couldn't legitimately refuse to be the chief caregiver. And even though Nan didn't particularly like her parents (much less love them), she concurred that she was the only one lacking a good reason not to be the chief caregiver. Hence she acknowledged her duty to take on that role.

Importantly, all of the sibs felt equally obliged to their parents, even though only one became the chief caregiver. And the sib who finally took on that demanding role had been more emotionally distant from her parents than any of the others had been. Chapters 2 and 3 showed that the *bottom line* of what families are all about is the shared obligation to help out whenever money, services, or goods are needed. These powerful "moral obligations" exist regardless of how little or how many emotional satisfactions family members do or do not share with one another. Two British researchers recently asked a sample of older persons if they "felt closer" to their relatives after those caregivers helped them out with their material or service needs. At the same time, the caregivers were asked if, after providing the needs of the older persons, they "felt closer" to them. "The most common response [from both caregivers and elderly alike] was to say that helping made no difference to their feelings towards each other."[57] In other words, the sense of we-ness, or bonding, shared by family members didn't seem to depend very much on feelings of liking and/or loving. Instead, the idea that "we are family" had emerged chiefly from the obligations to *give and receive* that had bound them together for many decades.

Elder Abuse   There is a dark side to the notion of family obligations to the elderly. Suzanne Steinmetz reports that sometimes caregivers such as Nan who are duty bound to help out their disabled elderly parents also get violent with them.[58] All of us have been in stores or other public places where we've witnessed young adults slapping or hitting their kids out of sheer frustration—"They're misbehaving and embarrassing me." But the disabled elderly seldom appear in public. Hidden from view, someone as ill as Lester can be extremely annoying to Nan, or even to his wife Amelia. Nan feels very frustrated at having to take care of her father when she'd much rather be pursuing her own life. She's also angry at her sibs for failing to pitch in for his care as much as they'd promised. Hence when Lester "misbehaves," Nan sometimes loses control and slaps or punches him. Afterward Nan feels deep shame and guilt, but a week later it happens again. Amelia's the only one who sees it, but she doesn't say a word. Amelia's afraid that if she says anything, Nan wouldn't be able to continue as Lester's chief caretaker. If that happens, Amelia fears she'll once again have to play that role, and she simply doesn't have the energy to do it.

Apparently, there is sufficient hidden violence toward the elderly in the United States to worry the American Medical Association. For several years the AMA has been urging pediatricians to be alert to signs of abuse among children, and to follow up on suspicions of child assault. The AMA recently issued a similar directive to physicians who treat elderly patients such as Lester.[59]

CONCLUSION—THE OBLIGATION OF LIFELONG REINVENTION

The numbers of later life citizens like Amelia and Lester have been growing and will continue to grow rapidly in industrial societies. The National Institute of Aging (NIA) was organized during the late 1970s as part of the official U.S. response to their physical, mental, and emotional needs. A major mission of the NIA is to study the coping strategies of older persons. During the past several years a number of researchers have turned their attention and energies to that important question.[60]

Some researchers have also begun to wonder about the aging of persons who are currently in their middle and early years. Nor have they forgotten later life people like George Bush and George Burns who are striking examples of the New Aging. Growing numbers of persons are now living into their later 80s and beyond, and many are leading healthy and active lives. Furthermore, millions of aging boomers expect to be considerably more vigorous and innovative during their later years. As researchers view the "life-course revolution" that's been occurring for almost all ages, some are thinking less about coping and more about choice and control.[61]

"Coping" pivots around the idea of reacting effectively to unforeseen circumstances. The unexpected can include a dread disease such as AIDS, breast cancer, MS, or Alzheimer's. Or it might be the elimination of one's job, a pregnancy, or the sudden death of a parent, partner, or friend. There is no doubt that the more effectively persons learn to cope with the vagaries of life, the better off they are and the better they feel about themselves. By contrast, the notion of "control" takes us an important step beyond coping. Coping asks, "How do I/we deal with the changes that have happened *to* me/*to* us?" Control asks, "How do I/we *make* changes happen?"

Earlier chapters talked about the basic human need of people to belong—to be part of a primary group and thus experience a sense of we-ness. We also discussed something called me-ness, especially its growing significance for women. Chapter 11 said that a large part of me-ness is the desire to exercise control. Just as the need to belong is a basic human feature, control is equally a "basic feature of human behavior." Control of one's life course has many names: "self-directedness, choice, decision freedom, agency, mastery, autonomy, self-efficacy, and self-determination."[62] Control is important for many reasons, not least of which is that the more control people believe they have the *healthier* they are both physically and mentally.[63]

Promoting the health of persons in their later years is NIA's all-encompassing objective. On the other hand there is no doubt that unexpected ill health (e.g., cancer, AIDS) causes anyone to feel out of control. But on the other hand researchers are also asking, "How can we assist later life people to develop a sense of mastery over their lives, thus helping them to generate good physical and mental health?" Those researchers are searching for ways to help today's older persons make the changes in their lives that they themselves desire.[64] Increasingly, however, researchers are beginning to understand that achieving control, like producing physical fitness, is ideally a lifelong process.[65] Monika, now in her 20s, intends to stay physically fit throughout her lifetime. She knows that waiting till age 45 to join a health club won't do it. The fitness she expects to have during her 60s, 70s, and 80s will simply be an extension of a lifelong pattern of keeping fit. She wants fitness to be as much a part of her lifestyle as "eating right," meaningful work, and satisfying primary relationships.

By the same token, the more Monika is able to make desired changes happen in her early and middle years, the more likely she is to keep on doing so during her later years. She takes very seriously the point made early in the chapter, that an important part of loving oneself is the obligation to take charge of one's life course as fully as possible. Monika hopes to develop a pattern—a lifestyle—of control and mastery over both her work and her relationships. She intends to experience lifelong life-course *re*-creation and *re*construction. As a

result, she hopes to enjoy a high degree of physical and mental health throughout her years, including her later ones. She's keenly aware also that a sense of me-ness is difficult to separate from a sense of we-ness, and from responsibilities to the adults and children who are part of her primary groups. Hence she knows that as she and her post-boomer generation age into middle and later years, their life courses will inevitably be marked by the struggles inherent in forever trying to balance the obligations to oneself and to others.

NOTES

1. Skolnick, 1991, pp. 14ff.
2. For example, Turner, 1962, 1985, 1990; Donald Hansen, 1988; Modell, 1989; Cowan, 1991.
3. Baltes and Baltes, 1986; Friedman and Lackey, 1991, p. 157.
4. Mirowsky and Ross, 1989.
5. Swidler, 1980.
6. Obviously, the obligation to "manage one's life course" must be balanced with the obligation to love one's neighbors and to look out for the interests of the broader social fabric, or public household, as described in Chapter 11. Just as obviously, the larger society has an obligation to provide structural opportunities enabling persons to take charge of their lives. Rather than impose greater social control, society needs to provide greater opportunities for personal control.
7. Duvall, 1962.
8. Aldous, 1978.
9. Elder, 1981a, b; O'Rand and Krecker, 1990.
10. Turner, 1962, 1985, 1990.
11. Rodgers, 1973; Aldous, 1978; Mattesich and Hill, 1987.
12. James White, 1991, p. 238.
13. Ibid., pp. 189ff.
14. Turner, 1985, uses the term *gestalt* to describe the image that the "role" of mother conveys.
15. White, pp. 6, 7.
16. Skolnick, p. 14.
17. Cowan, 1991, p. 5.
18. Ibid., p. 5.

19. Bumpass, 1990.
20. Cowan, pp. 8ff.
21. McCubbin and Figley, 1983a; Chilman, Nunnally, and Cox, 1988.
22. Nevertheless, Chapter 16 discusses recent work by researchers arguing that children may not merely be acted upon. Children very often make things happen around them. They too help to invent their social environment.
23. Nathanson, 1991.
24. Solberg, 1990.
25. Jack Katz, 1988.
26. Boxer, Cook, and Herdt, 1991, p. 60.
27. Nathanson.
28. Buchmann, 1989, p. 29.
29. Boxer et al., p. 63.
30. Ibid., p. 61.
31. Ibid., p. 71.
32. Waldman and Springen, 1992.
33. Buchmann, p. 8.
34. Ibid., p. 48.
35. Ibid., pp. 52ff.
36. Stacey, 1990.
37. Dinnerstein, 1992, p. xi, italics added.
38. Gerson, 1985.
39. Buchmann, p. 182; Modell.
40. Buchmann, p. 181.
41. Chapter 16 shows that the large increases in teen-age childbearing are occurring among pre-high-school graduates, many of them disadvantaged and/or black. They too are ignoring the script of adulthood, which says that childbearing should follow high-school graduation and especially marriage.
42. Gottman, 1982.
43. Buchmann; Modell.
44. Swidler, 1980; Skolnick, p. 161.
45. Sheehy, 1976.
46. Stacey; Weitzman, 1985.
47. Skolnick, pp. 161, 162; Beck, 1992.
48. Passuth and Bengston, 1988; Matilda Riley, 1988.
49. Harris, Fine, and Hood, 1992. See also Greeley, 1992.
50. Skolnick, pp. 163ff.
51. Riley, as quoted in McLeod, 1992, p. 12.
52. Ibid.
53. Moen and Wethington, 1992.
54. Abel, 1991, p. 165.
55. Kaye and Applegate, 1990, p. 8.
56. Ibid., p. 139.
57. Qureshi and Walker, 1989, p. 166.
58. Steinmetz, 1988.
59. Tamar Lewin, 1992.
60. In addition to Steinmetz; Qureshi and Walker; Kaye and Applegate; Abel; and Steinmetz, see Mancini, 1989; Dwyer and Coward, 1992; and Ade-Ridder and Hennon, 1989.
61. Rodin, 1990.
62. Ibid., p. 1.
63. McDowell and Newell, 1987; Cohen, 1990; Syme, 1990.
64. Abeles, 1990.
65. Berg, 1990.

CHAPTER 15

THE RESPONSIBILITIES OF PAID WORK AND HOME WORK

By now you should have no trouble guessing what reinventing responsibility means when it comes to paid work and housework. Chapter 7 used the label Big Change to describe the twentieth-century women's employment revolution. And Chapter 10 talked about increasing numbers of women accepting the obligation to love oneself. "Being responsible" and "taking care of oneself" mean, among other things, achieving economic autonomy. But for men residing with women, responsibility means nudging the pendulum in the opposite direction. It means loving one's partner enough to participate fully in the everyday demands of the household, whether routine chores or the complexities of parenting. This chapter explores some of the struggles inherent in enlarging the work responsibilities of both men and women.

"For Moms who have a lot of love, but not a lot of time . . .," declares the colorful Sunday supplement ad. As the background digital clock glows 7:55 a.m., an equally glowing 9-year-old sits holding a spoon of instant oatmeal in her mouth, her school lunch packed in a brown sack on which her name is inscribed, and an apple alongside. Standing slightly behind Nikki, her smiling (and flawlessly beautiful) "Mom" bends calmly to tie a bright ribbon on her left pigtail. Mom is dressed in business attire and has a briefcase dangling from her shoulder. Professional papers peek discretely from the briefcase. Front and center of the picture is the cereal box clinching the ad's message: The way for a woman to resolve the conflicting time demands inherent in being a good mother and a good professional is to microwave her child's instant oatmeal!

Next, *Business Week* sports a headline asserting that educated women are "America's neglected weapon."[1] Weapon against what? Against America's falling behind in the global economic competition identified in Chapter 14. Recall that fundamental structural changes are occurring in the economies of virtually every industrialized nation. Many manufacturing jobs, as well as other kinds of male-dominated occupations, are simply disappearing. "Male-dominated" refers to occupations in which the percentages of men far exceed the percentages of women. (Nursing is an example of a "female-dominated" occupation.) Managerial and executive positions have long been male dominated.

In recent years companies have cut costs through *downsizing*, which means they're eliminating the jobs of many managers and executives. Growing numbers of well-educated white men thus face something they never expected—layoffs and job insecurity. Top bosses cut jobs in order to compete effectively not only in the United States but in the world economy as well. If their companies don't compete effectively, top bosses discover they're not immune from pink slips either.[2] The *Business Week* article says that to be competitive companies need and want the best available talent. That educated U.S. women represent an expanding pool of overlooked talent in the worldwide race to be competitive.[3]

THE DREAM: (1) WOMEN'S EDUCATIONAL ACHIEVEMENTS

The *Business Week* article was based on a study done by a researcher from the U.S. Department of Education. Clifford Adelman followed a national sample of women and men from their 1972 high-school graduation through the mid-1980s.[4] He divided his study into two parts: (1) the educational experiences and (2) experiences in the paid labor force. Recall from Chapter 6 that ever since the Jacksonian era the American Dream has held forth the hope that people who work hard will eventually succeed. In particular, people believe that education is the "open sesame" door to success. Nevertheless, we learned that the Dream became a reality much more often for white men than for black men. Black men's educational opportunities were unequal to those of white men.[5] And once black men got into the job market, they were the last hired, were paid less than white men, and were the first fired.

What aroused Adelman's curiosity is the degree to which the Dream is turning into reality for *women*, both white and black. In today's global economy, are women who go to school and do well able to translate their academic achievement into occupational achievement? Or, like many black men, are most women being excluded from the Dream? If women *are* being excluded, what does that mean, Adelman asks, for America's economic competitiveness and well-being? What Adelman found was that, "In terms of general access and attainment in higher education, the issues of women's educational equity in the United States is largely passé. That battle has been won fair and square."[6] But Adelman quickly adds, "Labor market equity, sadly, is another issue."

To support his conclusion, Adelman cites a study sponsored by the Volvo corporation comparing the United States with several West European countries in terms of women's education and employment patterns.[7] At a conference discussing the Volvo study, author Kristin Keen said, "Americans are missing something . . . you're not utilizing women as well as you have prepared them. . . . In most of Europe, the problem is precisely the opposite." Keen said that European women tend not to receive the same quality of education as do American women. In other words, European women face much greater *educational* discrimination than do their American sisters. These researchers do not mean to imply that U.S. women no longer face any educational discrimination. For example, a recent national study comparing U.S. high-school boys and girls reports that teachers pay more attention to boys than to girls, girls are not encouraged to take math and science courses, girls' reports of sexual harassment are on the upswing, textbooks ignore or stereotype girls, boys' athletic events get more attention than girls' events and so on.[8] As painful as the U.S. situation is, however, American women appear to face relatively less educational discrimination than do European women.

Once in the paid labor force, however, most European women do better than most U.S. women: They achieve higher job status and they earn higher income. The term *job status* refers to the amount of prestige that most citizens assign to a particular occupation. Studies in the United States, for example, reveal that a Supreme Court justice is perceived as having more status, or prestige, than virtually any other occupation.[9] Among the very lowest occupations in terms of perceived status is ragpicker. Physicians have high status, engineers have somewhat less, bricklayers are somewhere in the middle, janitors are far down the list, and so forth. Although higher status jobs tend to generate more dollars than lower status jobs, the connection is far from being one to one. For example, top corporate executives and physicians earn far more than Supreme Court justices, yet they have relatively less status and prestige. In the eyes of the community, high-school teachers and librarians possess more status than bricklayers even though they usually earn less money. And although drug pushers earn vast sums of money, most citizens perceive them as having very little job status.

As part of his argument that U.S. women are achieving educational equity with men, Adelman compared the average class standing among 1972 high-school graduates who went on to any type of post-high-school training. "Class standing" is based on student grades: Graduates who'd achieved higher grades during their four years of high school had a higher class standing than students who'd gotten lower grades. Adelman's numbers show that no matter how one slices the students into categories, *women outperformed men in class standing achievement by an average of at least ten points.* Whether he combined students from all

racial/ethnic and social status backgrounds or examined whites only, blacks only, Hispanics only, or those from lower, medium, or higher social status backgrounds only, women had achieved significantly better high-school grades than men.

Next, Adelman compared only those women and men who had taken the three kinds of high-school courses generally required for college entrance—math, science, and foreign language. He found that "women outranked men [in class-standing] ... by a minimum of 20 percent."[10] Finally, Adelman compared the SAT (Scholastic Aptitude Test) and ACT (American College Test) scores among students who had taken those same three kinds of required courses. He found that the differences between females and males in SAT and ACT scores were negligible, at least among whites.

Having shown that among 1972 graduates, women's high-school academic performance was superior to that of men, Adelman next examined their college grade point averages (GPA). Among the 1972 graduates who went on to earn a bachelor's degree by 1984, and within each of the six major fields of study—science and math, engineering and computer science, humanities, social sciences, education, and business—women had achieved significantly higher grade point averages than men.[11] Thus, women high-school graduates from the class of 1972 continued outperforming men academically in college just as they had in high school.

Adelman also found that over time women are more likely than men to actually obtain a bachelor's degree (Table 15-1). Among 7,768 1972 high-school seniors who said they planned to get a bachelor's degree at some future point, by 1984 37 percent of the men had not yet done so (percentages rounded to whole numbers). In contrast, 32 percent of the women had not yet done so. Forty-nine percent of the

TABLE 15-1

U.S. Men and Women High-School Graduates Who Planned a Bachelor's Degree in 1972

Highest degree earned by 1984	Planned bachelor's degree,%	
	Men	Women
None	37.1%	32.2%
Certificate or license	0.9	1.7
Associate's	5.7	6.1
Bachelor's	44.1	49.3
Master's	7.5	9.2
Doctor's or first professional	4.6	1.2
All bachelor's and higher	56.2	59.7

N=7,768
Source: Adelman, 1991, p. 48.

women who in 1972 planned to have a bachelor's degree actually had one by 1984; only 44 percent of the men did. By 1984 60 percent of the 1972 women high-school graduates had a bachelor's degree *or higher*, compared with only 56 percent of the 1972 male graduates.

THE DREAM: (2) WOMEN'S LABOR FORCE EXPERIENCES

Adelman, along with many other researchers, has shown that women are doing what they're "supposed" to do when it comes to the education side of the American Dream: They work hard in high school and college, and they become well educated. Adelman remarks, provocatively: "It is not merely that women are equally qualified [with men]—they are better qualified."[12] If they indeed are better qualified, then it is logical to expect that women should at the very least get the same payoffs as men in terms of having good jobs and being reasonably well paid. The reality is that women do not do as well as men when it comes to reaping the rewards of their educational inputs.

Unemployment

Between ages 25 and 32 among persons from the high-school class of 1972, women were consistently more likely than men to experience longer periods of unemployment. Even when men and women with the same educational attainments were compared, women still reported more months of unemployment during those years. Women with college degrees were more likely to be unemployed than men with college degrees. Indeed, women with degrees were more likely to be unemployed than women who merely held certificates or licenses, for example, practical nurses, technicians, and real estate agents.[13]

Keep in mind that the definition of "unemployment" is the one used by the U.S. Department of Labor—the person is actively seeking paid work but is unable to find it. If a person is neither employed nor looking for paid work, she or he is classified as being outside the labor force (i.e., nonemployed). Many women (and now many men also) get discouraged after looking for a job for many months, and stop looking. They thus are technically no longer unemployed. For economic support they must look to their erotic friend if they have one (spouse, cohabitor), to their family (blood, social), to public assistance, or to some combination thereof. Thus, to discover the *total* number of women (or men) who at any point in time are to some degree economically dependent, we must add those who are *un*employed to those who are *non*employed.

Differences in Earnings

When women manage to get a job and hold on to it, they tend to be paid less than men. Adelman took a slice of the 1972 high-school graduates that he called "consistent [serious] labor market participants."[14] These were men and women who, first, were employed and had earnings during 1985. They also had a constant or continuous employment record since 1979. Instead of zigzagging in and out of the labor force, they had gotten in and stayed in. Labor-force continuity, or consistency, is crucial when trying to understand women's earnings. It makes little sense to compare the earnings of women who have an enter/exit (zigzag) employment history with those of men who remain in the labor force on a constant basis. For that reason, Adelman compared the earnings of men with women who were equally "serious" about paid labor. Table 15-2 shows what he found out. On the average, men were earning over $6,000 more than women *without children*. It has often been said that women earn less than men because of child-care responsibilities. Yet even when women have no children to care for, and even when they work as consistently as men, they still earn barely 76 percent as much as men do.

Plainly, however, children do make a substantial difference in young women's earnings, even among consistent workers. Women workers with children were earning almost $4,000 less than women workers without children (Table 15-2). In other words, having children meant women earned only 79 percent as much as women who were childless. Even more striking is the difference in annual earnings between men and consistent women workers with children—over $10,000. These women earned barely 60 percent of what the men did.

These numbers do not imply that every man is paid more than every woman who has the same job and works just as consistently. The numbers give us a general picture of gender differences in earnings. Moreover, the differences are not limited to the high-school class of 1972: Virtually every study reveals that in the United States men tend to earn more than women.[15] There are exceptions, of course. Table 15-3 shows earnings of workers in a variety of occupations. For most of the occupations men's average earnings are greater than those

TABLE 15-2

1985 Earnings of U.S. High-School Graduates from 1972 Who Had Been in the Labor Force Consistently, 1976–1985

Group	Mean years of work experience	Mean earnings in 1985
Men	8.0	$25,022
Women without children	7.8	18,970
Women with children	7.5	15,016

Source: Adelman, 1991, p. 23.

TABLE 15-3

Average 1985 Earnings for 1972 U.S. High-School Graduates Who Had Been Consistent Participants in the Labor Force

Occupation	Earnings		
	Men	Women (without children)	Percent difference
All	$25,000	$18,970	43.4%
Science, technology, and health:			
Computer programmers*	23,536	26,134	32.3
Computer systems analysts	34,091	32,797	24.2
Electrical engineering techs*	21,305	26,681	14.5
Engineers (all)	38,804	36,942	6.7
Engineering and science techs (NEC)	28,139	17,969	23.8
Scientists	28,975	21,053	28.8
Pharmacists	32,312	27,987	35.3
Physicians	39,054	32,458	25.0
Health technicians	22,237	20,998	75.0
Economists	34,770	33,594	31.8
Research work (NEC)*	18,708	19,086	56.4
Human services:			
Social workers	18,391	16,942	68.6
Elementary school teachers	21,403	19,661	87.0
High school teachers*	17,538	18,130	50.7
Other teachers (NEC)	19,254	16,009	67.7
School administrators	26,268	18,622	56.5
Therapists	24,168	20,858	75.0
Managers, human and health services	23,782	19,205	63.9
Business, finance, and management:			
Personnel and labor relations	34,895	31,552	56.8
Accountants	31,082	28,484	37.3
Bookkeepers	14,740	14,258	95.2
Buyer or purchasing agents*	23,385	31,783	39.0
Bank, financial, and insurance managers	34,386	26,383	40.3
Managers, wholesale and retail	23,365	19,002	25.3
Managers, manufacturing	32,879	31,930	22.8
Managers, communication industries	30,074	23,508	48.3
Real estate agents	31,017	30,516	28.9
Estimators and investigators	23,123	17,476	66.0
Production controllers	22,333	18,380	53.1
Others:			
Editors and reporters*	20,873	25,438	54.3
Lawyers	33,671	28,667	54.3
Police officers	28,376	21,444	15.4
Computer equipment*	17,534	18,581	67.9

NEC=not elsewhere classified.
*Women earning more than men.
Source: Adelman, 1991, pp. 60, 61.

of women, as we would expect. However, in seven occupations women earn more than men. In three of them (research work, high-school teachers, computer equipment operators) the differences are not very great. The largest differences are for electrical engineering technicians and buyers or purchasing agents.

Table 15-3 also lists the percentage of women working in a particular occupation. In four of the occupations in which women earn more than men, women make up the majority of workers. Hence those occupations are not male dominated. In the other two, women make up one-third of the workers.

Table 15-4 supplies a much broader landscape than 1972 high-school graduates. It shows the connection between education and earnings for the entire U.S. adult population in 1990. Many of the women covered in the table are in their middle and later years, have large numbers of children, or have been employed merely as "casual" workers, and so on. Regardless of their educational achievements, U.S. women usually earn around half, or slightly more than half, of what men earn. Even among persons with five or more years

of college, women earn only 56 percent of what men earn. It is clear that the promise of the American Dream has not yet become reality for the great majority of women.

It has not become reality even though both the percentages and the numbers of women in the labor force have increased dramatically during the past several decades. For example, in 1940 almost 70 percent of U.S. marriages were what Chapter 10 called *head-complement* arrangements: He was employed; she was not.[16] By 1990, that figure had dropped to about 20 percent. Demographers tell us that, "Dual-worker families [mostly senior-junior partner arrangements] are now the dominant family model among workers in the labor force."[17]

Economic Well-being

Thus far we've looked at unemployment and differences in earnings to underscore the conclusion that, in spite of academic achievements, women do not reap their fair share of benefits from their labor. We turn now to a third sign of that same conclusion. A major goal of having and holding a good job is what

TABLE 15-4
U.S. Mean 1990 Income by Educational Attainment, Sex, and Race for Persons Aged 18 and Over

Characteristics	Total	Fewer than 4 years high school	High school 4 years	College (years)		
				1–3	4	5 or more
Total	$20,393	$11,045	$17,072	$20,864	$31,256	$42,880
Male	26,833	14,240	22,521	27,009	40,636	52,429
Female	14,259	7,859	12,406	15,258	21,549	29,477
White	21,126	11,489	17,520	21,364	31,854	43,466
Black	14,624	8,901	13,878	17,553	26,610	33,683
Hispanic origin*	14,628	10,281	14,644	18,739	25,911	36,201

*May be of any race.
Source: U.S. Bureau of the Census, *Current Population Reports,* P-20, No. 462, issued May 1992.

Victor Fuchs calls *economic well-being*.[18] He defines economic well-being as the degree of access persons have to "goods, services, and leisure." In 1960, U.S. women of all ages spent an annual total of 572 hours in paid work, 1,423 hours in routine housework, and 266 hours in child care, for a total of 2,261 hours.[19] By 1986, those first three numbers were 997, 1,222, and 197, respectively, for a total of 2,416 hours. In short, women today are spending less time in housework and child care but far more time outside the home in paid work. Putting all three types of labor together, we can say that women are laboring more hours now than they were several decades ago.

Given that today's women labor (at both paid work and domestic work) more than yesterday's women, is their economic well-being greater than it was? Fuchs reports that for most women the answer is no. Today's women do not seem to have greater access to goods, services, and leisure than yesterday's women. Instead, says Fuchs, women's economic well-being has not changed at all or has actually declined, except for one major exception: Women who are white, young (ages 25–44), not married, and well educated (more than twelve years of schooling). Chapter 14's Monika is an example of the kind of woman Fuchs is talking about. Some within this slice of today's advantaged women may have been married before, some might be cohabiting, and some might have children living with them. In any case, this particular category of women is better off economically than were women before the Big Change of the sixties and seventies. But their improvement is an exception to the general rule.

ACCOUNTING FOR DIFFERENCES IN EARNINGS

A number of sociologists, economists, and psychologists, along with many feminists, have tried in a variety of ways to explain why men generally earn more than women and why

women's economic well-being has not increased, even though they're laboring harder.[20] If women are indeed better qualified than men as measured by educational achievement, why doesn't the Dream work for them? Social scientists usually offer two types of explanations for the persistent gender difference.

Structural Sexism

One explanation goes by the label of *structural sexism*. From this macro or mountain-top view, economic discrimination against women is built into the marketplace. Simultaneously, the discrimination is reinforced by government and by conservative religion. Take the issue of women in combat. A 1992 presidential commission came out against it.[21] Their major objection, they said, was their fear of women being taken captive by the enemy. Whatever the reason, the fact that this official rule is built into the structure of the military workplace hurts a woman's chances to increase her earnings no matter how talented she is or how hard she works. For example, a lieutenant (male) who does combat gets a bonus called "combat pay." A female lieutenant who is equally qualified is barred from earning that bonus. She is thus being discriminated against because of something over which she has no control. During years when the military is fighting, her annual income will be lower than that of fighting male lieutenants. This economic inequity is compounded when lieutenants come up for promotion. Lieutenants who've had combat experience are likely to be deemed more qualified for additional responsibilities than lieutenants without such experience. As a result, men with combat experience are likely to be promoted sooner and thus paid more than noncombatants. In effect, the structure (i.e., the rules) of their workplace means that military women, never having had a chance to be combatants, will probably earn less than men with otherwise identical qualifications.

Within the civilian labor market, Adelman

notes that one example of economic discrimination (sexism) is based on the belief that women are likely to have high job turnover, that is, they will quit very soon after being hired.[22] Employers thus pay women less, even women who actually stay at their jobs as long, and as consistently, as men. Even if women are paid the same as men at entry-level jobs, the women may not be promoted as readily as men because employers believe that women are not well suited to certain kinds of occupations. Monika (Chapter 4), for instance, graduated from college and took a job as a management trainee. Since the company she worked for received government contracts, it was required to pay her as much as a man hired for the same position. After a couple of years, however, it dawned on Monika that the men who had come in when she did (and were no more qualified than she) were being promoted faster and thus earning more.

When she tried to find out why, she discovered an unwritten but potent company policy—women were unsuited for, and thus should not be promoted to, jobs requiring travel away from home for several days at a time. The policy was based on the idea that given the stresses and strains of prolonged travel (including being away from their families), women don't make effective business negotiators. When Monika protested that she should at least be given a chance to try, her supervisor reluctantly promoted her. But her promotion came two years after the promotions of the men she'd come in with. That meant she'd already fallen behind them in terms of annual salary, not because she was less qualified or less motivated, but merely because of her gender.

Gender Segregation and Comparable Worth
Unlike Monika, many women continue to enter occupations that are segregated or typed by gender. The result is that no matter how talented they are, or how hard they work, they can only earn what those occupations pay. For

instance, Adelman reports that "dog pound keepers" earn higher annual average salaries than nursery school teachers.[23] Because being an attendant at a kennel or pound is perceived as a male job, men are much more likely to do it than women. Being a nursery school teacher is defined as a woman's job. The fact that being a pet attendant pays more than being a nursery school caregiver contributes to the earnings differences by gender reported in Table 5-4.

The fact that some jobs are stereotyped as women's jobs and thus get lower pay than men's jobs leads some women to avoid them. When Monika first interviewed at her company, she was encouraged to take a job as an administrative assistant. That position is paid less than management trainee, even though persons in both jobs do virtually identical things. Monika rejected the job as assistant (most of whom were women), and instead entered the male-dominated job of trainee. A number of feminists have argued against the structural sexism inherent in stereotyping certain jobs by gender and then rewarding "women's jobs" less than "men's jobs."[24] Preschool children are obviously more important than pets. Hence, advocates of what's called *comparable worth* argue that nursery school teachers should be paid at least the same wages as pet attendants. Currently, most firefighters ("men's work") earn more than most librarians ("women's work"). But advocates of comparable worth argue that since what librarians do is just as important as what firefighters do, their salaries should be the same.

Fuchs notes that not all feminists endorse the policy of comparable worth, and that economists fiercely debate its basic premise. Some economists, he says, believe that market forces should be left alone to determine the level of earnings a particular occupation can command. Other economists believe that it's possible to come up with a set of guidelines regarding, say, librarians and firefighters, or pet attendants and nursery school caregivers.

Those guidelines would state that because certain matched occupations are equally valuable and important to society, they should command the same earnings. Whatever the outcome of that debate, the idea of comparable worth is one response to one pervasive type of structural *sexism*—the fact that occupations stereotyped as women's jobs tend to earn considerably less than men's jobs.

Glass Walls, Glass Ceilings   A few years ago the term *glass ceiling* became a popular way to describe the discrimination women face when it comes to upward promotion. Women like Monika can peer through the ceiling to positions such as middle manager or senior executive, but the ceiling is difficult to crack. More recently, researchers have added the expression *glass wall* to our vocabulary.[25] Monika's job experiences illustrate both ideas (glass ceiling, glass wall), and reveal why it's often hard for women to move upward. Specifically, before anyone gets promoted he or she usually experiences a variety of *lateral* job moves. These are jobs that have different responsibilities but pay the same salaries and have the same status. Lateral moves supply a person with a wide range of information, contacts, and skills, thus preparing him or her for promotion. Compared with men, women are less likely to be given the opportunity to move frequently in a lateral position. They face walls through which they can see but through which it is hard to move. In Monika's case, her supervisors would have preferred to put her in the administrative assistant slot and keep her there indefinitely.

Monika knew, however, that if she were ever to break through the ceiling and become a manager or senior executive she first had to cut through the walls, and so she did. Before her promotion she sought for, and got, a wide range of lateral-type moves. Recent government data suggest she is not alone. In 1981, 27 percent of all managers in American business

were women. By 1991, that figure had risen to 41 percent.[26] However, during those ten years the number of women senior executives in U.S. businesses shifted from 1 to only 3 percent. Furthermore, the percentage of U.S. companies with women chief executive offices (CEOs) is less than that. At age 44, Carol Bartz is an actual CEO who "throughout her career . . . has refused to be overlooked because of her gender.[27] Although she does not call herself a "feminist . . . [Ms. Bartz says that] women have to perform better than men to 'get the titles.' "

Similar feelings about inequities facing career women in the marketplace emerged from a 1992 Lou Harris poll of 400 women executives in corporations with annual sales of $100 million or more.[28] Among those executives, 53 percent said that women do not have the same chance as men to be promoted; 63 percent said that if a woman is promoted her salary will be lower than that of a man who is promoted at the same time; 56 percent said that women face a "glass ceiling . . . beyond which they never seem to advance"; and 51 percent said that if their company had to choose between an equally qualified man and woman for promotion it would choose the man (36% said they weren't sure about that).

Socialization into Traditional Gender Roles

In addition to the sexism existing in the larger society, social scientists offer a second general explanation for the persistent tendency of most women to earn less than most men.[29] Earlier chapters stated that many girls and boys are taught—and thus are socialized into—traditional gender roles by parents, teachers, politicians, clergy, the media, and so forth. Chapter 14 said that Brenda grew up with traditional ideas regarding paid work, housework, and parenting, illustrated by Figure 2-1. The most significant difference between her and her brothers was that the brothers expected to be economically autonomous persons. Each brother expected and wanted to be able to provide a reasonable, or adequate, lifestyle for himself and for any children for which he might one day become responsible. Although each was aware that his wife might occasionally "have to go to work to help out," none ever expected to have to depend on a woman for support. By contrast, Brenda learned and fully accepted the traditional idea that it was okay for her to depend on someone else (her husband) for support, especially if she had children at home.

Because Brenda had been gender traditional, she didn't see much need to take any post-high-school training. Her high-school grades had been quite good—much better in fact than her brothers' grades. And although she enjoyed her premarital job in a local factory where her brothers also worked, she and they viewed their employment quite differently. The brothers perceived their jobs as means to help them become the chief providers for their families. Brenda defined hers as a way to earn money for nice clothes, a car, and her own apartment. After she married Mal, she kept her job until she got pregnant. Then she dropped out of the labor force to raise her family.

Part of the reason for Brenda's norms and behaviors can be traced to her parents' expec-

tations for her, compared with the expectations her parents held for her brothers. Adelman reports that when 1972 high-school graduates were asked how much education they believed their parents wanted them to get, he found different results for women and men. Table 15-5 shows that the parents held lower educational aspirations for their daughters than they did for their sons. Brenda's parents wanted her brothers to attend the local vocational college to learn a skilled trade, but they were quite content merely to have her finish high school. They were especially pleased for her to marry Mal because he was professional machinist. They believed him to be a "good catch" (i.e., a good provider).

It's plain to see how Brenda's growing-up experiences—her childhood and adolescent socialization—helped shape her into becoming a traditional woman. Furthermore, as she made her transition into young adulthood her parents and her friends, both just-friends and erotic friends, reinforced her traditional ideals and goals. Brenda exemplifies why some sociologists say that women tend to earn less than men. During her early married years, Brenda would not fit even within row 3 of Table 15-2. Although she was employed at various times after her children were born, she was not what Adelman called a serious or consistent member of the paid labor force. As a result, when

TABLE 15-5
Parents' Educational Aspirations for 1972 U.S. High-School Graduates as Perceived by the Graduates

Degree or educational level desired for child	For sons		For daughters	
	Father	Mother	Father	Mother
Graduate	16.1%	17.0%	9.5%	9.7%
Bachelor's	42.9	51.6	40.5	39.0
Some postsecondary education	31.2	22.7	36.5	39.0
No postsecondary education	9.8	8.7	13.5	12.3

Source: Adelman, 1991, p. 6.

Brenda did take a paying job she earned much less than women with children who were consistent workers, and much less than men and childfree women.

Structure and Tradition   When women like Brenda are counted, say in Table 15-4, it seems their traditional gender roles are one reason why women's earnings usually turn out to be lower than men's earnings. Because they have not learned the importance of being economically autonomous, they tend not to participate as consistently and as seriously as men in the paid labor force. Nevertheless, socialization into traditional gender roles can't be the whole story! Tables 15-2 and 15-3 revealed that many women who are child-free and who work just as consistently as men still earn less than men—Monika, for example.

Clearly, discrimination in the marketplace, as well as segregating work into men's jobs versus women's jobs, contributes to women's lower earnings. Hence, inequities in women's earnings are the result of a complex combination of structural features existing in society, as well as features that have been an intimate part of women's own lives since childhood.

Table 15-3 showed that a few women manage to overcome both structure and tradition. But recall that six of the seven occupations in which women do earn more than men are not typical women's jobs. The women in them have chosen to bypass women's work in favor of occupations usually perceived as men's work—work that is paid better than women's work. Having entered the world of men's work, they almost surely encountered many forms of gender discrimination, just as Monika did. But like Monika, many of them probably want to be economically autonomous. Hence, like her, they struggle against discrimination. For some women at least, the result is a 1985 level of earnings comparable to, or even greater than, that of men.

Children and Women's Paid Labor

The reason we stress the date (1985) is that the women in Table 15-3 are child-free. But because they're young, a number of them are likely to bear at least one child. When that happens, will the women now earning more than men find themselves earning less? Will women who already earn less than men fall even further behind? How many will land in row 3 of Table 15-2 by earning less than child-free women as well as men? Will some women become unemployed, or drop out of the labor force entirely, or start to zigzag in and out? Children figure into women's economic disadvantage from both a structural and a socialization standpoint. They're a critical element explaining the persistent differences between women's and men's earnings. Fuchs goes so far as to claim that their "greater desire for and concern about children ... [is] the biggest source of women's economic disadvantage."[30] Whether or not it's in fact the biggest, children obviously play a major part, as we learned from Table 15-2.

To help win World War II, the federal government urged American women to work in defense industries. The government provided child-care facilities at the very places mothers worked.[31] This monumental structural change in the workplace was introduced almost overnight, and it greatly facilitated mothers' employment. Just as rapidly, when the "boys" came back to claim their jobs, the on-site child-care facilities were closed and women were no longer welcomed in the labor force. During recent years, in response to the growing numbers of mothers in the paid labor force, many of whom are solo parents, a number of companies have aimed at becoming *family friendly.*[32] Among other things, family-friendly companies might offer on-site child care along with flexible work schedules, family leaves, and so on. Such programs are examples of structural changes in the workplace enabling women to work on a more consistent basis.

After dropping out of the labor force, some career women seek to reduce the potential impact of "lost earnings" by trying to keep up with their field at home.

Another proposal for structural change that for a while received wide media attention was nicknamed the *mommy track*.[33] Under that proposal, companies would create unique career paths for women (men were not mentioned) who wanted to divide their time between being managers and being mothers. This proposal suggests a significant structural change. Simultaneously it tries to bridge that change with the traditional idea that women have been socialized into the unique identity known as *mother*. A number of feminists, however, objected to the proposal on the grounds that it would reinforce the popular stereotype that women tend to be less committed than men to consistent and demanding careers.[34] A second objection was that "mommy-track" managers would invariably earn less than men; hence the proposal would do nothing to narrow the earnings gap between the genders.

Lost Earnings Regardless of whether women drop out of the labor force for structural reasons ("I have to"), or because of their socialization ("I want to"), they tend to pay a heavy price in terms of lost earnings. A recent study by two economists found that women who take a break from the labor force (for whatever reasons) earn significantly less than women (and men) who stay in. What is striking is that "the negative effects of a break on earnings are quite persistent, being discernible even twenty years after the last break ended."[35] The authors add that women whose labor force participation is "intermittent" (shifting in and out of the work force) are likely to have significantly lower lifetime earnings.

Nevertheless, some career women do stay out of the labor force for an extended period in order to have children. "Extended period" is defined as longer than a year. When a number of women who took extended leaves were recently interviewed, they reported that the single biggest obstacle they faced when returning to their companies was their colleagues' skepticism about their work commitment.[36] Their colleagues included women who had *not* stayed out for an extended period to have children, as well as men. The colleagues doubted the returning mothers' seriousness about reinvolving themselves in the heavy demands and incessant pressures of their careers. Incidentally, it's vital to keep in mind that virtually all of the women had a man (usually a spouse) to support them at the time they exited their careers. Solo parents rarely if ever possess the exit option.

Economic Autonomy and Control Sociologists are busy trying to learn much more than we presently know about women who exit their careers in order to have children.[37] One of the most important questions is, how do they feel about the likelihood of facing a serious earnings gap once they reenter their careers? Some of the women who exit might respond that for them the bottom-line issue is neither earnings nor job status. They might say that the basic issue is their own economic autonomy. Although they're sacrificing money and prestige, in their view staying out of their career for a while does not undermine their long-term capabilities to care for themselves and their child(ren) independently of a man, if it ever came to that. They might add that they still believe strongly in what Chapter 10 called the obligation to love oneself, and that pursuing a career is indeed one way to express that love. Nevertheless, they also believe that for them at this point in their life course loving one's neighbor means caring full-time for their child(ren). "When my children enter school," they might say, "will be time enough for me to

reenter my career and concentrate on loving myself once again." At least for the present, they may feel the best way to take control of their lives, and thus to experience emotional and physical well-being, is to concentrate on child caregiving.

Varied Life Choices To be sure, some women consider any paid work as foreign to loving themselves. For them, taking care of oneself means picking a husband who can provide enough money so they don't ever have to enter paid labor and be away from their children. Taking care of oneself also means hanging on to that husband for life. These days, such husbands are almost always located in high-paying occupations such as physician or corporate executive. The couple's affluence enables the wife to be a full-time mother and homemaker. Chapter 10 described these as head-complement marriages. Before the 1960s, having that sort of marriage was thought to be the ideal way to live. It was the unquestioned goal of the vast majority of North Americans.

Today, however, this ideal is for the most part held by persons who are devoutly religious, as well as affluent. Their denominational label, whether Protestant, Catholic, or Jewish, is far less important than how strongly they hold to the traditional teachings of their own religious group.[38] Such persons believe that the essence of the Judeo-Christian tradition is that the mother should love her children more than herself and willingly sacrifice her own occupational interests. Because such women never enter paid labor, they never have earnings nor do they wish to. Nevertheless, they feel very much in control of their life because it's giving them exactly what they want. It would not make sense to include women who don't want paid jobs in, say, Table 15-4. Their behavior provides no evidence to support the conclusion that men earn more than women.

From another perspective, some women

would prefer not to be employed, but their life circumstances require it. Certain solo parents, for instance, might feel forced into paid labor either because they don't have an erotic friend or because their child support may be inadequate or nonexistent. Likewise, public assistance may be insufficient or not considered a viable option. Even if a woman does have a partner, he may be unable and/or unwilling to support her and her children at what she perceives to be a reasonable level. The woman then reasons that loving her children means earning money for them. She never defines her paid work as an expression of loving herself.

Brenda's sister, Angie, works because she feels she has to, not because she wants to. She's employed as a secretary so that she and her husband can meet their numerous monthly bills. Because she's in a "woman's job," she doesn't earn a great deal of money. She quit her job when she had a baby, but soon had to take another job to meet expenses; she'd much rather have stayed at home. At different times her husband's earnings were high enough for her not to have to work. But those times are getting rarer. In order to take care of (love) her children, she needs to work outside her home. Because she's now usually employed full-time and year around, she fits within row 3 of Table 15-2—a consistent (but unwilling) worker with children.

Brenda and Angie—Different Identities Both Brenda and Angie were socialized into not being full-time workers. They learned instead to be full-time mothers and homemakers. Nevertheless, economic realities led both of them to change their behaviors from being nonemployed into being a full-time paid worker. Chapter 14 described how Brenda's behavioral changes were part of a genuine transition. Alongside her behavior, her own identity shifted from "traditional woman" to "autonomous worker." She no longer viewed herself as requiring a man to support her and her children; she perceived herself as an equal

partner with Mal. Mal and his mother viewed things very differently, however, and they blamed her for the dissolution phase and divorce that eventually followed.

Brenda's friends affirmed the "new Brenda," and her transition to autonomous worker was accomplished. Even when Mal's earnings became quite sufficient to meet their lifestyle demands, she kept on working. Her goal was to be able to take care of herself and her children just as well as Mal could take care of himself and the children. For Brenda, that's what loving herself as much as her neighbor meant. Making the transition to economic autonomy increased her sense of control over her own life, and thus enhanced her sense of well-being.

Angie, on the other hand, never made that sort of transition. Although she began to play the role of worker as consistently as Brenda, that was not the "real Angie." She strongly preferred to quit the labor force and be a homemaker. Thus, on the one hand her earnings provided some sense of control (and well-being) because she and her husband could now pay their bills. On the other hand, being forced to do something she didn't want to do made her feel that a major realm of her life was out of control. Consequently, Angie had a lot of stress symptoms and was often physically ill.

Autonomy among African-American Women
Although many African-Americans suffer severe economic discrimination, there is at least one striking exception that is probably connected to the matter of women's economic autonomy. During the early 1960s, black scholar Jeanne Noble identified what she called the "Negro woman's role as a working citizen."[39] Her argument was that at least since 1865, white discrimination against black men prevented many of them from being consistent workers and family providers even though they wanted to. As a result of this discrimination, black women had to enter paid labor even though they didn't want to. Like most white

Working mothers may be dropping out of the labor force because they are unable to afford caregivers.

women of those times, they preferred to have a man who could support them and their children. But to ensure the survival of their families, they entered the labor force.

Noble suggests that after generations of playing the *role* of paid worker, many black women by the 1960s had come to internalize the *identity* of "autonomous worker." That is, they defined themselves as wanting to be able to take care of themselves and their children, just as any man would. By contrast, said Noble, most white women at that time didn't feel that way because they didn't have to—there was almost always a man around who could earn a reasonable wage. By 1967 the median earnings of U.S. black professional women ($6,209) were discernibly higher than those of white professional women ($5,910), and the same as those for black professional men ($6,208).[40]

In spite of the many disadvantages of being black and female, professional black women were doing comparatively well even before the advent of minority affirmative action programs of the late sixties and seventies. Feeling keenly the need to be able to take care of themselves and their children may have been one factor spurring them to choose nontraditional jobs in the first place. And once there they, like Monika, did their best to try to resist the discrimination that would adversely affect their earnings.

This same sort of racial difference persisted among U.S. 1972 high-school graduates by the time (1985) they reached age 32. Adelman reports that "whether or not they had children, black and Hispanic women who earned bachelor's degrees had higher earnings than the white women" with the same level of education.[41] Table 15-6 shows the ways in which well-educated black women are continuing the labor force patterns that Noble identified several decades ago.

White Women's Prospects The intriguing question is whether the earnings of well-edu-

TABLE 15-6

**Race, Years of Employment, and 1985 Mean Earnings
for U.S. Women Graduates of High-School Class of 1972
Who Had Earned a Bachelor's Degree**

	White	Black	Hispanic
Women without children:			
Employment (years)	7.44	6.95	6.42
Earnings	$21,091	$24,394	$21,586
Women with children:			
Employment (years)	7.07	7.19	6.91
Earnings	$16,617	$18,538	$19,960

Source: Adelman, 1991, p. 63.

cated white women will eventually catch up with the earnings of their black sisters. Up to now, two key factors have contributed to the lower earnings of white women compared with black women. First, whites married men who were able to hold steady jobs. Second, they stayed married to those men. But we learned that the structure of the labor market is shifting drastically for white men. They are increasingly subject to unemployment or to underemployment, (i.e., taking a job below one's level of education or skills). Mal, for instance, though trained as a skilled machinist, was forced to take a clerking job (Chapter 14). White women thus can no longer count on their men for economic support the way they once could.

Earlier chapters showed that growing numbers of white women are marrying for the first time at a later age, meaning they've had to care for themselves (and any children) well into their late 20s or early 30s. Moreover, the divorce revolution (Chapter 13) means that many white women who might count on marriage (or remarriage) for long-term support tend to be severely disappointed. In addition, growing numbers of white persons are cohabiting, and there's no evidence to suggest that women married informally can depend on their partners for economic support in quite the same ways as formally married women. Furthermore, contemporary erotic friendships are marked by what earlier chapters called *permanent availability.* Instead of being locked into relationships (whether formal or informal), growing numbers of white women and men have the option of choosing whether to stay or leave. Because of the spreading cultural idea that women are obliged to love themselves, more and more women like Brenda are in fact choosing to leave.

In short, white women (and men) are having to learn to live with uncertainty in the labor market and also with uncertainty in the erotic friendship "market," in many of the same ways that black women (and men) have lived with uncertainty for many decades. Over time we may expect that the current earnings gap between educated white and black women is likely to narrow.

MEN AND THE WORKINGS OF THE HOUSEHOLD

Let's return now to the broader question of the earnings gap between the genders. Specifically, how do inequities in the doing of household chores and parenting contribute to that gap? Chapter 14 said that Monika (a well-educated woman in her 20s) was well aware of the uncertainties inherent in today's relationships, and in today's labor market. During the two years she'd cohabited with Aaron, they'd experienced ongoing conflicts over household chores. Before they moved in together, Monika frequently visited the small house that he rented with a woman housemate. It seemed plain to Monika that Aaron and his housemate participated equally in required housekeeping chores. They each did their share of cleaning, dusting, vacuuming, washing, cooking, and so on. They figured out who did what and when by means of what Chapter 11 called discussion and problem-solving. Thus, it had never occurred to Monika that domestic work would be any sort of big deal between them.

But after several weeks into their informal marriage, Monika became aware that increasingly she was doing more work than Aaron was. In fact, each week that went by he did less and less. He simply ignored the dust on the furniture, the dirt on the floors, the ring in the bathtub and the piles of soiled clothing. If he ran out of socks or underwear, he merely washed out several pair for himself, never bothering to ask Monika if he might do the same for her. Still, she kept her frustration to herself until she came home to discover that on his assigned cooking night he hadn't bothered to prepare anything. Monika, as we learned, was very much into healthy foods and fitness; she was furious to see him watching Monday night football munching on junk food when he was supposed to be stir frying vegetables.

Monika blew up, initiating the series of continual struggles between them over what Lydia Morris calls "the workings of the household."[42] Monika wanted to know what was so different about living with her (his erotic friend) and living with his former housemate (*just* a friend): "You didn't love her or even sleep with her," screamed Monika. "Why then did you treat her better than you treat me?" Aaron wasn't sure what to say. Two years later, when they had terminated their relationship, he still hadn't figured it out. But then neither had Monika. Nor, for that matter, have sociologists figured it out.

Facts about Housework

Todd Gitlin says that the most long-lasting outcome of the tumultuous sixties has been the *women's movement*.[43] First among its goals was to open women's access to the labor market and thus eventually move women toward economic autonomy.[44] Virtually everyone assumed that as women did more work outside the home, men would do more domestic work and child care.[45]

But by and large it hasn't worked out that way. Researchers have been extraordinarily surprised to discover a number of doggedly persistent "facts."[46]

First, housework remains defined as women's work. A major difference between housework and other "women's jobs" such as nursery school caregiver or librarian is that the latter are paid, but housework is not. While some men are currently being attracted into paid jobs previously defined as women's work (e.g., nursing), why would any man want to enter *unpaid* women's labor? Although the annual market value of the average homemaker's tasks is placed at around $50,000, who would be willing to pay that much?[47] Even upper-class households rarely if ever pay their full-time domestic help anything near that figure.

A second fact is that most women do more domestic work (both routine chores and child caregiving) than most men. Some studies suggest that across marriages in general, women do two to three times more of the routine tasks (cleaning, dusting, shopping, washing, meal preparation, and so on) than men.[48] Even when wives have paid jobs, they still tend to do more housework and parenting than their husbands. When employed wives are compared with nonemployed wives, a national study reports that the former spend almost as much time on both routine chores and parenting as the latter—27 hours per week versus 38.5 hours, or 70 percent as much time.[49]

Third, even though domestic work in general is perceived as women's work, some tasks carry less stigma than others and are often known as either shared tasks or male tasks. These include such things as bill paying, financial and insurance matters, car buying, gardening, and car and household maintenance and repairs. A number of studies show that men usually tend to do more of these "male" tasks than either employed or nonemployed wives.[50] Career wives, however, tend to do more of them than employed wives who are not in careers.[51]

Women's achievement was the major reason most observers once expected that men would eventually do as much homework as women. Most sociologists and feminists believed that as women entered the labor force they would be able to use their education, job status, and earnings as resources negotiating men into doing more domestic work.[52] And in a few cases today that might be true. Rosanna Hertz, for instance, says that the dual-career couples she studied are "more equal than others."[53] She means that the women and men from those well-educated professional and business couples seemed to share household tasks more equitably than, say, dual-employed working-class couples.

Women's Second Shift Arlie Hochschild's study suggests a similar conclusion. She did in-depth interviews with fifty white, middle-class, dual-employed, married couples.[54] She reports that only about 20 percent of the husbands did as much housework as their wives. But among this 20 percent, the wives were well educated and thus earned about as much as their husbands. The remaining 80 percent of the husbands earned more dollars than their wives. Most of those husbands did less than half as much housework as their wives did; a few did less than a third. Hochschild says that the great majority of employed wives in the United States do their paid work and then come home and do the bulk of unpaid labor. She describes women's unpaid labor as their *second shift*. By contrast, most men have but one work-shift per day. And indeed, not all studies of dual-career marriages report that men share equally in household tasks. Some researchers say that even career wives work harder at home than their career husbands do.[55] Moreover, most of the work that career husbands do at home is connected with parenting. According to these studies, even career men tend to concentrate less than their career wives on routine chores.

Models for Domestic Work On the basis of her study of couples with a child under age 12 and the wife employed at least part-time, L. Lein says there are at least four different models by which women and men view household work.[56] First is the *add-to* model, where the woman simply adds paid work to her previously ongoing home work. Because home work is perceived as women's work, the husband does virtually nothing around the house. Second is the *helping-out* model, where she retains prime responsibility for domestic tasks but he pitches in when she comes up short on time or energy. Although it's Angie's job to take the kids to day care on her way to work and pick them up on her way home, her spouse might occasionally fetch them if she has to work late. Both these models fit under Hochschild's notion that most employed women have two work shifts per day.

Lein next identifies a third, or *specialist*, model. Each partner is fully responsible for a particular household task. He concentrates, say, on dishwashing, laundry, repairs, paying bills, and financial matters. He does "his things" while she concentrates on different household tasks—"her things." Finally, Lein describes the *partners* model. This would fit under what Chapter 10 called the equal-partner relationship. Instead of stereotyping household chores as women's work or men's

Expressing his identity as *caregiver,* this man is not only attending to a baby, he is also modeling what a "real man" is for his little girl.

work, these couples perceive all chores merely as tasks that must be done. Rather than a task being gender *specific* (cleaning up is her work; repairing toasters is his), each task is viewed as gender *neutral.* If no task (including parenting) is defined automatically as hers or his, how do the partners figure out who does what? They figure it out either by discussion and problem-solving and/or by conflict and negotiation.

Piecing Together the Puzzle

While that sounds simple enough, Chapter 11 showed how difficult problem-solving can be, and also how emotionally wrenching negotiation can become. A number of studies report that even educated professional women find it very difficult to negotiate equitable task sharing with their partners.[57] Recall that Monika

was hesitant to say a word to Aaron about what she viewed as his negligent behavior. She certainly hadn't planned to blow up. She'd hoped that at some point they could quietly discuss a pattern of fair task sharing similar to the one he'd had with his just-friend. But suddenly they were fighting about cooking versus his wanting to watch football. He told her this was an important game and he couldn't see why she was making such a big deal about him not cooking.

Next day, after they both cooled off, Monika began their negotiations by reminding Aaron they were both professionals earning comparable salaries and that they were already contributing equally to household expenses. She was confident they could figure out fair arrangements as to who would do which household tasks and when. Although she wasn't entirely satisfied with what Chapter 11 called the *outcomes* of their negotiations, she was willing to go along with them. The rub was that after several weeks, Aaron would forget to do what he'd agreed to, or he'd delay doing it longer than she thought he should, or he'd do a job (e.g., cleaning) in what Monika defined as a sloppy and thus unacceptable fashion. Monika perceived his forgetfulness, stalling, and sloppiness as strategies for opposing what she wanted from him. She viewed those indirect strategies as silent conflict behaviors. Hence Monika and Aaron would periodically try to resolve their conflicts through *re*negotiation. For a while things would be okay again. But later Aaron would repeat his silent conflict strategies, and once again they'd be forced to renegotiate their chores. After a couple of years of living with these sorts of conflicts, her sense of we-ness, and his too, became significantly eroded. Each partner eventually perceived they'd made a transition into what Chapters 5 and 11 called a dissolution phase. As their erotic friendship continued to wind down, they began to realize there was no way to move on to a fresh maintenance and change phase. Hence they began to think about separating, and eventually they did.

Piecing together the puzzle as to why most men (even the well educated) participate less than most women in chores and parenting is important for a number of reasons. One major reason is that sharing home work more equitably would probably help narrow the gender earnings gap. It would be narrowed because women would have fewer constraints on their time, and thus would have greater freedom to choose nontraditional male jobs and also careers that are time demanding. Both kinds of occupations pay more than women's work. Once in those occupations, they'd be freer to work on a more consistent basis. They'd also have more time to work longer hours and to travel. Even in Sweden and Norway, where first-class care for preschool children is made

readily available to all citizens at little or no cost, women remain more involved than men in both chores and parenting.[58]

Every puzzle has several key pieces, and if they can be identified and fitted together, the other pieces fall into place. Kristine Baber and Katherine Allen suggest that one key to piecing together this puzzle is what Chapter 11 called "effective negotiation." Both Monika and Aaron are skilled negotiators in their paid occupations, yet they were unable to work out mutually acceptable outcomes regarding home work. Thus there must be a second piece, and previous chapters called it "economic autonomy." Autonomy fits under what Chapter 11 called the context of discussion and negotiation: It's one of the things couples bring with them into the give-and-take processes of figuring out what to do. Monika did view herself as an economically autonomous person, unlike Angie, who was merely playing the role of paid worker but never genuinely viewed herself as one. Like Brenda (and Brenda's brothers), Monika felt strongly that she had the responsibility to be able to take care of herself and her children, if any. But this piece of the puzzle didn't assist her negotiations with Aaron. Indeed, for both Monika and Brenda, the fact they were so determined to be autonomous contributed to their inability to resolve their conflicts.

Householder and Caregiver Identities There must thus be a third piece to our puzzle, and to find it we compare Aaron with Marshall (Chapter 10). When Kate (an autonomous person) and Marshall had conflicts over home work, they were able to resolve them reasonably effectively. One reason they could is that alongside his identity as autonomous worker, Marshall had an identity as *householder*, and also an identity as *caregiver*. By contrast, Aaron never had those identities even though he grew up learning that boys do things around the house. His father did chores regularly, and

Until they get into it, most persons don't realize that equal-partner couples with children face incessant, unremitting demands on their time.

as a small child Aaron started doing them too. And he proved he could do chores when he lived by himself and later with his female housemate.

Nonetheless, Aaron had the same connection to *home* work that Angie had to *paid* work. She played the role of paid worker, but that was neither who she was nor who she wanted to be. Aaron had played the role of householder, but that was never part of his identity: "Doing housework is not me!" The role of child caregiver was not part of his identity either. Marshall, on the other hand, developed both identities, even though his father had never lifted a finger around the house. Since Marshall perceived himself to be a householder, he did about as much home work as Kate during the many years they were informally married. And when they married formally and had a child, he did more than merely play the role of parent—he also fully expressed his identity as caregiver to their child.

Although Marshall had not grown up with those identities, he experienced a transition into both of them as a young adult. Just as Brenda made her transition to autonomous worker as a result of unexpected social circumstances, the same was true for Marshall. In his case the circumstances were Kate's very tough negotiations with him over home work soon after they began cohabiting. Like Monika (and many women), Kate was upset that her partner was not doing his share around the house. During their struggles over the issue, she was somehow able to communicate that for today's men, "loving one's neighbor as oneself" means taking on both identities.

There is no doubt that virtually all women strongly possess the identities of householder and caregiver. Their commitment to both identities is part of the reason they don't negotiate more assertively with men over home work. And it's part of the reason some women avoid nontraditional, high-demand jobs and do not work more consistently at jobs they do have.

Kate communicated to Marshall that loving a woman means taking on and then expressing both identities. The more he did that the freer she became to express her identity as autonomous worker. In effect, her me-ness is reinforced by their we-ness. Kate added that most women have always loved men in that fashion. By being both householder and child caregiver, women freed men to be paid workers.

Fitting these several pieces together moves us closer toward solving the puzzle of gender inequities in household task sharing. If women and men are to achieve reasonably equitable patterns of chores and child care, then a whole range of context factors must be in place. Among these are the identities that the genders carry with them into their discussions and negotiations about home work. Besides the identities they already possess as householder and caregiver, women must possess the identity of autonomous worker. Added to the identity men already possess as paid worker must be the identities of householder and caregiver. Underlying the two latter identities is the conviction that a man who expresses them is loving his partner in ways that were foreign to most men during the past. Finally, the couple's negotiations are made easier to the degree that their outside world is *family friendly*. That means less gender discrimination in the marketplace, more companies with flexible policies toward families, and more high-quality caregiving centers for children.

HOME WORK AND LABOR FORCE OPTIONS

To be sure, there are no guarantees that couples will be able consistently to resolve conflicts over home work effectively, even if women and men do share balanced identities. Certainty is never possible because, among other things, unforeseen factors (e.g., promotions, layoffs, new job options) always have a

way of intruding. Nor does our discussion imply a rigid formula regarding paid work and home work. There is no longer any ideal model for couples to follow, as there was during the 1950s. Today's couples are free to make an almost endless range of choices regarding paid work and home work during their life course. At certain times both may be employed and chores may be divided on a fifty-fifty basis. Later on, even though both are employed, they may negotiate a pattern in which he or she does more home work than the other. Or one partner may become unemployed either by choice or layoff and accordingly they may shift their patterns. They may agree, for example, that for a time he (or she) will be the "house-spouse" or "house-partner."[59] In short, couples may negotiate one set of mutually satisfactory patterns of home work and paid work at one time and a different pattern later on.

In addition to reconstructing home work, some couples and solo parents may for a while pursue the option of reconstructing their paid work via self-employment. Being one's own boss tends to enhance flexibility in organizing chores and childcare. Flexibility is increased even more if the paid work is done at home. A number of recent studies document the prospects, problems, and trends in home business—what some researchers call the *invisible work force*.[60] For instance, women who start their own business (whether in or out of their home) tend to encounter numerous obstacles, including getting credit from male bank managers.

One observer describes barriers encountered by self-employed women as *the brick wall*.[61] A very different type of nonconventional choice is made by women high-school graduates who don't want college but do wish to escape traditional low-paying women's jobs. These women opt for high-paying men's jobs such as carpenter, police officer, machinist, electrician, and so on. Recent studies show that these women face a great deal of discrimina-

For some women, job diversity means taking on formerly all-male, physically demanding, and dangerous tasks. The well-educated woman may choose to take on formerly all-male, intellectually demanding tasks.

tion from their male peers and supervisors.[62] They are also the workers most likely to be laid off during economic downturns.

Tough Choices

Tough choices always have important consequences and so must be carefully weighed. Before their child was born, Kate wondered whether she should take an extended leave beyond the six weeks of paid maternity leave provided by her company. Marshall had asked his company for a *paternity* leave so that when

Kate went back to work he could stay home for several months. However, his small firm already had two persons out on family leave and thus couldn't spare him. Kate sought advice from one of her colleagues about the wisdom of taking an extended family leave. Her colleague reminded Kate that their company was in the midst of planning expansions into international markets. "If you stay out of the loop now," warned the colleague, "you're likely to be overlooked for promotion into the new jobs" (with their greater challenges and earnings) that accompany expansion. Kate and

Marshall discuss the problems and tough choices facing them. After considerable agony they arrive at a solution they hope will work. When her six-week leave is up, she returns to her career. He then takes on ultimate responsibility for their infant, including day-care arrangements and staying home from work when the child is ill. Whenever and wherever possible, he cuts back on work duties and tries to spend as much time as possible with their child.

Recent studies of managers and executives (men like Marshall) report that it's just as difficult for them to be *chief caregivers* to children as it has been for career women.[63] Among other things, the men resented how frequently children's needs unexpectedly intruded on their plans and time schedules. Men also found challenging the emotional nurturing of children—how to cultivate emotional intimacy on a deep level. Reconciling intimacy with child discipline was especially perplexing for these highly disciplined career men.

Even though friends had warned Marshall and Kate ahead of time how difficult it is for couples to maintain two careers *and* have children, neither had any idea that it would be as arduous and stressful as it actually became. Nonetheless, whenever a new problem arose knocking holes in their prior problem-solving, they quickly scrambled and usually managed to figure out a new solution. The fact that they both worked for family-friendly companies contributed greatly to their creative problem-solving. That resource, alongside their own energy and resourcefulness as well as the particular kind of love just described, led them to believe they could do all of the following *at the same time:* maintain their erotic friendship, maintain both careers, and be responsible parents.

Commuter Relationships Although Kate and Marshall have not yet had to face the issue of a "commuter relationship," they sense it

looming in the distance. This is defined as an erotic friendship in which the work demands of both partners force them to be separated on a regular basis for intervals (usually a week at a time) during which they maintain two residences.[64] In the past it was very common for career sales*men* to leave home each Sunday evening and get back on Friday. Usually they stayed in hotels rather than maintain a separate residence. That sort of behavior is now also becoming common for career sales*women*, but in addition, some dual-career couples find it necessary to maintain two households.[65]

Kate and Marshall, for instance, currently live in the eastern United States. But the expansions planned by her company are into Asian markets. Office rumor is that the company will be asking managers promoted to executive positions in charge of the expansions to relocate on the West Coast. If Kate is offered a promotion and asked to move, she and Marshall would face a number of tough decisions. If they agree she should move, and Marshall continues in his occupation, they would have a commuter relationship. Among many other things, they would have to negotiate how often they get together, and where, and for how long. Additionally, which of them would keep their child with him or her, and for how long each time? How would the parent who has the child manage to balance career and caregiving demands without the active participation of the partner? That would be especially vexing for Kate because she would be required to spend extended periods outside the United States cultivating new markets in Asia.

In light of that reality, Marshall ponders the option of quitting his job, moving with Kate, and looking for a new job on the West Coast. In effect, he would become what many women have been for decades: *a trailing spouse*. Recently, growing numbers of men have found themselves in that situation and, in the words of one, " 'It's a very strange, unusual experi-

ence.'"[66] Severely complicating their shared
decision-making regarding these issues is
what Kate's male supervisors have told her
about the realities of doing business in Asia.
Her supervisors report that they themselves
often have trouble being taken seriously by
their Asian counterparts. Such discrimination,
they suspect, would probably be worse for women.[67] Several researchers report that Asian
businessmen (compared with American men)
are much more likely to *not* take women executives seriously, to trivialize them, and to negotiate with them in a demeaning and often intentionally unfair manner.[68]

Naive Expectations

While griping about their current problems
with their friends, Kate and Marshall admit
they were once extremely naive about the
pains of having dual careers and children at
the same time. But they're not alone. Baber and
Allen cite a number of studies showing that
most well-educated persons are in the same
boat: Many college women and men are
"naive about the dilemmas involved in integrating work and family."[69] The studies report
that college women in particular expect to
"have it all" and on their terms: They want to
have an emotionally satisfying formal marriage that endures, a challenging and rewarding career, and children. Their naivete is analogous to that of persons scaling Mount Everest
for the first time. Climbers making it to the
summit and back (some do not) admit that no
matter how prepared they were, they'd had no
idea how painful and wrenching it would be.
A recent study of U.S. college women says that
their peer culture exercises much greater influence on women than anything they learn in the
classroom.[70] Part of what the college peer culture does is mask the trouble and pain that
women (and men) will later experience in trying to manage a relationship, careers, and children all at the same time.

Mixed Cultural Messages   There are many
complex reasons why equal-partner relationships such as Kate's and Marshall's are extraordinarily difficult to maintain indefinitely.
Besides structural sexism, too few family-
friendly firms, and too few quality caregiving
facilities, there is also the matter of prevailing
cultural values. Specifically, cultural messages
regarding women's employment continue to
be mixed. Recall that Chapter 4 said that in
spite of the fact that premarital sex is an almost
universal behavior in North America, no
politicians or opinion-makers are publicly stating that responsible sex is a good thing and
everyone should feel free to enjoy it. The 1992
elections did, however, reveal a remarkable
shift in cultural messages regarding abortion.
For the first time ever, a politician could say
that "a woman's right to choose is a good
thing," and still be elected president.

Few if any opinion-makers are saying
openly that every woman should expect to be
economically autonomous throughout her life
course, in the same ways that men expect autonomy. In 1992, for example, the United States
was experiencing a "weak labor market,"
meaning that jobs were disappearing and few
new ones were being created. The U.S. Labor
Department was trying to figure out why
women were dropping out of the weak labor
market at a higher rate than men.[71] Economists
offered several explanations, and one of them
was, " 'It's still socially acceptable for women
to be dependent on someone else.' "[72] As a result of that belief, when jobs get scarce, nonemployed women seem more likely than nonemployed men to stop looking for paid work.

To assert that a woman should *not* be dependent—that she *should* be economically autonomous—is not yet a culturally acceptable
message. It's not yet endorsed in a popular,
widespread manner by respected opinion-
makers. Consequently, even though college
women expect to "have it all," only a relative
handful perceive the importance of being eco-

nomically autonomous. Nor do most college women as yet fully expect their men to possess the identities of householder and caregiver. Furthermore, not only do college men generally *not* possess those identities, they don't expect their women to possess the *autonomy* identity. This kind of scenario described Monika and Aaron. And because she went into that relationship naively believing they could work things out ("we love each other"), she encountered a rude awakening.

The Hazards of Scaling Back Expectations Sometimes women who experience the sort of pain endured by Monika scale back what they'll settle for.[73] They reason that next time, instead of having it all at once, perhaps they'll go for only part. Monika, for example, would like to have a child out of her next erotic friendship. But she doesn't want to be a solo parent. And because she wants to have a relationship that endures (she wants to keep her partner around), she wonders if she should lower her expectations for his home-work performance. In addition, she reasons that their negotiations would be greatly simplified if, for a few years, she left her strenuous career and took on a less demanding job. Although she'd keep on working, she would in effect become what Chapter 10 called a junior partner to her man: "When my kids are older," she thinks, "I might reenter my demanding career."

As she ponders those sorts of options, she reflects on the many solo parents she knows. Because most of those women had been junior partners (or complements), she concludes, first, that scaling down her expectations is no sure bet against losing her relationship. Second, when she compares those former junior partners with her solo-parent friends who'd been *equal* partners, she arrives at something quite fascinating: The former equal partners are much better off financially than the solo parents who were once junior partners. The reasons they're better off can be traced to their

previous choices. Monika's equal-partner friends had opted for nontraditional "men's jobs." But her junior-partner friends went into "women' jobs" paying less than men's jobs. Next, her equal-partner friends had worked consistently over time. But her junior-partner friends had zigzagged in and out of the labor force.

As a result of their choices, by the time both sets of solo parents were living without men, the former equal partners tended to have considerably higher earnings. They were thus much better able to manage the stringencies of supporting a household on one income instead of two. In addition, the equal partners were better able to cope with the irregularities of child-support payments from their former male partners. Chapter 13 showed how unreliable many U.S. men are when it comes to child support. Monika observed that junior partners (to say nothing of complements) faced serious problems in paying their monthly bills because support money from their former male partner was so unpredictable. Counting on that money usually got the women into financial trouble. By contrast, since equal-partner women earned more money, they were less desperate when child support was tardy, or when it was merely a partial payment, or when it never even arrived.

Work and Erotic Friendship Trajectories It became plain to Monika that work (paid and unpaid) and erotic friendships (formal or informal) follow trajectories that intercept each other throughout a person's life course.[74] We're familiar with the idea of a "trajectory" from newspaper accounts of guided missiles such as the Tomahawk. We're told that the missile's path (i.e., its trajectory), can be controlled with enormous accuracy. A political cartoon from the 1991 Persian Gulf War had two reporters casually remarking that a Tomahawk missile made a left turn over the downtown corner where they stood, and then a right turn several blocks down the street. It's laughable to think that anyone could ever control the path of either their erotic friendship (formal or informal) or their work (paid or unpaid) with anywhere near that kind of certainty. A major reason such control is impossible is that the two paths invariably intercept one another. Missiles intercepting missiles blow up. In the case of the women we've looked at (e.g., Monika, Helga, Kate) the intercept of their work and relationship paths has often been volatile. And the main reason it tends to be volatile is because another person's trajectories are intersecting at the same time. The man is trying to control his work and relationship paths at the same time the woman is trying to control her's.

In the case of Kate and Marshall, her work and relationship paths bumped severely into his at the time of their child's birth. As the paths came together, the only way the couple could keep things from blowing up (as they had with Monika and Aaron) was through strenuous problem-solving and sometimes torturous conflict resolution. Using those means, Marshall and Kate were able to keep their relationship proceeding within a maintenance and change phase. Ideally we should be able to show each partner's work and relationship paths on video. If we did, we would see that this couple's work and relationship paths had been intersecting for many years. Somehow they'd managed the rough spots in the same ways as now—through problem-solving and conflict-resolution. To be sure, their child's birth makes the current intercept particularly stressful. Finally, the video would also show that in future each partner's work and relationship paths will continue to intersect, and that rough spots are inevitable along with the accompanying struggle.

A separate video could show how drastically work and relationship trajectories have changed in North America since the 1950s. The major difference is that at that time there was (for most white citizens) very little intercept between his and her trajectories. Throughout his life course he did his paid work with few if any bumps of interference from her expecting him to do any chores or child caregiving. Throughout her life course she did her home work largely apart from interference either by the demands, or the opportunities, of paid work. A major part of the legacy of the 1960s' and 1970s' Big Bang is a dramatic shift away from those separate and distinctive life-course trajectories. Today the reality is much more complex. His and her work and erotic friendship trajectories continually impinge on one another throughout the life course. Very often the bumps result in bruises that may, or may not, heal.

CONCLUSION

Monika longs for a computer program called "Awesome" that could guide her through the difficulties of negotiating the conflicting demands of paid work, chores and child care, and loving oneself as much as one's partner. She's aware that her problems are compounded by what's out there in the larger society. One is the structural sexism of the labor market. Another is the absence of high-quality child caregiving centers readily available to all citizens. A third is the relative lack of family-friendly companies. For these and other reasons most women, after a few years in the labor market, are earning less than most men. That is so even though most women actually outperformed most men in school. In addition, even though women are laboring a total of more hours annually than women from the 1960s, most of today's women have not experienced a rise in their economic well-being: Most don't have greater access to goods, services, and leisure than yesterday's women.

Nonetheless, Monika has learned that a few of today's women are indeed better off economically than 1960s' women of similar social circumstances. These include younger, well-educated women who are not currently married. Because she fits each of those categories, she perceives herself as being economically well off. But that's not enough for her. From among the several prospects who could potentially become her partner in an erotic friendship, she wonders which one would give her most of what she wants. However, she's no longer as naive as she was when she began living with Aaron. She's keenly aware of the struggles and pains involved in trying to "have it all," and she feels better prepared for those struggles.

Ideally, she hopes she can find a man who fully accepts her identity as autonomous worker and is thus prepared to solve problems and negotiate conflicts in that context. Simultaneously, she wants the man to feel that to be a responsible partner he must love her as much as he loves himself. Specifically, that means he possesses the identities of householder and child caregiver. Those male identities too, she feels, must be part of the context of their relationship. Given her hopes and expectations, she senses that her chances may not be very high of actually having it all—of having a partner with whom she can indefinitely negotiate mutually satisfactory outcomes to paid work and chores and child care. But she feels she has to try.

NOTES

1. Gene Koretz, "America's neglected weapon: Its educated women," *Business Week*, January 27, 1992, p. 22. That same theme is developed in imaginative detail by Driscoll and Goldberg, 1993.
2. During one week in January 1993, the chief executive officers (CEOs) of IBM, Westinghouse, and American Express were forced to resign because of shareholder dissatisfaction with their performance. (See Leslie Wayne, "Shareholders exercise new power with nation's biggest companies," *The New York Times*, February 1, 1993, p.

A1.) A few months earlier, the CEO of Sears had been replaced on similar grounds.
3. Koretz (see note 1).
4. Adelman, 1991.
5. Staples, 1981a.
6. Adelman, p. 1.
7. Keen, 1989.
8. *The AAUW Report*, 1992.
9. Wegener, 1992.
10. Adelman, p. 4.
11. Reported in Koretz, from U.S. Department of Education data.
12. Adelman, p. 21.
13. Ibid., p. 18.
14. Ibid., p. 19; Scanzoni, 1978, pp. 11, 12, passim.
15. Fuchs, 1988.
16. Ahlburg and De Vita, 1992, p. 25.
17. Ibid.
18. Fuchs, p. 76.
19. Ibid., p. 78.
20. Adelman, p. 21; Baber and Allen, 1992, pp. 196, 197.
21. Ricks, 1992. But in April 1993, the U.S. government ordered the armed services to let women fly aircraft and be stationed on surface warships during combat: See *The Gainesville, Florida, Sun*, April 28, 1993, p. A1 (from *The New York Times*). Less than a year later, the government took an additional step toward gender equity by allowing women to participate in ground combat support units (engineering, maintenance, etc.) that had formerly been considered "too risky" for women. See *The New York Times*, January 14, 1994, p. A10.
22. Adelman, p. 21.
23. Ibid. See also Reskin and Hartmann, 1986.
24. Fuchs, pp. 122–129.
25. Lopez, 1992.
26. U.S. Bureau of Labor Statistics, reported in Segal and Zellner, 1992.
27. Mieher, 1992.
28. Vamos, 1992.
29. Baber and Allen.
30. Fuchs, p. 140.
31. Karen Anderson, 1981.
32. Shellenbarger and Trost, 1992; Driscoll and Goldberg, 1993, pp. 298ff.
33. Schwartz, 1989.
34. Bielby, 1992.

35. Jacobsen and Levin, 1992, p. 11.
36. Wadman, 1992.
37. Gutek and Larwood, 1987; Rose and Larwood, 1988; Grossman and Chester, 1990.
38. See Scanzoni, 1989a, for a discussion of religious orthodoxy and policies for families. See Kaufman, 1991, for a study of young women who convert to orthodox Jewish groups and thus accept their strong gender traditionalism.
39. Noble, 1966, p. 535; Scanzoni, 1977, pp. 228 ff.
40. Ibid., p. 230; see also Jones, 1985.
41. Adelman, p. 26. See Sokoloff, 1987, for added perspective on comparing black and white professional women.
42. Morris, 1990.
43. Gitlin, 1987.
44. Kraditor, 1968.
45. Scanzoni, 1972.
46. See Baber and Allen, pp. 205ff., for a thorough and excellent summary of these kinds of studies. Also see Godwin, 1991, for contrasting explanations of spouse housework involvement. See also Shelton, 1992.
47. Baber and Allen, p. 205.
48. Ferree, 1990.
49. Blair and Johnson, 1992.
50. Baber and Allen, p. 207.
51. Scanzoni, 1978.
52. Scanzoni, 1972, 1978.
53. Hertz, 1986.
54. Hochschild, 1989.
55. Gilbert, 1985; Berardo, Shehan, and Leslie, 1987; Ferree, 1988.
56. Lein, 1984.
57. Baber and Allen, pp. 209–213.
58. Moen, 1989.
59. Some years ago the expression "househusband" gained wide media attention. It captured the idea of a man devoting full time to chores and child care. For a realistic picture of such situations in Great Britain, see Wheelock, 1990.
60. Beach, 1989; Boris and Daniels, 1989; Lozano, 1989; Winter, 1992a, b.
61. Annetta Miller, "The brick wall," *Newsweek*, August 24, 1992, p. 54; Marsh, 1992a.
62. Rosen, 1987; Molly Martin, 1988; Rimer, 1992; and "Women in construction still waiting for respect," *The New York Times*, September 29, 1992, p. B12.
63. Shellenbarger, 1991.
64. Gerstel and Gross, 1984; Winfield, 1985; Elaine Anderson, 1992.
65. Shortly after former Vice President Quayle left office in January 1993, his spouse began using her own surname, Marilyn *Tucker* Quayle. She then became employed as an attorney in Indianapolis, and the couple established a commuting relationship between that city and Washington, D.C. See *The Gainesville, Florida, Sun*, February 25, 1993, p. A12.
66. Joann S. Lublin, *Wall Street Journal*, April 13, 1993, p. A1.
67. Marsh, 1992b.
68. Condon, 1985; Lo, 1990; Cherry, 1987; Bornoff, 1991.
69. Baber and Allen, p. 216; Eckenrode and Gore, 1990.
70. Holland and Eisenhart, 1990.
71. Harper, 1992.
72. Ibid.
73. Gerson, 1985.
74. Heise, 1990.

CHAPTER 16

RESPONSIBLE BIRTHING AND PARENTING

Chapter 1 began by describing a great debate over what's happening among today's families: "As people go about changing families, are they being responsible or irresponsible?" In particular, as adults busily care for themselves, are they just as busily caring for their children? Throughout this book we've said that reinventing responsibility means paying close attention to one's neighbor, especially children. And not just one's own biological children. Chapters 2 and 3, for instance, said that children are a chief reason for constructing a *social family*—a family that exists across several households. This chapter, moreover, talks about *blended families*. At the very least, that label identifies a child sharing a household with an adult to whom she or he is not linked by blood.

Throughout the book we've said that the prevailing cultural belief is that children thrive best within the the Benchmark or Modern Family—two legally married adults residing in one household with their own natural children. Nevertheless, in Western societies the unmistakable trend is away from the Modern Family.[1] Growing numbers of children and adults are living in varieties of postmodern families. Asking, "Is that trend good for children?," implies, first, that the Benchmark did indeed work for children, and second, that as Pulitzer prize winner Anna Quindlen puts it, "all other options [are] suspect and second-rate."[2]

Chapters 16 and 17 explore what kinds of families "work" for children. All of us are aware that having and taking care of children are viewed as positive and loving things to do. No one would ever say that harming children is okay. The strange paradox is that many adults do indeed harm children in a number of ways. What's more, historians tell us that's nothing new.[3] It seems that at least since the Colonial period, many adults cared for and yet harmed children at the same time. Because the majority of children have for 200 years lived in Benchmark families, it follows that the Benchmark does not guarantee responsible parents. To be sure, most parents have not meant to hurt children. But why this strange contradiction? Why do adults (both in and out of Benchmark fami-

TABLE 16-1
Total Fertility Rates and Expected Lifetime Births per 1,000 Married Women, 1970–1988

| Year | Total fertility rate* | Lifetime births expected by age | | |
		18–24	25–29	30–34
1988	1,932	2,128	2,260	2,175
1985	1,843	2,183	2,236	2,167
1980	1,840	2,134	2,160	2,248
1975	1,774	2,173	2,260	2,610
1970	2,480	2,375[†]	2,619[†]	2,989[†]

*Births per 1,000 women aged 15 to 44 over their lifetime under current fertility levels.
†1971 data.
Source: Adapted from Teachman, Polonko, and Scanzoni, (rev. ed.), forthcoming. Data from: U.S. Bureau of the Census, 1992. *Statistical Abstract of the United States: 1991*, table 99.

lies) love and sacrifice for children on the one hand but inflict damage on them on the other?

PRONATALISM

To begin to answer that question, we look first at *pronatalism.* Pronatalism refers to a number of simple but deeply ingrained ideas. The basis of pronatalism is the belief that having children is a moral obligation, much like the moral obligations to love oneself and to love one's neighbor discussed in earlier chapters. Lee Rainwater's research led him to express the obligation this way: "One shouldn't have more children than one can support; *but one should have as many children as one can afford.*"[4] At the same time, that obligation is softened by today's prevailing cultural belief that children are "emotionally priceless."[5] Thus, alongside the belief that a moral person *should* have children is the idea that children are *fun.* People perceive that children provide a great deal of unique personal satisfactions—they supply rewards found nowhere else! Thus the payoff for sacrificing lots of money on children (instead of taking an exotic vacation every year) is that: "Kids make you feel good; put a smile on your face; make life seem worthwhile!"

Lately, however, those smiles have gotten increasingly expensive. Sneakers that once cost ten dollars now carry a prestige label and sell for ninety dollars. According to Steven Nock, today's young adults view children as a high-priority, "big-ticket" consumer item.[6] To afford the wide range of other consumer items they want, young adults do two things: They lower their expectations about how many children they'd like to have and they limit the number of children they actually do have. Table 16-1 shows the steady decline between 1970 and 1988 in the number of births that women *expect* to have. Although expecting to have fewer children is no guarantee of actually having fewer, there seems to be a connection. Specifically, Table 16-1 shows that in the United States the number of children born to married women aged 15 to 44 (the total fertility rate) has also dropped considerably between 1970 and 1988.

Women's Employment and Children

But the financial drain of children is not the sole reason that women's fertility levels have been declining during recent decades. Since the Big Bang, the obligation to have children has been significantly modified by women's growing awareness of the moral obligation to love themselves. Chapter 15 said that one way some women seek to express that love is

TABLE 16-2
Percentage of Women in the Labor Force by Marital Status and Age of Children, 1960–1989

Marital status	Percentage in labor force			
	1989	1980	1970	1960
Married husband present	57.8	50.1	40.8	30.5
No children under age 18	75.5	46.0	42.2	34.7
Children aged 6–17 only	73.2	61.7	49.2	39.0
Children under age 6	58.4	45.1	30.3	18.6
Divorced	75.5	74.5	71.5	—
No children under age 18	72.5	71.4	67.7	—
Children aged 6–17 only	85.0	82.3	82.4	—
Children under age 6	70.5	68.3	63.3	—

Source: Adapted from Teachman, Polonko, and Scanzoni, (rev. ed.), forthcoming. Data from U.S. Bureau of the Census, 1992. *Statistical Abstract of the United States: 1991,* table 643.

through paid employment. Table 16-2 reports dramatic increases over the course of three decades in the proportions of women in the paid labor force. Especially striking is the increase among married women living with their husbands *and* with children under age 6. This figure went from less than 20 percent in 1960 to almost 60 percent in 1989, a threefold increase. In a study that looked at employed mothers with even younger children (under 3 years of age), 38 percent of the mothers (husband present) were in the paid labor force in 1978 and 56 percent in 1990 (numbers rounded).[7]

To be sure, many women are employed *because* children are so expensive. Chapter 15 showed how Angie had to work outside her home (even though she didn't want to) to help pay her children's bills. Other women such as her sister Brenda, and Kate (Chapter 15), limit their childbearing because they want to be free to pursue additional schooling and/or an occupation, usually a career. Regardless of whether they work because they *have* to, or because they *want* to, employed women tend to have fewer children than nonemployed women.[8] Angie said she couldn't afford any more children. Her time was taken up earning money to help support the children she already had. Brenda said she wanted no more

children so she could go to school and enter a career.

Postponing Children   The notion of *postponement* is another way to explore the question of women's employment and children. Table 16-3 compares trends in being child-free between 1970 and 1990. Whether we look at all women (left side of table), or only at women who have ever been married (right side), the trend is clear and unmistakable: Today's women are much more likely than yesterday's women to choose to have their first child at a later age.

For example, in 1970 some 36 percent of women aged 25 to 34 were child-free. By 1990 that percentage had almost doubled to 68 percent. The percentage of child-free ever-married women aged 25 to 34 also almost doubled—from 24 to 46 percent. In short, not only do today's women put off their first marriage until they are older, many women also postpone bearing their first child until their late 20s or their 30s. Chapter 10 described how Kate, after many years of being married informally, decided to formalize it and have her first child during her late 30s.

Among the many reasons growing numbers of women are choosing to postpone parenting for as long as possible is the desire for freedom—freedom to attend school and/or work

TABLE 16-3

Percentage of All Women and Ever-married Women Who Were Child-free at Selected Ages, 1970–1990

Year	Percentage of all women				Percentage of ever-married women		
	25–29	30–34	35–39		25–29	30–34	35–39
1990	42.1	25.7	17.7		29.3	16.8	12.2
1986	40.7	23.9	16.6		27.3	15.1	11.5
1980	36.8	19.8	12.1		25.3	13.7	8.0
1975	31.1	15.2	9.6		21.1	8.8	5.3
1970	24.4	11.8	9.4		15.8	8.3	7.3

Source: Adapted from Teachman, Polonko, and Scanzoni, (rev. ed.), forthcoming. Data from various issues of *Current Population Reports,* Series P-20.

at a paying job.[9] Chapter 15 showed how child-free women in certain occupations earn as much as men. By comparison, women with children tend to suffer a salary penalty. Table 16-3 suggests that growing numbers of women put off childbearing so they can first establish themselves in their careers, thus minimizing that penalty.[10]

Contraception, Control, and Childbearing
The capability to control childbearing and to plan for children when the "time is right" requires two major components. First and foremost, women and men must be highly motivated. "Doing what comes naturally" may be fun, but its consequences can send one's life spinning totally out of control. During the Great Depression of the 1930s, married couples got extraordinarily motivated to limit family size because there simply were no jobs by which men could support their children. Using merely the ancient techniques of withdrawal and low-tech condoms, they were highly successful in lowering the sizes of their families.[11] However, the control of childbearing is much easier and a lot more pleasurable in the presence of a second major component, namely, sophisticated means of contraception.

Table 16-4 reveals that most of today's women have added sophisticated and effective means of contraception to their motivation to control pregnancies. In 1965, only two-thirds of married women aged 15 to 44 used any sort of contraception at all. By 1988 the figure had risen to 82 percent. The Pill was first made available during the early sixties and instantly became very popular, as the 24-percent use figure for 1965 indicates. As information about its potentially harmful side effects became known, however, the proportion of married women using the Pill dropped to the 15-percent use figure shown for 1988. Pill use has been especially curtailed by women past age 30.

The contraceptive method whose use rose most dramatically between 1965 and 1988 is *sterilization.* Its use rose from 6.5 to 44 percent, an almost sevenfold increase. Sterilization is most commonly used by women with at least one child who want a birth-control method that is foolproof and free from side effects.[12] Kate, for instance, had her tubes tied at the time of her child's delivery. The row labeled "Other methods" in Table 16-4 includes condoms, diaphragms, jellies, creams, and suppositories, as well as withdrawal. Finally, Table 16-4 reveals a doubling of the abortion rate for married women between 1965 and 1988. The fact that abortions were first made

TABLE 16-4
Percentage of Married Women Using Contraception and Abortion Rate, 1965–1988

Method	Percentage by year			
	1988	1982	1976	1965
Contraception*	82.1	81.0	68.8	64.1
Sterilization	44.0	40.9	13.9	6.5
Pill	15.1	13.4	32.9	24.0
IUD	1.5	4.8	9.2	1.1
Other methods	21.5	21.9	12.8	32.5
Nonusers[†]	4.8	5.0	—	—
Abortion rate[‡]	27.1[§]	28.8	24.2	13.2[¶]

*Among currently married women aged 15 to 44.
[†]Excludes those noncontractively sterile, pregnant, postpartum, or seeking pregnancy.
[‡]Abortions per 1,000 women aged 16 to 44.
[§]1987 data.
[¶]1972 data.
Source: Adapted from Teachman, Polonko, and Scanzoni, (rev. ed.), forthcoming. Data from U.S. Bureau of the Census, 1991. *Statistical Abstract of the United States: 1991.*

legal and thus safe during the 1970s for all women has contributed a great deal to the reduced fertility rates shown in Table 16-1.

CHILD-FREE—AN ALTERNATIVE TO PRONATALISM

In recent years some persons have adopted a child-free lifestyle.[13] Many were initially postponers, as in Table 16-3. In their 20s they fully expected that one day they would have a child. Recent government data, for example, reveal that "nearly two-thirds of childless wives in their early thirties expect to have at least one child."[14] Chapter 9 said that the longer cohabitors stay together, the more families and friends are likely to ask, "When are you getting serious?" Similarly, because pronatalism is so powerful in North American culture, the more years couples postpone children, the greater the pressure they feel from families and friends to have children. Chapter 15 said that Monika, almost 30 years old and doing very well in her career, intensely desired to have a child someday. But she didn't want to be a solo parent. Some of her friends—career women in

their mid to late 30s without an ongoing erotic friendship—were taking the *Murphy Brown* route (Chapter 10). They allowed themselves to get pregnant or else adopted a child. In either case, they became solo parents.

Because Monika frequently helped out with her friends' child-care needs, she knew how drastically children change parents' lives.[15] In particular, she began to note her friends' feelings of losing control of their lives. Those circumstances made her increasingly appreciative of the freedom and benefits of not having to be responsible for children. She began to wonder if she ought to remain child-free on a permanent basis: "Should I be child-free as a way of life?" She was, in effect, considering whether she should set aside her pronatalism in favor of something else.

About that time she met Ian, a divorced father whose former spouse had custody of their child. As Ian and Monika constructed their erotic friendship, he made it clear to her that he wanted no more children. Although at first she resented his inflexibility, she gradually changed her mind. Instead of merely wondering about a child-free lifestyle, she turned to embrace it fully. The visits with Ian's child, plus helping out with her friends' children, convinced her she was currently getting all the emotional pleasures she needed from children.

Persons like Monika choosing to be child-free are ignoring the pronatalist norm to "have as many as one can afford." Hers is not a particularly popular choice. People who reveal they've chosen to be child-free are subject to a great deal of criticism and gossip.[16] They're often accused of being selfish and greedy and of not contributing to society. They're almost always pitied, and sometimes it's rumored that child-free persons are emotionally unhealthy and unstable. Nevertheless, a tiny but slowly enlarging minority of women do intend to remain child-free. Between 1967 and 1976, the percentage of all U.S. wives aged 14 to 39 intending to remain child-free rose from 3.1 to 5.4. By 1990, 9 percent of all women aged 18 to 34 intended to remain child-free.[17]

Furthermore, government figures show that the better educated a woman is the more likely she is to ignore pronatalism and to intend to be child-free.[18] That's not at all surprising. Chapter 15 said that well-educated women like Monika are often in careers. Careers demand great amounts of time, thought, and energy, which makes it difficult for any career person to be a responsible parent and responsive partner all at the same time. The impact of children on career women was widely discussed in the national press during the early months of 1993. President Clinton attempted to appoint to his Cabinet two highly successful career women with small children. In both cases he was forced to withdraw their nominations owing to political problems stemming from their previous child-care arrangements.[19] By contrast, at least two other career women who were child-free and unmarried were easily confirmed as Cabinet members.

Being Responsible by Being Child-free   The great majority of women—whether in careers

Child-free couples can spend a lot of time taking care of each other and sharing leisure activities.

or not, or married or not—do bear at least one child. Jean Veevers says that most persons reject a child-free lifestyle both because they believe they *should* have children (pronatalism), and also because they perceive children to be enjoyable. But she argues that most of us ignore the reality that not all women or men are cut out to be parents. Some persons have the motivation to be responsible parents but do not have the capability. Others have the capability but not the motivation. Some persons have neither.

Importantly, whether a person has a career is not the key factor in determining responsible parenthood. For example, historical studies show that children were abused long before anyone ever heard the term "career women."[20] Contemporary studies show that full-time mothers are no less likely than any other parent to abuse their children.[21] Veevers proposed a test for parenthood, much like a driver's test. She said that adults not passing the parent test should seriously consider a child-free lifestyle. Those adults should think about being child-free mostly for the sake of their unborn children. When it comes to children, says Veevers, perhaps the most responsible goal for some persons is not to have any!

"But," someone asks, "what does 'responsible' mean?" At the very least, it means what the chapter opened with: "Do good to children, and don't do them any harm." The difficulty with pronatalist beliefs is that they nudge many people into parenthood who shouldn't be there. Many persons become parents without ever thinking about it: "Everybody has children; why not me?" The problem is that some within the "everybody" turn out to be less than responsible. Unfortunately, there is as yet no valid parenting test to predict whether, say, Phyllis or Ed will be a responsible parent. One reason there isn't is because there's widespread disagreement over what "responsible" means. In plain English, what does it mean to do good? What does it mean to do harm?

RESPONSIBILITY AND CHILDREN'S DEVELOPMENT

Researchers use the label *development* to describe how a child changes over a wide range of dimensions—emotional, social, mental, and physical. We expect and want children to mature; we define change as a *good* thing. Lack of development is perceived as something *bad* or unfortunate, as in the case of a child with a disease or a mental or physical impairment. We consider it a tragedy, for instance, when an infant is born addicted to heroin, cocaine, or alcohol, or worse yet, is HIV infected.

Children's development is vital for two obvious reasons. First, it is good for the child. The more the child changes from a helpless and dependent infant into a strong, independent, and resilient person, the better off she or he will be. Western culture holds that the more autonomous the person becomes the greater the sense of control she or he will have over her or his life. Chapter 11 said that a sense of control provides feelings of personal well-being. Second, most citizens believe that child development is good for the rest of us. Chapter 11 talked about social responsibility, the public household, and the social fabric. We believe that children who experience healthy development will be the ones best fitted to contribute to the larger society.

Although everyone agrees that healthy child development is good for both the child and society, there's a lot less agreement over how to achieve that goal. How much of the child's development, for example, is genetically determined? If everything about a child is already contained in her or his DNA makeup, then the surrounding adults don't have much to do except sit back and watch the child mature. But even people who believe in strong genetic influences know they can't be totally passive toward the child. Robert Bellah and colleagues say that to have a "good society" adults must pay attention to children.[22] At the very least, that means seeing they receive good nutrition, medicine, sanitation, and exercise. But it also means providing emotional nurture, intellectual stimulation, and guidelines for behavior: "Don't' touch the burners"; "look both ways when crossing the street", "brush your teeth", "pick up your toys"; "play nicely with your friends"; "be flexible and cooperative"; "figure out a better way of doing it," and so on.

In short, most people believe that whatever the influence of genes, parents and other adults also have considerable impact on children's development. The big questions are, how much impact? and how long does the impact last? "As the twig is bent, so grows the tree," has been an American folk saying for generations. That saying conveys the belief that parental influence is so great that it shapes the child's entire life course. A biblical proverb makes the same promise to parents: "Train up a child in the way he should go, and when he is old he will not depart from it."

Until around the mid-twentieth century, there were extremists on both sides of the heredity–environment controversy.[23] People on the heredity side said that genes were much more important for a child's eventual life-course development than parental and other kinds of social influences. Sigmund Freud and some of his followers, for example, believed that "anatomy determines destiny." Thus, the biological fact that a woman bears children meant that the full range of a woman's behaviors throughout her life course was established at the moment of her conception. On the opposite side, people who believed in culture and learning claimed that the person's social environment was far more crucial than her or his biological inheritance.

Socialization—How Long Does It Last?

Since mid-century most people have come to accept the idea that it's not *either/or*. Instead, it's *both/and*. The way a child turns out is viewed as the result of both genes and social environment. Instead of bickering about which is more important, researchers now agree that both are vital, even though they themselves might concentrate on either genes or environment.[24] For example, social and behavioral scientists concentrate on what's called *socialization*—the effects of parental and other social and cultural influences on children.[25] Until very recently, most students of socialization believed that parental influence was extremely important, and also that it was

very long lasting. They believed that whatever children learned by ages 5, 11, or 16 would stay with them for a lifetime.

However, earlier chapters (especially 14) showed that as they became adolescents and adults, persons (such as Brenda) may ignore their earlier training and choose to behave in highly unpredictable ways. No matter what children learn, as they move through life they can, and in fact do, significantly shift what they believe and how they behave across many important dimensions. Today, researchers are busy trying to answer two further questions: What parts of childhood socialization may last for a long time, and what parts might lose their influence?[26]

In the meantime, everyone agrees that responsible parenting means enhancing the development of children. The disagreement arises over what may or may not enhance child development. In the North America of the 1990s, "responsible parenting" is fiercely debated in the news media, on TV talk shows, and by clergy and politicians. There are at least three specific areas over which controversies rage: (1) adolescent childbearing, (2) adult choices and transitions, and (3) child discipline.

ADOLESCENT CHILDBEARING

Although Table 16-1 shows that U.S. fertility rates have been declining in general, it also masks an opposite trend. That is that since 1970, childbearing among unmarried women under age 20 has risen substantially. That demographic fact must be put in the context of several other findings: (1) Teenage marriages seem on the verge of "disappearing" (Chapter 10). (2) Teenage sexual activity has been rising to record levels (Tables 4-2 and 4-3). (3) Compared with 1970s' adolescents, a higher proportion of today's teens are using contraceptives. Many, however, are using what Table 16-4 calls "other" methods. These are low-tech methods (condoms, diaphragms) that tend to be ineffective in preventing pregnancies.

Although rates of teenage childbearing have been increasing rapidly among whites, the rates continue to be higher among African-Americans.[27] Black teenage "welfare mothers" have been the focus of considerable public controversy. Some politicians, charge that out-of-wedlock teenage childbearing (illegitimacy) is a root cause of the "breakdown of the black family."[28] They add that illegitimacy is also to blame for poor school performance, drug abuse, and delinquency and crime. Many U.S. citizens, middle-class blacks as well as whites, believe that children bearing children is an *irresponsible* thing to do. They're convinced that teenage women, virtually all of whom are poorly educated, find it extraordinarily difficult to contribute effectively to their children's personal and social development.

Images of Unwed Mothers

Constance Nathanson says that until recently there were only two major contrasting images of adolescent motherhood: "Young women are alternatively portrayed as willful sinners or innocent victims."[29] During the century preceding the 1960s, the tendency was, says Nathanson, to think of unmarried mothers as victims. The prevailing belief was that such women had been exploited by unprincipled men who'd extracted sex from them after false promises of marriage. The community believed that those suffering women should be pitied and every effort made to minister to their needs and those of their "bastards." There was a clear understanding, however, that the women must be penitent for their misdeeds. In exchange for the help of family, church, and community (i.e., social workers), they would never again allow themselves to be taken advantage of by men. Even though they'd been "soiled," they would earnestly seek a husband who could act as father to their unfortunate offspring.

This victim image was altered by two major social forces. One force was the redefinition of sexuality emerging from the 1960s. Earlier chapters (4–7) showed that beginning with the sixties, sex began to be perceived less and less as an exchange medium used by women for marriage. Sex was redefined as something women and men did on a casual basis or as the boundary of an erotic friendship. In either case, the earlier social exchange between sex and marriage evaporated. One result was that some brand new terms surfaced in American culture. Among these was "sexually active teenager." If the teenager was in fact choosing to be sexually active, then the historic presumption of innocent victim necessarily vanished.

The Birth Control Movement Nathanson states that the second force altering the victim image was the creation of the birth control movement.[30] Before the 1960s, an unmarried woman who had sex on a regular basis but failed to be penitent about it was perceived to be a "willful sinner" and called nasty terms such as "whore" and "slut." Liberals of the 1970s realized that those labels had gotten out of date. The liberal response to changing sexual patterns was to invent the birth control movement. Nathanson adds that freshly minted, highly effective contraceptive methods—the Pill in particular, but also the intrauterine device (IUD)—became major pillars of the movement. Chapter 4 pointed out that liberals and other opinion-makers never asserted that nonmarital sex is a positive thing. Yet they refused to call unmarried, sexually active women willful sinners. Instead, the movement's chief policy was and is to communicate the following message to adolescents: "It would be better if you didn't have sex, but if you do, be certain to protect yourself against pregnancy and diseases."

The reality, remarks Nathanson, is that the birth control movement has failed to reverse the trend toward increasing numbers of babies being born to adolescent mothers: "The rise in teen birth rates continued in 1989 by an additional 6 to 8 percent."[31] By 1990, "The birth rate for women aged 18-19 years rose 5 percent. . . . For teenagers 15-17 years of age [the birth rate in 1990] increased by 3 percent."[32]

Welfare Mothers as Hedonistic   Because neither *victim* nor *sinner* seems an appropriate label to describe these growing numbers of young mothers, Nathanson states that fresh cultural images are emerging. She quotes an unnamed talk-show host saying, " 'I don't mind paying to help people in need, but I don't want my tax dollars to pay for the sexual pleasures of adolescents who won't use birth control.' "[33] In short, *hedonistic* seems to be the new label that many citizens are now applying to the behaviors of unmarried teenage mothers, many of whom are black. Instead of using contraception and getting a job, they are perceived as having one baby after another simply to get fatter welfare checks. At the same time, many of these mothers are defined as irresponsible toward their children. Like Sondra in Chapter 11, they are perceived as being unable to enhance their children's development.

The Social Context of Adolescent Childbearing

Nathanson has no quarrel with the conclusion that many poorly educated teenagers (white and black) have a very difficult time being responsible parents.[34] Her disagreement is with politicians and citizens contending that if adolescents would only use birth control, many of society's problems would be solved: poverty, crime, substance abuse, delinquency, child abuse, and so forth. Throughout this book we have said that the broader social context in which a person lives both hinders and helps the choices that she or he makes. Nathanson argues that the social context surrounding dis-

An adolescent mother gets her high-school diploma with her child in her arms.

advantaged teenage women strongly influences their choices regarding sex, contraception, parenting, and education. Her view is that unless their social context is changed by "enlarging the opportunities of women to *gain control of their lives*," adolescents will continue having children and go on facing enormous difficulties in being responsible parents.[35]

Changing their social context to give adolescent women greater control over their lives means stirring up a mix that includes pronatalism, traditional gender roles, and sexuality, alongside educational and economic opportunity. Nathanson's reasoning goes something like this: Presently, females get cultural messages that every "good women" must have a child to achieve complete fulfillment. Next, sex retains a tinge of the taboo, and it remains unusual for a teenage girl to be in complete charge of her own sexual and contraceptive life. Finally, working- and lower-class girls go to public schools that are often inadequate and do not stretch either girls or boys to develop their full personal and workplace potential.

According to Nathanson and a number of other researchers, the upshot of these cultural and social conditions is that many disadvantaged women define childbearing as their sole means of taking charge of their lives.[36] One of the most rewarding choices a girl can make is to have a baby. After all, she's merely doing what every good woman is supposed to do. As far as she's concerned, motherhood seems her only avenue to personal satisfaction and social status. Unfortunately, her quest for personal autonomy usually results in her life spinning more out of control than it was before.

Nathanson's recipe for social change and personal autonomy begins by targeting what she calls adult sexual hypocrisy. Opinion-makers, she believes, should assert that what Chapter 4 called *responsible sex* is a good thing. The route to responsible parenthood begins with responsible sex. But the route also includes reevaluation of the cultural belief that everyone should have a child. In particular, the idea that a woman requires a child to fulfill her destiny needs to be scrutinized. In its place, the child-free lifestyle should be endorsed as a legitimate cultural option for all persons from all social classes.[37] Furthermore, what earlier chapters called *economic autonomy* must be advocated for women just as it is now for men. That means that each women would be able independently to take care of any child for which she is responsible. For those things to become realistic cultural goals, says Nathanson, better schools and less marketplace discrimination against women are required.

In sum, Nathanson describes the transition between a woman's childhood and adulthood—her adolescence—as a "dangerous passage." The passage is difficult enough for any woman without adding the burden of parenting. Helping women achieve greater control over that passage requires a number of significant cultural and structural shifts. Nathanson

and other observers believe that until and unless those changes are addressed, many young women will continue to find their perilous passage complicated by children with whom they are ill prepared to cope.

ADULT CHOICES AND TRANSITIONS

A second aspect of responsible parenting debated by citizens, politicians, and researchers pivots around the question of what Chapter 14 called adult life-course *transitions*. Critics on the fixed-philosophy side of Figure 1-1 have no doubt that children are suffering because growing numbers of adults are failing to behave according to the rules of the Benchmark Family. Due to that suffering, conservatives believe that the *social fabric* (Chapter 11) is unraveling.[38] The majority of citizens (those in the middle of Figure 1-1) are puzzled and anxious. They worry about the short- and long-term effects on children of the varieties of choices being made by today's adults.[39] These choices include having sex and children outside of formal marriage, employment of mothers with young children, growing use of day-care centers, divorce, child-free lifestyles, informal marriage (heterosexual and homosexual), blended (step) families, and so on and on.

A prominent figure during both the Reagan and Bush administrations, William J. Bennett asserts that "illegitimate births" are one proof of America's decline.[40] Bennett makes his charge on the basis of recent government data that reveal that the same trend we just talked about for teens is also seen among adults—steady increases in the numbers of *un*married women *of all ages* bearing children.[41] Although unmarried black women are more likely than unmarried white women to have a child, the rate of increase is now faster among whites than among blacks.[42]

Government researchers add that the rate of increase in unmarried childbearing is actually faster among women who are 25 to 39 years old than it is among all women who are younger than that.[43] Some of these "mature" women are like Monika's friends: never-married, childless, well-educated, and in careers—the *Murphy Brown* route. Others may be divorced; and some, whether divorced or never-married, may have had children previously. Even though some women may currently have an informal marriage, any children born to them are counted as "illegitimate." After a while, of course, some women who bear illegitimate children get formally married.

Solo Mothers

In short, the picture of adult unmarried childbearing is like a mosaic—a lot of overlapping images that are difficult to sort out. The picture gets even more complicated due to the increasing numbers of married mothers who get divorced. *Solo parent* is the label used to describe women living with children but no husband. Chapter 13 reported how growing numbers of children are living with solo mothers, some of them previously married and some never-married. The thorny question that's debated by researchers, politicians, and TV talk shows is the effect on children of growing up with a mother *with no male in the household.*

After summarizing the scores of studies done on this question, Frank Furstenberg states that phrasing the issue in those terms—"no male in the household"—can be highly misleading.[44] Throughout Sondra's life course, described in Chapter 11, she was an unmarried adolescent mother who subsequently cohabited, married, divorced, and became part of a social family. During some of those years there was a man living with her and her children, and during other periods she had a boyfriend who spent many days and weekends with her and her children. Furstenberg reports that, "Close to 15 percent of *all* children will go through at least two [formal] family disrup-

tions by late adolescence. . . . If cohabitational unions were included, the figure would be significantly higher."[45]

The Ideal Research Design The "ideal" study of the effects of solo parenting would compare two categories of children: children whose biological parents were married and living together at the time of the child's birth and were still doing so eighteen years later, and other children. However, the trend is that fewer and fewer children are located in the first category, and this trend is accelerating, particularly among whites: "Half or more of all children will spend some time living in a single parent family. At least a quarter will enter a stepfamily, and about half of these children will see the breakup of this new family unit before the end of their teens."[46] In short, one of the major consequences of adult freedom to continually invent and reinvent erotic friendships is that decreasing numbers of children spend their first eighteen years living with both biological parents.

Since there is no ideal study of solo parenting nor is there ever likely to be one, what do "imperfect" studies tell us? Obviously, no one disagrees with the common sense folk wisdom that "children are better off when raised by parents whose relationship is stable, warm, and mutually supportive."[47] Beyond that, however, researchers disagree sharply among themselves. For instance, how important is the child's age at the time when the parents separate and/or divorce? Some studies report that preschool children suffer more than do older children, whereas others say that grade- and/or high-school children are more traumatized. There does seem to be agreement that the point of separation, that is, when one parent actually moves out, is usually more painful for children than what precedes or follows.[48]

Another unsettled question is the gender of the child. Some studies say that boys' emotional and social development is more negatively affected than girls'. Other researchers are not so sure. Although some boys may feel greater pain than some girls at the time of actual separation, there may be a "sleeper effect" for some girls.[49] The girls may suffer a painful reaction several months or years later. By that time the boys' negative reactions may have worn off.

This potential gender difference points to yet another unsettled question—how long do negative effects persist? Some researchers say that the effects of parental separation and/or termination last a long time. They claim that children exposed to those kinds of parental behaviors don't do as well in their educational and occupational careers. These researchers add that such children are also more likely than other children to pass through their own separation and divorce.

The Economics of Solo Mothering But Furstenberg warns that some of the long-term disadvantage associated with divorce may be spurious. Up to this time, the majority of children growing up in solo-mother households have had parents with relatively less education and job status. Moreover, Chapter 13 showed that after divorce, many solo mothers experience sharp declines in their standard of living. Hence, if children from solo-mother households have long-term problems, the problems may be caused more by the children's relative economic disadvantage than by anything else.

In recent years there have been many studies of solo mothering both in North America and Europe.[50] The studies conclude that solo mothers struggle very hard to be responsible parents in the face of continual economic harassment of one sort or another. Chapter 13, for instance, reported that many solo mothers cannot count on steady child-support payments. Some fathers not only fail to send money to their nonresident children, they also maintain very little contact with them by phone, letters,

or visits. The mothers' efforts to find and hold a job are complicated by the high costs of child care and child illnesses. The jobs mothers do find often pay low wages, and their hours are often reduced unexpectedly and/or they encounter repeated layoffs.

Experts offer a variety of suggestions that might alleviate solo-mothers' economic difficulties. Among these is the option on which Sondra unexpectedly stumbled. Chapter 11 showed how she became part of a *social family*. The bottom line of a social family (like a blood family) rests on shared obligations to give and receive money, goods, and services. As a result, the burdens and anxieties Sondra faced in combining paid employment with solo motherhood were lightened considerably.

Blended Families

Chapters 10 and 11 reported that many solo mothers eventually become formally married, either for the first time or the second (or third) time. And some solo mothers opt to cohabit. In either case, having two incomes instead of one (or having merely one male income but a considerably larger income than hers was) generally means that the woman and her children are economically better off than they were before. Sometimes the man also has children living with him, and so the family consists of her and his children.[51] In some cases the woman gives birth and their children are added to his *and* hers, or only to hers *or* his. In other instances only his children live with the couple. Most often, however, his children live in a separate household with their mother.

An Image Problem In any case, say Marilyn Coleman and Lawrence Ganong, "Stepchildren have an image problem."[52] Popular culture often portrays them like Cinderella—neglected, ignored, or mistreated. However, most studies of children in blended families (just like certain studies of children living with solo parents) reveal that "stepchildren, on average, fare comparably to children who have not experienced parental remarriage."[53] Sometimes stepchildren do indeed suffer a great deal of emotional pain. One of the sources of their suffering is the unique spin that "blended adults" tend to place on conflicts. Money, for instance, is a sore spot in all erotic friendships. But stepchildren hear their parents fight by complaining that, "You're spending more money on your kid(s) than on mine!" Another area of blended family conflict that has a unique spin is discipline: "You're much harder on my kid(s) than yours—sometimes you go so far as to physically abuse them!"

Furthermore, one of the adults may sexually abuse his or her partner's child. Most frequently, the man sexually abuses the woman's daughter. Perhaps the most sensational examples of alleged sexual misconduct inside blended families emerged from the 1993 charges and countercharges flung back and forth between Woody Allen and Mia Farrow. On the one hand, Allen acknowledged that he was having an "affair" with the college-age adopted daughter of Farrow and her former spouse, orchestra conductor Andre Previn. But he vehemently denied sexually molesting the 7-year-old girl he and Farrow had jointly adopted.[54]

For these and many other reasons, Chapter 10 showed that divorce rates for remarriages are going *up* at the same time that remarriage rates are going *down*. Coleman and Ganong say that one reason blended families experience serious strife is because many solo mothers viewed the man as a meal ticket. Mothers perceived him as the solution to their severe economic difficulties.[55] Hence some solo mothers marry in spite of misgivings they feel about the man. Coleman and Ganong suggest that one way to keep solo mothers from feeling constrained to marry is to enhance both their education and their employability. Mothers

who perceive themselves as economically autonomous (Chapters 11 and 15) are less likely to feel they have to marry (formally or informally) merely to supply economic resources to their children.

Male Role-Model Deficit Another reason that solo mothers sometimes marry in spite of unease and misgivings is their fear that their children will grow up without a man around. The pervasive cultural belief is that the children, especially boys, will grow up with a role-model deficit. Because of the prevalence of pimps and drug dealers, as well as distorted male images sold by the media, the charge is that many of today's boys (African-Americans in particular) have no positive male role models: They lack the opportunity to live with a strong, decent, honorable, and hard-working man able to shape them into his image.[56] Consequently, the fear is that the boys are unable to form what Wade Mackey calls the *man-child bond.*[57] Boys who lack this bond never learn how to behave "properly" at home, in school, in the work force, and toward women. A comparable fear is that girls growing up without a resident father fail to learn "appropriate" behaviors toward men.

Frank Mott recently did a very comprehensive study of the effects of father absence on children's development.[58] He looked at a national sample of some 1,700 children (about a third of whom were black) born between 1979 and 1983. Between ages 5 and 8, the children were tested on their mathematics and reading skills, and their mothers were asked questions about their children's behavior problems. Mott found many of the same things reported by earlier studies: Father absence seems to affect boys more negatively than it does girls, and white children more negatively than black children. Part of the explanation for the racial difference can be traced back to the ideas discussed in Chapters 2 and 3. Black solo mothers

Some fathers who don't live with their children spend a lot of time being a positive influence in their lives.

are more likely than white solo mothers to be part of social families that provide bottom-line help in the form of money, goods, and services.

Most important, Mott found that father absence by itself was not the most crucial reason these children were having problems. Instead, things such as the limited education of their mothers and their mothers' limited incomes (many of them were on welfare) were the main factors. Because advantaged solo parents (black or white) such as Murphy Brown are well educated and well paid, their children are much less likely to suffer from father absence.

Solo Fathers

Although growing numbers of children do not live with the same (or any) father for eighteen years, a few children spend most of their first eighteen years living only with their fathers (whether biological or social).[59] Chapter 13 reported that currently about 10 percent of solo parents are men, and that this figure hasn't changed much over the last decade. Geoffrey Greif found that solo fathers differ from solo mothers in some important ways.[60] They are usually better off economically. In addition, friends and families feel sorry for and take pity on solo fathers much more than they do solo mothers. Thus solo fathers have a more comprehensive network of helpers who cook meals, clean house, do child care, and so forth.

On the other hand, says Grief, solo fathers and mothers face similar worries because of the absence of an opposite-gender role model: Do girls growing up with solo fathers but no resident women experience a deficit? Do those girls fail to learn how a woman is "supposed" to behave? Do the girls fail to see how a man is "supposed" to behave toward a woman? And do boys living with solo fathers fail to receive the emotional support and nurturing that, some believe, only a mother can provide?

Homosexual Parents

Just as some mothers marry for a meal ticket or out of fear of a male role-model deficit, some homosexuals marry heterosexuals for social acceptance and respectability. Alan Bell and Martin Weinberg's massive study of homosexuals reported that 20 percent of the men and 30 percent of the women had been previously married.[61] Available research shows that very often homosexuals marry because they're not fully aware of their homosexuality, they've not yet come to accept it, and/or they're unwilling to accept it.[62] Chapter 4 said that largely as a result of those formal marriages, some 2 million gay men are fathers. The number of lesbian mothers may be double that figure.

Many heterosexuals find the linking of "homosexual" with "parent" to be quite distasteful and even dangerous for the children. Martha Kirkpatrick says that, "Homosexuality has long been considered antithetical to childrearing."[63] That belief is indeed ironic because in the past, virtually all adults who took care of children (e.g., teachers, governesses, maiden aunts, bachelor uncles, schoolmasters) had never been married, and many of them "may have been homosexual, at least in thought if not in deed."[64] In spite of culturally pervasive fears for the children of homosexuals, available evidence points toward a rather simple conclusion: Heterosexual and homosexual parents treat their children in "remarkably similar" fashion: Neither category of adults is better (i.e., more responsible) nor worse than the other.[65]

Research evidence also arrives at a second simple conclusion: The children of homosexual parents are neither better off nor worse off than the children of heterosexuals. A "striking feature" is that both sets of children are very similar, and there is no evidence of "pathological" behaviors among children of homosexual parents.[66] In short, the fact that a parent is gay, lesbian, or straight is nowhere nearly as important for the child's well-being as, say, the parent's education and income and how much the parent nurtures the child and seeks to enhance his or her feelings of autonomy.

In recent years, some lesbians who've never borne children have adapted the *Murphy Brown* strategy of having children without men.[67] Among heterosexuals, that strategy usually implies having intercourse but neither expecting nor wanting the impregnating male to be the child's social father. However, says Lillian Faderman, instead of intercourse, prospective lesbian mothers prefer getting pregnant by means of artificial insemination. Gays and lesbians wishing to become foster parents or adoptive parents often find their way blocked by state laws prohibiting known homosexuals from either option. Kirkpatrick reports that when the Boston press discovered that a gay couple had in 1985 been approved to be foster parents, the resulting uproar forced the state to back down. The state then devised a new policy requiring that foster children be placed only in "normal" or "traditional," that is, heterosexual, settings.[68]

Florida is one of a number of states prohibiting openly homosexual persons from adopting children. The 1992 request of a gay couple to adopt a child was denied on the grounds that the "child would be deprived of an 'opposite sex role model.' "[69] The couple, aided by the American Civil Liberties Union, challenged the state in court. In 1993 a circuit judge ruled against the state, saying "[the law] encourages homosexuals to lie and is an unconstitutional invasion of privacy."[70] He was the second judge in two years to rule against the state on this issue. The state was unsure whether to appeal to a higher court or simply grant homosexual couples the right to adopt.

The judge's concern about deception is on target. Researchers estimate there are large numbers of homosexuals who do not "come out" (admit they're gay or lesbian) because of their fear of reprisals.[71] Among these are losing one's job and/or being denied promotions. In 1993, for example, a military person who was homosexual and who did a good job had nothing to fear as long as she or he "stayed in the closet." Being honest and coming out meant that the person was thrown out of the military.[72] Similarly, some responsible persons who are homosexual conceal that fact so they can serve as foster and/or adoptive parents. Furthermore, a certain proportion of solo parents living with their biological children conceal their homosexuality for fear of losing child custody. Finally, researchers estimate there are a substantial number of married adults who, though homosexual or bisexual, remain living with their spouse and biological children until the latter grow up.[73] Researchers label all of these, and a range of comparable situations, as "invisible" gay households.[74]

If we sum up all of these varied situations, there appear to be far more children living with adult homosexuals than most citizens realize. And according to Dr. Michael E. Lamb, a psychologist and a chief government researcher: " 'What evidence there is suggests there are no particular developmental or emotional deficits for children raised by gay or lesbian parents. . . . These kids look O.K.' "[75]

Available evidence, said Chapter 4, suggests that persons do not choose to be either homosexual or heterosexual. Sexual orientation seems to be more a matter of what a person *is* or *isn't*. However, coming out versus remaining hidden is indeed a choice facing homosexuals, often an extremely painful choice. Chapter 14 talked about homosexual adolescents making the transition to viewing themselves as gay or lesbian. Their transition also involved having significant others (parents, friends) view them, as well as accept them, in that light. Judging from the 1993 struggles over homosexuals in the military, many U.S. citizens would prefer that gays and lesbians remain locked in the closet. Those citizens view the trend toward increased homosexual openness as one more lifestyle choice (alongside other adult choices such as divorce, solo parenthood, blended families, being child-free, and so on) that is destroying The Family.[76]

Children's Coping, Control, and Well-being

Recall that we are considering the chapter's second broad controversial issue—the impact of adult choices, transitions, and lifestyles on children's development. Underlying that issue is the wish, "If only it didn't have to be. . . ." All of us at one time or another have nostalgic longings for things to be the way they used to be. There seems little doubt that the experience of having the adults in one's life go their separate ways and/or choose new partners is difficult for any child, just as it is for the adults themselves. However, it appears highly unlikely that adults, women in particular, would wish, or even be able, to reverse the major trends emerging in recent decades.

Previous chapters talked about drastic shifts in national and global economies, expanding occupational opportunities for women, and the unwillingness of men and women to be caught indefinitely in the dissolution phases of erotic friendships, whether formalized or not. Because none of these changes is expected to disappear, it seems likely that today's and tomorrow's children will continue to grow up with very different experiences than yesterday's children. In view of these and other realities, the "sociology of children" was recently established as "a new field and section within the American Sociological Association.[77] In the past, most researchers wondered about what adults do to and for children, that is, their socialization. For example, if an unmarried woman bears a child, or an adult gets divorced, or a mother enrolls her child in day care, what happens to the child?

A number of today's researchers are asking questions with a somewhat different spin.[78] First, how do children cope with their social environment, for example, living with a solo parent, or in a blended/stepfamily, or with a homosexual parent? How do children react to the unexpected and unforeseen events of their lives, for example, parents who go their separate ways? Specifically, Warren Brown and Waln Brown want to know why some children succeed despite the odds.[79] Other researchers want to explore things like "resiliency" or "invulnerability" among at-risk children.[80] Bonnie Robo goes so far as to suggest that, "For some children and adolescents the divorce process might encourage healthy development."[81] Although parents going their separate ways is difficult for almost all children, Robo says that some of them may nonetheless "experience the divorce as a growth-enhancing process, albeit a painful and initially distressing event."

Chapter 14 explored comparable questions for adults: As they age, how do adults cope with, or respond to, unforeseen and unexpected happenings? But Chapter 14 added that an important step beyond adult coping is control: "How do I / we *make* changes happen?" In similar fashion, the second thing some researchers are asking about children is this: How do children create, construct, and shape their own lives?[82] Chapter 14 said that adults who feel in relative control of their lives also feel good about themselves—they are emotionally better off and physically healthier. The same principles apply to children: Children who sense they have some degree of control over their lives are likely to feel better about

themselves. They are also likely to be physically healthier and, according to some researchers, be better students.[83] Myles Friedman and George Lackey add that students with a sense of control are less likely to drop out and more likely to participate effectively in the rapidly changing job market described in Chapter 15.

Cocoons, Gardens, and Children   The older issue about what gets done *to* children by adults viewed children as relatively passive: How do adults harm or hurt children? The two newer questions about coping and control assume that children are active—What can they do *for themselves?* What can they do to try to make their own lives better? In this new view, says Sylvia Blitzer, children are seen as social agents.[84] Up to now, the dominant image of children has been like that of a caterpillar in a cocoon. The helpless child is viewed as experiencing a lot of maturational changes until the magic moment when she or he breaks through the cocoon as an adult. At this point (age 18? 21?) he or she starts "flying," that is, finally taking charge of his or her own life.

Besides the cocoon imagery (if no one disturbs the cocoon the maturing butterfly/child will be okay), a second and similar imagery was often applied to children. In this image, the Benchmark Family was like a walled garden surrounding children and keeping them secure from negative external forces. Researchers who study children's coping and control are now beginning to doubt the imagery of a "mythic 'walled garden' of 'Happy, Safe, Protected, Innocent Childhood' that all children ideally inhabited."[85] It seems that yesterday's children were not as shielded from life's pains and uncertainties as the imagery of a cocoon or a walled garden might imply. Chapter 12, for example, reported that woman abuse has been with us for centuries even though it's only recently been uncovered. And Chapter 17 shows that the same conclusion holds for child physical and sexual abuse. Harry Hendrick says that Britons and North Americans have shared a common belief in the cocoon/garden imagery for at least 200 years. Citizens believed that the best and most ideal place for a child to develop is within the safe and sheltered Benchmark Family.[86]

A major goal of Benchmark parents, adds Hendrick, was to "control childhood." The chief means used to control children's lives was physical punishment, as described later on in this chapter. In particular, girls and boys were expected to conform to behaviors that were appropriate to their own gender. A second priority was helping children cope with life's uncertainties in preparation for the time when they would become independent adults. But according to Allison James and Alan Prout, it never occurred to most parents that their children might need to develop a strong sense of control over their lives *right now*.[87] Most parents would not have understood that the following statement had anything to do with their own children and adolescents: "It is important to realize that control is prerequisite to improving quality of life; indeed it is necessary to life itself."[88] Instead of worrying about developing their children's own sense of control, most parents seemed preoccupied with getting children to conform to adult authority and control.

Children as Perverse   There's a reason parents were preoccupied with getting their children to "behave properly." The reasons, says Hendrick, is that most adults view children in at least two ways. One view is that because children are innocent and helpless they require the protection of a cocoon or walled garden. The other view is that children also have a perverse side that resists superior adult knowledge and experience. By resisting adults, children are likely to endanger themselves and disrupt the lives of the adults. Furthermore, resistance is viewed as a bad omen for the future—if children don't learn to conform, how can they make it as adults? And if they don't make it, then won't society suffer?

According to Hendrick, viewing children as slightly perverse influences how parents treat children. In this view, The Family is like a field on which is played out the struggle between parents and children for control of children's lives. The older a child becomes the more control (especially during adolescence) he or she wants over his or her own life. Parents resist whenever and wherever they can, trying to retain as much control as possible. They believe it's in the child's best interests for them to do so, even if the child feels otherwise. Yet all the while parents sense their battle is a losing one. Eventually their children will indeed become independent adults. The big questions are, how much freedom should parents give to children, and at what ages?

This view of parent-child struggle assumes that both biological parents live with the child during its first eighteen years. The father is believed to be the main source of the firm discipline and physical punishment necessary to control the child.[89] The mother is seen as the fountain of nurture and emotional support necessary to balance the father's strong hand. The father is the role model for perseverance, strength, dependability, and economic success. The mother is the role model for compassion, forgiveness, intimacy, and personal sacrifice. Left undisturbed, that straightforward model of parent-child relations would probably have persisted indefinitely.

That model is being eroded partly because of recent adult efforts, especially by women, to get more control over their own lives. As today's adults make certain life-course choices, today's children are surrounded by a very different social context than existed during the 1950s, the pinnacle of the Modern Family. Many of today's children do not live indefinitely with the same two parents, and/or they may live with only one parent for a while, and so on. Even if they live with two adults, growing numbers of small children spend many of their waking hours in day-care centers (looked after mostly by women) because both adults are employed. Some critics worry that because of the many changes springing from adult choices, parents' (and teachers') capabilities to control (and nurture) their children are being undermined.[90] Because of adult choices, today's children appear to be living in a different world. Still, it's not quite certain—does this "different world" help or hurt their quality of life?

Benchmark Limitations on Children One way to try to answer that question is to make an analogy between children's and women's lives. Since the 1960s, persons on the left side of Figure 1-1 have worried that the Modern Family had a lot of negative impacts on women. One of its major impacts was to limit women's choices and to minimize the amount

of control and autonomy they had over their own lives.[91] In similar fashion, some researchers are now beginning to wonder about the negative effects that the Benchmark Family might have had on children. Just as it stifled women's autonomy and did little to enhance their sense of control, did it impose similar kinds of limitations on children? As varieties of families become increasingly common throughout society, some researchers are raising new questions, questions stemming from the possibility that springing children from the "cocoon" or "garden" may not be all bad.[92] Is it possible, they ask, that what's happening might somehow create opportunities for some children to take greater control over their own lives? And over the long haul, would that result in an improvement in the well-being of some children?

The chief objection to children's autonomy that immediately pops into everyone's mind is that children and adolescents don't have the

Children's day care experiences—just like their home experiences—can be either positive or negative.

experience and maturity necessary to control their own lives. Most of us believe there's too much risk they'll hurt both themselves and others. We say that small children are especially prone to harm if given too much freedom. Robin Leavitt studied small children in day-care centers and begins her report by reminding us that, "Child care is not simply a pedagogical or technical issue."[93] She adds it is also a political and social issue. By that she means that adults fight over how much autonomy and control children of any age should have. That issue is at the heart of many political conflicts in the United States between citizens located on the left and right sides of Figure 1-1. At what age, for example, should adolescents be required to get parental permission to get condoms, use the Pill, or have an abortion?

Leavitt spent five to ten hours a week for several years observing what went on in day-care centers between the children and their adult caregivers. "What went on" was precisely the same thing that goes on within many families, whether Benchmark or not. She observed ongoing contests and struggle between the children and adults. Most of the time, says Leavitt, the children lose. By "lose" she means that whenever a child's actions strayed outside the guidelines set by the center, the caregiver immediately imposed what Leavitt calls "extractive power" on the child. She defines that as power that "treats children as property or things to be managed, directed and controlled."[94] By contrast, "empowering caregiver" is the term Leavitt uses for the adult who appreciated the child for himself or herself. That sort of adult tried to share power by allowing the child the "freedom to create and construct" his or her life in the center.

Children's Autonomy Neither Leavitt nor anyone else is suggesting that children and adolescents be allowed to do whatever they want whenever they wish. Instead, Leavitt says that responsible adults want to know

under what conditions children's autonomy can flourish. That question is more basic (and complicated) than asking the usual questions such as: Does the child live with one or two parents, and for how many years? Is the parent male or female? Is the child's mother divorced or never-married? Does the child live in a blended/step family? Is the child living with adults who are "merely cohabiting? Are the adults homosexual? Does the child attend day care? Is the child's mother in a career? The reason why it's so vital for a child to be autonomous, to participate in creating and constructing her or his own life, is because of the kind of world in which she or he lives *right now.*

First, for example, participating in the control of his or her own life means that he or she will be a healthier child and adolescent, both emotionally and physically. Second, autonomous children and adolescents are better prepared to counteract the deadening effects of most schools bent on enforcing student conformity.[95] Third, adolescents who are struggling to be autonomous will be better able to cope with and to manage the hazards of contemporary erotic friendships. That is particularly true for women facing the onslaughts of sexual harassment and/or assault, as well as pregnancy and motherhood. Finally, today's and tomorrow's adult world of complex erotic friendships and shifting employment opportunities demands persons well versed in the arts of what Chapter 11 called problem-solving and negotiation. Being proficient in those arts is a chief component of what autonomy is all about.

PHYSICAL PUNISHMENT AND CHILDREN'S AUTONOMY

Trying to understand more about children's autonomy brings us to the last of the three children's issues being hotly debated during the 1990s. People on the right side of Figure 1-1 press the offensive when it comes to the first two issues—adolescent childbearing and adult choices. For example, former Vice President Quayle (the *Murphy Brown* incident) and social critic Bennett define both issues as social ills to be cured by returning to "old values." By contrast, people on the left side of Figure 1-1 press the offensive when it comes to the third issue—physical (corporal) punishment of children. Progressives worry about it for a number of reasons. One thing that concerns them is whether force has a negative impact on children's autonomy. Another thing they worry about is the connection between force and children's physical and sexual abuse.

"Sensible" Spankings

Throughout most of the twentieth century, some progressives have argued that spankings and other forms of physical force are not healthy for children.[96] Religious conservatives have strenuously objected to that view; they hold that spankings are part of the divine will. James Dobson, a nationally recognized conservative religious expert on such matters, argues that spankings "should be reserved for the moment a child (between the age of 18 months to 10 years old) expresses to parents a defiant 'I will not!' or 'You shut up!' "[97] The key question, says Dobson, is, "Who is going to win?" Dobson believes that the lifetime health of the child requires that the parent win. To win, Dobson asserts that the parent must sometimes spank "according to very carefully thought-out guidelines." As part of the guidelines, Dobson recommends applying a "neutral object" such as a switch or paddle to the child's buttocks.

Historian Philip Greven objects to the prevailing cultural view that "sensible" spanking is necessary for healthy child development. He admits that a number of secular experts agree with Dobson that parents must distinguish between " 'legitimate violence' " toward children and "unacceptable violence"—abuse that is excessive and inappropriate."[98] But Greven

and a few other researchers assert that it is impossible to distinguish between legitimate and nonlegitimate violence toward children. Greven claims that, "All levels of violence against children, including all the varied forms of physical punishments, are hurtful and harmful."

Greven states that his own well-intentioned and loving parents used corporal punishment on him, and he admits that he's done the same thing to his own children on at least a few occasions. He adds that writing his book was a way to express the anguish he feels between two conflicting viewpoints. On the one side is the view held by most citizens that physical punishment results in healthier children and an orderly society. On the other side is the minority view that physical force hurts both children and society. Greven believes that one reason the United States is among the most violent societies in the world is its widespread acceptance of corporal punishment.

According to Greven, the chief reason corporal punishment is so universally endorsed in the United States is because of its evangelical religious heritage. Greven cites the case of a 23-month-old boy who was paddled to death by his fundamentalist parents.[99] The State of West Virginia sentenced the parents' preacher to jail for "involuntary manslaughter and conspiracy to commit the unlawful wounding" of the child. Although the preacher never touched the child, the judge said she had incited the parents to use extreme and unnecessary force. The preacher's lawyers appealed her conviction on the grounds that the U.S. Constitution guarantees religious freedom. In this case, the lawyers argued, religious freedom means, first, that preachers have the right to exhort parents to use corporal punishment on their children. Second, it means that parents must have the ultimate right to decide whether and how much force to use on their child. The U.S. Supreme Court refused to listen to their appeal, and the preacher's conviction stood.

The question of how much force is legitimate to use on children remains unsettled among both religious and nonreligious people. Greven notes that the illustrious Dr. Benjamin Spock, who has been writing advice books for parents on baby and child care since 1945, has recently shifted his position on physical punishment.[100] Although Spock once cautiously endorsed "sensible" force, he now rejects it, for the reasons stated at the beginning of this section: possible negative emotional impacts on the child and possible encouragement of child (and woman) abuse.

Undermining Children's Autonomy and Well-being Greven believes that corporal punishment does indeed have negative emotional impacts on children. He argues that, among other things, force produces anxiety and fear, anger and hate, apathy, melancholy and depression, paranoia, and so on. Force, he claims, also undermines a child's autonomy— it weakens the child's sense of control over his or her own life.

People who disagree with Greven (e.g., Dobson) say that force itself does not harm children; emotional harm is wrought only if the punishment is excessive and unnecessary. Furthermore, advocates on the right side of Figure 1-1 take the matter a step further by asserting that today's parents are not tough enough! They believe that many of society's ills such as lack of order in the public schools, drug and alcohol abuse, and delinquency and crime are in part the result of parents being afraid to use appropriate physical force on their children. They criticize Dr. Spock and other media figures for undermining parents' courage and resolve to use necessary force. They argue that if parents consistently applied the wise and prudent use of corporal punishment to their children, the children would become good students, honest citizens, and productive adults.

Physical and Sexual Abuse Greven and others on the left side of Figure 1-1 believe that whatever its emotional impacts, physical force

legitimates the widespread physical and sexual abuse of U.S. children documented in Chapter 17.[101] Their reasoning begins with the point made in Chapter 12 that at one time husbands had the legal rights to use physical force on their wives and also to compel them into sexual intercourse. Husbands had those rights because of the religious teaching that they are responsible to God for their wives' behaviors. A "good husband" must answer to God if his wife goes astray. He is thus charged with the sacred duty to shape her into a devout and godly woman. Whenever possible he should avoid force. Unfortunately, force sometimes becomes the last resort, but when it does, it must never be excessive.

The last twenty years of research, said Chapter 12, have revealed that over the centuries those teachings helped to reinforce the cultural idea that a wife, cohabitor, or girlfriend may occasionally be fair game. That is, there are certain times when she is defined, albeit reluctantly, as a *legitimate target* for the man's physical force, for example if she "flirts" and/or is "sexual" with another man. But the fact is that because many men (and some women) believe it's okay for her to be a target on certain occasions, men make her a target on many occasions. Men appear to believe they have the ultimate right to decide when to use force on their erotic friends. In recent years, many states have acted to limit men's rights. Men—whether husbands, cohabitors, or boyfriends—who use physical force on their partners can be charged with assault and battery. Men who compel their female partners into sex can be charged with rape. North American society is slowly drawing a formal line that men are not supposed to cross: Because women have control over their own bodies, men can no longer confront them with physical or sexual coercion.

Greven and other advocates make comparable arguments regarding children. If children are defined as legitimate targets for force on *certain* occasions, they will inevitably become targets on *many* occasions. Those advocates believe that a cultural climate that permits any sort of violence toward children encourages the indiscriminate violence known today as physical and sexual abuse. They argue that all "physical assaults against children are abusive and . . . often cut to the core of life itself."[102] They want the same type of line drawn to protect children that is now being drawn for women's protection. Their hope is that this line will make the use of *any* sort of physical coercion of children culturally unacceptable.

Force, Autonomy, and Children's Best Interests

The majority of citizens both in the middle and on the right of Figure 1-1 are not at all convinced about the merits of nonviolent child rearing. Greven acknowledges how difficult it would be for the United States to emulate Sweden, which in 1979 passed a law (carrying no criminal penalties) stating that " 'A child may not be subjected to physical punishment or other injurious or humiliating treatment.' "[103] Some progressives believe that humiliating a child by any means undermines the child's sense of autonomy. As the sense of control declines, so do his or her feelings of well-being. Because these advocates believe that instilling a sense of autonomy is the most responsible thing a parent can do for a child, they are eager to encourage and assist parents to adapt an autonomy perspective. The advocates believe that such a perspective is the first step on the road toward eventually convincing parents to do nonviolent child rearing.

Throughout Europe and North America, many of those advocates have placed the ideal of children's autonomy under broader headings such "children's best interest" and "children's rights." In 1989, for example, the United Nations adopted a document called the *Convention on the Rights of the Child.* By 1990

enough nations around the world had signed it to give it the status of an official U.N. Treaty. However, James Lucier, a conservative spokesperson, is proud of the fact that the U.S. government chose *not* to sign it. He severely criticized the document because he objects to the core idea of children's rights.[104] Advocates for children's rights hold that if families are not doing what's best for the child, then governments have both the right and responsibility to intervene on the child's behalf. What matters most, they claim, is the best interests of the child.

Parental Accountability   What worries conservatives such as Lucier is what's missing in the U.N. document—the "idea of rights for families. The child is seen as an autonomous being, with the family as a mere caretaker."[105] Up to now, says Lucier, parents had the last word in controlling their children's lives. They didn't have to glance over their shoulders worrying that outsiders were checking them out. Children's rights' advocates say that's precisely the problem—parents are accountable to no one for how they treat their children. In particular, advocates worry that many parents undermine their children's sense of autonomy and well-being through physical, mental, and sexual abuse; but outsiders have no way to finding that out until, in many cases, it's too late. The advocates propose that we try to create ways of making parents accountable for their children's well-being.

Jeffrey Blustein says it boils down to a case of parental autonomy versus children's autonomy. He states that the parents "right . . . to raise their children in accordance with their own notions of childrearing" may clash with the child's well-being.[106] What happens then? In 1992, a 12-year-old Florida boy sued his biological mother for "divorce."[107] He claimed she'd neglected and mistreated him and caused him to live in deprivation and poverty. There were years, he said, when he didn't hear from her even at Christmas. Hence he petitioned the court to allow him to be adopted by his current foster parents. His biological mother fought back, but the judge ruled against her. The judge made the boy the adopted child of his new parents.[108] Afterwards the boy said "he hoped his case would encourage other young people to take action to gain their happiness."[109]

For many decades most states have claimed the right to remove children from the custody of their biological parents in obvious cases of parental neglect and/or abuse. What is unique about this case is the fact that the boy, not the state, initiated it. The state in fact opposed it. In an attempt to exercise greater control over his own life he decided that he no longer wished to have any formal ties with his biological mother. Conservative critics responded angrily that "the case has substantially weakened the traditional ties that bind families and set a dangerous precedent," and the mother's lawyer complained that the ruling would have a "sinister impact. . . . 'We have decided to place children's wishes over the preservation of the family.' "[110]

Following that incident, the boy's adoptive father (an attorney) went next to the legal aid of a 12-year-old Florida girl suing for the right to escape her parents and live with her grandmother. The girl complained that her "stepfather sexually abused her, her mother betrayed her and her father abused alcohol, smoked marijuana and ignored her emotional needs."[111] Moreover, the national press is reporting additional incidents of children going to court in various efforts to assert their own rights, that is, their control and autonomy, thus limiting their parents' autonomy.[112] Harry Hendrick describes similar kinds of incidents occurring in Great Britain. He asserts that these incidents reflect something new that's emerging in Western societies: the willingness of some adults to "listen to children's grievances and campaign on their behalf."[113]

The Big Picture

The Big Picture goes something like this. Advocates on the right side of Figure 1-1 claim that the two-parent, formally married, heterosexual family is what's always best for children. They also hold that the parents should have ultimate autonomy in shaping their children, including the measured use of physical force. The state should reluctantly interfere in only the most extreme and obvious cases of neglect and/or abuse.

Progressives claim that what's best are families that enhance children's autonomy—families that encourage their childrens' feelings that they are participating in the invention and control of their own lives.[114] They add that regardless of whether there are one or two parents, whether they're formally married, or whether they're straight or gay, parents should be accountable to their community for their parenting.

Some parents, for example, might wish to practice nonviolent child rearing but fear they'll be unable to manage their children's unruly behavior. Citizen volunteers from the community might be able to assist them in figuring out how to elicit their children's cooperation without hitting them. Those parents and volunteers might belong to what Chapters 2 and 3 described as social families. The result would be that adults outside the household might actively participate in parenting with the parent(s). Advocates hope that this belief in active involvement would somehow gradually replace the current cultural belief that the family is a private domain into which outsiders can venture only reluctantly.

CONCLUSION

It remains to be seen whether the progressive agenda is merely unrealistic sentimentalism. Right now, when it comes to children the "high moral ground" is firmly occupied by conservative social critics such as William Bennett. Among other things, they charge that today's women are being selfish, first by postponing marriage, and next by delaying children, thus bearing merely one or two. And, say the critics, women and men who delay childbearing so long that they end up being child-free are being extraordinarily narcissistic. Women, the critics charge, are sacrificing their duties to themselves and to society on the altar of their jobs and careers. At the same time that the critics assert that married women *should* have as many children as they can afford, they charge that unmarried, poorly educated teen-age women (mostly black) *shouldn't* have any children at all. Their prescription to avoid teen parenting—as well as teen choices about contraception and abortion—is to avoid sex.

As they grope for the high moral ground of their own, progressives zero in on the matter of children's physical punishment and what it tells us about adult respect for children's autonomy and children's rights. They charge that in the past, many stable families abused children emotionally, physically, or sexually. In many ways, they assert, private families can be places where children's feelings of control, autonomy, and well-being are undermined. To achieve healthy child development, the bottom line is not the number of adults in the household, whether the mother's employed, whether she's been divorced or never-married, whether the parents are straight or gay, and so on. The bottom line is rather whether the parent(s) is/are participating with the child in enhancing his or her sense of invention of, and thus control over, his or her own life. Feelings of autonomy, they believe, are the key to a child's sense of well-being right now, as well the key to the child's participating effectively in the complex world she or he will face tomorrow.

Some advocates for children's rights carry the matter a step further by asserting that parents are accountable to their community and society for how well they nurture their children's autonomy. The implications of campaigning politically for the "rights and best interests of the child" are indeed far reaching. One is that children themselves should be able to sue to be free from parents they perceive as not acting in their best interests. Another is that the community should take a more active role by participating with parents in their child rearing.

What the future holds for the competing conservative and progressive agendas regarding children looms murky at best. It appears unlikely that most adults will give up the sense of autonomy and well-being that springs from inventing their own life courses, even if conventional wisdom holds that children would be better off if they did. It seems just as unlikely that most adults will soon recast what child rearing is all about, and will accept the notion that children—to say nothing of outsiders—should have a significant say in their parenting.

NOTES

1. Espenshade, 1985.
2. Anna Quindlen, "Playing perfect pattycake," *The New York Times*, April 13, 1994, p. A15.
3. Blustein, 1982; Greven, 1991.
4. Rainwater, 1965, p. 150, italics in original. See Cheal, 1991, Chapter 3, for a contemporary critique of pronatalism.
5. Skolnick, 1991, p. 35.
6. Nock, 1987; see also Scanzoni, 1975.
7. Kamerman and Kahn, 1991, p. 6.
8. Teachman, Polonko, and Scanzoni, revised edition forthcoming (originally published 1987).
9. Ibid.
10. Schwartz, 1992.
11. Teachmen et al.
12. Ibid.
13. Veevers, 1980; Polonko, Teachman, and Scanzoni, 1982; Houseknecht, 1987.
14. Ventura and Martin, 1993, p. 3.
15. Cowan and Cowan, 1992.

youth in his informal family is an example of expanded contemporary images about incest.[9] A number of prominent persons are now acknowledging that they were victims of childhood sexual abuse from either blood or social relatives. Hoping to bring the "last taboo" out of the closet and into the light of public discussion, these figures include Roseanne Arnold, Oprah Winfrey, La Toya Jackson, and former Miss America Marilyn Van Derbur.[10]

The third type of sexual coercion law is similar to the second except that it focuses on adults external to the child's blood and social families. Those adults are also prohibited from vaginal/anal intercourse with children, fondling children's genitals, having oral sex with them, or exposing themselves indecently to children. Besides strangers coercing children in these ways, recent reports describe alleged sexual coercion by adults known to the children—teachers, day-care workers, scout leaders, clergy, neighbors, and so on.[11] In one such case, a Catholic priest "pleaded guilty to having sex with members of parish boys' clubs from 1983 to 1991."[12] His defense was that he had been a "sex addict" who had now overcome his affliction with God's help. A Federal judge sentenced him to prison for eight years.

Professional Disagreements Describing these three kinds of laws prohibiting child sexual coercion is simple and straightforward. Researchers and counselors agree that sexual coercion of any kind undermines a child's sense of autonomy. The child is likely to suffer reduced feelings of well-being, that is, less emotional and physical health.

However, researchers and counselors differ sharply among themselves on a number of more specific matters. For example, is one kind of sexual coercion worse for the child than another? Some professionals believe that the worst kind is sexual intercourse between a parent and her or his biological child. Other professionals believe that the amount of physical force accompanying the sexual coercion is

the big question. Still others claim that if the adult doesn't touch the child (e.g., the adult and child masturbate in each other's presence), the harm is less than if the child is touched (e.g., each masturbates the other). Age is another big question: Is sexual coercion more harmful for adolescents or for younger children?

Another major issue over which professionals disagree is how to define child sexual coercion/abuse. Because researchers define it in different ways, they often come up with different figures regarding both its incidence and its prevalence.

Incidence of Child Sexual Coercion "Incidence" means the number of cases of sexual abuse that occur among those at risk during a specific period. One study that examined official U.S. government reports concluded that during 1986 there had been 132,000 cases, or an *incidence rate* of 20.9 cases per 10,000 children under age 18.[13] The 20.9 figure was the highest reported since 1976 (the first year such information had been collected). This does not mean that there actually was more child abuse in 1986 than there had been in 1976. One reason the rate seemed to go up was that a bigger net was cast. Later definitions of "incidence" were expanded to include a broader range of adults who could be potential abusers. Specifically, a 1981 national study looked only at natural and social parents.[14] But a study done later in the decade included in addition *all adult caretakers* (e.g., teachers, clergy, scout leaders, day-care workers).[15] If the earlier studies had included all adults of social and blood families, they might have found that the incidence of child sexual coercion hadn't changed much at all.

Prevalence of Child Sexual Coercion Prevalence means something different from incidence. The *prevalence* of child sexual coercion means the proportion of children who have *ever* been sexually coerced from their birth to age 18. Although some studies report that as few as 2 percent of girls have ever been abused, other studies say that the figure is more like 62 percent. Likewise, some studies place the prevalence figure for boys at 2 percent, but others place it as high as 30 percent.[16] Many other studies lace the figures for both genders somewhere between those highs and lows.

One reason the prevalence figures roam all over the map is because different researchers investigate different kinds of sexual activities. One study of college students asked them to report any kinds of sexual *intrusion* (oral, vaginal, anal) done to them while they were children. Men reported 1.4 percent intrusion, and women 1.8 percent.[17] If sexual abuse is defined in that narrow sense, its prevalence would not seem very large. When those same students were asked to report about a broader range of coercive activities (e.g., kissing, fondling, genital exposure), the prevalence figures climbed substantially. For men the figure went up to 5 percent and for women it was 11.9 percent.

Many other problems seriously affect the accuracy of both the incidence and prevalence numbers. One is that many studies of child abuse are done with college students. Would samples of noncollege youth aged 18 to 24 reveal higher, lower, or the same levels of childhood sexual abuse? Another problem is how frequently the sexual coercion occurred while the child was growing up. A 15-year-old boy may report that he was once confronted by his uncle exposing himself. But a 17-year-old girl may report that ever since puberty hardly a week went by when the men in her household didn't fondle her breasts and buttocks.

Honesty is another problem that affects the accuracy of numbers of reported child abuse incidents. Do people lie when asked if their mother or father or teacher sexually coerced them? If they lie out of guilt and/or embarrassment, do they tend to say abuse never happened when in fact it had? Or do they claim it did happen when in fact it didn't? A connected problem is the capability to recall abuse experiences. The sexual coercion may have been so painful that the person repressed it and thus "forgot" all about it. The events described in the *Newsweek* cover story mentioned earlier began when the Souza's 24-year-old daughter, Shirely Ann, had a recurring dream that she was being raped by her parents. Her dreams reminded both her and her sister, Sharon, of repressed childhood experiences—alleged sexual abuse by their parents. Gradually those reminders led Sharon to pay attention to her two small daughters. She then came to believe that her parents had abused them too.

Connected with the problems of honesty and repression of unpleasant experiences is how children interpret, or perceive, what adults do with them. Knudsen says that because the adult is an authority figure, the child may figure that whatever the adult does is okay. That's especially true, adds Knudsen, if the child feels the behavior is pleasurable. And if the child believes the behavior is acceptable and/or pleasurable, the child may never report it to anyone, especially not to a researcher.

As a result of this and the other problems just discussed, official estimates of the incidence and prevalence of child sexual coercion may be far too low. However, we can arrive at some reasonably safe estimates about what's going on today. First, as far as incidence is concerned, Knudsen concludes that each year at least 150,000 U.S. children are "tricked or coerced" into some kind of sexual activity with adults.[18] Second, as far as prevalence is concerned, sometime during their childhood 20 to 40 percent of girls and 5 to 10 percent of boys can expect to have some sort of unwanted sexual experience.

Sexual Coercion by Adolescents

So far we've been talking about what adults (aged 18 and over) do to children (under age 18). But Lois and Robert Pierce say that researchers often overlook the sexual coercion that adolescents inflict on other adolescents and on younger children. These authors go so far as to argue that sexual coercion within families "occurs *most often* among persons of . . . the same generation."[19] To be sure, many preteen siblings engage in mutual exploration and experimentation that is not coercive. And because increasing numbers of blended households contain children who are not blood linked, those children are perhaps more likely to define sexual experimentation as okay "cause she/he is not my *real* sister/brother."

But sexual exploration that began as voluntary may gradually become coercive. One of the sibs may wish to stop it but the other insists they continue. In many cases the sibs had not previously engaged in voluntary sexual activities. Whether or not the activities had ever been voluntary, Pierce and Pierce report that the adolescents in their study were now using threats and/or actual force to coerce their sibs (blood or social) into sexual activities. Males accounted for 81 percent of the adolescents they studied. The coercive sexual activities ranged from exposure and genital fondling to oral, anal, and vaginal intercourse. The authors add that most of the adolescents who'd been sexually coercing their sibs reported that they themselves had been sexually abused by adult family members.

Besides adolescent sexual coercion within families, Chapter 12 described the sexual harassment that some adolescent boys inflict on girls at school. Sexual assault goes beyond harassment, and two separate assault instances got enormous national media publicity during 1993. In the first case, a New Jersey court convicted four high-school boys, all athletes, of sexually assaulting a mentally retarded female classmate.[20] In the California case, eight high-school male athletes, members of a clique called the Spur Posse, were arrested and charged with unlawful intercourse and rape.[21] The alleged victims were girls ranging in ages from 10 to 16. All charges against the boys were later dropped.

Though they differed in specifics, in both in-

stances the boys' aggression was justified by the same set of beliefs about girls. In both states the boys claimed "the girls wanted it." Moreover, in both communities a number of adults (mostly men) were sympathetic with the boys' justification. Some of the men asserted that those kinds of sexual episodes are inevitable. Their feelings seemed to be that, "After all, boys will be boys." A father of one of the California boys was quoted as saying, "Nothing my boy did was anything that any red-blooded American boy wouldn't do at his age."[22] Finally, in the State of Florida, officials estimate that they "will receive 13,000 reports annually of children [mostly girls] who are sexually abused by other youngsters [mostly boys]."[23] In response, the 1994 state legislature passed a bill requiring cases of child-on-child sex abuse to be reported to a central registry.

Prosecuting Child Sexual Abuse

In both the New Jersey and California cases, the prosecutors' efforts to get convictions faced enormous community and legal obstacles. One is that some professionals believe it is not in the best interests of the youthful victim, child or adolescent, to go to court. Researchers and counselors who oppose prosecution believe that having to testify in court only makes the child feel worse about her or his victimization.[24] The court experience, say opponents, requires that the child recreate the pain and suffering that she or he is trying to forget and thus is unhealthy for the child's immediate well-being and long-term development.

Those who favor prosecuting persons accused of child sexual coercion see it very differently. They believe that successful prosecution (as in the New Jersey case) "clearly establishes the child as the innocent victim."[25] Punishing the wrongdoer sends a message to the community that "an adult [or coercive adolescent] cannot violate or exploit the relative weakness of children." Conviction also means that the court can order offenders not merely to jail, but also to treatment programs that might perhaps prevent repetition of their offenses.

Some researchers have tried to find out how much, if at all, the court experience actually harms alleged child sexual abuse victims.[26] Thus far the results are mixed. All professionals agree on one thing, however: If a child is compelled to testify in court, infinite care must be taken to make the experience as nonthreatening for him or her as possible. At the same time the rights of the accused (adolescent or adult) must also be protected. For example, when Mi Farrow accused Woody Allen of sexually molesting their 7-year-old adopted daughter, a team of experts (pediatricians, social workers, nurses) was assembled to determine if formal charges should be filed against Allen. Although Farrow produced a videotape of the child saying certain things, the experts unanimously agreed there was no substance to her charges. Allen, they concluded, had not sexually abused his daughter.[27]

In a 1988 case a woman (Kelly Michaels) was sentenced to forty-seven years in prison for sexually abusing children at the day-care center where she worked. In 1993 the New Jersey Court of Appeals ruled that she had not received a fair trial and overturned her conviction. The Appeals Court said that the judge in the original trial had appealed to the children's "suggestibility."[28] Specifically, the judge questioned the children alone in his chambers while the jury watched on closed-circuit TV. He also played games with the children, held them on his lap, and whispered into their ears while encouraging them to whisper in his ear.

What worried the Appeals Court and some professionals is that adults (therapists, prosecutors, judges) may manipulate highly impressionable children, getting the children to say things about the accused that are not true. Of particular concern is the testimony of a group of children who all know each other claiming that (a) certain adult(s) molested them. The concern is that if one child makes such a claim, there'll be a snowball effect: Others in the group will follow suit because they fear being different. The children's fear is heightened if they sense that powerful adults are encouraging them to "tell us what happened," even if there's nothing to tell.

A Child Abuse Establishment   For instance, as a result of a large number of children accusing him, a North Carolina owner of a day-care facility was convicted of ninety-nine counts of child sexual abuse. But defense lawyers claimed that state-employed therapists convinced the children that they had been abused.[29] A Public TV two-hour documentary on *Frontline* that investigated the case before it ever came to trial suggested the same thing.[30] Richard Gardner is a professor of psychiatry who often serves as an expert witness at child sexual abuse cases in the United States. He claims that over the past two decades, "a child abuse establishment" has grown up. This "establishment" consists of certain counselors, prosecutors, and judges who encourage "charges of child abuse whether they are reasonable or not."[31] Gardner illustrates his claim via the North Carolina case.

The *Frontline* documentary interviewed counselors hired by some of the parents whose children belonged to the group saying they'd been sexually coerced. These private counselors found no factual basis for the charges. But all of the counselors paid by the state claimed that the children had been coerced. *Frontline* noted this striking contrast between the privately paid and state-paid counselors, and hinted that the contrast might be explained by the fact that the state counselors are part of an establishment more concerned for their own career interests than for the children's or defendants' interests.[32]

Gardner enlarged his criticism of the establishment by talking about Raymond and Shirely Souza, the grandparents profiled in the

Newsweek cover story. After personally examining them, he concluded that none of the charges against them was true, that they had not sexually coerced their grandchildren. Gardner argued that the prosecutor had managed the impressions of the children, thus leading them to say things that weren't factual. Gardner also testified as an expert witness before the New Jersey Appeals Court in the Kelly Michaels case just cited. He examined the alleged victims, the accusing parents, and Ms. Michaels, and concluded that Michaels was innocent, that counselors and prosecutors had manipulated the children into saying things that had no basis in fact.

Gardner acknowledges that many thousands of cases of actual child sexual coercion do occur annually in the United States, and that the great majority go unreported. Some cases are more tragic than others. In Oregon, for example, a man who knew he carried the AIDS virus sexually molested a number of preteen girls and boys in his neighborhood.[33] Besides bearing the emotional scars of sexual coercion, those children also face the possibility of an early and horrible death. In Florida, authorities certified that a *month-old* infant girl was raped.[34] Though not fatal, her injuries were described as extreme. And in a Delaware case, a father who signed a confession that he had repeatedly raped his 3-year-old daughter was never brought to trial.[35] State laws designed to protect the rights of the accused meant that his confession could not be used as evidence. Hence the prosecutors concluded it would be impossible to gain a conviction on the basis of a 3-year-old girl's testimony.

All professionals and concerned citizens (regardless of their viewpoints) feel profound anguish over the confused and contradictory picture of child sexual coercion in the United States. One sentiment that unites them all was expressed by Pulitzer Prize winner Anna Quindlen. Her comment on the Appeals Court decision in the Michaels' case was: "From the moment a child says something disquieting to a parent, all involved—parents, investigators, psychologists, lawyers, judges—need to proceed with an unusual degree of sophistication and caution."[36]

PHYSICAL ABUSE

Dean Busby claims that the sexual abuse of children is distinct from, and not equivalent to, their physical abuse.[37] In one sense that's quite correct. The behaviors described here under sexual abuse (e.g., fondling, exposure, intercourse) are not the same as beating, punching, slapping, and so on. But in another sense they share more than many people realize. For instance, a child may be physically and sexually assaulted at the same time.[38] Or the same child may be abused in a *physical* way at one time and in a *sexual* way at another. Busby himself talks about Sigmund Freud's well-known 1919 essay connecting child beating with sexual perversion.

Another thing that sexual and physical abuse share in common is that they've always been part of human societies.[39] It wasn't until the nineteenth century, however, that any organization existed to guard U.S. children against either type of abuse. During the late 1800s the Society for the Prevention of Cruelty to Animals felt compelled to take up the case of Mary Ann, who was being viciously abused by her foster parents. No other public organization, including churches, would intercede on her behalf. The resulting publicity and subsequent public outrage led to the formation of the New York Society for the Prevention of Cruelty to Children.[40]

Before the 1930s, labels such as "violence against children" simply did not exist. Caseworkers and medical professionals called it merely "harsh discipline."[41] Indeed, child abuse got only minimal attention from the media and professionals until the 1960s. During that decade it generated more interest and

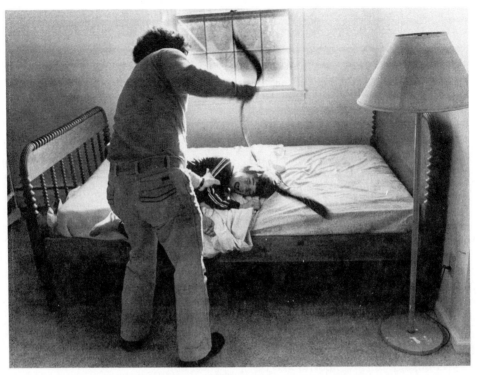

Some researchers believe that using objects such as a belt to spank a child is an example of severe or perhaps even very severe violence.

got more notice than ever before. Some medical professionals even coined a term to describe what was going on: "battered-child syndrome."[42] Recall from Chapter 12 that it wasn't until the 1970s that researchers began to pay serious attention to woman abuse. The same thing applies to child abuse. During the seventies, "the literature on parent-child violence exploded."[43]

Chapter 16 reported that most citizens draw a sharp distinction between child abuse and "necessary" physical punishment. And Chapter 12 stated that many citizens make an analogous distinction when it comes to woman abuse. Murray Straus and his associates label that distinction, for both women and children, as "minor violence" versus "severe violence."[44] They argue that minor violence is not child

abuse. Minor violence, according to them, occurs when a parent pushes, grabs, shoves, slaps, or spanks the child, or throws something at him or her. Only severe violence counts as actual child abuse.

Rates of Violence Toward Children

In their 1985 survey, Straus and associates report that among U.S. families with a child aged 17 or younger, nearly all of the children had during that year been exposed to some sort of parental violence, either minor or serious. It appears, in short, that the vast majority of U.S. parents with children under age 17 have at least once used some degree of physical force on them.

Among older adolescents, the violence rate

Physical aggression against children is part of what some experts call a pervasive "culture of violence."

drops markedly. During 1985 for every 1,000 adolescents aged 15 to 17, about 340 had been exposed either to minor or serious violence from their parents.[45] The total number of U.S. adolescents aged 15 to 17 who were exposed to either type of violence during 1985 was estimated to be almost 4 million.

The reported rates for serious violence alone are much lower. According to Straus, abuse does not occur until the parent kicks, bites, punches, beats up, chokes, or assaults the child with a knife or gun. Those kinds of behaviors are defined as serious or severe because any one of them can cause serious injury. Straus assumes that by contrast, minor violence (shoving, slapping, etc.) is less likely to result in serious injury. Straus adds a further distinction between what he calls "severe violence" and *"very* severe violence" toward a child. He says it's very severe if, in addition to any of the severe behaviors, the adult also uses

culturally approved objects such as a belt, paddle, or hairbrush.

In 1985, for every 1,000 children aged 17 and under there were 110 reported cases of both severe and very severe violence (what Straus defines as child abuse). The total number of assaulted children was estimated to be around 6.9 million. However, only 23 of the 110 cases per thousand were very severe. In the same year, for every 1,000 adolescents aged 15 to 17 there were 70 reported cases of both severe and very severe cases of abuse. Twenty-one of these were defined as very severe. The total number of both types of assaulted adolescents was estimated to be around 800,000.[46]

Official Reports of Abuse and Neglect   During 1990, the National Committee for Prevention of Child Abuse (NCPCA) did a fifty-state survey of official (governmental) child abuse and neglect statistics. *Neglect* means that the parents have failed to provide children with the bare minimums of food, clothing, shelter, medical care, and education. It also includes abandonment and inadequate supervision. NCPCA defines abuse in the same way as Straus—parental violence that results in injury. NCPCA says that in 1990 there were 2.5 million official reports of child abuse *and* neglect compared with 789,000 official reports in 1980.[47] This means that in ten years there was more than a threefold increase in the numbers of official reports of neglect and violence.

Paula Jaudes and Leslie Mitchel acknowledge that those official numbers don't mean that child abuse by itself increased that much. A major reason the 1990 numbers are higher is because today's "officials" (teachers, nurses, physicians, police, social workers, etc.) are much better trained than they were years ago to look for and report the outward symptoms of child abuse.[48] For example, before the 1980s, if a child came to school with "bruises, lacerations, swollen areas, or marks on the child's face, head, back, chest, genital area, buttocks, or thighs, or specific lesions such as human bites, cigarette burns, . . . puncture marks, or missing hair," teachers, coaches, and counselors would conveniently look the other way.[49] Even if the child went to a hospital emergency room with those symptoms, or even with broken bones, the parent's version of what happened ("my kid fell off his chair") was accepted without question.

By contrast, today's officials are immediately suspicious of such injuries. If they can't question the child's parents or caretakers, they will report the injury as a potential child-abuse case. Or, if the official questions the parent in depth and he or she presents a story that does not explain the injury, the incident is also reported as a potential case of child abuse. For instance, Jaudes and Mitchel tell about official alertness in the case of a gym teacher noticing that 6-year-old Ellen had unusual marks on her arms and legs. Fearing the marks were

caused by a belt, the teacher called the child protective services, who investigated the incident and then involved the police. The mother admitted using a belt to discipline Ellen. Years later, at age 24, Ellen had become a mother herself. She told her physician that her 1-year-old son David was clumsy and had backed into a lit cigarette. After the suspicious physician notified officials, Ellen admitted that she'd once gotten so angry with David that she'd " 'slapped him across the room.' "

In a separate story, 5-year-old Nancy was knocked unconscious by her father while trying to rescue her little brother from the midst of a violent battle between her drunk and drugged-out parents. The father told the neighbors (who'd called police) that it was an accident. Examination in the hospital revealed that Nancy had a long history of being physically assaulted. The girl reluctantly admitted that "Mother and Daddy get crazy when they drink or take pills." In this case it was the neighbors' willingness to notify officials that rescued Nancy. In the past such incidents were often treated by neighbors as none of their business.

Underreporting   In spite of growing sensitivity and alertness on the part of neighbors and officials toward physical child abuse, many researchers believe that official statistics continue to underrepresent both its incidence and prevalence.[50] For one thing, the 2.5 million *officially* reported cases for 1990 fall far short of the 6.9 million abuse cases estimated by Straus's 1985 household survey. One reason for the difference is that in some cases the abuse may not cause actual injury, or may cause injury too slight to be detected. In other cases the injuries may be significant enough to be detected (e.g., bruises, black eyes, welts) but outsiders may simply miss them or not perceive them as abuse. Third, outsiders may be well aware that the injuries are caused by abuse but may ignore what's going on.

In sum, there are very likely many more cases of injury due to child abuse than come to official notice. Furthermore, many adults undoubtedly lie when researchers ask if they assault their own children. Consequently, the 6.9 million figure itself is probably also low. The number of U.S. children who are abused each year, whether or not they're actually injured, is almost certainly much higher than that.

Social Factors Associated with Physical Abuse

Economic Disadvantage Straus and Smith do not pretend that there's any magic bullet explaining why parents and other adults abuse children either physically or sexually. But on the basis of their studies of U.S. households, they suggest some social factors that often tend to be connected with physical abuse. One of the most important is the social and economic position of the parent(s). Throughout the twentieth century, official statistics have consistently shown that abuse and neglect are more common among economically disadvantaged persons. As family income goes *down*, the likelihood of reported physical abuse goes *up*. Although some degree of child abuse occurs at "all social levels, from paupers to royalty."[51]

Race If child abuse is in fact more likely to occur among disadvantaged persons, then it should come as no surprise that child abuse appears to be more common among black families than among white families.[52] The proportion of black adults and children living below the poverty line, or just above it, is greater than it is for whites. And many employed blacks (without college degrees) are likely to be earning less than whites at the same job level. Chapter 12 said that economic disadvantage was also one reason for the greater incidence of woman abuse found among blacks compared with whites.

Gender Chapter 12 also said, first, that beyond household walls (in bars, on the streets, in leisure and work activities), men are much more violent than women. Second, within households, men are much more likely to abuse women than the other way around. It is therefore surprising to learn that "women are at least as violent as men against their own children."[53]

Straus and Smith say that one reason women abuse children as much as men is that women experience a whole lot more "time at risk." Because most women spend many more hours each day attending to children than most men, they're more likely to feel greater levels of frustration and anger over the children's unruly behavior. Assaulting their children is one potential outcome of those feelings. That's especially true, add Straus and Smith, if the woman would rather spend time doing something besides child care, namely, being employed. By contrast, a woman who *wants* to be a full-time homemaker is less likely to feel frustrated and angry over her children's unruly behavior. Hence she's less likely to abuse them.

Mother's Employment To explore those issues further, Straus and Smith compared full-time homemakers with employed mothers. In their 1975 national study they found that the child abuse rate for homemakers was "half again higher" than the rate for employed mothers.[54] It thus appears that during the 1970s a number of homemakers felt frustrated at having to stay home and care full-time for their children. However, the 1985 national study showed no difference in child abuse rates between homemakers and employed mothers. To explain the change from 1975, Straus and Smith say that during the 1980s increasing numbers of married women were entering paid labor. Hence the number of "frustrated homemakers" had probably declined substantially since the seventies. Mothers who

Displays like this one help bring child abuse out of the closet and into the light of public discussion.

were homemakers during the eighties were more likely to feel that, "This is my choice and I like it!" In short, by 1985 the total number of U.S. homemakers had dropped significantly, and mothers who'd chosen to stay home had less pent-up frustration and anger to release through physically assaulting their children.

Personal Control and Physical Abuse

A number of researchers say that these and other social factors make the point that physical abuse is not *solely* the result of being mentally or emotionally sick, as some citizens believe.[55] Assaulting children is in part, at least, connected with the social circumstances in which a person lives. For example, we could suggest that part of the reason Ellen and her parents were abusers was because they shared the same social conditions. Ellen's parents were economically disadvantaged. Likewise, Ellen and her husband were economically strapped, and she was a frustrated full-time homemaker.

To be sure, part of the reason some adults assault children has to do with emotional needs that counselors are trained to handle through intervention strategies.[56] But social situations are also significant. It seems that adults who feel out of control of their own lives are more likely to physically assault children than adults who feel that their lives are relatively under control. Hence for some adults, assaultive behavior is in part a combination of *both* social circumstances *and* personal feelings. For these adults, preventing further abuse would require more than therapy. It would also require a change in the *social* conditions of their lives, enabling them to achieve a greater sense of personal control.

Violence by Children

Earlier in this chapter, and in Chapter 12, we talked about adolescent sexual aggression toward both siblings and outsiders. Straus and his associates also studied physical violence among siblings, and also children's violence toward their parents.

Against Siblings　In 1975 they found that for every 1,000 children aged 3 to 17, 800 reported either minor or severe violence against a brother or sister.[57] The number of siblings physically assaulted was estimated to be about 50 million. Of the 800 children, 530 reported using severe violence, as defined previously.

Among adolescents aged 15 to 17, the violence rates during 1975 were lower. For every 1,000 of them, 640 reported either minor or severe sibling violence. The estimated number of siblings assaulted was placed at around 7 million. Of the 640 children, 360 said their violence was severe.

Against Parents　During 1975, 180 out of every 1,000 children aged 3 to 17 reported using either minor or severe violence against their parents. The estimated number of assaulted parents was put at almost 10 million. Of the 180 children, 90 said they used severe violence.

Finally, among older children the 1975 violence rates were again lower. Among every 1,000 children aged 15 to 17, 100 reported being violent toward parents. The number of assaulted parents was around 1 million. Of the 100 children, 35 said they used severe types of violence.

These numbers led Straus and Gelles to conclude that *"children are the most violent people of all in American families."*[58] They remark that at first the numbers surprised, even shocked, them. Popular culture does not picture children as violent. But if we think back to our own childhood experiences, most of us recall how frequently siblings fought with each other, to say nothing of being violent toward outside children. A trip to the local school playground reveals that not much has changed in this regard.

Straus and Gelles suggest that adults communicate contradictory messages to children

about violence, in much the same ways they give out hypocritical messages about sex (Chapters 4 and 16). On the one hand, children are told to play nicely, share, and don't fight. On the other hand, most adults seem to believe that children's fighting is inevitable, and they tacitly accept it. Parents wink at and often overlook violence, as long as kids aren't hurt and parents don't have to get involved. Furthermore, if the children are male, there's actually a subtle, but genuine, encouragement of violence. The boy gets the message that, after all, "I have to protect myself." Being able to fight well and to win is part of the boy's development, part of his becoming a man.[59]

CRADLES OF VIOLENCE

Let's add up all of the coercion/violence (sexual and physical) that adult erotic friends do to one another (Chapter 12). Next, add up all of the sexual and physical violence that parents do to children. (Forget for a moment what outside caregivers such as clergy and teachers do to children.) Next, add up all of the physical and sexual violence that children do to other children within their families. (Forget for a moment what they do to outside children.) Next, add up all of the physical violence that children do to parents. Finally, add in what Chapter 14 reported—the physical abuse of older persons by midlife and younger persons. The sum we get from all these entries is captured by a message that's becoming increasingly, though reluctantly, accepted as valid: Families are cradles of violence.

Some social critics target TV shows and Hollywood movies because of their graphic, and excessive, scenes of violence. This fake violence, say the critics, stimulates real violence by children and adults. While that may be true, few public voices target families in quite the same way. Little attention is paid to the reality that families are usually the first social setting where small children are coerced, physically and/or sexually. Children from noncoercive homes may find themselves coerced at day care, on playgrounds, or elsewhere either by children who are being coerced at home and/or by adults who, very likely, were coerced as children. As they mature, many children not only experience coercion from parents and sibs, they also *observe* coercion between other sibs, between their parents, between their parents and sibs, and between midlife and older family members.

Consequently, what some researchers call *minor* types of physical coercion are as much a part of most U.S. families as anything else we might think of—love, affection, money, sex, companionship, teaching, caring, and so on. In addition, *serious* physical violence and/or sexual coercion seem to be very much a part of many families as well. Virtually everyone agrees that serious violence and sexual coercion are negative features of families. No one would disagree that those features should be rooted out, in much the same way that family poverty should become history. However, there are as many disputes over how to prevent serious violence and sexual coercion as there are over how to end poverty.

The tangle begins with Greven's belief (described in Chapter 16) that physical and sexual abuse stem from the same root. Most adults, he says, believe that children occasionally require *nonexcessive* physical punishment. Those adults feel that appropriate punishment is essential to teach children right from wrong and to help control their often unruly behavior. But Greven's complaint is that "appropriate" is almost impossible to define. Hence, many adults stray into realms of excessive force and/or sexual coercion. The only solution, he claims, is to swear off child coercion in much the same way that the pacifists described in Chapter 12 renounce war. He believes there should be a cultural and social line drawn around children—similar to the line being drawn around women—declaring them out of bounds from any sort of force *period*.

A Radical Suggestion

Jenny Kitzinger's view is that such a boundary would be a useful first step. However, she favors what she calls an even more radical approach.[60] Her complaint is that most strategies aimed at preventing child abuse (sexual, physical) are based on ideas such as childhood innocence, children as passive victims, adults protecting the weak, and so on. Recall that Chapter 16 said that Western cultures image the Benchmark Family as a cocoon or walled garden that surrounds and protects the developing child. But Kitzinger worries that, "Such paternalistic approaches can, in fact, act *against* children's interests."[61] In explaining what she means, she points out that media ads focus on parents and on what they can do to safeguard their child. Parents are warned that since any child can be abused, they must guard and protect their children from potential assaults. Occasionally, certain ads will target adults advising that if they're abusing children, they should get professional treatment to help them stop it. Or a bumper sticker reads, "1-800-96-ABUSE—Let's call a Halt to it."

Few media ads target children. And those that do tend not to alert them to the fact that the persons most likely to assault them are the very persons they live with (parents, siblings, others). Interestingly enough, immediately following its story on the Souzas' alleged child abuse, *Newsweek* devoted more than half a page to an essay called, "How to safeguard your own children." Parents were warned that teachers or janitors might sometimes touch their children, and what parents should, or should not, do about it. The essay never discussed the fact that children are most vulnerable to assaults from their own parents and siblings, persons already within the walled garden or cocoon.

Kitzinger is *not* saying that parents and other adult caregivers should stop being alert and sensitive to potential assaults on children.

But she goes a step further by advocating programs that " 'empower' children to help themselves. "[62] Kitzinger describes some of these types of programs currently found in Great Britain. She says that children in the programs are trained to reject the idea that they are weak and vulnerable victims. The children are trained, first, to believe that they can resist abuse, and, second, how to do it. The programs "urge children to be assertive, to express their own feelings and to develop a sense of control over their own bodies."

In her research on abused children, Kitzinger found that in the past many of them had actively tried to resist coercion (via scratching, kicking, striking back, and so on), or at least they *wanted* to. In any case, her studies do not support the prevailing cultural images of children being mute, passive, or unquestioning in the face of sexual and physical coercion. Few if any children, Kitzinger claims, enjoy or wish to be coerced in any way. Kitzinger is one of those advocates identified in Chapter 16 who believe that encouraging children to be autonomous persons should be the most important goal of parenting. A big part of taking control of one's own life as a child is being able to effectively resist any form of coercion.

Kitzinger reports that the training programs she describes are opposed by advocates from the right-hand side of Figure 1-1. Their chief objection is that the programs undermine parental rights and authority. Children are trained to resist coercion from all adults, including their parents. Hence the critics worry that children will fail to appreciate the difference between what parents "must" do in order to discipline them, and what parents "shouldn't" do. For example, one critic complained that the programs do not help children grasp the distinction between a "bad touch" by a parent and a spanking they deserved because they'd done something naughty or dangerous.[63]

Empowering Children via the Community

Kitzinger readily admits that there are limits to empowering children. For one thing, children have fewer alternatives, resources, and power than parents and other caregivers.[64] But Chapter 16 reported that some advocates of children's rights and interests argue for greater parental accountability to their community. Those advocates believe the community could supply at least some of the alternative resources most children currently lack. Over the years a number of studies have revealed that the more private or isolated families are from their communities the more likely they are to maltreat their children.[65] Noel Cazenave and Murray Straus tested that idea on their 1975 national study. They found that the more years families had lived in their neighborhoods, and the more children they had, the less violence (both minor and severe) they reported. The authors claimed that being in the neighborhood for a longer time, and having more children, meant that a family was more embedded in the community.

The authors reasoned that being *embedded* meant at least two things. First, families had built up support networks that could, for instance, help out with financial needs and child care. Because their networks helped them feel more in control of their lives, the parents had fewer frustrations to take out on their children. Second, those same support networks were made up of outsiders who over the years had gradually learned a great deal about what was going on within families around the neighborhood. Consequently, those outsiders might warn parents who were abusing children (physically or sexually) to stop. The authors discovered that the effects of community supports and pressures were especially noticeable among African-Americans. Being part of a network, and/or what Chapters 2 and 3 called social families, played a significant role in reducing the likelihood of black parents abusing their children.

It would seem that community networks and social families are one means to help empower children against adult coercion, whether from parents or outsiders. That would be especially true for preschool and preteen children who might be too young for the kinds of assertiveness training programs described by Kitzinger. Community adults could help supply the alternatives and resources that most children lack, especially if they're younger. Not only could community adults help empower children, they might also be able to lessen conservatives' anxieties about children going too far in resisting legitimate parental control. For example, community adults might often find themselves in the role of reinforcing parental authority, and/or mediating between parents and children. Those adults, in short, would be an outside check on children trying to resist to the point of being irresponsible and perhaps destructive. Being a check on children would occur alongside their role in restraining parents and outsiders who are coercing children.

CONCLUSION

These particular strategies for responding to child coercion are but a few among many advocated by a number of professionals and concerned citizens. While there is no single best strategy, the idea of empowering children fits with the overall theme of this book.

The theme is that *autonomy*, that is, control over one's life, is extraordinarily important for a number of basic reasons. But control does not imply irresponsibility or excessive individualism. Autonomy simply means the capability to make responsible choices. Most often those choices occur within a context of negotiation and problem-solving that includes other parties, for example, parents, children, or out-

siders. Furthermore, that sort of shared decision-making takes place within a broader social, educational, or economic environment that could either be hostile, neutral, or positive for one or more of the parties.

There seems little doubt that the sooner children learn how to struggle with autonomy, the better their lives will be, both now and later on when they are adults. A large part of becoming an autonomous child is learning how to spot and resist coercion. A second part of autonomy is being able to count on outside help to resist coercion when one is confronted by overwhelming odds.

NOTES

1. Laura Shapiro, "Rush to judgment," *Newsweek,* April 19, 1993, p. 54.
2. Busby, 1991.
3. Knudsen, 1991, p. 17.
4. Ibid.
5. Marlise Simons, "The sex market: Scourge on the world of children," *The New York Times,* April 9, 1993, p. A3.
6. Knudsen, p. 18.
7. Davis, 1949.
8. Knudsen.
9. Laura Shapiro, "Suffer the children," *Newsweek,* March 29, 1993, pp. 56, 57.
10. Nina Darnton, "The Pain of the Last Taboo," *Newsweek,* October 7, 1991, pp. 70–72.
11. Evelyn Nieves, *The New York Times,* April 6, 1993, p. A9.
12. "Priest pleads guilty to sex abuse," *The New York Times,* April 15, 1994, p. A12.
13. American Humane Association, 1988, cited by Knudsen.
14. National Incidence Study, 1981.
15. National Incidence Study, 1988.
16. Knudsen, p. 20.
17. Haugaard and Emery, 1988, cited by Knudsen.
18. Knudsen, p. 21.
19. Pierce and Pierce, 1990, p. 99, italics added.
20. Robert Hanley, "4 are convicted in sexual abuse of retarded New Jersey woman," *The New York Times,* March 17, 1993, p. A1.

21. Jean Seligmann, "Mixed messages," *Newsweek*, April 12, 1993, pp. 28, 29.
22. Anna Quindlen, "Good guys should step forward," New York Times News Service, from *The Gainsville, Florida, Sun*, April 20, 1993, p. 8A.
23. Sally B. Kestin, *The Gainesville, Florida, Sun*, April 10, 1994, p. 2B.
24. Whitcomb, 1991, pp. 181, 182.
25. Ibid., p. 181.
26. Ibid.; Lyon and Mace, 1991; Mac Murray, 1991.
27. Richard Perez-Pena, "Abuse inquiry dropped in Woody Allen case," *The New York Times*, March 19, 1993, p. A9.
28. Evelyn Nieves, "After 5 years in prison cell, a day-care worker is set free on bail," *The New York Times*, March 31, 1993, p. A10.
29. Sheila Turnage, "North Carolina sex scandal," *The Atlanta Constitution*, January 28, 1993, p. A3.
30. *USA Today*, August 19, 1991, p. 3a.
31. Gardner, 1993. Other observers call this establishment a "cottage industry/profession" (see Haugaard and Repucci, 1988, p. 148).
32. For her efforts in producing the 1991 *Frontline* documentary, filmmaker Ofra Bikel won an Emmy and also an Alfred I. duPont-Columbia University *Silver Baton* award (*Newsweek*, July 26, 1993, p. 52).
33. David Foster, Associated Press, from *The Gainesville, Florida, Sun*, November 29, 1993, p. 4A.
34. Lise Fisher, "Infant, 4 weeks old, raped," *The Gainesville, Florida, Sun*, May 4, 1993, p. 6B.
35. Michael deCourcy Hinds, *The New York Times*, November 6, 1992, p. B10.
36. Anna Quindlen, *The New York Times*, March 31, 1993, p. A13.
37. Busby, p. 335.
38. Gomes-Schwartz, Horowitz, and Cardarelli, 1990.
39. Greven, 1991.
40. Pfohl, 1977.
41. Busby, p. 345.
42. Kempe et al., 1962.
43. Busby, p. 345.
44. Straus and Smith, 1990b; Straus, 1991.
45. Straus, p. 22.
46. Ibid.
47. Jaudes and Mitchel, 1992, p. 3, italics added.
48. Jaudes and Mitchel add that another reason the total number of reports of abuse and neglect was much higher in 1990 than in 1980 was the sharp increase in poverty and homelessness in the United States during those years. Increases in poverty and homelessness account for much of the rise in the incidence of child neglect.
49. Ibid., p. 4.
50. Ibid.
51. Straus and Smith, 1990b, p. 249.
52. Ibid., p. 250; Hampton and Gelles, 1991.
53. Straus and Smith, p. 247; Wilking, 1990.
54. Straus and Smith, p. 248; see also Gelles and Hargreaves, 1990.
55. Busby.
56. Gelles and Conte, 1990.
57. Straus, p. 22.
58. Straus and Gelles, 1990, p. 106, italics added.
59. Stearns, 1979, pp. 142–143.
60. Kitzinger, 1990, p. 176.
61. Ibid., p. 167, italics in original.
62. Ibid., p. 171.
63. Ibid.
64. Ibid., p. 174.
65. See Cazenave and Straus, 1990, p. 31, for a review of those studies.

PART FOUR

THE QUEST
FOR RESPONSIBILITY

CHAPTER 18

PUBLIC POLICIES FOR FAMILIES

"The United States should put a man on the moon by the end of the decade." So said President Kennedy during the early 1960s as he envisioned a bold, new, long-range, national policy goal. Because virtually everyone agreed with his vision, citizens immediately set about inventing programs aimed at achieving that goal. In *Megatrends*, John Naisbitt said that before organizations or societies can get anywhere, they have to have a *vision* of where they want to go.[1] Once they do that they're ready to design the specific programs and strategies that will eventually get them to their goal, whether it's the moon or something else. Absence of a vision, said Naisbitt, is a sure recipe for failure.

A VISION OF THE MODERN FAMILY

The "great debate" that launched Chapter 1 is in fact a divergence over competing visions. Recall that David Popenoe, representing citizens on the fixed-philosophy (right-hand) side of Figure 1-1, charges that the nuclear family is breaking up. Hence, his vision is the restoration of the nuclear, or *modern*, family to its for-

mer preeminence. In its purest and most ideal form his vision of the Benchmark Family is a man and a woman who had never had sexual intercourse with anyone before their first (and only) formal marriage. And they never have sex with anyone else after marriage. They do not divorce, so remarriage and blended families are nonissues. They have children (being child-free is not an option), and the mother refrains from paid labor while the children are preschoolers. His steady earnings and her wise stewardship of money enable their private and independent household to be economically self-sufficient. After their children enter school she might consider part-time employment, although it will never interfere with *being there* for her children.[2]

Advocates of the Modern Family vision believe that it is the surest and shortest route to social responsibility. They hold, for instance, that poorly educated, unmarried, adolescent women having babies (who, like their mothers, then grow up to be "constant drains" on society) is just about as far from the ideal as one can get. Some of those advocates argue that the way to "cure" these women's irresponsibility is to take away their welfare benefits after two years. A few go even further and argue that such women should be given no benefits, period.[3] They reason that in the absence of government money, women will wait until marriage to have children. Then, being in the Benchmark, they will be able to take care of themselves and their children—they will have become "responsible" citizens.

Although not all persons in the center of Figure 1-1 (the majority) agree about the specifics of welfare reform programs, there seems little doubt that most share that same broad vision of the Modern Family. It is just as certain, however, that every year growing numbers of persons are falling short of the ideal in one way or another.[4] Nevertheless, says Philip Cowan, the majority of citizens are "struggling hard . . . to make decent families."[5]

A CONTEMPORARY VISION

Margaret Mahoney concurs with Cowan and offers a contemporary, or *postmodern*, vision of a national policy for families. Representing the process-oriented category of Figure 1-1, she wants to replace the Benchmark Family with "the *concept* of family."[6] For many decades, black (and some white) citizens of South Africa dreamed of the concept of democracy. They held a vision—a policy goal—of replacing *apartheid* with a democratic government. By 1994 their dream was becoming a reality. The fact that the specific patterns of their new government are very different from those of the United States, Canada, and England matters not a whit. What unites all democracies is not the patterns and programs about organizing and running a government, but rather the shared vision of effectual citizen participation in their political destinies.

The Concept of Family

If that is the concept of democracy, what then is the concept of family? Mahoney pinpoints

the core issue when she asserts that *"the need to belong to something larger than oneself is innate and compelling."*[7] By "something larger than oneself" she's describing what earlier chapters called a *primary group*. By definition, this means a group in which one feels a unique sense of belonging and bonding. The bonding can also be described as a sense of we-ness. "We-ness" means that "I matter to others in the group and they matter to me. I'm important to them and they're important to me." Primary groups supply a sense of identity and security. They are marked by boundaries distinguishing "us" from "them." The boundary can enclose groups as small as a dyad, yet be considerably larger as well. Persons can, moreover, belong to more than one primary group at a time.

Moral Obligations If that is what we mean by "family," then the vision or long-range policy goal is to facilitate meaningful citizen participation in primary groups. "Meaningful" means being able to get what one needs, as well as to give what one should. "Giving what one should" means that primary groups impose moral obligations—they require the sorts of responsible behaviors described throughout this book. The "quest for responsibility" means trying to take care of the adults and children in one's primary group at the same time that one tries to take care of oneself.

Vitality and Variety Mahoney assures us that, "The endurance and universality of the concept of family testify to its strength and vitality." There is, in short, no danger that "family" will ever disappear. Mahoney's vision of family policy is based on the idea that there's always been a concept of family and there always will be.

But just as certain as its vitality is its variety, the idea that "family patterns vary and compositions alter."[8] There never has been, nor will there ever be, one best way to construct and organize families. Mahoney reminds us that the "need [to belong] is demonstrated over and over again by groups that refer to themselves as 'family.' . . . Children play 'family,' and *elders reinvent it when it does not exist.*"[9] Hence, advocating a contemporary or postmodern national policy for families is actually to endorse and ancient view. Since time began, people in all cultures have continually *re*invented varied and imaginative ways to fulfill their need to belong to family.

The Broader Social Structure

National policy, we just said, should facilitate that reinvention. "Facilitate" means that a society (i.e., its citizens) is obliged to construct the sorts of structural patterns as well as cultural beliefs that contribute to personal responsibility. Throughout the book, we've said that the term *structure* refers to the broader social arrangements that exist around us. Examples include specific programs about jobs, educa-

tion, day care, welfare, housing, public safety, taxes, medical care, retirement, housing, family leave, physical and sexual abuse, and so on. Many advocates have written a great deal about programs aimed at helping families meet basic economic needs.[10] They argue that quality education for all citizens (women and men, whites and minorities) would represent a major step toward helping families. They also believe strongly in equal job opportunities for women and minorities. Family leave programs and affordable, high-quality day care are an additional part of their agenda.

Their arguments are based on the changing nature of the occupational system, not merely in North America but throughout the industrialized world. They contend that today's citizens must be prepared to fit into a *global economy* that looks to be very different from the one experienced by our parents and grandparents. Foundational to all of their arguments is the belief that economic well-being precedes

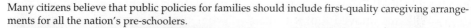

Many citizens believe that public policies for families should include first-quality caregiving arrangements for all the nation's pre-schoolers.

everything else. Those advocates contend that unless family members have quality education and are able to get good jobs, they'll be hard pressed to be responsible for the material and emotional needs of the adults and children in their families.

THEMES ABOUT CONTEMPORARY FAMILIES

Earlier chapters described a number of hypothetical case studies of women and men struggling to reinvent the concept of family in a responsible manner. These included Helga, Hans, and Kurt; Kate and Marshall; Monika; Sondra, and so forth. *Mrs. Doubtfire* was a 1993 movie that humorously communicated several key insights about contemporary, postmodern families. Robin Williams and Sally Fields portrayed a married couple with three children. Williams dearly loved his children, but it was clear that in Field's perception, their erotic friendship was in an irreversible dissolution phase. She was a very successful interior architect; he had trouble holding any kind of job. At her request, Williams moved out of their house, but he was deeply troubled that their separation / divorce might somehow harm their children. The remainder of the movie turns on the critical matter of how to take care of children when the adults are no longer able to maintain an erotic friendship. Deceiving both Fields and the children, Williams goes to the ridiculous lengths of dressing in drag and becoming their nanny. As their nanny, Williams benefits the children enormously, and both they and Fields develop warm affection and deep respect for "her."

Eventually, of course, he's found out, but not before he's landed a job as host of a TV children's show called *Mrs. Doubtfire*. "She" plays a loving grandmother who, besides entertaining with puppets, also raps with the children. During one of those rap sessions, *Mrs. Doubtfire* brings up the subject of adults in the children's lives going their separate ways.

She informs them that "there's no longer one kind of family anymore," and goes on to describe the many different kinds of families in today's world. She tells them that one kind of family is not necessarily better or worse than another, and not to feel badly no matter what kind they're in. Her eloquent words follow a scene in which Williams and Fields agree that although they can never again be erotic friends, they can be just-friends who are totally committed to the shared care and well-being of their children.

Women's Autonomy

What insights can we glean from this story? What insights can we get from the case studies and research information found in earlier chapters? How does this range of insights fit into a postmodern vision of public policy for today's families? What kinds of specific programs might be offered to help achieve these general goals?

The insight, or theme, that's perhaps been most fundamental to the entire book is women's autonomy. Like the Sally Fields' character, today's woman must be able to provide economically for herself and her children, if any. As endearing and loving as the Williams' character was, women simply cannot rely on men's good intentions. To achieve outcomes that are beneficial to them (and children, if any) they must be able to negotiate effectively with men from a position of strength, that is, economic autonomy.

Earlier chapters showed that striving for autonomy has a broad range of implications for women's lives. These include matters such as "responsible" sexuality, physical abuse, sexual harassment and assault, and so on. Autonomy flows from the moral obligations to love oneself as much as one's neighbor (partner, children, kin)—something women have not historically done. As many conservatives see it, women's autonomy touches a very sensitive nerve. Critics charge that *individualism* is running rampant throughout North American and other Western societies. They claim that today's citizens care solely for their own self-interest. Unlike their forebears, they care little about children, spouses, kin, and the larger community and society. However, this charge vastly oversimplifies how complex things actually are. In the past, women did indeed love their neighbors more than they loved themselves. Men, on the other hand, sought to balance their individualism with altruism. That gender difference was the chief reason the Benchmark Family worked.

More recently, increasing numbers of women are beginning to take seriously the notion that one should love oneself *as much as* one's neighbor. Women (such as the Fields' character) are now seeking to balance their altruism with their individualism. The task of balancing women's, men's, and children's interests is difficult indeed. Trying to balance those often-competing interests means that challenges and conflicts are normal. Consequently, the processes of problem-solving and negotiation have become pivotal and essential for today's families and relationships.

Me-ness as a Basic Human Need Another way to describe concern for oneself is to talk about a sense of *me-ness*. "Me-ness" is simply another way to describe autonomy, that is, control over one's own life. Researchers are finding that the more control (autonomy) that people believe they have over their lives, the healthier they are, both physically and emotionally (see Chapter 14). Indeed, we can say that autonomy is a basic human need. Thus, alongside the vital need to belong described above (we-ness), we can place the equally vital need for control (me-ness).

In the past, women lacked the same amount of control over their lives that men had. For the most part this was because men had much greater access to job opportunities. Today, women are entering the labor market in ever-increasing numbers. Younger, well-educated

women who are child-free tend to earn as much as men. The rapidly shifting character of national and international labor markets seems likely to further expand women's economic opportunities. As women pursue those opportunities, they gain a greater sense of me-ness. Inevitably this spills over into their relationships with men and also with children (we-ness). In effect, the pursuit of me-ness very often fails to mesh with the quest for we-ness.

Male Identities Because that is so, many observers fear that children's interests suffer. However, the *Doubtfire* character illustrates several themes addressing children's interests. Specifically, Williams keenly expressed what Chapter 15 called the identities of *child caregiver* and *householder*. Historically, women have possessed both identities. Today, increasing numbers of women are in addition taking on the identity of autonomous worker. If that is a vital policy objective for today's families, then it becomes just as imperative to state a comparable policy objective for men: Namely, to add the identities of child caregiver and householder to their historic identity of autonomous worker. Doing so is not a guarantee of anything. However, men possessing those identities can at the very least be expected to become more personally involved with children's interest than men who do not. Progressives have argued for years that the ongoing, responsible reinvention of postmodern families requires that men, as much as women, must expand not only their behaviors but their core identities as well.[11]

Beyond Blood Ties and Beyond the Household

Children's interests are addressed not only by expanding the range of male identities but also by enlarging our vision of two additional elements: (1) the physical location of family and (2) genetic or blood ties. Earlier chapters made the point that the concept of family cannot be limited to persons and households connected by genes. Nor can family be limited to any one particular physical household. *Social families* are constructed out of clusters of households that cultivate a sense of we-ness even though they do not share genetic ties. The bottom line that binds them is their exchanges of tangible things—money, goods, and services. Those are the same kinds of obligations that bind persons and households linked by genes. Sometimes, persons across gene-linked households don't even like each other. Nevertheless they help out, because they feel obligated to do so.

But not always! They may be too poor to help out—they have few tangible resources to give. For over a century, disadvantaged African-Americans, living in separate households and not linked by blood, have formed their own social families as a means of economic survival. White researchers and policy-

makers roundly condemned those efforts as *deviant*. Presently, growing numbers of white women are becoming solo parents. Like black women before them, many are finding it exceedingly difficult to meet their children's basic tangible needs, to say nothing about their emotional needs.

Social Families as a Policy Goal   Hence, is the climate right to make the enhancement of social families a major public policy goal? Some advocates argue that at the very least, we ought to make the development of *mutual support networks* a public policy goal.[12] Some of those networks provide exchanges of money, goods, and services quite apart from achieving a perception of themselves as "being family." Other support networks do eventually move on to achieve a sense of themselves as family.[13] The rationale for making social families a policy goal is this: As they empower households

Solo mothers maintaining a social family within one household.

to gain tangible resources, they simultaneously meet human need—they achieve a sense of belonging and bonding not now enjoyed by many citizens.

In addition to solo mothers and disadvantaged dual-adult households, other clusters of citizens could benefit from making social families a policy goal. One example is the middle-class household with two employed adults and children. Their being part of a social family could make an enormous difference in their being able to meet the unremitting demands of a constantly overbooked schedule. Another example is senior citizens who lack blood kin and thus do not have a ready-made we-group. Other senior citizens may lack a sense of being in family because of a variety of circumstances. They may, for example, reside great distances from blood relatives. Whatever the circumstances, social families provide some senior citizens a sense of belonging and identity (see Chapters 2 and 3). Just as persons sometimes ignore their obligations to older blood kin, they occasionally ignore their obligations to kin afflicted by a serious illness. AIDS victims are a particular case in point. Whatever the illness, social families often emerge as the only source of the patient's emotional and tangible support.

In general terms, urban industrial societies have long been characterized as places where many citizens fall through the cracks. For numerous reasons they feel isolated, alone, and abandoned.[14] Making social families sometimes in which governments have a stake could have a substantial payoff. The payoff might consist of material well-being, and also emotional and physical health. Thus, both individuals and the larger society could profit from such a policy initiative.

Independence and Privacy The major obstacle to social families is, of course, that the vast majority of Americans envision households, or dwelling units, that are both independent and private. Moreover, they equate The Family with that type of household. In terms of our cultural ideals, we believe that the husband and wife should not look to outsiders for economic resources, emotional support, or help in the care and discipline of their children. The Modern Family often achieved that ideal because wives devoted themselves totally to the needs of the household and its inhabitants. For growing numbers of citizens, however, the ideal is becoming increasingly elusive. Furthermore, the ideal is being scrutinized. For instance, what were and are the implications of independence and privacy for the physical and sexual abuse of women and children?

Some progressives argue for a strategy that they believe would, first, protect women and children from abuse, and second, contribute to children's overall well-being. Their strategy is twofold: (1) expand the community's role in child-involvement, and (2) make parents more accountable to the community for the general well-being of children in their own household (see Chapters 16 and 17). During the seventeenth- and eighteenth-century Colonial era, said Chapter 6, the ideal of household privacy and independence simply did not exist. That ideal blossomed with the urbanization and prosperity of the nineteenth and twentieth centuries. The Colonial Puritans, for example, believed strongly in the biblical notion that "I am my brother's/sister's keeper." Among other things, that meant that neighbors kept an eye on each other to make sure they "did right" by their family members. Although that practice may have sometimes led to excessive *in*trusion, the current situation is one of excessive *ex*clusion. Citizens, even the police, hesitate to interfere when their neighbors, within their own private households, physically and sexually abuse children and women. To counter that isolation, the U.S. Advisory Board on Child Abuse and Neglect argues that if we are to solve the problem of child maltreatment, "it is critically important that we view it from an environmental [community] perspective rather than strictly as an individual [household] phenomenon."[15]

Social Families and Children Interests
Quite apart from the issues of abuse, today's adults are making many kinds of choices that inevitably affect children's lives. There is no certain answer regarding how best to meet the varied needs of children being affected by the many choices adults are making about their relationships. Furthermore, in future it appears that choices will be increasingly forced on adults. Just as the 1930s' Depression forced engaged couples to choose whether to have sexual intercourse, the shifting global economy will force many couples to make many sorts of agonizing choices. In certain instances their choices may mean that for a time their children will be living with only one adult. It may also mean that the parent with whom they reside would bring a new adult into their household.

In any case, given that growing numbers of adults are likely to be continually making a wider range of relationship and occupational choices than ever before, what can be done to foster children's well-being? Expanding our vision beyond the singular household to social families may become part of the response. Alongside the rationales just discussed, a major reason for social families would be the emotional support they provide to "their" children. In the black community, social families were quite frequently a source of emotional support and encouragement for children who otherwise lacked those benefits.[16] Part of that encouragement often came in the form of positive adult role models.

In sum, promoting social families as a crucial policy goal could have significant implications for children's well-being.[17] Social families could serve as cushions for children caught up in fluctuating adult relationships. Social families would share responsibilities for being alert to instances of abuse and/or neglect. And they would also pay close attention to "their" children's economic and emotional needs, irrespective of whether the children reside with one or two adults.

Informal Marriages

Having argued that social families should, in effect, be given the same legitimacy as blood-linked families, what about formal marriage? In Sweden, said Chapter 9, formal marriage continues to hold a somewhat higher legal priority that informal marriages (cohabitation). At the same time, in terms of Scandinavian public policies regarding adults and children, the differences between formal and informal marriages are markedly narrowing. In Scandinavia (and the rest of the Western world), rates of legal marriage are declining, and growing numbers of childen are growing up in households where the adults are informally married.

In North America there is overwhelming support, both legally and culturally, for the notion that formal marriage is a better situation than singleness and/or cohabitation. Marriage is thought to be more desirable for children because of its presumed permanence, which gives children a stable life experience. Current trends, however, indicate that growing numbers of couples are cohabiting at one point or another in their life courses. Many of these couples have children living with them. Some of the children came out of previous formal marriages, but growing numbers of children are being born to never-married women who may later cohabit and/or marry formally. Even though most U.S. citizens eventually marry formally, rates of first marriages and also of remarriages have been gradually declining. Furthermore, there is no indication that these trends are likely to be reversed any time soon.

Until recently there were few if any public policy supports for cohabiting couples, whether heterosexual or homosexual. The recent emergence of *domestic partnership* ordinances in several cities (and a few private companies) supplies a certain, but limited, degree of social legitimacy to informal marriages (see Chapter 9).[18] Perhaps the chief public policy question about informal marriages is the degree to which they fulfilled the basic human needs described above. These include material and tangible needs, as well as intangible needs. Do informal marriages supply a sense of we-ness? What about a sense of me-ness? How do informal marriages enhance their children's economic and emotional well-being? In response to these kinds of questions, Chapter 9 suggests that there appear to be many more basic similarities than differences between formal and informal marriages. One researcher even argues that among today's very youngest couples, formal marriages appear to be no more stable than informal marriages.[19]

Erotic Friendships German sociologist Lerhe Gravenhorst coined the term *erotic friendship* to mean that in the entire Western world there is growing social acceptance of "coupling" apart from formal marriage.[20] In North America, heterosexual cohabitors, as well as boyfriends/girlfriends, no longer need to conceal the fact that they are ongoing sexual partners.[21] Nevertheless, it is still quite common for others to inquire when they plan to get "serious," that is, to marry. In Scandinavia, even that question is no longer relevant. Throughout the West, the label "erotic friendship" is an umbrella notion that covers formal marriages, informal marriages, and also girlfriends/boyfriends. The reality is that increasing numbers of adults and children live within various expressions of erotic friendships throughout their life course. Faced with that reality, what are policymakers to do?

The official Scandinavian response, as well as the response of most European societies, has been to focus on the human needs issue. If erotic friendships, like social families, are becoming increasingly common, what specific strategies and programs can be designed to support them in meeting their tangible and intangible human needs? Their broad policy goal has been, "Let's try to help meet human needs regardless of the kind of primary group in which adults and children find themselves." The fact that the group is a social family, or a particular expression of an erotic friendship, becomes less significant than the overriding issue of the basic human needs of its adults and children.

STRUGGLING OVER POLICIES AND PROGRAMS

Advocates on the left-hand side of Figure 1-1 argue the contemporary notion that policies and programs should assist people in constructing varieties of families that work best for them.[22] By contrast, advocates on the right-hand side argue the notion that governments must foster a social climate that makes the Benchmark Family work.[23] They believe the fact that growing numbers of citizens are unable to make The Family work indicates a basic flaw in the persons themselves. How often have we heard or read something like this: "If people only had greater moral fiber and a willingness to sacrifice, they could make The Family work."

The official North American response to the many ways in which persons are constructing varieties of primary relationships has so far been ambivalent at best. Even so modest a statement as the Equal Rights Amendment (ERA) has yet to be added to the U.S. Constitution, although a number of states have added ERA to theirs. During her 1993 examination for the U.S. Supreme Court, Judge Ruth Bader Ginsburg asserted that ERA should be "added to the [federal] constitution, at least for its 'symbolic' value."[24] The major reason it's not been added is because of intense and effective opposition to ERA among advocates on the right-hand side of Figure 1-1.[25] During the

Former U.S. Surgeon General Dr. C. Everett Koop, though a religious conservative himself, often took a pragmatic approach to public policies. For example, he strongly advocated condom distribution programs to prevent the spread of HIV infection.

1970s their struggles against ERA helped crystallize their emergence as a potent political force. In describing a wide range of conflicts between progressives and conservatives since that time, James Hunter titles his book, *Culture Wars: The Struggle to Define America*.[26] And indeed, conservative spokespersons acknowledge that during recent years, a " 'civil war of values' has heated up."[27]

Up to now many advocates on the left-hand side of Figure 1-1 have hesitated to get sucked into disputes over values that belong to competing visions such as "The Family" versus "the concept of family."[28] Advocates would much prefer to limit themselves to less volatile matters such as quality education and full employment. Daniel Bell says it's plain enough why advocates shy away from struggles over values: "Wars of truth, wars of ideology, wars of passion are not negotiable. . . . [As a result, those wars] only polarize a society."[29]

For instance, the policy statement that all varieties of *responsible* social families and erotic friendships constructed by person are equally viable and legitimate is simply unacceptable to advocates on the right-hand side of Figure 1-1. Likewise, encouraging women's autonomy as a policy goal is not something those advocates are likely to endorse. The *Murphy Brown* furor illustrates how uncomfortable they are with the idea of women living and parenting outside of legal marriage (see Chapter 10). The notion of a woman being able to "make it" economically and socially apart from a man is not part of their vision of The Family. Their view is clear and unambiguous: "The fabric of society itself and the foundations of our culture are built upon the family, and tampering with its legal definition must necessarily tear that fabric and undermine those foundations."[30] Or, as Bell puts it, "The reigning fear of the right is the destruction of the family."[31] What about citizens on the other side, as well as the majority located in the middle of Figure 1-1? In a *New York Times* opinion page essay, Katha Pollitt commented on a 1993 census report showing gradual increases in childbearing among white, well-educated, never-married, adult women.[32] She claims that advocates on the right-hand side of Figure 1-1 will use that trend as evidence for the alleged continuing moral decline of American society. But she responds that to reverse that particular trend, as well as reverse the many other social trends described in this book, "We'd have to . . .: Restore the cult of virginity and the double standard, ban birth control, restrict divorce, kick women out of decent jobs, force unwed pregnant women to put their babies up for adoption on pain of social death, make out-of-wedlock children legal nonpersons. None of this will happen, so why not come to terms with reality?"

Struggles over public policies and programs for families will continue to be waged in the light of these two very different visions of what the future should hold. There probably won't ever be any single definitive legal or political outcome. Skirmishes favoring first one side and then the other will probably continue. Meanwhile, increasing numbers of ordinary citizens appear likely to join the ranks of those trying to figure out what works best at inventing responsible families, and then simply do it.

NOTES

1. Naisbitt, 1984.
2. See William R. Mattox, Jr., "A lesson for Alison," *Wall Street Journal,* April 28, 1994, p. A12. Mr. Mattox is vice president for policy of the Family Research Council, a conservative organization that seeks to influence governmental policy and programs in the direction of the Benchmark Family. He states that on the national "Take Your Daughter to Work Day" he is indeed bringing his daughter Alison with him to his job in downtown Washington, D.C. Nevertheless, he tells Alison that her mother, who is a well-educated and talented woman, currently has a higher calling than merely being in the workplace. And that is to remain "at home teaching you."
3. Jason DeParle, *The New York Times,* April 22, 1994, p. A1.
4. Bumpass, 1990.
5. Cowan, 1993, p. 550.
6. Mahoney, 1986. Cited in *Work and Family Responsibilities Achieving a Balance.* New York: Ford Foundation, 1989, p. 3, italics added.
7. Ibid., italics added.
8. Ibid.
9. Ibid., italics added.
10. From among the many cited in this book, see Cherlin, 1988; Kahn and Kamerman, 1988; Kamerman and Kahn, 1988, 1991; Anderson and Hula, 1991; Cherlin, 1991; DaVanzo and Rahman, 1993; Driscoll and Goldberg, 1993.
11. Pascall, 1986.
12. Cochran et al., 1990.
13. Rivers and Scanzoni, 1994.
14. Durkheim, 1951; William Wilson, 1989.
15. "Neighbors Helping Neighbors," 1993, p. 18.
16. Scanzoni, 1977; Berry and Blassingame, 1982.
17. "Beyond Rhetoric," 1991; "Neighbors Helping Neighbors," p. 18.
18. Wisensale and Heckhart, 1993.
19. Schoen, 1992.
20. Gravenhorst, 1988.
21. Among heterosexuals, exceptions might exist among a few occupations (e.g., clergy). Many more exceptions exist among homosexuals, most notable of which is the military.
22. Otto, 1970; Cowan, 1993; Stacey, 1993. And see Chapter 1 of this book.
23. Bauer, 1986; Christensen, 1990a,b.
24. Joan Biskupic, "Ginsburg wants ERA," from *The Washington Post,* published in *The Gainesville, Florida, Sun,* July 22, 1993, p. A1.
25. Boles, 1979: Mathews and De Hart, 1990.
26. Hunter, 1991.
27. "Who we are and what we stand for," August 1993, *Focus on the Family,* Colorado Springs, Colo., p. 10. The *Special Statement* also reports (p. 10) that "Dr. [James] Dobson sees the North American culture wallowing in skepticism and relativism under the thin pretense of freedom and individuality."
28. See Scanzoni, 1983, 1989a, for a discussion of this matter.
29. Bell, 1990, p. 75.
30. "Who we are and what we stand for," p. 11.
31. Bell, p. 69.
32. Katha Pollitt, "Bothered and bewildered" *The New York Times,* July 22, 1993, p. A13.

BIBLIOGRAPHY

The AAUW Report. 1992. "How schools shortchange girls." American Association of University Women Educational Foundation, and Wellesley College Center for Research on Women, Wellesley, Mass.

Abbey, Antonia. 1991. "Misperceptions as an antecedent of acquaintance rape: A consequence of ambiguity in communication between women and men." In Andrea Parrot and Laurie Bechhofer (eds.), *Acquaintance rape: The hidden crime.* New York: Wiley, pp. 96–112.

Abel, Emily K. 1991. *Who cares for the elderly? Public policy and the experiences of adult daughters.* Philadelphia: Temple University Press.

Abeles, Ronald P. 1990. "Schemas, sense of control, and aging." In J. Rodin, Carmi Schooler, and K. Warner Schaie (eds.), *Self-directedness: Cause and effects throughout the life course.* Hillsdale, N.J.: Erlbaum, pp. 85–94.

Adams, Evelia V. R., and Paul L. Adams. 1990. "What is a woman's family? Fluctuations in definitions, structure, and functions." In Jeanne Spurlock and Carolyn B. Rabinowitz (eds.), *Women's progress: Promises and problems.* New York: Plenum, pp. 9–21.

Adams, Margaret. 1976. *Single blessedness: Observations on the single status in married society.* New York: Basic Books.

Adelman, Clifford. 1991. "Women at thirtysomething: Paradoxes of attainment." Washington, D.C.: U.S. Department of Education, Office of Research.

Ade-Ridder, Linda, and Charles B. Hennon (eds.). 1989. *Lifestyles of the elderly: Diversity in relationships, health and caregiving.* New York: Human Sciences Press.

Ahlburg, Dennis A., and Carol J. De Vita. 1992 (August). "New realities of the American family." *Population Bulletin,* vol. 47, no. 2. Washington, D.C.: Population Reference Bureau.

Alanen, Leena. 1990. "Rethinking socialization, the family and childhood." In Nancy Mandell (ed.), *Sociological studies of child development. Vol. 3.* Greenwich, Conn.: Jai Press, pp. 13–28.

Aldous, Joan. 1978. *Family careers.* New York: Wiley.

———. 1987. "American families in the 1980s: Individualism run amok?" *Journal of Family Issues* 8:422–425.

———. 1991. "In the families' ways." *Contemporary Sociology* 20:660–662.

Alexander, Jeffrey C. 1988. "The new theoretical movement." In Neil J. Smelser (ed.), *Handbook of sociology.* Newbury Park, Calif.: Sage.

Alexander, Pamela, Sharon Moore, and Elmore R. Alexander III. 1991. "What is transmitted in the intergenerational transmission of violence?" *Journal of Marriage and Family* 53:657–668.

Allan, Graham. 1989. *Friendship: Developing a sociological perspective.* Boulder, Colo.: Westview.

Allen, Janice. 1991. "The development of primary

relationships among nonkin as 'relatives.' " Unpublished paper. Gainesville: University of Florida, Department of Sociology.

Ambert, Anne-Marie. 1989. *Ex-spouses and new spouses: A study of relationships.* Greenwich, Conn.: Jai Press.

American Humane Association. 1988. *Highlights of official child neglect and abuse reporting, 1986.* Denver American Humane Association.

American footnotes. 1991. Washington, D.C.: American Sociological Association, September.

Anderson, Elaine A. 1992. "Decision-making style: Impact on satisfaction of the commuter couples' lifestyle." *Journal of Family and Economic Issues.* 13:5–21.

———, and Richard C. Hula (eds.). 1991. *The reconstruction of family policy.* New York: Greenwood.

Anderson, Karen. 1981. *Wartime women: Sex roles, family relations and the status of women during WW II.* Westport, Conn.: Greenwood.

Aneshensel, Carol S. 1992. "Social stress: Theory and research." *Annual Review of Sociology* 18:15–38.

Aquilino, William S. 1990. "The likelihood of parent-child coresidence: Effects of family structure and personal characteristics." *Journal of Marriage and Family* 52:405–419.

Askevold, Odd Helge. 1990. "Support for lone parents in Norway." In Elisabeth Duskin (ed.), *Lone-parent families: The economic challenge.* Paris: OECD Publications, pp. 241–252.

Atwater, Lynne. 1982. *The extramarital connection: Sex, intimacy, and identity.* New York: Irvington.

Avineri, Shlomo, and Avner De-Shalit. 1992. "Introduction." In S. Avineri and A. De-Shalit (eds.), *Communitarianism and individualism.* New York: Oxford University Press, pp. 1–11.

Babchuck, Nicholas. 1965. "Primary friends and kin: A study of the associations of middle-class couples." *Social Forces* 43:483–493.

Baber, Kristine M., and Katherine R. Allen. 1992. *Women and families: Feminist reconstructions.* New York: Guilford.

Backhouse, Constance, and Leah Cohen. 1982. *Sexual harassment on the job.* Englewood Cliffs, N.J.: Prentice-Hall.

Bahr, Stephen J., Gabe Wang, and Jie Zhang. 1991. "Early family research." In S. J. Bahr (ed.), *Family research—a sixty year review, 1930–1990.* Lexington, Mass.: D.C. Heath, pp. 1–23.

Baltes, Margaret M., and Paul B. Baltes (eds.). 1986. *The psychology of control and aging.* Hillsdale, N.J.: Erlbaum.

Bart, Pauline B., and P. H. O'Brien. 1985. *Stopping rape: Successful survival strategies.* Elmsford, N.Y.: Pergamon.

Bates, Alan P., and Nicholas Babchuck. 1961. "The primary group: A reappraisal." *The Sociological Quarterly* 2:181–191.

Bauer, Gary L. (ed.). 1986. *The family: Preserving America's future.* Washington, D.C.: White House Working Group on the Family.

———. 1991. "Just say 'no' to safe sex propaganda." *Washington Watch,* December. Washington, D.C.: Family Research Council.

Baxter, Leslie A. 1988. "A dialectical perspective on communication strategies in relationship development." In Steve Duck, Dale F. May, and Stevan E. Hobfoll (eds.), *Handbook of personal relationships.* Chicester, N.Y.: Wiley, pp. 257–274.

———, William W. Wilmot, Christopher A. Simmons, and Andrea Swartz. 1993. "Ways of doing conflict: A folk taxonomy of conflict events in personal relationships." In P. J. Kalbfleisch (ed.), *Interpersonal communication: evolving interpersonal relationships.* Hillsdale, N.J.: Erlbaum, pp. 89–102.

Bayer, Alan E. 1968. "Early dating and early marriage." *Journal of Marriage and Family* 30:628–632.

Beach, Betty. 1989. *Integrating work and family life: The home-working family.* Albany: State University of New York Press.

Bechhofer, Laurie, and Andrea Parrot. 1991. "What is acquaintance-rape?" In A. Parrot and L. Bechhofer (eds.), *Acquaintance rape: The hidden crime.* New York: Wiley, pp. 9–25.

Beck, Melinda. 1992. "The New Middle Age." *Newsweek,* December 7, pp. 50–56.

Bell, Alan, and Martin Weinberg. 1978. *Homosexualities: A study of diversities among men and women.* New York: Simon & Schuster.

Bell, Daniel. 1990. "Resolving the contradictions of modernity and modernism, Part II." *Society* 27:66–75.

Bell, Norman W., and Ezra F. Vogel. 1960. "Toward a framework for functional analysis of family behavior." In N. W. Bell and E. F. Vogel (eds.), *A modern introduction to the family.* New York: Free Press, pp. 1–33.

Bellah, Robert N., Richard Madsen, William M. Sullivan, Ann Swidler, and Steven M. Tipton. 1985.

Habits of the heart: Individualism and commitment in American life. Berkeley: University of California Press.

———. 1991. *The good society.* New York: Knopf.

Beneke, Thomas, 1982. *Men on rape.* New York: St. Martin's.

Bennett, Neil G., Ann Klimas Blanc, and David E. Bloom. 1988. "Commitment and the modern union: Assessing the link between premarital cohabitation and subsequent marital stability." *American Sociological Review* 53:127–138.

Bennett, William J. 1993. "Quantifying America's Decline." *Wall Street Journal.* March 15, p. A12.

Berardo, Donna H., Constance L. Shehan, and Gerald R. Leslie. 1987. "A residue of tradition: Jobs, careers, and spouses' time in housework. *Journal of Marriage and Family.* 49:381–390.

Berg, Cynthia A. 1990. "What is intellectual efficacy over the life course? Using adults' conceptions to address the question." In J. Rodin, Carmi Schooler, and K. Warner Schaie (eds.), *Self-directedness: Cause and effects throughout the life course.* Hillsdale, N.J.: Erlbaum, pp. 155–182.

Berger, Raymond M. 1990. "Men together: Understanding the gay couple." *Journal of Homosexuality* 19:31–49.

Berman, William H. 1985. "Continued attachment after legal divorce." *Journal of Family Issues* 6:375–392.

Bernard, Jessie. 1964. *Academic women.* University Park: Pennsylvania State University Press.

———. 1969. *The sex game: Communication between the sexes.* London: Leslie-Frewin.

———. 1972. *The future of marriage.* New York: World.

———. 1981. "The good-provider role: Its rise and fall." *American Psychologist* 36:1–12.

Bernardes, Jon. 1986. "Multidimensional developmental pathways: A proposal to facilitate the conceptualisation of 'family diversity.' " *Sociological Review* 34:590–610.

Berry, Mary Frances, and John Blassingame. 1982. *Long memory: The black experience in America.* New York: Oxford University Press.

Besharov, Douglas J. 1990. "Improved research on child abuse and neglect through better definitions." In J. D. Besharov (ed.), *Family violence: Research and public policy issues.* Washington, D.C.: AEI Press, pp. 42–52.

"Beyond rhetoric: A new American agenda for children and families." 1991. *National Commission on Children.* Washington, D.C.: U.S. Government Printing Office.

Bielby, D. D. 1992. "Commitment to work and family." *Annual Review of Sociology* 18:281–302.

Billingsley, Andrew. 1968. *Black families in white America.* Englewood Cliffs, N.J.: Prentice-Hall.

Blair, S. L., and M. P. Johnson. 1992. "Wives' perceptions of the fairness of the division of household labor: The interaction of housework and ideology." *Journal of Marriage and Family* 54:570–581.

Blau, David M. 1991. *The economics of child care.* New York: Russell Sage Foundation.

Blau, Peter M. 1964. *Exchange and power in social life.* New York: Wiley.

Blitzer, Silvia. 1991. " 'They are only children, what do they know?' A look at current ideologies of childhood." In Spencer E. Cahill (ed.), *Sociological studies of child development, Vol. 4, Perspectives on and of children.* Greenwich, Conn.: Jai Press, pp. 11–28.

Blood, Robert O., and Donald M. Wolfe. 1960. *Husbands and wives.* New York: Free Press.

Blumenthal, Sidney. 1993. "Adventures in babysitting." *The New Yorker.* February 15, pp. 53–62.

Blumstein, Philip, and Pepper Schwartz. 1983. *American couples: Money, work, sex.* New York: Morrow.

Blustein, Jeffrey. 1982. *Parents and children: The ethics of the family.* New York: Oxford University Press.

Bohmer, Carol. 1991. "Acquaintance rape and the law." In A. Parrot and L. Bechhofer (eds.), *Acquaintance rape.* New York: Wiley, pp. 317–333.

Boles, Janet K. 1979. *The politics of the equal rights amendment: Conflict and the decision process.* New York: Longman.

Booth, Alan, and David Johnson. 1988. "Premarital cohabitation and marital success." *Journal of Family Issues* 9:255–272.

Boris, Eileen, and Cynthia R. Daniels. 1989. *Homework: Historical and contemporary perspectives on paid labor at home.* Urbana: University of Illinois Press.

Bornoff, Nicholas. 1991. *Pink samurai: The pursuit and politics of sex in Japan.* London: Grafton Books.

Bott, Elizabeth. 1957. *Family and social network.* London: Tavistock.

Boxer, Andrew M., Judith A. Cook, and Gilbert Herdt. 1991. "Double jeopardy: Identity transitions and parent-child relations among gay and lesbian youth." In Karl Pillemer and Kathleen McCartney (eds.), *Parent-child relations throughout life.* Hillsdale, N.J.: Erlbaum, pp. 59–92.

Bringle, Robert G., and Bram P. Buunk. 1991. "Extradyadic relationships and sexual jealousy." In Kathleen McKinney and Susan Sprecher (eds.), *Sexuality in close relationships.* Hillsdale, N.J.: Erlbaum, pp. 135–153.

Brown, Thomas. 1988. *JFK: History of an image.* Bloomington: Indiana University Press.

Brown, Waln K., and Warren A. Rhodes. 1991. "Factors that promote invulnerability and resiliency in at-risk children." In Warren A. Brown and Waln K. Brown (eds.), *Why some children succeed despite the odds.* New York: Praeger, pp. 171–177.

Brown, Warren A., and Waln K. Brown (eds.). 1991. *Why some children succeed despite the odds.* New York: Praeger.

Brownmiller, Susan. 1975. *Against our will: Men, women, and rape.* New York: Simon & Schuster.

Bruborg, Helge. 1979. *Cohabitation without marriage in Norway.* Oslo: Central Bureau of Statistics.

Buchmann, Marlis. 1989. *The script of life in modern society: Entry into adulthood in a changing world.* Chicago: University of Chicago Press.

Buckley, Walter. 1967. *Sociology and modern systems theory.* Englewood Cliffs, N.J.: Prentice-Hall.

Budd, Linda Gail Stevenson. 1976. "Problems, disclosure, and commitment of cohabiting and married couples." Unpublished dissertation. Minneapolis: University of Minnesota.

Bullis, Connie, Carolyn Clark, and Rick Sline. 1993. "From passion to commitment: Turning points in romantic relationships." In P. J. Kalbfleisch (ed.), *Interpersonal communication: Evolving interpersonal relationships.* Hillsdale, N.J.: Erlbaum, pp. 213–236.

Bumpass, Larry L. 1990. "What's happening to the family? Interactions between demographic and institutional change." *Demography* 27:483–498.

———, and James A. Sweet. 1989. "National estimates of cohabitation." *Demography* 26:615–625.

———, ———, and Andrew Cherlin. 1991. "The role of cohabitation in declining rates of marriage." *Journal of Marriage and Family* 53:913–927.

Burchinal, Lee G. 1964. "The premarital dyad and love involvement." In Harold T. Christensen (ed.), *Handbook of marriage and the family.* Chicago: Rand McNally, pp. 623–674.

Burgess, Ernest W., and Paul Wallen. 1953. *Engagement and marriage.* Philadelphia: Lippincott.

Burgess, E. W., Harvey Locke, and Mary Thomes. 1963. *The family: From institution to companionship.* 3rd ed. New York: American.

Burt, Martha. 1991. "Rape myths and acquaintance rape." In A. Parrot and L. Bechhofer (eds.), *Acquaintance rape.* New York: Wiley, pp. 26–40.

Busby, Dean M. 1991. "Violence in the family." In Stephen J. Bahr (ed.), *Family research: A sixty year review, 1930–1990, Vol. 1.* New York: Lexington, pp. 335–385.

Butterfield, L. H., Marc Friedlander, and Mary-Jo Kline. 1975. *The book of Abigail and John: Selected letters of the Adams family.* Cambridge, Mass.: Harvard University Press.

Buunk, Bram. 1983. "Alternative lifestyles from an international perspective: A trans-Atlantic comparison." In E. D. Macklin and R. H. Rubin (eds.), *Contemporary families and alternative lifestyles.* Beverly Hills, Calif.: Sage, pp. 288–330.

Buunk, Bram P., and Barry van Driel. 1989. *Variant lifestyles and relationships.* Newbury Park, Calif.: Sage.

Byers, Sandra E., and Larry Heinlein. 1989. "Predicting initiations and refusals of sexual activities in married and cohabiting heterosexual couples." *Journal of Sex Research* 26:210–231.

Caldwell, Cleopatra Howard, Angela Dungee Greene, and Andrew Billingsley. 1992. "The black church as a family support system: Instrumental and expressive functions." *National Journal of Sociology* 6:21–40.

Canary, Daniel J., and Laura Stafford. 1993. "Preservation of relational characteristics: Maintenance strategies, equity, and locus of control." In P. J. Kalbfleisch (ed.), *Interpersonal communication: Evolving interpersonal relationships.* Hillsdale, N.J.: Erlbaum, pp. 237–259.

Cargan, Leonard, and Matthew Melko. 1982. *Singles: Myths and realities.* Beverly Hills, Calif.: Sage.

Carter, Peter J. 1992. "An exploratory study of decision-making among three non-traditional sets of couples: Gay, lesbian, and heterosexual cohabitors." Unpublished MA thesis, Department of Sociology, University of Florida, Gainesville.

Cazenave, Noel A., and M. A. Straus. 1990. "Race, class network embeddedness, and family violence: A search for potent support systems." In

M. A. Straus and R. J. Gelles (eds.), *Physical violence in American families.* New Brunswick, N.J.: Transaction, pp. 321–340.

Cheal, David. 1991. *Family and the state of theory.* Toronto: University of Toronto Press.

Cheatham, Harold E., and James B. Stewart. 1990. "Retrospective and exegesis: Black families reconceptualized." In H. E. Cheatham and J. B. Stewart (eds.), *Black families: Interdisciplinary perspectives.* New Brunswick, N. J.: Transaction, pp. 395–399.

Cherlin, Andrew J. 1988. *The changing American family and public policy.* Washington, D.C.: Urban Institute Press.

Cherry, Kittredge. 1987. *Womansword: What Japanese words say about women.* Tokyo/New York: Kodansha.

Chilman, Catherine S., E. W. Nunnally, and M. Cox (eds.). 1988. *Variant family forms.* Newbury Park, Calif.: Sage.

Chrisman, Robert, and Robert L. Allen (eds.). 1992. *Court of appeal: The black community speaks out on the racial and sexual politics of Clarence Thomas vs. Anita Hill.* New York: Ballantine Books.

Christensen, Bryce J. 1990a. *Utopia against the family: The problems and politics of the American family.* San Francisco: Ignatius Press.

——— (ed.) 1990b. *The retreat from marriage: Causes and consequences.* Lanham, Md: University Press of America.

Clanton, Gordon. 1989. "Jealousy in American culture, 1945–1985: Reflections from popular literature." In D. D. Franks and E. D. McCarthy (eds.), *The sociology of emotions: Original essays and research papers.* Greenwich, Conn.: Jai Press.

Clive, E. M. 1980. "Marriage: An unnecessary legal concept?" In J. M. Eekelaar and S. N. Katz (eds.), *Marriage and cohabitation in contemporary societies.* Toronto: Butterworths, pp. 71–82.

Cochran, Moncrief, Mary Larner, David Riley, Lars Gunnarsson, and Charles Henderson, Jr. 1990. *Extending families: The social networks of parents and children.* New York: Cambridge University Press.

Cohen, Ira J. 1989. *Structuration theory: Anthony Giddens and the constitution of social life.* London: Macmillan.

Cohen, Sheldon. 1990. "Control and the epidemiology of physical health: Where do we go from here?" In J. Rodin, Carmi Schooler, and K.

Warner Schaie (eds.), *Self-directedness: Cause and effects throughout the life course.* Hillsdale, N.J.: Erlbaum, pp. 231–240.

Coleman, James S. 1961. *The adolescent society.* New York: Free Press.

Coleman, Marilyn. 1993. "Editor's note." *Journal of Marriage and Family* 55:525–526.

———, and Lawrence H. Ganong. 1990. "Remarriage and stepfamily research in the 1980s: Increased interest in an old family form." *Journal of Marriage and Family* 52:925–940.

———, and ———. 1991. "Stepchildren: Burying the Cinderella myth." In Warren A. Brown and Waln K. Brown (eds.), *Why some children succeed despite the odds.* New York: Praeger, pp. 41–54.

Collins, Randall. 1975. *Conflict sociology.* New York: Academic Press.

Collison, Michelle N.-K. 1992. "A Berkeley scholar clashes with feminists over validity of their research on date rape." *The Chronicle of Higher Education,* February 26, pp. A35–37.

"Condom roulette." 1992. *Washington Watch.* January. Washington, D.C.: Family Research Council.

Condon, Jane. 1985. *A half-step behind: Japanese women of the '80s.* New York: Dodd, Mead.

Cooley, Charles H. 1909. *Social organization.* New York: Scribners.

Coser, Lewis. 1956. *The functions of social conflict.* New York: Free Press.

Cott, Nancy F. 1977. *The bonds of womanhood: 'Woman's sphere' in New England, 1780–1835.* New Haven, Conn.: Yale University Press.

———. 1979a. "Eighteenth-century family life as revealed in Massachusetts divorce records." In N. F. Cott and Elizabeth H. Pleck (eds.), *A heritage of her own: Toward a new social history of American women.* New York: Simon & Schuster, pp. 107–135.

———. 1979b. "Passionlessness: An interpretation of Victorian sexual ideology, 1790–1850." *Signs* 4:162–181.

Cowan, Carolyn Pape, and Philip A. Cowan. 1992. *When partners become parents: The big life change for couples.* New York: Basic.

Cowan, Philip A. 1991. "Individual and family life transitions: A proposal for a new definition." In P. A. Cowan and Mavis Hetherington (eds.), *Family transitions.* Hillsdale, N.J.: Erlbaum, pp. 3–30.

———. 1993. "The sky *is* falling, but Popenoe's

analysis won't help us do anything about it." *Journal of Marriage and Family* 55:548–553.

Cuber, John D., and Peggy B. Harrof. 1965. *The significant Americans: A study of sexual behavior among the affluent.* New York: Appleton-Century.

Dahlerup, Drude. 1986. "Introduction." In D. Dahlerup (ed.), *The new woman's movement: Feminism and political power in Europe and the U.S.* Newbury Park, Calif.: Sage, pp. 1–25.

Danigelis, Nicholas L., and Alfred P. Fengler. 1991. *No place like home: Intergenerational home sharing through social exchange.* New York: Columbia University Press.

Darling, Carol A., David J. Kallen, and Joyce E. VanDusen. 1984. "Sex in transition, 1900–1980." *Journal of Youth and Adolescence* 13:385–397.

Darnton, Nina. 1991. "The pain of the last taboo." *Newsweek.* October 7, pp. 70–72.

DaVanzo, Julie, and M. Omar Rahman. 1993. *American families: Trends and policy issues.* December 16. Santa Monica, Calif.: The Rand Corp.

Davis, Kingsley, 1949. *Human society.* New York: Macmillan.

DeMaris, Alfred, and Vaninadha Rao. 1992. "Premarital cohabitation and subsequent marital stability in the U.S.: A reassessment." *Journal of Marriage and Family* 54:178–190.

D'Emilio, John, and Estelle B. Freedman. 1988. *Intimate matters: A history of sexuality in America.* New York: Harper & Row.

Demos, John. 1982. "The changing faces of fatherhood: A new exploration in American history." In Stanley H. Cath et al. (eds.), *Father and child: Developmental and clinical perspectives.* Boston: Little, Brown, pp. 425–445.

Denfeld, David, and Michael Gordon. 1971. "Mateswapping: The family that swings together clings together." In Arlene Skolnick and Jerome Skolnick (eds.), *The family in transition.* Boston: Little, Brown, pp. 463–475.

Denmark, F., J. Shaw, and S. Ciali. 1985. "The relationship among sex roles, living arrangements and the division of household responsibilities." *Sex Roles* 12:617–625.

Dinnerstein, Myra. 1992. *Women between two worlds: Midlife reflections on work and family.* Philadelphia: Temple University Press.

DiTomaso, Nancy. 1989. "Sexuality in the workplace: Key issues in social research and organizational practice." In Jeff Hearn, Deborah L. Sheppard, Peta Tancred-Sheriff, and Gibson Burrell (eds.), *The sexuality of organization.* London: Sage, pp. 56–70.

Dizard, Jan E., and Howard Gadlin. 1990. *The minimal family.* Amherst: University of Massachusetts Press.

Dobash, Russell P., and R. Emerson Dobash. 1983. "The context-specific approach." In David Finkelhor, Richard J. Gelles, Gerald T. Hotaling, and Murray A. Straus (eds.), *The dark side of families.* Beverly Hills, Calif.: Sage, pp. 261–270.

—— and ——. 1990. "How theoretical definitions and perspectives affect research and policy." In D. J. Besharov (ed.), *Family violence: Research and public policy issues.* Washington, D.C.: AEI Press.

Dobson, James. 1992a. "Dare to discipline in the '90s." *Focus on the Family,* September, pp. 2–5.

——. 1992b. "Spanking: Harmful or helpful?" *Focus on the Family,* February 13, p. 5.

Donnelly, Marguerite. 1991. "The impact of women's name change at marriage: Implications for relational development: A research proposal." Unpublished paper. Department of Sociology, University of Florida, Gainesville.

Douvan, Elizabeth. 1977. "Interpersonal relationships: Some questions and observations." In George Levinger and Harold Raush (eds.), *Close relationships: Perspectives on the meaning of intimacy.* Amherst: University of Massachusetts Press, pp. 17–32.

Dralle, Penelope Wasson, and Kathelynne Mackiewicz. 1981. "Psychological impact of women's name change at marriage: Literature review and implications for further study." *The American Journal of Family Therapy* 9:50–55.

Driscoll, Dawn-Marie, and Carol R. Goldberg. 1993. *Members of the club: The coming of age of executive women.* New York: Free Press.

Duncan, Greg J., and James N. Morgan. 1985. "The panel study of income dynamics." In G. H. Elder (ed.), *Life course dynamics.* Ithaca, N.Y.: Cornell University Press, pp. 50–74.

Durfield, Richard. 1990. "A promise with a ring to it." *Focus on the Family,* April, pp. 2–4.

Durkheim, Émile. 1951. *Suicide.* Translated by John A. Spaulding and George Simpson. New York: Free Press.

Duskin, Elisabeth (ed.). 1990. *Lone-parent families: The economic challenge.* Paris: OECD Publications, Social Policy Studies No. 8.

Duvall, Evelyn M. 1962. *Family development.* 2nd ed. Philadelphia: J.B. Lippincott.

Dwyer, Jeffrey W., and Raymond T. Coward (eds.). 1992. *Gender, families and elder care.* Newbury Park, Calif.: Sage.

Ebaugh, Helen Rose Fuchs. 1988. *Becoming an ex: The process of role exit.* Chicago: University of Chicago Press.

Eckenrode, John, and Susan Gore (eds.). 1990. *Stress between work and family.* New York: Plenum.

Eco, Umberto. 1988. *Foucault's pendulum.* New York: Ballantine.

Edwards, John. 1991. "New conceptions: Biosocial innovations and the family." *Journal of Marriage and Family* 53:349–360.

Egan, Timothy. 1992. *The New York Times.* September 25, pp. A1, A11.

Ehrmann, Winston. 1964. "Marital and nonmarital sexual behavior." In Harold T. Christensen (ed.), *Handbook of marriage and the family.* Chicago: Rand McNally, pp. 585–622.

Ekeh, Peter. 1974. *Social exchange theory.* Cambridge, Mass.: Harvard University Press.

Elder, Glen H. 1981a. "History and the family: The discovery of complexity." *Journal of Marriage and Family* 43:489–520.

———. 1981b. "Social history and life experience." In Dorothy H. Eichorn, John A. Clausen, Norma Hann, Marjorie P. Honzik, and Paul H. Mussen (eds.), *Present and past in middle-life.* New York: Academic Press, pp. 3–31.

Ellis, Desmond P. 1971. "The Hobbesian problem of order: A critical appraisal of the normative solution." *American Sociological Review* 36:692–703.

Ermisch, John. 1990. "Demographic aspects of the growing number of lone-parent families." In Elisabeth Duskin (ed.), *Lone-parent families: The economic challenge.* Paris: OECD Publications, Social Policy Studies No. 8.

Espenshade, Thomas J. 1985. "Marriage trends in America: Estimates, implications, and underlying causes." *Population and Development Review* 11:193–246.

Estep, Rhoda, Dan Waldorff, and Toby Marotta. 1992. "Sexual behavior of male prostitutes." In Joan Huber and Beth E. Schneider (eds.), *The so-*

cial context of AIDS. Newbury Park, Calif.: Sage, pp. 95–112.

Etzioni, Amitai. *A responsive society: Collected essays on guiding deliberate social change.* San Francisco: Jossey-Bass.

Faderman, Lillian. 1991. *Odd girls and twilight lovers: A history of lesbian life in twentieth-century America.* New York: Columbia University Press.

Falk, Candace. 1984. *Love, anarchy, and Emma Goldman.* New York: Holt, Rinehart & Winston.

Farber, Bernard. 1964. *Family: Organization and interaction.* San Francisco: Chandler.

Faris, Ellsworth. 1937/1957. "The primary group: Essence and accident." Reprinted in L. A. Coser and B. Rosenberg (eds.), *Sociology theory.* New York: Macmillan, pp. 298–303.

Feagin, Joe R., Anthony M. Orum, and Gideon Sjoberg (eds.), 1991. *A case for the case study.* Chapel Hill: University of North Carolina Press.

Ferree, Myra M. 1988. "Negotiating household roles and responsibilities." Unpublished paper presented to annual meeting of National Council on Family Relations, Philadelphia.

Ferree, Myra M. 1990. "Beyond separate spheres: Feminism and family research." *Journal of Marriage and Family* 52:884–886.

Finch, Janet. 1989. *Family obligations and social change.* Cambridge, Mass.: Basil Blackwell.

Fine, Mark A., and Andrew I. Schwebel. 1991. "Resiliency in black children from single-parent families." In Warren A. Brown and Waln K. Brown (eds.), *Why some children succeed despite the odds.* New York: Praeger, pp. 23–40.

Finkelhor, David, and Kersti Yllo. 1985. *License to rape: Sexual abuse of wives.* New York: Free Press.

Firth, Robert. 1936. *We, the Tikopia.* London: George Allen & Unwin.

Fitzpatrick, Mary Anne. 1988a. *Between husbands and wives.* Newbury Park, Calif.: Sage.

———. 1988b. "Negotiation, problem-solving and conflict in various types of marriages." In Patricia Noller and Mary Anne Fitzpatrick (eds.), *Perspectives on marital interaction.* Philadelphia: Multilingual Matters, Ltd., pp. 245–270.

———, and Diane M. Badzinski. 1985. "All in the family: Interpersonal communication in kin relationships." In Mark L. Knapp and Gerald L. Miller (eds.), *Handbook of interpersonal communication.* Beverly Hills, Calif.: Sage, pp. 687–726.

Fletcher, Ronald. 1988. *The Shaking of the foundations: Family and society.* London: Routledge.

Fogarty, Michael P., Rhona Rapoport, and Robert N. Rapoport. 1971. *Sex, career, and family.* Beverly Hills, Calif.: Sage.

Folberg, H. Jay. 1980. "Domestic partnership: A no-fault remedy for cohabitors." In John M. Eekelaar and Sanford N. Katz (eds.), *Marriage and cohabitation in contemporary societies: Areas of legal, social, and ethical change.* Toronto: Butterworths, pp. 346–356.

Fortes, Meyer. 1969. *Kinship and the social order.* Chicago: Aldine.

Fox, Kenneth. 1986. *Metropolitan America: Urban life and urban policy in the U.S.—1940–1980.* Jackson: University of Mississippi Press.

Francoeur, Robert T. 1983. "Religious reactions to religious lifestyles." In Eleanor D. Mackin and Roger H. Rubin (eds.), *Contemporary families and alternative lifestyles.* Beverly Hills, Calif.: Sage, pp. 379–399.

Freese, Pamela. 1991. "The union of nature and culture: Gender symbolism in the American wedding ritual." In P. Freese and John M. Coggeshall (eds.), *Transcending boundaries: Multi-disciplinary approaches to the study of gender.* New York: Bergin & Garvey, pp. 97–112.

Friedan, Betty. 1963. *The feminine mystique.* New York: Norton.

Friedman, Myles I., and George H. Lackey, Jr. 1991. *The psychology of human control: A general theory of purposeful behavior.* New York: Praeger.

Frohnmayer, John. 1991. "A litany of the taboo." *Old Oregon.* Eugene: University of Oregon.

Fuchs, Victor R. 1988. *Women's quest for economic equality.* Cambridge, Mass.: Harvard University Press.

Furstenberg, Frank F. 1990. "Divorce and the American family." *Annual Review of Sociology* 16:379–403.

———, and Andrew J. Cherlin. 1991. *Divided families: What happens to children when parents part.* Cambridge, Mass.: Harvard University Press.

———, and Graham Spanier. 1984. *Recycling the family: Remarriage after divorce.* Beverly Hills, Calif.: Sage.

Gadlin, Howard. 1977. "Private lives and public order: A critical view of the history of intimate relations in the United States." In George Levinger and Harold Raush (eds.), *Close relationships: Perspectives on the meaning of intimacy.* Amherst: University of Massachusetts Press, pp. 33–72.

Gagnon, John H., and William Simon. 1973. *Sexual conduct: The social sources of human sexuality.* Chicago: Aldine.

Ganong, Lawrence H., Marilyn Coleman, and Dennis Mapes. 1990. "A meta-analytic review of family structure stereotypes." *Journal of Marriage and Family* 52:287–297.

Gardner, Richard A. 1993. "Modern witch hunt—child abuse charges." *Wall Street Journal,* February 22, p. A10.

Garfinkel, Irwin, and Sara S. McLanahan. 1986. *Single mothers and their children: A new American dilemma.* Washington, D.C.: Urban Institute Press.

Garrison, Marsha. 1990. "The economics of divorce: Changing rules, changing results." In Stephen D. Sugarman and Herma Kay Hill (eds.), *Divorce reform at the crossroads.* New Haven, Conn.: Yale University Press, pp. 75–101.

Gecas, Victor. 1989. "The social psychology of self-efficacy." *Annual Review of Sociology* 15:291–316.

Gelles, R. J. *The violent home: A study of physical aggression between husbands and wives.* Beverly Hills, Calif.: Sage.

———, and Jon R. Conte. 1990. "Domestic violence and sexual abuse of children: A review of research in the eighties." *Journal of Marriage and Family* 52:1045–1058.

———, and Eileen F. Hargreaves. 1990. "Maternal employment and violence toward children." In M. A. Straus and R. J. Gelles (eds.), *Physical violence in American families.* New Brunswick, N.J.: Transaction, pp. 263–277.

Gerson, Kathleen. 1985. *Hard choices: How women decide about work, career and motherhood.* Berkeley: University of California Press.

Gerstel, Naomi, and Harriet Gross. 1984. *Commuter marriage: A study of work and family.* New York: Guilford.

———, and ———. 1987. "Introduction and overview." In N. Gerstel and H. Gross (eds.), *Families and work.* Philadelphia: Temple University Press, pp. 1–21.

Gerth, Hans H., and C. Wright Mills (eds.). 1958. *From Max Weber: Essays in sociology.* New York: Oxford University Press.

Giallombardo, Rose. 1966. *Society of women: A study of a women's prison.* New York: Wiley.

Gidycz, Christine A., and Mary P. Koss. 1991. "The effects of acquaintance rape on the female victim." In A. Parrot and L. Bechhofer (eds.), *Acquaintance rape.* New York: Wiley, pp. 270–283.

Gilbert, Lucia A. 1985. *Men in dual-career families: Current realities and future prospects.* Hillsdale, N.J.: Erlbaum.

Gilligan, Carol. 1982. *In a different voice: Psychological theory and women's development.* Cambridge, Mass.: Harvard University Press.

Gitlin, Todd. 1987. *The sixties: Years of hope, days of rage.* New York: Bantam.

Glendon, Mary Ann. 1989. *The transformation of family law: State, law and the family in the U.S. and Western Europe.* Chicago: University of Chicago Press.

Glenn, Norval D. 1993. "A plea for objective assessment of the notion of family decline." *Journal of Marriage and Family* 55:542–544.

Glick, Paul C. 1988. "Fifty years of family demography: A record of social change." *Journal of Marriage and Family* 50:861–873.

———, and Graham B. Spanier. 1981. "Cohabitation in the United States." In Peter J. Stein (ed.), *Single life: Unmarried adults in social context.* New York: St. Martin's Press, pp. 194–209.

Godwin, Deborah D. 1991. "Spouses' time allocation to household work: A review and critique." *Lifestyles: Family and Economic Issues* 12:253–294.

———, and John Scanzoni. 1989a. "Couple decision making: Commonalities and differences across issues and spouses." *Journal of Family Issues* 10:291–310.

———, and ———. 1989b. "Couple consensus during marital joint decision-making: A context, process, outcome model." *Journal of Marriage and Family* 51:943–956.

———, and ———. In preparation. "Marriage and marriage-like relationships: Demographic, interactional, and cultural issues."

Goleman, Daniel. 1992. *The New York Times,* December 2, p. B7.

Gomes-Schwartz, Beverly, Jonathan M. Horowitz, and Albert P. Cardarelli. 1990. *Child sexual abuse: The initial effects.* Newbury Park, Calif.: Sage.

Gonsiorek, John C. 1991. "Conclusion." In John C. Gonsiorek and James D. Weinrich (eds.), *Homo-sexuality: Research implications for public policy.* Newbury Park, Calif.: Sage, pp. 244–248.

———, and Michael Shernoff. 1991. "AIDS prevention and public policy: The experience of gay males." In J. C. Gonsiorek and J. D. Weinreich (eds.), *Homosexuality: Research implications for public policy.* Newbury Park, Calif.: Sage, pp. 230–243.

Goode, William J. 1956. *After divorce.* New York: Free Press.

———. 1963. *World revolution and family patterns.* New York: Free Press.

———. 1976. "Family disorganization." In Robert K. Merton and Robert Nisbet (eds.), *Contemporary Social Problems.* 4th ed. New York: Harcourt, Brace, Jovanovich, pp. 513–554.

Gottman, John M. 1982. "Temporal form: Toward a new language for describing relationships." *Journal of Marriage and Family* 44:943–962.

Gravenhorst, Lerke. 1988. "A feminist look at family development theory." In David Klein and Joan Aldous (eds.), *Social stress and family development.* New York: Guilford, pp. 79–101.

Greeley, Andrew. 1992. *Sex after sixty: A report.* Chicago: University of Chicago, National Opinion Research Center.

Green, G. Dorsey and Frederick W. Bozett. 1991. "Lesbian mothers and gay fathers." In John C. Gonsiorek and James D. Weinrich (eds.) *Homosexuality: Research implications for public policy.* Newbury Park, Calif.: Sage, pp. 197–214.

Greenblatt, Cathy Stein. 1983. "A hit is a hit is a hit . . . or is it? Approval and tolerance of the use of physical force by spouses." In D. Finkelhor, et al. (eds.) *The dark side of families.* Beverly Hills, Calif.: Sage, pp. 235–260.

Greif, Geoffrey L. 1985. *Single fathers.* Lexington, Mass.: Lexington Books.

Greven, Philip. 1991. *Spare the child: The religious roots of punishment.* New York: Oxford University Press.

Grossman, Hildreth Y., and Nia Lane Chester (eds.). 1990. *The experience and meaning of work in women's lives.* Hillsdale, N.J.: Erlbaum.

Gubrium, Jaber F., and James A. Holstein. 1990. *What is family?* Mountain View, Calif.: Mayfield.

Guerrero, Laura K., Sylvie V. Eloy, Peter F. Jorgensen, and Peter A. Andersen. 1993. "Hers or his? Differences in the experience and communication of jealousy in close relationships." In P. J. Kalbfleisch (ed.), *Interpersonal communication: Evolving interpersonal relationships.* Hillsdale, N.J.: Erlbaum, pp. 109–131.

Gulliver, Paul H. 1979. *Disputes and negotiations: A cross-cultural perspective.* New York: Academic.

Gupta, Giri Raj, and Steven M. Cox (eds.). 1987. *Deviance and disruption in the American family.* Lexington, Mass.: Ginn & Co.

Gutek, Barbara A., and Laurie Larwood (eds.). 1987. *Women's career development.* Beverly Hills, Calif.: Sage.

Hage, Jerald, and Charles H. Powers. 1992. *Post-industrial lives: Roles and relationships in the 21st century.* Newbury Park, Calif.: Sage.

Halem, Lynne Carol. 1982. *Separated and divorced women.* Westport, Conn.: Greenwood.

Hampton, Robert L., and R. J. Gelles. 1991. "A profile of violence toward black children." In R. L. Hampton (ed.), *Black family violence.* Lexington, Mass.: Lexington Books, pp. 21–34.

———, ———, and John Harrop. 1991. "Is violence in black families increasing? A comparison of 1975 and 1985 national survey rates." In R. L. Hampton (ed.), *Black family violence.* Lexington, Mass.: Lexington Books, pp. 3–18.

Hansen, Donald A. 1988. "Schooling, stress, and family development: Rethinking the social role metaphor." In David Klein and Joan Aldous (eds.), New York: Guilford, pp. 44–47.

Hardey, Michael, and Graham Crow (eds.). 1991. *Lone parenthood: Coping with constraints and making opportunities.* New York: Harvester/Wheatsheaf.

Harper, Lucinda. 1992. "Women account for bulk of decline in work force, but it's not clear why." *Wall Street Journal.* November 11, p. A5.

Harris, Diana K., Gary A. Fine, and Thomas C. Hood. 1992. "The aging of desire: Playboy centerfolds and the graying of America; a research note." *Journal of Aging Studies* 6:301–306.

Hatchett, Shirley J. 1991. "Women and men." In James S. Jackson (ed.), *Life in black America.* Newbury Park, Calif.: Sage, pp. 84–104.

Haugaard, Jeffrey J., and R. E. Emery. 1988. "Methodological issues in child sexual abuse research." *Child Abuse and Neglect* 13:89–100.

———, and N. Dickon Reppucci. 1988. *The sexual abuse of children: A comprehensive guide to current knowledge and intervention strategies.* San Francisco: Jossey-Bass.

Hayes, Cheryl D., John L. Palmer, and Martha J. Zaslow (ed.), 1990. *Who cares for America's children? Child care policy for the 1990s.* Washington, D.C.: National Academy Press.

Heaton, Tim B., and Stan L. Albrecht. 1991. "Stable unhappy marriages." *Journal of Marriage and Family* 53:747–768.

Heise, David R. 1990. "Careers, career trajectories, and the self." In J. Rodin, Carmi Schooler, and K. Warner Schaie (eds.), *Self-directedness: Cause and effects throughout the life course.* Hillsdale, N.J.: Erlbaum, pp. 59–84.

Hendrick, Harry. 1990. "Constructions and reconstructions of British childhood: An interpretive survey, 1800 to the present." In Allison James and Alan Prout (eds.), *Constructing and reconstructing childhood: Contemporary issues in the sociological study of childhood.* New York: Falmer Press, pp. 35–59.

Hertz, Rosanna. 1986. *More equal than others: Women and men in dual-career marriages.* Berkeley: University of California Press.

Hewlett, Sylvia Ann. 1991. *When the bough breaks: The costs of neglecting our children.* New York: Basic Books.

Hicks, Mary W., Sally L. Hansen, and Leo A. Christie. 1983. "Dual-career/dual-work families: A systems approach." In E. D. Macklin and R. H. Rubin (eds.), *Contemporary families and alternative lifestyles.* Beverly Hills, Calif.: Sage, pp. 164–193.

Hill, Wayne, and John Scanzoni. 1982. "An approach for assessing marital decision-making." *Journal of Marriage and Family* 44:927–941.

Hochschild, Arlie (with Anne Machung). 1989. *The second shift: Working parents and the revolution at home.* New York: Viking.

Hofferth, Sandra. 1985. "Updating children's life course." *Journal of Marriage and Family* 47:93–116.

Holden, Karen C., and Pamela J. Smock. 1991. "The economic costs of marital dissolution: Why do women bear a disproportionate cost?" *Annual Review of Sociology* 17:51–78.

Holland, Dorothy C., and Margaret A. Eisenhart. 1990. *Educated in romance: Women, achievement, and college culture.* Chicago: University of Chicago Press.

Holmes, Ronald M. 1989. *Profiling violent crimes: An investigative tool.* Newbury Park, Calif.: Sage.

Houseknecht, Sharon. 1987. "Voluntary childlessness." In Marvin B. Sussman and Suzanne Steinmetz (eds.), *Handbook of marriage and the family.* New York: Plenum, pp. 369–395.

Howard, Judith A., Philip Blumstein, and Pepper Schwartz. 1986. "Sex, power, and influence tactics in intimate relationships." *Journal of Personality and Social Psychology* 51:102–109.

Howard, Ronald. 1981. *A social history of American family sociology.* Westport, Conn.: Greenwood.

Hunter, James Davison. 1991. *Culture wars: The struggle to define America.* New York: Basic Books.

Ihinger-Tallman, Marilyn. 1988. "Research on stepfamilies." *Annual Review of Sociology* 14:25–48.

———, and Kay Pasley. 1987. "Divorce and remarriage in the American family: A historical review." In K. Pasley and M. Ihinger-Tallman (eds.), *Remarriage and stepparenting: Current research and theory.* New York: Guilford, pp. 3–18.

Intons-Peterson, Margaret Jean. 1988. *Gender concepts of Swedish and American youth.* Hillsdale, N.J.: Erlbaum.

———, and Jill Crawford. 1985. "The meanings of marital surnames." *Sex Roles* 12:1163–1171.

Island, David, and Patrick Letellier. 1991. *Men who beat the men who love them: Battered gay men and domestic violence.* New York: Haworth.

Jacobsen, Joyce P., and Laurence M. Levin. 1992. "The effects of intermittent labor force attachment on female earnings." Paper presented to American Economics Association. Memphis: Rhodes College, Department of Economics.

Jacobsen, Linda A., and Fred C. Pampel. 1989. "Cohabitation versus other nonfamily living arrangements: Changing determinants from 1960 to 1980." Unpublished paper, Department of Consumer Economics and Housing, Cornell University, Ithaca, N.Y.

Jaffe, Dale J. 1989. *Caring strangers: The sociology of intergenerational homesharing.* Greenwich, Conn.: Jai Press.

James, Allison, and Alan Prout. 1990. "Re-presenting childhood: Time and transition in the study of childhood." In Allison James and Alan Prout (eds.), *Constructing and reconstructing childhood: Contemporary issues in the sociological study of childhood.* New York: Falmer Press, pp. 216–238.

Jaudes, Paula, and Leslie Mitchel. 1992. *Physical child abuse.* 2nd ed. Chicago: National Committee for Prevention of Child Abuse.

Jenks, Richard J. 1987. "Swinging: A replication and test of a theory." In Giri Raj Gupta and Steven M. Cox (eds.), *Deviance and disruption in the American family.* Lexington, Mass.: Ginn, pp. 145–150.

Jewell, K. Sue. 1988. *Survival of the black family: The institutional impact of U.S. social policy.* New York: Praeger.

Johnston, Janet R. 1988. *Impasses of divorce: The dynamics and resolution of family conflict.* New York: Free Press.

Jones, Charles, Lorna Marsden, and Lorne Tepperman. 1990. *Lives of their own: The individualization of women's lives.* Toronto: Oxford University Press.

Jones, Jacqueline. 1985. *Labor of love, labor of sorrow: Black women, work, and the family from slavery to the present.* New York: Basic Books.

Joshi, Heather. 1990. "Obstacles and opportunities for lone parents as breadwinners in Great Britain." In Elisabeth Duskin (ed.), *Lone-parent families: The economic challenge.* Paris: OECD Publications, pp. 127–150.

Joyce, James. 1914. *Dubliners.* New York: Modern Library, 1969 ed.

Kahn, Alfred J., and Sheila B. Kamerman (eds.). 1988. *Child support: From debt collection to social policy.* Newbury Park, Calif.: Sage.

Kalbfleisch, Pamela J. 1993. "Looking for a friend and a lover: Perspectives on evolving interpersonal relationships." In P. J. Kalbfleisch (ed.), *Interpersonal communication: Evolving interpersonal relationships.* Hillsdale, N.J.: Erlbaum, pp. 3–10.

Kallen, David J., and J. Stephenson. 1982. "Talking about sex revisited." *Journal of Youth and Adolescence* 11:11–23.

Kamerman, Sheila B., and Alfred J. Kahn. 1988. *Mothers alone: Stategies for a time of change.* Dover, Mass.: Auburn.

———, and ——— (eds.). 1991. *Child care, parental leave, and the under 3s.* New York: Auburn.

Kanin, Eugene J. 1957. "Male aggression in dating-courtship relations." *American Journal of Sociology* 63:197–204.

———. 1984. "Date rape: Unofficial criminals and victims." *Victimology* 9:95–108.

Katz, Jack. 1988. *Seductions of crime: Moral and sen-*

sual attractions in doing evil. New York: Basic Books.

Kaufman, Debra Renne. 1991. *Rachel's daughters: Newly orthodox Jewish women.* New Brunswick, N.J.: Rutgers University Press.

Kay, Herma Hill. 1990. "Beyond no-fault—New directions in divorce reform." In Stephen D. Sugarman and Herma Kay Hill (eds.), *Divorce reform at the crossroads.* New Haven, Conn.: Yale University Press, pp. 6–36.

Kaye, Lenard W., and Jeffrey S. Applegate. 1990. *Men as caregivers to the elderly.* Lexington, Mass.: Lexington Books.

Keen, Kirstin. 1989. Education for European competence. Brussels: *The European Round Table.* February.

Keller, Daniel P. 1989. *The prevention of rape and sexual assault on campus.* Goshen, Ky.: Campus Crime Prevention Program.

Kempe, C. H., F. N. Silverman, B. F. Steele, W. Droegemueller, and H. K. Silver. 1962. "The battered-child syndrome." *Journal of the American Medical Association* 181:17–24.

Kennedy, David M. 1970. *Birth control in America: The career of Margaret Sanger.* New Haven, Conn.: Yale University Press.

Kingsbury, Nancy, and John Scanzoni. 1993. "Structural-functionalism." In Pauline Boss, William Doherty, Ralph LaRossa, Walter Schumm, and Suzanne Steinmetz (eds.), *Sourcebook of theories and methods about families.* New York: Plenum.

Kinsey, Alfred C., Wardell B. Pomeroy, and Charles E. Martin. 1948. *Sexual behavior in the human male.* Philadelphia: Saunders.

———, ———, ———, and Paul Gebhard. 1953. *Sexual behavior in the human female.* Philadelphia: Saunders.

Kirkendall, Lester A. 1961. *Premarital intercourse and interpersonal relationships.* New York: Julian Press.

Kirkpatrick, Martha A. 1990. "Homosexuality and parenting." In Jeanne Spurlock and Carolyn B. Rabinowitz (eds.), *Women's progress: Promises and problems.* New York: Plenum, pp. 205–222.

Kitzinger, Jenny. 1990. "Who are you kidding? Children, power, and the struggle against sexual abuse." In Allison James and Alan Prout (eds.), *Constructing and reconstructing childhood: Contemporary issues in the sociological study of childhood.* New York: Falmer Press, pp. 157–183.

Klassen, Albert D., Colin J. Williams, and Eugene E.

Levitt. 1989. *Sex and morality in the U.S.* Middletown, Conn.: Wesleyan University Press.

Klemer, Robert H. 1959. *A man for every woman.* New York: Macmillan.

Knapp, Mark L., and Gerald R. Miller (eds.). 1985. *Handbook of interpersonal communication.* Beverly Hills, Calif.: Sage.

Knudsen, Dean D. 1991. "Child sexual coercion." In Elizabeth Grauerholz and Mary A. Koralewski (eds.), *Sexual coercion: A sourcebook on its nature, causes, and prevention.* Lexington, Mass.: Lexington Books, pp. 17–28.

Koeppel, Liana B., Yvette Montagne-Miller, Dan O'Hair, and Michael J. Cody. 1993. "Friendly? Flirting? Wrong?" In P. J. Kalbfleisch (ed.), *Interpersonal communication: Evolving interpersonal relationships.* Hillsdale, N.J.: Erlbaum, pp. 13–32.

Kohn, Barry, and Alice Matusow. 1980. *Barry and Alice: Portrait of a bisexual marriage.* Englewood Cliffs, N.J.: Prentice-Hall.

Kondo, Dorinne K. 1990. *Crafting selves: Power, gender and discourses of identity in a Japanese workplace.* Chicago: University of Chicago Press.

Koretz, Gene. 1992. "America's neglected weapon: Its educated women." *Business Week,* January 27, p. 22.

Koskoff, David E. 1974. *Joseph P. Kennedy: A life and times.* Englewood Cliffs, N.J.: Prentice-Hall.

Koss, M. P., C. A. Gidycz, and N. Wisniewski. 1987. "The scope of rape: Incidence and prevalence of sexual aggression and victimization in a national sample of higher education students." *Journal of Consulting and Clinical Psychology* 55:162–170.

Kraditor, Aileen S. 1968. *Up from the pedestal.* Chicago: Quadrangle.

Krause, Harry D. 1990. "Child support reassessed: Limits of private responsibility and the public interest." In Stephen D. Sugarman and Herma Kay Hill (eds.), *Divorce reform at the crossroads.* New Haven, Conn.: Yale University Press, pp. 166–190.

Kurdek, Lawrence A., and J. Patrick Schmitt. 1986a. "Early development of relationship quality in heterosexual married, heterosexual cohabiting, gay and lesbian couples." *Developmental Psychology* 22:305–309.

———, and ———. 1986b. "Relationship quality of partners in heterosexual married, heterosexual cohabiting, and gay and lesbian relationships." *Journal of Personality and Social Psychology* 51:711–720.

———, and ———. 1987. "Partner homogamy in married, heterosexual cohabiting, gay and lesbian couples." *Journal of Sex Research* 23:212–232.

Ladewig, Becky, Stephen J. Thoma, and John H. Scanzoni. 1988. "Sociobiology and the family: A focus on the interplay between social science and biology." In Erik E. Filsinger (ed.), *Biosocial perspectives on the family.* Newbury Park, Calif.: Sage, pp. 188–207.

Landale, Nancy S., and Katherine Fennelly. 1992. "Informal unions among mainland Puerto Ricans: Cohabitation or an alternative to legal marriage." *Journal of Marriage and Family* 54:269–280.

LaRossa, Ralph, Betty Anne Gordon, Ronald Jay Wilson, Annette Bairan, and Charles Jaret. 1991. "The fluctuating image of the 20th century American father." *Journal of Marriage and Family* 53:987–998.

Lasch, Christopher. 1977. *Haven in a heartless world: The family besieged.* New York: Basic Books.

Lash, Joseph P. 1971. *Eleanor and Franklin.* New York: Norton.

Laumann, Edward O., R. Michael, S. Michaels, J. Gagnon. 1994. *The Social Organization of Sexuality.* Chicago: National Opinion Research Center.

Leavitt, Robin Lynn. 1991. "Power and resistance in infant-toddler day care centers." In Spencer E. Cahill (ed.), *Sociological studies of child development. Vol. 4. Perspectives on and of children.* Greenwich, Conn.: Jai Press, pp. 91–112.

Lee, S. C. 1964. "The primary group as Cooley defines it." *Sociological Quarterly* 5:23–34.

Lehmann, Jennifer, M. 1990. "Durkheim's response to feminism: Prescriptions for women." *Sociological Theory* 8:163–187.

Lein, L. 1984. *Families without victims.* Lexington, Mass.: Heath.

Lenzer, Gertrud. 1992. "Sociology of children section interfaces with other groups." *ASA Footnotes,* December, pp. 6–7.

Leonard, Diana. 1990. *Sex and generation: A study of courtship and weddings.* New York: Tavistock.

Levine, Carol. 1990. "AIDS and changing concepts of family." *The Milbank Quarterly* 68:33–58.

Levinger, George, and Ted L. Huston. 1990. "The social psychology of marriage." In Frank D. Fincham and Thomas N. Bradbury (eds.), *The psychology of marriage.* New York: Guilford, pp. 19–58.

Levinson, David. 1989. *Family violence in cross-cultural perspective.* Newbury Park, Calif.: Sage.

Levinson, Marc. 1992. *Newsweek,* December 7, pp. 36–40.

Levi-Strauss, Claude. 1957. "The principle of reciprocity." In Lewis A. Coser and Bernard Rosenberg (eds.), *Sociology Theory.* New York: Macmillan, pp. 84–94.

Lewin, Bo. 1982. "Unmarried cohabitation: A marriage form in a changing society." *Journal of Marriage and Family* 44:763–774.

Lewin, Tamar. 1992. "AMA asking doctors to note abuse of elderly." *The New York Times.* November 24, p. A7.

Lewis, Lionel S., and Dennis D. Brissett. 1986. "Sex as God's work." *Transaction—Social Science and Modern Society,* 23:67–75.

Liebow, Elliott. 1967. *Tally's corner.* Boston: Little-Brown.

Lindsey, Karen. 1981. *Friends as family.* Boston: Beacon Press.

Lips, Hilary M. 1991. *Women, men, and power.* Mountain View, Calif.: Mayfield.

Lo, Jeannie. 1990. *Office ladies, factory women: Life and work at a Japanese company.* Armonk, N.Y.: M.E. Sharpe (East Gate Book).

Locke, Harvey J. 1968. *Predicting adjustment in marriage: A comparison of a divorced and a happily married group.* New York: Greenwood.

Lockhart, Lettie L. 1991. "Spousal violence: A cross-racial perspective." In R. L. Hampton (ed.), *Black family violence.* Lexington, Mass.: Lexington Books, pp. 85–101.

London, Kathryn A. 1991. "Cohabitation, marriage, marital dissolution, and remarriage: U.S., 1988." Hyattsville, Md.: National Center for Health Statistics, *Advance Data, No. 91-1250,* January 4.

Long-Laws, Judith, and Pepper Schwartz. 1977. *Sexual scripts: The social construction of female sexuality.* Hinsdale, Ill.: Dryden.

Lopez, Julie Amparano. 1992. "Study says women face glass walls as well as glass ceilings." *Wall Street Journal.* March 3, p. B1.

Lovejoy, Nancy C. 1990. "AIDS: Impact on the gay man's homosexual and heterosexual families." *Marriage and Family Review* 14:285–316.

Lozano, Beverly. 1989. *The invisible work force: Transforming American business with outside and home-based workers.* New York: Free Press.

Lucier, James P. 1992. "Unconventional rights: Children and the United Nations." *Family Policy* 5:1–16. Washington, D.C.: Family Research Council.

Luckey, Eleanor, and Gilbert Nass. 1969. "A comparison of sexual attitudes and behavior of an international sample." *Journal of Marriage and Family,* 31:346–379.

Lyon, Eleanor, and Patricia Goth Mace. 1991. "Family violence and the courts: Implementing a comprehensive new law." In Dean D. Knudsen and JoAnn L. Miller (eds.), *Abused and battered: Social and legal responses to family violence.* New York: Aldine De Gruyter, pp. 167–180.

Mackey, Wade C. 1985. *Fathering behaviors: The dynamics of the man-child bond.* New York: Plenum.

Macklin, Eleanor D. 1983. "Nonmarital heterosexual cohabitation: An overview." In Eleanor D. Macklin and Roger H. Rubin (eds.), *Contemporary families and alternative lifestyles.* Beverly Hills, Calif.: Sage, pp. 49–74.

Mac Murray, Bruce K. 1991. "Legal responses of prosecutors to child sexual abuse: A case comparison of two counties." In Dean D. Knudsen and JoAnn L. Miller (eds.), *Abused and battered: Social and legal responses to family violence.* New York: Aldine De Gruyter, pp. 153–166.

Mahoney, Margaret E. 1986. Cited in *Work and family responsibilities: Achieving a balance.* New York: Ford Foundation, 1989.

Makepeace, James. 1989. "Dating, living together, and courtship violence." In Maureen A. Pirog-Good and Jan E. Stets (eds.), *Violence in dating relationships.* New York: Praeger, pp. 94–107.

Malamuth, Neil M. 1981. "Rape proclivity among males." *Journal of Social Issues* 37:138–157.

Malone, Susan. 1993. "Sorority as socially constructed family." Unpublished manuscript, Department of Sociology. University of Florida.

Mancini, Jay A. (ed.). 1989. *Aging parents and adult children.* Lexington, Mass.: Lexington Books.

Manniche, Erik. 1985. *The family in Denmark.* Helsinger, Denmark: IDC Press.

———. 1991. *Marriage and non-marital cohabitation in Denmark.* Family Reports No. 20. Uppsala, Sweden: Uppsala University.

Marciano, Teresa Donati. 1990. "Hiding the priest and sharing the struggle: Wives and other partners of Roman Catholic priests." Paper presented at the annual meeting of the Society for the Scientific Study of Religion.

Markowski, Edward Mel, James W. Croake, and Jane F. Keller. 1978. "Sexual history and present sexual behavior of cohabiting and married couples." *Journal of Sex Research* 14:27–39.

Marsh, Barbara. 1992a. "Gay women starting own businesses." *Wall Street Journal.* July 1, p. B2.

———. 1992b. "Gender gap overseas." *Wall Street Journal.* October 13, p. R20.

Marsiglio, William. 1991. "Male procreative consciousness and responsibility: A conceptual analysis and research agenda." *Journal of Family Issues* 12:268–290.

———, and John Scanzoni. 1992. "Sexual behavior and marriage." In Edgar F. Borgotta and Marie L. Borgotta (eds.), *The Encyclopedia of Sociology. Vol. 4.* New York: Macmillan, pp. 1754–1761.

Martin, Molly. 1988. *Hard-hatted women: Stories of struggle and success in the trades.* Seattle: Seal Press.

Martin, Ralph G. 1983. *A hero for our time: An intimate story of the Kennedy years.* New York: Macmillan.

Martin, Teresa Castro, and Larry L. Bumpass. 1989. "Recent trends in marital disruption." *Demography* 26:37–50.

Masheter, Carol, and Linda M. Harris. 1986. "From divorce to friendship: A study of dialectic relationship development." *Journal of Social and Personal Relationships* 3:177–189.

Masnick, George, and Mary Jo Bane. 1980. *The nation's families: 1969–1990.* Boston: Auburn House.

Mathews, Donald G., and Jane Sherron De Hart. 1990. *Sex, gender, and the politics of ERA: A state and the nation.* New York: Oxford.

Mattesich, Paul, and Reuben Hill. 1987. "Life cycle and family development." In Marvin B. Sussman and Suzanne Steinmetz (eds.), *Handbook of marriage and the family.* New York: Plenum, pp. 437–469.

May, H. F. 1959. *The end of American innocence.* Chicago: Quadrangle.

McAdoo, Hariette P., and Marie F. Peters. 1983. "The present and future of alternative lifestyles in ethnic American cultures." In Eleanor D. Macklin and Roger H. Rubin (eds.), *Contemporary families and alternative lifestyles.* Beverly Hills, Calif.: Sage, pp. 288–307.

McChesney, Kay Young, Vern L. Bengston. 1988.

"Solidarity, integration, and cohesion in families: Concepts and theories." In V. L. Bergston (ed.), *Measurement of intergenerational relations.* Newbury Park, Calif.: Sage, pp. 15–30.

McCubbin, Hamilton I., and Charles R. Figley. 1983a. "Introduction." In H. I. McCubbin and C. R. Figley (eds.), *Stress and the family. Vol. I. Coping with normative transitions.* New York: Brunner/Mazel, pp. xxi–xxxi.

——, and ——. 1983b. "Bridging normative and catastrophic family stress." In H. I. McCubbin and C. R. Figley (eds.), *Stress and the family. Vol. I. Coping with normative transitions.* New York: Brunner/Mazel, pp. 218–228.

McDowell, Ian, and Claire Newell. 1987. *Measuring health: A guide to scales and questionnaires.* New York: Oxford.

McLeod, Don. 1992. "Matilda Riley's revolution." *AARP Bulletin* 33:12.

Merton, Robert K. 1957. *Social theory and social structure.* New York: Free Press.

Meyering, Ralph A., and Elizabeth A. Epling-McWherter. 1986. "Decision-making in extramarital relationships." *Lifestyles: A Journal of Changing Patterns* 12:115–129.

Midelfort, H. C. Erik. 1972. *Witch hunting in southwestern Germany 1562–1684—the social and intellectual foundations.* Stanford, Calif.: Stanford University Press.

Mieher, Stuart. 1992. "Baby boomers begin taking the top jobs at many companies." *Wall Street Journal.* November 6, p. A1.

Mill, John Stuart. 1869. *The subjugation of women and other essays.* London: Oxford University Press.

Miller, Brent. 1992. "Adolescent parenthood, economic issues, and social policies." *Journal of Family and Economic Issues* 13:467–475.

Millman, Marcia. 1991. *Warm hearts and cold cash: The intimate dynamics of families and money.* New York: Free Press.

Mintz, Steven, and Susan Kellogg. 1988. *Domestic revolutions: A social history of American family life.* New York: Free Press.

Mirwosky, John, and Catherine E. Ross. 1989. *Social causes of psychological distress.* New York: Aldine de Gruyter.

Mizruchi, Ephraim H. 1964. *Success and opportunity.* New York: Free Press.

Modell, John. 1988. "Institutional consequences of

hard times: Engagement in the 1930s." In D. Klein and J. Aldous (eds.), *Social stress and family development.* New York: Guilford, pp. 175–192.

——. 1989. *Into one's own: From youth to adulthood in the United States, 1920–1975.* Berkeley: University of California Press.

Moen, Phyllis. 1989. *Working parents: Transformations in gender roles and public policies in Sweden.* Madison: University of Wisconsin Press.

——, and Elaine Wethington. 1992. "The concept of adaptive family strategies." *Annual Review of Sociology* 18:233–251.

Money, John. 1988. *Gay, straight, and in-between: The sexology of erotic orientation.* New York: Oxford University Press.

Montgomery, Rhonda J. V. 1988. "Family sociology." In E. F. Borgotta and K. S. Cook (eds.), *The future of sociology.* Newbury Park, Calif.: Sage, pp. 105–119.

Morgan, Edmund S. 1966. *The Puritan family: Religion and domestic relations in seventeenth century New England.* New York: Harper & Row.

Morgan, Leslie A. 1991. *After marriage ends: Economic consequences for midlife women.* Newbury Park, Calif.: Sage.

Morris, Lydia. 1990. *The workings of the household: A US-UK comparison.* Cambridge, Mass.: Blackwell.

Moschetti, Glen J. 1979. "The Christmas potlatch: A refinement on the sociological interpretation of gift exchange." *Sociological Focus* 12:1–7.

Mott, Frank L. 1992. "The impact of father's absence from the home on subsequent cognitive development of younger children: Linkages between socio-emotional and cognitive well-being." Paper read at the meeting of the *American Sociological Association.* Ohio State University, Department of Sociology, Columbus.

Moynihan, Daniel P. 1965. "Employment, income and the ordeal of the Negro family." *Daedalus* 20: 745–769.

Mozny, Ivo, and Ladislav Rabusic. 1992. "Unmarried cohabitation in Czechoslovakia." *Czechoslovak Sociological Review* 28:107–117.

Muehlenhard, Charlene L., and Jennifer L. Schrag. 1991. "Nonviolent sexual coercion." In A. Parrot and L. Bechhofer (ed.), *Acquaintance rape.* New York: Wiley, pp. 115–128.

Murstein, Bernard I. 1974. *Love, sex, and marriage through the ages.* New York: Springer.

Naisbit, John. 1984. *Megatrends*. New York: Warner.

Nardi, Peter M. 1992. " 'Seamless souls': An introduction to men's friendships." In P. M. Nardi (ed.), *Men's friendships*. Newbury Park, Calif.: Sage, pp. 1–14.

Nash, Roderick. 1971. *The call of the wild 1900–1916*. New York: Braziller.

Nathanson, Constance A. 1991. *Dangerous passage: The social control of sexuality in women's adolescence*. Philadelphia: Temple University Press.

National Incidence Study. 1981. *National study of the incidence of child abuse and neglect*. Washington, D.C.: U.S. Department of Health and Human Services, National Center on Child Abuse and Neglect.

National Incidence Study. 1988. *Study of national incidence and prevalence of child abuse and neglect*. Washington, D.C.: U.S. Department of Health and Human Services, National Center on Child Abuse and Neglect.

Neighbors Helping Neighbors. 1993 (September). *A new national strategy for the protection of children*. Washington, D.C.: U.S. Department of Health and Human Services, Administration for Children and Families, U.S. Advisory Board on Child Abuse and Neglect.

Noble, Jeanne L. 1966. "The American Negro woman." In John P. Davis (ed.), *The American Negro reference book*. Englewood Cliffs, N.J.: Prentice-Hall, pp. 501–559.

Nock, Steven L. 1987. "The symbolic meaning of childbearing." *Journal of Family Issues* 8:373–393.

Noller, Patricia, and Mary Anne Fitzpatrick. 1990. "Marital communication." *Journal of Marriage and Family* 52:832–843.

Nye, F. Ivan. 1976. *Role structure and analysis of the family*. Beverly Hills, Calif.: Sage.

———. 1979. "Choice, exchange, and the family." In Wesley R. Burr, Reuben Hill, F. Ivan Nye, and Ira L. Reiss (eds.), *Contemporary theories about the family. Vol. II*. New York: Free Press, pp. 1–41.

Ogburn, William F. 1927. *Social change with respect to culture and original nature*. New York: Viking.

Olson, David H., and Harold McCubbin. 1983. *Families: What makes them work?* Beverly Hills, Calif.: Sage.

O'Neill, Nena, and George O'Neill. 1970. "Patterns in group sexual activity." *Journal of Sex Research* 6:101–112.

———, and ———. 1972. *Open marriage*. New York: Evans.

O'Neill, William L. 1967. *Divorce in the progressive era*. New Haven, Conn.: Yale University Press.

———. 1969. *The woman movement: Feminism in the United States and England*. New York: Barnes and Noble.

O'Rand, Angela M., and Margaret L. Krecker. 1990. "Concepts of the life cycle: Their history, meanings, and uses in the social sciences." *Annual Review of Sociology* 16:241–262.

Otto, Herbert A. 1970. "Introduction." In H. A. Otto (ed.), *The family in search of a future: Alternate models for moderns*. New York: Appleton-Century-Crofts, pp. 1–10.

Owen, William Foster. 1993. "Metaphors in accounts of romantic relationship terminations." In P. J. Kalbfleisch (ed.), *Interpersonal communication: Evolving interpersonal relationships*. Hillsdale, N.J.: Erlbaum, pp. 261–278.

Parsons, Talcott. 1965. "The normal American family." In S. Farber, P. Mustacchi, and R. Wilson (eds.), *Man and civilization: The family's search for survival*. New York: McGraw-Hill, pp. 31–50.

Pascall, Gillian. 1986. *Social policy: A feminist analysis*. New York: Tavistock.

Pasley, Kay, and Marilyn Ihinger-Tallman. 1987. "The evolution of a field of investigation: Issues and concerns." In K. Pasley and M. Ihinger-Tallman (eds.), *Remarriage and stepparenting: Current research and theory*. New York: Guilford, pp. 303–314.

Passuth, Patricia M., and Vern L. Bengston. 1988. "Sociological theories of aging: Current perspectives and future directions." In James E. Birren and V. L. Bengston (eds.), *Emergent theories of aging*. New York: Springer, pp. 333–355.

Peplau, Letita Anne. 1991. "Lesbian and gay relationships." In John C. Gonsiorek and James D. Weinrich (eds.), *Homosexuality: Research implications for public policy*. Newbury Park, Calif.: Sage, pp. 177–196.

Perlman, Daniel, and Beverly Fehr. 1987. "The development of intimate relationships." In D. Perlman and Steve Duck (eds.), *Intimate relationships: Development, dynamics, and deterioration*. Newbury Park, Calif.: Sage, pp. 13–40.

Peterson, Jean Treloggen. 1993. "Generalized extended family exchange: A case from the Philippines." *Journal of Marriage and Family* 55:570–584.

Peterson, Richard R. 1989. *Women, work and divorce.* Albany: State University of New York Press.

Peterson, S. A., and B. Franzese. 1987. "Correlates of college men's sexual abuse of women." *Journal of College Student Personnel* 28:223–228.

Pfohl, S. J. 1977. "The discovery of child-abuse." *Social Problems* 24:310–323.

Phillips, H. P. 1966. *Thai peasant personality: The patterning of interpersonal behavior in the village of Bang Chan.* Berkeley: University of California Press.

Phillips, Roderick. 1988. *Putting asunder: A history of divorce in Western society.* New York: Cambridge University Press.

Phoenix, Ann. 1991. *Young mothers?* Cambridge, Mass.: Basil Blackwell.

Pierce, Lois H., and Robert L. Pierce. 1990. "Adolescent/sibling incest perpetrators." In Anne L. Horton, Barry L. Johnson, Lynn M. Roundy, and Doran Williams (eds.), *The incest perpetrator: A family member no one wants to treat.* Newbury Park, Calif.: Sage, pp. 99–107.

Pirog-Good, Maureen A., and Jan E. Stets. 1989. "The help-seeking behavior of physically and sexually abused college students." In M. A. Pirog-Good and J. E. Stets (eds.), *Violence in dating relationships: Emerging social issues.* New York: Praeger, pp. 108–125.

Pitts, Jesse R. 1964. "The structural-functional approach." In Harold T. Christensen (ed.), *Handbook of marriage and the family.* Chicago: Rand McNally, pp. 51–124.

Pleck, Elizabeth H., and J. H. Pleck. 1980. "Introduction." In E. H. Pleck and J. H. Pleck (eds.), *The American man.* Englewood Cliffs, N.J.: Prentice-Hall, pp. 1–52.

Pleck, Joseph H. 1980. "Man's power with women, other men and society: A men's movement analysis." In Elizabeth H. Pleck and J. H. Pleck (eds.), *The American man.* Englewood Cliffs, N.J.: Prentice-Hall, pp. 417–433.

Polonko, Karen, Jay Teachman, and John Scanzoni. 1982. "Assessing the implications of childlessness for marital satisfaction." *Journal of Family Issues* 3:545–573.

Pomeroy, Wardell B. 1982 (rev. ed.). *Dr. Kinsey and the institute for sex research.* New Haven, Conn.: Yale University Press.

Popenoe, David. 1988. *Disturbing the nest: Family change and decline in modern societies.* New York: Aldine De Gruyter.

———. 1993. "American family decline, 1960–1990: A review and appraisal. *Journal of Marriage and Family* 55:527–555.

Prout, Alan, and Allison James. 1990. "Introduction,"and "A new paradigm for the sociology of childhood? Provenance, promise, and problems." In Allison James and Alan Prout (eds.), *Constructing and reconstructing childhood: Contemporary issues in the sociological study of childhood.* New York: Falmer Press, pp. 1–34.

Qureshi, Hazel, and Alan Walker. 1989. *The caring relationship: Elderly people and their families.* London: Macmillan.

Rainwater, Lee. 1965. *Family design: Marital sexuality, family size and contraception.* Chicago: Aldine.

———, and K. K. Weinstein. 1960. *And the poor get children.* Chicago: Quadrangle.

———, R. P. Coleman, and Gerald Handel. 1959. *Workingman's wife: Her personality, world and lifestyle.* New York: Oceana.

Rapoport, Rhona, Robert N. Rapoport, and Z. Strelitz. 1977. *Fathers, mothers and society: Toward new alliances.* New York: Basic Books.

Raush, Harold L. 1977. "Orientations to the close relationship." In George Levinger and H. L. Raush (eds.), *Close relationships: Perspectives on the meaning of intimacy.* Amherst: University of Massachusetts Press, pp. 163–188.

Reid, Helen M., and Gary Alan Fine. 1992. "Self-disclosure in men's friendships: Variations associated with intimate relations." In Peter M. Nardi (ed.), *Men's friendships.* Newbury Park, Calif.: Sage, pp. 132–152.

Reilly, Mary Ellen, and Jean M. Lynch. 1990. "Power-sharing in lesbian relationships." *Journal of Homosexuality* 19:1–30.

Reisman, Judith A., and Edward W. Eichel. 1990. *The indoctrination of a people.* Lafayette, La.: Huntington House.

Reiss, Ira L. 1960. *Premarital sexual standards in America.* New York: Free Press.

———. 1967. *The social context of premarital sexual permissiveness.* New York: Holt.

———. 1990. *An end to shame: Shaping our next sexual revolution.* Buffalo, N.Y.: Prometheus.

Renzetti, Claire M. 1992. *Violent betrayal: Partner abuse in lesbian relationships.* Newbury Park, Calif.: Sage.

Reskin, Barbara F., and Heidi I. Hartmann (eds.). 1986. *Women's work, men's work: Sex segregation on the job.* Washington, D.C.: National Academy Press.

Rhode, Deborah L., and Martha Minnow. 1990. "Reforming the questions, questioning the reforms: Feminist perspectives on divorce law." In Stephen D. Sugarman and Herma Kay Hill (eds.), *Divorce reform at the crossroads.* New Haven, Conn.: Yale University Press, pp. 191–210.

Richardson, Laurel. 1985. *The new other woman: Contemporary single women in affairs with married men.* New York: Free Press.

———. 1988. "Secrecy and status: The social construction of forbidden relationships." *American Sociological Review* 53:209–219.

Ricks, Thomas E. 1992. "Panel decides against women being in combat." *The New York Times.* November 4, p. A4.

Riessmen, Catherine Kohler. 1990. *Divorce talk: Women and men make sense of personal relationships.* New Brunswick, N.J.: Rutgers University Press.

Riley, Glenda. 1991. *Divorce: An American tradition.* New York: Oxford University Press.

Riley, Matilda White. 1988. "On the significance of age in sociology." In M. W. Riley, Bettina J. Huber, and Beth B. Hess (eds.), *Social structures and human lives: Social change and the life course, Vol. I.* Newbury Park, Calif.: Sage, pp. 24–45.

Rimer, Sara. 1992. "A test for women who build cars." *The New York Times,* October 12, p. C1.

Rindfuss, Ronald R. 1991. "The young adult years: Diversity, structural change, and fertility." *Demography* 28:493–512.

Risman, Barbara, and Pepper Schwartz. 1988. "Sociological research on male and female homosexuality." *Annual Review of Sociology* 14:125–147.

Rivers, R., and J. Scanzoni. 1995. "Social families among African-Americans: Policy implications for children." In H. P. McAdoo and J. L. McAdoo (eds.), *Black children: Social, educational, and parental environments.* Newbury Park, Calif.: Sage.

Robinson, I., and D. Jedlicka. 1982. "Change in sexual attitudes and behavior of college students from 1965 to 1980: A research note." *Journal of Marriage and Family* 44:237–240.

Robo, Bonnie E. 1991. "Children of divorce: Some do cope." In Warren A. Brown and Waln K. Brown (eds.), *Why some children succeed despite the odds.* New York: Praeger, pp. 7–22.

Rodgers, Roy H. 1973. *Family interaction and transaction: The developmental approach.* Englewood Cliffs, N.J.: Prentice-Hall.

Rodin, Judith, 1990. "Control by any other name: Definitions, concepts and processes." In J. Rodin, Carmi Schooler, and K. Warner Schaie (eds.), *Self-directedness: Cause and effects throughout the life course.* Hillsdale, N.J.: Erlbaum, pp. 1–18.

Rose, Suzanna, and Laurie Larwood (eds.). 1988. *Women's careers: Pathways and pitfalls.* New York: Praeger.

Rosen, Ellen Israel. 1987. *Bitter choices: Blue-collar women in and out of work.* Chicago: University of Chicago Press.

Rosenberg, Morris, and B. Claire McCullough. 1981. "Mattering: Inferred significance and mental health among adolescents." In Roberta G. Simmons (ed.), *Research in community and mental health,* Vol. 2. Greenwich, Conn.: Jai Press, pp. 163–182.

Ross, Catherine. 1991. "Marriage and the sense of control." *Journal of Marriage and Family* 53:831–838.

Rothman, Ellen K. 1984. *Hands and hearts—A history of courtship in America.* New York: Basic Books.

Rubin, Lillian B. 1976. *Worlds of pain: Life in the working-class family.* New York: Basic Books.

———. 1985. *Just friends.* New York: Harper & Row.

———. 1990. *Erotic wars: What happened to the sexual revolution?* New York: HarperCollins.

Rusbult, Caryl E. 1987. "Responses to dissatisfaction in close relationships: The exit-voice-loyalty-neglect model." In Daniel Perlman and Steve Duck (eds.), *Intimate relationships—development, dynamics, and deterioration.* Beverly Hills, Calif.: Sage, pp. 209–238.

Russell, Diana E. H. 1982. *Rape in marriage.* New York: Macmillan.

———. 1984. *Sexual exploitation: Rape, child sexual abuse, and workplace harassment.* Beverly Hills, Calif.: Sage.

———. 1991. "Wife rape." In A. Parrot and L. Bechhofer (eds.), *Acquaintance rape.* New York: Wiley, pp. 129–139.

Samar, Vincent J. 1991. *The right to privacy: Gays, lesbians, and the constitution.* Philadelphia: Temple University Press.

Scanzoni, John. 1970. *Opportunity and the family.* New York: Free Press.

———. 1972. *Sexual bargaining: Power politics in American marriage.* Chicago: University of Chicago Press.

———. 1975. *Sex roles, lifestyles and childbearing: Changing patterns in marriage and the family.* New York: Free Press.

———. 1977 (rev.; orig. 1971). *The black family in modern society: Patterns of stability and security.* Chicago: University of Chicago Press.

———. 1978. *Sex roles, women's work and marital conflict.* Lexington, Mass.: D.C. Heath.

———. 1982 (rev.; orig. 1972). *Sexual bargaining: Power politics in American marriage.* Chicago: University of Chicago Press.

———. 1983. *Shaping tomorrow's family: Theory and policy for the 21st century.* Newbury Park, Calif.: Sage.

———. 1989a. "Alternative images for public policy: Family structures versus families struggling." *Policy Studies Review* 8:599–609.

———. 1989b. "Joint decision-making in the contemporary sexually based primary relationship." In David Brinberg and James Jaccard (eds.), *Dyadic decision-making.* New York: Springer-Verlag, pp. 251–267.

———. 1991. "Balancing the policy interests of children and adults." In Elaine A. Anderson and Richard C. Hula (eds.), *The reconstruction of family policy.* New York: Greenwood, pp. 11–22.

———, and Cynthia Arnett. 1987. "Enlarging the understanding of marital commitment via religious devoutness, gender role preferences, and locus of marital control." *Journal of Family Issues* 8:136–156.

———, and Greer Litton Fox. 1980. "Sex roles, family and society: The seventies and beyond." *Journal of Marriage and Family* 42:743–756.

———, and Deborah D. Godwin. 1990. "Negotiation effectiveness and acceptable outcomes." *Social Psychology Quarterly* 53:239–251.

———, Deborah D. Godwin, and Denise Donnelly. 1993. "Comparison and contrasts between marrieds, cohabitors and unmarried non-cohabitors." *International Journal of Family and Marriage* 1:1–20.

———, and ———. 1992. "Heterosexual behavior patterns." In Edgar F. Borgotta and Marie L. Bor-

gotta (eds.), *The encyclopedia of sociology,* Vol. 2. New York: Macmillan, pp. 822–831.

———, and ———. 1993. "New action theory and contemporary families." *Journal of Family Issues* 14:105–132.

———, Karen Polonko, Jay Teachman, and Linda Thompson. 1989. *The sexual bond: Rethinking families and close relationships.* Newbury Park, Calif.: Sage.

———, and Maximialliane Szinovacz. 1980. *Family decision making: A developmental sex role model.* Beverly Hills, Calif.: Sage.

Schaap, Cas, Bram Buunk, and Ada Kerkstra. 1988. "Marital conflict resolution." In Patricia Noller and Mary Anne Fitzpatrick (eds.), *Perspectives on marital interaction.* Philadelphia: Multilingual Matters, Ltd., pp. 203–244.

Scheff, Thomas J., and Suzanne M. Retzinger 1991. *Emotions and violence: Shame and rage in destructive conflicts.* Lexington, Mass.: Lexington Books.

Scheuble, Laurie, and David R. Johnson. 1993. "Marital name change: Plans and attitudes of college students." *Journal of Marriage and Family* 55:747–754.

Schmitt, Eric. 1993. *The New York Times.* January 13, p. A1.

Schneider, Beth E. 1992. "AIDS and class, gender, and race relations." In Joan Huber and Beth E. Schneider (eds.), *The social context of AIDS.* Newbury Park, Calif.: Sage, pp. 19–43.

Schneider, David M. 1984. *A critique of the study of kinship.* Ann Arbor: University of Michigan Press.

Schoen, Robert. 1987. "The continuing retreat from marriage: Figures from 1983 U.S. marital status life tables." *Sociology and Social Research* 71:108–198.

———. 1992. "First unions and the stability of first marriages." *Journal of Marriage and Family* 54:281–284.

———, William Urton, Karen Woodrow, and John Baj. 1985. "Marriage and divorce in twentieth century American cohorts." *Demography* 22:101–114.

Schroeder, Leila Obier. 1986. "A rose by any other name: Post-marital right to use maiden name." *Sociology and Social Research* 70:290–293.

Schwartz, Felice N. 1989. "Management women and the new facts of life." *Harvard Business Review* 69:65–76.

Schwartz, Felice N. 1992. *Breaking with tradition: Women and work and the new facts of life.* New York: Warner.

Sears, Hal D. 1977. *The sex radicals: Free love in high Victorian America.* Lawrence, Kan.: Regents Press.

Seeley, John R., R. Alexander Sim, and Elizabeth W. Loosley. 1956. *Crestwood Heights.* New York: Basic Books.

Segal, Amanda Troy, and Wendy Zellner. 1992. "Corporate women." *Business Week.* June 8, pp. 74–78.

Seidman, Steven. 1991a. "The end of sociological theory: The postmodern hope." *Sociological Theory* 9:131–146.

———. 1991b. *Romantic longings: Love in America, 1830–1980.* New York: Routledge.

"Sexual behavior among high school students—U.S., 1990." *Morbidity and Mortality Weekly Report.* Atlanta: U.S. Centers for Disease Control.

Shapiro, Laura. 1993a. *Newsweek.* March 29, pp. 56–57.

———. 1993b. *Newsweek.* April 19, pp. 54–61.

Sheehy, Gail. 1976. *Passages.* New York: Bantam.

Shellenbarger, Sue. 1991. *Wall Street Journal.* September 12, p. B1.

———, and Cathy Trost. 1992. *Wall Street Journal.* September 22, p. A2.

Shelton, Beth Anne. 1992. *Women, men and time: Gender differences in paid work, housework and leisure.* New York: Greenwood.

Shostak, Arthur B. 1987. "Singlehood." In Marvin B. Sussman and Suzzanne K. Steinmetz (eds.), *Handbook of marriage and the family.* New York: Plenum, pp. 355–368.

Silva-Ruiz, Pedro F. 1992. "Family formation and dissolution in Latin America." Paper presented at International Conference on Family Formation: Perspectives from East and West. Taipei, Taiwan: Academica Sinica.

Simmons, Roberta G., Susan D. Klein, and Richard L. Simmons. 1977. *Gift of life: The social and psychological impact of organ transplantation.* New York: Wiley.

Simons, Marlise. 1993. *The New York Times.* April 9, p. A3.

Sipe, A. W. Richard. 1990. *A secret world: Sexuality and the search for celibacy.* New York: Brunner/Mazel.

Sklar, Fred, and Shirley F. Hartley. 1990. "Close friends as survivors: Bereavement patterns in a 'hidden' population." *Omega* 21:103–112.

Skolnick, Arlene. 1991. *Embattled paradise: The American family in an age of uncertainty.* New York: Basic Books.

Smith, Audrey D., and William J. Reid. 1986. *Role-sharing marriage.* New York: Columbia University Press.

Smith, Dorothy E. 1993. "SNAF as an ideological code." *Journal of Family Issues* 14:50–65.

Smith, James, and Lynn Smith. 1970. "Co-marital sex and the sexual freedom movement." *Journal of Sex Research* 6: 131–142.

Smith, Michael Peter. 1989. "Urbanism—medium or outcome of human agency?" *Urban Affairs Quarterly* 24:353–358.

Sokoloff, Natalie J. 1987. "The increase of black and white women in the professions: A contradictory process." In Christine Bose and Glenna Spitze (eds.), *Ingredients for women's employment policy.* Albany: State University of New York Press, pp. 53–72.

Solberg, Anne. 1990. "Negotiating childhood: Changing constructions of age for Norwegian children." In Allison James and Alan Prout (eds.), *Constructing and reconstructing childhood: Contemporary issues in the sociological study of childhood.* New York: Falmer Press, pp. 118–137.

Somenstein, Freya L., Joseph H. Pleck, and Leighton C. Ku. 1991. "Levels of sexual activity among adolescent males in the United States." *Family Planning Perspectives* 23:162–167.

Spiegel, John. 1960. "The resolution of role conflict within the family." In Norman W. Bell and Ezra F. Vogel (eds.), *A modern introduction to the family.* New York: Free Press, pp. 361–381.

Sponaugle, G. C. 1989. "Attitudes toward extramarital relations." In Kathleen McKinney and Susan Sprecher (eds.), *Human sexuality: The societal and interpersonal context.* Norwood, N.J.: Ablex, pp. 187–209.

Sprecher, Susan. 1989. "Influences on choice of a partner and on sexual decision making in the relationship." In Kathleen McKinney and Susan Sprecher (eds.), *Human sexuality: The societal and interpersonal context.* Norwood, N.J.: Ablex, pp. 115–138.

Spurlock, Jeanne. 1990. "Single women." In Jeanne

Spurlock and Carolyn B. Rabinowitz (eds.), *Women's progress: Promises and problems.* New York: Plenum, pp. 23–33.

Spurlock, John C. 1988. *Free love: Marriage and middle-class radicalism in America, 1825–1860.* New York: New York University Press.

Stacey, Judith. 1990. *Brave new families: Stories of domestic upheaval in late twentieth century America.* New York: Basic Books.

———. 1993. "Good riddance to 'the family': A response to David Popenoe." *Journal of Marriage and Family* 55:545–547.

Stack, Carol. 1974. *All our kin—strategies for survival in a black community.* New York: Harper & Row.

Stack, Steve. 1992. "The effect of suicide on divorce in Japan." *Journal of Marriage and Family* 54:327–334.

Stannard, Una. 1977. *Mrs. Man.* San Francisco: Germain Books.

Staples, Robert R. 1976. "Race and family violence: The internal colonialism perspective." In Lawrence Gary and Lee Browns (eds.), *Crime and its impact on the black community.* Washington, D.C.: Howard University.

———. 1981a. *The world of black singles: Changing patterns of male/female relations.* Westport, Conn.: Greenwood.

———. 1981b. "Black singles in America." In Peter J. Stein (ed.), *Single life: Unmarried adults in social context.* New York: St. Martin's Press, pp. 40–52.

Stearns, Peter N. 1979. *Be a man! Males in modern society.* New York: Holmes and Meier.

———. 1989. *Jealousy: The evolution of an emotion in American history.* New York: State University of New York Press.

Stein, Peter J. 1981. "Understanding single adulthood." In Peter J. Stein (ed.), *Single life: Unmarried adults in social context.* New York: St. Martin's Press, pp. 1–20.

Steiner, Gilbert Y. 1981. *The future of family policy.* Washington, D.C.: Brookings Institute.

Steinmetz, Suzanne K. 1988. *Duty bound: Elder abuse and family care.* Newbury Park, Calif.: Sage.

Stellway, Richard. 1990. *Christiantown USA.* New York: Haworth.

Stets, Jan E. 1991. "Cohabiting and marital aggression: The role of social isolation." *Journal of Marriage and Family* 53:669–680.

———, and M. A. Straus. 1990a. "The marriage license as a hitting license: A comparison of assaults in dating, cohabiting and married couples." In M. A. Straus and R. J. Gelles (eds.), *Physical violence in American families.* New Brunswick, N.J.: Transaction, pp. 227–244.

———, and ———. 1990b. "Gender differences in reporting marital violence and its medical and psychological consequences." In M. A. Straus and R. J. Gelles (eds.), *Physical violence in American families.* New Brunswick, N.J.: Transaction, pp. 151–166.

Stevenson, Howard, and Warren A. Rhodes. 1991. "Risk and resilience in teenagers who avoid pregnancy." In Warren A. Brown and Waln K. Brown (eds.), *Why some children succeed despite the odds.* New York: Praeger, pp. 79–91.

Straus, Murray A. 1972. "Foreword." In Richard J. Gelles, *The violent home.* Beverly Hills, Calif.: Sage, pp. 13–17.

———. 1979. "A sociological perspective on the prevention and treatment of wife-beating." In M. Roy (ed.), *Battered women.* New York: Van Nostrand Reinhold.

———. 1990. "The national family violence surveys." In M. A. Straus and R. J. Gelles (eds.), *Physical violence in American families.* New Brunswick, N.J.: Transaction, pp. 3–16.

———. 1991. "Physical violence in American families: Incidence rates, causes, and trends." In Dean D. Knudsen and JoAnn L. Miller (eds.), *Abused and battered: Social and legal responses to family violence.* New York: Aldine De Gruyter, pp. 17–34.

———, and R. J. Gelles. 1990. "How violent are American families? Estimates from the national family violence resurvey and other studies." In M. A. Straus and R. J. Gelles (eds.), *Physical violence in American families.* New Brunswick, N.J.: Transaction, pp. 95–112.

———, and Christine Smith. 1990a. "Family patterns and primary prevention of family violence." In M. A. Straus and R. J. Gelles (eds.), *Physical violence in American families.* New Brunswick, N.J.: Transaction, pp. 507–526.

———, and ———. 1990b. "Family patterns and child abuse." In M. A. Straus and R. J. Gelles (eds.), *Physical violence in American families.* New Brunswick, N.J.: Transaction, pp. 245–261.

Sugarman, David B., and Gerald T. Hotaling. 1991. "Dating violence: Prevalence, context and risk-markers." In M. A. Pirog-Good and J. E. Stets (eds.), *Violence in dating relationships.* New York: Praeger, pp. 3–32.

Sugarman, Stephen D., and Herma Kay Hill (eds.). 1990. *Divorce reform at the crossroads.* New Haven, Conn.: Yale University Press.

Sundstrom, Gerdt. 1987. "A haven in a heartless world? Living with parents in Sweden and the United States, 1880–1982." *Continuity and Change* 2:145–187.

Swain, Scott O. 1992. "Men's friendships with women: Intimacy, sexual boundaries, and the informant role." In P. M. Nardi (ed.), *Men's friendships.* Newbury Park, Calif.: Sage, pp. 153–172.

Swidler, Ann. 1980. "Love and adulthood in American culture." In Neil J. Smelser and Erik H. Erikson (eds.), *Themes of love and work in adulthood.* Cambridge, Mass.: Harvard University Press, pp. 120–150.

Syme, S. Leonard. 1990. "Control and health: An epidemiological perspective. In J. Rodin, Carmi Schooler, and K. Warner Schaie (eds.), *Self-directedness: Cause and effects throughout the life course.* Hillsdale, N.J.: Erlbaum, pp. 213–229.

Tallman, Irving, and Louis N. Gray. 1990. "Choices, decisions, and problem-solving." *Annual Review of Sociology* 16:405–433.

Tanfer, Koray. 1987. "Patterns of premarital cohabitation among never-married women in the U.S." *Journal of Marriage and Family* 49:483–497.

———, and Marjorie C. Horn. 1985. "Contraceptive use, pregnancy, and fertility patterns among single American women in their 20s." *Family Planning Perspectives* 17:10–19.

———, and Jeannette J. Schoorl. 1992. "Premarital sexual careers and partner change." *Archives of Sexual Behavior* 21:45–65.

Tannen, Deborah. 1990. *You just don't understand: Women and men in conversation.* New York: Morrow.

Taubin, S. B., and E. H. Mudd. 1983. "Contemporary traditional families: The undefined majority." In E. D. Macklin and R. H. Rubin (eds.), *Contemporary families and alternative lifestyles.* Beverly Hills, Calif.: Sage, pp. 256–270.

Teachman, Jay D., and Karen A. Polonko. 1990. "Cohabitation and marital stability in the United States." *Demography* 69:207–220.

———, Jeffrey Thomas, and Kathleen Paasch. 1991. "Legal status and the stability of coresidential unions." *Demography* 28:571–586.

———, Karen Polonko, and John Scanzoni. Forthcoming (rev. ed.; orig. 1987). "Demography of the family." In Marvin B. Sussman and Suzanne Steinmetz (eds.), *Handbook of marriage and the family.* New York: Plenum, pp. 3–36.

Thomas, Keith. 1959. "The double standard." *Journal of the History of Ideas* 2:205–215.

Thomas, W. I. 1918–1920 (with Florian Znaniecki). *The Polish peasant in Europe and America.* Chicago: University of Chicago Press.

Thompson, Edward H., and Patricia A. Gongla. 1983. "Single parent families: In the mainstream of American society." In E. D. Macklin and R. H. Rubin (eds.), *Contemporary families and alternative lifestyles.* Beverly Hills, Calif.: Sage, pp. 97–124.

Thompson, Linda. 1993. "Conceptualizing gender in marriage: The case of marital care." *Journal of Marriage and Family* 55:557–569.

Thomson, Elizabeth, and Ugo Colella. 1992. "Cohabitation and marital stability: Quality or commitment." *Journal of Marriage and Family* 54:259–267.

Thornton, Arland. 1989. "Changing attitudes toward family issues in the United States." *Journal of Marriage and Family* 51:873–893.

———. 1991. "Influence of the marital history of parents on the marital and cohabitational experiences of children." *American Journal of Sociology* 96:868–894.

T'ien, Ju-K'ang. 1944. "Female labor in a cotton mill." In Kuo-Heng Shih (ed.), *China enters the machine age.* Cambridge, Mass.: Harvard University Press, pp. 178–195.

Tong, Rosemarie. 1984. *Women, sex, and the law.* Totowa, N.J.: Roman & Allenheld.

Trost, Jan. 1979. *Unmarried cohabitation.* Vasteras, Sweden: International Library.

———. 1990. *Scandinavian families.* Family Reports No. 15. Uppsala, Sweden: Uppsala University.

Turner, Jonathon H. 1988. *A theory of social interaction.* Stanford, Calif.: Stanford University Press.

Turner, Ralph H. 1962. "Role-taking: Process versus conformity." In Arnold M. Rose (ed.), *Human be-*

havior and social processes: An interactionist approach. Boston: Houghton-Mifflin, pp. 22–40.

———. 1985. "Unanswered questions in the convergence between structuralists and interactionist role theories." In H. J. Helle and S. N. Eisenstadt (eds.), *Microsociological theory 2.* Newbury Park, Calif.: Sage, pp. 23–36.

———. 1990. "Role change." *Annual Review of Sociology* 16:87–110.

Valverde, Mariana. 1989. "Beyond gender dangers and private pleasures: Theory and ethics in the sex debate." *Feminist Studies* 15:237–254.

Vamos, Mark N. (ed.), 1992. "Business Week/Harris Executive Poll." *Business Week.* June 8, p. 77.

Vance, Carole S. (ed.), 1984. *Pleasure and danger: Exploring female sexuality.* Boston: Routledge & Kegan Paul.

Ventura, Stephanie J., Selma M. Taffel, William D. Mosher, and Stanly Henshaw. 1992 (November 16). "Trends in pregnancies and pregnancy rates, US, 1980–88." Vol. 41. Hyattsville, Md.: National Center for Health Statistics, p. 6.

———, and Joyce A. Martin. 1993 (February 25). "Advance report of final natality statistics, 1990." Vol. 41. Supplement. Hyattsville, Md.: National Center for Health Statistics, p. 9.

Vera, Hernan, and Joe R. Feagin. In preparation. "Racism as inflicted anomie: The black middle-class case." Gainesville: University of Florida, Department of Sociology.

Veevers, Jean. 1980. *Childless by choice.* Toronto: Butterworths.

Wadman, Meredith K. 1992. "Mothers who take extended time off find their careers pay a heavy price." *Wall Street Journal.* July 16, p. B1.

Waldman, Steven, and Karen Springen. 1992. "Too old, too fast?" *Newsweek.* November 16, pp. 80–88.

Wallace, Ruth A. (ed.). 1989. *Feminism and sociological theory.* Newbury Park, Calif.: Sage.

Waller, Willard. 1938. *The family: A dynamic interpretation.* New York: Dryden.

Wallerstein, Immanuel, and Joan Smith. 1990. "Households as an institution of the world-economy." In Jetse Sprey (ed.), *Fashioning family theory: New approaches.* Newbury Park, Calif.: Sage, pp. 34–50.

Wallerstein, Judith, and Joan Kelly. 1980. *Surviving the breakup: How parents and children cope with divorce.* New York: Basic Books.

Walsh, Robert H. 1989. "Premarital sex among teenagers and adults." In Kathleen McKinney and Susan Sprecher (eds.), *Human sexuality: The societal and interpersonal context.* Norwood, N.J.: Ablex, pp. 162–186.

Ward, Russell A., and Glenna Spitze. 1992. "Consequences of parent-adult child coresidence." *Journal of Family Issues* 13:553–572.

Warshaw, Robin, and Andrea Parrot. 1991. "The contribution of sex-role socialization to acquaintance rape." In A. Parrot and L. Bechhofer (eds.), *Acquaintance rape.* New York: Wiley, pp. 73–82.

Watkins, Susan Cotts, Jane A. Menken, and John Bongaarts. 1987. "Demographic foundations of family change." *American Sociological Review* 52:346–358.

Weeks, Jeffrey. 1985. *Sexuality and its discontents: Meanings, myths, and modern sexualities.* London: Routledge & Kegan Paul.

Wegener, Bernd. 1992. "Concepts and measurement of prestige." *Annual Review of Sociology* 18:253–280.

Weil, Mildred. 1990. *Sex and sexuality: From repression to expression.* Lanham, Md.: University Press of America.

Weinrich, James D., and Walter L. Williams. 1991. "Strange customs, familiar lives: Homosexualities in other cultures." In John C. Gonsiorek and James D. Weinrich (eds.), *Homosexuality: Research implications for public policy.* Newbury Park, Calif.: Sage, pp. 44–59.

Weitz, Shirley, 1977. *Sex roles.* New York: Oxford.

Weitzman, Lenore J. 1974. "Legal regulation of marriage: Tradition and change." *California Law Review* 62:1169–1288.

———. 1981. *The marriage contract: Spouses, lovers, and the law.* New York: Free Press.

———. 1985. *The divorce revolution: The unexpected social and economic consequences for women and children in America.* New York: Free Press.

———, and Mavis Maclean. 1992. *Economic consequences of divorce: The international perspective.* New York: Oxford.

Weston, Kath. 1991. *Families we choose: Lesbians, gays, kinship.* New York: Columbia University Press.

Whitcomb, Debra. 1991. "Improving the investigation and prosecution of child sexual abuse cases: Research findings, questions, and implications for public policy." In Dean D. Knudsen and JoAnn L. Miller (eds.), *Abused and battered: Social and legal responses to family violence.* New York: Aldine De Gruyter, pp. 181–190.

White, Jacquelyn W., and John A. Humphrey. 1991. "Young people's attitudes toward acquaintance rape." In A. Parrot and L. Bechhofer (eds.), *Acquaintance rape.* New York: Wiley, pp. 43–56.

White, James M. 1991. *Dynamics of family development: A theoretical perspective.* New York: Guilford.

White, Lynn K. 1990. "Determinants of divorce: A review of research in the eighties." *Journal of Marriage and Family* 52:904–912.

Wheelock, Jane. 1990. *Husbands at home: The domestic economy in a post-industrial society.* New York: Routledge.

Wiersma, Gertrude E. 1983. *Cohabitation, an alternative to marriage: A cross-national study.* Boston: Martin Nijhoff.

Wilking, Virginia N. 1990. "Mothers who abuse their children." In Jeanne Spurlock and Carolyn B. Rabinowitz (eds.), *Women's progress: Promises and problems.* New York: Plenum, pp. 143–157.

Williams, Constance Willard. 1991. *Black teenage mothers: Pregnancy and childbearing from their perspective.* Lexington, Mass.: D.C. Heath.

Williams, Kirk R. 1992. "Social sources of marital violence and deterrence: Testing an integrated theory of assaults between partners." *Journal of Marriage and Family* 54:620–629.

Wilson, Barbara Foley. 1989. "Remarriages and subsequent divorces: United States." *Vital and Health Statistics,* Series 21, No. 45. Washington, D.C.: U.S. Government Printing Office.

———, and Sally Cuningham Clarke. 1992. "Remarriages: A demographic profile." *Journal of Family Issues* 13:123–141.

Wilson, P. S. 1980. *Man, the promising primate: The conditions of human evolution.* New Haven, Conn.: Yale University Press.

Wilson, Patricia, and Ray Pahl. 1988. "The changing sociological construct of the family." *Sociological Review* 36:233–272.

Wilson, William Julius. 1987. *The truly disadvantaged: The inner city, the underclass, and public policy.* Chicago: University of Chicago Press.

Winfield, Fairlee E. 1985. *Commuter marriage: Living together, apart.* New York: Columbia University Press.

Wingert, Pat, and Eloise Salholz. 1992. "Irreconcilable differences." *Newsweek.* September 21.

Winter, Mary (ed.). 1992a. "At-home income generation, part one." *Journal of Family and Economic Issues* 13:3.

——— (ed.). 1992b. "At-home income generation, part two." *Journal of Family and Economic Issues* 13:2.

Wisensale, Steven K., and Kathlyn E. Heckart. 1993. "Domestic partnerships: A concept paper and policy discussion. *Family Relations* 42:199–204.

Woodworth, Melvin R. 1989. *The solemnization of non-marital intimate relationships.* Unpublished dissertation. San Francisco: San Francisco Theological Seminary.

Wright, P. H. 1982. "Men's friendships, women's friendships, and the alleged inferiority of the latter." *Sex Roles* 8:1–20.

Yankelovich, Daniel. 1981. *New rules: Searching for self-fulfillment in a world turned upside down.* New York: Random House.

Zabin, Laurie Schwab, Rebecca Wong, Robin M. Weinick, and Mark R. Emerson. 1993. "Dependency in urban black families following the birth of an adolescent's child. *Journal of Marriage and Family* 54:496–507.

Zartman, I. W. 1978. "Negotiation as a joint decision-making process." In I. W. Zartman (ed.), *Negotiation process: Theories and applications.* Beverly Hills, Calif.: Sage, pp. 66–86.

Zelnick, Melvin, and John F. Kantner. 1980. "Sexual activity, contraceptive use and pregnancy among metropolitan area teenagers." *Family Planning Perspectives* 12:230–237.

———, ———, and Kathleen Ford. 1981. *Sex and pregnancy in adolescence.* Beverly Hills, Calif.: Sage.

Ziskin, Jay, and Mae Ziskin. 1973. *The extra-marital sex contract.* Los Angeles: Nash.

PHOTO CREDITS

NAME INDEX

SUBJECT INDEX